"DARK AT THE TOP OF THE STAIRS"

By

JOHN DARK

From the bottom.

To the top

The memoirs of an International Film Producer

Published 2007 by arima publishing

www.arimapublishing.com

ISBN 978-1-84549-223-6

Printed and bound in the United Kingdom

Typeset in Garamond 11/14

arima publishing
ASK House, Northgate Avenue
Bury St Edmunds, Suffolk IP32 6BB
t: (+44) 01284 700321

www.arimapublishing.com

This book is dedicated to the families,
Scott, Dark and Pieck.
Especially to the Pieck who became a Dark.

And in memory of my darling

Vicki

Foreword

"There's no business like show business/ Like no business I know," sang Liza Minnelli.

We were in the Kempinski Hotel in Toronto, Canada. It was Saturday, and it was party night.

As on every Saturday night we were gathered to enjoy one another's company. We were in town making a movie, and it was one of those movies where everybody loved everybody else. It happens. There were many reasons why. First of all the story was based on a tap dancing school, and the sounds of taps echoing around the studio brought a happy air to the day to day business of movie making. Secondly, it was being directed by the veteran director Lewis Gilbert, who always worked in a quiet and happy environment, and thirdly, the cast was headed by Liza Minnelli, who in complete contrast to her reputation was a dream of a professional. A darling person who looked after the rest of the cast like the head girl at a boarding school. I should also add that we had not only a talented cast, but also a special lovely bunch of people.

There was Britain's much-loved Julie Walters, then from America Ellen Green who starred in movies like "Little Shop of Horrors", followed by Andrea Martin who was such a success in "My Fat Greek Friend's Wedding", Robyn Stevan, a young Canadian actress I had spotted on an in-flight movie. There was also Jane Krakowski, who wooed audiences around the world as the saucy secretary in "Alli McBeal", and London when she starred in the stage production of "Guys and Dolls". Bill Irwin, a talented mime actor from New York, and Carol Woods an amazing singer, who starred in numerous Gospel shows. Finally, Sheila McCarthy, one of Canada's leading actresses who had played Liza's role in her country's stage production of "Cabaret".

There we all were, crammed into Liza's suite, and with Peter Howard at the piano, she entertained us. The rest of the cast would do their party pieces, but it was Liza who sang the night away in a sort of "you ain't seen nothing yet" mode.

Sitting by my old friend and mentor, Lewis Gilbert, and looking across the room at my darling Dutch wife, I turned to Lewis and said, "It doesn't get much better than this."

Lewis replied, "You know, boy, I've made a few films in my life but I don't think I have ever had so much pleasure as on this one." I raised my glass to him: "Thank you", I said, and sat back to take in the scene, and marvel at my luck in having one of the world's great talents singing just for my friends and me. It was like a Hollywood scene – the backstage musical, where a bunch of people would get together and sing just for themselves. Listening to Liza belting it out I also thought back to how I loved her mother, how my childhood had been so influenced by the Andy Hardy films, and "The Wizard of Oz".

5

Was it films like this that made me want to be in movies? Was it all those hours spent in darkened cinemas, disappearing into another life, another world that gave me the wish to be in movies? I was too young to know exactly what I wanted to do. I think that it probably was to be an actor, for that is what I saw, but I don't think I ever said, "I want to be an actor".

It was always "I want to be in films". I yearned for the excitement of this strange world. It was Lewis who, decades later, said, "John you never lost your sense of excitement, and I don't think, please God, you ever will."

I never have. Sitting there, I thought back.

So many memories. . .

CHAPTER 1
A CHILD IS BORN

I was born on April the seventh 1927. My father was Stuart Dark, and my mother Eva Scott. I was christened John Stuart Alan.

CHAPTER 2
THE DARK PAST

I always thought the most illustrious thing about the Dark family was that at one time they owned Lord's Cricket Ground. They in turn sold it to the MCC (or to give it its full title, The Marylebone Cricket Club). My brother Peter and I were never cricket enthusiasts, agreeing with Lord Mancroft that cricket "was a game which the English, not being a spiritual people, have invented to give themselves a concept of eternity". We used to fantasise as to how many blocks of flats we could have built on this large plot of land situated in one of the more expensive parts of London.

My great, great, great grandfather was one of a number of brothers who came from the West Country and did very well for themselves. James Henry Dark bought the cricket ground in 1835, but in 1865 assigned his interest to the Earl of Dudley and others. At the same time he was assigned certain premises Nos. 30, 31 and 32 St. John's Wood Road for a peppercorn rent. He and his family were also given access to the cricket ground through the garden gate. It was sold to the MCC about forty years later. Actually Peter and I were not direct descendants, but came from his brother Francis. He and another brother, Ben Dark, started the cricket bat and ball business, still talked about in hushed tones by the cricket historians and enthusiasts. The curator at Lords only recently told us that a Dark bat would be worth thousands if you could find one.

Another brother, one John Dark (!), owned the street cleaning contract for Paddington and Marylebone, and it was he who added an 'e' to the family name as there were five panels on the watering carts! He prospered, making the old North Country saying, "Where there's muck there's money" once again true.

The Lords' family house was truly a family house with my great great grandparents, my great grandparents, my grand parents, and all my great aunts and uncles all living there at one time or another. My grandfather described *his* grandfather as "fundamentally a tough, unimaginative person who wasted his money buying rubbish that neither he, nor any other person, could possibly want, drinking far too much …" (a Dark trait, I'm afraid!) "… and persistently reading. He was the only man I ever knew who read a book without caring what sort of book it was. When he died at the age of ninety, he was reading alternately Lamb's 'Tales from Shakespeare' and the Civil Service catalogue!"

The Darks were an extremely prolific family. When my great grandfather was alive, he had sixty-one first cousins still living. The result was that the comfortable fortunes left by the first generation, once divided amongst all the family, severely reduced their living standards. They had enough, though, for many of them to live an idle and unproductive life.

My great grandfather was a man who was only really happy working with his hands, and when he was left the family business and had to reluctantly become a business man, an occupation he was totally unsuited to, it didn't take him long to run it into the ground.

I really did not know my grandfather, Sidney Dark. On rare occasions, I would be taken to town to see him and my grandmother. I would be scrubbed, polished, and constantly reminded to mind my p's and q's. Then we would be off to my grandparents' elegant flat in the centre of London. I was never very comfortable there. My grandfather would pop in, kiss my mother, ruffle my hair, exchange a few pleasantries, and then disappear to his study, leaving us to the tender care of his wife, my grandmother, known to me as Granny Nell. I am sure the last thing she wanted to do was to entertain my mother and myself. For a start, I don't think she approved of my mother, and secondly small boys were better left to nanny in the nursery. She was not unkind, but terribly grand, polite but distant; in complete contrast to my maternal grandmother, whom I adored. Both grandmothers shared one thing: they both dressed in long dresses right down to the ground. Granny Nell, though, had large strings of pearls, and expensive jewellery adorning her short body. The arrival of tea was a particular terror. My grandmother poured the tea, and dispensed the sandwiches and cakes like the Pope holding High Mass. Little boys are not very adept at holding cups, saucers and plates whilst attempting to drink and eat, not helped in this case by my grandmother's ever-watchful eye. I am still the clumsiest of people, and can leave a trail of crumbs after eating half a slice of toast. You can imagine what a state I was in as a young boy, trying to balance all the various china and silver whilst eating a meringue!

My grandmother's character I think is best summed up by an incident that happened after my grandfather had died. She had moved to The Onslow Court Hotel, a pleasant hotel in Kensington, which was mainly frequented by elderly well-off ladies, whose main occupation was to gossip and viciously criticise one another. During her stay, horror struck. A serial killer was found to be amongst the guests. He had killed two of the fellow female guests, disposing of their bodies by dumping them in a bath of acid. Ah, now the guests really did have something to talk about, but Granny Nell was beside herself with fury. "What I want to know is," she'd say in her most regal tones, "whatever did he see in them"!

Their marriage was not at all happy. Of course I was not aware of this whilst I was young, and it is true that most of my information comes from my mother who reciprocated her mother-in-law's dislike. So I have always taken her views with a pinch of salt. However, I don't think there is any doubt that the marriage was far from successful. I don't think there is any doubt either, though, that my mother loved my grandfather – and probably a bit too much!

Sidney Dark was a tall distinguished man, well over six feet and in complete contrast to his own father who was small (unfortunately, I took after my great grandfather). When I got older I had always presumed that my grandfather's standard of living came from inherited money and it was only after reading his autobiography "Not Such a Bad Life", that I learnt that by the time he left school the family fortunes had been completely dissipated. His father's incompetence had seen off the last remaining pounds. My grandfather's way of life had been totally achieved by his own talents. Considering that for most of his life his main occupation was that of a journalist and author, not the highest paid of professions, it shows what a prolific writer he was. Unable through lack of funds to go to university, he went as a clerk to Paris, a city that he came to love, and where he learnt to both write and speak French fluently. Returning to England and unable to sell any of his writings, he got a job as a singer, which, though, he hated, did bring in a few pounds. Eventually he started work on the Daily Mail, and then the Express, where he was to stay for seventeen years and where he was the theatre critic for something like twelve of those years. He knew the great man of the English theatre, Henry Irving, and the great lady, Ellen Terry. His friends were theatrical folk, and I presume that is where he met my grandmother as she had been, hard though it is for me to believe, a minor actress for a short time. He was on close terms with all the leading producers, people like CB Cochren, and playwrights like George Bernard Shaw.

After this, he spread to further fields, covering things like the Versailles Treaty at the end of the First World War during which he became acquainted with many French and British politicians. His fellow writers were also his close friends, including H.G. Wells, but his greatest friend probably was William Orpen, the portrait painter, who painted most of the great figures of the period including my grandfather.

After nearly twenty years, he left Fleet Street and the hurly-burly of the daily newspaper world for the calmer waters of the weekly. He first edited a literary magazine, "John O 'London's Weekly", and I am sure this move allowed him more time for his own books. During the following years he published a large number of novels, including "The Man Who Would Not Be King", and travel books, one on London and one on Paris, as well as numerous religious works, and several translations from the French. Over his lifetime he wrote thirty-one books. On top of this he was a constant contributor to the newspaper and magazine industry, and a popular lecturer. G.K.Chesterton wrote about him, "Mr Sidney Dark is probably a man much younger than the Victorian, and certainly more modern. He is not only an acute critic familiar with all the latest literature and philosophy, he is also a very active and energetic man of the world, editing libraries and managing literary business of the most practical sort." His last major appointment was as editor of "The Church Times". I have never been able to find out when religion hit him. I think he had always been fairly religious, but something happened in his life because in his book he writes about "a personal tragedy----which materially altered the course of my life", but he goes no further than that. He goes so far as to say, "It was a sorrow no man can write about." I think by "no man" he actually means one man, himself.

His autobiography doesn't even give a glimpse of his feelings. His family only gets a casual mention. When his son, my father, enlisted in the war when he was still underage, he is mentioned, but nothing else. The event is recorded, but there is nothing about the torment and the worry that he must have suffered. Nor does he say whether he tried to stop him. Was he the typical Englishman with an over-developed stiff upper lip? Was he only able to vent his feelings in prayer? Was religion his drug? What was it that changed the course of his life? Was it a woman? Whatever it was, it didn't affect his natural humorous nature. One of his colleagues wrote of him at that time saying, "He was a man of engaging personality; large of build, generous and self-indulgent to match. He used to breeze into the office around 10a.m., smoke endless cigarettes, and lunch at great length; but he somehow gave the paper a new vitality, as well as a political slant to the left. He was a theatrical and an ebullient character and would shed tears of grief or laughter when dictating what he would term his 'deathless prose'. He could be capital company with an expansive but well worked repertoire of outrageous jokes and anecdotes". Seemingly whatever it was lay hidden deep inside him, and his religious beliefs were expressed publicly only in an academic manner.

There was a mercenary side to his joining "The Church Times". He was paid eighteen hundred pounds a year, a staggering sum in those days, so I can understand that decision. Not being religious, I find it hard to understand what draws people to theology and its philosophy. Is it the fear of death? Or maybe the fear of living? You believe what you are brought up to believe, so if I were brought up to believe God was a crocodile then I would worship crocodiles, and could then declare war on the people who worship frogs!

I was forced to church when I was young, twice on Sundays when I was at school, though, only for weddings, funerals and christenings when I was at home. I can honestly say that if there were any religious feelings inside me they were quickly squashed by the Anglo-Catholics and the Church of England. Is there anything more boring than a Church of England service? A collection of people gathered in a cold church with wooden seats listening to some boring old man intoning some indecipherable gibberish, broken now and again by some equally dreary piece of music. Then comes the high spot, the top act, as it were, the sermon. One is forced to sit and listen to the "old fart's" ramblings, to sit dutifully, quietly and, however one might disagree, not to say a thing. Probably the only time you do pray is around about here – pray that it will all finish. I always wished they had one of those hooks that pulled unsuccessful comics off the stage. "Dearly Beloved brethren —" Whoosh --- out would come the hook, and off with the vicar.

A strange man, Sidney, a man of contrasts, for not only was he religious but he seemed to enjoy the pleasures of the flesh. Again, he was a successful man but did not like the successful, even though his main friends numbered amongst them. He preferred the unambitious man, with his cakes and ale. He was a lover of good books, good wine, and good painting, yet despised the trappings of the rich. He was also a Socialist and was always for the underdog. He disliked the Labour party under Ramsay MacDonald, a collection of people he could not abide, calling them all puritans. I am sure he would have got on well with New labour, firstly because they number amongst them some good drinkers, then their leader, Tony Blair, is a religious man, and thirdly and most importantly, they do seem to care.

Over the years, he built up a wonderful library, and a fine collection of paintings. Sadly, all that disappeared. On his death, after providing for my grandmother, he left everything to his daughter, Enid. He knew better than to leave anything to his son. Enid in turn, on her death, left it to her daughter Pam, who has never been heard of since. All I recall ever knowing about Pam was that at one time she had run off with a Roman Catholic priest, and this was at a time when it wasn't even fashionable! My aunt Enid was the older of the two children, a very tall, very thin, elegant Victorian lady, lightly made up, and dressed very conservatively but smartly. She was adorned with few, but very good, pieces of jewellery. Possessed of a melodic voice, and an impeccable English accent, she was a typical upper-class woman of her period.

I remember one night, shortly after I had come out of the army, I was on my way to Victoria station when I spied her striding along towards me. "Darling," I shouted (I very early learnt the lingua of show biz). "Darling," I repeated. Pulling herself up to her very full height she rounded on me, "You are a very rude man---oh, my God, it's John." I was truly relieved that she recognised me, even if belatedly, and before she struck out with her personal weapon, her umbrella. It is hard for me to think that even the most sex-starved of men would have dared to approach this large, regal, indomitable woman! Mind you I was relating my thoughts about my aunt to my father one day saying how dignified she was to which he replied, "You should ask her about the times when we were children and we used to fart under the bed clothes to see whose smelt the worst!" The idea of my aunt farting was too much to even contemplate, never mind the thought of comparing the quality!

Enid had been married to Paddy Hobson, a doctor, by whom she had two children, the eccentric Pamela and the conservative son, Ashley. He was at Dartmouth Naval College and passed out, after winning the King's Sword, just as the war started, so after a few days' leave he was on active service. He had a pretty bloody awful war being the First Lieutenant in submarines, towing vital fuel to the beleaguered island of Malta. Somehow he came through the war unscathed, much to the relief of the whole family, only to die of some common disease in, I think, Gibraltar.

Though she lived alone, her constant companion, and I presume lover, was a senior Anglo-Catholic priest. Not that it is easy to imagine either of them having sexual organs never mind actually using them! Father Mortlock was a pompous bore heartily disliked by my father. The last time I saw him he was presiding over my father's funeral. How Stuart would have hated it. Bad enough that the Anglo-Catholic service with its complex procedures droned on interminably (we all had to watch Enid to see when we should sit and when we should stand!), but that Mortlock was sending him on his way was the final straw! During the service, I could not help but smile when I recalled a story my father told me. He, my father, was working for a publishing group, probably Odhams, and there was a large ecclesiastical conference coming up. Knowing my father's connections with the Church through *his* father, he was instructed to organise the press coverage. In the company was a really top writer and she approached my father asking if she could cover the forthcoming event. Now, here was a problem; for, talented though she was, she suffered from one great drawback ---- she swore. These were the days when only navvies and sailors swore, and then only with one another. Gentlemen may have passed the odd curse, but never in mixed company. As for ladies swearing, it was unheard of. When my father pointed this out to her as delicately as possible she replied, "Oh don't be so bloody silly, don't you think I know how to behave when I have to?" And as she promised to control her fruity language my father relented. And indeed everything did go well till she was introduced to Mortlock. "And which is your parish, Father?" she asked.

"St Mary's in Kensington."

"Oh, so it's you that wakes me up every Sunday morning ringing those fucking bells!"

Whilst the funeral continued its complicated way, bells ringing, incense wafting, hymns singing, psalms intoning whilst we all bobbed up and down in sync with my aunt's leadership, I thought back on the father I did not really know.

He was born somewhere at the turn of the century. He had a very unhappy childhood. His early schooling was with a private tutor, a man whom he adored and whose photograph he was to keep until the day he died. His mother, though, had different ideas, and thought he should be like all the other sons of society friends. So he was duly dispatched to Tunbridge School, a place my father hated with a passion and demonstrated this dislike by running away three times. Three times he was sent back. Seemingly, he had very little home life even in the holidays. His father was too busy working and his mother too busy enjoying the social life of London. Money was no problem, and as long as he kept out of the way, he was never short of funds. This I am sure was the cause of his lack of understanding about the value of money. Five pounds or fifty pounds was all the same to him, a trait that he was to demonstrate frequently during his life.

While still at school, and the First World War in full swing, he and a few of his school chums joined the army. I don't know at exactly what age, but I do have a photograph of him as a private soldier where he looks about twelve! Shortly after joining, he was commissioned in the London Scottish Regiment, probably because he was a "gentleman" and no doubt because he would have been made to join the OTC (Officers' Training Corps) at school. It was only in the early 80s that I learnt from his old friend, Sydney Lawrence, that my father rose to the rank of Captain before being reduced to the ranks for fiddling the mess funds. He was soon, though, re-commissioned on the field because of his extraordinary bravery.

I had mixed emotions at this piece of information; both pride and sadness. I knew he couldn't survive without a drink or a smoke. I knew he thought tomorrow would never dawn. I knew of his lack of monetary understanding. I knew all this, but what I didn't know was that he was brave. Now that was something new, a surprise, for in civilian life he was a weak man. Yes, I felt proud when Sydney told me of his bravery. I also felt tears. I wanted to cry for this sad, sad man who only in battle could distinguish himself, and find in himself the pride that he was unable to find in life.

After the war was over in 1918, civilian life beckoned, a life unknown to him. So far, all he had experienced was school and the army, and the freedom offered was full of temptations, most of which he indulged to the full. Somehow, Stuart got a job with the League of Nations in Geneva. I don't know what he was supposed to be doing there, but I am sure he was having a good time. This pleasant period was enhanced when he met my mother, and they fell in love. They married back in England and settled down to lead a normal British middle class life.

My mother dearly loved him, I am sure, but she was also in love with the Dark family. Ever the snob, in complete contrast to Stuart, she revelled in being a Dark and not a Scott. However, her life was to be far from happy, even with the arrival of my brother Peter, and four years after, me. Stuart's drinking got worse and worse, and his irresponsibility led to the bills piling up. His father used to get him odd jobs on various papers and magazines. He told me of one job that was right up his street.

He used to work for the weekly "John Bull", and they ran a weekly competition, the prize being "A Millionaire's Weekend in London". Someone mistakenly put my father in charge, meeting the contestants and spending the two days with them! He would accompany them to the best hotels and restaurants. Invariably the winners were simple people, with simple tastes. Fish and chips, and brown ale, and maybe a port and lemon for the wife were the height of their desires. It took several months for the company to realise that the bills for champagne and caviar were actually only being eaten by their representative.

One day my mother was at home and was surprised by a knock on the door, but she got an even bigger surprise when the deliveryman handed her large wreath with a card on it, which read "With Deepest Sympathy – the directors and staff, Odhams press". Apparently the firm had put their foot down, and refused any more advances of salary until he started paying back some of the loans. So in desperation he went to them and said despite their ruling, he just had to have an advance as his wife had died and he needed the money to pay for the funeral expenses!

He was one of the world's misfits, really only happy in the army. Here he always had the companionship he enjoyed, leaning over a bar with a pint and a cigarette, chatting up the barmaid and swapping stories with his mates. No real responsibility, a pay packet at the end of the week. The army clothed you and fed you, even did your thinking for you, and if you ran out of money there was always a friend who'd buy you a drink and give you a cigarette, and sadly that was all he was really interested in. That is why, I suspect, at the outbreak of the Second World War he was first in the queue to join up again. Not being accepted from the Officers' reserve because of his age, he joined up, for the second time, as a private soldier. He served throughout the whole war, until he was demobbed in 1945 as a Sergeant. He was to end his days working in a menial civilian capacity with the Territorial Army. The closest he could get to the real thing. At a young age, he died of cirrhosis of the liver in the Hampstead Hospital.

I think of him with great fondness, wishing I could have helped him, wishing that he had known his grandchildren. I cannot help contemplating his childhood and how different his life would have been if his father's religious philosophy had included giving and showing the love his son so dearly craved.

CHAPTER 3
THIS HAPPY BREED

I always thought that the most illustrious thing about the Scotts was that we had a relative who, in order to wean her babies, used to draw monsters on her boobs!

The oldest known Scott ancestor, David Scott, a baker, dates back to 1817. At the age of fifteen his sixth son left England for India and became a Volunteer for the Bengal Pilot Establishment. Rising through the ranks, he eventually became a Pilot on the River Hoogly guiding ships into the busy port of Calcutta. This was my great grandfather.

On his return to England, after twenty-five years service, he married and had six children. Sadly he ended his days in Bedlam, an institution for the mentally deranged. It is thought his illness was caused by the ordeal of being shipwrecked off the coast of Bombay.

 His second son, my grandfather, had a good private education at Aske's Hatcham Academy for the Sons of Gentlemen, but I am not sure what he did after this. I know that at one time he bought a sweet shop in which he didn't seem to have much interest, but left it in the hands of his children, all seven of them! So the venture was short lived, and once the children and their friends, including the dog, ate their way through the stock, that was the end of that.

I know they also had a pub, but oh my God, keep that quiet! In Victorian days, it was rated only slightly higher than owning a brothel. I can remember the last time we quizzed my mother about it. She and my Aunt Winnie were having lunch with us when we broached the subject. It brought howls of denial from both of them (even, though, this was in the 80s when it was, if not fashionable, at least respectable to be a publican), and were so strong I thought, "Methinks you doth protest too much".

However, I know it's true, for I remember Wendy, my mother, telling me the story of how at school they had to bring a pair of stockings for the domestic science lesson on washing. The other girls brought nice silk stockings but my mother brought woollen ones with the sawdust from the pub floor ingrained in them! Humiliation! I think this type of incident in her childhood made her the snob she later became.

My father was the only one who got on with my grandfather. (Something to do with the fact that they were both drinkers?) He told me a story about how the old man (I never heard him referred to by any other name until my mother was in her 80's) was doing a building job for a doctor, which necessitated taking up all the floorboards in the upstairs bedroom. They both went off for a liquid lunch, and on his return my grandfather fell through the open floor to the surgery below and on top of a patient who was being examined! The poor man came in with 'flu and went out with two broken ribs!

When my mother left my father, we moved to my grandparents' house in Brockley, South London. Of the seven children, all but one was still living at home. The one who had flown the nest was Dudley, or Duds when he was referred to at all. He was the eldest, the odd one out, the black sheep. He was a chauffeur and perhaps this made him an outsider, or perhaps it was just his unfortunate personality. The only thing about him I related to was that he was married to a woman called Olive, whom I took to be Popeye's girl friend Olive Oyl! The wonderful thing was that when I did meet her I was not all that disappointed as she certainly had a strong resemblance to the cartoon character.

After Duds came my mother, christened Eva, but always referred to by all (except her parents, brothers and sisters) as Wendy, and she has been Wendy to my brother and me since we were teenagers. She was an extremely bright, bird-like creature with a sharp brain. She was ambitious to raise herself up the social scale, and would have been horrified to be judged lower class; despite the fact that my grandfather always insisted he was "lower middle class". I think that there is no doubt that, though she loved my father, in marrying him there was the added attraction of marrying upwards. She was devoted to her two sons, but she was also very demanding. Like many single mothers who put all their love and affection into their children, she expected the same thing in return from them. Happiness always eluded her. She never liked her daughters-in-law, and was very, very difficult with them. She adored her grandchildren but once they got older, she was unable to keep their affection.

Next in line came George. Dear Uncle George was a quiet, kind man and the only one of the family who worked with his hands. For most of his life, he worked for the De Havillands aircraft company. What he did exactly I have no idea, but whatever it was I am sure he did it wonderfully. He married a lovely woman, a well-educated, cultured lady, Winnie Phillips. Phillips, being her maiden name, was used to avoid confusion with my actual Aunt Winnie, my mother's sister. They had the most wonderful sixty years of marriage, with three children (twin boys and a girl). Their kindness to me as a child has stayed firmly in my head, and in my heart.

After George came my Aunt Winnie, a small plump, warm person who adored me and spoilt me very badly. She was the scandal of the family having had a long-standing affair with a married man, who was not only married but also a socialist! The fact that he was also a successful businessman only compounded the felony. Despite the family feeling, I rather liked him. He was always very kind to me. He was the sales' director of Weston Biscuits at one time, and when I was at boarding school, he used to send me tin boxes of chocolate biscuits. I wouldn't have cared if he had been a member of the IRA!

Then came Bo, or Borance, whose real name was Harold,, though, no one remembers where his nickname came from. Bo was quite a strange guy; if you didn't know you would have sworn he was gay. He spoke with an affected accent, and all his hand gestures were effeminate. He sewed, made lampshades, or did some other work normally performed by women in those days. Yet the opposite was true, as he always seemed to have a good-looking girl around, eventually marrying the most enchanting person, Vana, who was the double of Greer Garson, the 40s film star. A fun personality, my Aunt Vana was something special. I remember in my 30's getting pissed at a family party, going up to her and saying, " You know, Vana, I'd really like to fuck you"! The next day, through my hangover, the memory returned and, though, the sentiment was true, it was hardly the thing to say to one's married aunt. So I rang her to apologise, and she responded, "Oh darling, I've never been so flattered." A lovely lady.

The last of the boys, Jack, was the complete opposite of Bo. A man's man, solid, no nonsense, a minor entrepreneur. He seemed to live comfortably, though not ostentatiously. Here again the male Scott luck was in when he married my Aunt Vera, another warm, cuddly, happy person, everybody's ideal aunt. I adored her, and I still remember my last sight of her before she died tragically early of cancer. She was lying in bed waiting for the ambulance to take her to the hospital, when I peeked in at her. Without raising her head, she just looked at me and winked her good-bye to me.

The last of the seven was my Aunt Doreen. This was the tough one. When my mother went out I always hoped it would be Winnie who would look after me, not Doreen. There was no getting around her; bedtime was on the dot, no mucking about. With Winnie, I could spin it out for hours, but Sergeant Doreen was a stickler for discipline – bath, bed, lights out, and goodnight. It's funny to think that when she had two children of her own, she completely changed and seemed to spoil them rotten.

That just leaves my darling grandmother. I don't know her real name, I don't want to know her name, she was always granny to me. I think back with great longing and I still miss her after all these years. She was a simple woman, not terribly affectionate, but so very kind. With my parents divorced, and my mother and the rest of the family out to work all day, she and I shared the days together. She was my security, my warmth, my safe haven. She was always there, day or night. When I got older we used to go the cinema together, and she called me her little husband. I suppose the six children were glad to get us both out of the house.

I still remember her cooking the most wonderful meals. "You know, John," she once said to me "there are people who eat things out of tins!" I remember her sitting down after Sunday lunch whilst the others did the washing-up, reading the Sunday newspaper, from which she liked to read out little tit-bits. "Fancy that," she once exclaimed, "it says here that lobsters lay several hundreds of eggs at a time." She put down the paper and reflected, "You wouldn't think they would be so expensive, would you?"

She died when I was abroad, and I am glad I didn't see her at the end.

So there I was, a child of divorced parents, with a grandmother, three fathers and three mothers! How lucky I was to have been so loved by so many. I think a couple of lines from a poem by Noel Coward best sums up my feelings.

"How happy they are I cannot know
But happy am I who loved them so."

CHAPTER 4
MEMORIES OF ME

My earliest recollections are few. I remember my grandfather digging a fishpond in the garden. I remember Rex, the dog, and the day Sadie, my grandmother's parrot, escaped and was in a tall tree shrieking her lungs out. I can also dimly recall being a "boat boy" helping to "fumigate" the congregation in the local Anglo-Catholic church with incense. I don't think my mother was at all religious; it was just a question of keeping in with my paternal grandfather. My memory of it is far from religious, for it is of sitting still in the service and peeing my pants!

My only other memory was my mother and aunts standing around a "copper" (not a policeman, but an early version of a washing machine). It was virtually just a large container, rather like a dustbin, with a heater underneath. The clothes were added to the hot water and soap and pummelled around with a wooden stick. Doing the family washing, scarves tied around their heads whilst they discussed the latest row between their parents.

I gleaned later in life that there was constant friction between my grandfather and the rest of the family. Poor man, I have always had sympathy for him. Fancy being up against your wife and six children! The end was especially poignant. They had decided to leave him, but because of my grandmother's fear of him, they decided not to give him any warning. I don't know why she was so scared. I presume it was that he ill treated her. They had found a house to rent way on the other side of London, literally from the South to the North. On the appointed day, both my grandmother and I were taken off to friends for the day. After my grandfather left for work, the moving truck arrived and the contents of the house laden on to it. With the shortage of time, there was little finesse in the packing, no time to take the curtains off the rails – they were cut off with scissors, leaving the rings and two inches of material hanging on the rails! By mid-day, the van was loaded. The last item to be put on board was Sadie the parrot, a scene aptly expressed by the lyrics of the old song, "Off went the van with me home packed in it/ I followed on with me old cock linnet"! By the time my grandfather returned that night, the house was empty of wife, children and furniture, just his own personal things remaining. He never saw his wife again and only saw his children when he was close to dying.

So we moved to 109 Osulton Way, Finchley: a small, semi-detached house at the end of a long road leading down to Hampstead Garden Suburb. Surrounded by fields at that time, although later, like all dormitory areas of London, they were developed into massive housing estates. The house was quite small, with four bedrooms and one bathroom. My grandmother had one, my mother one, the two aunts in the other, and we blokes – my three uncles, myself, and in the holidays my brother Peter, in the fourth. How we all fitted in I have no idea, but I have no memory of being squashed, or in any way being uncomfortable.

Life proceeded peacefully, though, my grandmother was still terrified by the thought that one day the dreaded "old man" would return and exact his revenge. Whenever practical, she would sit in the pantry. I am not quite sure why, but perhaps she thought it would give her some protection if he came snooping by.

Both Peter and I were obedient kids (I think!): Peter because that's how he was, and I, as I have said, adored my grandmother and don't think I ever went against her. On refection I do not think I was disobedient to anyone, not because I was a goody-goody (far from it) but because I was a coward. I hated to be in someone's bad books, and I disliked being out of favour. I wanted the world to love me, and, though I would push my luck as far as it would go, I would quickly retreat when punishment loomed. I am afraid I don't think a lot has changed over the years.

My brother, Peter, is nearly four years older than I am. I don't think he was as close to the Scott family as I was – mainly, I think, because he was sent away to boarding school (courtesy of my paternal grandfather) at the tender age of six or seven. Thank God my grandfather's generosity didn't extend to me! However, my time was to come.

First though, there was nursery school. A not unpleasant experience, and a place where I was happy to be. I enjoyed the percussion band and had ambitions to be the conductor, already demonstrating my Aries character of wanting to be the leader, and to boss everyone about. It also started my lifetime pleasure in drumming, one of my early heroes being Gene Krupa, the famous 30s jazz drummer.

About this time my other lifelong pleasure started to dawn. Sex!

I used to lie in bed, hearing Betty, the sweet cleaning girl, vacuuming, thinking, "I'm going to go and pull her knickers down." I never got any further, and that was the end of my fantasy. A short and not very inspiring thought, but strong enough to remain in my mind all these years. Poor Betty would have been horrified as she always thought what a sweet little boy I was.

The fun of nursery school soon gave way to the horror of school proper. In my case a local Catholic one. A place in which I never felt comfortable, and where I fear I didn't learn too much either. Lessons, mostly taken by nuns, commenced with prayers and ended with prayers. Consequently you finished one lesson's prayers and almost immediately started again. There were some nice nuns but the majority certainly weren't out to win a popularity competition! You would have thought that they would make their religion attractive to children, radiate happiness and warmth. The opposite was true, as their faith seemed based on hardship, misery, and boredom. If you believe in God you must admit that one of His greatest gifts to man was humour. Yet when have you ever seen a religious painting, sculpture or whatever depicting people smiling? If Jesus was the Son of God, all I can say is that he never seemed to be very happy in that relationship.

The only good thing about the school was that I had to go there by bus and was given my bus fare every day. Now, if you were lucky the conductor was too busy to get round to everybody, so he would stand on the platform when the bus was about to pull up and collect the money as you got off. The knack was to jump off before he took up his position, and while the bus was still travelling. My family could never understand why I was always covered in bruises. All that to save a penny (less than half a present pence).

I hardly ever saw my father and I could honestly say I didn't miss him. I didn't know him, so what you don't know you don't miss. He was a shadowy character in my life, and I found his lurking absence rather exciting. Anyhow, I had a whole family to love me, and as my brother was away most of the time, a whole family to spoil me like an only child. Still it was rather fun every so often to remind one of my uncles, usually Bo, that if he weren't nice to me I would tell my father. God, kids are devious.

There was one time when my father actually arrived on my birthday, and he brought with him a toy motorboat, powered by a torch battery. I can see it now, a white cabin cruiser, whose deck came off to reveal a small motor and battery. I loved that boat, more because he gave it to me than because of anything else. It's a strange thing that for years to come, whenever I had been away for some time I would hunt through the cupboards to find it on my return. I would look at it, and then put it back. I am sure a psychologist would have a ball with that, but I guess their conclusions would be wrong. I wasn't unhappy that he wasn't there; I think I just wanted some evidence that he did exist.

Well, very soon he was to re-enter my life. Life was changing, things were moving on. George and Jack got married and left the Finchley nest. Bo and the two aunts bought a house where they and my grandmother were to live. My mother, Peter and I were to set up home on our own ... well, not quite on our own because my father was to come back and live with us.

The new abode was a very pleasant flat in a modern block behind Park Royal station, back from what was then called the Western Avenue, and is now the A40. This allowed my mother to get to her job in central London comparatively easily. My mother, father, and I went to inspect the flat. Peter was away at school. I remember looking out of the window of the flat and my father coming up to me and saying, "You've had a very stupid father."

And I replied, "Well, I've got a very sweet one now." Even at that age, I had the gift of the gab!

He wasn't sweet for long, though. On the appointed day, the day we were all to move in, he didn't turn up. So there we were, just the three of us. Once again, I don't recall any great disappointment. I mainly felt sad for my mother, but then I seem to have spent most of my life being sorry for her. In fact, one of my earliest memories is of her getting ready to go to a dance, dressed up in a long evening dress. Whilst I powdered her bare back, she cried her eyes out. I really don't know why, but it was probably because she had no partner. I remember Bo telling me how fed up he was of her constant tears. Her problem was she couldn't live with my father, and she couldn't live without him! No other suitor appeared, and she found life very difficult without male company, which probably explains why I had so many "uncles" over the years.

At this time, though, her main problem was money. I imagine my mother had always reckoned on having the salaries of both of them when she signed the lease on the apartment. If I remember correctly her salary was five pounds a week, and even taking into account the value of money in those days, it was not a hell of a lot. She had to find other ways of making money, like addressing envelopes and making palm crosses for sale at religious shops at Easter time. She started designing knitted articles and sold them to the various women's magazines. I always swore I'd never marry a woman who knitted because every time I asked my mother a question she would say "twenty-one, twenty-two, twenty three --- what did you say, darling?"

My education was her real worry. She wanted to send me to Christ's Hospital, a leading public school that was maintained by a charity. Parents paid whatever they could afford. The only trouble was that I was way behind the standard required. The people at the school suggested to my mother that I be sent to a "crammer", and gave her the name of a woman they recommended. This woman had a small school in Tuffnel Park miles away from where we lived so I had to live with her, together with another boy.

The school/home was a large Victorian house complete with basement. The schoolroom was on the ground floor, and the two boarders' bedrooms were on the second floor. I had never been away from home before and the whole place struck terror in my heart. The "crammer" was an eccentric old lady who looked exactly like Old Mother Riley. For those of you who are too young to remember this classic Music Hall act I'll explain. She had grey hair combed back into a bun at the nape of her neck, spectacles perched on her nose, and dressed in navy blue serge with a skirt reaching almost down to the ground. She was both a comical and an intimidating figure for a young boy. She was horrified that I had brought my favourite soft toy with me, my monkey, and was about to take it away until stopped by her maiden daughter, an unattractive woman, but a lifesaver for me at the time.

I suppose there were about twelve pupils in the school, including us two boarders. I don't remember much about the actual schooling, but do recall the terrible food. I ate in the basement and was served by the cook and the maid. My pet hate was the potatoes. I have no idea what she did to those boiled roots, but I can still smell them. They were quite revolting, and I used to smuggle them into my pocket and put them down the loo later!

After a short while she closed the school, as it was getting too much for her, and moved to a smaller house. My mother prevailed upon her to keep me on, and so I became the only pupil she had. I was therefore more in contact with her, and was taken out on shopping expeditions. She strode about as though she was off to a fire, and puffed the entire time. To go out with her was an experience as she caused comment wherever we went. I tried to walk behind so people wouldn't think that I was with her, but she soon put a stop to that. As a treat I was taken to the ABC café (ABC stood for the Aerated Bread Company), a rather dismal place, like pre-historic present day motorway cafés. I was not asked what I wanted, but given tea and a meringue. I can still see these two white blobs, a yellow gash of mock cream cementing the two together.

I am sure in her time she must have been a great educator, but by the time I arrived, she was past her shelf-life. However, I was to take the blame. I was staying with George and Winnie when my mother arrived with a face like thunder bringing the news of my failure to pass the entrance exam. She was furious with me, and in the end I ran away in tears, and hid somewhere in the woods behind the house. After a little time, my aunt found me, wrapped her arms around me and consoled me. Later on in life I would remind her of this and she always used to say, "Poor little chap, it wasn't his fault." A remark I was to hear later on in life when I screwed up on my first job in the film industry.

My mother was such an active person, full of ideas, full of energy, always on the hunt for something, some way to earn a pound or two. However, life was far from poor; we had a nice flat with constant hot water, two bedrooms and a kitchen with a fitted refrigerator, a big item in those days. There was a miserable old caretaker; however, he did keep the gardens very nicely. We always had someone who came in to clean, and the first was an Irish girl who lived in with her small baby. I was always trying to get into her knickers, very unsuccessfully I might add, but as I was only about ten, it was hardly surprising.

One day I didn't feel well, and my mother said I didn't have to go to school. However, as the day wore on I started to feel better, and randy. I tried to indulge in some sort of sexual activity with this girl, but she responded by reminding me that I was supposed to be ill, and she would tell my mother when she got home that I had been lying about being sick. That evening when my mother came home I actually got worse. The doctor was called, who in turn rang for the ambulance and I was rushed to hospital with an inflamed appendix. Before the ambulance pulled away from the flat, the Irish girl, with tears streaming down her face, came and kissed me good-bye. "Serve you right if I die," I thought unkindly.

But soon all thoughts of her disappeared as off I went off in the ambulance. Those were the days when parents weren't encouraged to stay with their children, and certainly not given rides in the ambulance. "If you like, you can come to the hospital tomorrow," she was told. So there I was, alone with the nurse, and as she bent down to make me comfortable, I looked up at her and it hit me.

I was in love!

I gazed at this divine creature, in her starched uniform and white frilly bonnet and my stomach churned, not with the rumbling appendix, but with the explosion of pure and unrelenting love. As she chatted to me, made me comfortable, and stroked my brow I was lost in a haze of total devotion. There was nothing sexual about this feeling, but neither was it platonic. It was not the love that one has for a sister or a mother; this was deep all encompassing pure, virginal love of a man for a woman, though in this case the man was only ten!

I always thought this girl must have felt something, for days later she actually came and visited me in the ward. I can still see her now walking down the ward towards me, her frilly white cap perched on her head, her blue cape flapping as she walked, and her smile when she saw me. I still can feel the pain in my stomach as I realised that it was she, and she was with me. Alas, a week or two later I was released and I never saw her again, but she was my first love and oh how I wish I could have met her later in life so I could have told her how she stole a young boy's heart.

My mother always tells the story of how she couldn't afford a taxi to pick me up from the hospital, so we came back home by bus and tube. I lost so much weight after the operation, that as I walked up the stairs of Park Royal station my shoes fell off my feet. I used to think that this was a really sad story, and rather enjoyed my mother recounting it. Of course, at the time I was not aware of any deprivation in my life. I was not aware that we were hard up, and of course compared to most people we weren't. There is no doubt that my mother had a tough time, but we were never hungry. It was just that every shilling had to be counted and every avenue explored to make a little extra money. I describe it as a sort of genteel poverty. Money was spent on appearances, on education, and on keeping a warm, comfortable home.

My mother worked for a very aristocratic gentleman by the name of Captain Wallace, and his occupation, other than being a retired soldier, was letting out shooting boxes. If a party wanted to bang off at some grouse, or pheasants, or go for a week's shooting in Scotland, they would first go to Wallace. There was only he and my mother in their dignified offices in Pall Mall, very close to St. James Palace. He had a thriving business up until the war came in 1939, when humans took over from the birds! Wallace was the complete Victorian English gentleman, upright of appearance, moustached, elegant with his bowler and cane. Extremely pedantic, he always referred to Walt Disney as Walter Disney. My mother asked him if he referred to the cartoon character as Michael Mouse! I never heard the answer to that but I expect he had never heard of him anyhow. This was the basic income my mother had, and I think she enjoyed dealing with the upper classes who indulged in this form of entertainment.

Whilst she was busy helping to keep down the bird population, somewhere around 1936/37, another tradition loomed: Prep School! Penitentiary for young boys! A peculiar British institution where at a tender age boys and girls are dragged away from their homes and their loved ones and handed over to complete strangers to do with what they will. In my case, I was incarcerated at Woodbridge School in Suffolk, an Anglo-Catholic public school, with a prep school annex.

The one thing that this place did for me was to develop very quickly my total hatred for school. I had had a brief period at a stage school, which I loved, but in those days, a child's happiness was not considered, and it was off to be trained as an English gentleman. It was not cruelty on our parents' part, it was just, well, everybody did it. I am sure the fact that my mother worked also affected her decision, as she didn't want me to become a "latchkey child". Whatever the reason, it was wrong for me, just as it had been wrong for my father. All it did was to turn me into a rebel, and for the whole of my limited school life it was me against them, and as they had all the weapons on their side, I always lost. Maybe that is why I have always been scared of authority. They've got you by the balls and if you don't want them twisted you'd better comply. What I've learnt is if you are right, fight, but if there is any doubt lie down and eat shit.

My mother could not really afford for me to be at a boarding prep school so she scrimped, saved, and sacrificed to keep me there. One of the consequences of our financial situation was that she was never able to afford the clothing insisted upon by the school. You would be horrified to read the seemingly never-ending requirements. There were clothes for the summer term, and the winter term, clothes for the various compulsory sports, clothes for bedtime, even a travelling rug was an essential requirement, even though we did precious little travelling.

My mother's inability to comply gave the most wonderful ammunition to my personal pet hate, the school matron, the "Mrs Danvers" of Woodbridge. She was a vicious, lying sadist and if she didn't like you (and I was number one on her hate list), she made your life hell.

One of her more charming pastimes at the beginning of each term was to demonstrate to the whole dormitory the pathetic circumstances of my life. "Look," she would declare, "how many underpants white are required? Six. How many did Dark bring? Four." And on she would go down the whole list to humiliate me as much as she could.

She would frequently report me to the house master (Mr Riddell) for minor crimes I had not committed. Though minor, they still warranted a beating of six of the best, four if you were lucky. The only benefit was when you displayed your wounds to the rest of the dorm, you acquired a sort of hero status. As I was beaten more than anyone else, and held the school record of sixteen strokes over one weekend, I achieved notoriety, though I would have happily traded this for one less painful!

That wasn't too long in coming. My mother had a friend who was an "agony aunt" who had heard from an English woman living in New York that she was looking for a "pen friend". She passed this on to Wendy, and they started up a correspondence. She was a widow with one child, and anxious to come back to England, but as this was in 1938 my mother did all she could to deter her, explaining that Europe could very soon be involved in another war. However, she wasn't to be persuaded, and Bo and Wendy met mother and daughter at Southampton. Making her first (and last) visit to me at school, Wendy brought them down to Woodbridge. The mother was a funny little plump thing, but the daughter was something else with long dark hair, long legs, and at thirteen, the biggest pair of boobs you've ever seen. Now, it seems American girls matured more quickly than the English ones. Our female visitors at school were mainly middle class mothers, with no or little make-up, conservatively dressed, accompanied by daughters with braces and figures like ironing boards. It was not usual for a prep school boy to be seen out with such a well-moulded girl!

We hit it off from the beginning. She was very extrovert, and talked in a loud strong American accent. I managed to convince the two mothers to stay behind, and made sure that as many boys as possible saw me with this delicious creature. So, after touring the grounds of the prep school, I moved on with her to the senior school where the first eleven were playing a visiting team. It was a bright sunlit day, and as we rounded the boundary many an eye turned on my guest. Woodbridge was bowling and unfortunately one of the school's fielders was so intent on looking at her that he missed the simplest of catches. And that is how I became notorious for the school losing a needle match. The joke in the school was that it was the first time a match had been lost by a pair of "bouncers"!

That was the start of my friendship with Peggy. She was my childhood sweetheart, and would in time, become much more. But back to school. After her visit, things became a little easier. I don't think it had anything to do with my new found "fame". I think in the end Riddell started to twig, because I remember so well, when pleading my innocence of talking after lights out, his saying, "You are asking me to believe something that I find very hard to contemplate", and then letting me off without a beating.

Looking back in later life, I think the matron and Riddell must have been having an affair, though why this should make her hate me so much I have no idea. One thing is for certain: I have met plenty of unpleasant people in my life but no one as miserable, or so hateful as this woman. Oh how I would have loved to have met her in adulthood.

All this gave me my loathing for boarding schools, those places run for the most part by people who themselves have been institutionalised and who spend their lives in these academic prisons as part teachers, part warders. Where the inmates have no right of appeal but just have to take the punishment that is handed out. Of course there are some decent teachers, and I came across one in my public school, The Reverend Chester-Master, a thoroughly good, decent man, but he was one amongst so many. I hear things have changed a lot, and I know my nephew James, who was at Winchester, seems to have lived a completely different life.

The only good thing about the place was that we would quite openly under our bedclothes, but leaving nothing to the imagination, have a J. Arthur (or a Joddrell, a Barclays or even a Levy and Frank). We never touched each other, and didn't even take much interest in what the others were doing. It was just an accepted practice. I have to say despite all that has been said to the contrary, I never came across any homosexual practices at either my prep or public school. What I did find out was that women were just as interested in sex as men. This was when I was taken in hand (literally) by one of the local girls. It was she who introduced me to the joys of heterosexual sex, and to whom I shall be forever grateful. The trouble was finding partners, not easy when you are, like, twelve!

But apart from this I hated school. On the other hand, my brother rather liked it, but then he and I were so different. As I said earlier, he was four years older than I was and always away at school, so we would only meet at the holidays when I would give him a pretty rough time. I would tease him constantly until even he, the gentlest and patient of people, could take no more of my taunting and so would hit me. I would then fall on the floor and play dead. He would take no notice for a while. "I know you're not hurt…" or "you can't fool me this time …" he would say, then when I didn't flicker an eyelash, "John …John …are you all right?" Poor chap, he always thought he had killed me. He would bend down and shake me, calling my name until after a long time I would relent, utter a low groan and open an eye.

Didn't seem to matter how many times I did it, he would always fall for it. No wonder he liked boarding school!

Holidays were very boring. Where we lived was a concrete jungle, and, though it was very middle class, with expensive houses and tree-lined streets, there was nothing to do. Thank God, they built a cinema at Hanger Lane (now famous for its gyratory system) where I saw every film shown, but as they only changed the programme once a week, it still left the other six days. Other than this, there was nothing. I really don't know how my brother and I amused ourselves. Now and again, we would make up little shows to entertain my mother when she came home at night. We would always wait for her at Park Royal station, take the short walk back to the flat, have dinner, and then show time. My brother played the piano, and I would sing (very badly) to Peter's accompaniment, a tradition that lasted into our 70's. Whenever there is a family gathering and a piano, off we go. I have to say the voice has not improved!

There was roller-skating, where once again Park Royal station was the focal point, having an extremely smooth surface. It was as good as any rink, but not really appreciated by the passengers, or the stationmaster, known by us as Spider. I seem to have spent a good part of my life in dispute with Spider, and clearly, in the holidays he symbolized the teacher, the authority that needed to be attacked. He was a horrid little man, with a Hitler moustache, one of those people who have a little power and try to make the most of it. Like clipping tickets; he had to clip tickets, unless (of course) he was talking to a mate, or just didn't feel like it. The trouble was you never knew which mood he was in, and woe betide you if he was in a clipping mood and you didn't have it ready! This was a serious criminal act! So you can imagine how he felt about roller-skating. I feel sad now when I see signs up banning skateboarding from all the nice smooth sloping areas. Where are the kids supposed to go?

We did have one or two holidays, I seem to remember. You know, proper holidays when you went away somewhere. Once we went on a camping holiday near Skegness. What my mother had to put up with to entertain my brother and myself, with the three of us bundled into a tiny tent on some dreary piece of the English coastline. Not knowing any better, Peter and I thought it was paradise. We were once on holiday with some distant relatives, the McClareys. Bertie was a regular officer in the Royal Air Force and was a fat, pompous man. Later I found he was also a man who could laugh at himself. He used to recount the story of being in Glasgow during the war when some Black Watch squaddies passed him without saluting. "Gentleman of the Black Watch," he shouted after them, and as they turned he continued, "aren't we proud of our Royal Air Force?"

"Aye, sir," came the reply.

"So, shall we salute it, then?" And they duly saluted each other. Bertie was rather pleased with this reaction, so some days later when a party of American GI's went past without any acknowledgement, he repeated, "Gentlemen of the American army, aren't we proud of the British Royal Air Force?"

The GIs were stunned for a second until one said, "Sure, buddy, put it there," and shook Bertie warmly by the hand!

I can't recall any other holiday, and anyhow the war was not far off, so holidays were not even thought about. All the talk was whether there would be a conflict or not. At school we were put to digging trenches to be turned into air-raid shelters. Life was becoming rather exciting. I never thought about the dangers, the sadness, and the deaths, but rather what a change it would make. Anything had to be better than that dreary institution, and I secretly hoped that the whole place would be bombed, and the teachers killed !

We were staying with a friend of my mother's in Oxford when war was actually declared. Everyone expected London to be flattened by Germany's bombers. We had all seen the scenes in the newsreel of the dive-bombers attacking places like Warsaw, and that same treatment was what we all expected. Shortly after Chamberlain's declaration, the air-raid sirens went. "Wow," I thought, "action."

My mother started to shiver but our hostess said, "Do come and look." And in the garden next door we saw the neighbours running down to their air-raid shelter dressed in oil skins, tin helmets and gas masks! It was such a comical sight that we all burst out laughing, and the fears the adults had were soon dispelled. The bombs were to come later.

And come they did, but this was after a long period of inactivity. The phoney war, as it was known, lasted so long that people became cocky and life was lived without a thought for the possible actions. My mother and I had been to the West End of London to see "Night Train to Munich" when the raid started just after the film ended. We were directed to a departmental store's basement, where we spent the night sleeping on the piles of Oriental carpets. This was the first of the raids on the London docks and the East End.

Life suddenly changed, as the raids became a nightly event. The tenants of the flat where we lived were organised into fire watching teams. My mother and I, together with Peter when he was at home, were one team. Our viewing post was at the top of the block, in a room at the side of a roof garden. We had an amazing view overlooking London. It was appalling quite how beautiful the raids were. London was ablaze and the sky lit up with its bright orange glow gave an amazing background to the fireworks display put on by the German air force. At that age, I had no fear whatsoever. The only thing that scared me was a chimney on the roof that I kept on glimpsing out of the corner of my eye, for to me it just looked like a man standing there. My imagination was much more terrifying than any physical fear.

When we were not on fire duty, we stayed in our flat. We were lucky that we lived on the ground floor. My mother decided that the cupboard in the kitchen, which was situated under the back stairs of the flats, was the safest place. So as soon as the sirens went we were bundled into this small area. I was usually asleep and resented being woken up. Poor Wendy was terrified, and started shaking as soon as the sirens went off and stayed that way until the all clear sounded. The only time I felt any fear was when one night my mother suddenly announced, "I can smell gas."

We had some of the Scott family staying with us at the time, and this threw us all into panic. Everyone started searching for their gas masks, until my mother suddenly realised that the smell was coming from the refrigerator which had sprung a gas leak.

Around this time I had another bout of hospital. Nothing dramatic, in fact it was so mundane as to be embarrassing. In-growing toenails! I had to have both my big toe nails removed. Later in life I have had to have this twice more, and the last time I just had a quick local anaesthetic and they were whipped off. But back in those days I had a general anaesthetic, and was in hospital for two weeks! I was put into the men's surgical ward and, because of the talent of their brain surgeon, the ward was full of men with tumours and other brain diseases. On the ward rounds, the surgeon and his retinue would wend their way down the various beds, listening to all the gory, serious and often terminal details of the patients. When he got to me he would mutter, "Oh, young Dark, in-growing toenails." And would hurry on. So humiliating!

On leaving hospital, I returned home, and though I was allowed to walk, I had the front of a pair of shoes cut out to accommodate the bandages on my feet. One night we had a bad incendiary bomb raid right over the top of us. My moment had come! Somehow or other I had won myself a stirrup pump. These pumps were issued by the government to the ARP people (Air-raid Precautions), and were a very simple, lightweight pump for use against small fires. So here were the fires, and here was I with my pump. How my mother let me out of the flat I don't know, but out I went to save the neighbourhood. As I walked down the street a man came out of a house, and said, "Are you the fire brigade?" What a prat he must have been. Anyone looking less like the fire brigade than a thirteen-year-old boy with a stirrup pump on his shoulder, carrying a bucket of water, and shod in cut-away shoes, I can't imagine! However, at the time I believed I was Red Adair. The man took me into his house, and opened the door to the sitting room which I quickly saw was on fire. He shoved me into the room and slammed the door shut. The fire had just caught the curtains, and was travelling pretty fast, with parts of the carpet and furniture also ablaze. I had the most marvellous time, tearing down the curtains, and frantically spraying the room – a schoolboy's adventure come true.

During this time I used to see Peggy on and off. Travel was difficult, and as she lived some distance from us, and with me being away at school, our meetings were pretty infrequent. We still got on really well despite the fact that she defended her virginity with ferocity. You have to understand this was the 40s, long before female contraception, when it was a case of "nice girls didn't". So this was an ongoing battle. We had our share of petting but as soon as I got near the "Holy Grail" the barriers came down, and not the panties! God, how men of my age envy the guys of today. They have no idea how difficult it was to get one's leg over. How we used to study the art of seduction – set the room right, have the light switch at hand; put the condom (in those days called a "French letter") under the cushion. For everything to go smoothly, she should not know what was happening. Any sudden movement could break the moment, and bring her back to reality. Any distraction could pierce the fog of desire, and the brain would again take control. The whole thing had to be a study in silent and smooth action. Nothing could disturb the gradual build-up, and the tide of passion had to continue to rise without interruption. Never mind if you had cramp in your left leg, or your right arm had gone to sleep, because a change of position could put you right back where you started, and hands removed, skirts straightened and a request made to put the light back on! Oh, to have been born later in life!

For some reason, I was taken away from Woodbridge. Probably through lack of money, for as soon as war was declared Wendy's job ended, and, though she managed to get a position in some minor civil service department, it couldn't have paid much. Anyhow, I was sent to the London Polytechnic School. This was something like a present day grammar school. I don't know whether it was partly subsidised or not, but it certainly had to be a lot cheaper than a public school, especially as the school had been evacuated to Somerset, and the cost of the children's board was paid for by the government.

The idea was that I would stay with an elderly cleric and his wife, who were friends of my grandfather. They lived in Minehead, the town where the school was temporarily situated. Just before I was due to leave, a cable arrived asking how old I was. When they got the reply (I would have been about twelve or thirteen) they quickly cancelled the arrangement as they felt that they were too old to look after someone so young. This created a flurry of activity as my mother took a quick trip to Somerset to find some little nook for me to stay. She settled on some people who had a riding stable in a small, typical Somerset village near to Minehead, Dunster. The people who owned the stable were what my mother would call "the right class". I would have called them "a pain-in-the-arse". There was the "horsy" mother with her two young children. The husband was away in the services so his brother carried out the stable work. He was quite different, speaking with a broad Somerset accent and more working-class than his haughty sister-in-law. We all lived in the house except for him, who had a few rooms over the stables. Life was grim. She didn't attempt to hide her dislike of me, and as the two children were much younger than I was, I was virtually on my own.

The polytechnic shared the local school in Minehead, so they used the buildings in the morning and the refugees in the afternoon. Thus we only had half-days at school, which normally would have been paradise, but with nowhere to go and nobody to go with, life was lonely. The boys who lived in Dunster were bussed in every afternoon, and then bussed back at the end of the school day so we couldn't even indulge in the numerous activities of a seaside town. And, though Dunster was a beautiful place, it was hardly a hive of activity. Despite living on a riding stable, I was never offered a ride on a horse. Only if a horse was to be moved down to the fields or back was I allowed to handle them, and even then I was supposed only to lead them, no riding. Mind you, I used to cheat and ride them bare back, until I was caught, when a stop was put to that. The only friend I remember was a young girl who worked as a maid at one of the large houses. She can only have been about fourteen, but she was a bright little thing who was not averse to going the whole way. The trouble was finding the place to do it, so we never did manage it, though we got close. I can still remember the ecstasy of the whole thing. Once again, my relationship with this "gal" was soon discovered, so an end was put to that also.

As I said earlier, the government paid for our housing and keep, but my mother used to pay extra so that I could be looked after as well as possible. In spite of this, my hostess at some stage decided she needed my room in the house (probably couldn't stand the sight of me any longer), so moved me over to the stable block to share with her brother-in-law. This had no running water, or electricity. I washed and bathed in the house, but for reading, I had to make do with a candle. The brother-in-law was a nice old boy, and actually I got on better with him than any of the others in the family, but he was hardly the companion for a young boy.

The only bright spot was Sunday afternoon when I went to tea with the cleric and his wife who were initially going to have me in their house. They were a pair of real darlings, quite elderly, but wonderfully kind to me. In the summer, we would have tea on the terrace, where we would feed the numerous birds that flocked around, seemingly unafraid, and who now and again would eat out of your hand. After tea, we would go to church, where the cleric, though long retired, because so many priests had been called up, was pressed into conducting the occasional service. As I had to catch a bus back to Dunster I used to leave early, which always seemed to be in the middle of his sermon. "You know, "he once said to me, "when I see you walking down the nave I have a tremendous job not to shout out 'Bye, John, have a nice week'!" I think it was through them that I got away from Dunster. I think they must have told my mother what was going on and she moved me to a house in Minehead.

This was something else: a small terrace house in the back streets of Minehead, owned by a darling woman and her husband, Mr and Mrs Searl. I have no memory of him at all and I don't think I ever saw him as he went out early and came back late. Either that or his personality was so weak that it made no impression on a young boy. There were two other boys living in the house, two brothers who shared a sort of hut in the garden whilst I had a large room in the house. There was no bath in the house, so Mrs Searl would give me sixpence every week to go to the public baths, but as these were housed in the same place as the swimming pool, it was my swimming that improved whilst my hygiene deteriorated! Maybe because of this I also found it hard to make school friends! Although I like to think that it was just because we came from different backgrounds, and had little in common. The two boys in the house were nice enough but they had each other, and at school, though I wasn't bullied or even teased, I just found myself alien to them all. The masters I found not only to be as unpleasant as the others I had met in my short life, but also small-minded. They could only see so far. For instance, the reason you needed to learn languages was so that you could get a job as a Customs officer! Woodwork, metalwork, mechanical drawings were the important things. So, no stars to aim for there; no aims, no ambitions but only the bottom rungs.

Once again, help was at hand, and once again from the same place, from my elderly cleric friend. They had again written to my mother to say that the school was doing me no good, that they had connections with Wellington School in Somerset, and could arrange for me to get a bursar's scholarship. So one day Mrs "Cleric" and I travelled to the school where I was interviewed by the headmaster, Mr Price.

Wellington was a minor public school and was an attractive complex with large playing fields, swimming pool, and tennis courts. It also had the almost obligatory cloisters. The school was a combination of the new and the old, which also went for the dormitories. The new ones were very pleasant and these were the ones shown to new parents. The old were pretty disgusting and hidden away on the top floors! There was also a big hall (known as Great Hall) used for assemblies in the mornings, and for prep in the evenings by the boarders. It had an exceptionally lovely modern chapel. It is best known now for being Lord Jeffrey Archer's old school. When asked where he went to school he would always reply, "Wellington", giving the impression that he had been to the famous military college of the same name.

Life at Wellington was slightly more bearable than Woodbridge. I can't say I liked it, but it was made a lot better by my having a good friend, Peter George. His father was in the diplomatic service so, like my parents, he never visited the school. What made Peter of special interest to me was that he spent his holidays with his aunt and uncle who were on the stage. This put him in the glamour brigade for me, as I had always had an interest in what we now call "show business". When I went to visit them in the holidays, I was in seventh heaven. His aunt and uncle were originally Music Hall artists, Ernest Butcher and Muriel George, but with the demise of the Music Halls were now going "legit". Muriel George had cornered the market in "cook parts". The last time I saw Ernest Butcher was in the original London stage production of "Guys and Dolls" where he played the father of the Salvation Army girl. Peter was very bright, unlike me who held a comfortable position second from bottom of the class. I was the clown, and never could resist making a joke at the teacher's expense. Consequently I spent most of my time outside in the corridor, which together with the fact I cribbed Peter's work during prep in the evenings, probably explains why I never learnt anything.

After my fourteenth birthday, I was legally permitted to take up full-time employment, so in the Easter holidays I took myself off to Ealing Studios to get a job. The war was on so it was a lot easier than at any other period to get film work. I seemed to have arrived at the right time because they offered me a post in the camera department. I came back home on a wave of excitement. I had always wanted to be in the film industry and now I was on my way. This euphoria was not, however, shared by my mother, or by my grandfather, and an unholy row developed. In the end I threatened, "You can send me back but you can't make me work." However, despite this, they sent me back.

So back to Wellington, but not to work. My behaviour deteriorated even further, and when I was hauled up in front of Mr Price, I told him that I wanted to leave because I was going into the film business. There was not a lot he could say to that, but I think the final straw for him was when I was caught in the Art Room with a girl, and a town girl to boot. So it was decided, for the benefit of the school I am sure, that I should leave.

So I left. Walking out of the school for the last time, I looked back a. and thought, "Thank God I'll never have to pass through those portals a. longer will I have to put up with the petty discipline, the pressure of exams, the unhappiness. I'm on my way; I'm going to be a cameraman!"

Sadly, it was not to be. As soon as I got back home, I went off to Ealing only to be told that the job had gone, and there were no other vacancies. Disaster. There I was at fourteen years of age, unemployed, untalented, and certainly unwanted. My mother had a field day with all this. She had already told me, "Don't you ever blame me for leaving school. It was your decision, and your responsibility."

Well, I never have, if for no other reason than I still think it was the right decision for me at that time. I do not say I often wish that I were better educated, but I hope I have, to some extent, made up for it by reading and having worked on a newspaper. Looking back, I am so very grateful to have been allowed to take responsibility for my own life at that early age. I had always said I would never send my own children to boarding school, but at thirteen, my youngest son Daniel decided he wanted to go to boarding school. However, after two terms he rang me in tears, saying, "You've got to get me out of this horrible place." So I did immediately. Sadly, he left school at sixteen, and I feel guilty about that, although he says that, like me, he is grateful he was allowed to leave. Education is the most precious thing, but it is not for everyone. We should be pleased that it is right for the majority, whilst allowing that there are a few of us who have to let life be our tutor. I was also lucky in that I could speak well, and, though my hand-writing was awful, I had enjoyed English lessons, and could string words together, unlike so many children who leave school without having absorbed the most basic scholastic skills. I once said to Cyril Howard, the Managing director of Pinewood studios, that I had got used to the fact that the post boys could neither read nor write, but now they couldn't even talk outside of a few grunts! The pity is that so many English children just don't want to learn, and are often not helped in this matter by their parents, unlike the Asian community who are so eager and so ably supported by their parents. It won't be long before the English are doing the menial work whilst the Asians occupy the professional and managerial positions. I suppose then the English will bleat that they never had a chance and that the Asians have taken their rightful jobs.

At the time, the only unemployed person I was worried about was myself. However, help was soon at hand. We lived next door to a cameraman, Jack Whitehead, who very kindly got me an interview at Gainsborough Studios in Shepherds Bush. There were no vacancies in the camera department, but there was the possibility of a job in the sound department, so I met up with Brian Sewell, the head of that department. He was a very tall, very thin man with a long neck, which housed the most enormous Adam's apple. This completely threw me, for I was so absorbed watching this bobbing ball that I took in little of what he said. It ended by him saying that they would let me know. Weeks went by and I heard nothing, so desperate and fed up I got a job with a local builder looking after his shop. In my second week there, a letter came from B.C. Sewell offering me a job at two pounds a week as a sound loader, whatever that was, to start immediately. I was off, and this time for real. I was on my way. Such happiness.

CHAPTER 5
YOUNG & EAGER

Monday March 19, 1942, I entered through the main doorway of Gainsborough Pictures for the first time. Only departmental heads, senior technicians, producers, directors and stars were allowed through the "Executive Entrance" so from then on I entered through the workers' entrance, where I would have to "clock-in and -out".

The studios were situated in a working-class residential street, Lime Grove, Shepherd's Bush, a huge white-faced block with a flat roof, towering nearly 90 feet from the ground, opposite a state school and the public baths. It was a very uninspiring place to find a film studio. However, this didn't in any way depress my enthusiasm or excitement.

With my heart thumping I reported for duty to the Sound Supervisor, Brian Sewell, known by his staff as "Collar and Cuff" – so named because of his long gaunt neck and his conservative way of dressing. I was to find out that he was not really interested in film at all, other than from a technical aspect. He was a boffin, and not a creative person. I suspect he was brought in through the equipment supplier rather than through the normal movie channels.

The first "talkie" was "The Jazz Singer" in 1927, and even by the 40s soundmen had not yet built up their own fraternity. The original sound technicians came from various sources, often from studio electricians, or from the record industry and, as in Sewell's case, the equipment manufacturers.

My job was as loader in the sound department. Let me explain. In those days sound was "photographed" onto 35mm film, in appearance exactly the same as the film that went through the picture camera. However, it was a specially made film with very fine characteristics suitable for all of the three sound systems being used in the UK. There was Western Electric, RCA, and a British system, British Acoustic. Our studio used the latter. They all shared the same set-up, though the actual photographing of the sound onto the film differed.

When sound first came in, the sound engineer (or Recordist, or Sound Mixer) was housed in a special soundproof box. They used to tell of how in one studio that was plagued by birds, at the start of each shot the Mixer would come out of his booth, fire a pistol to scare them away, and stop the chattering during filming! By the time I joined, the booth had been discarded and replaced by headphones. On the set, the mixer was supported by the boom operator and his assistant. Microphones in those days had a very narrow field of response, and therefore were directional and had to be precisely pointed at the actor who was speaking, thus the need for two men on the boom.

The senior man controlled the overall movement, following the artists by either swinging the boom, or extending or decreasing its length by turning the operating handle. The assistant, by the use of two connecting cords, favours the microphone to the left or right to be precisely in front of the artist who is talking. In other words "on mike". From the set, the sound was passed to the recording rooms, which housed the sound camera controlled by "the sound camera operator". These cameras took one thousand foot rolls of film, which were housed in magazines. When exposed, it was handed to the "sound loader" whose job it was to take out the now exposed film, pack it up in paper, place it in a film can, and then tape it around so no light could filter in. At the end of the day, this would be taken to the laboratory for processing.

This was a drama for me as I was born with two left hands, and just about the clumsiest person ever to have lived. Overnight the laboratory would process the film and first thing the following morning, both the picture footage and the separate sound film would be returned from the processing plant to the cutting rooms where the editors would synchronise the sound with the picture. The two pieces of film, the sound and picture, would remain separate until the very end, until the movie was ready to be sent to the cinemas. The last print to be checked is the combined picture and sound, known as the married print.

My tutor was a pretty young, Jewish girl, Barbara Levy, who was leaving to get married. She was a sweet girl, but in a hurry to get out and get on with her life, so my training was pretty sketchy, and probably was the reason why she did not spot my total unsuitability for the work! My colleagues were very welcoming, very kind and very solicitous of my well-being. Not only was I fourteen, but I was small of stature and young looking for my age. There were the usual initiation wind-ups, like being sent for a bucket of sprocket holes, and to the lab for a film stretcher. They actually had one made up, an enormous heavy piece of equipment which I had to carry across the roof of the adjoining film laboratory, but apart from this kind of thing everybody in the studio could not have been nicer to me, and once again I was spoiled.

The various recording rooms were spread all around the studio, and it took me some time to find my way around the maze of corridors, stairs, lifts and stages. As it was built in the middle of a busy suburb, the studio had no back "lot", or area around the studio for shooting exteriors. In Hollywood, all the major studios had enormous areas for exterior shooting, though they were whittled down when the companies, desperate to make money, sold them off for real estate development. Crossing the stages was the best, seeing the sets being built, from tubes of scaffolding, wood, paint and plaster. The brilliant skilled tradesmen created anything the designers and directors required.

One of the first films I saw being created was "We Dive at Dawn" for which they had built the complete and exact interior of a submarine. Built on rockers so the set could be moved to give the impression of navigating underwater, I didn't realise at the time what a nightmare it was for the cameraman. He had such little space for his lights. Normally there is a rail above the set for the lamps, but here the set was completely covered, built in the same size and shape as an actual "sub". Nowadays this is not so much of a problem as the speed of film has been increased so much, but in those days, it must have been a struggle. Sensibly they had one of the best lighting cameramen on the Gainsborough payroll, Jack Cox, who was not only a first rate technician, but one of the nicest of people. He was always so good to me, took time out to explain things and always encouraged me to get ahead.

I especially remember the road sets. In those days, we rarely went out on location, so the exteriors were built in the studio. There were roads winding through the countryside, fields of grass and trees. I remember the smell of the turf, the crunch of the cork pellets used as gravel, the magic of the lights suddenly going on and the sets coming alive. I still haven't lost that sense of wonder.

Mind you, I never stood around gawping. I was so enthusiastic I flew from here to there without lingering, especially if I had to cross a stage where they were shooting. I was petrified of the assistant directors and just prayed that I would never be spotted as I sped across. The first assistant director is the one in charge of the shooting, is the controller and the disciplinarian, and is the man who gets everything ready for the director. Usually visitors see the Assistant and think he is the director, for his voice is heard above all others, his authority is obvious and his presence pre-eminent. His job actually is a lot more complicated than it seems, but more about that later. I was terrified that one of them would spy me and I would come in for a tongue-lashing. One AD (Assistant director) I was especially scared of was Dougie Pierce, a well-spoken Sergeant-Major, who stood no nonsense and was completely in control of the mass of chaos and confusion that seemed to ebb and flow around him. Little could I have thought that many years later Dougie would be my production manager.

Very soon I was on my own, darting around like an over active bumblebee. We had our busy days, when it was all go and others when there wasn't anything happening. My main base was in a certain recording room. On quiet days, I would sit listening to all the "old men" talking about what had happened on pictures they had worked on in the past. They all seemed to love Jessie Mathews, felt sorry for George Formby who at that time was one of the biggest film comics in England, but was ruled by his wife, who controlled all his money and just gave him a few shillings pocket money every day. They used to tell stories about Arthur Lucan and his dreadful wife, Kitty O'Shea. Lucan did an act as "Old Mother Riley" (he was an early Dame Edna Everage) and was quickly brought in to cheap British films. His character was a rumbustious, aggressive Irish woman and his wife Kitty played his daughter. Kitty was neither talented nor attractive, but she thought herself both. Though middle-aged, she dressed in frills and lace in a sort of Baby Jane style. But if you wanted Arthur you had to have Kitty, and not only Kitty but also her latest protégé/lover who also had to be found a part. She was a bitch, and over the years I have met many who knew them and I have never heard anyone say a nice word about her. He was a lovely man, and his only problem was, he loved her.

I couldn't get enough of these stories and I used to ply them with questions. I was so lucky because the sound camera operator in this room was a very attractive woman, Edith Kanturick, the widow of a cameraman who had been killed whilst working on a film. I suppose the studio gave her a job out of sympathy (and perhaps so they didn't have to pay her compensation?). She used to attract some of the top men in the studio, and through her, I became acquainted with many talented people. The top designers, cameramen and production managers all used to pop in and pay court. I guess they would have liked to give me sixpence to go out and play, but they were in my work place and Edith made sure they included me in their conversations. I was to learn a lot from these super people.

My only regret was that I didn't meet the actors. At that time, Gainsborough had what was in effect a repertory company. There was Margaret Lockwood, Phyllis Calvert, Jean Kent, Stewart Granger, the brooding James Mason, and the utterly delectable Patricia Roc. Frequent visitors were Johnny Mills, Eric Portman, Dulcie Gray and her husband, Michael Denison. These were the days of the Rank Charm School, which included pupils like Diana Dors and Derek Bond to name just two. I would see actors going to and from the stages, even catch a glimpse of them working, but I never stopped to watch. Somehow, I realised that this wasn't my place. I would be embarrassed to catch their eye, or even let them feel I was watching. "Clear the eyeline" is a constant cry of the 1st AD, which clears the onlookers from the actor's gaze. Even now, I try to be as inconspicuous as possible when watching a scene on the set. Of course, a number of people have to watch very carefully, but the idly curious are just another problem for the actor. So they were still mystery people to me, people to be worshipped from afar, but I was excited to be close to them, seeing them waiting on the side of the set, drinking tea and making idle chatter with their fellow artists or members of the crew. How I longed to be one of the crew, to be actually involved in the making of the film, to be a member of that select company. I always thought of it like aircrew and ground crew in the air force. I was definitely ground crew but how I longed to get my wings.

During my time as loader, the studio was making various films like "The Young Mr Pitt", starring Robert Donat and Robert Morley, and directed by Carol Reed with whom I was to work years later. There was also a musical, "I'll Be Your Sweetheart", a story about the early days of music publishing, starring Margaret Lockwood and Vic Oliver, with stunts arranged by one of Britain's boxing champions, Dave Crowley, whom I was to meet in different circumstances years later in Rome. There was also a wonderful film, "The Rake's Progress", starring Rex Harrison and his wife at that time, Lilly Palmer. Ken Annakin was directing one of his "Huggets" films, which starred, amongst others, Petula Clark. She was one of the few performers I did get to know, but not for long as her father kept a very close eye on her and I am sure he didn't think a scruffy kid from the back rooms a suitable friend for her. She was a sweet girl, and I am pleased by her continuing success and that she is still going strong in her 70's. I think back with great warmth to the days I used to hold her hand behind the set.

There always seemed to be an Arthur Askey film, and nearly always with the same cast: Evelyn Dall, Max Bacon and Anne Shelton. They were all under contract to the bandleader, Ambrose. In fact, Max Bacon was his drummer, and only later developed into a comic. Askey, of course, was a big name on the radio and in the variety theatre. They say comics fall into two categories: those who are manic-depressives and those who are never off. Askey belonged to the latter group. He was always in character, making jokes, continuously repeating his catch phrases ("I thang yow…"; "Before your very eyes") which was quite fun for the first few days, but by the end of the eighth week the crew and cast could have happily strangled him.

Anne Shelton was a sweetheart, almost literally as she came second only to Vera Lynn, who was known as "the Forces' sweetheart" during the war. I have never been able to understand why Anne should have been second. She was prettier, and a much better singer. I can only think that Vera Lynn was so ordinary that blokes away from home could relate her to their wives and girl friends. Anne used to play the halls. It was after the" Music Hall period" and known as variety, or vaudeville as the Americans called it. We would take a box at the Shepherd's Bush Empire to see her. She would always have us around after the show to have a drink and a chat. I remember meeting her mother ("call me Clem"), the typical wonderful Jewish mom. No wonder her show stopping song was always "My Yidisha Momma." (Later in the army I was amazed that this song always brought the house down, considering that the vast majority were gentiles.) Both mother and daughter were so pleasant. There was no side; they were just fun folk who were lucky that she had such a wonderful voice. Though Anne was an amazing singer, the material she had to sing in the films was unforgettably bad. I think these few lines from "King Arthur Was a Gentleman" will give you the flavour. Anne is the station announcer at Waterloo station, and she sings over the Tannoy:

"The Five Forty Choo Choo
To Waterloo Choo Choo
Choo's into Platform Sixteen
It's bringing your boy in
So get 'Ship a-hoying'
Your soldier or your Marine
There may even be a little AC two
In Air Force blue."

And so on!
Arthur's usual style of song was:
"Got a Bee in my Bonnet
And a honey on my mind …"

it would start – he had a thing about bees, having had a big success with his song *"Buzz, buzz Honey Bee/ Buzz if you like but don't sting me."* (Cole Porter eat your heart out!)

He actually made a film with us called "Bees in Paradise" about an island populated only by women. This was one of the few times that the studio went out on location. In those days it was no easy task as the equipment was so heavy and cumbersome, especially the recording department. The sound truck that housed it all was like a Pickford's pantechnicon. They went to the South coast resort of Torbay, got themselves nicely settled onto the beach and started shooting. Unfortunately, they had an unwelcome inquisitive onlooker! A German plane attracted by the mass of equipment on the beach must have thought the second front was about to start and machine-gunned them all! Luckily, no one was hurt, and the story made all the news headlines the next day.

If Arthur Askey was a big name, then Tommy Handley was even bigger. His weekly radio show ITMA (short for "It's That Man Again") was the most popular of all the radio shows, and the whole country would tune in to hear it once a week. It was regarded by the government as the biggest morale booster the country had at this very dismal time. Years later I got to know one of the main characters in the show, Jack Train, who played the drunken Colonel ("I don't mind if I do, sir!"), who told me that the BBC paid them practically nothing, something like twenty pounds a week! Even allowing for inflation this was a miserable sum for the top comedians in the country. He also told me that when they went out on tour all they could afford was the usual theatrical digs. These were pretty basic, with the loo outside. He said, "You'd have to pass through the kitchen and no matter the time of day or night, the family was always eating." Once he related, "I was having trouble flushing, kept pulling the chain, until I heard a voice outside, 'You have to surprise it!'"

I was excited when I heard that we were to make a film of the show, but even more excited by the fact that as they broadcast on Tuesdays we were going to work Sundays and have the Tuesdays off. Excited because we were going to get double time for working the Sunday!

Now all this came about because of the Unions. At that time in the studios, they were all powerful. In earlier days, companies had worked the crews at all hours with no overtime payments. If you were lucky, you might get a free supper or a shilling or two. There is no doubt that the "workers" were exploited and it is easy to see why the film Unions were formed. There were five Unions: Equity, the actors' group; the Electrical Union (ETU) which obviously covered all the electricians (usually known as "sparks"); the Association of Cine Technicians (ACT), which represented the camera, sound, production and art departments; The National Association of Theatrical and Kine Employees (NATKE) which looked after the rest: all the craft grades, plasterers, carpenters, riggers etc. as well as make-up and hair artists and anybody else they could cajole into joining. I think the fifth Union, the Film Artists Association (FAA) that represented crowd artists and stand-ins, came later.

In the 40s, during the war, the Unions were flexing their muscles, and handing power down to little dictators called "shop stewards". Traditionally the main activists in the ACT were in the sound department. I am not really sure why but possibly because they came in from other already unionised industries, or they had more spare time, or they were just more bloody-minded than the other technical people. Sound people also suffered an inferiority complex at this time, which was to last for many years. When sound first came in, they were the gods, they ruled the set. But as soon as someone worked out that you could always alter sound later, their power disappeared overnight. Anyone who has seen that wonderful film "Singin' in the Rain" knows how it's done.

At the Bush our ACT steward was a boom operator by the name of Charlie Wheeler. Charlie was a loud, vulgar Cockney troublemaker, whose every other word was fuck, but in his case pronounced "p'uck" owing to the fact that he usually spoke out of the side of his mouth. He rarely did any real work but just concentrated on Union affairs, which the studio management seemed to tolerate. I think this was in the mistaken belief that if he were not called upon to work, he would be better behaved. What happened in reality, though, was the opposite. With so much time on his hands, he was able to sniff out any possible contraventions of the Union agreement, and as these were written so loosely they could be interpreted in various ways. He was never at a loss at making trouble. Never was the saying: "The devil finds work for idle hands" more true.

The President of the Union, Anthony Asquith, a top director, and son of Lord Herbert Asquith, one time Prime Minister of Britain, frequently worked at the Bush. Mr Asquith, or Puffin to his friends, was the opposite of Charlie. He was softly spoken, well educated, and a kind, charming, talented man. When he and Charlie got together, it was like some rather poor Music Hall act. Once they were in the recording room where I was, and Charlie and he were having an argument about one of the management.

"'E's a bleedin' fiddler, that's what 'e is."

"Oh, I don't think you should say that, Charlie," Asquith remonstrated.

"What?" asked Charlie.

To which Asquith replied, "That he is a fiddler."

"A fiddler!" exploded Charlie "A fiddler? No, 'e is a double bass plucker p'uker, that's what 'e is!"

Puffin Asquith used to come to the studio in a blue boiler suit, its trouser legs much too short for his legs. I don't know whether he wore this to show his solidarity with the workers or because he felt comfortable in it. He certainly directed some wonderful films including "Pygmalion", "The Way to the Stars", and "The Importance of Being Ernest" amongst many.

Charlie spent a lot of his time in the poor studio manager's office, or in the personnel manager's room. I was all right with him as I was the bottom of the whole technical pile, and therefore to be looked after and protected against the evil management, even though I was not a member of the Union because of my age, but this was soon to change. Anyhow, on "ITMA" Charlie had negotiated the deal and very happy I was with it too. Sunday was a nice easy day with only the one unit shooting, so plenty of time to listen to all the stories about "the old days", and plenty of time too to listen to what was happening on the floor. The room was fitted with a speaker, which relayed the pick-up from the microphone on the floor. So here we had England's greatest entertainers working, rehearsing, fooling about or just chatting, for our personal and exclusive entertainment. It doesn't matter how experienced an artist or crew member is they always forget the ever-listening ear of the microphone. You would be surprised how much the sound crew know about people's personal lives.

One day on the floor, they were a boom assistant short so they sent for me to join the crew. This was certainly a big day for me, and I watched the scene closely. The boom operator was the infamous Charlie Wheeler, and after a quick "hello", he disappeared muttering something about going to the "orfice". The set was an upper class sitting room in a London penthouse. The husband enters, throws his coat on the chair by the door, and crosses to the couch where his wife is sitting, kisses her, walks over to the window and stares out. He then moves over to the cocktail cabinet and pours them a drink, comes back and joins her on the couch, all the while talking non-stop. Whilst the cameraman was lighting the set, the mixer, Sid Wiles, helped me get the cumbersome boom into position. The boom is the bane of a cameraman's life. Wafting around in front of all of his carefully placed lights, it casts its evil shadow so that he has to adapt his lighting continually to accommodate the intrusion. How the old time cameramen must have hated the introduction of sound.

Soon the lighting was over and the director started to rehearse the artists. Of course, we had not seen anything of Charlie since early morning. Messages were sent, phone calls made and eventually he was found in the personnel manager's office. Suddenly the director decided to go for a take. Make-Up and Hair rushed in to put the final touches to the actors, last minute adjustments were made to the lighting. Just as the Assistant called for the "red light", Charlie rushed in. "What's it? What's 'appening?"

I slowly explained the movements of the two actors, and Charlie took up his perch on the raised boom, with me standing below with the two mike cords. "All quiet now, stand-by and roll 'em", the Assistant called. "Speed … mark it" and the clapper board went in. "Artists test one, take one." Bang went the clapper.

"Right. Action!" the director shouted and the scene commenced. The actor came into the room, threw his coat on to the chair, crossed to the couch, kissed his wife, walked over to the window and then to the cocktail cabinet. The boom, though, went back to the couch, travelling in the opposite direction from the talking actor.

"Cut," shouted the mixer.

Bang, a thump in my back, Charlie had kicked me in the back, and as I turned he shouted at me, "You're off mike, you prick!"

Around about this time my father left his present wife and came back to live with us. Though he was in the army, he seemed to get a lot of leave. I don't think he had much of a job and I suspect that they were quite pleased to get him off camp. With both my mother and myself at work, and Peter abroad in the army, he was at home all day on his own. Alone and with no money was a recipe for disaster. He thought it a good idea to have an allotment, grow badly needed food, and give him something to do. He found a place on some waste ground very near us, my mother bought some gardening tools, and he did actually start the thing off. However, it wasn't long before it all came to a halt as he sold the tools in order to buy some beer! And so it went on. Before I was allowed to smoke at home I used to hide the cigarettes in my room, and there were no prizes for guessing who had taken them when I found them gone. Of course, neither of us could say anything. My mother would find items of her clothes gone, which he had taken to pawn. Even pieces of furniture would disappear and my mother and I would have to make visits to the pawnshop to retrieve them. It was not an easy time.

At the studio, on orders from the accounts department, Brian Sewell checked on my accounting. Disaster! I was twenty-nine thousand feet of sound film short!

Now, how this happened I have no idea, and nor did anybody else. Thank God, nobody even thought for a second that I had stolen it, presumably because being such a small industry, someone trying to flog thousands of feet of sound stock would soon be found out. I felt sure my career in films had ended. The strange thing was that everybody rushed to my defence. The consensus was that I had not been properly trained, which I am sure was not true. The fact of the matter was I was just plain incompetent.

Years later, when I was a producer at Pinewood I had the pleasure of having a drink with the lady from the accounts department who had uncovered my crime, Eve Rowe. By this time, she had retired and lived in one of the small cottages that are in the grounds of the studio. Going over it with her she talked about me then as, though, I were a different person (which of course in a way I was). "Poor little chap," she said, "it wasn't his fault."

What to do with me, though? I had so much support amongst my fellow workers, ably supported by Charlie, that they didn't dare sack me. However, it still left the question of what was to be done with me. I couldn't be demoted because there was no lower position, they used to say the studio cat was rated higher than me, so I was kicked upstairs, up to the dubbing theatre.

Well now, this was something else. Maybe it wasn't the floor, or the shooting crew, but it was involvement in the actual making of a movie and a hell of a lot more interesting than putting film into a can! Let me explain that dubbing is the completion of the sound work on a film. When a picture comes "off the floor", it goes to the editing department where the editors, in close co-operation with the director, start to put all the various pieces of film together. Any one scene may have numerous "cover" shots, and the editor initially, and the director ultimately, decides which will be used. The running order is laid out and it is quite possible that the last scene was shot first, and the first scene last. Possibly even this running order will be changed many times before the movie is completed.

When the picture is first assembled, it is known as "the rough cut" and will be run for the sound editors, and the music composer. At this stage, the sound track just has the dialogue on it; all the other sounds will be added during the dubbing. But first these sounds have to be created, so in close co-operation with the director, they map out their first thoughts and requirements. When the movie is finally assembled to the satisfaction of the directors and producers they all return to fine-tune their needs.

Let me say here that things have changed enormously over the years. Firstly, in the days of "The Studio" people were under contract to the studio and had to obey the wishes of the man in charge. This was the era of the Goldwyns, the Cohens, and the Zanucks etc. At the Bush we had Ted Black and Maurice Ostrer, and they would see the "fine cut" and insist on any changes they thought necessary.

Nowadays leading directors negotiate a clause in their contract giving them the final decision on the "final cut": a clause the studios fight to retain. That is why writing about films is so difficult because the only rule seems to be "there are no rules."

The technical side has also changed. What I have written about here was in the days of "optical sound" when the sound was photographed onto film and before the advent of revolutionary "magnetic recording". However, the system may have changed, but not the operation. For the most part, the dialogue comes from the floor shooting, though at times this has to be re-recorded afterwards, usually because of a technical fault. This especially happens from location shooting when there may be a wind blowing, planes flying overhead etc.

Some directors hate post-synching (this used to be the technical description), insisting on direct sound, some don't care, and a few actually prefer it and like to replace all the dialogue thinking that they can improve the performances in the controlled environment of a specially adapted recording stage.

In "optical" days, lip-synching was a nightmare. The dialogue to be replaced would be cut up into small pieces, both picture and sound cut to be in synch with each other. This film and track would be played in the recording room for the artist to both see and hear. Chinagraph pencil marks would be made on the picture to indicate to the actor when he should start speaking. After watching it a few times, the sound would be cut off or put through headphones to the actor, depending which system they liked best, and he would speak the line, which would be recorded. The sound editor, the sound mixer and finally the director would say when they had a "take" with which they were happy regarding quality, synchronisation with the picture, and the performance. In changing the dialogue track it isn't just the dialogue itself that has to be recreated, but also all the pertaining sounds, like footsteps, the clink of a glass, and all the sounds that were recorded at the time the scene was shot and which are naturally on the "dialogue track".

In my early days we would make all these sounds effects ourselves, and what fun that was. One of my early attempts, for which I got one of my many bollockings, was for "We Dive at Dawn". We needed some splashes to come after the explosions of the depth charges, so I found an outside walkway from the studio to the laboratory, where I placed a big tub of water at the bottom, rigged the mike up and pushed over a great pile of old iron. It worked a treat and the mixers gave it the thumbs up. It was a fine summer's day, and a certain studio executive, a very dapper little man who always wore a fresh orchid in his buttonhole that he grew in his office, was having his afternoon nap, and was rudely awakened by a rush of water through his open window! His orchids certainly got watered that day.

When I first arrived at the dubbing theatre, I was working for two guys; the head dubbing mixer, Bill Salter, and his assistant, Les Hammond. They made me very welcome, and I started out doing odd jobs like getting the commentary box ready, for the war was on and we used to do a lot of work for the Ministry of Defence and all the three services. Even I had to be cleared by security, which made me feel very important. I was to learn a lot from these films and for a time was quite an authority on naval gunnery. We also made some films for the British Medical Council; and one in particular I remember was about surgery and chest disease. I especially recall it as the surgeon wanted an extra close up and brought the lung to the studio in a biscuit tin!

We also worked on numerous short films made by the studio's documentary unit, Gaumont British Instructional (GBI). One series in particular was very popular, "The Secrets of Nature" which today would be a television series on the Discovery Channel. These films were made by a very upper class, formidable lady, Mary Field, who always reminded me of my aunt Enid. I was also to meet a few years later one of their rising directors, Lewis Gilbert.

Life in the dubbing theatre had numerous side benefits, one of them being that as it was the largest theatre in the studio, producers, directors and especially cameramen, liked to see their rushes (the previous day's work) on the big screen. So I was able to see the work of all the various pictures in production. And there is no better way of studying film technique than in watching the daily rushes. They were usually run during our lunch hour so as not to impede progress on our dubbing schedule, so I would grab a sandwich from the canteen and then belt back to the theatre to watch. When we were not busy, the executives would run the various cuts, so I was able to study the development of the film. I also used to listen in on their deliberations, their ideas, their conversations, arguments and even rows. No film school could possibly have given me better training. My nephew spent four years at university in both the US and Britain learning the film trade but I am sure six months working in a studio would have been much more beneficial. I was very, very lucky.

The other benefit was that we were responsible for recording the music, and as there was no acoustically acceptable recording stage in the studio, we used to go out, mainly to HMV at Abbey Road of Beatles' fame. The recording was very simplistic, usually three microphones, one sky high at the back, and the other two positioned depending on the piece to be recorded. Nowadays for a large piece, it is quite usual to have multiple mikes being recorded onto up to forty-eight separate tracks for mixing down later.

The musical director at the Bush was a very short cockney man, Louis Levy, who was a bundle of energy. Apart from his position at the studio, he also had a radio programme "Music From The Movies". He rarely conducted the orchestra himself, but when he did, there was a marked difference. His speech was not of the quality of his music, though.

One time we had a very distinguished composer, Hubert Bath, who was conducting his own score for a film called "Love Story" which featured his "Cornish Rhapsody". Hubert, a delightfully vague, slightly absent-minded gentleman of the old school was certainly not used to the hurly- burly of film recording when as much work had to be packed into each session as possible, and costs didn't enter his head. He was put out, to put it mildly, whilst studying his score to get a blast over the Tannoy from the musical director, "'ubert, 'ubert, what the bleedin' 'ell's going on darn there?"

I enjoyed working with the orchestras, and again learnt so much watching and listening.

Looking back, the real trouble was that Bill was not a very good music recordist. I loved him dearly but he really was not creative enough for the job. As long as he didn't overload the track, he was happy. God knows what he would have made of today's music recording studios, which are purpose-built with enormous recording desks and enough switches and knobs to terrify an astronaut. Trained specialists in music recording operate them and do nothing else. Bill was expected to do everything connected with post-production – sound, post-synch, effects dub and music.

When the film is finally cut, and the sounds tracks prepared, dubbing could commence. This consisted of bringing all the various sounds together in synch with the picture. Here again the limitations of optical sound are demonstrated. On completion, the finished combined track was sent to the lab, and could not be heard until the following day. Today, with magnetic, it can be heard immediately and any errors or changes made. In my day we would record the whole reel (up to a thousand feet) in one go, and if there was an error it all had to be stopped and started again from the beginning.

Now, about this time two things happened. Firstly, as I had reached sixteen, I was invited into the Union. When I told my mother, she nearly died! To her and the rest of the family, Unions were organs of the Communist party or the devil, which, to them was the same thing. Incidentally, she was much more concerned with this than that I had been abused by one of her best friends! When I told Charlie that I wasn't sure, I thought he would burst a blood vessel. "You ain't got no p'uckin' choice, mate. You're either p'uckin' in or you're p'uckin' out ... out the p'ucking door." So I joined. I was to laugh later when people were queuing up to get into the film business and couldn't because they weren't Union members. It was the old thing; you couldn't get a job without being a member, and you couldn't be a member without a job.

The other thing that happened was that the studio was a mixer short, so Les Hammond was promoted leaving Bill short of an assistant dubbing mixer. Bill somehow or other convinced Brian Sewell to give me a chance. You can imagine how proud I was. There I was, sixteen years of age, in a senior technician's job. Now I would be in close working relationship with the editors, the producers and directors. For the first time, the executives of the studio would have to recognise me, even call me by my name.

Sixteen, cocky and confidant, and in love with what I was doing, I was to start on the desk as assistant to the senior mixer. Amongst other films, together we dubbed "The Man in Grey", "Madonna of the Seven Moons", "A Home of One's Own", a lovely film "Waterloo Road", starring Johnny Mills, Stewart Granger and Joy Shelton. One picture I particularly remember is "The Adventures of Tartu" with Robert Donat, a gentle and courteous person with whom I spent several days whilst he was post-synching his part. He was not a well man but was such a brilliant actor, and I felt so privileged to be working with the man who was "Mr Chips". When we came to dub the picture, the American producer was astounded to find this little boy in the position of dubbing mixer. I don't think the war had affected Hollywood as much as London, and of course the only reason I was in the position was because of the war. This guy just could not get used to the fact that his movie was in the hands of one so young. Luckily, I had a natural aptitude for the job so he very quickly forgot my age, and discussed his requirements with me as he would have done with any adult.

Bill Salter was like a father to me, and taught me the job as we went along. The only trouble was that his wife used to keep him on a very short leash. She would give him so much "pocket money" every day. It was another "Formby" saga. I still cannot believe how grown men can accept such a situation. Is it really their wives, or is that actually they are mean, and this is a good excuse never to have any money? I wonder. He was always, as the Cockneys say, "on the cough", always borrowing two shillings, or half-a-crown. At the start I used to give it to him, but as I rarely saw it back I soon got wise and confessed to being penniless. He was also a pipe smoker, except when he was smoking other people's cigarettes. When we were dubbing I would sit on his right hand side, and at first I would keep my cigarettes between us. However, this was too close, as he would just help himself. Therefore I switched and kept them on my right hand side, well away from his grasp. But he would wait until I was in a particularly difficult spot, using all my fingers and thumbs on the faders, when he would lean across me and take a cigarette. Between him and my father, most of my income was going on cigarettes! Yes, he was a mean old sod, but I loved him.

My friend, Charlie Wheeler, was not too happy about my elevated position, especially as I now ranked above him. This put him in a quandary, for one of his most repeated calls was for "the rate for the job", and, though I had been given a small raise, I was getting nothing like the Union agreed wage. Every time this was brought up at a Union meeting, he managed to worm his way out of it. He didn't want the job himself, but neither did he like me being in a position above him. I do not think I should have got what was after all a man's wage, but it just shows the hypocrisy of so many Union officials. They bend the rules to suit themselves; the very thing they are always accusing the management of doing. I was to come across this many times in my career.

The war was still being waged, and life was dismal. My brother Peter was in the army. He went to Sandhurst to learn to be a tank officer but as soon as he was commissioned, he was sent to the infantry! We knew he was in Italy and we, like so many others, worried about him. Entertainment was sparse. The black-out regulations were very stringent, and people generally tried to get back home from work before the black-out, and before the night raids. The radio was our great companion, and provided news and entertainment. Winston Churchill now and again broadcast to the nation, and everything stopped whilst the nation listened to him. That wonderful stirring voice raised our morale and our hopes. We who lived through that time will never forget how this man kept us all together, restored our pride and confidence. Despite the raids, people still went to the cinema. I tried to see everything, and grew up on a diet of Judy Garland, Mickey Rooney, Red Skelton, Abbot and Costello, Bob Hope and so many others.

There were few guys of my age at the studio – they were all at school! So all my friends were much older than me. They often used to come back to my mother's flat where we would have some great parties.

My mother loved it all; at last there was some zest back in her life, for there were some good-looking men around. One of these was a tall, handsome New Zealander, a former fighter pilot who was invalided out after being shot down. He had taken his release in the UK, as he wanted to gain more experience in his profession as a film recordist. He had a great personality, and he was soon on close terms with the stars at the studio. He also took a big shine to me, and often came home where my mother soon fell under his spell.

The war was on; people would always be dropping in at home, some staying over if they had missed the last bus. Others would be on leave and passing through on their way home or on their way back. People bunked down where they could and you could wake up in the morning and find strangers sleeping on your floor. There was a small gang of us: Mickey Hobbs, the mixer from the sister studios at Islington; Gerry Synnet, who had never been in the film business before but was employed as a sound camera operator; Lloyd Coleman, an Aussie; our leader the Kiwi ex-pilot, Ralph Becker; and an ex-RAF type whose name I can't remember because we always called him "Penguin". (Pilots who, for one reason or another, were no longer allowed to fly were called "penguins" because they had lost the power of their wings.)

Becker was a man who exuded fun, and he was always the first one to suggest what we should do, he was always the centre of attention and if someone had lost, or had some money stolen, he would be the first to put his hand in his pocket to start the whip round. He was very generous but he would give me the oddest presents – a few clothes-hangers and sunglasses are two things I remember.

One day he decided it was wrong that we paid for our own cinema tickets and that we should have passes. He arranged an appointment with J. Arthur Rank, our heavenly father. I went to town with him and waited in the secretary's office whilst he was inside with "the man". He came out having procured cinema passes for the whole gang! No one else in the studio, just us. I still don't know how he wangled it.

At the studio, he continued to be more and more popular. Unfortunately, whenever Ralph did a recording job there always seemed to be some technical trouble. First of all it was put down to him using different equipment. Even after questions started to be asked, they somehow were glossed over by his strength of personality and his ready answers, or excuses. Rumours started, one of them being that he was married to a doctor, another that he had been decorated and awarded the DFC.

I was once on the roof of the studios with Ralph waiting to record a flying bomb, a frequent occurrence. We spotted one and started recording. We heard the engine cut out and watched as it glided down into the centre of London, and exploded. "Christ," shouted Ralph, "that's my flat."

I tried to point out to him that it was impossible to judge from that distance, but he wouldn't hear of it. He dragged me out of the studio, hailed a cab and we sped of to Kensington. We arrived at his block of flats at the bottom of Church Road near to the High Street, and he was right! We dashed inside his flat on the ground floor, and, though there was a lot of muck around, there didn't seem to be any life-threatening damage. When we got to his open front door, Ralph called out to his wife, informing her that I was with him. She replied, "Hold on, I'll just put something over my head."

We went into the sitting room and she was standing there with a sheet over her head! Ralph introduced us and we talked about what had happened, and how lucky they had been. We eventually left and at no time did she take the sheet off! It was quite unnerving, shaking hands with the unseeing! Even with the Klu Klux Klan you see the eyes.

Soon other questions were asked. Phyllis Calvert, one of Gainsborough's leading stars, asked to see my mother because, after Ralph had been to her house several times, she noticed things were missing. Others began to come forward, and so eventually investigations were made.

It was discovered that he had never been in the Air Force, never mind being a decorated pilot, he had never worked in Australia in the film business, and as far as could be found out had no experience of recording. What makes talented, charming men act in such a stupid way? What makes them tick? He could have done anything; he had the cheek, the impudence, the confidence to get a job in a film studio, to bluff his way onto the set, pick up the headphones and put them on his head without having the faintest idea what he was doing. With his personality and his connections he could have done anything, and I am sure would have ended up as a producer. So once having got into the studio why did he wreck it by stealing worthless articles and small amounts of money? Why?

As soon as he was found out, he disappeared. I was to hear no more about him until years later when I read of a perjury case in the newspaper, about a man who had been prosecuted for stealing a camera, but had been acquitted because he produced a receipt for the article. Some time later a legal student was studying the case and noticed that the stamp had not been issued until after the date on the receipt. Ralph was once more sent back to prison

After this excitement, things became a lot duller. Work took over and we were busy dubbing "The Wicked Lady". We did not see the director during the dubbing, and, though this was not unusual in those days, on this particular film, there was a special reason. It had not been a happy film, and the director had been found, let us say, wanting. So much so that James Mason, attired in his highwayman's outfit, in a moment of total frustration hit the director, Leslie Arliss, on the jaw. This caused quite a scandal and made headlines in all the national newspapers. The following day, in front of the whole crew, he apologised, and Mr Arliss graciously accepted. However, nothing much changed and the film continued its erratic and sad way. The management were far from happy, not so much by Mason's fisticuffs but because of what caused such a professional actor as James Mason to behave in such a (dare I use the word) cavalier way. Mr Arliss was discouraged from attending the dub.

Despite all this, "The Wicked Lady" was to be Gainsborough's biggest box-office success and is still shown today on television channels around the world. It was remade in the 80s and, despite an amazing cast, "laid a big egg". This was probably because of its director, the ill mannered, Mr Michael Winner. Just think what James Mason would have made of him!

I had a bunch of mature friends, and had discovered the joys of drink. At the wrap I would move to the pub at the end of the road, "The British Prince", and spend several hours boozing. Nobody ever queried my age, or referred to my youth. Once I was pulled up in front of the studio manager (I think this was Albert Fennel who later became one of the producers of the highly popular and acclaimed television series "The Avengers") who gave me a good telling of. "You seem to hang around the pubs of Shepherd's Bush making remarks about the studio," he complained.

To which I replied in my cockiest manner, "What I do in my spare time is no concern of yours."

He should have fired me on the spot and I'm sure the only reason he didn't was because they needed me.

I had put in a request to be transferred to the production department and been refused as there was no trained person to take over my role in the dubbing theatre. This was a big blow to me as I had now spent enough time in the theatre, and I could see I was much more suited to being an assistant director than a sound recordist. However, it did strengthen my position in the sound department, and I did get some satisfaction in knowing that I was doing a good job. In addition, my eighteenth year was beginning to dawn and that meant there was only one place I was going – the army.

The end of the war with Germany was nigh, and a call came through from the newsreel company (Gaumont British News) that they wanted to film the King's victory speech, and they wanted a features sound crew to cover it for them.

We reported to Buckingham Palace and together with the camera crew and electricians, set up in the King's study. Brian Sewell came with us, for no other reason I suspect than he wanted to be there. Thinking he had better do something, as there was no actual job for him, he started ordering us all about, which led to a great deal of confusion. We had a long established system of which he was not conversant. Through his interference something went wrong and we weren't picking up any sound. In the middle of all this the King entered. He was obviously in a very happy mood, totally at ease, and with no trace of the stutter which had hounded him all his life. There was a certain amount of panic as we were still "silent", but luckily, the King's entrance had cast a spell over Sewell, who remained stock-still and best of all, silent. We quickly found the problem, put it right, and we were ready to go.

The King took his seat before the camera, gave us a few words so we got the proper level, and we were in business. As soon as the cameras and sound began rolling, he started making the pauses to cover his stutter. I could see his legs under the desk tighten whenever he came to a tricky spot. Poor man, he had not wanted to be King, he had never dreamt he would be, and yet England could not have had a better monarch through those ghastly years. When it was finished, he graciously thanked us all and went on his way. To a happy victory lunch, I hoped, with all his family.

We were told we could also go off to eat and return later to clear up the equipment. Off we went to Soho for our victory lunch. After a boozy meal, we came out only to find that some clever shopkeeper was making and selling ice creams. We hadn't seen these for over four years, so we quickly bought large cones. We then hailed a taxi. "Side door, Buckingham Palace, please," we cried.

To which the cab driver replied, "I don't take drunks!"

It took some time to convince him that we really did want the side entrance to the palace, but he still watched us carefully as the police quickly admitted us.

We had been told that the declaration of peace would be made at mid-day, but it didn't happen. We heard that Churchill had a great lunch, with a large amount of wine and brandy, and instead of making the announcement, he went to sleep. So in the end his broadcast was not made until later on in the day.

Then began two wonderful days of celebration: two days of drink and debauchery. London was alive with happy people out to have the time of their lives after all the years of war, of worry, of deprivation and horror. Everybody was your friend. I just went along with the general wave of happiness. I remember starting at the Ritz Hotel bar and ending up two nights later in a pub in the East End. I also remember an affair with a girl from Grey's in Essex who I kept in touch with for a while. Such heady days.

Soon back to work, and very quickly, the manila envelope arrived demanding my presence at Britannia Barracks, Norwich.

CHAPTER 6
O.H.M.S.

Norwich station, and greeted by an infantry Sergeant looking and sounding just like Richard Attenborough in the film "Guns at Batasi". For the first time I began to know what it is like to be a number, a thing, an object. For after all it was the job of these guys to take us back to zero, and to eliminate our personality. To take an influx of individuals and weld them into one common "thing": a soldier, one who responds to an order without question or hesitation, one whose only pride is in being a soldier, of belonging to the regiment, to the country and to the monarch. I am not going to say much about this basic training as it has been written about non-stop.

All I would say was overall, I didn't find it too bad, and in actual fact was surprised by what we were allowed to do, rather than what we must not do. I think I expected it to be like boarding school, and when I realised that I could drink, smoke and swear I was happily surprised. It didn't seem to matter what we were doing, after a very short while there would be a break for what was known as a "spit and a draw". Cigarettes were the staple diet and you could buy so many per week from the NAAFI tax free. These were the days when even nice people smoked!

I found the NCO instructors to be strict, but very fair, almost fatherly, in complete contrast to so many movies depicting them as obscene shouting sadists. We came from all walks of life but we all seemed to get on really well. Maybe it was because we were all in the same boat, and we only had one another to help us through it all. So the army taught us our first lesson – how to depend on your mates. Mind you, I did find the table manners a bit disgusting, and when they served the jam straight on the table, rather than on a plate or dish, I thought, "Oh my God!" and actually didn't eat for the first two days, relying on some pretty foul, but slightly better food from the NAAFI. However, once training started I would have eaten a horse, and probably did!

In general, I found the officers to be a dreary lot. I guess here you got the bottom of the pile, for a posting to a basic training camp with a six-week turnover was hardly likely to attract future Montgomerys or Alexanders.

We went through all the tests to find out for what we were suitable. I took the mechanical aptitude test and created history by being the first person out of all the thousands that had been through the same exam to score zero! I was told that they usually gave you one for turning up, but I was caught in the door on the way in! It is a wonder they didn't post me to The Royal Electrical Maintenance Engineers. I had two interviews with two different officers, on different days, to assess me. A year later, when I was travelling alone and had to carry my own papers to my next command, I read them and fell about laughing, as they had written the exact opposite of each other. To one I was immature; to the other I was very mature. To one I seemed a very responsible person, to the other the opposite. It proved how impossible it must be to judge an individual whilst sitting behind a desk interviewing a queue of men at the rate of one every ten minutes.

It was decided that owing to my slight size and scrawny body I should be sent to a special physical training camp. So after two weeks I was sent to Kingston barracks near Richmond in Surrey, which was great in one way as home was just a bus ride away. That was the good news. The *bad* news was that I thought they would kill me with the training! From dawn to dusk, under the watchful glare of Army Physical Training Corps Sergeants, who looked like clones of Arnold Schwarzenegger, we were put through our paces: exercises, obstacle courses, route marches, forced marches carrying a full pack, march a mile, run a mile. Just as you thought you couldn't go on, they'd take you back into the barracks shouting: "Hold on, you can make it," and straight through and out the back to start again! The only reason I didn't lie down at the side of the road was not because they might shoot me, which would have been a relief, but because if you failed you were set back two weeks and had to go through it all again! Eight weeks later, I left Kingston and returned to Norwich a much fitter man. Now in my 70's I smile to think how much it would cost to go to such a "health clinic", and have such trainers! And there was I complaining about it all. It was tough, but it stood me in good stead when I went through basic training, battalion training, and advanced training, as I never had any trouble keeping up. I can't say I liked it, but it made a five-foot five inch wimp feel pretty good when he ended a route march carrying two extra rifles for chums who couldn't manage it.

During my time there, the first post-war election was held. The British public kicked out our great war-leader and brought in a Socialist government with a massive majority. The election results were announced on the barrack square with the whole camp on parade, and there was a massive cheer when Labour's victory was announced. When it became known that I supported the Conservatives I was regarded as some sort of freak. There was no animosity, no attacks, just surprise – rather like finding a bacon sandwich in a kosher restaurant!

My training continued, first with the Royal Fusiliers. To my horror, I had to participate in the first Lord Mayor's Show after the war. It was a complete cock-up. I think the army organisers had forgotten how to do this after having been "otherwise engaged" for the past five years. We marched with one band in front of us and another at the back, both much too close, resulting in our section marching to two different beats. Naturally, we got the blame and our promised weekend leave pass was cancelled.

I was then posted to the Royal Norfolk's, back to that rainy, windy god-forsaken East Anglian county. Now, I'm sure it is a wonderful place, but when you have marched over every inch of it, been drowned in its never ending rain, frozen in its snow, struggled through its mud, cut into slices by its saw-edged wind which blows its way, unimpeded by not even a mole hill, it doesn't make you fall in love with the place! As I marched, or ran, I used to think, "There are people who come here for a holiday!" It didn't help!

I was in a newly formed battalion, in which there were a number of NCOs recently released from Japanese prisoner-of-war camps. I remember one in particular, Sergeant Rice, nicknamed "Tupenny", a wonderful chap. He had not recovered from the hell of his imprisonment and so if we didn't perform the way we should, instead of giving us a verbal thrashing, he would cry. There was not a man amongst us that did not feel for him, and we would all pretend that nothing unusual was happening while he stood in front of us weeping.

One day I got a letter from my brother who, after going through the whole of the Italian campaign, had been posted to Kenya. Whilst going through some Army papers he discovered that an elder brother could claim a younger one and asked me if I would like to join him in Africa. I would have joined him in Siberia, anything to get out of where I was.

Meanwhile we trained to become a mobile fighting unit ready to fly off to anywhere in the world when there was an outbreak of trouble.

One day I was told the Commanding Officer wanted me. God had called! I had never even seen him, never spoken to him. I reported to his office where I had a cheerful greeting from his Sergeant-Major clerk. "What the fuckin' 'ell you bin up to, then?" he solicitously enquired.

"Sir?" I queried.

"Go to Africa, you! Why, those n------ will bloody eat you for breakfast."

I was ushered into the presence of the Commanding Officer, my Company Commander, my Platoon Sergeant and others. We had been trained not to look an officer in the face, so I marched smartly to his desk, saluted and looked at the picture on the wall above his head.

"I have been asked to advise whether you would be suitable for employment with African troops in the East African Command, and despite the excellent report I have from your Company Commander, looking at your size, your height and your weight, I don't think it would do you any good to be put in such an environment," he announced.

I didn't know whether I was supposed to make any comment, so I used the all encompassing word "Sir" which can mean anything the listener likes to make of it.

"Very well, Dark, you can go."

I saluted, did an about turn and marched out, feeling pretty pissed off.

Outside the Sergeant-Major glowered at me, probably because I had caused him a lot of paper work, and said, "Well, how did it go?"

I replied, "At least he knows my name."

"And so bloody well do I, and don't you forget it."

He wasn't the only one to know my name. It had been firmly planted in my Company Commander's brain, for, though I had met him only once, it seemed to be the only name he knew. When anything needed doing, my name always came up. He even put me up for the company boxing team. Flyweight, which was quite appropriate, as that was just about all I could fight: flies!

The Company P.T. instructor, a Corporal with the usual irritating high-pitched voice, outlined the training schedule to me. "Now, Dark," he'd squeak. "Reveille o-five-thirty hours, at o-six-hundred hours a nice little run to warm you up for the day, and at o-seven-hundred…" But I was still stuck at o-five-thirty hours.

However, God once again came to my rescue. Despite the C.O.'s unhelpful position, army custom and practice overcame his objections. I was ordered to a transit camp in Dorset, where I waited until I was told to report to a ship going to Mombassa. So I packed my kit, hopped on the usual army three-toner and off I went. No one said goodbye, no one wished me luck. So kit bag over my shoulder, up the gangplank I went and into the ship.

I was expecting a drab functional troop ship but instead was greeted by a curved, carpeted staircase, surrounded by cut mirror. Whilst taking all this in I heard: "Bloody 'ell you're the first squaddy I've seen on this ship." Turning, I saw a cheerful Cockney Private. "'Ere, give that to me," he said, taking my kit bag, "and follow me, mate. It's all Officers and Warrant Officers 'ere, and one or two Sergeants who were the lowest till you come along."

I learnt that he was part of the ship's company, that the ship was the "Dominion Monarch", and that the ship held a mixture of passengers, mainly civil servants and their families, and military personnel either returning or taking up a new posting. It was also carrying Italian prisoners-of-war who were being repatriated back to their homeland.

My sleeping quarters were not as luxurious as the entrance would have indicated, but still they weren't bad, with bunk beds instead of the usual hammocks on most troop ships. My new mate showed me over the rest of the military area, and I was surprised to see a tiled swimming pool, which he informed me the troops were allowed to use once we got into better weather.

The greatest surprise was the food. Used to the rationing in England, and army cooking, I now found myself sitting at a table with mounds of butter and white bread instead of the grey national loaf I was used to. I had the meal of my life.

Soon we were under way, and I watched the lights of England gradually disappearing. Without any sadness or homesickness, I turned my face to the future, wondering what it would hold for me. I was both excited and apprehensive at the thought that I was a lone squaddy heading into the unknown. Things had already taken a turn for the better, with no one to shout or scream at me, no one to tell me when to get up, when to go to bed. I was my own person, be it only for a short while.

The trip was amazing. I had a small job watching over the Italian P.O.W.s which was quite fun as it gave me something to do. I also used to spend a lot of time on my own at the very aft of the ship, watching the wake, and daydreaming. I had been entrusted with my own papers and was surprised and delighted to see a note from my company commander saying, "This young soldier is deserving of promotion."

As soon as the weather got better, the Italians gave impromptu concerts. You can imagine their happiness at going home, and with their talent for music these evenings were magic affairs. Opera under the stars.

As we approached Naples harbour, I could see that the whole bay was filled with Italians welcoming their boys home. Every vantage point was covered, every window was occupied with happy smiling, cheering folk. It was an amazing sight, especially when the first Italians stepped foot on their homeland, and a tremendous cheer went up. Looking back, I wish I had already known and loved the Italian people as I do now. At that time, I had never been out of England, and had hardly ever met anyone who was not English, and so like many of my race I was suspicious of them especially as only a short time ago they had been the enemy.

Once past Naples, the weather was warm and the swimming pool was opened. I wondered what I had done to be suddenly switched from the hell of an infantry battalion in the wilds of windswept Norfolk, to the delights of cruising through the Mediterranean. It was all due to my brother and I don't think I ever really thanked him for changing my life. I think he was marvellous to have "claimed" me, especially as he was commissioned and I was a rather pathetic Private. I'm not sure if I would have been brave enough to have done the same for him. I have always tended to keep my family as far away from my working life as possible.

Down we travelled through the Suez Canal, through the Red Sea and into Mombassa. From Mombassa we took the Kenya and Uganda Railways and Harbour train up to Nairobi. This climbed from sea level to 1,675 metres (5,495 feet) without ever going through a tunnel. It was a single line, so there were various double areas along the route to allow the opposite on-coming train to pass. The civilians on the train had private rooms, which were very good because they had no corridor and consequently were bigger than the usual sleeping compartment. You may well ask how you got up and down to the dining car without a corridor. Well, it was quite simple, you just got off the train when it stopped and walked down the outside, and you performed the same ritual at the end of your meal. The train attendants on the other hand climbed along the outside of the train whilst it was travelling to make up the bunks. These were comforts I wasn't to know until years later, for now it was hard wooden seats and no air-conditioning.

At the beginning of the journey, the army issued us lower military personnel with enough rations for the journey. These included a handful of dried tea, but there were no apparent means of getting the necessary hot water. The old hands knew the score though. When the train stopped, they took a billycan, or whatever utensil they could find, and rushed up to the engine where there was a tap on the side of the locomotive, which gave boiling water. However, this was the water from the boilers that fed the engine. The drivers, mostly Indians, did their best to stop their tanks being emptied. A fair amount of screaming and verbal abuse ensued, usually ending with the driver getting down to physically defend his machine. By this time, however, with luck the tea was already brewing. It was all part of a game, of course, as the amount of water taken was hardly likely to be enough to stop the train, but it gave the Indian drivers a good excuse to lay into the British troops. However, after it was over, there was always a lot of laughter from both sides.

Nairobi railway station, and my dear brother was there to welcome me. After the initial greetings, he looked at me and said, "The first thing we've got to do is get you some proper clothes." I did indeed look a mess. There I was in the ill fitting outfit supplied to me in England; large baggy shorts, floppy tropical shirt, a hot beret and regulation boots and puttees. If I had been him I would have disowned me on the spot.

The next day I was measured for a smart, properly tailored new uniform. It was typical of the army that nobody in the East African Command wore the uniform issued in England, and as soon as they arrived, like me, they were given the proper clothing and made to look like proper soldiers. I wonder whatever happened to all those Blighty outfits? What did it all cost? Didn't anyone ever query it? That is the Army, Mr Jones!

Initially I was sent to a transit camp. I knew I was in the right place as soon as I saw the large notice outside the camp's orderly room which said: "All Other Ranks must report their personal servants to the Adjutant's Office."

Next day I was sent to an office in town, where a young wild, red headed captain, Tiger Smith, interviewed me. I subsequently learnt that he was in the same mess as my brother. I was to get to know him quite well, but at the time he was the voice of authority and I treated him as I would any other officer. I entered his office, giving my best salute, and looked over his head.

"Careful, old chap, got the most bloody awful hangover, and can't take all that stamping about. Just quietly take a seat, there's a good fella."

He shuffled some papers aimlessly around his untidy desk. "I don't know about you, but I'd like a cup of tea," and shouted in what I supposed was Swahili to some unseen person outside. "Now, let's see, what would you like to do, old son?" he enquired. I was not used to being asked my opinion on anything, much less my personal choice of occupation, so was struck dumb. "Let's see," he went on, "there are several jobs going, but they are all up-country and I presume you want to be near dear old Peter." An African soldier appeared with two giant mugs of tea. "Ah, saviour," he said and took several large swallows. I tried mine but it was impossible to drink as it was boiling hot, a fact, which didn't seem to affect him at all as he proceeded to gulp his down. "Ah, that's better. Now, there is a job on the camp staff at the Guards' Company for the H.Q. at Giri Giri, not far out of town, just past Muthaga in fact. Do you fancy that, eh? Don't know what you have to do exactly, march about, I suppose, looking ominous, something like that."

I hadn't yet received my new uniform, so was sitting there, all five foot five of me, in my ill-fitting clothes behind a mug of steaming tea and looking about as ominous as the dormouse in Alice in Wonderland. However, I thought it sounded good, and being close to Nairobi was a definite plus, so I quickly agreed.

"Great, let's give it a bash. If you don't like it, come back and we'll see what we can do." Somehow I managed to down the tea, and express my thanks. He wished me the best of luck and said he was looking forward to seeing me up at the mess. He was a wonderful character and quite unlike any officer I had met. I left his office in a daze. I was being treated like an equal and even asked what I would like to do!

I had the weekend off before reporting to my new assignment on the Monday so hurriedly bought a civilian shirt and, with my new drill trousers, I looked a lot better than the pathetic creature that had arrived at Nairobi railway station. We stayed the weekend at Peter's mess, an incredible place staffed by Italian prisoners-of-war. The Italian Captain in charge had been a restaurant manager in his own country, and had managed to attract professional chefs and waiters from amongst his fellow prisoners. Consequently the food was magnificent and the place was run with the usual efficiency and fun that the Italians always bring to their restaurants and cafés. We had a wonderful weekend with Peter taking me out to the game reserves, and to Brackenhurst for tea, a lovely hotel outside Nairobi. Life was unbelievable – but reality was at hand.

Reality came in the shape of Regimental Sergeant-Major Bill Bailey of The Royal Artillery, a thickset man, with jet-black hair, sporting a Clark Gable moustache. As I stood in his outer office and listened to him tearing a strip off some poor unfortunate soldier I thought, "Well, all good things have to come to an end."

Once I was in his presence, he eyed me up and down with some apprehension. Though I was now kitted out in some sort of reasonable manner, the uniform I had been issued with still hadn't been starched or ironed, so I was far from looking my best, especially in comparison with him in his immaculate highly starched tailored uniform, complete with a polished Sam Browne. Poor man, there he was, a regular Warrant Officer, the most senior non-commissioned rank in the British army, responsible for looking after over a thousand African troops, plus God knows how many Europeans. He was probably expecting a senior Drill Sergeant to assist him in running this important camp, and what he got was me! A conscripted Private, small in stature, scruffy in dress, and unable to speak the local language.

He explained to me that the camp housed the various guard companies that serviced the Command Headquarters as well as all the various auxiliary people, like cooks, batmen and drivers, who were all Africans. It also accommodated the British Other Ranks who worked at the H.Q., mainly clerks, draughtsmen, accountants, bookkeepers, signallers, and general office workers. These were transported into the offices of the HQ close to Nairobi city each day.

The British camp staff consisted of a Major and a Lieutenant, who for some reason had their offices at the other end of the camp, than "himself", the RSM and me. He told me that we would not see much of the officers as the Major spent most of his time at the officers' mess in Muthaga, and the Lieutenant was married to a local European girl, and spent most of his time off-camp with his new wife. I got the impression that this suited him fine. In our offices we had an English-speaking African Warrant Officer as company clerk, but the person who kept the whole thing together under RSM Bailey was the African Regimental Sergeant-Major, an impressive, tall, good-looking Somali with over thirty years' service in the army. He was decorated by both the British and the Germans, having served under the latter in the First World War. I was handed over to his tender care, and he treated me with great courtesy and kindness. He spoke excellent English, and he and the office Sergeant-Major were the only two Africans on the camp with whom we were allowed to speak in English. Therefore, I had to learn the language in a hurry! Apparently he commented on my size, complaining that the replacements were getting smaller and smaller! Despite this I was immediately given my first stripe, and became a Lance Corporal.

The African soldiers were housed in barrack rooms made out of flimsy local material where they slept on boards. They kept them smart and clean, with their kit laid out in the same way as the British infantry, though, with much less equipment and in a much simpler manner. The structure of the Africans was also the same as the British with the exception that they did not have any officers. They had their own RSM, and then each company had its own Warrant Officer, then Sergeants and so on down. I had to get used to the fact that even as a Lance Corporal I ranked above the African RSM. These were still the days of the Raj, and the white man ruled.

I soon got into the swing of things, and started to pick up the language. It isn't generally known that each tribe has its own language, so a common one had to be found so that everybody could communicate with one another. That language was Swahili, of which there were two types: the one spoken at the coast known as Safi Swahili, and the one spoken up-country which was a much simpler version that could be picked up by an African peasant in a short space of time – or even a British conscript! I learnt to communicate in about two weeks, mainly because, at the beginning, one could speak it without the use of grammar. For example, the verb "to go" in the future tense was "I soon go", past tense "I finish go". However, some of the British found even *this* a bit too hard. One day going past the medical room I heard the British orderly saying to his assistant, "Safisha this (clean this), tumia maji moto (use hot water) but not too bloody moto or the fuckin' fing'll break!"

I was soon taking parades, mounting the guard and fulfilling the role of Drill Sergeant. Strutting around the camp as I had seen it in the movies, I always saw myself as playing a part, and in actual fact think this is the closest I ever got to being an actor!

I began to like the Africans more and more. They had the most enormous sense of humour, were good natured and kind. They were good soldiers too, and actually seemed to like the bullshit part of the job. Guard duty outside the camp was the favourite; in fact, it was so popular that if they were disciplined, they were taken *off* guard duty, in contrast to the British who were put *on* it. They liked parading up and down outside the camp, looking very important as they eyed the local girls. Dressed in their parade uniforms, boots shining in the sun, looking like they had just stepped out of the bandbox, they were a sight to be proud of, and they knew it.

Other things were very different too, like going out on a route march. Fifteen minutes after leaving camp, we would stop so the Askaris could take their boots off! On the way back, we would stop so they could put them back on and return to camp as smart as we had left. They also preferred to play football without boots, as their feet were as hard as any boot that could be produced, and anyhow found any type of footwear uncomfortable.

As time went on my relationship with the RSM Bailey got closer and I began to discover what a remarkable man he was. He ran a tight ship and insisted on total discipline, but he cared about the people in his charge. He got on well with the

African troops and especially with their NCOs and Warrant Officers. He had a great sense of humour and, though I was still pretty scared of him, we did have a lot of laughs.

Our Commanding Officer left and our Lieutenant Tremaine was made up to Captain, and became our Commanding Officer. This was good news, as we got on really well and we had something in common as well. The movies!

Before the war he had been manager of the Tussaud's Cinema, in Marylebone Road. He was a total movie buff and was also the film critic on the local radio station. He and I used to spend hours talking about films. In fact, that's just about all we did talk about. He was happy to leave the running of the camp to Bill so he could spend most of his time at home, or chatting to me. When his demob number came up, he took local release. His cinema, next door to the famous wax works museum, had been bombed during the Blitz and never replaced, but I think the main reason he stayed was that his wife did not like the thought of cold, still rationed, servant-less England, and I suppose who could blame her?

No such fears worried my brother when his time was up, and he returned to the UK and to civilian life. This coincided with my being made up to Sergeant, which was lucky as until then I had spent most weekends with Peter, and with his absence, my life could have become pretty dreary. As it was, my membership of the Sergeants' mess, and the friends I made there was to occupy all of my spare time.

I do not know who was the most excited about my being made Sergeant, Bill or me (now I was one of the elite I was allowed – off-duty, mind you – to call him Bill). As soon as I got the news, Bill had the stripes all ready, had a tailor standing by, and in a few moments I became a full Sergeant with the stripes on my arm to prove it. It was a proud moment, and, though I was the only one in my family not to have been commissioned, I am very proud to have held such a rank. The other thing that made me proud was my friendship with Bill. He was the best friend a man could have, and I think about him often, and pray that his life turned out well.

Bill took me straight to the mess, to celebrate the occasion. It was a night to remember, not only for my promotion, but also for the start of my drinking days. The mess was the focal point of our social lives; and most nights there was a party. Other camps would come over and we would entertain them, and then we would go to theirs. We were especially friendly with the Military Police (a very sensible precaution!) and I think some of the most drunken nights were in their company. Overall, they were a lovely bunch of guys, and quite unlike my previous opinion of them. Of course, they had their assholes amongst them and I remember one who gave me a ticket for some minor traffic offence whilst I was parked outside their mess. That was soon put right!

About this time Giri Giri was being closed down and we were moving to the new Command Headquarters in Nairobi. Apart from all the offices, there was to be a Senior Officers' mess, a Junior Officers' mess, and a Sergeants' mess. This was not a popular move, as we had got used to being on our own. At Giri Giri there was no Officers' mess and after about four in the afternoon we had the place to ourselves. The good thing was that a lot of the accommodation was new, and of a much better standard than the old. Our mess was completely new and we had a lot of say in fitting it out, with Bill and me having a free hand in its construction.

Before this, I had worked out that it was good to be in charge of things which could add to one's comfort. I engineered myself to be O/C of the Personal Servants Company and also the accommodation for all British ranks. Consequently I had the best two batmen in the command, and the best room. I did a deal with the Transport Officer, got him some nice accommodation and a wonderful batman, and in return he gave me the use of a staff car with a driver. One day in my official capacity as Camp Sergeant, I came across some nice bedroom furniture, which had been off-loaded into a large storeroom. It did not take long to get a few chaps to help me get it fitted into my bed-sitting room. The place was now complete, and I was happy. The African RSM would come to my room in the early morning and check what parades I would take that day, and invariably not having got to bed till the early hours, I would ask him if he would look after that problem, and go back to sleep.

One morning I was rudely awakened by an irate Captain Quartermaster. "Dark," he shouted, "I've been looking for you everywhere. What the hell are you doing in bed at eleven o'clock?"

Oh my God, I thought, it must be the new one out from England, not used to our little ways. "Late guard duty, sir," I replied sitting up in bed. If he had checked, he would have found the only guard duty I had done was propping up the mess bar.

He gazed around the room at the furniture. "What the bloody hell is this furniture doing here? We've been looking everywhere for it, it's for Flag House. For the General's fucking bedroom," he screamed. Then, pulling himself together, "Where did you get it?" he demanded.

"It was here when I came, sir."

"Well, you can just bloody well get it out," he insisted.

"Don't think it's that easy, sir. It's all been fitted in, and I think they had to cut bits of it to get it all in."

"Cut bits of it! That's best mahogany!" Rubbing his hands over the polished surface, he seemed on the verge of tears. Then almost to himself, "We had to write it off. Lost in transit. There was a hell of a fuss about it."

"Oh well, that's all right, then," I said.

"No, it's not all fucking right. I'm going to look into this, and you haven't heard the last of it." – But I had!

In the same way, we got our new cooker in the mess kitchen, and the large refrigerator in the bar. Both destined for the Senior Officers' mess but somehow in the confusion of the move were diverted to the Sergeants' mess. The thing about the army is that nobody ever seems to know where anything goes. Millions get lost every year and nobody seems to have a clue where they have gone. Months, if not years, after I left the army, I got a letter asking me to return the two rifles I still had in my possession. As I hadn't seen a rifle since I first left the UK at the start of my African tour, I had no idea what they were talking about. I ignored the letter and never heard another word.

Another example: I once decided to teach myself to drive so whilst out mounting the guard I took over the driving. I made the classic mistake of the learner, and put my foot on the accelerator instead of the brake, driving the three-toner right up a tree. In damaging His Majesty's property, I was not only driving without a licence, without permission, but also driving on duty. It was with shaking boots that I reported this to the Transport Officer. "Oh, don't worry about that, old boy, we'll write it off. It was due for scrapping anyhow, so we'll just bring the date forward a bit." And that was the end of that.

One of our friends, a handsome Sergeant-Major, used to take a convoy up to Addis Ababa every so many weeks. This convoy was heavily provisioned in case of any breakdowns on the journey. It was not very long before this young Warrant Officer realised that nobody ever asked him to account for these extra provisions, so he used to sell them. One day someone shopped him and he was court-martialled. His defence was that the provisions, food, petrol, etc. had all been returned and he challenged the prosecution to submit the relevant documents to the court. Of course, they couldn't. A more guilty man never went into court, but it was an "innocent" one who came out.

Shortly after changing camps, the Mess Sergeant was demobbed, and I was asked to take over his job. I suppose they thought that, as I spent so much time in it anyhow, I might as well run it! It had many perks, one being that as there was no boss, you could be anywhere at any time. There were financial advantages too. In addition, I was rather keen on the catering business, especially after seeing what the Italians had done in my brother's mess, so I accepted.

Bill then took me aside and explained the real reason he wanted me to take the job. The mess was in serious debt, due to the previous Mess Sergeant fiddling the books because of problems back home. Bill had taken pity on him because if he had charged him it would have meant the guy's release being halted, a spell in the glasshouse (army prison) and a dishonourable discharge, resulting in him having a hell of a time getting work in civvy street. He asked if I thought I could do anything about reducing the debt.

Now, ours was a very busy mess with all the various command personnel as members, and I was determined to turn it into the best Sergeants' mess in the British Army. The first thing, though, was to pay off the debt. I arranged parties, functions and general entertaining so we could start paying it off. We had a Goan Sergeant-Major accountant who helped a lot, and taught me many of the wrinkles. For instance, there were always lots of empty bottles that did not have a refund value, but did have a value to an Indian trader in town, although what exactly he did with them I don't know. Every week a pile of empties was returned to him in exchange for money. Then there was the unexplained profit created by the allowance for spillage on both spirits and beer. With a big clientele, and an efficiently run bar, it all soon mounts up. To help further, at the beginning, after a certain time of night, we would serve smaller tots. As we worked on twelve tots to a bottle where the average pub works on something like twenty-six, they weren't exactly short changed. I also appeased my conscience by thinking it was better for their health! There were many such dodges, and within six months, the money was repaid and the mess put on an even keel.

I could then turn my attention to improving the standard of the mess. The first thing I did was to improve the food so I bought only the best of raw food from the town. I also managed to obtain a very good cook. We refurbished the furniture and improved the bar. I was very, very lucky to have a wonderful African bartender from Uganda, an Acholi who are the sister tribe to the Watutsi, the very tall tribe. Sadly, the Acholi and the Watutsi were almost wiped out by the Amin regime. My chap was over six foot six, and is the reason why he was called M'Refu (the tall one). He kept the bar spick and span, was always polite, honest and very hard working. On top of this, when I had drunk far too much he would pick me up and take me back to my room and to bed!

One of the results of the success of the mess was that the income kept increasing. We used to throw a free night every so often, but still the profits grew. I got used to the fact that I never bought a drink or a packet of cigarettes, and I reckoned that the benefits were legitimately mine. However, one day Tremaine said he wanted a quiet word with me. "Look, John," he said, "do me a favour and draw some of your pay. You haven't drawn any for months, and it's a bit embarrassing!"

Life could not have been better. A leisurely wake up call in the morning by my No. 1 personal servant, with a cup of tea, shower, shave, and then get dressed in a newly ironed, newly starched uniform. Over to the mess for a light breakfast, then down to town for the mess shopping at the leading grocer's, Atma Ram's. Then to Torrs, probably the best hotel in town at that time, for coffee, back to the mess to open up at mid-day, and then have a morning session with the chums, after which everyone went back to work, have a late lunch, then a siesta. There would then be a change of uniform for the evening and off to the mess for an evening of booze and fun. I never in the whole of my life drank so much, laughed so much, or had such an easy, lazy time. I had plenty of money, great friends, very little responsibility, and actually enjoyed what little work I did. I turned the mess into something special and the other camps were always trying to be invited. We served the best food, had the best-looking mess, our service was impeccable and the wine flowed regularly and freely.

Weekends were often spent in the game reserve, or at one of the outlying hotels. Though I had a staff car, the use of army transport for personal use was only to be used within a certain radius of Nairobi. However, like most things in the East African Command, nobody took much notice. On more than one occasion, I would be dining at an out-of-town restaurant way outside the permitted area, and see the provost-marshal at another table. We just didn't look at each other!

One of my other pleasures was the cinema, and there were two in the centre of town. Going to the cinema in Nairobi was like going to the opera in London. The civilians wore evening dress, every cinema had a bar where you met to have a few drinks before the show started, and again afterwards, to discuss the film you had just seen. Of course, this was a whites only audience, though there were times when the Africans were allowed to see a carefully selected film. One Empire day, after a parade through the main streets of the capital, there was a special showing for the Askaris of an old George Formby film. This was a great success, and afterwards I spoke to a few of them. They all said they thought it was marvellous, and that they had never appreciated before what a wonderful King they had – riding motorbikes through flames, crashing cars, singing and making funny jokes. No, there was none greater than Bwana Kingi George. To them "George" meant the King, and on reflection, Formby did not look dissimilar to George VI. Anyhow, Formby did wonders for the British monarchy in Kenya!

My Swahili had now greatly improved, thus allowing me to have a wonderful relationship with the African soldiers. I would often sit in the evenings with them swapping stories, tales of England, and what it was like there always fascinated them. However, there was a distance between us, a little like the divide between officers and non-commissioned ranks, no matter how friendly you were.

We were required to give lectures and organise discussion groups each week under an organisation called the Army Bureau of Current Affairs (ABCA). Pamphlets were sent from Whitehall detailing topics that we should cover, and with the new Labour government, they were often of a left wing character. Trying to explain what a Trades Union was to a group of African soldiers was bordering on the impossible, so we usually let them talk about what worried them. Once they asked why pencils had "Made In England" on them.

I replied, "Because they are."

"Oh no, they're not," they chorused. "We know where they're made." It transpired that in Naivasha, there was indeed a very small pencil factory and as far as they were concerned that was where all the pencils in the world were made! Similarly, because blood donor vans circulated the camps, a frequent question was, "Why do the white men steal our blood?"

Africa is a very superstitious place, and in those days the witch doctor was someone to be recognised and honoured, to the extent that the army allowed us a small allowance to pay for their services when conventional medical treatment failed. There were many instances when the witch doctor found the solution. The ones I saw weren't dressed in skulls, monkey skins and ostrich feathers but were rather scruffy looking, and in European clothing. One funny old boy used to sit on the side of the road selling individual cigarettes. He would have one bowl for the smokes and another for the money. Most of the time he was not there, so people would help themselves, and pay the right price. He never lost a cent. Word had it that if you didn't pay a snake would come and bite you! Scared as I was of snakes and very superstitious, I understood his success.

Africa was full of life and excitement for me. I loved the journeys into the game reserves, which had only just recently been created, and long before there were more tourists than animals! I loved the sounds at night and the African haze during the day. Above all, I loved the people and the different tribes ranging from the warrior Masai to the trader Kikuyu. They were all different and all fascinating. Some people mistakenly think their philosophy is the same as ours – or, even worse, that it is below ours: It is simply different.

War between the tribes has been going on for centuries and I don't see it ending quickly. It is often brutal, but to me a whole lot more understandable than the war between the Northern Irish tribes.

In our camp we had tribes from Kenya, Uganda, Tanganyika (now Tanzania), Sudan and Somalia. The smartest soldiers were from Northern Uganda and they formed the core of our top guard squads. Indeed most of the Ugandans were somehow a bit special, and certainly one in particular.

I don't recall where or how I met her, but she was a nurse in the operating theatre at the local African hospital. She came from Uganda and was a member of the Buganda tribe, a good-looking, proud and dignified people. The women dressed in distinctive style, with colourful long dresses stretching from just above the breasts down to the ground, and tied at the waist. Unlike most of the Kenyan tribes, they didn't wear a scarf around their hair, but held their uncovered heads high and proud. Her name was Mary, a name maybe "as plain as any name can be" as the song goes, but the name belied the person. She was very petite, slim, with strong breasts, and an adorable little face, which was always wreathed in the biggest smile in Africa. She was a heart-stopping poppet, a chattering, lively, fun-loving person. We started the most passionate, romantic and dangerous affair. I say "dangerous" because this was in the days of the Raj, the days of white supremacy. Black people were not allowed into the European hotels, bars, or restaurants; a modified form of apartheid although not as brutal. In the army, fraternisation, or any personal contact with Africans (or Indians for that matter) outside of one's duty, was not only frowned upon but was subject to military discipline, and any contravention severely punished.

However, we used to meet sometimes in the countryside, sometimes at houses of friends, but mostly in her room at the hospital, which was situated some way from the main buildings, in a block built for about twenty nurses. The whole of this compound was surrounded by barbed wire, with a main gate guarded by a hospital employee. I would leave at night dressed like a commando on a night raid, with cap comforter, blackened face, and a pair of wire cutters at my side. I would creep up to the wire, snip it back, crawl through, and be off to paradise! On the way back I would repair the fence as well as I could, and hoped that the breaks would not be noticed. This went on for many months and I got more and more frustrated with the manner in which we were forced to carry on our affair. She would calm me down and say we shouldn't waste our time together in frustration, but just enjoy each other whilst we could. Of course, it couldn't continue. The night came when I was woken up with a bright light shining down on me. Above me stood two Africans and a white man, whom I later found out was a doctor. There was a moment of dreadful silence, then the white man said, "I think you had better get dressed and get out of here."

One of the Africans found my pay book in my shirt, which he handed to the European, he wrote down my name and number. I took one fleeting glance at Mary, sitting up in bed holding the bedclothes close to her.

I was in the shit and I spent the rest of the night worrying about what would happen to us both. They would probably sack her, for it was the rule of any hospital that lovers were not permitted. As for myself, I could see me spending the rest of my life breaking stones in the military prison in Burbura!

I spoke to Bill about it the next day, and although we discussed whether we should get Tremi to try to stall things at the Provost Marshal's office, Bill was for not saying a thing and seeing what happened. Twenty-four hours went by and I heard through my contact that Mary had indeed been fired and deported back to Kampala. A further twenty-four hours passed and still no repercussions from the military authorities.

However, Mary was back!

We met outside the camp and she told me that she had been escorted out of Kenya, but when they left her at Kampala, Uganda's capital, railway station, she just crossed over and caught the train back to Nairobi. After a joyful reunion celebration, we cuddled together in the long grass and I told her how worried I was about my own situation. "Stop worrying," she said, "'cause nothing is going to happen."

"Why do you say that?" I asked.

"I'll tell you, we were very lucky because the doctor that came that night, well, he was having happy time with the nurse in the room next door, so he's not going to say anything." I couldn't believe my ears, or my luck. Someone was looking after me again.

For a while we continued meeting, until one day she told me tearfully that she had decided to go back home. "There is no future for us. I love you, John, but this is no life and one day you will leave and return to your country. I am a nurse and I can work at home with my own people."

I didn't try to dissuade her. She was right, I was just a liability to her, and, though I loved her, I knew I couldn't keep her.

She said, "There is just one thing I want, your watch. I want you to give it to me so every time I hear it ticking I can hear your voice, and every time I look at it I can see your face." I took the watch off my wrist and gave it to her. As I left, I looked back at her for the last time, silhouetted against a giant African moon, holding my watch up to her ear.

Today I look with horror at what is going on in Uganda, that poor country of very special people. I worry about what may have happened to her, for, though so many years have gone by, she still holds a very special place in my heart.

After she left, life was never quite the same. My time was nearly up and soon I would be returning to the UK. We had demob numbers, and as they got closer and closer, so the excitement increased. One day Bill came to me and said that several public and private companies were seeking to engage ex-army personnel with experience in handling African labour. These included road construction, tsetse fly and mosquito prevention, and jungle clearance for the ill-fated Socialist government's groundnut project.

Someone had the brain-wave to cultivate jungle land and grow peanuts on it. It was the joke of the colony. However, they were offering big money to supervise the labour. They had brought people out from the UK but none of them could either speak the language or knew how to deal with mass African labour. The idea was that we went "up-country" for several months, during which time our wages would be banked. There was nothing to spend money on, as the company supplied all our living expenses. We would then come back to civilisation, go off to one of the fleshpots of the world, spend all our money, and come back penniless, ready to start all over again. What a life! Nevertheless, at the time it sounded good to me.

Bill wouldn't get his demob for another six months and suggested I deferred mine so we could go together. I got Tremi to draw up the necessary papers and when they were ready, I entered his office, picked up the pen, bent down poised to sign. Then stood up and said, "I don't think so. I think I'll go back to the movies."

I often wonder what would have happened if I hadn't changed my mind at the last second. I suppose I would have been a bum, washed up in some far-off place, unknown and unloved. Who knows?

My number came up and I was due to go home on the next ship. To celebrate, I went out one afternoon with another Sergeant, a lovely Cockney guy who was a barber in civvy street, Sergeant Herbert. After drinking in the New Stanley bar until we were pissed out of our skulls, we poured ourselves out into Delamere Avenue and hailed a taxi. Unfortunately, for us, a couple of MPs were passing at the time. Up until then the lowest rank in the Military Police was Sergeant, and as we knew most of them, we didn't worry them and they didn't worry us. However, things were changing and there had been talk of a British regiment coming out. These two young, enthusiastic red-caps were different, and were Lance Corporal MPs. They pulled us up for wearing shorts after dark, a minor offence. However, we didn't like their tone, so told them to fuck off, and climbed into the cab and up to the mess. Back there the party continued until the two MPs and the Duty Officer arrived in the mess to arrest us. As I have said before, you are never charged for one thing in the army. There was always a list: In this case, drunkenness, improperly dressed, insulting behaviour, failure to stop when requested by the Military Police, and so it went on. They put us under open arrest, which meant we could not leave the camp and were confined to our rooms, though this was treated with a certain amount of leeway.

I realised that whatever happened, I was going to miss the boat – literally! The army always takes its time, and I would be under close arrest until the court-martial. Tremi gave me a right bollocking, but said he would have a word with the provost-marshal. My preparations for departure continued, even though I was still under open arrest. When the day of departure came, I was in a quandary, as I still had not heard anything. However, Bill took me to Nairobi Railway Station where the provost-marshal himself met me. "Well, Dark, I suppose we'll have to let you go." And he officially released me from arrest.

With a huge sigh, I boarded the train, a free man. The euphoria of "getting away with it" made me forget the fact that I was leaving. I heard the band playing "Auld Lang Syne", and it struck me that although I was going home, I was also leaving. It was the end of an episode in my life, an episode full of friendship, experience, and love. However, it was goodbye to Africa, to the African people, goodbye to so many friends, black and white. Above all, it was goodbye to an amazing man, a great friend, a man I would never forget, whom I never saw again, but who has remained in my thoughts over all the years. I would like to think that he watched some of the films I made. I always wanted him to sit there and see my name. He was always very proud of me for some reason, and I would have liked him to know that I didn't do too badly, even though I didn't join him on a wayward life up-country.

As I looked out of the carriage window at the passing African scenery, I thought, "I'll be back."

The journey back to England was hell.

The troop ship from Mombassa was never allowed to go to Britain, as the conditions were so bad the troops used to walk off it. However, knowing that people would put up with anything to get home, the buggers would ply it up to Egypt and back. We spent four weeks getting up to Port Said, and to give an idea of how slow this was, it took "The Dominion Monarch" only two weeks to make the whole trip from Portsmouth to Mombassa.

The troop decks were crowded and stifling hot. I was issued with a hammock, which, with my two left hands, was a disaster. I did try but either I would tie it too tight and have a sort of suspended ironing board, or too slack so ended up like a jack-knife kissing my own arse. So I quickly found a place on deck, and, though hard, it was a bloody sight less dangerous than a badly tied hammock guaranteed to collapse at any moment.

In Egypt we went by train alongside the Suez Canal, and then by ferry to an enormous transit camp, mainly staffed by German Prisoners-of-war and by a group of very unpleasant officers. The Commanding Officer was a certain Colonel Kat, famous at the beginning of the war for making his troops shout out, "Hi Di Hi" when saluting an officer! I kid you not. When returning the salute, his officers had to reply, "Ho de Ho"! This person was obviously a nutter. Whilst I was there, he had his dog on bread and water for entering the Sergeant's mess!

I was at the camp office one evening when a large parade came marching along, and I enquired of the Duty Sergeant who these troops were. I was told they were the defaulters. It seemed that if Kat saw you, he put you on a charge, so the thing was to keep out of his sight! The word would go round when he was out and about, and people would scatter in all directions. He must have thought he was running an empty camp, because he never saw anyone! Was he stupid, or what was his problem? I have to say, though, in his defence that the camp ran like clockwork. Was this because of him? Or the German P.O.W.s?

Mind you, he was preferable to the kind of British officer on the camp staff. Most of the officers I came across during my three and half years were, on the whole, pretty good types, but these were a different breed. If anyone had thought about staying in, and making the army their career, these men would soon have knocked it out of them. The sad thing about the army is that if you get a lousy officer there doesn't seem to be much that anyone can do about it, at least not anyone without a commission. They weave their evil way without any interference from above. Why? Don't their commanders see the damage they do? The worst thing about them is their rudeness, their sarcasm, knowing that a soldier could not answer back. They used their positions to vent their own sadism. I wonder what they found to do in civvy street? Prison warden?

I was stuck in this bloody awful Egyptian transit camp where I was a lone Sergeant. The camp was shipping battalions and companies *en masse*, and there didn't seem to be a space for little me. Finally, I twigged, went and saw the camp orderly clerk and slipped him a few quid. I was on the next boat "The Empire Ken", a name I shall never forget.

My feet had barely touched the deck when I heard over the ship's Tannoy: "Sergeant Dark to report to the troop ship Commander." The ship was under the control of the RAF, and I reported to an RAF officer who, much to my surprise, told me that I had been made Troop Deck Sergeant of B1 deck.

"I thought this ship had come from India", I said.

To which he replied, "It has."

So I asked, "Where is the Sergeant who did the job before?"

He rather shakily replied, "We wish we knew."

Wish we knew? I thought. Wish we knew? What the hell did that mean?

I was soon to find out.

My deck was of entirely Scottish troops – rebellious, unpleasant, raucous, foul-mouthed. I had no doubt they had had my predecessor over the side. I would have been lost dealing with any British troops, but this lot were beyond my comprehension. I could understand half they were saying, literally, as every other word was "fuck".

I left them alone as much as I could, but there were a few rules and regulations that had to be obeyed. I tried, "Look chaps…" which was immediately imitated in a Scottish attempt at an upper English accent "Oh, look chaps" and several of them would camp around "Och, mind me fuckin' handbag, chaps!"

Once they got tired of that, I tried again. "Look, we're all going back to be demobbed, so why don't we make the most it, eh? Just do what they ask. It's only for a short time and then we'll be home."

There was a bit of quiet after this, until one squaddy shouted out, "But we're nay goin' to take orders from no Sassenach."

"Aye, that's right," they chorused.

"Well, that's a problem, because I've got to give you some. That's how it works, even if I don't want to give you orders."

"Well, then fuckin' don't," they interjected,

"But the army …" I went on.

"Fuck the army."

I got nowhere, but somehow I muddled through. I was determined not to put anyone on a charge. All I needed was to be held up in the army attending a court-martial or whatever! Apart from anything else, if I had charged any of them, I would have lost what little authority I possessed, and quite possibly my life. I never ever went out on deck, so somehow I arrived in Southampton alive!

And went off to Aldershot to get demobbed.

Now there are two things the army does really well: they get you in quickly and they get you out quickly. It worked like a conveyor belt. "Hats, trilby, brown – one. Suit, grey, two-piece – one…" and so on till you were kitted out in a set of civilian clothing. Off to get your pay, which gave you money till the end of your leave, calculated on the number of days you had spent in the service, and how much overseas; a nice little sum to keep you for about a week.

Then off home. Back to the great anti-climax that all returning service men seem to suffer. From the London railway station, a taxi. Who is going to get the tube on this special day? Arrive at the flat, run across the lawn to my waiting mother. That was good. It all went downhill from then on.

I don't know what I expected, but I guess I didn't expect that everyone would go on living their normal routine. I unpacked, and gave out the presents and the food I'd brought to still rationed England, food which I had lugged up and down ship's sides, carried into far-flung desert camps, stored in tents, lugged onto railways, army trucks and God knows what. After getting a small thank you, it was put away in a cupboard, never to be mentioned again. That was that.

My mother had made friends with three men who shared a flat upstairs, and we went out that evening to the pub. At least we can have a decent pint of British beer and a laugh or two, I thought. Another mistake. I felt completely out of it. My mother had much more to say to them than to me. I didn't know what they were talking and laughing about. I was an interloper, an intruder, a stranger, not part of their lives and their activities. They talked about radio programmes I had never heard of, of friends I did not know.

God, I thought, why didn't I stay in a family I knew, and where I was known?

I don't know whether Wendy was having an affair with one of the two older men, but she sure wanted to. So, feeling like the spare prick at a wedding, I got into Britain's best bitter. Even that didn't taste the way I had dreamt it would be. God, how I missed the mess and all my friends.

Next day, down to the studio, complete in my uniform, proudly displaying my three stripes, and my East African bush hat. I received warm greetings from old friends but they were busy with their jobs. "It's nice to see you back, Johnny", and off they went to their various tasks. Bill Salter was up in the theatre with a new Assistant home from the war.

Charlie Wheeler greeted me: "Well, you're p'uckin' back, then", and went on to explain that according to government ruling they had to give me my job back. Well, they had to give me *a* job. There was no way I was going to get back as Assistant to Bill, even though he wanted me. So, I got a start date from "Collar and Cuff" and I started again as a sort of general dog's body. "Fuck," I thought, "I should have stayed in Africa."

Whilst I was away in the army, my mother had bumped into Peggy, with whom I had lost contact, and got her telephone number. So I rang her and asked her home for tea. She asked if she could bring a friend. To which I, of course agreed, but was rather put out when this friend turned out to be a rather glamorous Captain in the

Canadian Army. Peggy was a suitable partner for him, looking very glamorous and sophisticated. I thought, "Christ, I'm not going to have much of a chance here!"

Nevertheless, the next day I rang her up and made a date which turned out to be the start of our courting. She had the prettiest little flat in Victoria, was elegantly dressed and groomed and looked and sounded (having totally lost her American accent) like the successful English career woman that she was. I was a scruffy, lowly film technician. She didn't seem to care, and our relationship picked up as though we had never been out of touch. It was a happy time and we used to spend many romantic hours on the Thames at places like Maidenhead, and Thames Ditton with a rented rowboat, which most of the time was tied up under a tree. We did all the things young lovers do, the theatre, movies, concerts.

I thought we should get married, asked her, and she agreed. Wow, I thought, what a catch. We had a small and simple wedding, my Uncle Bo gave her away, and Peter my brother was my best man. We had the reception at my mother's flat and a small dinner party at a local roadhouse. My mother never stopped bitching about it, how it had come at the most inconvenient time, and that she really could not afford the two blankets she had given us as a present.

We rented a small furnished house in Hampstead Garden Suburb, a middle-class, predominately Jewish district. We had great fun playing house and drinking large quantities of gin and Merrydown cider. The combination was quite lethal, but we were young and could take it. Life got even better when some friends gave up their flat in Hampstead and said we could take over their lease. This was post-war Britain, and housing was at a premium. We were not only lucky to get the flat but we did not even pay key money, which was a payment for just taking over the rental. It was a large flat in a block over a parade of shops. Ours was over a bakery, and we soon were organised by ringing down, ordering the bread, and lowering a basket out of the window! Life was magical, but a cloud was on the horizon.

The management of the studio had changed since I left. Ted Black and Maurice Ostrer had gone and in had come Sidney Box, his wife (Muriel) and his sister, Betty, together with another producer, rumoured to have been Box's florist, Tony Darnborough. They were a motley crowd, and were not respected by the people in the studio who thought they were very unprofessional. It was not particularly successful. Sidney Box got the job on the basis of one film he had produced, "The Seventh Veil", with James Mason and Ann Todd, but now as head of the studio he was finding it hard going.

One film, "Quartet", sticks in my mind. This was four separate stories, each with a different director and different cast, and based on short stories by the master, Somerset Maugham. Someone had the idea to get him to introduce each story. The day came and the great man was met at the gate by the producers, and personally escorted through the trials of make up and wardrobe, ushered onto the hushed set, and introduced to the director and senior technicians. He was seated in front of the camera whilst the final adjustments were made to the lights, the director quietly explained that there would be no rehearsal, just a voice test to get a level, when the tea trolley arrived on the set, and the shrill voice of the young third assistant piped up, "Tea's up, Somerset!"

"Quartet" was a great success, but sadly was one amongst many flops, so their regime was short lived. There was a general meeting on stage four where Sidney Box informed us that the studio was going to close. "It's the same for me as it is for you, boys." With that he got in his car with his wife and his personal chef, and went straight to Denham studios to continue his career, which didn't last much longer. It was that nice woman, his sister, Betty Box, who became a very successful Independent producer.

So there I was, a married man, with a flat, no furniture, and no job.

Luckily, Peggy had a job as secretary to Edward Martell, an influential member of the Liberal party, who was a member of the London County Council, a wealthy and influential politician and businessman. He is probably best known as the man who insured the deposits of the Liberal prospective members of parliament. The party put up a candidate in nearly every constituency, so it cost the insurance company a packet as most of the candidates lost their deposits. The insurance companies swore that they would never cover politics again! After leaving the Liberal party, Martell started up his own party, The Anti-Nationalisation Party, which had a brief but noisy existence, then after a few years fizzled out. He is also known for setting up a fund for Winston Churchill who was going through a bad financial time after the war.

Martell was a strange man, and obviously besotted with Peggy. She never let me tell him we were married, though it did eventually leak out. When he did find out we were married, he could not have been nicer to me. He did me many good turns, and was always amazingly generous, although I think that if I had left Peggy he wouldn't have seen me again. He would do anything to keep her happy, even if it meant being helpful to me.

It was a strange relationship, which I don't understand to this day. He was obviously in love with her, but it was not sex. I am convinced they were not having an affair. Was it unrequited love? Whatever it was, I am grateful to him for all the many things he did to help us.

I hope the meeting I had with *his* wife helped him out of the shit too.

She became suspicious, and asked to meet me. I found her a charming woman, and we had a very pleasant tea together at the Ritz. What I thought would be an ordeal turned into a pleasant meeting. She asked me directly whether they were having an affair, and I explained what I thought their relationship was. She returned to her husband a much happier woman, and I never heard another word about it, and never saw her again.

So, we had Peggy's wages, and I kept myself busy decorating the flat whilst looking for work. It was hard as it wasn't just the Bush that had closed down. Complexes were shutting down all the time and fewer and fewer British films were being produced. At one point there was only one film being made, "The Little Ballerina" – the feature's debut of the young director, Lewis Gilbert.

Once a month there was a meeting for the unemployed technicians which probably were some of the biggest meetings the Union ever held. There was a lot of talk, but of course very little action. What could they do? Anyhow, they used to give us tea and a biscuit at the end, and it was a good opportunity to meet old friends.

Out of the blue the phone rang and it was from Vic Films, offering me a job on a film being made in Italy. The job was as fourth member of the sound crew. Back to the bottom again, but never mind, it was a job, it was a film and it was money.

We gathered at Northolt aerodrome, and took off in a clapped-out aircraft. It had obviously been used for carrying troops, had no inner lining, the seats were of the most basic, and the noise was alarming. I didn't care. I had never flown before so had nothing to compare it with, and I was just thrilled to be in the air and on my way to Italy.

On arrival in Rome, we were split up into various hotels, and after unpacking, we enquired where the restaurant was, only to be told that this hotel did not have a restaurant! The company had not yet given us any money so we were unable to go out and buy ourselves anything. However, after a moment's conversation, and in a typical Italian way, the problem was solved; they would take us to a nearby restaurant and tell the owner to send the bills to the hotel.

We had come from highly rationed England, and the sight that greeted us stopped us in our tracks. We just stood and looked at the piles of food arranged in the centre of the room. It was a gourmet's Aladdin's cave. What a meal! We ate our way through things we hadn't seen for years: steaming plates of spaghetti covered in rich meat sauces, strange fish we did not recognise, steaks, chops, game and fowl washed down with numerous bottles of the finest Chianti. After amazing desserts, we were served coffee and Sambucca (my introduction to my favourite liqueur).

If *we* were amazed, so were the restaurant staff. This was 1948 and they had not seen many English civilians since before the war, and certainly none who spent this kind of money, currency control being in effect at this time. They probably wondered if this was a sign that the good days were coming back. God knows what the final tab was, but nobody ever mentioned it. I wish now I had had the Beluga caviar!

The next day we waited for someone to tell us where and when to start work, but nothing happened. So after hanging around all morning, we went off again to the restaurant for another gigantic meal, returning to sleep it off and be ready for the evening bout. This went on for a couple of more days, which we spent sightseeing in between our gourmet meals. I fell in love with Rome then, and have been in love with it ever since. My only problem was that it was boiling hot, and the only suit I had must have been made out of old army blankets, as it was as thick as a rug, and I had to keep pretending I was not hot at all!

Eventually someone did turn up, but instead of telling us when we would start, he said that the Italian crew wished to throw a welcoming party for the British crew. The next night a coach picked us up and took us to a banqueting hall where we had a fantastic party. Full of food and enormous quantities of booze, we all loved each other. So much so that the next day our contact appeared again, and was assured by us all that we had had one of the best nights of our lives. He said that as the Italians had been so generous we, the British, should return the compliment and that we should throw a party in their honour that night. So off we went again, same coach, different restaurant. It was a great party, with an orchestra, and the usual mounds of food and drink. There were toasts of friendship, Viva Italia, Viva Ingletere. Mind you, the same person was paying for both parties!

The film was an Anglo-Italian co-production entitled in English "Honeymoon Deferred" and in Italian "Due Molia Soni Tropo" ("Two Wives Too Many"). The picture was to be shot in English, with a mainly English cast, which included Sally Anne Howells, Griffith Jones (an old Gainsborough stand-by) and an Irish actor, Keiron Moore. A fine actress, Lea Padovani, and numerous small part players represented the Italians. The director was Italian, who had one big disadvantage on this film; he spoke no English! The producer was Jo Janni, an Italian who had lived in England since 1939. He later produced some fine films, including "Romeo and Juliet", "Darling" and "Far From the Madding Crowd", but this was not to be one of his successes!

Two days later, we actually left Rome. I had a huge hangover, as, after getting my pay and expenses, I went out on the town, out on a spree ending up in a nightclub entertaining most of the showgirls. We journeyed to the other side of Italy to a place called Soli (the sun).

My first sight was of umbrellas. Everyone was carrying one, and very soon, we found out why. It poured, and it poured. At the hotel, I was allocated a room sharing with the chief make-up artist, John O'Gorman. We became friends on that night and remained friends until his sad death many years later. Thank God for John, who made me laugh so much. Our room was not only dismal, not only dank, but you could actually see the water running down the wall behind the bed.

The next day there was a bit of a kafuffle, and it was decided we would move down the coast to Pescarra, a seaside town on the Adriatic. This was certainly a lot better, and we were ready to start work. On the first day, we all had to get to know how we all worked, and how to give the director what he wanted. There were two production managers, one English and one Italian. The first assistant, Gus Agosti, was a bilingual Italian who lived and worked in England and was a very experienced and successful First. Under Union arrangements at that time, there had to be a double technical crew, so every man was duplicated. The director, quite rightly, insisted on his own director of photography, who insisted, again quite rightly, on his own crew. So *they* all worked, and the British camera crew spent most of their time, other than the odd Second Unit shot, sitting on their backsides.

As the picture was being shot in English, the English sound crew worked and we all got on really well with the Italians. Very quickly, I started to pick up the language, and found myself able to hold my own in the shouting and arm-waving departments.

The Italian cameraman was a delightful character, but also a temperamental martinet. Whilst he was lighting no one was allowed on the set other than his crew, his gaffer and sparks. Which was all very well but as soon as we started to rehearse there were big boom shadows everywhere. This showed up the difference between

Italian and English film making. The Italian audience had been trained not to worry about sound quality. Their cinemas were badly equipped at that time. In the South lots of people were dependent on the travelling 16 mm shows. As they imported most of their films, dubbing them into Italian very badly and, as nobody seemed to complain, the shooting crews took little interest in obtaining a clean and clear track. The cameraman was king, and the sound crew just had to pick around as best it could. The producers wanted as much direct sound as possible, thereby saving post-synching at the end, but the directors, egged on by the cameramen, couldn't understand the importance of sound when shooting. After all, they pointed out, "It can be done later." The rest of the crew followed this lead and English and American artists found it most disconcerting to hear members of the crew chatting to one another whilst a scene was being filmed.

A mainly English cast, and an Italian crew, with the exception of the sound team, was asking for trouble, but apart from a few good-natured wrangles it somehow or another jogged along.

The main problem was that the director could not communicate with his artists. They had trouble trying to understand what he was saying to them, even though Gus Agosti did his best to translate. The director would get very frustrated, which made him shriek and scream. Something not taken seriously by fellow Italians, but not appreciated by the English cast.

On top of this, the continuity girl was an English matron who obviously hated all foreigners, especially Italians, and this director in particular. She would sit all day long making snide remarks, until the Italian crew rebelled and refused to work unless she was removed.

The British camera crew was headed by Geoffrey Faithful, a cameraman used to working on really low budget 'B' films. He was a pain- in-the-arse, and led his crew in being as difficult as possible. I think the company knew these people would have little to do, only taking them in order to obtain British Quota, and so hired the cheapest they could get. They had too much spare time on their hands, and used it to make as much trouble as they could. I was embarrassed by their behaviour. Sadly, this was not the last time a British crew gave me that feeling when working abroad.

I was nonplussed on the first day to see an Italian policeman sawing a piece of wood and acting in every way like a stand-by carpenter, until I found out that he was indeed the carpenter, and was just adding a little crowd work as well. The Italians in their wisdom did not bother recruiting local crowd artists or small bit players but just used members of the crew.

We were shooting a scene in which the local police due to a misunderstanding had locked up our two stars, Sally and Keiron. It was a small room and I could not help wondering why we had come all this way and spent all this money to photograph a small set, which could have been built for a few pounds back at the studio. However, that was not my concern, and I got on with my menial job.

Soon we were ready. "Quiet … Silenzio …Azione", and in burst the Mayor, making a grand exuberant entrance, closely followed by the Priest, apologising to the couple for the terrible error of their being locked up.

The actor playing the part of the Mayor was a well-known Italian character actor, a small, rotund, and heavily moustached, grey-haired man. An amateur, a tourist guide by profession, played the part of the Priest but he had the distinct advantage over the professional actor – he could speak English.

Flinging his arms wide, "As the Mayor of Poppi," the actor started, "I make…" and fumbled for the next line.

"Cut!"

Once more someone gave him the lines. Off we went again, the Mayor always acting to the full, bursting in, hands in the air. "As the Mayor of Poppi, I make many apol….apol…" And he would start again, "As the Mayor of Poppi…." Then lapsed into Italian, "Dio mio, quale le parole? (what are the goddamn words?)"

"Cut, Cut. Stopa."

After several attempts at that, someone had the bright idea of writing his dialogue phonetically on a board at the side of the camera. We started again. "As the Mayor of Poppi-----" he then peered in the general direction of the board and took off his spectacles, for, apart from speaking no English, he was short-sighted!

The next idea was to get the tourist guide who was playing the Priest to prompt him, and time was spent shielding the Priest from the camera whilst he was giving the lines to the Mayor.

"Action!"

"As the mayor of Poppi, I make much apol- …" The priest prompted. "… apologises for…" The Mayor turned on him and gave him a blast of Italian.

"Stop. Stop," shouted the director. Then started a real Italian verbal fight, the gist of which was that the actor playing the Mayor resented being prompted by the man playing the Priest pointing out that he was not a real actor, but merely a pathetic guide.

"I," he proudly exclaimed, "I am an actor, a famous actor and have no need for some snivelling peasant telling me what to do."

The director was eager to point out that, though he may be an actor, he couldn't speak the lines. To which the actor quite rightly replied that the director didn't know the lines either.

"I am the director, not some bastard actor, and I don't *have* to know the lines." Of course, all this in full flowing, screaming Italian.

We eventually got through the day, mainly by shooting on the Mayor's back and leaving it to be dubbed by an English actor in post- production.

The next location turned out to be even more fun.

We were to shoot a flood sequence, and the site chosen was on the landside of a large dam. Arrangements had been made with the water authorities to co-operate by opening the floodgates so that the water, fully under control, would come down through the set and follow a pre-determined course. It was a multi-camera set up, as it was a one-off shot. There would be no chance of a second take, so every precaution had to be taken to see that there were no hiccups. We, the sound crew, were there just to record a guide-track (which allows the editors to have something to go on when they come to lay the various sound tracks, and to pick up the various noises for use in the ultimate dub). It was a difficult set-up down in a boulder-strewn ravine, and all the equipment had to be manhandled down from the road above.

There was a telephone link between the assistant director and the man at the dam and when all was ready and the cameras were running, the order was given to open the floodgates. Just as it was given, one of the cameras had trouble.

"Cut ... blocca l'aqua", and the dam order was duly rescinded. Off we went again.

Cameras turned. "Right, aqua," to the dam operator.

"Cut!" A cloud had appeared from nowhere.

"Stop the water."

This went on several times and long arguments developed between the director and the cameraman, with everyone getting very twitchy, including the dam operator, who was heard to ask why they didn't make up their minds.

At that the director grabbed the phone and screamed at the poor man. This must have been the final straw, for the next thing I saw was the director throwing the phone on the floor, and telling Gus "Gira" (Turn over), but before the necessary instructions could be given, we heard a rushing sound, and looking up saw a torrent of water coming down towards us.

Afterwards we found out that the man on the dam had got fed up with it all, and just opened up the gates. The water came hurtling down, completely out of control, smashing everything in its path. Luckily everybody was able to scramble up the sides or on to the large boulders. The set was smashed to smithereens and the water created its own channel.

Despite the director jumping up and down and screaming "Gira", not a camera turned. The camera crews were more interested in saving their cameras and themselves. The water stopped, the day was ruined, and a very unhappy and disconsolate director was last seen that day walking very determinedly along the rim of the dam towards the control room. I don't think he killed him, 'cause I guess we would have read about it, or would we? He did come from the South!

From Pescara we headed into the Southern mountains, to a tiny walled village perched on the top of a hill, Colli-Al-Fortuno. This place hadn't changed much over the centuries, and was quite medieval. It possessed little electricity, some piped water, and all the laundry was still done in the public area. It had a couple of shops and that's all, not even a café.

Because of the shortage of accommodation, most of the English crew were sleeping in a ward in a new hospital in a nearby village. There were about twelve of us in this one ward, but I could not have cared less, as it was clean, warm, and comfortable, quite apart from the fact that we got an extra living allowance for the "unusual conditions"! There was a small hotel also in this village where some of the Italian members stayed and some of the more senior of the British. The hotel staff had been briefed about having English guests and to give them whatever they wanted, however strange. They were told they liked tea, not coffee, they liked boiled cabbage, they didn't like garlic, and they ate fried potatoes with everything. The art director came down and in his fluent Italian proudly asked the waiter for two three-minute boiled eggs. The waiter just shrugged and reappeared a little later with two steaming boiled grapes on a plate! The words for "egg" and "grape" were very similar ("uva" and "uve").

We really started to work long hours, which was great because of the overtime. The terrain was very rugged and tiring, and we would get back at night just wanting to fall into bed, but were kept up by the camera crew to whom we had to give all the details for their overtime sheets. For, though they weren't working, they got the same hours extra as us. Mind you, I didn't envy them their inactivity, as they had nothing to do (other than bitch). There was nothing in the village, and as they themselves were very boring people, they couldn't have had much fun entertaining one another. On the other hand, we were having fun, and, though, the work was tough, we were all getting on well, except for the director and his leading British artists. I found the village fascinating, though could not believe that people could still live in such conditions. When we first arrived there was a "fair" in the main square consisting of one roundabout, and one shooting gallery, but it was a great piece of set dressing, and we shot happily away for three or four days. Then one morning we arrived to find the "fair" was already packed and being loaded onto a truck. Consternation! The "fair" was well established in the film. The man explained that he had his schedule and he was off to his next village. Then began a lot of screaming, a lot of pleading and in the end they had to buy him out of his dates, and compensate him for loss of earnings and the damage to his reputation. He had never earned so much money in his whole life, bless him.

Many people in the village made money working as crowd artists, or as cleaners or porters. There was the police (one), and the telephone operator (one), who had to be "looked after", if you know what I mean. Communications were very difficult, and once when I wanted to ring the next village, the only phone was in the shop with the operator, who timed my call with a little sand filled egg-timer! At this same shop, we used to buy amazing thick slices of home cured ham between enormous chunks of local baked bread. Fabulous. They sold more cigarettes and wine than they could believe. They loved us, and we loved them.

Peggy decided she would like to come out, and I rented a room in a newly built flat in a nearby village. This was typical post war, hurriedly built, shoebox architecture. What I did not realise at the time was that they had no running water, and everything was done with buckets. Also, that the electricity came on and off with a mind of its own. But what it did have was a wonderful warm Italian family.

I got permission to go up to Rome to collect Peggy. The production manager, Jack Hanbury, had met her when we left London, and I think he was quite taken with her, which may have helped. It was an amazing bus trip, which took forever as it wended its way up from the deep South to the Eternal City, seemingly stopping at every village en route. We arrived at a grotty suburb, and I got myself to our hotel in the centre, and thence to the airport, ready to meet her plane, which (surprise,

surprise!) was late. So I sat in the bar getting more and more happy. By the time she arrived, I was really gone, which probably explains why my Italian sounded so fluent. I took her to the restaurant we had first gone to, and she was further surprised by the way the restaurant staff greeted me.

Back in the South, we enjoyed living with the small Italian family. We became friendly with them and their friends, especially the young schoolmaster who spoke passable English, much better I am sure than my Italian. So we were sad when the time came to leave and we were off to Rome. There were emotional goodbyes, kisses and tears, promises to visit one another. In fact, our schoolmaster friend did come to Rome to see us, but it was not a success. Out of his village, he was lost, and he admitted to us that he felt like a fish out of water. We had a lovely meal together and he went home, back to where he was someone.

Rome was wonderful – such a city. You live the history books, you eat in some of the best restaurants in the world, you fall in love with the Roman girls, and you sit and drink your coffee and watch the world go by in the Via Veneto. On top of this you shop. After the austerity in London, the Roman shops were full of so many wonderful things that we were like kids in a candy store, wide-eyed and small pocketed. We did have a little money and we bought some wonderful things for our flat.

Soon it all ended, and we were bound back for England. The film was going to be finished at Walton but I was only contracted for the location. We arrived at Northolt aerodrome late at night, and the accountant was there to pay us off. So there I was out of work again. I turned to Peggy, kissed her and said, "Happy Christmas" for it was the twenty-fourth of December.

CHAPTER 7
WHAT HAVE I DONE TO DESERVE THIS?

Work got even tougher to find, and the money I had made in Italy dwindled quickly. On top of this, Peggy was pregnant so her income would be ceasing (there was no such thing as maternity benefits in those days) and things looked grim.

I started to look for work outside of films. I had various jobs; one was selling silk stockings door to door. I sold one pair – to the man in the adjoining territory, who bought a pair off me! So at least we could say we had sold something!

I sold refrigerators door-to-door in the middle of a freezing winter but became fed up with the cold and the slamming doors. I realised that I was useless as a door-to-door salesman, and found it a soul-destroying occupation, which explains why I am a sucker now for any poor sod that comes knocking on my door.

After that, I wangled a job at Barker's departmental store in Kensington where a friend already worked. At least it was warm in there. I was sent to the lace-curtain department. A mistake. As you may remember, I am not very good at maths, nor at measuring things. I thought the gods were smiling on me with my first sale, as the customer picked up a remnant, which had the sizes and the price on the label, so all I had to do was to wrap it up and take the money. But the gods must have been teasing me, for I found out that I couldn't wrap parcels either. I thought if I took a big enough piece of paper, I couldn't go wrong. I tore off an enormous sheet from the roll on the counter, and carefully laid the yard or two of net in the centre, duly wrapped it over and over, tied it together with several yards of string, and made it into a nice firm, if large, parcel. The women looked surprised but, being a well-bred English woman, did not make a fuss. I watched her stagger out of the department with this ugly looking bundle, trying to tuck it under her arm, and to my horror saw the back of the parcel slowly open, rather like a flower opening its petals, and the remnant quietly drop to the floor. I hurriedly hid.

Hiding was one of the skills my friend told me I should acquire as quickly as possible. The commission being so small, he said, it's not worth the worry, so the art is not to sell anything. (Mind you, this was before shopkeepers came up with the idea of labelling all their staff.)

The first lesson was, whenever possible, never be behind the counter. There you were trapped, but not only that, you were unable to take advantage of another trick, which was to look like a customer. If you saw a customer approaching, you should be looking at material yourself, never ever make eye contact, ignore any sort of approach like hand waving or "excuse me" or even "can you help me?". If they still approached, you should suddenly look at your watch and hurry off in the opposite direction. I discovered some people were very determined, and insisted on actually buying something. We used to have stands in the department, which showed off various materials, and I can remember being chased around one several times by a committed purchaser.

Apart from the bore of actually serving someone, I also was desperate to dodge the client who, armed with sheaves of notes, and bunches of samples, wanted to know if they had a window five foot two and a half inches by six feet seven and eighth inches, allowing for a double hem, how much it would cost if the material was ten shillings and eleven and a half pence a yard. This, remember, was before pocket calculators, and before decimalisation. The customer invariably stood over you, watching your pathetic mathematical calculations and sometimes even correcting your numbers. I used to panic until I thought up a good wheeze. I thought that if I gave a price wildly lower than what they were expecting, they would be happy, and not query the figure. That was all right as far as it went, but after the gleam of greed had left their eyes, I then had the problem of how much material to give them. So I applied the same principle and gave them much more than the reckoning or the cost.

One woman came in and wanted a piece of curtain material for her pantry window (a pantry?), and she ended up with enough material to furnish the whole house!

Another problem I had was getting the material off the roll. I am sure you have seen these guys in shops holding the roll in one hand, the end of the material in the other and bouncing the roll up in the air as they pull the material off the roll. Do I have to say more? One of the reasons I can't play tennis is that when I throw the ball up in the air to serve, I can never see where it has gone, and by the time I have located it, it is bouncing on the ground! So, seeing me trying to bounce a large and heavy roll of material so that I could unwind it was a spectacular sight. You have to bounce it just right: too high, you lose it, too low, and there isn't time to release the material. I would throw it up and when it came down give it a hard yank, which usually meant the roll ending up on the other side of the counter, and me spread-eagled across the counter in a vain attempt to catch it.

The stands were my ultimate downfall. They told me to dress the centre displays, which entailed getting out the rolls of different net and throwing them gracefully over the pillars of different heights. I had seen my colleagues do it, unravelling a length, tossing it over the stand, placing the rest of the roll on the floor and making a few adjustments. They all thought they were Cecil Beaton! I don't quite know what happened, but as I pulled a suitable length off the roll, and threw it, I moved forward, tripped on the edge of the stand, and fell into the heap of pillars. I lay there swathed in pink net and fallen display columns, looking up at the departmental buyer as he looked down at me, shaking his head sadly, and said, "I don't think, Dark, you are really cut out for the retail trade." My career as a shop assistant came to an end after ten days!

Once again, work had to be found. There was no money in the bank, no food in the larder, and worst of all, no cigarettes! Not even the odd dog-end in an ashtray.

At a Union unemployment meeting, I met a couple of chaps who told me of work at HMV's television factory at Hayes in Middlesex. The money was much more than anything else I had heard of. I hurried down, and somehow managed to talk myself into work. My job was to be a tester, a trouble-shooter and, as such, I would be at the end of the production line and would test the television sets to see they were working correctly. By now you will have got the message that I am not the most technical person in the world, nor am I proficient with my hands, so they must have been *mad* to employ me. Anyhow there I was, having my first taste of factory life.

I found the people amazingly friendly, and very hard working. I had heard the stories of British laziness but I saw none of it there. A whistle was blown mid-morning for a short break, and blown ten minutes later for the resumption of work. A hooter was blown to start work, when there would be a rush for people to clock in, as if you were more than two minutes late you were docked fifteen minutes. As this was a collective figure, once I was late I couldn't see the sense of rushing. In order to retain some sort of dignity, I would always saunter in regardless of how much it cost me. I was pulled up once by the foreman who very nicely told me it was not usual to greet everyone on the line individually with "good morning". I replied that I thought it a shame to abandon one's manners in a HMV factory.

It was the same with lunch. We were allowed one hour exactly, and I discovered that, apart from there being several canteens, there was also an executive restaurant. That is for me, I thought, and after the second day I took my lunch with the managers and senior technicians of the plant. They used to question me about what I did, but I truthfully replied that I was in television, but….., and then I would shrug, and look away. "Ah," they would say, "we understand", and I was never questioned again, as they obviously thought I was in some form of hush-hush research.

About this time my son, Gregory, was born. We lived just around the corner from the Elizabeth Garret Nursing Home in Haverstock Hill, a wonderful place that had just been brought under the control of the National Health Service and was therefore free. When the contractions started, all we did was grab the case and walk up to the hospital, much to the disbelief of the night staff who said we were the first ever to arrive on foot.

Like all fathers, I guess, having your first child is a magical moment, and at the risk of upsetting my daughters and the rest of the female population, I have to say that having a son first is an added bonus.

These were the days when fathers were not encouraged to be with the mother in the delivery room, in fact the further away the better! Actually, I have to agree with them. I do not want to be anywhere near and I am pleased to report that I have managed to escape this ordeal. It is a time for doctors, nurses and midwives, not an agitated, nervous male, dying for a cigarette, or a drink, possibly both. Who wants to see the love of his life stretched out in pain, writhing in agony, or so sedated she doesn't know whether you are there or not? I know this is all old hat, and both my sons have attended the births of their children. Well, bully for them. I like to be left with my dreams, dreams that it was the stork that came, and that the process of childbirth has absolutely no connection with sex!

So, now I had a son to look after and bring up, and I was grateful to have a job, pathetic though it was. It was a long journey to and from Hayes, and a long and tiring day at work. The novelty of factory life had long gone, so when I answered an advertisement from Underwood, Elliot and Fisher to sell adding machines, and after a short interview got the job, I was not sorry to leave. I often felt sorry for the nice people that I met there, especially when I realised that is where they would most likely spend the rest of their working lives. I also genuinely hoped that I hadn't done too much damage to HMV's television reputation!

I was now back in a business suit, and once again back in the sales world, which I really didn't like but hoped that this time it would be better. The company was a famous name in the office equipment market, and the people I worked with were a charming bunch. My Sales Manager especially was a pleasant man. He had decided to have a big recruitment drive and had acquired about twelve new salesmen. We were an odd bunch and there didn't appear to be a constant characteristic amongst us, except that we all seemed to share an over-developed sense of humour. After a brief training period learning how the machine worked, and the range of goods we had to sell, we were off.

In today's world of pocket calculators, it is hard to imagine how large and cumbersome adding machines were then. Ours worked manually or by electricity, both were clumsy and heavy. We were allocated our territories and I was given the EC1 area, that part of the City that runs along the South bank of the Thames.

At that time London was still an active port and the streets were lined with warehouses, shipping, and import and export offices. I am not too bad at selling if someone has asked me to call, but cold selling isn't my thing. One was greeted by either an austere, elderly secretary, or a snotty kid right out of school. Whoever they were, they always seemed to be able to humiliate you. The worst were the open plan offices where everybody would look you up and down whilst you were interrogated, and usually ejected by a junior member of staff. I didn't have a tough skin, so my way of coping with it was simple: I just did not to call! I spent most of my time in the law courts or on flush days in the pub with my fellow salesmen who shared my feeling. It was hardly surprising, therefore, that they decided to hand the adding machine division over to their old and experienced typewriter sales staff, and we were all given notice.

Shortly after this I bumped into an old friend, Bollu Ilnicki, a Polish musician who had been the conductor of the Anglo Polish Ballet Company. I got to know him when he spent time with us at the studio on a government grant, studying the relationship between music and film. He was a delightful, quiet, serious and cultured person, and what he ever made of Louis Levy God alone knows. Unable to find work in England in the music world, he had opened an interior decorating firm with a number of his Polish friends, and after sharing a cup of coffee and finding out that I was unemployed, he suggested that I come and work for him. His accent was not very good and he felt that an Englishman would be a help in the business. I am afraid that did not turn out to be the case!

My fellow workers were, once again, the most charming bunch of people, most of them educated and, like Bollu, unable to find work in their own professions. It was amazing that none of them seemed to be bitter, or harped on about what they had been in Poland before the war. They had taken to their new work with as much concentration and dedication as they had to their previous professions. They were marvellous painters, decorators, carpenters etc. Unfortunately, neither Bollu nor his delightful wife had a clue when it came to finances, or indeed coping with living on very little money. They both had come from wealthy families and were not used to coping with shopping, or domestic life in general. Any money that came into the firm, Bollu took as his own, irrespective of the fact that there were bills to be paid, both domestic and business. It would be off to the Savoy Grill for dinner, and another bottle of champagne! Consequently, every Friday there would be a mad panic to raise the money to pay the staff. I remember well hearing a noise outside my home, going out of the front door and looking down the stairs to see Bollu carrying a sofa on his head. I helped to get it into our sitting room, where he collapsed onto it. After catching his breath, he explained that he couldn't afford to pay me that week, so had brought me a couch! After a few weeks of this, I had to point out to him that I was having a hard time getting into the flat with all the furniture, even though I was getting thinner due to the lack of food!

I knew that life could not continue in this way, and one night I said to Peg, "Let's get out of here."

"But where would we go? "she asked.

"I think we should go to Africa, where I speak the language, and know a lot people. It's got to be better than this."

"But how could we afford to go?"

Which was a good question. We had no money other than my pathetic weekly wage, which was unreliable, to say the least. Then an idea struck me: We would sell the key to the flat. This, as I have remarked before, was at a time when housing was at a premium and, by law, property owners could not evict you from rented unfurnished property, so people "sold the keys", as it were. As we were going abroad, we had no use for our furniture so decided to sell this with the keys, which was ideal for someone starting a home. The first step, though, was to get the landlords' permission. As they were a very large property company, I had my doubts that they would agree but, much to my surprise, they did, and after several false starts we eventually got a buyer.

In the meantime I had put an advertisement in the "East African Times", and had a reply from The Muthaga Club in Nairobi, a very up-market establishment, offering me a job as assistant club secretary, and Peggy as a secretary to the club secretary, with a good salary for both of us, plus accommodation. Things looked wonderful, and I started to look into booking our passage on the ship quickly finding a Union Castle boat sailing at the right time. The only problem was that I had to put down a deposit to confirm our booking. As the money had not come through from the sale, I went to my mother to borrow it, which she turned down with the excuse that if anything went wrong in Africa she could never be blamed!

She was a dab hand at thinking up excuses not to help me. In the end, I borrowed it off my old friend, Bollu Ilnicki. I hate to think it, but I am sure the boys weren't paid that week!

The sale came through, the ship was booked, Bollu's loan repaid, and an uncle of mine who lived in the country took our darling Corgi, Michael. Everything was organised. Then the blow fell!

The Muthaga Club heard we had a child and withdrew their offer. It was too late to change anything so we said our good-byes. The night before we left, I went to have a farewell drink in our local pub, and the landlord asked me what I was going to do once I got to Kenya. I replied I had no idea. "Well you should look up my firm Ind Coope and Allsops. They are about to open a big new brewery there." Thanking him for this tip, I walked slowly down Haverstock Hill and bid farewell to London and that part of my life.

The next day we were driven through drizzling rain to Tilbury docks and the Union Castle ship that was to take us to Kenya. The first thought that passed through my mind when I saw her was of the troopship that had taken me from Mombassa to Egypt. It was a very old lady, and without any of the sleek glamour of the "Dominion Monarch". When we found our cabin, I thought there was a mistake as it was a narrow corridor with two bunks on one side, leaving just enough room to stand up. The answer to where Gregory was going to sleep was to bring in a cot, which stood in the narrow space. We pondered as to how the three of us were going to live in that minute space for a month.

The next day Peggy and I with Greg in our arms watched as we left the docks and slowly moved down the Thames and out into the open sea. We were off, back to a country I knew, but with no job and about a hundred pounds in my pocket. You had to be only twenty-three years young!

The voyage turned out to be one long one. The ship was very old, soon to be scrapped, as air transport would soon take over. These ships of the Union Castle line that had served the British Empire for decades were, like the Empire itself, coming to an end, and were no longer plying their trade of carrying the servants of the King to the furthest reaches of the British controlled areas of the world. Apparently, "Port Out, Starboard Home" gave us the word "Posh". We were one of the last voyages and whether it was this that made the journey so enjoyable, or whether it was because there was by chance a collection of fun people, I don't know. When you first get on board, you think, "Oh my God, who are these ghastly people?", but when you leave at the end you kiss, cry, and swear to be in touch very soon. Of course, you never see them again! The food helped, of course. Like on most ships, we never seemed to stop eating, and we were determined to make up for all the lost meals in England.

I have always been scared of who would be sitting at one's table on cruises. Well, we came up trumps with a family of three: mother, father and grown-up daughter.

He was a retired Colonel and type-cast, from his grey moustache, to his clipped British accent. Life had to be conducted according to tradition, and only certain things were discussed in front of strangers, or indeed friends. His wife seemed to spend most of her time trying to make sure that their daughter never by deed or word did anything to upset her husband. The daughter was also a caricature, a caricature of her role as the only child still living at home with Mummy and Daddy. She was not very attractive, and did little to help herself by making the most of the attributes she had. She had a good figure but as she wore clothes suitable for an older woman, it was not until I saw her in a bathing suit that I realised it. She wore no make-up, but that was probably because of Daddy.

Poor girl, she had probably already realised that she wouldn't find a husband, and was destined to be a spinster all her life. Nevertheless, she was also a bit of rebel and fought against her parents, trying to stop her father completely suffocating her personality. Sadly, she was losing, and we not only felt for her, but also liked her. They were very sweet people, but they inhabited another planet. Whenever the daughter opened her mouth, the mother would look in alarm, the father would cough in apprehension, but undeterred she would keep on talking.

For the most part her conversation would be on safe ground: the weather, the ship sweep, and the food. At the end of her discourse, there were sighs of relief from the aged parents, but there were times she would start talking about an actor, an actress, a play, or a radio programme. These were dangerous areas, which created lots of coughing, table tapping and eye twitching. When she broached topics like the upcoming divorce of Laurence Olivier and Vivien Leigh, there would be a sharp kick under the table. Peggy and I were excessively polite to the parents, and for that reason alone I think they decided not to ask to change to a different table. It didn't help matters when they found out that I worked in the movies. They never went to the cinema, but they did have a radio, though they had never heard of the popular light entertainment shows. God knows what they would have made of England in the new millennium!

When the weather got warmer, the crew built a swimming pool out of timber and canvas. Parties were held on the open deck and we celebrated both Christmas and the New Year on board.

Peggy and I went down below decks to wish the crew a Happy Christmas, ended not only having one of the best parties of the trip (with one of the best hangovers to prove it!) but also winning the friendship of the crew, and from then on were even more spoilt!

The ship limped along and we stopped frequently, which was fun until we got to Egypt where there was a lot of anti-British feeling so were not let ashore. I bought a fez off a bumboat and was strongly denounced by an old Colonel who accused me of contributing to the enemy! However, when Gregory, our two-year-old son, won the fancy dress competition, as King Farouk (in an outfit made from two table napkins sewn together and the fez), he apologised.

I had spent some of the time on the voyage swotting up on my Swahili, but not getting very far, even though I enlisted the help of various passengers who spoke the language fluently. Therefore it came as some surprise to me that shortly after landing at Mombassa, I found myself telling the porters where to put our luggage. It all came back.

The train journey up to Nairobi brought back memories. This time, we were in the first class compartments and able to experience the fun of getting off the train and haring up to the dining room. We settled into a hotel in Nairobi, and I contacted my old Commanding Officer "Tremi", who was employed as a warden at the local prison. He was very keen for me to join him, and gave me a tour of the whole place, including the gallows. Happily, I was saved the embarrassment of turning his offer down because the Senior Officer said I was not tall enough for the job.

I had not had any further response from my advertisement so I decided to call at the new brewery my English pub landlord had described. I had a very pleasant meeting with a Mr Taylor who had owned the only competition to the main brewery, Tuskers. During my army days, no one, but no one, ever drank his beer and it was mostly consumed by either the Asians or the Africans, who couldn't get hold of Tuskers, the main local brew of the colony. He had sold out to Allsop's who, he explained to me, had just built a brand new brewery under the guidance of a top Danish brewer. They were due to launch their new locally produced beer, Allsop's White Cap, onto the market in a few weeks' time. He explained that the actual marketing of the beer would be handled through a major importer, Smith Mackenzies, and he there and then made an appointment for me to see its Managing director. I can't remember his name, but he was a tall grey-haired man with piercing eyes and was the type of executive who loves to intimidate you. Later his secretary told me how much she hated him for he was a bully. I had experienced some tough Sergeant-Majors in my time, so he didn't worry me, and when he offered me the job, I even got to like him. The job was to market this new locally brewed beer for the first time in Kenya, Tanganyika (now Tanzania), Uganda and Zanzibar. A bit different from EC1!

I was back in business, the beer business.

We quickly rented a furnished house about ten miles from the centre. This was a bad move as we did not know how bad the road became in both the very dry season and the rainy season. Either we had big ruts, deep holes and dust, or we had mud. However, the house was quite cute, we got ourselves a houseboy, and life looked good.

I was not too popular when I cashed a cheque at the office and it bounced. I had somehow miscalculated, or whatever, so there I was with no money and in the shit with the company. I told the company's accountant that there had been some mistake, and hurried to the only people I knew who would help me, my old Sikh grocer, Atma Ram. He lent me the money with just a little to spare, and I paid off the company. Peg and I had a pretty lean and hungry time that month.

Work was fun. I mean, to be paid for being in bars was my idea of heaven. Tuskers had had it all their own way for too long and everybody was glad to see a new kid on the block. I was paid a basic salary and commission on each case of beer, but as they hadn't really worked it out, and nearly all sales were repeat orders, the commission kept growing.

After visiting all the clubs, pubs, hotels and shops in Nairobi, I took off on my launch trip. I had a lovely driver, James, which I thought was the right and proper name for a chauffeur. We headed out of town and to the top of the escarpment where you look down on the Rift Valley. You can see for ever, and it seems you are looking down on the whole world, a world of green and brown, with a small patch of blue, and an even smaller one of pink: lake Naivasha and the flamingos. We followed the wonderful road built by the Italian prisoners-of-war and one of the few decent roads in the whole territory. Down, down into the valley with a stop at the "The Bell", then on to Nanyuki, stopping at large hotels as well as tiny shops.

It soon became very clear that both the Asian and African traders were delighted to see me. Tuskers had treated them very badly over the years and they were so happy that at last they would be able to buy European type beer. The Africans brew a sort of beer of their own, "pombe", brewed out of maize, which is drunk as soon as it is made. It is very strong, with lots of pieces of debris floating around in it, and really has no relationship with what we know as beer. However, over the years that is all they had and there is no doubt that even after they were able to buy the real thing, "pombe" was still made and drunk, as it was very cheap and in the end gave you the same effect. Now they had a choice, and I was there to give it to them. Where I would sell say ten, twenty, thirty, even fifty cases a week to a large hotel, a small Indian trader would take hundreds. If I did come across any opposition then James and I used to spread it around that Tuskers made you sterile! One of my best customers was a man from the Masai tribe. Now, at that time the Masai were still the warrior tribe and therefore had the best land for grazing their cattle. They existed on a mixture of blood and milk supplied by these cows and it sure seemed to agree with them as they were amongst the most handsome, and best physically built men I have ever seen. They were very independent, and did not even let doctors into their areas, but there was one thing that they really liked and that was European beer! They would order crates of it, and pay in cash. This wasn't selling; this was just taking the money!

My tour continued, through the various towns and villages, ending up at The Mawingo hotel, a little piece of paradise in the foothills of Mount Kenya, right on the Equator, which years later was acquired by a group headed by that lovely man, William Holden. Here one relaxed in one's bungalow by the light of a burning log fire, and wake up in the morning to watch the elephants crossing the skyline. You could eat your way through never-ending courses of food, and amble around in the beautiful gardens. I could not believe that I was being paid for this!

I returned to Nairobi with a full order book of repeats. Everybody very pleased, and I, quite unjustifiably, was hailed as Super Salesman.

Back home, our house-boy had taken a few days off and had returned with his two-year-old daughter, who was about the same age as Greg. She was a shy little thing, filthy dirty and covered in sores. Soon she was in the bath with Greg, her one dress burnt and her sores treated. She and Greg became great playmates, and when

Peggy went on a quick trip to England, she came back with a whole bunch of the cutest clothing. She was eating the same food as Greg so she started to fill out, and her laughter and high spirits were wonderful to see. She soon got used to us and there was no doubt she was one of the family. Several months later her father asked if he could go home for a few days. To which, of course, we immediately agreed. We packed all her stuff up carefully and sent them on their way. After a week they returned, but gone was the laughter, gone were her clothes, and her skin was again covered in sores. "What has happened? Where are her clothes?" we wanted to know.

He just shrugged his shoulders and said, "Oh, a cow eat them."

We were dismayed and, try as we might, we could not get the child back to how she had been. What happened in that one week? Did she perhaps realise that her life was never really to be the same? Soon after this, they both left, and we felt a terrible loss.

We bought some land, which had been cultivated to a certain extent. It also had several rondavels, which are typical African huts built out of mud and straw. Ours had metal windows, cement floors, and in the main one a stone chimney and fireplace. There was water from the mains but no electricity. We bought the bare necessities of a table, two chairs, some oil lamps, and a bed. The land was situated near the game reserve, and right in the middle of nowhere.

The first night the three of us slept together in the same bed. Greg was soon asleep but Peggy and I clung to each other as we listened to the jungle sounds surrounding us. Then I heard the door slowly opening and felt Peggy tense up. I lit the oil lamp, but there was nothing, no one, and the door was firmly shut. I just turned the lamp low and lay down, but again the same noise of an opening door. I looked up, but nothing. Once again, the door was shut. This went on the whole night. Later an old Kenyan hand told me that it was bush-babies. They make exactly the same noise as an opening door. God, we were such innocents.

It truly amazes me, looking back, that Peggy not only agreed to live in such a place but also to my best recollection seemed to enjoy it. It is not as though she was an adventurous person, or even a country lover. She was a City girl, and used to the amenities of civilised urban living. To compound it all, I was often away on my travels. How she stayed there alone, with just Greg for companionship, and the servants (who lived several yards away), I shall never know. She was, and I think still is, a very brave woman. Years later, talking to an old friend from those days, she told me that she would never get over the shock of seeing Peggy coming out of a mud hut dressed to the nines looking like something from a "Vogue" photograph.

After being assured by the doctors in both England and Kenya that it would be impossible for Peggy to have another child, Vicki arrived. Once again proving the fallibility of medical science. As we lived out in the wilds, the doctors put Peggy into the hospital before the child was due but any euphoria quickly went because of the anti-climax of getting to the hospital each day and finding out that there was still no sign of arrival. So much so, that when our baby girl *was* born, and I arrived to be given the news, my only response was, "You know the bloody carburettor fell off the car!"

Now in her 50's, Vicki to this day holds this against me, thinking this response was an indication that I didn't want her. Well, the truth is that I don't know that I wanted any of them. Except for the last, that is, but that is another story. I love them all to bits now. But at the time, I think I was too selfish to want them. That, together with the worry about whether I could afford them or not, made me very dubious. I had just had an experience of how much they could cost. Gregory caught tic-typhus, a very dangerous disease caused through infected tic bites. Luckily, a new anti-biotic had just come on the market which treated this disease successfully. Before you just sweated it out and you might recover, though the chances were slim. Thank God for the treatment, but being new it was hideously expensive, and it soon drained the coffers. At the time, you don't give these things a thought, as all you have in your mind is his recovery and his return home. This was at the time when parents were not allowed in the hospital, not even to visit. I can still remember his howls on the day we left him there with strangers. Thank God times have changed, and the medical profession realises what unhappiness is caused by this forced separation at a time when the child is most in need of its parents.

We were both excited when Princess Elizabeth and her husband visited, and we were amongst the crowds standing on the pavement in Nairobi to greet them. Listening to the African onlookers, I realised what a mistake the British Foreign Office had made: The Africans were very disappointed, because they said she looked just like any other white woman, and where was her crown? Why didn't they send a troop of the Household Cavalry, and an open landau? That would have done more good than any groundnut scheme, and would have done a lot to balance what was to come.

First, though, the news that would put an abrupt end to their visit. Whilst they were up at Treetops, at Thika, the sad news came that the King was dead. Poor Elizabeth, now Queen Elizabeth, had to fly back to England and the heavy responsibility of state would fall on her frail shoulders. Looking back, I remember what a great King he had been, a reluctant King, and a shy nervous man, who nevertheless stood strong and firm, and with Winston Churchill gave such compassionate leadership during the dark days of war. I remember one cartoon on his death showing a working man putting a wreath on the King's headstone, with a note, "To the Gentlest of Georges".

What a great Queen she has been. Her children may have misbehaved, they may not have always done the right thing, but the Queen has never put a foot wrong. She is a wise woman who has been able to help an array of Prime Ministers. She has been the main reason for keeping the British Commonwealth together. I have such admiration for her.

So, with a new Queen, and a new baby, called after the Queen's grandmother, Victoria (but always known as Vicki), life took on a normal domestic routine. We had a wonderful houseboy, Peter, from Uganda, and his wife (another Mary) joined us to help with the children. They were a wonderful couple and we soon became very fond of them. We gradually started to build more, the ground was yielding up an abundance of fruit and vegetables, and the job was going well. Yes, life was good.

Until along came the Mau Mau.

The Mau Mau were practically entirely recruited from the Kikuyu tribe. We had none working on our land, though we were actually situated on the side of a Kikuyu reservation. They were also the most prolific tribe in the Nairobi area.

Everything changed.

No longer could we leave the doors and windows open at night, guns had to be purchased and one was forced to enrol in the local patrols. The sadistic racialists came into their own at this time, and after they entered my property, interrogating and hitting our lovely Ugandans, I had a notice put up banning the local vigilantes from my land.

They were scary times. Lying awake in bed at night, one would try to analyse every noise. We put suitcases all around the rooms, so if they did break in they would, hopefully, fall over them and give you a chance to fight back. Our kitchen was outside, so when the houseboy came in we would have to cover the door with a gun, as it was a favourite ploy of the Mau Mau to come in behind the domestic staff. Our Ugandans were afraid of them, as we were, though were equally afraid of the local *white* patrols as well. There was a strict curfew, and any African caught after hours was arrested.

I went out on those patrols myself and soon found out how difficult it was. In the dark you couldn't tell which tribe anyone one was from, and there was little time to take action if they were members of the Mau Mau. The rule was to hit first and ask questions later, and sometimes, I am afraid, an innocent person got hurt. The whole thing was a mess, and very frightening.

Our home was not only very isolated, not only right in the middle of a Mau Mau area, but it was also almost impossible to make secure. So we decided to move out and into a hotel, where we once again began to sleep through the night. I always remember this hotel for one of those stupid incidents that stick in your mind. One of the hotel guests had bought himself a new car, and as it had already got dusty from the bad roads, the hotel boy asked if he could wash it whilst the owner was away for the day. The proud possessor of this brand new car willingly agreed, but warned the African to be very careful. So you can imagine his horror when he returned that evening to find his prized possession covered in scratches. In Kenya, the domestics clean saucepans and such like with a handful of sand, the early brillo pad, and this is what this African had used. He wanted to do a good job, and get it really clean, so he copied what his mother did. Poor owner, poor African.

One day, Peggy was in town with the baby visiting a friend who worked at the Town Hall. She left Vicki, then about three- or four-weeks' old, in the lobby. This was a large, cavernous place, always busy, and policed by the local force. Her friend attempted to get her to stay longer but Peg made her excuses and left. Thank God she did! For when she got back to the pram, she saw that the covers had been pulled over the child's head, and stones placed on top of her face, in an obvious attempt to suffocate her. After this, I thought it best to send the three of them back to England for a holiday (what in colonial times was known as "leave").

I moved into Torrs Hotel in the centre of town and changed my job. There had been a change in the management and they wanted to change my terms of employment, which were certainly not to my benefit! So I told them what they could do, and got a job with a small firm of importers, where my main job was running a small factory manufacturing Vaseline products. This made all my friends howl with laughter. They all knew the joke about the man knocking on a door in the East end of London, which was opened by a woman with her hair in curlers and a fag sticking out of the corner of her mouth. "Good morning, madam," the man says. "I am from the Cheeseborough Manufacturing Company, and we are carrying out a survey on how many people use our Vaseline products. Tell me, madam, do you keep Vaseline in the house?"

"Oh yes, dear, wouldn't be without it," she says.

"Would you mind telling me what you use it for?"

"Oh no, luv, I don't mind. We use it for sex, see. "

"For sex, yes." The man ticks the form on his clipboard. "For sex, and, er, would you mind telling me, how exactly you use it?"

"Well, it's like this, see: Bert – that's my old man – well, on a Sunday, like, 'e goes down to the boozer, takes on a skinfull, then when they throw him out at two o'clock, 'e comes 'ome and I have lunch ready for 'im. Then, like, after lunch we go up to the bedroom, see, and we get out the Vaseline and we rub it on the door handle so the kids can't get in the room!"

So there I was, the butt of every joke, but it was a nice little number and I had a good time with the people that worked with me. Most of them were Somalis, hard workers, and pleasant to be with.

At this time, I could tell from Peggy's letters that she was not keen on coming back and I decided to join her back in Britain.

I arrived back on the day before the Coronation. The streets were decked out in bunting, there was a buzz in the air and I was glad to be back in time for the crowning of Elizabeth the Second.

Peggy had rented a furnished flat in Earl's Court, and I set about trying to find a job.

Now, I have no idea why I did not at this time try to get back into films. I suppose I thought it was still in the doldrums, but there you are, I didn't, which was pretty bloody stupid.

In my conversations with Edward Martell we discussed various things, including, of all things, football forecasting. The football pools were the big thing of the time. Everyone dreamed of becoming a millionaire, and every newspaper, magazine, and sporting paper had their own football forecaster who would predict the results of the fifty odd matches to be played the following Saturday, and on which the pools were based. A newspaper placard started it. We were walking down Fleet Street and I saw this "Evening News" sign: "Our Forecaster the Best. Read the Evening News." I quizzed Martell on how they knew, and he told me that the "Sporting

Life" gave a cup each year to the best forecaster, and that they printed a table each week showing how the various papers had fared.

"The trouble is," he went on, "the table comes out too late. With newspapers it is the immediate that is needed."

And that's how it started.

We took the top office at 223 The Strand, right by "The Griffin" and opposite the Law Courts, and below us was a secretarial company. We registered the name "The press and General Research Service". The idea was to set up a system that would enable us to inform a newspaper two hours after the results of how their forecaster had fared that Saturday. It was set up in such a way that it gave forecaster eight chances of being successful. We had four tables, one for the most correct forecasts, the most away wins, the most draws, and the most points based on one point for a correct home win, two for an away win, and three for a correct draw. Then having these results for the week and the accumulated total for the season doubled this. It was hard not to come up on top of one of these tables some time during the season. Especially as certain papers cheated like crazy and forecast practically every other match as a draw thus ensuring that they could proclaim to the British punter that they had the best forecaster by far!

Speed was essential, as we had to get the information to the Sundays very quickly, as they were important possible clients. We sold the service on a contract basis. They signed a contract with us to receive the information each week, and they paid us whether they used these facts or not. At that time, there were forty-four national forecasters, and we sold the service at two pounds per week. In the end, we had about half of these giving us an income of four hundred and forty pounds – not bad for a few hours' work.

We had trouble at the start in working out a system that would get us the information in the time. In the first week we certainly didn't meet the target in any way, and we had to keep coming up with different systems. Of course, in the present age of computers, it would be a simple matter, but in the old manual days it took a lot of thinking to come up with the right idea. After several weeks, we did it, and business thrived.

We moved from the furnished flat in Earl's Court, to an unfurnished and expensive one in Allan Street, just off High Street Kensington, and settled back into life in central London.

I was so chuffed that I began to think of other services we could offer newspapers, and came up with the idea of issuing a daily analysis of the news.

The first thing any newspaper man does is to read the rival publications, so why not help them, I thought, and compare the amount of space each national paper devoted to every story covered that day. To have that information on an editor's desk by ten o'clock on the day they were printed seemed like a good idea. I began, and very quickly discovered how hard a job it was going to be. Firstly, I had to hire staff to help and I took on four people to work through the night. Then we would start with the early editions, measure each story printed, and compare it in column inches with each of the other papers, and if I remember correctly, we covered eleven national papers. It was a daunting task and I should have given it up straight away, but I did not and I persevered over many weeks to get it right and in time. Eventually it came out and ran for two weeks, but it was clear that this service was the last thing any one wanted at the time.

However, I was approached by the Gas Council to set up a press cutting agency of the airwaves.

There are several press cutting agencies where clients are sent any mention of their name or product when they are printed, but no one at that time had started one covering radio and television. The trouble was that it was a very expensive operation to set up, and although the Gas Council were willing to sign up as a client, they were not able to fund the setting up cost. So, sadly, I had to let it go, for not only did I not have a penny, I owed money everywhere, and had grossly overspent. What with the flat, the furniture, the office, the staff, and the equipment, I was in the shit!

The first thing I did was to go round the various people I owed money to and explain to them that if they made me bankrupt, they would get nothing but if they would hold fire then I would pay them back every penny. They all agreed, and were more than kind to a young idiot.

All agreed, except one: the landlord of the flat who quickly put the bailiffs in.

This was the real low point of my life. The caretaker of the flats, with whom I had numerous rows in the past, soon found out and made sure that every one in the block knew. No one ever came and shook my hand, or indicated in any way that they were sorry. No, they gave sidelong glances and chatted amongst one another about it, sometimes making an unkind remark. I have hated Kensington ever since, which is very unfair, but the place just brings back such sad recollections. It also reminds me what a fool I was, and what a lesson I learnt.

It took me years, but I paid off every debt in full and I never allowed myself to get into such a state again. Since that day, I have never had anything on hire purchase. If I could not afford it, I did not have it. I got rid of mortgages as soon as I could, much to the horror of my accountant. I am sure I have been a nuisance to all my family with my worries about money, but I have never recovered from strangers coming into my home to threaten to take away my furniture and personal belongings. I am sure it was a good thing to happen to me, and it knocked out any cockiness I had left.

A change had to be made. But what to do? I still had the football service, which Peggy and I could run on our own, but that was the only plus as we had no home and many debts, plus two kids. I got rid of the office, and we borrowed some money from Martell and bought a house (we must have seemed mad, but as it turned out it was the perfect solution), which was an enormous old building in East Molesey, right by Hampton Court. It had been a nursing home, and in the sitting room, you could still see where the heads of the patients had rested against the wall. It was big, but it was in the most ghastly state, and when my mother first saw it, she burst into tears. It cost twenty six thousand pounds, and in addition to the house, it had a self-contained flat at the top. In one swoop we had a home, and a potential income.

Our furniture soon got lost in the flat so it was a quick trip to the local auction rooms to pick up some cheap bits and pieces. Poverty stricken or not, somehow we managed to bring our housekeeper from town with us, who insisted on serving dinner as, though, we were living in the Dorchester Hotel.

We had a house, a flat, an income and a lot of debts.

So?

So, a job had to be found. Once again, I never thought about the movies, but another avenue opened up. Edward Martell was connected with a group of local and weekly papers and he got me a job on The Brixton Free press, as a sort of odd job man, from driving the delivery van to covering local weddings, funerals etc.

From this, I was then co-opted into what was to be the first new national daily newspaper for years, "The Daily Recorder". It had been a weekly political paper, but the owner W.J. Brittain and Martell had dreams of turning it into a daily. The offices were in Farringdon Street, and it was going to be printed at the works in Brixton. Here again I did everything including covering certain events and even writing the odd comments column. Large journalistic and administrative staffs were taken on, and it was very exciting to be in the middle of what seemed like such a fantastic enterprise. Exciting but doomed. If I had had trouble with my press survey, this daily was in real deep, deep shit.

Despite many trial runs, from the first day it was a disaster. For example it was decided that a special copy should be printed on high quality paper for The Queen, to be delivered by hand first thing in the morning to Buckingham Palace. Well, Her Majesty, and the rest of the British public, didn't get it on their breakfast trays, that's for sure, not even on their luncheon table, although if they had they still been at home they should have had it on their tea trolley, together with the first editions of the evening papers.

When they did get a chance to read it, they found they would have found that they could enter a competition in order to win the major prize of two seats to the moon! "The Daily Recorder" had reserved two seats on the first passenger flight, although they never printed with whom they booked the seats! If this wasn't enough to confuse them, then the puzzle page would have certainly done the job, as the wrong crossword clues were sent out! The best, though, was when the Foreign editor was sent to Berlin to cover an international conference, got pissed the first night and just sent back two words of copy: "It's war!" And was never heard from again!

Well, it certainly was not going to be victory for Mr Brittain, and, though Martell and I had worked our balls off, it was all to no avail. After about ten days, the whole venture collapsed. I had enjoyed myself, and was able to pay back Martell a little for all he had done to help in the past.

A few weeks after the collapse of "The Daily Recorder" there was a national newspaper strike. Peggy and I quickly saw this as an opportunity to make some money, and we decided to print our own paper, "The Strike Special".

The first thing we learnt was that the public was only interested in sport, especially the racing. In those days BBC radio did not give out certain information. They would give the anticipated runners, and the first three winners, but not the names of the "also-rans". Neither did they give out the odds, but sort of pretended that no one bet!

The second thing we realised was that we could not do it on our own, so we co-opted our neighbours, Pat O'Neill, who was a Professor at London University teaching Japanese, and his wife, Di. He was on vacation and as eager as us to make some cash. So, we had the staff and all we had to do was get the information. But where?

Our first attempt was through a bookie, as bookmakers were desperate to co-operate as their livelihood depended on getting the information out to the punters. So, there we were in our sitting room, with miles of paper tape, as in those days the information came through on what was known as ticker-tape, which was paper about a quarter of an inch thick. We managed to get this tangled around the furniture, and indeed ourselves in trying to find the various race meetings, the horses, the odds and all the other information needed by the deprived racing fraternity. We worked all through the night and into the day and eventually got something out in the early afternoon. We then hawked this around the various newsagents in the area. One thing we had determined was that we would not sell on a sale-or-return basis: they either paid for what they took, or they didn't get it. This was a big obstacle at the beginning, and a great many refused to take it on this basis.

Back at the house, an irate bookie phoned us, complaining that we had the horses down as being trained by the jockeys and ridden by the trainers! Such is ignorance. Apart from this mistake, we also realised that we could never make it work with the bookies' tape, so after a few discreet phone calls, we got a friend in Fleet Street to agree to get the information for us. I used to travel up to town and meet him in a back street off Fleet Street, where he would hand me the necessary information. Of course it was illegal as it came through agencies like Reuters. Illegal or not, I used to justify my behaviour by thinking of all the little people dependent on this information, and that as we only covered a very tiny part of Surrey, I couldn't see that Reuters were likely to lose any money. Actually, they did ring us up after some days and enquired where we were getting our information. We told them we had agents at each racetrack. This seemed to satisfy them, and we never heard another word.

I would get the contraband details and drive like hell back to the house, where we would type it all up on stencils, as luckily we had a large double Roneo machine, which we had bought for the Football Results Service. We would print all through the night as many copies as we could, then set off on our rounds to the shops, the bookies, and the street newspaper vendors. Gradually all the newsagents who had been so uppity at the beginning started calling up and ordering, in fact in the end we had to *ration* the number of copies we allowed each customer.

We spent the days collecting new paper, getting other sports news from other sources, and handling the incoming orders. There was little time for sleep, though

Pat and Di did manage to conceive their daughter Pella on our couch! Time was so short that we did not have time to count the money, but just threw it into a drawer.

One day the gasman arrived because we hadn't paid the bill. "Just help yourself," we cried, opening the drawer. Another day Vicki was out playing in the garden, fell over and money poured out of her pockets. She had been helping herself and no one had noticed.

We celebrated our last day with our one and only scoop. We had this hot news from someone very close to the horse's mouth. We had all the billboards made, which we displayed at all our sites around the area, and especially at the local railway stations. The news was so dramatic that no one believed us, and it wasn't till hours later that the BBC confirmed what we had been saying, "Churchill Resigns Today".

Sadly, we couldn't gloat in the next day's edition for the nationals went back to work.

It was all over. There was just time to count the money, split it up, and go to bed. There was just one passing thought before I went to sleep, "What the fuck am I going to do now?"

CHAPTER 8
BACK TO THE FUTURE

"Why?" said Peggy, "don't you go back into films?"

This stopped me in my tracks. Why hadn't I thought about that? I always loved it, so why had I been screwing around all these years? But, and it was a big but, what about the Union? Was I still a member? In those days, a Union card was the most precious thing you could possess, and you couldn't even get a job sweeping the stages without one. I had an idea. I wrote to the infamous "Charlie p'uckin' Wheeler".

Back by return of post came his reply saying he had checked up and when I had been unemployed I had lodged my card at head office, meaning that, though I had not paid any subscriptions over the intervening years, I was still a full member. That was good news. He then came up with a great idea to follow it up. Why didn't I move over to the production side? I had always wanted to go in that direction and now was the time to do it, and if I agreed he would arrange to have my status in the Union changed, allowing me to get a job as an Assistant director. For this was something else that was controlled by the Union. You couldn't change from one department to the other without their okay. So, good old Charlie, for all I had said about him, had come up trumps. He single-handedly changed my life, and I have been forever grateful.

It wasn't long before I was invited to an assistant directors' branch meeting, and I was surprised to find that I was the only person there not working. The business had certainly changed since I was last involved. Anyhow, it wasn't long before that situation changed and I got a call from Rank Film Services at Pinewood Studios to start straight away as Third assistant director. This was the commercials' arm of Rank's, where they made both television and cinema advertisements.

1955 and once again I entered a film studio for work and my life in production began.

Now, the title of third assistant director sounds very grand, but actually it is a glorified callboy, the bottom of the chain: calling the artists from the dressing-rooms, getting numerous people cups of tea, taking the call sheet around the studio, and assisting the First and the second assistant director. On a few joyous occasions, one was allowed to work on the floor, controlling crowds under the direction of the first assistant.

The second assistant works as a liaison between the floor and the office. He prepares the call sheet for the following day for the first's approval. He studies the script, the breakdown, and the schedule so that he can list the scenes to be shot, the artists required, and gives instructions to the various departments listing the day's requirements. For instance, it might be to the special effects' department asking for fire, or to the art department for a specific set requirement, and so on.

The second prepares this document, though it is the first who, in consultation with the director, approves it, and signs it as his responsibility. However, it is the second's responsibly to make sure that everyone is supplied with this information, especially the actors. Often an actor wanted for the following day will not be at the studio, so the second has to ring him up and make sure that he knows what time he is required and in what scenes he will be working. This is to ensure that the artist knows his lines when he turns up.

Calling actors can be a nightmare experience. The first thing one is taught is that you must talk to the actor directly, and not trust anyone else to give him the message. Now, this is okay for reliable, home-loving actors, but as we all know, not all of them are like that, and a second can spend hours hunting through the clubs of London trying to track down a certain artist. Good seconds get to know the habits of the members of the cast: know their haunts, their girlfriends and mistresses. Even the best of them go through the ordeal of waking up in the middle of the night, trying to remember if they have called a certain actor. Once I rang an actor, Paul Whitsun-Jones, a very respected and reliable person, and said "It's Johnny Dark here, scenes so and so to so and so, seven thirty tomorrow morning, see you then." Seven thirty the next morning, no Paul. I rang his home, no reply.

About eight o'clock the phone rang, "Paul here."

"Where are you?" I asked. He was at the Radio Luxembourg Studios. Why? He was in a series there called "Johnny Dark"! Another lesson learnt. Be precise, be repetitive, and remember you cannot be too careful. Because if the artist does not turn up, or he doesn't know what he is supposed to be doing, it is your neck that will be on the block. Luckily, I got Paul to Walton before he was needed.

I was yet to reach those dizzy heights, as I was busy getting the tea at Pinewood. Lowly though the job was, it was made worse by the fact that I was waiting on people who had been my juniors at the Bush. However, nobody took advantage of this turn of events. In fact, I think most people thought it was a good idea for me to have changed departments. I was never really a technician, and though I enjoyed my time as a Dubbing Mixer, I never did know how it worked. I think I had a good ear, and a good sense of the relationship of sound to film, but how and why the sound increased when I pushed a knob, I had not the faintest idea. I must say Brian Sewell did give me a glowing reference when I left the Bush.

Working on commercials was not the most prestigious employment in movies, but it was fun, with very little pressure, a small cast, and time seemed to be of no importance. We would take at least a week to shoot a three-minute commercial. Things are a bit tighter now, but in those days no one seemed to care. This was especially true when we worked on one of the big productions, like our monthly cinema show called "Tips". This was a number of household hints interspersed with advertisements. Wow, big time. There was a large set, with a well-known personality hosting the programme, and usually a crowd of anything up to forty people. We never got a shot in before lunch, and perhaps just two in the afternoon. Where all the time went, I have no idea.

Of course, in commercials, so many people have a say. There are hours and hours of meetings prior to the shoot, from which a storyboard is finally completed. As every shot has been studied, all he has to do is put into reality what has already been agreed. Then there is the agent, who is responsible to the client for delivering the commercial, and as his livelihood depends on the client, he has to make sure that he is delivering what he has proposed. Just like justice, he has not only to deliver but must be seen to deliver. So he will take an active part in the shooting, mostly for show, as few of them have the technical knowledge to make any constructive criticism.

After the agent comes the client, the man picking up the tab. He has to be kept happy at all costs, so when he wants to play, he has to be indulged. They all like looking through the camera, especially if it is on a crane. They can be swooped up in the air to get a bird's eye view of the whole set, but looking through the camera is not always the easiest of things if you are not used to it. The eyepiece has to be adjusted to one's own optic, and the actual mount of the camera positioned to what is to be actually shot. Camera operators are highly trained technicians and one of the few top men on the set. After having been so visibly involved, once having landed back on the ground the client feels duty bound to offer up some comment, which usually is for something either out of shot, or just technically impossible. It is rather like me inspecting the inside of a jet engine and asking where the carburettor is!

All of this, of course, takes time, but as I said, no one seemed to care, though it was extremely frustrating for the director who had to wait patiently while the agent and the client discussed each shot.

The directors we had then were themselves a strange bunch. This was 1956, commercials were still in their infancy, and were before they had attracted real talent. None of the directors we had was ever heard of again, unlike the later ones who were to become top Hollywood feature directors, like Ridley and Tony Scott, and the great Alan Parker.

We would also get rare visits from executives of the company, who spent most of their time in the rarefied grand offices in Mayfair. They were referred to as the producers, and were extremely nice, pleasant gentlemen. I stress "gentlemen" for that is what they were, "toffs". They always reminded me of Senior Officers from Command H.Q. visiting their troops: polite, but distant. These gentlemen were there to find the clients, and to raise the money, and as we always seemed to be busy, they were obviously doing a good job. I rather liked them.

About this time, I had my first brush with the Unions. We had made a Christmas short wishing the customers at the Rank cinemas a Happy Holiday. The start of the film was a series of shots of people working at Pinewood, from the carpenters to the camera crews, and the commentary said, "The management and staff of Rank's Pinewood Studios stop for a moment to wish you a Happy Christmas." There was a great to do about this because the Extras' Union, The Film

Artists Association, made a formal complaint that the real people had been used when they should have been members of their Union playing the part of the Pinewood workers.

Well, of course, it was all nonsense, and the next thing would be they were demanding that you could not use real people in a newsreel! It went to the works committee and a big meeting was held in one of the larger stages for the whole of the Pinewood staff, not just the Film Services part. There the debate ranged back and forth, until a show of hands was called for to censure the people who had dared to take part, and to raise a serious objection with the management for allowing such a thing to happen. Well, it was obvious that the motion had been lost, but the platform declared that it had been carried. I wasn't about to put up with that, so I leapt up and demanded a recount. With the backing of the majority of the members, the platform had to reluctantly concede. I went around personally and counted the show of hands. I cannot remember the exact figures but the motion was well and truly defeated. The works committee, the shop stewards, and Union organisers had to leave hurriedly, in full retreat. This was not the last time that I came across the total dishonesty of Union officials, their arrogance, their power and their lack of real interest in their members. Back at Screen Services, I was a sort of hero, and the boys came out of it without any form of Union punishment.

After six months at Pinewood, the company offered me a year's contract with slightly more money, which I promptly turned down. I was happy where I was, but desperate to get on and to get back into the mainstream of filming. I also had learnt a thing or two, the main one being that there was plenty of work around. So, when they said I had either to sign the contract or leave, I decided to leave.

I was used to unemployment. However, this time it was only to last a couple of days.

I got a call from Walton Studios for a few days' work on a filmed television series, "Aggie". Now, before I left Pinewood I had got my local shop steward (if you can't fight 'em join 'em!) to sign me off as a second assistant. With one signature I leapt up the first rung of the ladder. So there I was on the set at Walton Studios, working on a series that was soon ending. It had been shooting for some time and so had an established crew. I was there only because their Second had gone off to pastures green. Now, I had never actually done the job, and I certainly had no experience of a filmed TV show. Where I had been used to shooting a few seconds a day, there we were doing anything from six to ten minutes.

I worked under an established first assistant, Denis Batera, and I inherited a third, Ted Wallace. They were, like the rest of the crew, very nice to me, especially the young production manager, Basil Somner, who later in life became the supervising production manager for MGM at their studios in Borehamwood.

After a few days Basil called me and said that his company was starting a new show and that he would like me to join it as the second assistant. He offered me what seemed a wonderful salary and I went home to celebrate once again being solvent with a future. I would be able to increase my payments to all my creditors.

We kept the Football Results Service running, which boosted our income, and as we ran it from home, we had very little overhead expenses.

The show I was to work on was called "Sailor of Fortune" and was about three guys on a battered old boat travelling around the world and getting into a different adventure each week. It seems unbelievable now, but we never left the studio. Somebody had picked up some stock shots of a boat at sea, which we matched by building a replica in the studio. The boat was rigid, and if it needed to rock, they would just move the camera. The scripts bordered on the pathetic, but there was a good cast headed by Lorne Greene who became famous later on for being the lead in a major American television series "Bonanza". He was backed up each week by Rupert Davis who himself became well known in the UK for his weekly portrayal of Maigret, and the last of the trio was Jackie McGowan, a superb Irish actor, but who like so many of his countrymen, had a taste for the hard stuff and was sadly to die at a very young age.

The cast and the directors did their best to put some sparkle into the show but it was a hard slog for them. I learnt then there's not a lot you can do without the right script. However talented the director, or charismatic the actor, they cannot make a silk purse. I remember taking my second wife to the London premiere of the remake of "The Jazz Singer" starring Neil Diamond. After about fifteen minutes into the film she leant over and whispered, "That's the worst actor I've ever seen."

I replied into her ear, "And that is probably the most renowned actor in the world today: Laurence Olivier." Without the right script even the best can't rescue the show.

Still, at this stage, script and acting were not my concern. Getting everything on the set at the right time was, and learning what was expected of me. I had taken Ted Wallace with me as Third, and I was given a new First who was a nice chap but very weak, and not the person to do that job. He was later to go into insurance which I am sure was a much better industry for his talents. The producer was a young Canadian, a very nice man whom we didn't see much of. His associate producer was an old-time production man, Ted Holiday, who was a bit of a rough diamond and who, as far as I could see, left most of the work to the production manager, Basil.

I soon found one of my jobs was dealing with the crowd. The first assistant, in consultation with his director, would tell me how many people they would need for the following day. A row would then often develop with the production office who would say that the budget couldn't stand that number and it would have to be cut. Eventually a compromise would be made. There was never enough, and the maximum use had to be made of each person.

Crowd, in my days, was supplied by Central Casting, an organisation set up by the Producers' Association with the co-operation of the Extras' Union. Nowadays this is handled through private agents, but the system is the same: You would instruct Central Casting of the numbers and types required for instance six tough males, young and Latin-looking, twelve flashy girls to play hookers, six policemen and so on. If uniforms or special clothes were called for, then in advance of the call they would have to attend a wardrobe fitting at one of the costumiers in town. A small fee was paid for attending these fittings. Some of them would specialise, especially in police, and they would have their own uniforms, their own police cars, and motorbikes. Then there was the "well-dressed crowd", people who had their own evening clothes, smart suits, evening gowns etc. They are paid extra for, as it were, hiring their own property. The "crowd" were paid in accordance with an agreement between their Union and the Producers' Association.

This agreement also covered stand-ins, the people who take the place of an artist whilst the set is being lit, enabling the actor to be free to be in make-up, or to go over his lines, by himself or with a fellow actor.

All this was quite straightforward, but trouble arose over the "special action" money, which was supposed to cover something other than just being one of the herd. For example, a waiter serving at a table in foreground would quite rightly get an extra payment. Now, everyone on the call always thought that they had a reason for a "special action" payment, and it was the Second who had to fight the good fight every night. Usually these were settled there and then, but any unresolved dispute was taken to arbitration at Central Casting.

At the end of each day the Second had to sign off the crowd chits before the cashiers would pay them out, and each night the second was surrounded by this shrieking mob wanting to catch their bus and get home, but also wanting to get as much money as they could possibly screw out of him. It was a game, and after a time you got to know the wily ones, the ones who always tried it on, the older craftier ones who always kept at the back, tried not to be seen so they wouldn't be noticed and therefore stand more chance of a re-call the next day.

In the early days of filming, the crowd were obtained from Archer Street, where the waiters would congregate waiting for hotel or restaurant jobs, and consequently there were many professional waiters in the crowd. At times like Ascot you knew that many of your regulars would be unavailable, and you also knew that straight afterwards you would be the recipient of some champagne, smoked salmon or caviar, which had somehow made its way from Royal Ascot to Walton Studios!

There was one fat little mid-European who always seemed to get on the call, and once there always seemed to pop up where you didn't want him. He also had a talent for finding reasons why he should be paid more money. Once we were shooting some scenes on a set of a platform at the Gare du Nord station in Paris and whilst we were busy setting up, this little fellow appeared in front of me, "And me, what, Mister John, what would you like me to do, eh?"

I looked around, saw a newspaper kiosk and thought, Ah, just the place, "You go into that kiosk there."

"I go in the kiosk," he asked, "and you want that I sell the papers, right?"

"Yes, go in the kiosk, and stay there."

During the course of a busy day, I have to admit that I was aware of a voice in the distance saying, "Paris Soir", "Le Monde". When I came to sign the crowd off, our friend appeared with a chit for hundreds of pounds.

"What's this crap?" I asked him.

He pulled out a long piece of paper on which he had written down all the scenes, numbered, with the different takes, and what he had said in each one!

Now, under the agreement a Crowd Artist is paid for every word spoken, and even more in a foreign language. Yep, he had well and truly screwed me. Of course, I would not pay, and it was the only time when I had a case go to arbitration. A settlement was reached, and I suspect he was a very happy man. On future calls I used to say to him, "Isaac, no talking, not a word, understand? Don't even open your mouth to breathe!"

We tried to shoot one half-hour episode per week. You have to remember that it was a lot more difficult in those days as equipment was heavier, and stock was slower, so set-ups took much longer to achieve. The poor directors had a tough time trying to improve the quality and still keep to schedule.

It was the same before television, when we had the double bills. The second movie, known as a "B" film, was also shot on a very tight schedule. I remember one director at the Bush who used to leave all the entering and exiting shots until last. Then he would line the actors up outside the door, and do all their entrances with out stopping the camera. "Right, action," he would shout. "Number One…" and the first actor would come in, say his line, and he then had to walk past camera … "Number Two…" and so on. They would then move around to the inside and do their exits. Afterwards the editor would cut them in to fit the scene.

The same director always used to take a shot of the clock. "You never know when it might come in useful," he would say!

On the "Sailor of Fortune" series we had one director, John Guillermin, who really tried hard to improve the material. He was a very highly-strung person and sometimes it was just too much for him. I can see him now kneeling down on the set, and banging his head on to the studio floor. He was always behind schedule, and always in trouble with the front office, but unlike so many "B" or TV directors who kept to the schedule, he had talent. A talent that eventually took him to Hollywood where he directed such films as "The Towering Inferno", "The Blue Max", and "Death on the Nile" amongst many others.

I loved the job, and was always first in at the studio and the last to leave. Strangely, that has remained the same all over the years, and whatever position I have held, I have always had my first cup of coffee with the Security Man. It is not necessarily something to be proud of, and I admire those producers and executives who can roll up about ten, take a long lunch and leave for town about five, but that ain't me.

I also found that trouble used to come early in the morning. If an actor goes sick, or if there has been an accident, or some other reason why the day's work has to be rescheduled, you are there on the spot to cope with the problem. An alteration to the set needs to be completed by the swing gang, but confirmation is needed first from the laboratories that the previous day's rushes are technically okay. I say technically, as the lab boys do not make judgement on the artistic content. That comes later when the director and producer view the rushes. But at times like this, risks are taken and, to save time, a set alteration can be made prior to the director's viewing, based on a lab report.

There are so many things that can delay the start of shooting, and as the old adage goes, time is money. If you are on the spot, you can often save a lot of money.

I received a call at home one evening from John Guillermin saying that he had just had a new idea, and that he needed a chimpanzee on the set for the following morning! Where was I going to get a chimp from at that time of night? Of course I rang all the zoos, and was not exactly surprised to get no reply. I tried the bigger pet shops, the circuses, everywhere I could think. This went on for hours and I was beginning to get desperate when I had an idea and rang directory of Enquiries for the number of a certain television "animal presenter". My luck was in: he was not ex-directory, so I rang him and got him out of bed. He was very nice about it, and agreed to be at the studios at eight-thirty the following morning, complete with chimp. As the crew and cast assembled for the start of work, I proudly walked on the set with the chimp. John turned, took one look, and said, "Too big." And that was the end of that.

We finished shooting thirteen episodes, and it was agreed to shoot a further thirteen, but to move to another studio. This was the Danzigers' studios at Elstree – a real bitch for me as Walton was a short bus ride from home, but Elstree was one of those cursed cross-country runs, a safari through the concrete of the outer suburbs of London.

I bought an old Vauxhall from a friend, and when I say old, I mean ancient, as not only did it not have any heating, the clock was a wind-up job. However, it was a good old reliable "tank" and I can't remember it ever letting me down. I used to give various people lifts, including a Boom Operator, Ted Belcher, who was a religious nut. He had this disconcerting way of talking directly to God. He would get in the car first thing in the morning and it would start. "I see God has given us a lovely day, John. Shall we thank Him?"

"I'm busy driving, Ted."

"Yes, God," he would continue, "John has to concentrate on his driving". He would bow his head and in a flat monotone voice say, "I ask You, God, to protect him in this task, especially as there are so many children on the roads this morning." Then he would try and convert me, to bring me into God's arms. Well, I never knew I had been out of them actually. I was never very religious, but early in the morning I was certainly not in the right frame of mind to be converted into a born-again Christian.

His continual conversations with God used to send me crazy, and my language used to get worse and worse, which only resulted in Belcher saying, "Ignore that, Lord. He doesn't really mean it."

"Yes, I do," I would scream.

It was to no avail and in the end I told him in no uncertain terms that he either stopped trying to save me, or he would have to walk to work. I guess he reckoned that one lost soul was small payment for transportation to the studio.

Even at the studio it didn't stop. Once a particular scene necessitated the boom to be cranked up high, so that Belcher was standing several feet above the proceedings. It was one of those days when nothing had gone right. The director was in despair as, in take after take, something went wrong. It seemed he would never get it "in the can". At last, it was coming together; the actors hadn't fluffed, the camera hadn't jammed, the lights hadn't flickered. The crew froze in concentration as the scene gradually entered its final phase. Suddenly a load of leaflets started to flutter down over the set. The actors looked up in surprise, and the director, tearing his hair out, shouted "Cut, cut, what the fucking hell …?"

He grabbed one of the fluttering tracts and read in amazement, "Jesus will save you. Jesus will save….", and looked up at Ted Belcher smiling down at him. "You, you threw these – you … you fucking idiot, I'll kill you … I'll fucking kill you, you raving, idiotic lunatic. You … you …" Words and expletives failed him.

Ted smiled down and said, "God will forgive you, my son." The director collapsed on the floor. It was just one of those days!

Years later I bumped into Ted in the street. Not surprisingly, his film career had ended and he was selling eggs outside his terraced worker's cottage in Molesey. He said the eggs' business was only a sideline, and his main occupation was performing a Punch and Judy show. Now, it just so happened that it was one of the children's birthdays in a few days, so I booked him to appear. He turned up with his Punch and Judy theatre and puppet characters. But he also brought with him an enormously fat woman totally dressed in black. I could not think what role she could play, as certainly there was no way she was going to fit into the Punch canvas puppet tent. He explained she was the singer and this added a new dimension to the traditional Punch and Judy show.

So, with a certain amount of apprehension we gathered the children together, the theatre was set up, and Ted announced that Aunty Alice was going to sing.

Aunty Alice, without any accompaniment, stepped forward, opened her arms took an enormous breath, thus expanding her already over-ample bosoms like two inflatable beach balls, and launched into a song which made up in volume what it lacked in melody.

The children sat transfixed by this penetrating sound, the cat beat a hasty retreat into the garden, whilst the adults cowered in the kitchen, covering their ears. This massive black bubbling blob reached off-key heights rarely obtained by any other human. The children sat still and mute as "Uncle" Ted thanked her and told the children that it was time for Punch and Judy. Punch appeared and started talking, but in Ted's voice! So thinking that Aunty Alice's caterwauling has made him forget to put the swizzle in his mouth (the thing that gives the characters that unique sound to their voices). I crept close to the tent and whispered, "Ted, you've forgotten the swizzle."

Unaware of my aside, the audience suddenly saw Punch disappear, to be replaced by Ted's moon face peering over the edge of the stage. "No, I don't use them any more. You see, I swallowed three of them."

A big wail went up from one of the younger children, "Uncle Ted has swallowed Punch," he screamed.

"No," said an older one with great glee "he's swallowed all three!" An even bigger wail went up, and even the best endeavours of Aunty Alice and the other adults could not pacify the children.

It was no better with the reappearance of Punch, Judy and the Policeman, for they all spoke just like "Uncle Ted" which was quickly pointed out by the "know-all" in the party (my mother said you get one at every party).

I am afraid Ted's popularity took a big dip and in the end, he and his cast ended up by playing to Aunty Alice, our housekeeper, and the dog!

Before he left, Ted, of course, had a word or two with God. I was always very embarrassed when he put his arm around me and had one of his intimate conversations with the Deity, with Whom he was obviously on good terms. He spoke with great respect, and yet with great ease, as he asked God to look after us, and see that the children had a good time. Nothing was too small to ask for, whether the washing machine had broken, or if one us had a cold. I couldn't take the mickey out of him as he had such faith. On reflection, I think he was a lot more sincere than most of the clergy I have come across. He was a simple man, who tried to share his friendship with God with others.

Danziger studios were newly built, financed by the two brothers who gave the studios their name. They were hotelkeepers (owning at that time the Mayfair hotel in the West End) and I suppose they went into the business as they could see the potential growth of television.

The six stages at the studio were small and not suitable for feature productions, but ideal for television filmed series. I stress film, for at that time taped shows had not come in.

Apart from building the studios, the Danzigers also became producers and made several series, and a few "B" films, which I think also ended up going straight to the box. After several years they realised it was not their business and the studios were closed, never to open again. When we rented the studios, the brothers had no connection with us other than to be our landlords.

When we changed studios, we also changed the first assistant director. Our new one was a lively little anxious Cockney. I found him a nice bloke and easy to work with. I had built up a great relationship with Basil, the PM, over the previous months, and I had kept the good, kind, hard working and efficient Ted Wallace with me as Third, so we had a nice little team. However, I detected that the three lead artists were not too happy with the new man's bossy manner, and one day Lorne said to me, "John, I'm going to talk to the front office about you becoming the First."

Well, this was a bolt from the blue. But, sure enough, on the Friday, the First told me that he was leaving that night, and he didn't know who would be taking over the job. We shook hands and left good friends, and indeed were to meet many times in the future. The same day Ted Holiday asked me whether I would like to take over as First.

Can a duck swim?

I was where I had always wanted to be. From the time I first started to work, I not only admired the first assistants but I longed to be in that position. It is the First who controls the floor and the set, and is responsible for the control, the discipline, and the management of all that goes on. He is both responsible to the director and the producer, and is the Production Company's representative on the floor.

But he is much more, as his personality, and his manner set the atmosphere. He can lighten the tension with a difficult director, or tactfully push a slow one. It is his responsibility to see that everything from the star to the tiniest prop is on the set at the right time.

He is also in control of the crowd, as with his second and in consultation with the director, he agrees the numbers and types, and "dresses" the crowd into the scene after the director has his set-up with the principals. All those busy people walking around in the background are not just doing their own thing, but are following the instruction of the first as to where and when they are to go.

Certain scenes can be tricky, for instance a dancing scene where the camera is moving around photographing the two principals the crowd must be directed so the other dancers do not cover the principals yet do not leave them isolated. All this is worked out by the First. Remember also that the scene is usually with dialogue and therefore there can be no music. The principals and crowd have to remember that they are dancing to a waltz or a foxtrot, and must hold the pre-arranged tempo in their heads. Again, the feet of the dancers might make too much noise and upset the recording of the dialogue, so the Assistant must ensure that the crowd have some felt on the soles of their shoes.

A First will be concerned with the schedule, and in many ways held to account for how the day has progressed. The job really is what you make of it. Sadly, the majority shout a lot, call for the "red light" and that is that. A top Assistant controls every aspect of the shoot, and is a vital and important member of the crew.

In France, the first is solely what the job says, he is the assistant to the director, whereas in the UK and the States the first has a much wider role.

So there I was, in less than a year back in the film industry, a first assistant, and I was determined to be one of the best. The morning after the first day Lorne came and congratulated me. He said the floor was run properly for the first time since he had been on the show.

However, this was not the associate producer's view. "Too serious, John, got to lighten it up, mate." Well, at least I got called "mate", a definite step forward. That day I had a good time making jokes and, as Ted asked, "lightened it up". The next day Lorne said to me, "That was the best day of all, some fun for a change."

But Ted's comment was, "Now, that was going a bit too far, lad, it's a serious business, you know."

Well, I thought, the best thing I can do is just make my own judgement and hope for the best. I received no more advice and we settled down to a happy time.

The day starts very early. Though the actual commencement of shooting begins normally at half-past eight, many things have to be done before this. The first to arrive are the make-up artists and hairdressers, in order to be ready for the artists. The assistant directors are there to greet them and to report that they are actually in the studio. They keep a check on their progress so that they are ready to walk on the set at eight-thirty. The girls are normally the first to be made up, as they take longest, unless it is a speciality make-up, like the Elephant Man. At around the same time the wardrobe department arrives.

There may well be a new set, in which case some of the art department will be there, plus the props and certain of the construction crew. The camera assistants and the sound crews will be in to get the equipment ready.

At half-past-eight, the cast and crew are ready on the set, and the director gets his first set-up. With the camera crew, he walks the cast through the scene, and lays out the various camera positions. Once this has been finalised, the stand-ins take over from the principals and the lighting cameraman starts to light the scene.

This is a good moment to explain the roles of the camera crew. The lighting cameraman, sometimes called the director of photography, but usually referred to as "the cameraman", only comes second to the director in the pecking order. His job is to instruct his leading electrician, known as the gaffer, as to what lamps to use and where to place them.

The individual who actually looks through the camera and follows the scene is the camera operator, and his assistant is the focus puller whose job is to keep the camera in focus when it is moving about. He is also responsible for the care of the camera.

Finally there is the clapper boy. Everyone has seen the clapperboard going in, but not a lot of people realise what it is for. Firstly, it is to identify the production, the director, and the cameraman. It will have a set-up number on it and the take number. The clapper itself is used to synchronize the sound track with the picture. Not till the very end of the film process will the sound and picture be put together on one piece of film, so after the film is processed the editors will "synch" the two by watching where the clapper joins the board, and where the bang of the clapper is heard.

Once the cameraman has completed his lighting, the director takes over, the principals relieve the stand-ins, and rehearsals commence. The First will call for the "green light" and ask for quiet.

One of the first directors I assisted was John Guillermin and, as I said before, he was a very nervous, highly-strung person, and could not bear any sort of noise or disturbance whilst he was rehearsing. Often, in order to save time, the cameraman will quietly move around adjusting the odd light, but not with John. With him "quiet" meant "stand still, don't move, don't talk, don't even whisper, and only breathe if necessary". The slightest noise would make him turn and glare at me and I couldn't wait to put up the "red" which meant that no one could go in or out.

Modern studios have automatic locks on the doors to prevent any movement in and out, but in the old days they had to rely on people respecting the red and green lights. The bigger budget pictures used to use doormen, nearly always old boys who had retired from a more active job in the business, but they were one of the first victims of modern technology. However, the "red light " is something to be treated with caution: abuse it and it rebounds on you, because people stop respecting it. Many people have to go in and out, and you stop them for too long at your peril. A balance has to be reached, even if you risk the wrath of a director like John Guillermin.

I remember years later attending a party in the boardroom at Shepperton Studios to celebrate the start of a new picture, "Death on the Nile". It was one of the usual, happy pre-production parties, and I was certainly pleased to see John again, because although he was a difficult bastard, I was actually rather fond of him and I respected him. After our meeting he was swept away to meet various people, but some time later came back and wanted to know what was making me laugh. "Nothing really, John," I replied, "it's just that I was looking at the gathering around you, and thinking that they all believe you're a really nice guy."

He just gave me that sidelong glare I knew so well and said, "They'll learn", and walked away with a smile on his face!

We were getting near to the end of the series, and I suggested to the family that we go off for a week's holiday. We hadn't been away for years and this seemed a good time. I just hoped that I would soon find another job after I came back.

However, as so often happens, life had a different plan for me. The last one in the series was to be directed by a very experienced film director, Vernon Sewell, a bright, energetic upper class man always dressed in a double-breasted navy blue blazer with black buttons, who spoke with a slight stutter. He had been an assistant cameraman and a Film editor before becoming a director, so was technically very knowledgeable. He had directed the Second Unit on Michael Powel's "Silver Fleet", and had made numerous low budget films.

One day he told me that in the late 40s he had been contracted to the National Studios at Elstree, which at that time were owned by Lady Yule, widow of a jute millionaire who lived with her unmarried daughter. When a new project came in, Vernon was summoned, and the three of them would read the script together, Lady Yule as casting director, allocating the various parts. As there were always more than three characters, each of them would play several parts, reading the script aloud. On this basis the decision to purchase the script or not was made! This system would make any modern day movie executive blanche. Mind you, they were probably as successful then as they are today, with the interminable meetings, market research and numerous professional readers.

Vernon was unlucky coming in on the final one of the series in that everyone had their minds on other things: Lorne was busy getting ready to go back home, Rupert and Jackie were anxious to get on with their new productions and the crew were concerned with finding a new job. So, poor old Vernon had a bit of a hard time – especially as he was very worried about the script. As the producers were more interested in finishing on time than trying to improve the last script, he could get no help there.

Not finding much co-operation with the permanent cast, he rang Raymond Huntley, a highly experienced and well-known character actor, who had a large part in the last episode, to try to persuade him to use his influence to get the producers to agree a major script rewrite. Mr Huntley had taken the part on the basis of the existing script, and I am sure viewed the whole thing as one of those times when an actor just does it for the money. Vernon had no alternative but to resign, or shoot the show as it was written.

I have to say, I don't think it was any worse or any better than the other twenty-five.

We got through it on schedule, and on the last day Vernon told me that he was making a film on his yacht as well as in the studios and would like me to join him as first.

"When would that be?" I asked.

"N-n-n-next week," he stuttered. Bang went the holiday. As always, work came first. You took it while you could get it.

On the Monday, I went to town to meet Vernon's partner in Cresswell Productions Ltd, George Maynard, who was also the producer. He was a charming, silver-haired, well-groomed man with an easy and very pleasant manner. I also met the two accountants, who I was to find out later were both top production accountants, but did George's work between them on the side.

As usual with film companies, everyone I met was more than pleasant. They offered me a deal which I accepted, gave me the script told me to report to Vernon's yacht at Shoreham Harbour on the Wednesday, from where we would sail to Le Havre in France.

The film was "Rogue's Yarn", a "B" film about the owner of a yacht, who does away with his wife so he can marry his French mistress. His alibi is that at the time of the murder he was on his yacht in the English Channel on his way to Le Havre from the UK. The yachtsman leaves port, sets the automatic pilot, and then takes his dinghy to the shore where he collects his car and goes home and kills his wife. He charters a plane to fly him to France, where he takes a boat to pick up his yacht at sea. The whole thing was full of holes, but it was quite a fun thing, and in those days people didn't ask too many questions. The great thing for George and Vernon was that Vernon owned the main prop, the yacht, complete with automatic pilot.

I arrived at Vernon's yacht the "KuSika" at Shoreham. It was a wonderful, elegant vessel, with an outer and inner "bridge", a large stateroom, and full sized galley. Below were the cabins, including the master's cabin, a twin berthed luxurious room with an en-suite bathroom. Then there was the engine room: a magnificent sight with its two large, gleaming chromed engines. I was soon to find out how powerful they were.

I met the rest of the film crew. This only consisted of one cameraman, not known to me but who, I was told, worked out of the Brighton Studios. (I didn't even know there was a studio at Brighton.) His assistant, who was the son of the writer Paul Tabori, and the Continuity Girl, Jane Moscrop (who obviously had worked on other Vernon films), Fred Worsley (one of the accountants I had already met), Beanie the cook, and Bill, the ship's engineer.

It was a jolly crowd of eight film- and yacht's-crews who sat down to an excellent dinner that night.

Next morning, it was up anchor and away onto the high seas. The sea seemed calm, the sun was shining, and I looked forward to the trip. But as I heard the engines rev up, from where I was in the galley, it felt as though we were going to fly there rather than sail. The yacht seemed to leap out of the water, and I had to hang onto the kitchen sink to keep my balance. Looking out, I could see the harbour wall zooming past as we accelerated out of the harbour and into the sea. I was later told that Vernon had a theory that the "KuSika" only reacted to the helm when moving at speed.

He had already been in trouble with the harbour authorities over nearly drowning one of their divers. It seems the poor chap had just surfaced, and removed his helmet before getting out of the water when Vernon passed by, his wake filling the diver's suit with water and sinking him like at stone. Luckily, he was attached to a line and they were able to haul him out.

This was just the start of many of Vernon's "sea" stories. I loved the one about how, before the '39 war, Vernon had owned a coal-fuelled yacht. At the outbreak of war it was commandeered by the Navy. Further, Vernon was commissioned as a Naval Lieutenant and made Captain of his own yacht, which was a happy situation as he no longer had to pay for the yacht's upkeep, instead got paid for living on his own vessel! He spent the entire war on anti-submarine patrol in the English Channel. He always said he spent five and a half aggressive years at war – at war with the lords of the Admiralty! Their bureaucracy and his directness just did not gel. He once sustained some damage below the water line, so reported at the docks for repair and was told that he would have to wait several weeks. Vernon was the most ingenious mechanic, self-taught, and he was truly in his element when dealing with something mechanical. So, fed up with the idea of waiting around, he rigged up a mask and connected it to a bellows contraption. Donning the mask, he went below, mended the damage in a matter of days and returned to duty at sea. This created an avalanche of signals between the Admiralty and Vernon, and he was forced to return to the docks where he sat around for days. Eventually they were forced to admit that the repairs were excellent, but he was warned never to repeat such a thing in the future.

My favourite story, though, was that he had a new sailor posted to him, one of the world's great incompetents. If he could fall over something, trip over a rope, fall down a gangway, he would. Worse still was that he was known to drop the depth charges on the deck. Eventually Vernon called him and said, "L-l-l-look, to get posted to this type of vessel you m-m-m-must have h-h-had some pre-war experience of the sea."

"Yes, sir," replied the sailor.

"So, what ships were you on?"

"I was on the 'Queen Mary', sir," the sailor replied.

"What exactly did you do on the 'Queen Mary'?" Vernon enquired.

To which the sailor responded, "I operated a dish-washing machine."

At this, Vernon sent a signal to the Admiralty listing all the sailors many inadequacies, ending up, "So I feel there are only two courses open to my Lords: either you post him immediately, or you send me a dish-washing machine!"

The war was drawing to a close, and Vernon realised that during all the years of ploughing up and down the Channel they had never let off one of their depth charges. So, mustering his crew together, one day they decided to let one off. Woops! Up into the air sped the underwater bomb, splashed down into the sea, and Vernon and the crew waited ... and waited ... and waited. Vernon saw a Dutch freighter approaching which they frantically signalled to change course ... but still nothing. There never was an explosion! When Vernon got back to the docks Vernon had the charges checked and discovered that they were all charged for the Pacific!

Yes, our Vernon was quite a character. I soon found out that on his yacht he turned into a sort of Captain Bligh, and expected his passengers to be experienced sailors. I was the first to suffer his wrath.

On arriving at the outer harbour of Le Havre, he declared that we wouldn't start filming till the next day, so I asked if we could go ashore, a request he found incomprehensible. After a lot of "umming and ahing", with my pointing out that, come what may, we would have to dock the following day, he reluctantly, and rather bad temperedly, agreed.

"Right, then, get the anchor up," he commanded me. When I looked completely blank, he shouted sarcastically, "Raise the an-an-anchor, for'ard, that's the sharp end, down there, you'll find a chain and a lever by its side, lift that, and that starts the anchor m-m-m-motor." And disappeared to where I had learnt was known as "below".

I found the anchor chain quite easily, raised the lever, heard the motor start up and watched as the chain started slowly to move, gradually getting faster. I was rather pleased that I had accomplished this feat entirely on my own, and without help from anyone. Whilst I stood there ruminating on my mechanical achievement, I looked down and was amazed to see how filthy the mud was at the bottom of the harbour. It was black with a covering of green greasy slime, which glistened in the sun's rays. It also stank to high heaven.

My reverie was broken by a penetrating scream. Vernon appeared on the deck; puce of face and so contorted with rage he was unable to get a word out.

"Fer...fer...fer ...Oh Christ", and he charged down the deck and switched off the anchor motor.

He finally calmed down enough to explain that one is supposed to hose the mud off the chain before it disappears into the bowels of the vessel. The reason for this was brought home to us all, as the smell invaded the whole yacht for days.

I was in the shit, and that's what the boat smelt like. Vernon was rough on me for a while, and I realised that his vocabulary had been honed in his five years in the Navy. I felt bad and nearly suggested to him that he buy me a dish-washing machine!

After dinner that night we walked down to a small café, leaving Vernon and Bill behind, where we had a few drinks. On our return, we sat at the back of the yacht enjoying the summer night. Somebody started to sing, and we all joined in a rather pleasant, amiable singsong after which we retired to bed.

Next morning Vernon appeared in his usual dress of grey slacks, blazer, and navy blue cap, indicating his rank. "Number One", he beckoned me, "see me on the bridge", and I thought, "Oh God, another bollocking."

Outside I found Vernon pacing up and down. "Number One, I want to make one thing very clear: I will not tolerate drunken matelots aboard my vessel." I realised that the term "Number One" was being used in the naval sense, and not the film sense. I did not try and explain that they were neither drunk, nor matelots, but film technicians quietly amusing themselves. I realised that to him we were a modern day "press gang" and if I weren't careful Vernon would order Bill, the engineer, to give me twenty strokes of the cat!

That day we started shooting and Derek Bond, playing the murderer, flew over and met us in Le Havre where we did various shots of him arriving by plane, going out from the French coast, on the yacht itself, and arriving in Le Havre harbour and having his passport stamped. At the end of a few days, we had completed this Second Unit work, and were ready to sail back to England, joining the rest of the crew and cast. Derek Bond flew back and we set sail. Everything had gone well, and the naval displeasure had moved from me to the Continuity Girl, who had left her tap on in the cabin and emptied all the yacht's fresh water tanks!

Being back in favour, Vernon invited me to share his cabin and I had this wonderful bed complete with heated blanket. As we were leaving very early in the morning, Vernon told me that there was no need for me to get up. As I had the feeling that he would be much happier knowing I was safely tucked up "below", I happily accepted.

I was in a deep trouble-free sleep, when suddenly Bill was in the cabin shouting, "Quick, John, quick, on deck."

"Oh my God," I thought "we're sinking."

I could hear the yacht's hooter going, so quickly slung some clothes on, grabbed my shoes and tried to get into them on the run, out into the corridor and up the gangway onto the deck.

There was a certain amount of confusion with Vernon at the wheel shouting instructions to all and sundry, the camera crew with the camera (what dedication I thought), and a bemused Continuity Girl in her dressing-gown. Where were the lifeboats?

I then spied over the side a French fishing boat, obviously coming to rescue us. However, as Vernon came alongside them, the French fishermen seemed distinctly uncooperative, and far from keen on saving a lot of rich Brits. Where was their compassion and the code of the sea? I asked myself.

Vernon abandoned the wheel, leant over the rail, and spoke to them in voluble but excruciating French, which only served to increase their antagonism. Ignoring their protests, he pushed the Camera Assistant and the cameraman, complete with camera onto the boat. The fishermen, in turn, resenting this invasion of their territory, tried to push them back. Fortunately, the sea was as calm as a millpond but, even so, two boats next to each move a lot. And the two camera boys had trouble keeping their legs.

Thinking that we should follow, I gallantly went to help the Continuity Girl over the rail. "N-n-n-n-not you two, for Christ's sake," shrieked Vernon.

At that moment, the accountant, Fred Worsley, arrived on deck dressed in his pyjamas, slippers, Burberry raincoat, bowler hat and with his briefcase.

"Fred," Vernon shouted, "get on there and give them some francs."

"But I haven't got any," Fred responded.

"Well, give them something, and for fuck's sake, get on there," and manhandled him over the side and into the fishing boat.

This was too much for the French temperament – I think it was probably the sight of a bowler-hatted Englishman that was the final straw – and they started to physically attack poor Fred, who was only saved by the "KuSika" pulling away at high speed, causing a great swell and sending them all, invaders and defenders, onto their backs.

"What is going on?" I asked Bill.

He explained that after several miles out of Le Havre they came across this fishing boat. A delighted Vernon instructed the two Cameramen to get into the fishing boat and to photograph the yacht as it came steaming towards them. I was relieved that we were not sinking, and could well understand the reaction of the fishermen.

"Bit of luck, eh, N-n-n-number One?" Vernon shouted, steering the "Kusika" at high speed away from the fishing boat. "Now," he continued, "get the decks clear, get everyone b-b-b-below, you and I are going to the lower bridge."

Vernon was taking advantage of the appearance of the fishing boat and was going to film from the boat as the yacht ploughed towards them, seemingly with no one aboard, not even at the helm.

"Did you explain this to the fishermen?" I asked

"No time, no time. Fred and the boys will have to d-d-do that."

"But they can't speak French," I explained.

"Not important, old boy, not important, they'll manage."

We were some distance from the fishing boat when Vernon opened up the engines, turned the yacht, and headed in a direct line for the fishing boat. He pulled me down onto the deck where he had a mirror through which he could see the boat.

The fishermen didn't know any of this, and although they had calmed down after Fred had managed to explain to them in sign language that we were making a film, what he was unable to explain was that the yacht was going to head for them, and it would look as though no one was steering it!

As the yacht got nearer and nearer to them, they got more and more agitated and signalled for it to turn away. They then noticed there was no one on board, not even at the wheel, and they became frantic, crossing themselves the nearer it got. At the last minute, it just slipped past, narrowly missing them, with the wake once more sending them on their backs. Standing up, Vernon turned to me and said, "F-f-f-funny lot, the French: so b-b-bloody excitable"!

It all ended happily, as Fred gave them a lot of pound notes. After a lot of hand-shaking we pulled away …and their captain raised Fred's bowler hat in a final good-bye.

Back in England, we set up base in the Brighton studios. As I said, I was unaware there were any studios in Brighton – hardly surprising, as they were minute, and up until then had only been used for commercials.

We first shot the location work in and around Shoreham and Brighton whilst the sets were being completed in the two small stages. The London mob took up residence in a "kosher" hotel in Hove. I have no idea why we were in a Jewish hotel because none of us were of that faith, but probably because they gave the company a good deal. I wasn't even aware that it was kosher until one night when we asked the night porter if he could make us a bacon sandwich! However, it confirmed what a lot of people believed: that I was Jewish.

I look Jewish, and I am told I act Jewish, and I am even circumcised, a fact noted by certain close friends. I think I have also always wanted to be Jewish, but there you are, I ain't. My very special secretary, Diane, was a Jewish girl whose mother always used to complain that she, Diane, hadn't gone into the family button business. She used to deride her working in films, and especially working "for that yok, John Dark". One day she saw me on a television show and she rang Diane saying, "Well, he may not *be* Jewish, but he *looks* Jewish!" Diane never heard another critical word again! I was very proud.

All being together in the same hotel lent itself to some intense drinking. I loved the friendship, the camaraderie, the fun, and the laughter, leaning over the bar, swapping stories, experiences, dreams. Film people have such wonderful stories, so many actors can be so entertaining, and our group was no exception.

Amongst the cast a well-known character actor, played the detective, by the name of Elwyn Brook-Jones.

Like so many gays, he had a wicked wit and, as he was a heavy drinker, he used to keep us entertained to the small hours of the morning. Derek Bond was a hell of a nice man, and a very good-looking chap, who had been for a long time under contract to the Rank Organisation where he played support roles to people like James Mason and Stewart Granger. They tried to build him up, but he never really made it.

He told me one wonderful story of how Rank's publicity department arranged for him to make a personal appearance at their Southampton cinema. On the train going down, the publicist explained that just before arriving at Southampton they wanted him to lean out of the window so the photographers could get shots of him arriving, and when the train stopped, he would alight and be greeted by the Mayor of the city. So at the appointed time Derek leant out of the window and, as they approached, he saw the large banner: "Southampton Welcomes Derek Bond". The brass band started to play, and he started to wave. However, the train just kept going and sailed right past the assembled dignitaries with Derek waving good-bye! The train was destined to stop at Southampton Docks, not the city!

Derek used to stay for the early part of the evening but would disappear to bed fairly early, leaving the hard core made up of Elwyn, George Maynard, a pretty little blonde actress, Barbara, who was playing a small part in the film, and was also George's girlfriend, and myself. Every night was party night and George and I soon lost the employer/ employee relationship, becoming good friends.

I had a tough day's work, as there was no production manager and as George always seemed to be in the Oyster Bar I had to do two, and sometimes three, jobs. I had made Ted Wallace my Second but we didn't have a Third. Consequently we were busy people and not knowing any better, were happy just to get on with it. I had a telephone rigged up on the floor and used to deal with the administration side in-between takes. I don't want to exaggerate the problems, but this was a very small film, and this kind of situation would not have been possible on any sort of major feature. It was great training, though, and I think it is a bad thing that young people are trained on big pictures and have no idea how to operate on small budgets.

I don't know how much "Rogue's Yarn" cost but I would guess it was something under twenty thousand pounds. Imagine, this was a film with a foreign location, an English location and interiors in a studio. Being away from London, the cast, George, the art director and I had to be housed and fed. Vernon lived on his yacht berthed at Shoreham so there were no extra costs for him. The rest of the crew came from the Brighton-based boys who always worked at the studio. Of course, a few Union rules were, shall we say, bent. Used as they were to only working on commercials, the Brighton crew thought they were working on "The Ten Commandments", and what they lacked in experience they made up for in enthusiasm. They placed no restrictions on shooting, and indeed they would have been happy to go on shooting all night long if we could have afforded to pay for their suppers, never mind the overtime!

It was a happy time, and when it came to an end I was really sorry. I had got used to Vernon, and found him much easier once we got him back on land.

On returning to the office in London, George greeted me by telling me not to take anything else because there was another picture coming up. He suggested we discuss it at the "Duke of Wellington", situated at the Shaftesbury Avenue end of Wardour Street, right behind the back of the Queen's Theatre. In those days this was the film pub and was frequented by crew members and actors. If a rush call was needed you could nearly always find someone ready to work in "The Duke ...". I would hate to think how much of my time and money was spent there. Bunny, the landlord, was my banker, my message centre, my cloakroom attendant, my confidant, and my good friend. I got to know an awful lot of people in the business there.

Over numerous drinks George told me that he hoped to have this new picture very soon. But the main thing he wanted to discuss was for me to stop being an assistant director and become Cresswell's production manager.

I was quite flattered, but not really all that keen as I enjoyed being a first, and didn't really know whether I wanted to move from the floor to the office. He took me to Isow's for lunch, a famous restaurant in Brewer Street whose owner, Jack

Isow, had been imprisoned during the war for selling black market steaks. I don't expect he was any more guilty than plenty of other restaurant owners, and I imagine the resulting publicity pushed up his business several notches!

Over lunch George tried to talk me into taking the job. But it wasn't until he told me how much they would pay me that I gave in and accepted.

However, I quickly realised that I knew very little about the job, so I thought the only way around that was to find the best production secretary (now called "Production Co-ordinator") the budget could afford. Here I was lucky and I found a very experienced girl, Betty Parry, who was between major features. She was my guiding light throughout the shoot and we went on to make several films together.

First, though, was "The Strange World of Planet X". A story in which something happens, something goes wrong in the laboratory, and the insects in the neighbourhood grow into monsters.

My first job was to find someone who could create the special effects' work, and I found Les Bowie who was to become quite famous in the future as one of the senior technicians on "Superman" and who helped him to fly! At that time he had a small outfit with which he said he could easily enlarge the insects with microphotography, and then utilise this with back projection, which is a system whereby the background is projected onto a screen for the live action being photographed on the set: the enlarged insect is the background and the actors are the foreground. This is a very basic system used mainly in those days for car shots, trains, or any other moving object, and used successfully with animals in the Johnny Weissmuller "Tarzan" films.

We were to make the film for Eros films, a small English distributor specialising in support features, owned by two brothers, Sid and Phil Hyams.

Much has been written about the Hyams, and Phil in particular. Phil was the oldest, but out-lived his brother by many years and was over a hundred when he died, his obituary covering several columns in "The Times". I shall just restrict myself to what I have been told, and my own experiences.

Phil and Sid were Polish Jews, who started out as bakers. I was told that they got into the cinema business through a bad debt and by accident became cinema owners. Then, realising that there was more money to be made in making and distributing films, set up Eros Film Distributors. Also in the company was Phil's son, Norman, who, though he was a much better educated man than either his father or uncle (he was, I believe, a qualified architect), didn't have the same instincts for the film trade. Another important man in the company, John Saunders, was a man in complete contrast to the brothers and was a tall, good-looking, grey-haired man, every inch an Englishman. He was the company secretary, and very much the pounds and shillings man. He had his own company, Banner, a completion bond company, which is a company that insures the financial over-run of a picture, and guarantees that the film will be completed. Banner was very closely linked with Eros.

My first meeting with them was brief. I met them in their Wardour Street offices. The three Hyams shared an office and, with a minimum of preliminaries, Phil said, "No matter what happens, boy, you are not to go over-schedule."

"Or over-budget", jumped in Sid.

"Yes, or over-budget," echoed Phil. "*Especially* over-budget," he continued. "Don't care what happens, no excuses, got it?" That was my brief.

Vernon was not going to direct as he was tied up finishing "Rogue's Yarn", and preparing a new movie. The picture was going to be directed by an Associated British contract director, Gilbert Gunn, who I found a very pleasant fellow, but quite unlike a Film director, being rather shy and introverted, and more like a minor clerk than the top man on a film set.

This was 1957 and we were going to shoot at the National Studios in Borehamwood (known by most crews as "Bore 'em Stiff") and here I had my first meeting with the studio manager, Percy Dayton.

He had originally been a sound Boom Operator, but came to prominence when the Union started to become strong. Because he was the most militant of the shop stewards, in order to curtail his disruptive activities, the employers in their wisdom gave him a job in management. Percy overnight changed from a radical, militant Union official to a ruthless, dominant employer. He was so successful that he got the job of running the National Studios. He was a hard drinking, uncouth, vulgar man, but there was no doubt that he did run the studios well, had the Unions under control and therefore was able to offer independent producers a good deal. There is no doubt, though, that the studios largely operated for his convenience. Amazingly he had a telephone line fitted from the studio switchboard to the local pub, so if anybody rang for him, the studio operator could put them right through to him sitting cosily in the bar!

I soon realised that to get the right deal and co-operation, one had to get on the right side of Percy. These were the days when the studio employed the craft and electrical labour: the carpenters, plasterers, prop men, stagehands, and electricians were all on the studio permanent pay roll. The producer brought in the technical grades; the production personnel, the set designers, make-up artists and hairdressers. The studios were always trying to get the right balance, having enough labour to build the sets, but not too much as they had to be carried through the lean times. Consequently all producers and production managers worried about getting their sets up on time. When they got behind, the producers were in conflict with the studio management who were loath to take on extra labour. Overtime would be increased thereby increasing the cost to the producer, and this was compounded when there was more than one production shooting in the studio at the same time. You were not only in conflict with the studio but also with the other film. Accusations of preferential treatment were the norm and the situation was not helped by the fact that the studios made a profit on the labour. A production company was charged the hourly rate for the individual craftsman, plus a percentage to cover his fringe benefits (National Insurance, holiday pay) plus a loading for the studios. This meant that if you had a film with a big set budget you could often make a good deal on the renting of the stages, as the studio would see the profit they could make on the labour.

Now the arbitrator on all these matters was the studio manager, in this case, Percy Dayton. So I made it my business to become the best friend Percy had, which meant drinking vast quantities of alcohol but still be able to do my job. Now I can't say I objected to this, but I could have thought up a better boozing companion!

Forest Tucker, a minor star in his time, headed our cast. Forest was the usual giant of an American, ideally suited for the many times he had played cowboys. He was very proud of his physique, and especially the size of his dick, which he called Wilbur! Certain members of a haughty Surrey golf club never really recovered from the sight of Forest putting on the last hole with Wilbur as a club! He was an easy-going, laid-back actor, turned up on time, knew his lines and said them as well as could be expected. That was all that was required of him. The trouble was that we started to slip behind, and despite pulling pages out of the script we were having difficulty keeping up. Not having a producer (as George, when he did turn up, was more anxious to get to the bar than worry about the budget); not knowing any better, I would go on the set and ask Gilbert what he was up to. He would explain his shooting plan. "I'll do a master, then over- shoulders and then into the singles," he would explain.

"Oh, you haven't got time for that, Gilbert."

"Well, what would you suggest?" he'd enquire.

Taking hold of the viewfinder and backing up against the studio wall I'd say, "I think if you got back here, you could get it in one", and poor Gilbert would comply. He had been brought up in a tough studio where directors did as they were told, or their contracts were terminated.

My behaviour, though, was far from normal for a production manager. I was to find out later, but at this time all I had was my brief from the Hyams. When we did finish (on time and on budget!), the editors needed an extra scene. It was I who directed it. I was director, producer, and first assistant. Then, at the end, as the picture was under length, I wrote a pre-credit title sequence (something not heard of in those days) which started: "Ever inventive man ..." and I got a lot of stock shots of high speed trains, jet planes, nuclear bomb explosions, and cobbled them all together.

Whilst this was happening, Les Bowie was busy finalising the special effects. Soon I was able to ring up Eros and tell them the film was finished, and they could view the film whenever they liked.

It was Phil who came to see it. George didn't even manage to turn up for this, so it was my misfortune to have to attend the showing. Afterwards Phil said to me, "Well, boy, it's not the worst film I've ever seen, but what you need is more bleedin' beetles!"

CHAPTER 9
THE WAY AHEAD

This was 1957. Shortly after this George received a call from Gerry Blattner at Warner Brothers asking if he could recommend a production manager for a few weeks' work. As I was not being gainfully employed, George suggested to me that I go there until he had something new, like the next Vernon picture.

Before reporting to Blattner's office at the Associated British studios at Elstree, I checked up on him. He was the son of Ludwig Blattner, who at one time owned what were to become the National Studios. He also invented the Blattnerphone, the first electro-magnetic sound recording machine, which obviously was not a success and, sadly, he went bankrupt and eventually committed suicide. Prior to his death, Joe Rock, an American producer, bought the studios and made Gerry his manager. I do not know whether this was a kindly gesture or not, but Gerry remained a film executive all his working life, and eventually became head of Warners' UK operations, a post he held for many years.

Trying to gain entrance into the ABPC studios was like trying to get into Buckingham Palace. The security was very tough, and not for nothing was it known as the "salt mines". Luckily I was not on the ABPC pay roll and therefore did not have to go through the staff gate, where they timed you in and out. Working for Warners' meant I was free to enter and exit at will once my position had been established. This took several phone calls to confirm my position, and my signature to be taken and duly recorded into the security ledger.

I eventually got in and found Mr Blattner's office. Gerry greeted me most kindly, coffee was ordered, and he proceeded to tell me that his company was to embark on an enormous project and that he would like me to start planning the production. He then handed me a copy of a book entitled "The Nun's Story".

"Take it away and read it."

"Is there anything else I should know?" I enquired.

"No, that's all we've got so far."

Off I went to the office assigned to me, which was on the other side of the studio. I had hardly taken my coat off when the phone rang and a girl said, "Mr Blattner would like to see you in his office."

So, back I went into the outer office where the younger of the two secretaries told me to go straight in. On entering, I saw Gerry was with two men, whom he introduced as the company's production accountants, adding, "You've already met my secretaries". With the two secretaries, these made up the total Warner Brothers' production staff.

Gerry was a very short man, and rumour had it he had a raised floor behind his desk, but I have no personal evidence about that, and I was too shy to ask either of his girls. All I know is that he seldom strayed from behind his large desk. "A cable came from Burbank over the weekend," he announced. Gerry treated receiving a communication from the Los Angeles studios, I was to find out, as Moses treated the arrival of the Ten Commandments. "The cable reads 'Advise availability of British cameramen for Nun'."

"Okay, I'll go and check up", I said, and started to leave.

Gerry stopped me. I turned and waited, and the other two settled back in their chairs with a look of resignation. I sat on the edge of a chair expecting a quick instruction. "First of all, we have to consider exactly what this means."

Not very tactfully, I jumped in, "I think it's pretty obvious that they want a list of available Cameramen."

"Ah, that's what you think it means, but does it? Believe me, I have been dealing with the Coast for many years, and it is true that we are two countries separated by the same language. So let us consider this quietly." I was conscious that one of the secretaries was taking down every word. "'British': do they mean an *English-speaking* cameraman, a British *resident*, or a British *national?* ..." and so it went on. After a while, the other girl replaced the secretary, taking down the dialogue. In due course, the first secretary would return with the typed pages of the beginning of the meeting, and replace the second girl. We then discussed these pages, which in turn were recorded. This went on throughout the day, the two girls taking it in turns to take down and type up what we had discussed. In effect, it meant that at the end of the day we were still discussing what we had discussed at the start! It was a daily occurrence to be called over to Gerry's office shortly after arriving and spend most of the day there while he pontificated at length about this, that, and the other. He would ask your advice about something, you would reply off-the-cuff thinking this was just a casual chat, an idle enquiry, and the next thing was a cable to Burbank, "Dark advises ..."

As I never had time to read it in the office, I took the book home. I thought it was an amazing book, and would make the most wonderful film. However, it was written in the first person, the reader being privy to what was in the girl's mind, and it was difficult to anticipate how the screenwriter would transfer this into dialogue. I told Gerry that, to make any plan, I had to know a few details: like where they intended shooting, *when* they intended to shoot, whether they were shooting in colour or black and white etc.

To every question he would reply, "Plan it for all the alternatives." This was impossible. Even to get to a very preliminary pre-production plan one has to know a few things, like who is going to direct, where the main studio is likely to be, which countries are likely to be scouted and so on.

However, I need not have worried as I never got round to planning anything, because I spent all my days in Gerry's office.

Eventually a call came from George that I was needed back to start their new picture. I had mixed feelings as I would have loved to have worked on such a wonderful and prestigious film, but was glad to get away from the very pleasant, but, in my opinion, hopeless Mr Blattner. He kept his position, like so many other movie executives, by never making a decision. Mind you, that is an art in itself and is not to be sneered at, though it is an art I think the business could do without.

When I saw the film with the delectable Audrey Hepburn, my heart did ache a little, thinking how close I got to working on it, but I also realised how woefully inexperienced I would have been. So perhaps it was lucky for the talented Mr Fred Zinnemann, who directed the film, that I was called back to Cresswell Productions. Mind you, it was quite a shock to the system descending so quickly from Warner Brothers to the Hyams Brothers!

Back to the old gang and a new film. Not this time a 'B'-movie, but a first feature. A first for Vernon and George, and a first for Eros, and mine as a production manager. This was the picture that Vernon had been researching for years, and he had at last convinced the Hyams Brothers to put up the money.

"The Battle of the V.1." was the story of how the allies got hold of an actual "flying bomb" before they were ever launched against Britain. This resulted in the bombing of the factory in Peenamunde, and the failure of Hitler's much-vaunted secret weapon. It was an incredible true story of how a group of Polish underground fighters got their hands on an unexploded bomb, and smuggled it back to London. It had all the ingredients for an intriguing war film.

After starting to plan the production, the picture hit a problem and everything had to stop. As often happens, we were in the "on/off" pre-production saga. There are so many things that can go wrong and I think in this case it was that the Hyams were getting cold feet. This was a big undertaking for them, as they had never tackled anything so big or so costly, and they were obviously trying to spread their financial undertaking. Anyhow, we had a hiatus on our hands whilst the moneymen sorted out their problems.

George suggested that we make some commercials as he had some contacts, so some money changed hands, and we had a contract to shoot a series for Bird's Eye Frozen Peas. Although this was a come down from "The Nun's Story", it was slightly softened by the fact that I was to direct them!

My leading lady, the presenter, was Fanny Craddock, a well-known television cook, who, with her husband, did a weekly television show where she would cook in full evening dress. Her husband, dressed in a tuxedo, used to fluff around explaining the wines. Fanny was without doubt the star, and I think her old man was there just because you couldn't have Fanny without him. She had the reputation of being a tyrant, and the agent warned me that I would probably have trouble with her. So with some trepidation I went to meet her in her dressing-room on the first day.

She was a good-looking woman in her 50's I suppose, very elegant, and with most wonderful upper class voice sounding as though she had gargled with gravel. I liked her immediately and took to her fascinating way of speaking. As so often happens, she was the opposite of what I had been told. These people are often pussycats, it is just that they are professionals, and don't suffer fools gladly.

After the preliminary greeting we discussed what had to be done, she was anxious to get away as she had a personal problem. She had been booked for two days, but I told her I really thought we could get through in one. I explained that we had two one-minute commercials to shoot but they were both on the same set and once we were lit there would be few changes needed. In the end we finished with her before lunch on the first day. I made a friend, the agent was happy, the client over the moon and I delighted with a fat cheque.

We shot a few others and I soon became very bored. The actual filming of them was not too bad but it was the planning, the endless discussions with the agents and the clients, the endless pretentious prattle that went on at the numerous meetings that were held. We were forever going to lunches and discussing the merits of the latest proposals. Though the food was excellent, and the wine a delight, the conversation was banal in the extreme. I eventually blotted my copybook and asked not to return.

It happened at a meeting to discuss a thirty-second commercial for Four Square cigarettes. We were all gathered in the boardroom of a large agency: where about twenty of us sat around this amazing oval table, and were addressed by the Account Executive.

He explained that, though the pipe tobacco sold well, the cigarettes had never really taken off, and that they were launching a campaign to increase their popularity. One of his aides rose to explain to "silly me" why men smoked cigarettes, and after fifteen minutes of waffle he concluded that they smoked them because it was a virile and masculine thing to do. I wonder what they would think now, now that it is the young women who are smoking more and the men less.

Anyhow, after this, the head of the television department got up and unveiled his beautifully prepared storyboard. "As you can see," he started, "we dissolve in on a yacht anchored in still waters, probably a lake. It is a beautiful and tranquil scene, and as the yacht gently rises and falls, its sail gleaming white in the moonlight, we cut to a good-looking young couple lying on the deck. It is obvious that they have just, how shall I put it, had an experience. The boy sits up, lights a cigarette, inhales, leans over the side, and we cut to his reflection in the water as he looks down into the depths and the commentary says, '… but for *complete* satisfaction smoke a Four Square cigarette.'"

This is where I got the giggles, not so much for the line, but by the seriousness with which it was treated by the high-powered executives. Advertising is a serious business and not to be treated lightly! Also this was the late 50s, and some things were just not mentioned, like Tampax, or condoms, unlike now when they are sold over the air like Corn Flakes.

I pulled myself together as I listened whilst they proceeded to discuss the idea. A lengthy debate started about the couple, what they should look like, how old they were, and that they should look a really nice clean couple.

"Do you think she should be blonde or brunette?"

"Oh, brunette, blonde gives the wrong impression, you know, a bit flighty."

"Yes, right, she must not look trampy, just lightly made up, no excessive exposure of flesh."

"Yes, yes," they all agreed with the head man.

"I think a wedding ring," one suggested.

This idea was greeted with great enthusiasm. "Yes, that's a really good idea, Alan, a wedding ring." Alan reacted to the reception of his idea as though he had just come up with a cure for cancer! "That removes the problem of any suggestion of sleaze."

"Heaven forbid, this is a young married couple enjoying an evening on their yacht."

"Yes, but they should look as though they had just … *had* it."

"Yes, that is very important, but it must be done with great taste."

"Yes, with taste, but with just very subtle suggestion there, you know, so when the boy is looking in the water, the audience understands the implication of the voice over, '… but for complete satisfaction smoke Four Square cigarettes.'"

"Or," I chipped in, "it could say, 'For fuck's sake smoke a Four Square cigarette!'"

We lost the contract.

However, they made the commercial and, shortly after, this brand of cigarette ceased to exist!

I wasn't out of work for long, as the very next day it was announced that "…V.1." was on again, and there was the usual panic to get going quickly before the summer was over and the weather turned. All our precious pre-production time had gone whilst the money was straightened out.

The idea was to shoot the location work in and around Brighton and Shoreham, using the services and crew from the Brighton studios, and to shoot the main interiors at the National Studios in Elstree, using their craft personnel. Here was the first problem.

Under the agreement between the Unions and the Producers' Association, you could have only one base on a picture – which in our case would mean taking all the craft grades like carpenters, stagehands, painters and electricians from National Studios to Brighton, keeping them all in hotels and paying them special rates for being on location. We could not shoot the whole thing at Brighton, as the studios were not big enough, and we couldn't shoot the whole thing around Elstree, as the right locations just weren't there.

The first thing I did was to arrange a meeting in Brighton with all the various Trades Union officials, one from each of the three main Unions and one from the Producers' Association, in order to get their agreement to a two-studio base.

We met them off the Brighton Belle at Brighton railway station. The Brighton Belle was a Pullman train, all one class, and very luxurious with its ornate fittings and furnishings, staffed by liveried men who delivered a service in keeping with the surroundings. Many notable people who lived in Brighton would catch this train for the one-hour journey to London, and often Laurence Olivier would be seen having his favourite breakfast of grilled kippers whilst he was sped up to London. The passengers we met off the Belle that day were not as distinguished as the great actor, though they would have considered themselves in the same line of business as Sir Laurence. The awful truth was that in those days they exerted more power than he did.

George and I were there to greet them, and on the way we had to pass a very good oyster bar. It seemed only right to offer our guests half-a- dozen prime oysters and a glass or two of Chablis. It wasn't long before the Electrical Union organiser said, "Just want to get one thing straight from the start, right? You know what you are asking for is impossible, right? It is one of the principle rules of all Unions, not just us, but all film Unions, and I might add, signed by the Producers' Association. Right? In all agreements it firmly states that there is to be only one base for any picture, right?"

"Right," echoed the other two.

"Well," I said, "we'll get into that later. How about another half- dozen?"

Gradually the morning wore on and as it got to one o'clock and as we had a table booked at English's restaurant, we decided not to go to the studios until after lunch. Lunch was amazing, with the best food the establishment could offer, served with the most expensive of wines. At the end of the meal, over the large brandies, the NATKE organiser lent over to me and whispered, "John, the cigars."

So, the cigars came round and the same man took two. "One," he explained, "for Sir Tom" (Sir Tom O'Brian the President of NATKE at that time), and put it in his top pocket.

It was after five when we finished lunch, and as the pubs were open, we went to "The Caxton Arms", our favourite watering hole, and the party continued. With warm embraces all round, they eventually staggered on to the ten o'clock train to Victoria. The final word from the electrical Union organiser was: "Well, I can tell you, no trouble, no trouble at all, right?" And the others echoed, "Right."

And right it was. Our request for using both Brighton and National as main bases was granted. There was one more meeting at the National Studios where the local works council, now let down by their organisers, were demanding to go on the location. Percy Dayton held a meeting in his office.

"Well," said Percy, "to put it in a nutshell ..." then spoke for the next fifteen minutes! At the end he said, "Any questions?"

But when one of the shop stewards got up, before he could open his mouth, Percy said, "You can shut up for a start." And that was the end of that.

The Brighton boys were delighted. At last they were going to be allowed to work on a big movie, and their enthusiasm continued throughout the shoot. Obstacles are easy to overcome if you have the right spirit. It is a two-way thing, enthusiasm has to be nurtured, and boys and girls have to be made to feel an important part of the team, which indeed they are. Film-making is a team effort and every one has his or her place in the scheme. We sometimes forget when we want to go on shooting and the sparks want to go home, that our job is interesting, fascinating even, but sitting up on a rail tending an arc light is not only hot, not only grubby, but also very boring. If you can get the crew to feel involved in the making of a film, you are halfway there.

Sadly, this was not true of many of the old studio hands who had seen it all, rarely went to the cinema themselves, but just looked on it as a job and where you made the most money for the least amount of work. Protected by powerful Unions, they could make film-making very difficult.

At Brighton it was different. We had a collection of people busting a gut to work. They were paid in accordance with the Union agreements, so their work was well rewarded. As the Brighton studios rarely had the opportunity to offer them overtime, and with us shooting six days a week plus a lot of night work, they ended up with the biggest wage packets they had ever seen. Which was still a lot less than bringing studio staff from London.

The camera crew, the art department, the production staff, Make-up and Hair came from London. Basil Emmet, the lighting cameraman, had made many films with George and Vernon and was known by the crews as "Burn 'em up Basil" because of the amount of light he used. Our first assistant director was Dougie Hickox who later was to become a director in his own right, and much more successful than Vernon. When I met him years later, after he had directed several large films, I said, "I see you're a better director than you were an assistant." For he was not the best man to have on the floor. I realised afterwards that his mind was on directing, and he found the job of assistant tiresome, especially the boring bits like the schedule, the call sheet, and keeping the office informed as to what was going on. I think he spent most of his time mentally criticising poor old Vernon.

George left for Los Angeles to get some names to head the cast, whilst Vernon and I started scouting locations, casting the small parts and getting the rest of the crew together. We planned to use Shoreham's old gas works for the bombed Peenamunde factory. Standing derelict, the building was ideal for us, and the authorities were only too glad for us to knock it about even more. It was already fenced off, and with their permission, we could use as much explosives as we liked, as the gas had long been disconnected.

We set up our production office in an equally derelict farmhouse, Old Salt's Farm, which became the centre of our operation, housing not only the office but also almost all the necessary facilities like wardrobe, hair, and make-up.

I lent my car, the old Vauxhall, to the early construction boys in order to save money. Little did I realise at the time that they would also use it for carrying down their cement and timber, and eventually one day it just collapsed. So then I had no car. However, the company took pity on me, and the compensation was enough for me to buy a nearly new one, so that weekend I went home to Peggy and the children in a new shiny car. It was not the only thing to change, as we were gradually getting the house decorated, central heating installed, turning it into a fantastic residence.

George came back with a cast agreed, albeit not a cast that would get us into the front rank of movies. We had Michael Rennie (one of the old Gainsborough repertory company members), Patricia Medina, a very minor star born in England who had moved to Hollywood, Milly Vitale, an Italian actress, and Christopher Lee.

I had always thought that Michael Rennie, though very good-looking, was a very wooden actor with a flat voice, and was surprised he got as far as he did. He was a nice person and he went on and on working, even if he never reached the kind of star status he craved.

Patricia Medina seemingly never expected too much, but just accepted whatever was going around, whether it be an Abbot and Costello film ("Abbot and Costello in the Foreign Legion") or the Three Stooges ("Snow White and the Three Stooges"). She had been married to Richard Greene and after him to Joseph Cotton, so I guess she didn't have too much to worry about, alimony being what it was in the US.

Milly Vitale must have been about twenty-five at the time, and didn't seem to have any men around, probably because her mother never took her eyes off her.

In addition to the cast, George also brought back an American producer, Johnny Bash. Exactly what the deal was, I don't know, but as the movie progressed, everyone got more and more pissed off with him. He was one of those annoying Americans who always knows a better way of doing things. I subsequently found out that he had little experience, so it was no wonder that a lot of the time he was in conflict with the various members of the crew. Vernon didn't like him from the start, and as he also did not like the cast that George had put together, Johnny Bash was just the final pill that he did not want to swallow.

The budget was the usual nightmare. Nobody in the history of the cinema has ever presented a budget without the company saying, "But it *can't* be that much." With the Hyams it was even worse for they had never financed a picture of such a size. With "… the V.1." they were entering the big boy's league.

The problem was compounded by the fact that the company secretary, John Saunders, was also the owner of the completion bond company, Banner Pictures. John Saunders controlled the money for both companies, so for sure he wasn't going to allow me to go over by one dime, even though the film was woefully under-budgeted. It was very, very tight, bordering on the impossible, but George and Vernon had impressed on me the necessity of getting it down to a minimum or the Hyams would get cold feet and back off the deal. Looking back, I realise that it was my inexperience that made me think I could do it for the money. Somehow I convinced the Hyams family and John Saunders and after numerous meetings, we got the green light.

We had one bit of luck. During the hiatus period, Vernon had Ken Adams design the sets. Ken was to become the first designer of the Bond pictures, and in my opinion was one of the main contributors to the success of those films. So we had great designs ready, and were able to start building very soon after getting the "off". Several large exterior sets had to be built, the main one being a large square in the middle of a Polish city. Another was of a concentration camp and we were lucky to find an old disused mushroom farm, which gave us a collection of low, long buildings, so we only had to build the perimeter fence and the guard towers. It also gave us the interior sets we needed, as the concrete shelves, that used to house the mushrooms, exactly resembled the bunks in the camps.

Casting was well under way, and the crew engaged, so George and I rented a cute little house in the middle of Brighton and he, Barbara, and I moved in. Life was good. A pre-shoot party was held at the Café Royal by the Hyams to introduce the cast to the press, and for us all to get to know one another. As a kid, I had worked with Michael Rennie, but, as I explained to him, it would be impossible for him to remember the scruffy little kid that ran around the studio with cans of film stock in his arms. I think he was happy to be back in England making a movie. Patricia Medina was a bubbly sort of person who made a big effort to belie her age by being the life and soul of the party. I don't know whether she and Michael were having an affair during the movie, but they were certainly very close. I think they helped prop each other up, neither of them being very talented, and I suspect in their hearts, both of them knew it.

We started shooting outside on location in the countryside whilst the exterior and studio sets were constructed. One of the major problems was getting hold of German Second World War transport. Some enterprising companies had, at the end of the war, realised the potential of owning such stuff and bought it all up. The trouble was in maintaining it over the years. It used to rot outside in the English climate and receive little or no maintenance, and it was only when a film company had a war film and wanted a car, a tank, or whatever, that the machines were hurriedly made ready. By that time, they were often beyond the skills of any mechanic, and were horribly unreliable. They invariably broke down on the first day, and the director had to resort to all sorts of ruses to shoot travelling scenes – towing or pushing – and leaving the long shots to be filmed by the Second Unit when at last the vehicles were functioning.

Automatic firing guns were another problem. In a conventional weapon, it is the kickback of the bullet that re-cocks the weapon allowing the next bullet to be fired. With a blank cartridge, there is not the same power, the same explosion. At the time we were shooting, "gas guns" were the usual way out of the problem, but these had many disadvantages as not only were they unreliable, but there was always the problem of hiding the tube that went from the gun to the gas bottle. Vernon, though, had anticipated this, and using his undoubted mechanical skills and his amazing ingenuity, invented his own electrical firing guns. His demonstrations before production were, to say the least, impressive, and we all applauded him as he proudly strutted around spraying us with his rapid firing machine gun. In fact, all was well until they were handed out to the actors. Vernon gave them explicit instructions as how to use them, but the trouble was that, not only did the actors have to fire the guns, they also had to act out the scene, and it soon became clear that Vernon was more interested in the guns than in the artist! Though they were well-briefed military wise, artistically they were on their own. The strange thing about all props, but especially guns, is that they always work perfectly beforehand in rehearsal, but come the "take", nothing. Vernon's guns were no exceptions. However, he blamed the poor actor. "Cut," he'd shout. "Look, you've got to give the trigger a strong pull, not f-f-f-fucking grab at it. Try again." And so the day would progress.

Vernon only printed the takes in which the gun worked, often he would choose a take where an actor had fluffed, or miscued. "Print," he would yell despite the pleas of the actor. "D-d-d-don't worry about that, old boy. I can cut round that." And off he would stomp to the next set-up, leaving the poor unfortunate artist standing forlornly contemplating the end of his career. No wonder that eventually so many of them hated the guns. I suspect some of them hated Vernon too!

One of the early scenes called for a young boy fishing with his Polish father. He quizzes his father about the funny planes that fly over, and at that moment one of the early test flying bombs flies overhead. Its engine cuts out, and it dives down, whereupon the father grabs the boy in his arms and waits for the explosion, but nothing, it has not gone off. The father realises that this is the Polish underground's chance to get their hands on a complete bomb, so he sends his son off with a message, whilst he goes off to gather his comrades together. We then see the Germans hunting for the bomb. They are in their vehicle studying a map, and the recorded flight path of the V.1. They come across some boys playing football, and question them about the whereabouts of the flying bomb, but the boys all deny any knowledge of it. The senior German Officer gets out some chocolate and offers it to any boy who can tell them where it went. All the boys shake their heads, until the little boy that we saw earlier pushes his way through and tells the Germans that he can tell them where it went. When the German asks where, the boy insists that he give him the chocolate first. Whilst the other boys stand around looking horrified, the German smiles and hands over the chocolate. "It went that way", the boy responds, pointing in the opposite direction to the actual path the bomb had taken. The Germans grin, and tear off in their car, leaving the boy chewing on his chocolate with the others all crowding around him, slapping him on the back, the hero of the hour.

The morning the scenes were going to be shot I got a message that I was wanted on the set. Now, that means trouble. Whenever you are told you are needed on the set, you know something's wrong. Nobody is asking you down there to have some fun, to tell you some good news ... no, it's trouble.

This time the trouble was that the child cast in the part of the little boy burst into tears as soon as he got in front of the camera, and despite all the entreating, bribing and scolding of his "show biz mum" would not stop. Vernon, who was not used to children at the best of times, just said, "We'll have to re-cast." Which was fine, but it was a Saturday and the agencies were closed. Where was I supposed to find a small boy of the right age at this short notice? The next set wasn't ready, so we were stuck. I could think of only one solution. I suggested sending a car to my home to get my son, Gregory.

"Great idea," said Vernon, and turning to his Assistant, "Now, get rid of that ghastly child, and we'll shoot around him till young Dark turns up."

So a car was dispatched with the script so he could learn the lines on his way to Shoreham. I wasn't there when he arrived as I had to go to a meeting with the local council, but when I returned there was another urgent, and ominous, message to go to the set. When I got there, Vernon approached me with a face like thunder, "He can't do it, just mumbles, what's the matter with the wretched boy?"

All I needed was for my own son to be holding up the shooting. I went and got hold of Greg, took him away from the shoot, and told him in no uncertain terms to get on and do it, "Just say the lines out loud and stop fooling around, holding everything up and making my life even more difficult. Now, get in front of the camera and do what Mr Sewell tells you."

"Right, Vernon, shoot it," I said.

"But he hasn't had a rehearsal yet," Vernon objected.

"Well, I think you should shoot."

"Okay, if you say so." Turning to Dougie his Assistant, "Shoot."

I retired as far back as I could go, certainly out of earshot. I couldn't stand the tension of watching my five-year-old son bollocks the whole thing up. After a short while I heard the Tannoy speaker go, "Cut."

Vernon marched over to me. "Well, I don't know what you said, but it did the t-t-trick, he was b-b-b-bloody marvellous." So a relieved and proud father returned to the office. Greg spent the next three days on the set, was thoroughly spoiled, earned himself a few pounds to increase his piggy bank, and no doubt found it difficult to go back to the normal routine of his life.

The film progressed with the usual number of disasters. Two sides of the Warsaw square set were blown down, and the rest badly damaged by the high wind on one particularly stormy night. The special effects man nearly killed Michael Rennie and Christopher Lee, who was playing a German SS Officer. Vernon had briefed the special effects chief and agreed that he would signal him when to blow the charge that would simulate a bomb dropping. The special effects chief in turn instructed his assistant to watch the director holding his white handkerchief, and when he dropped his hand to pull the switch. Getting near to shooting, Vernon made a mistake in deciding to brief him twice. The trouble was that the poor assistant didn't hear these instruction and following orders pulled the switch, setting off the explosion right by where Michael was standing chatting to Chris.

Thank God, neither of them was badly hurt, but they sure had a nasty shock. Michael took it quite well, but Chris took longer to recover, and not being afraid to take advantage of a situation, kept moaning on about it.

I don't know whether this was why Vernon offered him a lift back to the studio at the end of shooting, but it was an offer which Christopher would have been wise to decline.

Mind you, the poor man was not to know that Vernon drove a bubble car! This was a three-wheeled vehicle, the front of which opened up, to allow the driver and passenger to enter or leave. It could only hold two people, who sat side by side on a bench seat. The steering wheel was fixed to the folding door, which you closed on yourself after entering. Vernon had it, he said, because it was so easy to park as it could squeeze between two stationery cars, and one could open the front and step out onto the pavement. The trouble was that it was only really built for short people, and Christopher Lee is a very tall man. His first reaction was to tell Vernon that he couldn't possibly fit into this strange mode of transportation.

"Nonsense," replied Vernon.

"But I'm too tall, I can't get my head in," remonstrated Christopher.

"No problem," replied Vernon, opening up the canvas roof, and pushing Chris into the midget car, then jumping in beside him, slamming the door shut and shooting off as fast as this motorised scooter could muster.

I don't know why, but Christopher put on his hat – I suspect it was because he was wearing a toupee and he was scared of it blowing off.

Whatever the reason, Shoreham was treated to the sight of this bubble car tearing through its streets with an SS officer in full uniform sticking out of the top as though he was in the gun turret of a tank.

If this were not bad enough, in the middle of Brighton, Vernon had an accident. Now, all actors are easily embarrassed but Christopher Lee especially so. He was without doubt one of the most conceited men I have ever met. He once rang me up at home in the middle of the night to tell me how many people had recognised him in Ruislip High Street that day! So here he was in a most undignified position, trapped, dressed in German Officer's uniform, his head stuck out of the roof of a comic contraption staring straight into the eyes of the woman driver of the car Vernon had driven into.

The poor woman promptly had hysterics!

Not only had she been crashed into, but was now staring at an SS Officer, who seemed to be sprouting from a green frog contraption!

Unable to escape, as the only door was now firmly jammed into the side of the other car, he was trapped, and had to suffer the humiliation of watching the crowd grow bigger and bigger, and witnessing his embarrassment. It was not the best position to greet one's fans, nor for one's self esteem, especially when they started shouting things like, "You're in a right horror there, Chris, mate", "Reckon 'e looks better on the screen", "'e's very dark ,ain't 'e. Fuckin' gypo, if you ask me" or from another who didn't recognize him, "Bleedin' Nazi".

Eventually they managed to part the cars, and Christopher anxious to escape, hailed a passing cab, and leapt in. The driver enquired, "Where to, mate? Nuremberg?"

Brighton was a pleasant place to live and work in, and the house that George and I shared was very comfortable, if a bit lonely. George had Barbara but I was on my own. This was soon to change as I had met a really cute girl when working on "Planet X", a young, dark-haired, South African actress. We had gone out a couple of times, and she was as keen as I was to celebrate our meeting in a positive and physical way. She had what was almost an arranged marriage in South Africa. He was a son from the neighbouring farm, a big, rugged, rugby player. They had married there but had come to London for their honeymoon. But after several nights of non-activity, and after using up all the excuses of post wedding, long journey, jet lag etc., she realised that it was never going to happen, and she was asking the court for the dissolution of her marriage because of non-consummation. She was still a virgin, and had to be medically examined. We used to joke that she had to go and show it to the judge.

One day in Brighton she called me. "He's just seen it," she cried down the phone.

"Great, get down here on the next train. I'll meet you at Brighton station."

We had a wonderful night after dinner at English's restaurant, and sinking several bottles of champagne. Afterwards I said to her, "Well, whatever happens, it's great to have been the first."

"That's what you think," she replied. "My lawyer was the first." And turned over and went to sleep.

She was a lot of fun, though, and we had some great times together. She was in and out of my life for a long, long time.

Of course, I was a married man indulging myself with other women. I know it is no defence, but I have met few men who didn't, given the opportunity. Some poor sod that works nine till five has precious little chance of getting away with it but, given the right circumstances, I have only come across two men who to my knowledge were always faithful by choice. Of course, most men won't admit it. It is rather like pornography – despite the fact that it is a multi-million pound industry, you never come across anyone who admits to buying it.

I guess the film industry is one of the better places for sex. Our working hours are erratic, you never know when you're going to finish, and you are in close contact with the opposite sex. In addition, the dressing-rooms are there, and the occupants not always reluctant to share the couch. (Which brings to mind that wonderful line of Hermione Gingold: "Oh for the comfort of the double bed after the hurly-burly of the chaise- longue!")

I make no excuses for myself except to say I have always viewed sex as the ultimate pleasure. Shared with someone you love, it's wonderful, but like a good dinner companion it can be wonderful even with a comparative stranger. Modern youth has it worked out, and I congratulate them, and envy them. As the Duke of Edinburgh said, "We were born too early." We pre-pill boys had it rough by comparison, and in my old age I look back at not what I did wrong, but wish I had done more. I'm with John Betjeman, the poet, who on his death bed was asked if he had any regret in his life. "Only one" he replied, "that I didn't have more sex"!

Even Vernon succumbed to the temptation, taking one of the more mature actresses back to his yacht, where he was living whilst we were on location. He plied her with drink, but instead of this making her amorous it had the opposite effect. She got very stroppy with him and ended up storming off the yacht.

Sadly for her, it was low tide and the vessel was lying in the harbour mud, and as she staggered down the gangplank, she staggered once too many times to the right and fell straight into Shoreham's best mud.

She refused all help, dragged herself out, and declined Vernon's offer of a shower and a change of clothes. She blamed him for the accident and insisted that he drive her to Brighton station in her bedraggled state, where she caught a train to London and was last seen hanging out of the window shouting obscene abuse at poor old Vernon. I think that put him off sex for life! He said to me some time later, "I d-d-don't need it any more, old boy, and I m-m-must say, it's an almighty relief!"

Soon it was back to Elstree, and the more easy going studio shoot: home at night, and weekends off. Soon after that, there was the end of picture "wrap party", where you say good-bye to all those people who, for a brief period, have been closer to you than most of your family, and many of whom you will never see again. One or two remained close, especially Doreen Jones, my secretary.

Into post-production, editing, music recording and dubbing, weeks of work putting the whole film together. Vernon had uncovered some never seen before "stock footage" of actual trains arriving at a concentration camp. These cut into the film gave it immense strength, and a sickeningly factual feel.

It was felt that a commentary should be given at the beginning of the film, to explain the significance of the Polish Underground's contribution to the defeat of Hitler's secret weapon. Many names were put forward, and then I suggested Churchill. He would be the ideal person, they said, but would he do it, and how do we get to him? I suggested that they leave that to me.

I knew that the old man was going through a difficult financial time, so much so that a fund had been set up to help him. The man who had started the fund, and was the main trustee, was Edward Martell.

I contacted Martell and told him we would like Churchill to do the commentary, and that of course he would be paid. If he wanted to do it, he just had to name his fee. Martell said he would think about it and if he agreed he would talk to the ex-Prime Minister next time he saw him. Weeks later, I was in my office when the phone rang, and it was Martell who said, "I am with Mr Churchill and he has a few questions for you." The next thing I knew I was speaking to that great British wartime leader and my hero. I don't think I answered his queries too well as I was tongue-tied and overcome just listening to that voice; that voice that I remembered so well from the dark days of the war, when we would all sit round the radio and listen to his wonderful and inspiring speeches. This was the great man, whom the British rewarded for winning the war by kicking him out of office.

After I put the phone down, I just sat there in total disbelief. George came in and I said, "You have no idea whom I've just been talking to", and then went on to explain. He was over the moon, and immediately rang Vernon to tell him the news. I quickly interrupted him, and told them both that he had not yet agreed and it was vitally important that it be treated with great confidence. Only when he had agreed could it be released through our publicity people.

A few days later, George went out with a reporter from "Photoplay", got pissed and told this guy the story. The following week they published a story that Churchill had rung me, and I had said to him, "Right, mate, this is what we would like you to do...." I nearly died with embarrassment. I phoned Edward Martell and grovelled. Needless to say, we never heard another word from the bulldog of Britain.

Moral: "Never go out drinking with the press."

The film eventually came out and it looked like a blown up B picture.

It is a truism that, give certain directors a budget of a few bucks and they will make a film looking like it was thousands, give those same directors millions and their talent will not live up to the budget. Dear Vernon just did not have it within him to take a super war story and turn it into a super film. Also the cast, who gave their usual wooden performances, didn't help. So sad.

The only good thing for me was that we didn't get Churchill, who would not have been happy at being associated with such a film.

Despite George's faux-pas, we had become great friends. We had enjoyed sharing a house, I got on really well with his Barbara, and he enjoyed drinking even more than I did. This was a problem. I found it hard to do my job, as he always wanted me to be out and about with him, into one bar or another. Being my boss made it even harder as he would say, "Look, I need to talk to you about something. Let's get out of the office so we can speak freely." Off to the nearest hostelry we would go, emerging several hours later.

On our return to London, he asked me to join him for another such talk, but this time it really was something important; he wanted me to direct the company's next picture. I was very flattered, and very excited. I floated home on a cloud of euphoria, disbelief, and terror! I had never really given directing much thought, and suddenly to be asked to take up such a challenging job resulted in an emotional cocktail of adrenaline, of happiness, and of apprehension.

Was I about to fall right on my face, or was I destined to be the next Carol Reed or David Lean? I had so little experience, but such high ambition. Was this the big chance?

I was never to find out. The next week George told me that he had been offered the chance to produce a very big movie for the Rank Organisation, "Ferry to Hong-Kong", to be directed by a young, successful director, Lewis Gilbert. He was obviously thrilled to pieces, never having produced a movie as big as this.

Putting his arm around me, he took me off to a nearby pub to celebrate in the time-honoured tradition. "Don't worry, John, you'll be coming with me. Lewis has asked me if I can recommend a production manager for a small film he is to make before the Hong Kong project. I naturally said I had the best, and I have arranged for you to meet him later today. Do this picture with Lewis, and then you can come to Hong Kong with me."

I vaguely remembered the name Lewis Gilbert, from Lime Grove. He used to direct documentaries and we dubbed them in between the feature films, though, I had no memory of actually working with him. He was by this time a very successful features director, with many films to his credit including "Reach for the Sky", "Carve Her Name with Pride", "The Admirable Crichton" and many others. I was proud and excited to be given the opportunity to work with him. Later that day we met.

He was a young, fair headed, quietly spoken man, with a wonderful open way of speaking. His parents were Music Hall artists, and Lewis was born in the proverbial "theatrical hamper". His father had died many years before, but his mother, Ruby, was still working. But at this time in films, in the crowd. Lewis had started as a child actor, working in many films, but especially enjoyed being one of Will Hay's boys. Will Hay was England's leading film comic in the mid-30s, and usually played a schoolmaster. However, it was Lewis's scene with Laurence Olivier that he was most proud of, and it was a happy choice that years later they played this scene at the British Academy Awards when he won the Lifetime Achievement Award.

He changed from being an actor and started life behind the camera as an assistant director. I think he got his first break in the RAF when he was stationed with the American film Unit.

We met in a small Soho café, and he explained the picture to me. He seemed to have assumed that I was already aboard. I was yet to meet the producer, Ian Dalrymple, and I found it a bit strange that Lewis was hiring the production manager, as this is always the job of the producer. I was to find out that Ian, who had been an editor, was not interested in the practical side of film making. He had bought the rights to the subject, asked Lewis to direct, and from then on Lewis would act as the producer as well as direct the film. I had little contact with Ian, though he was always most kind to me whenever our paths did cross, and I always found him charming. With Lewis on the floor, and Ian not interested, I was once again left alone to run things my way.

To my surprise and delight, the film was to be made for Eros. They knew me, and as I had brought in two films on time and under budget, they would look on me favourably. The film was called "A Cry from the Streets" and was to star the British entertainer, Max Bygraves, in a straight part. Two well-known Australian children were also cast, the boy, Colin Petersen, who had starred in "Smiley", and the little girl, Dana Wilson, who had played a leading role in the "Shiralee". Lewis handed me the script and warned me that we had to get going quickly as the Hong Kong picture was coming up fast. I took the script home and quickly read it. The plot centred on a deprived children's home, and the lives of various children living there. Including three children of a convicted murderer sentenced to death for killing their mother. A thirteen-year-old, whose mother (played by the brilliant Kathleen Harrison) was living with a drunken bully. There was also the young boy whose drug-addicted mother always promised to visit, but never came. Max played an electrician carrying out repair work at the home, who falls for the visiting Social Worker (played by Barbara Murray) and the two of them befriend the children.

Within a few days, I had a production plan and first budget, and after further meetings with Lewis, I met up with the Hyams brothers and John Saunders. As usual we went through the same routine, "It's too much", "Can't you get it lower?" and so on. This time, though, they were more relaxed: They were excited about having a Lewis Gilbert film and after two films nearly trusted me!

Eros were keen for me to use Walton Studios, where I had worked on the Lorne Greene series, so off I went to a meeting with the studio manager, J.K. Morris.

The studios were very run down and dilapidated, and used to exist on cheap 'B'-movies and filmed television series. The carrot offered to producers was that they would do a "package deal", including not only the stage rental but also the cost of the sets, based on the designs submitted by the producer's designer (in those days called an art director). On the surface, it looked like a good deal. The trouble was that the film was in the hands of the studio. As they were trying to make as much money as possible, they would try to skimp on the sets, thus creating constant friction between the producers and the studio. One of their ploys was not to put the sets up until the last moment, so that it was too late for the producers to insist on changes. Often when a designer walked on a bare stage the night before shooting was due to start, he would hear from the construction manager, "Don't worry, it'll be your'n in the morning."

Making my way up to JK's office, I noticed the rot growing on the walls. Well, I thought, we turned a mushroom farm into a studio; maybe they could change a studio into a mushroom farm! I met with JK and Wally Smith, his construction manager, got the prices off him for the stages, and left.

On arriving back at Wardour Street and the Eros offices, I was met by the disturbed Hyams brothers. It seemed that J.K. Morris had rung up and complained to them that I had just accepted the price he asked, and had not even attempted to bargain with him! I knew I was naive at the job, and realised I had to put up some sort of argument for my seeming incompetence. I explained that I had not accepted the deal, and in fact thought that Walton was the wrong studio. Sid asked me where I thought would be better. God knows why, for I hadn't till just very recently heard of the place, but I answered, "Twickenham". With a certain amount of scorn, I was allowed to go off and see what I could do there. I knew very well that I had to come back with something very special.

It just so happened that Twickenham was going through a bad patch, and hadn't had anything sizeable for years. The inexperienced, but delightful studio manager greeted me as though I was Samuel Goldwyn and was quite honest in telling me that he would do anything to get our picture into his studio. And he did. I reported to town with the best deal they had ever seen. It even got a small smile out of Phil.

That started a long-standing relationship with this small studio on the outskirts of London.

Our production offices were housed in wooden huts at the side of one of the two stages, not exactly luxurious, but very convenient. I wanted to get the best production secretary I could find. Betty Parry, who had worked on "Planet X" with me and who had nurtured me through my first picture (and, if there was any justice, should have had the PM's screen credit) was on another picture. Darling Doreen Jones who had coped with me through the V.1. film also was unavailable. Margarete Green came into my life.

She had a fine track record, and I took to her as soon as we first met. She was a fantastic person to have running your office and your production. Little known, and even less praised, a production secretary (or co-ordinator) has a very important role in the administration of a movie.

They must be knowledgeable about Trades Union regulations as they prepare all the engagement letters. The same applies to shipping and transport as they control all the various Customs and shipping lists. They complete a Daily Progress Report sheet showing the status of the picture, how far in advance, or behind the picture is, how many minutes and seconds have been shot that day, and since the film began, how much film and sound stock has been used, how much printed, and so on. The production manager signs this, but it is the co-ordinator that actually does the work. So for every good PM there is an even better co-ordinator, and for every bad one, an even better one is needed! Quite a few of them become production managers themselves, and very good they are too.

Maggie Green was rated one of the best, and I soon found out why. She was quiet, unassuming, never panicked, just worked steadily and kept me from making too many ghastly mistakes.

Lewis had already engaged two members of the crew, John Stoll and Harry Gillam. John, the art director, I had met at Walton. Although a born artist, a bohemian, he had great technical knowledge of the industry and was wonderful at his job. However, he was under-rated by the industry, mainly I think because he was so self-effacing. Like Lewis, he was free of any bullshit, just loved his job and lived life to its full. He always seemed to have a young lady in tow, whom he would take out to dinner and indulge his other two loves, food and drink. He was married to a talented painter of miniatures, and they seemed to be very happy, though their marriage could hardly be called conventional. He was a darling man and he became a life-long friend.

The other technician, Harry Gillam, was the cameraman (now known as the director of photography, the Lighting director, or the Cinematographer). He is not to be confused with the camera operator, who is the person actually operating the camera.

Directors are very dependent on their Cameramen, and take great care in choosing them. Harry had worked with Lewis on many movies, but as an Operator. This was to be his debut as the Lighting man. I already knew Harry as we had worked together on the Lorne Green show. He was a tall, lugubrious man, and Lewis and I often shared a laugh by recounting "Harry stories". He had a habit of sidling up to you on a Monday morning in the summer, and whispering in your ear, "Thirty-two and four for one hundred and two."

The first time this happened I had no idea what he was talking about. I eventually learned it was the cricket statistics from his weekend match! Then on other occasions he would stand beside you, wait for a while, then gently nudge you in the ribs. "I suppose you're stashing it away," he would mutter. Everyone else was a millionaire except Harry, he thought. He lived very simply, and never to my knowledge owned a car.

Working with Lewis was always fun, and when out looking for locations we would frequently stop for coffee or lunch. One of the first things his wife Hylda said to me was, "Make sure you feed him, or he'll get ratty." Ratty? In all the years I knew him, he rarely showed any sign of bad temper, irritation maybe, but never anything vicious or uncontrolled. I took Hylda's advice and kept him fed. Not for him the smart restaurant, he was just as happy in a "greasy spoon". He was no drinker, but he enjoyed a pub lunch, where he'd have half a glass of beer, and that was that. I don't think I ever saw him drink more than a couple of glasses of wine. After lunch we would carry on, but it wouldn't be long before it was "tea time", when he would often say, "Well, it's getting late. Let's call it a day, and carry on tomorrow." He took it easy, I realised, because he knew what he wanted, and best of all, knew what he could use. Though he appeared laid back, even lazy, he was totally responsible, aware of not only his duty to bring the script to the screen, but also to make the film as efficiently and cost effectively as possible. He made decisions and then stuck to them. If I were to say that I soon came to love the man, it would only embarrass him, as he was not one to show affection.

He was the complete professional and could not understand directors that made a lot of fuss. He told me that he met my old friend John Guillermin on a plane. John told him how he hated making films, and how he even hated turning up at the studio. Lewis found this baffling for, he said, "You know, John, it's not as though the job is difficult!"

Well, he didn't make his life easier when he decided not to use children from stage schools. "It doesn't matter what we do to them, how much make-up we use, or how we dress them, they will never look like the kids I see playing in the streets. Get me some East End kids, John."

I thought, this is just the job for Bushel!

I had met Ted Bushel on "The Battle of the V.1." He had been one of Jock Easton's stunt team, and somehow or other had become close to George and myself. He was not a trained stunt man, and really didn't know the techniques of the job, like how to fall, take a punch, or how to land. He just did it. In addition, he was tough! Because of that we got some amazing shots of Ted in "…V.1." being blown up, blown over, and generally mutilated in numerous ways.

Ted was an amazing person, stocky of build, about 5′10″, thinning fair hair, and a battered face, scarred all over with razor slashes, the legacy of a gang fight many years before. Not for nothing was he known as the toughest man in Soho, and yet he was not a violent man, and would go to great lengths to avoid a fight. He could be gentle and kind, and later on in our relationship, when working with Orson Wells, Ted was the only person Orson would allow to take his young daughter out for walks. He was always superb with my own children, and looked after me personally for many, many years. Yet he was not somebody to be trifled with.

One day George and I were in a group of people drinking in our usual watering hole, "The Duke of Wellington", when some stranger kept trying to butt into our conversation. Ted very politely told him we were having a private conversation, but he was not to be put off and kept on pestering us. Ted put himself in front of the man and gently pushed him backwards. The poor mutt then made his big mistake. Grabbing Ted by his collar, he pulled him around to face him. Whereupon Ted just let the momentum of the pull continue as he drove his fist straight into the man's face, who went flying out of the open doors to land just outside the Stage Door of the Queen's Theatre. An ambulance was sent for, and he was carried off to the Middlesex hospital.

Bunny, the landlord, came over and told Ted that, though it wasn't his fault, because of the likely police enquiry, he was banning Ted from the pub until it all blew over. A couple of weeks later, Ted was walking down Wardour Street, just after opening time, and in need of a little pick-me up. Passing the "Duke", he thought, what the hell, and went in. The place was deserted except for the two Irish barmen getting the place ready for the busy day ahead. One of them approached Ted, "What'll you be having?"

"A pint of best," replied Ted.

As the barman was filling the glass from the pump, the other barman came up and whispered, "You know he's barred?"

To which the first barman replied, "You fuckin' tell him!"

Ted lived in a council block behind King's Cross station, at that time one of the toughest areas of London, so was well qualified to find the kind of kids Lewis was looking for. An audition for the children was arranged by Ted to be held in the Church Hall belonging to the Reverend Hogg. On the appointed day, Lewis and I ventured into the King's Cross area. Despite directions we couldn't find the place, even after stopping and asking various people, for nobody seemed to have heard of the Reverend Hogg, never mind his Church Hall. That was until we stopped a little boy of about seven. "Never 'eard of 'im".

"The Reverend Hogg, from the church," we explained.

He suddenly got it, and with a big beam said "Oh, you mean *fuckin'ogg* (pronounced as one word)! Oh, fuckin'ogg is up there at the end of the road." And indeed that is where we found him.

The Church Hall was full of a motley crowd of kids, mums and a few unsavoury looking dads. Strict instructions had been given to Ted to make sure the mums didn't try to clean up the kids, although I don't think there would have been much chance of that, as these kids seemed to live on the streets, only going home for food and to sleep.

Lewis was delighted, and made his selection, but sadly had to turn away the majority, which didn't please some of the mothers or fathers who had tagged along in the hope of their kids making a few bob.

Ted was magnificent and dealt with all the parents. "That's all for now, mate, but we got more comin' up like, and I think the guvnor's saving your Jack for somefink special," he'd say, as he got them out the door.

From those chosen, Lewis also chose the ones he wanted to test for the three named parts, the others being just crowd. He chose a thirteen-year-old cocky kid, Charlie McShane, who turned out to be a natural. He was to give us a lot of grief during shooting, for he was always up to something. He had a terrible life, as he had no father and his mother lived with a drunken sot who used to bash her up on a regular basis. Charlie used to sleep with a milk bottle under his bed, and if his mum's lover came near him he would threaten to put it over his head. The man had the sense to leave him alone. Charlie had learnt to hit first, and, though one could understand his philosophy, it sometimes got him and us into trouble.

The other two kids were to be the brothers of Dana Wilson, the girl whose father was to be executed for killing their mother. Lewis chose Tony Baker, a solemn looking, tiny, fair haired, six-year-old, with a round open face and large blue eyes which seemed to look out in wonder at the world. It seemed as though he was always pondering on how he came to be in the jungle of King's Cross, and one wanted to pick him up and take him away from this ugly, cruel place. The other one was Ted's youngest son, five-year-old David, the opposite of Tony Baker, and an ugly, dirty imp of non-stop mischievous activity, whose cheeky grin kept you from wringing his neck.

The next question was how to control them. We decided to leave that to Ted. This wasn't the only thing left to Ted that day for John Stoll had decided to come along with us and was smitten with the buildings. These were the last of the slum areas of London, and whereas everyone else viewed them with disgust, filmmakers saw only the excitement.

"We should have a careful look around," John said, in that funny high-pitched voice of his.

To which I replied, "Well, I've got news for you, John, I ain't going anywhere until we get Ted"

"And I'm with John," echoed Lewis!

Ted had a flat in an old council building, three sides of a square, about four or five stories high, each flat opening up onto an open gallery.

"Now, just be careful 'ere," warned Ted. "The kids like to drop the odd milk bottle, so mind your 'eads."

The insides of the flats were like something from Dickens, except that they did have a running cold-water tap, and electricity, although I am not sure about loos as we didn't like to ask. John was over the moon, and all the way back kept on about the beauty of it all. In the end we used these flats in the title backgrounds, and all John Stoll's designs were based on them. "I don't think you'd find it very beautiful if you had to live in there, John," said Lewis.

When we started shooting, we bussed the kids in and back home at night. We had a few narrow escapes, like finding several of the boys with knives, old chains, and other vicious weapons. So Ted used to have security checks, one when they got on the bus in King's Cross, and another at the studio, for they were adept at hiding things and passing them from one to the other. Apart from this, they soon settled down and became part of the company.

The strange and wonderful thing about a film company is that cast and crew become like a family, very attached to one another. Quick to criticise each other, but let any outsider make a disparaging remark, they close ranks and defend the person they have just been attacking. I have seen this so often.

I remember in Malta we had two companies in the same hotel, Alan Parker's "Midnight Express" and our film "Warlords From Atlantis". There was a large horseshoe-shaped bar. Alan's crew would assemble on one side and ours on the other, and though many of them knew one another, there was little fraternising. During a shoot, everyone works very closely together, all striving for the same end. Usually the hours are very long, especially on location where you probably have a long journey from the hotel to the shoot and where you have you take maximum advantage of the weather. Any free time is usually spent with people from the company as there isn't time to make friends amongst the locals. So it is a very tightly-knit group, and the appearance of a stranger results in: "Who's that?" or "What's he doing here?"

That is why I hate going on other people's sets, however well I know them. Even in the studio, and even when you go back home at night, that close feeling still exists. It extends across the whole company, and it doesn't matter who or what you are, what colour or creed, you are one of "us".

That is why the King's Cross kids soon became part of the film company, the set their second home, and the crew and cast their second family. Indeed the real problem was how they would settle down when it was all over, for they were probably looked after better than at any time in their lives, and they all started to put on weight.

As they had an early start, we used to give them breakfast when they arrived, then at about ten the tea trolley would arrive and they would devour rolls, sandwiches, cakes and biscuits; lunch was at one, and tea at four. We engaged tutors to look after their education, and a nurse to see to any ailments or accidents. Even in those days, quite rightly, there were strict regulations regarding the employment of children; how many hours a day they could work and how many hours of tuition they had to have. The bureaucracy regarding their employment was such that usually one engaged children through a theatrical school, which held special licences. Here we had a different problem that I did my best to explain to the school's inspector, who was a clear example himself of a deprived education.

In the end we decided to enrol the two boys, Tony and David, in such a school. The thinking was that if they stopped the King's Cross crowd kids from working, we could manage, but if they stopped the two boys, once having started, we would be right up the creek. So we enrolled them in a theatrical school, the Corona School. We had to buy their school uniforms of grey union flannel shorts, shirts, ties, blazers, and caps. Little Tony could not believe it, his wonderful blue eyes bright with wonder, as he looked at himself in the wardrobe department's long mirror. No hand-me-downs, but new clothes just for him. David on the other hand had already filled his cap with water from the wardrobe sink, had somehow or other managed to get a big stain down the front of his new blazer (later found to be powdered dye) and was using his tie to lash himself to the wardrobe mistress's chair.

We never did get him fully dressed, and we had to forgo the publicity picture. Trying to keep a cap on David was rather like trying to cap a recalcitrant gushing oil well! Charlie McShane was not a problem, as he was due to finish school at the end of the term anyhow, and a grateful Head Teacher greeted a few weeks of absence with relief!

For the girls' dormitory scenes, where the girls were in bed most of the time, I persuaded Lewis to use children from the Theatrical School. This worked fine until I had an irate chaperone in my office in a high old temper. "You have to do something about that disgusting boy, Charlie. He keeps trying to get into bed with my gals."

When I had him up on the carpet he said, "Tell you what, guv'nor, give me a fiver and I'll keep me maulers off 'em!" I gave him the five pounds. I thought it was cheap at the price.

Very early one morning I was woken by the phone. It was Ted. "What is it Ted?"

"It's David," he replied. Being a born pessimist I always think the worst and I could see him spread out underneath a lorry somewhere, blood pouring everywhere. "It's 'is 'air."

"'is air?" I asked, bewildered.

"Yeah, 'is 'air, you know, the 'air on 'is 'ead."

Comprehension began to dawn. "Oh, his hair. What about his hair?"

"'E's cut it orf."

"He's done what?"

"'E's cut it orf, with the kitchen scissors."

So instead of having a five-year-old boy with hair falling down over his forehead and almost over his eyes, we now had the same boy but shorn of most of his hair. As we were shooting out of continuity, it would be difficult for the audience to comprehend why this young actor's hair kept changing its length. There was nothing for it but to call up Wig Creations, and have a quick toupee made for him. The managing director of the company said that David was the youngest actor for whom they had had to make a hairpiece!

His disgrace was short-lived, though, and all would be forgiven in a wave of warmth and sympathy for him. There was a scene where David was in bed on his first night in the orphanage, separated from his sister, and all alone. Lewis asked Ted how he was going to get David to cry the next day. "Don't worry about that, guv'nor, got it all worked out." The next day Ted took David to the toyshop at the corner of the road and bought him a little wooden sword that he had been admiring for weeks. Ted told Lewis that he would not bring the boy in until all was ready, with the scene lit, and the camera actually turning. Lewis gave Ted the wink and he brought David in, clutching the toy sword, dressed in pyjamas. As he put him to bed, he slipped a sixpence into the child's pyjama jacket pocket, and sat on the side of the bed.

"You like that sword, don't you, son?" Ted patted him on his chest. "Hey, what's this?"

"I don't know, dad."

Ted fished in the pocket and pulled out the sixpence. "It's a bleedin' sixpence, where did you get that from?"

"I dunno, dad, it were just there."

"Oh yes, you do. You bleedin' well stole it, that's what you done."

Ted picked up the little sword, broke it in two and quickly ran out of the shot, leaving the little boy sobbing his heart out. Well, he wasn't the only one. The whole crew cried; the tough old sparks on the rail, the grips, and the chippies, all of us. There wasn't a dry eye in the house, as our little monster turned into the darling of us all as he sobbed his heart out. Never was a little boy so spoiled after that.

With Dana it was different. She was an experienced actress (or so she thought), but when it was her turn to cry in the scene where she hears the news of her father's execution, she told Lewis in her strong Australian accent, "If you want me to blub, you'd better get that John Dark down here to give me a lathering."

I was duly sent to the location at the Children's Home.

"You've got to give Dana a good hiding."

"You're kidding. What's she done?"

"Nothing, she's got to cry and she says the only way she can do it is if you give her a smack on her bum."

"You are kidding!"

"No, I'm not, get on with it, we're ready to shoot."

Dana and I disappeared behind a big oak tree where I sat on the root and she lay across me. I gave her a couple of gentle taps.

"No, that's no good. Give me a good wallop."

So I did, and she sat in front of the camera and sobbed. As I said, it takes all sorts! I don't think today either of these methods would be acceptable.

We were the only picture filming at the studio, so we had the place to ourselves, although that's not saying much, as it only had two and a half stages, and they were pretty ramshackle. Still, it was a friendly place, and with the deal they had given us, it was the best game in town. Close to London, it made commuting easy. A nearby station provided public transport, and it was close to Richmond and the underground services. I would not pay the rate for the usual film chauffeured car but got two guys from outside the station, Ted and his brother-in-law, Billy Willmot: Billy a one in a million and who played a large part in my future life

The picture progressed happily in the usual Lewis Gilbert mode; one kid hanging round his neck, and a mass of unruly children in front of the camera. He was absolutely in charge, completely unruffled, oozing self-confidence and inspiring his performers. Max Bygraves was a much-loved English comic and singer, a pillar of the entertainment industry, and almost an institution, as there was hardly a Command Variety Performance without him. At home in the theatre, he was not so used to the movies, but with Lewis's quiet control and his own self-confidence, happy to leave himself in Lewis's hands, he gave a polished and sincere performance. There was no crap about him either, and in between set-ups, he could often be seen strolling up to the shops with a trail of kids in tow, buying ice-lollies all round.

Then our first major problem arose. Barbara Murray went down with the flu. Although shooting came to a halt, we didn't fret as our insurance policy covered all expenses until we started again. The insurance man arrived; we shared a few bottles of wine, and waited for Barbara to start again in a couple of days. Well, a couple of days passed and no Barbara, so the insurance company decided to send in one of their own doctors, whom she refused to see. Antibiotics would have put her back on her feet within a few days, but we discovered that a Dr Sharma, a homeopathic doctor, who would not prescribe antibiotics, was treating her. In the end we waited weeks rather than days. This case made the insurance companies change their policies. Now, if an insured actor refuses to accept a registered medical practitioner, the insurance company will not honour its obligations. At the time I didn't know that this same Dr Sharma would one day play a role in my personal life.

Whilst all this was going on, Lewis was in touch with George, and with Pinewood studios. At this time Pinewood had in-house crews: technicians who were under permanent contract. The rumour that a freelance production manager was coming in sent ripples throughout the whole place. Would this be the thin end of the wedge? The thought was: "Today it's a production manager, who will it be tomorrow?" And of course that is exactly what happened. Not long after "Ferry" was completed, no new contracts were given and Pinewood "went four wall" joining the rest of the industry in engaging crews picture by picture. producers and directors had long fought against the system of being allocated crews. The making of films depends on many people, and it essential that the top men have the right to choose their own people.

With George and Lewis continuing to insist that I be appointed, opposition came from both ends; the Unions *and* the lower management. Their objection was based on the fact that there were several experienced production managers available on the Rank payroll. These men had far greater experience than I did; in fact my credits looked pathetic in comparison to theirs.

Feelings were so strong that a deputation of Pinewood production managers went to see John Davis, the tyrannical Chairman of the Rank Organisation. They supported their argument by informing Davis that they had the total backing of the Studio production controller, Arthur Alcott. There is no doubt that they had a good case, and I was beginning to believe that I would lose out, despite the assurances of both George and Lewis. Eventually Lewis met John Davis and told him that unless he allowed him to have me, he would have to find another producer and director. Lewis was very powerful at this time, having made several successful films for Rank's, and John Davis felt he had to agree. I was in.

But not loved.

Mr Alcott found a good reason not to use me. He insisted that someone be sent to Hong Kong immediately, knowing that I was shooting the Bygraves picture. No casting had been completed, no dates had been fixed, and there were no deadlines to meet, so I think it was just a clever move of the Pinewood production department to get rid of me.

Lewis and I talked it over; and he thought we should not give them any ammunition. The present picture was well into its schedule, was well on budget, the sets were built, the casting complete, and there was not a lot left to do. We promoted our very experienced second assistant director and got him to take over from myself, leaving me free to go to Hong Kong.

First to Pinewood.

Not a happy experience.

The bar at Pinewood had always been the social centre of the studio, so before my meeting with Arthur Alcott I made my way there to see what old chums were about. As I went in, people turned round to see who had just entered. Noticing who it was, they rapidly turned their backs, muttering to their neighbours, and engrossing themselves in their drinks. I tried smiling and greeting certain people whom I had known since I was very young, but all ignored my greetings and even the barmaid seemed in no hurry to serve me. Eventually I did get a drink, which I took and sat in the corner, the ice in the vodka matching the bar temperature.

Leaving the chill of the bar, I reported to the production controller's secretary, Lorna Stevens, whom I had known since the Shepherd's Bush days. If I thought this might help, I was soon disillusioned. She was not even polite, in fact bloody rude, and made my wait in the outer office most uncomfortable. It was something of a relief to get to see the boss, who, though obviously not over the moon about my appointment, in comparison with his secretary, treated me like Santa Claus!

Lewis said he wanted to make the whole film in Hong Kong, almost unheard of in those days, but Rank's were opposed to this, and thought we should just shoot the exterior scenes, returning to the studio for the interior shooting. My role at this time was to go to Hong Kong, where both Lewis and George would join me, assess the situation, and then report to Pinewood. After various meetings with the accountants and travel departments, I left London.

J. D. greeting French actress Gaby Andre at London Airport for "The Strange World of Planet X" 1956

Son Gregory in "The Battle of the V.1" 1957

J. D. with The Singing Group for "Ferry to Hong Kong" 1958
Paula on the far right

Kenneth More and J. D. at a wrap party for "The Greengage Summer" 1960

J. D. aboard the Argos. "Jason and the Argonauts" 1963

J. D. with William Holden "The 7ᵗʰ Dawn" 1964

J. D. with Woody Allen. "Casino Royale" 1966

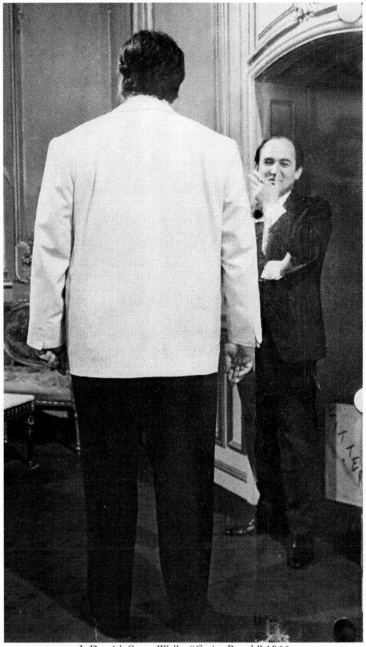

J. D. with Orson Welles "Casino Royale" 1966

J. D. with Ursula Andress "Casino Royale" 1966

J. D. with Hollywood gangster George Raft "Casino Royale" 1966

CHAPTER 10
CHINA GIRL

I settled back into my comfortable seat, sipping the welcoming glass of champagne, accepting a cigarette from the leather cigarette box handed to me by a white-gloved stewardess (now called flight attendants), and thanking her for the proffered light from her Dunhill lighter, I picked up the book and the script of "Ferry to Hong Kong".

It was the story of a man who was a waster, a bum and a tramp who is deported from Hong Kong on the Macao ferry. On arrival in this Portuguese territory, he is refused permission to land, and the Captain is forced to carry him back to Hong Kong, where the authorities also refuse him permission to land. For months, he lives on board the ferry, ploughing up and down the Chinese coast.

I have to say I thought the plot very thin, but I also thought that, knowing Lewis's talent, he had something up his sleeve to make it work. In any case, neither the story nor the script was my concern. My brief was, could it be made in Hong Kong?

I was really flying into the unknown, all I had was just two contacts: one was the Rank Far Eastern distribution chief, George Reardon, and the other was the Political Advisor to the Hong Kong Government. Not a lot to go on, but a start. This trip would be quite short – four or five weeks, I reckoned. But if it was decided to shoot the whole film in the East, I would be away for months.

I began to think of Peggy and the children, the happy farewell party at a local restaurant, and the many demands for presents on my return. Even in the tough times, I had always somehow or other found the money to send the children to private schools, as the local state schools (now called comprehensives) were of such a poor standard. The children were happy and were certainly doing well where they were. Peg had many friends. So I wasn't worried about leaving them. It was also a pivotal point in my career, and whatever it took, I had to do it.

The British Overseas Airways Corporation (now called British Airways) flight took thirty-six hours, for this was before the jet engine. It made many stops; Rome, Beirut, Baghdad, Calcutta, Kuala Lumpur. The route depended on which day you left. I don't think we ever flew more than five or six hours without landing to re-fuel. We would all troop off the plane, have free drinks in the airport lounge, and inspect the souvenir shops before re-boarding, enjoying our welcome back-on-board glass of champagne, with the elegantly lit cigarette. There was a charm in first class travel in those days that one doesn't get today. With all the luxury of modern day flights, and the competition between the airlines to outdo one another, they are unable to re-create the quiet, courteous service we had in those days. The girls looked like French models just out of a Swiss finishing school. They were well trained and well spoken, attentive in a quiet, reserved way, anticipating one's needs and anxious to make the journey as comfortable as possible.

At Calcutta we were taken by bus to a nearby hotel, where rooms with baths and showers had been booked so we could change into fresh clothes. The crews were changed frequently, and I think it was here in Calcutta that we first took on some Chinese cabin staff. This was my first sight of those delectable creatures, in the smart cheong-sam uniform, the classical Chinese split skirt dress, adapted for the BOAC uniform. From there the journey took on a new interest, and I really felt that I was actually going to the wonders of the East. If these adorable creatures were an example of what was to come, I thought, the future held out great possibilities. Little did I realise how prophetic these thoughts were.

The journey finally ended, and dramatically. In those days the runway to Kai Tak airport had not been extended out into the harbour, and was way before the brilliant new airport opened in 1998. Even after the runway was extended, landing was scary, but at the original airport, it was positively terrifying. In those days, the pilot had to fly those big aircraft between the tower apartment blocks, with little room to spare on either side. As you looked out of the aircraft window, you could see people in their apartments having dinner. It was a spooky and fascinating experience, almost as fascinating as, and a lot less frightening than, the journey between the airport and the hotel.

Bustling Hong Kong, with its crowded streets, car-filled thoroughfares, clanging trams, rickshaws weaving their way through the noisy traffic, food stalls spouting flames with sweating men busy frying aromatic delicacies, fruit barrows with their colours heightened by the hanging oil lamps; the crowds, the packed pavements of Chinese, dotted with the occasional European face, with everyone seemingly in a mad rush on their way to wherever. There were business men in neat suits, collars and ties, carrying the obligatory briefcase, elegant Chinese women in high-necked dresses, with shoes and bags to match, the classical amah in black trouser suit, hair plaited and hanging down the back, young office workers dressed in a mixture of Chinese and European styles, coolies with their classical round straw hats, others in just a vest and shorts. There were little men with yokes over their shoulders from which dangled round metal containers delivering God knows what to God knows who, diving down dark, dingy lanes with that strange Oriental shuffle, half walk, half run. It was a mad kaleidoscope of humanity, which changed every second.

Tired from the flight, I nevertheless felt the energy of the place and was so re-charged by it, that when I arrived at the hotel I felt quite fresh.

The Gloucester Hotel, where Rank's had booked me in, was housed on several floors of a major block with very pleasant large rooms and excellent service and facilities, its big drawback I was to discover later. Bright and early the next day, I made appointments with my two contacts.

George Reardon had been in film distribution for years, though what he knew about Hong Kong was amazingly limited. The average Englishman or woman there lived as though they were in a hot and humid English suburb, with Chinese servants. They seemed to actively dislike the Chinese, and spent a considerable amount of time complaining about them. Few of them had Chinese friends but lived together in claustrophobic areas, socialising with the same people and frequenting the same restaurants and clubs, some of which were closed to the Chinese. I soon realised that George Reardon was not going to be of much help to me, though he was always kind and eager to do anything he could. The trouble was there just was not much that he could do! Distribution has little similarity with production, and I needed to meet people who knew Hong Kong from the bottom up.

So, onto my next contact, the political advisor to the H.K. Government. Once again he was a jolly, nice, colonial English civil servant, but with a "If we can ever do anything for you, please let us know, but we are not really the right people for you", he suggested I try the Chinese film companies, particularly Run Run Shaw.

One thing I did not want to do was to get into bed with any one film producer, or one film production company. Although Hong Kong was the second largest film producing country in the world, only beaten by India, the films they produced were strictly for the domestic market, plus Macao, Taiwan, Malaya and Singapore. They were made on shoestring budgets, and in a manner completely at odds with Western methods. In order to survive, their producers had to be very sharp, and I felt I had to know what I was talking about before I approached any of them.

That evening I sat in my room wondering where to start. I looked at the list of requirements of the Pinewood budget department, which was endless. Film financing is very detailed and complex, unlike the outsiders' view of a big barrel of money that we dip into whenever we want.

Before a picture starts, the cost of every single person, every piece of equipment, from cameras to powder puffs has to be estimated and costed. Transport, limousines, trains, planes or ships, all have to be calculated. All financial aspects have to be estimated, including social security, local taxes, VAT, insurance, bank charges, interest, etc. In addition, there are set construction costs, props, wardrobe, make-up, electrics, grips, and so on. The list is endless. A film budget is pages long, and is the basis for controlling the costs for the duration of the production. Every week a detailed report is issued showing any changes, either up or down. On an independent picture, the production manager and the production accountant complete the budget, but in the large companies like the American majors and Pinewood, they have a budget department to handle this important task. However, these accountants can only be as good as the information they are given. So, where on a British or American based film they know the costs of the individual items, on a foreign location picture they are reliant on the information brought back to them.

I knew that Lewis was desperate to make the whole film in Hong Kong, so it was up to me to prove to Rank's not only that it could be done, but also that it could be done cheaper than in the studio in England. So, where to start? Who did I ask?

The night was young. There wasn't much I could do at that time, so I went out for a stroll. Walking down a busy road I saw a sign, "Maxim's Restaurant and Bar" which seemed inviting, so I entered. I found myself in an elegant centre of excellence, where a tall, Chinese waiter attired in a spotless, starched uniform greeted me. I said I just wanted to have a drink and he guided me to the bar, where several men were sitting and standing around, so I took a stool and ordered a drink. The man sitting next to me suddenly said in a rather plummy English accent, "It's a pity you can't get draft bitter here."

This is how I met John O'Connell. It turned out that he was a very rich man, a major shareholder in the Hong Kong tram company. He told me that he was looking around the world to see where to settle. Although he had only been in Hong Kong a few weeks, he already seemed to know more about it than most of the Europeans I had met so far. Naturally, he enquired what I was doing there, so I obliged and told him I was at a bit of a loss to know where to start. At that point, a chap sitting on a stool interrupted me, and said that he could not help overhearing our conversation, and that maybe he could help me. He had lived and worked in the colony for many years, and was a font of information, giving me names and addresses of the kind of people I needed to contact.

This was the start of my "Maxim's Connection". Whenever I was in trouble or needed help, I would hurry down to their excellent bar and would invariably find someone to help me. It was the meeting place for executives, their local. It was a place to relax after a hard day, to meet old chums, greet new ones, and chew the fat with whoever was in that evening. It also had one of the best Western restaurants in the colony, so that you could make an evening of it if you wanted. The service was amazing, the waiters being not only efficient but also charming. Through a casual meeting in the bar, I was asked to be on Hong Kong radio, where Tim Brinton, who later became a Conservative Member of Parliament, interviewed me. From this, the local press picked up the story, and soon the whole place was buzzing about the forthcoming film to be made in Hong Kong. Now I was really getting into my stride, so that when George Maynard arrived I was able to introduce him to numerous locals.

Up until then, I had behaved myself, being more interested in work than in play. But with his arrival, everything changed. After a tough day, I'd meet up with him, have a few drinks, have an amazing meal at one of the numerous restaurants, and then hit the town. This is when we met the Chinese girls, bar girls, hookers (now called sex therapists), call them what you like.

In fact, they were quite different from the hatchet-faced European or American ones, and to compare them would not only degrade them, but also misunderstand them. True they sold sex for money, but they also sold companionship and fun. They would also be faithful to you, maybe for a night, a week, a month, or however long it lasted, but during that time they would not sleep with another man. They would watch that you didn't get robbed by the barkeeper, the rickshaw man, the taxi driver, whoever. What they really wanted was "a long time man", someone they could look after and cherish, and they were almost motherly in some respects. They were never dull, bad-tempered or money grabbing, and made you feel that they also were having fun, and that you were the only man in the world. They talked in amazing picturesque, pidgin English, and were like attractive, chattering budgerigars, though most of them supported their families, they never discussed their problems, their heartaches, their ambitions or their hopes, except perhaps one – the hope that you would stay with them. Looking back now, I realise how sad it was, but in those days I just revelled in their company, enjoyed the sexual delights of these slim, tiny-waisted, elf-like women, who were anatomically different – if not sideways, as the joke goes! They were a male delight, and I look back with great warmth at the many happy hours I spent in their company.

Not long after, Lewis joined us. We started to scout locations, which was a great way of seeing the colony. From the Chinese border, through the New Territories, down through Kowloon and over to Hong Kong to Repulse Bay.

I had taken on a location manager, a local English resident who worked with Radio Hong Kong. He was a very pleasant, knowledgeable, chap with a fair command of Cantonese. Through his work on the radio, he knew a lot of people, and was useful in introducing me to both the European and Chinese Government officials like the Police, the Customs, and the various government bodies that we would need during the preparation and shooting of the film.

Lewis was anxious to screen-test some of the local actors. Being a major film producing company, Hong Kong had a great pool of local talent, but few spoke English, their films being shot in either Cantonese or Mandarin. Those who did either spoke it so poorly you couldn't understand it through the thick Chinese accent, or they could speak in a conversation, but as soon as they got in front of the camera and had to read a script, they became stilted and flat.

Lewis spent many days interviewing possible contenders, and selected the best for screen-testing. I hired a small studio, and a Chinese crew for a day's shoot. What I hadn't bargained for was the heat and the humidity, and the fact that the stage in the studio had no air-conditioning and was like an oven. The Chinese crew didn't even seem to notice it, but Lewis and I were knocked sideways, and ended up by taking it in turns to direct the artists.

We did find one good boy, a large handsome Northern Chinese actor and a couple of gorgeous girls, who could just about manage one or two words of passable English.

Lewis had to rush back to London to discuss the main casting with Rank's. He was keen to use Peter Finch as the tramp, and somebody like Burl Ives as the Captain. There was also a leading part for an English girl to play a school teacher, but at that stage no names had been discussed.

George and I were left to continue our work, and for me things were rapidly coming together. I thought that I could not only make the film in H.K. but also bring it in for a very good price. I was getting good quotes from the various companies, but I was also getting to understand the way of doing business.

Although it was a British Colony, the Chinese still kept to their traditional way of handling negotiations. One of the most important things I learnt was the importance of "face". Whatever you did, you must not let anyone lose face, and the very best thing one could do was to give face. When negotiating a price it was right to get the best price you could, but it had to be done in a way that did not belittle the other side. One could never bully, or be impolite to the senior person in front of his own people, but always had to treat them with dignity and respect. Of course they would do the same with you, and this often meant that the negotiations continued for much longer than in the West.

This question of face is not just in business but creeps into all facets of life. On meeting people care must be taken to ensure all are included in greetings and conversation and one must not turn one's back on a person. Put like this, one could say this is just good manners, but it is more. It can involve a glance, a look, or a tone of voice.

We had a Pinewood cashier known by the Chinese crew as "cold eye", and they complained to me that he made them lose face, as he would glare at them when he paid them. "We work for our money, he no give us present," they said. "We lose face."

Giving face, though, worked magic, and I soon found out that a little time spent in appreciating the Chinese ways, the Chinese philosophy, their likes and dislikes, paid massive dividends.

Never was face more demonstrated than when we went to Macao. We did not have much shooting to do there, but nevertheless it had to be set up, contacts made, and prices, laws, restrictions and customs all had to be investigated. In those days, the ferry journey took several hours, and the idea was to go in the evening, have dinner on board, and arrive in Macao the following morning. I had already made contact with the British Consulate there who told me that a Mr Whu would meet us off the boat, give us any assistance that we needed, and he, the Consul, would join us later that evening. We had a great evening on the ferry, and both woke up with huge hangovers, which probably accounted for the ridiculous Abbot and Costello comedy scene that followed. As we docked, I could see a small Chinese man waving a Union Jack flag to whom I waved back.

"Who is that?" enquired George.

"Whu," I replied.

"That one down there."

"That's Whu," I said again.

"That's what I'm asking, that one down there, with the flag," he said irritably.

"That is Whu."

"Jesus Christ, John, that is what I keep asking. Who is that little bugger waving at us?"

"That little bugger, I keep telling you, is Whu."

At which point George stamped off with a "fuck you", and we didn't talk again till on the quayside I was able to introduce him.

"George, I would like you to meet Mr Whu from the British Consulate."

"Well," explained George later that day when we were alone, "I expected a type of tall Englishman representing the Queen, not a Chinese. I mean, it's not the kind of thing a chap expects."

Macao in 1957 was an extraordinary place. A mere dot on the mainland of China, it was a mixture of decaying Portuguese architecture and Chinese decadence. Relics of Portuguese rule rubbed shoulders with the gambling casinos. One wall of the cathedral stood silhouetted against the sky as a reminder to glories long ago.

Large neon sings advertised the names of the various clubs – for at this time Macao's economy depended solely on fireworks, gambling and vice. Nowadays, with the introduction of the fast hovercraft, Macao has changed, and big hotels have been built for the many tourists that cross over to attend the horse racing and to gamble. In those days, the casinos were like something out of a 'B'-movie, and the whole place had a sinister feel, as in a cheap Oriental drama.

Our hotel had only a few rooms, and was one of the few buildings left over from the Portuguese and still habitable. It was situated right on the road by the sea and had a certain run-down charm, with its faded brocade furniture, high ceiling rooms, shuttered windows and ancient plumbing. It was pure Somerset Maugham.

One of our main contacts was a local banker, H.K. Lee, and after checking into the hotel we made our way to his office. Driving down the narrow streets in a pedicab we understood why the comical Mr Whu had advised us to use this form of transport rather than a taxicab. Unlike Hong Kong, there were no tall buildings, or tall Europeans, but just a maze of alleyways choked with people, all Chinese. It was a pretty terrifying and humiliating ride, with the two of us sitting side by side, with the driver pedalling away behind us. It was as though we were at the front end of a broom sweeping all in front of us. Ignoring the mass of traffic and pedestrians around us, our driver kept up a running commentary in pidgin English, mostly trying to sell us one or other of his family. Clutching our briefcases, we pretended not to hear the curses of the pedestrians we narrowly missed, or the cries of the other pedicab drivers trying to sell us various wares, "Got nice sister, good fucky" or "You want girl? Two girl? Boy?"; "Ah, you two shit bags, you want see exibish?" And so on.

Somehow or other we arrived at a watch shop, and coming to a halt with a flourish, the driver indicated we were at our destination.

"No," we chorused, "we want bank."

His eyes lit up. "Oh, you want wank", and started to move off. With a lot of yelling, we stopped him and showed him the card we were carrying. We paid him off and entered the shop, and after showing the card we were ushered into a passage leading to the back.

On going through, we found out that indeed there was an H.K.Lee, and this indeed was the bank. I never did find out why it was situated in this way, but then I never did find out why *anything* happened in Macao.

H.K. Lee was a delightful man, and we quickly got all our accounts opened and were issued with a cheque book, all in Chinese and further complicated by the fact that it was printed sidewise, our side being their top. George found it useful though, and paid his Pinewood bar bill with one! After concluding all our business, we were taken to lunch.

By then we were quite used to Chinese food, which is completely different from the food served in Chinese restaurants in the West. We really enjoyed the meal and especially the frog legs, which were so big I thought they were small chicken legs.

What did worry us was the "hawking". Everyone in the country seemed to spit, and all the offices were furnished with spittoons. If this was not bad enough, they also did it at meal times! In the middle of lunch H.K. would leap up and gob in the nearby pot. This is hardly conducive to enjoying one's meal.

After lunch we were bundled into a car, and driven through the streets until we arrived at a hotel. The road was so narrow, we all had to get out from one side of the car, as it wasn't wide enough to open both sides. We were ushered through a tiny dingy entrance, past a small counter, up some dark wooden stairs and into a room on the first floor. The room was sparsely furnished with several wooden chairs, a table laden with every type of drink you could think of, and the obligatory spittoon.

"Take seat, take seat. Have drink, have drink," H.K. said, indicating the array of bottles.

I had no desire to drink more, but seeing his enthusiasm and his obvious desire to please us, I asked for a very small brandy. H.K. muttered in Cantonese to one of his cronies, who duly poured me a full glass of brandy, the sight of which nearly got me to sign the pledge. George got the same treatment, and then they poured themselves drinks and sat down. There we were in this stark room, sitting on hard, straight chairs, looking at one another. "Yum Sing," said H.K. raising his glass.

"No, no, please no," I hastily interjected.

I had learnt about Yum Sing. You raised your glass as if offering a toast, and saying the words Yum Sing, raise the glass to your lips and drink the entire contents, after which you turn the glass upside down to prove that you have drunk every drop. I couldn't possibly drink a whole glass of brandy after having consumed various bottles of wine, and eight courses of local food. They all seemed to think my reaction was hugely amusing.

"Thank God, you got us out of that," whispered George.

At that moment the door crashed open, and ten girls paraded in. They all lined up whilst H.K. inspected them, rather like a Sergeant-Major inspecting his troops.

"Ah, this one very good. Look, big tits," H.K. exclaimed, going down the ranks of the young girls.

"Oh my God," George cried out, " I think they're for us."

This was quickly confirmed by H.K. "Look George, this one very good for you, you producer, you choose. You first, then John."

George gave me a despairing look, "I couldn't," he said, "I just couldn't. I'm dead on my feet."

"But," I said hastily, "you have to George, you have to, they have gone to all this trouble." Then I put in the clincher. "If you don't, it would make them lose face. Just think, George, just think that you are fucking for the Rank Organisation!"

My girl was a sweet thing, though, unlike the Hong Kong girls, spoke no English. Conversation being out, when I lay back on the bed I thought how wonderful it would be to just fall asleep. She soon had me forgetting that idea, and gave me the most incredibly erotic massage. When it was all over, and despite the fact that H.K. had told us that everything had been paid for, I gave her a more than generous present. She was so amazed that she stared at it for a short while, then came and wrapped her arms around me and kissed me on the lips, before darting out of the room with a happy laugh.

I met George outside, who looked the worse for wear. Gone was the incredibly smart, well-groomed, elegant Englishman. Instead, with his tie askew, his jacket over his arm, and his trousers creased everywhere but where they should be, he looked like a debauched tramp. "Jesus," he said tiredly, "I don't know what she was supposed to be, but I think she was a Turkish all-in wrestler." And got into the car and went to sleep.

That night we had dinner with the British Consul and his wife, who were very nice people, but deadly dull. It was a real feat of strength to get through the meal. We had both decided not to drink anything as even one more drink could easily have sent us both to sleep. I think they were surprised how well behaved we were. We were very unlike film people, the wife gushed. We assured her it was early to bed in order to get on with the work. She said she was pleased to hear it, as so many English people there did "the most disgusting things" and didn't behave like English gentlemen "at all"!

The next day, we were busy interviewing possible local help, and meeting with an undertaker, as the script called for a Chinese funeral procession. We had to find a location manager as well as accommodation for the company, which was not easy. In the end, they took us to a hotel that had the right number of rooms, but had been built when they were under the mistaken impression there was going to be a race track. Our hearts sank when we saw the place, especially when I pulled the cover off the iron bedstead in the dirty cell-like room, and saw the state of the pillow! What was I to do? It really was the only game in town. We left Macao without solving the problem.

Back in Hong Kong, I started to talk to a few of the local producers, which resulted in being invited to lunch at Run Run Shaw's house in Repulse Bay. Situated overlooking the sea, it was one of his more modest residences, but nevertheless was both opulent and comfortable, combining the best of Chinese and Western furnishings. Lunch was a long and amazing meal, a gourmet marathon, with seemingly never-ending courses, all served from golden dishes swinging out from golden pagodas. Each guest had his own wonderful looking Chinese girl to look after him, known by the locals as lotus blossoms. These girls were not hookers, but rather like the Japanese Geisha, there to both entertain and look after the guests. If you wanted, you could proposition the girl and she may, or may not, agree. My girl was quite beautiful, but I have to confess I never made the proposition. The food and the wine saw to that. I thought the meal would never end, and I tried to help it down by drinking. I only had to take one sip before my girl would top up my glass. I was scared to refuse any dish in case it caused my host, and my girl, to "lose face". When the meal did finally end, the last thing on my mind was sex. All I wanted was a pee!

Apart from one or two occasions like that, much to my sorrow we did not socialise much with the Chinese – except for one. We had become friendly with a government agency Englishman, George Tyler, who was often accompanied by one of the most striking people I had ever met. She was from the North of China and was the daughter of a Mandarin. The Communists had killed her parents and most of her family, but she, her sister, brother and a brother-in-law managed to escape to Hong Kong. Her brother soon left and lived in Japan.

Paula had made an unhappy marriage to a local European civil servant, which ended in their separating. She was a stunning vision with her jet-black hair swept back tightly against her head, her perfectly applied heavy make-up accentuating her Chinese eyes and high cheekbones. She was elegant in her high-necked cheong-sam, moulded to her ravishing figure of large bust, narrow waist and lithe legs. She was petite, but exquisite. Whenever we met her and George Tyler, after politely greeting us, she would sit in a corner not saying a word. So much so, that I would tease her about not talking, and she would just smile at me and say, "Chinese say, better to listen."

As the time for us to leave got nearer, we realised that we had better take advantage of the fantastic shopping there and take some presents back with us. George Tyler suggested that Paula accompany us to make sure that we not only went to the right shops, but also got the best prices.

She might not have spoken much before when we were out, but in the shops a torrent of Cantonese came out and shop assistants were quickly hurrying here and there at her bidding. We got incredible bargains: pearls for Peggy for half the marked price, toys for the children, clothes for the whole family, transistor radios and so on. She had been a great help to us, and George Maynard and I were both very grateful to her. I think we bought her a small present in appreciation, though it was difficult because she seemed to have everything.

George had the great idea of stopping off in Bangkok on the way home, on the pretext of seeing what film equipment they had for hire. The name and address of a local film company was found, cables sent, and off we went after several last good-bye parties with the favourites of the girls we had met.

Then we were off on the BOAC flight to the capital of Thailand. It was magical, and much more Oriental in flavour than Hong Kong, not having been exposed to such heavy Western influence, and our hotel was exotic, in both style and service. We called our contact who came straight round to the hotel, and on hearing that it was our first time in Thailand, insisted on giving us a tour of the city, which I found, much to my surprise, the most fascinating place.

With its strong Buddhist culture, Bangkok had many magnificent and well-preserved temples, quite unlike the ones in Hong Kong, which were pretty tatty. The buildings, with their classical double roofs were delightful, and the many monks in their saffron robes added a touch of colour. The enormous signs advertising the many massage parlours, and their claims of having hundreds of girls to choose from, were a forerunner of what Bangkok became famous for, but this was the 50s and long before the sex tourist industry had expanded.

Our contact insisted on taking us for lunch before visiting his studio, where on arrival we were led through a small room, which was equipped with the type of lighting used by still photographers, then on through another door, and into a perfect little screening room. We sat down, straight away the lights dimmed, and the projection started. It wasn't very long before we realised what sort of film we were watching. It turned out that he was one of the largest producers of blue films in Thailand, and he thought that we were two buyers interested in buying up the Western rights! On returning to the hotel, we found a telegram from Pinewood, forwarded from Hong Kong. All it said was, "Where are you?" Sadly we decided we had to go, and after one more pleasant night in that wonderful city, we left.

More drama at the airport. When we arrived in the country, we were told by Immigration that we had to check with the Police the following day. As we didn't know where to go, we went to the BOAC office for directions, but were assured by them it was completely unnecessary. Naturally we believed them. Wrong! Apparently we were missing one "chop" (an Eastern expression meaning a rubber stamp) in our passports. We did our best to explain, but the officer wasn't having any of it, and the next thing we knew, three armed police officers were escorting us to an office at the back, where a more senior officer inspected our passports. He too was unimpressed with our story.

"So, you prefer to listen to airline staff, rather than official immigration officer of the Thai government," he said menacingly.

We apologised profusely but seemingly to no effect.

As we were taken away by the waiting police, George muttered to me, "Maybe we should call the embassy." We were split up and led into separate bare rooms, with a single barred window, through which I could see our waiting aircraft. After a little time, we were led out again, back to the same officer whose attitude had completely changed. He handed back our passports with a large smile saying, "Have a nice journey, gentlemen." We bowed and scraped, shook his hands, thanked him and hurriedly left with waiting BOAC officials, who rapidly escorted us to the waiting plane, engines turning. We never knew what it was all about. It still seems strange that they made such a fuss over such a minor matter.

I settled back in my seat, and thought over the past weeks, trying to go over all the points, all the facts that I needed to be able to complete a budget in London. I also thought back to all the fun we had had, and what an amazing place Hong Kong was. I prayed that the picture would actually be made, and we would be able to go back and shoot the film.

My day-dreaming was interrupted by George asking me how much money we had drawn from Pinewood. I replied by asking him what the receipts amounted to, as he was keeping them. He looked worried and said he thought I was looking after them, and would I please check. Although I knew I didn't have them, I started searching in my pockets, but could only come up with a laundry bill, written in Chinese. Now we were in the shit. Having spent thousands of Rank's money, the two of us were returning without anything to show for it.

On arriving back at Pinewood, we were given a sour welcome from Arthur Alcott, and told to clear our expenses with Robbie, a dour Scot, and chief accountant of the studios. Retiring to our newly allocated office in the attic of the main block (the sort of office usually allocated to a lowly Assistant director), we carefully typed out "George Maynard and John Dark, 'Ferry to Hong Kong', Recce Expenses: Money Drawn £4,000, Money expended £4,056. Balance due to GM & JD: £56." We both signed it, and made our way to Robinson's office. Another dismal greeting from the Happy Scot as he took our expenses claim, glanced at it, and asked for the receipts. We handed over the Chinese laundry bill, which he eyed dubiously.

"Do you understand it?" we asked.

He inspected the grubby piece of paper with great interest, "No, I don't."

"Well," we said, "they were all like that, so we didn't bother to bring them!"

He bought it, and we had a dinner out on the proceeds. Nobody has ever believed this story, but it is absolutely true.

For the next few weeks, we were busy preparing the budget. Thank goodness the accountants were delighted with my report. They even went as far as to say it was the best they had ever had, and apparently so much so they approved it in record time. Only later did I find out why it had been so easy to get it approved.

No decision had yet been made as to the main casting, though Sylvia Syms seemed to be the hot contender for the English school teacher. We all agreed that we should take John Stoll as the art director. Both Lewis and I had enjoyed working with him on the Bygraves picture, but once again a fight had to be fought with Pinewood. However, Lewis was very much in John Davis's good books, who invariably gave in to him. Rank's allowed the producer and director to choose their own editor and their own cameraman, so Lewis decided on another technician from "A Cry From the Streets", Peter Hunt.

Peter had cut many films for Lewis, and was very well respected in the industry. We always thought he would become a top director himself. Peter cut several of the Bond films for Cubby Broccoli, after which Cubby gave him the chance to direct the next one. Sadly this was the one starring George Lazenby, and through no fault of Peter's it was the only one of Cubby's Bond films to flop. He directed one or two other movies but none of them ever came to anything. He went to the States but things didn't go his way there either and he eventually returned to the UK and disappeared.

However, at that time, we were young and we had our lives ahead of us. "Ferry …" looked a good stepping stone on our way to bigger and better things.

The only major technical position to be filled was the cameraman. After a lot of discussion, Lewis decided to ask Otto Heller, a mid-European, plump, dapper little man, who was a wonderful cameraman. He still spoke English with an amazing accent, and would pretend not to understand you when it suited his purpose.

There was one other position critical to the crew, that of first assistant. As there was no one Lewis really wanted, he agreed to take one of Pinewood's contract assistants. Lewis and George met with him first, mainly to see how he would get on with Lewis, but also to explain to him the character of the Chinese, and how important it was to treat them in a way that didn't make them lose face. They went into long explanations on the sensitivity of the Chinese, and how one had to be tactful in handling them. After about half-an-hour, they asked him whether he understood.

"I understand perfectly," he replied. "If they don't do as you tell 'em, kick 'em up the arse"!

Normally this would have been enough for Lewis, but realising how good Rank had been about all the other positions, he agreed to take him. This was a mistake. Not that he wasn't good, it was just that he wasn't the man for Lewis. He was the noisy, Sergeant-Major type, whereas Lewis liked a calmer approach to the job.

Choosing a person for the job of buyer was a worry. If we took someone from England, they wouldn't know where to go, or what to pay. On the other hand, if we chose a local person they would most likely rob us blind. After several meetings, and getting nowhere, George suggested Paula. After thinking it over, I queried whether she would want the job, as it didn't look as if she needed the money.

"Exactly," said George, "she doesn't, and that's what makes her right. We know she knows her way around, we've seen her in action getting the best prices, and she's got style." He then gave Lewis and me a hard look. "She would give us face," he said.

Lewis nodded. "With that first assistant, we could do with a bit of that!"

I agreed to talk to her when I got back. And with the budget approved, and the picture given the green light, I knew I had to get back to Hong Kong, and take John Stoll with me.

There was a mountain of work to be done.

We had to settle on a ship, and then convert it to our requirements. All the locations had to be finalised, local crew had to be found, and small- part casting completed. Offices and premises had to be found and furnished for the producer, PM, secretaries, publicity, accounts, wardrobe, make-up, hairdressers, etc. In addition banks had to be primed, transport organised and adapted to film requirements, local legal, fiscal, and Customs' problems to be discussed, equipment to be found and hired. The list was endless.

George and Lewis agreed that it was essential that I return as quickly as possible, but Pinewood took a different attitude, with Alcott insisting my place was there. I argued that as we were making the whole picture in Hong Kong, it was obvious I should be there.

"You are just trying to escape your responsibilities," he shouted. "Who is going to see the unit off? Who is going to see the company off? Who is going to be responsible for that, eh?" I could not believe my ears.

"Well," I replied, "considering you have a complete Production department here, and a complete transport department, including Tommy Green who meets everyone in and out at the airport anyway, I would have thought that was not too difficult a problem."

"But it's *your* responsibility," he cried.

"Okay, I'll tell you what, I will engage someone to see them on to the plane, someone I trust, and I will hold myself responsible, even if I am in Hong Kong."

But he wasn't having any of it, and in the end Lewis once again had to go to John Davies and have Alcott overruled. I go into all this in detail just to show not only the animosity at the studio: the middle management would go to great length to make my life as difficult as possible, even if it disrupted the making of the film. More was to unfold as we went along.

It was tough leaving home, Peg, and the kids, for such a long time. I promised to write often, and get some fantastic presents. With lots of tears on both sides, we said good-bye as the Pinewood car collected me to take me to the airport where I met up with John Stoll.

John, apart from being a talented designer, was a delightful companion. He was a lover of good food, good wine and women (good and bad!). With him alongside, the journey seemed much shorter. He enjoyed the service, the food, and especially the wine, in the first class cabin. No matter the time of day or night, whenever he was offered anything, even breakfast or tea, he would always say, "Could I have a little champagne?" We discussed the film, the script, and the possible casting, but in the main, we discussed his problems. He questioned me extensively about my previous trip. The ferry boat was a big worry to him – as it was to all of us.

John had discussed with Lewis having a paddle boat as he thought, quite rightly, that it would be visually more exciting than a propeller driven craft. I had told him that to my knowledge there wasn't that kind of vessel in Hong Kong, and although we could make enquiries when we got there, I was not optimistic, and reckoned it would have to be built. That would not be easy, for the ferry had to be practical, had to be seaworthy and, though John was a talented art director, he was not a marine engineer. Apart from this, the ship had to be equipped like a floating film studio, the design of which John said he would leave to me, as he didn't know what was wanted.

It was a great adventure and unique opportunity, as not many English pictures had been totally made in a foreign location at that time especially a location as far away from base as Hong Kong. Communications were bad in those days, as there were no cable links, no faxes, no satellite phones, and only a very unreliable and noisy radiophone link. To a large extent, we were cut off, and there were just the two of us to plan this epic-sized film.

Looking back now, I realise how inexperienced I was (maybe Rank's had a point?), but it was my inexperience and lack of training that allowed me to keep the budget so low. No one at Pinewood thought I could do it for the money. I also told them that I believed I could get all the heavy equipment locally, so all I was bringing out from the studio were the cameras, the sound equipment, certain specialised make-up, and sundries that I had ascertained were unavailable in the East.

It was the same with the ferry, and I had assured Rank's that we would be able to get such a ship at the price I had put in the budget, which was mainly based on a not very educated guess.

John and I discussed all these problems, but then he got fed up with talking shop, and he asked me to tell him again about the hotel where we were going to stay.

I had already told him where *I* was going stay, but I had sheaves of pamphlets from hotels in H.K for him to choose from, but he said he would stay at mine. This was the Luk Kwok hotel in Wanchai, which was a Chinese hotel on the water's edge in a Chinese part of Hong Kong Island. On the ground floor was the reception area, and a bar, a girlie bar. On the first floor, there were two large restaurants, one serving Chinese food, and the other decorated like a Wild West Saloon, serving both Chinese and Western food. On the next four floors were basic hotel rooms. The top two floors, though, had been totally modernised, with extremely smart, large, comfortable air-conditioned rooms, with amazing views over the harbour. The hotel had become famous when Richard Mason stayed there whilst he wrote "The World of Susi Wong", though I think that was before the upper floors had been renovated. Apart from being comfortable, with the best views in town, it was less than half the price of the Gloucester. It also provided the services of a room boy who looked after everything, including full room service; and when I say "full", I mean overflowing!

John's life was very well under control. Very soon after arriving, I arranged a little meeting where I introduced him to Ruby. They were to stay together until John's return to England at the end of shooting some nine months later.

I would meet John in his room in the morning. As he always seemed to be in the bath when I arrived, I would sit on his loo and talk over the day. We had decided on a shipyard which had a freighter we both thought would make a good base for the ferry. We were lucky in that shipping was at an all-time low, with the harbour full of abandoned ships, so we were able to get a good price. The shipyard was owned and run by a tough American who understood our problems, and was the sort of man that one felt one could trust. John set up his office at the shipyard, and as he could not get enough of the Chinese culture and way of life, soon had it decorated with several Chinese religious artefacts. Bells rang in the breeze of the fan, red paper, covered with Chinese script, flapped around like so much colourful fly paper, Buddhas nestled on the shelfs, and various Chinese gods looked down on their latest convert.

Soon the final designs for the ferry were finished, the price approved, the contract signed, and the ship pulled out of the water ready to be converted from a coastal propeller-driven freighter to a paddle-wheeled passenger ferry, the "Ferry To Hong Kong". I had to agree with the shipyard my various requirements, but first I had to make sure that the ship's generators were adequate, not only for supplying the ship's electrical power, but also for our lighting.

As at that time I had neither a cameraman nor an electrical technician, I had to make some wild guesses. I had discovered that the Chinese did not use any brutes, the top heavy arc lights, so I was intending to ship these out as soon as I knew Otto Heller's requirements. In the meantime, I had to "wing it" and pray.

Then, with the plan of the ship's cargo hold, I mapped out the various departments: camera (complete with dark room), sound, prop store, wardrobe (fitted with washing machines, drying cabinets and irons), make-up and hairdressing-rooms (fully fitted with mirrors, hot and cold water and barbers' chairs). Provision also had to be made for crowd artists, for their dressing areas and showers. More loos had to be built to accommodate the extra passengers the vessel would be carrying. Existing cabins had to be stripped out, repainted, furnished and turned into dressing-rooms for the principals. As the ship would be out at sea the whole day, everything had to be carried aboard, including the catering, dining areas, kitchens and large refrigeration rooms. It was indeed a floating film studio, and I have to admit I had great fun planning it all.

By this time I had spoken to Paula, and she was delighted to have been asked to help. She started work immediately with John, helping him find the research material he needed, translating for him with the Chinese shipyard workers, taking him around to see where properties could be hired. She was a busy girl, and John was delighted with her.

Meanwhile I was busy with the various production problems. I had taken on the same guy who helped me on my recce, and I engaged him as our local location manager. Every day I stressed to him that he was on no account to take any sort of back-hander. This was Hong Kong, and the commission, known locally as "the squeeze", was the norm, a way of life. I had discovered that in making a deal, you first haggled about the price, after which you haggled over "the squeeze". I used to follow this formula, but once I had agreed "the squeeze", I would instruct them to deduct the amount from the invoice. This was not popular amongst our suppliers, as they felt that not only was I an idiot for not taking the money, but I was also behaving in an undignified manner by not following the normal Hong Kong business ethics. In effect, everybody lost face. Maybe, but I insisted on this the whole time we were there.

My local chap, who shall be nameless, had, on my instructions, done a deal with a hotel for the use of their rooms by the various departments when we were shooting on land, and also for accommodating the crew and artists when they first arrived. I asked him how much squeeze he had got out of the deal.

"Nothing. Like you said, nothing," he said.

"Ah, come on, I want you to tell me so that we can go fifty: fifty," I continued.

"Okay, I got ten per cent," he quietly replied

"Right, you're fired."

I then took on John O'Connell, my plummy English friend whom I had met on my first day in the colony, and who I felt would never take a shilling. He was too English, too proud; also he did not need the money! He also liked and admired the Chinese, and could mix with them. This was strange for an Englishman, but then he was rather a strange chap. He stayed with us throughout, and did a bloody fine job. The firing of his predecessor went around like wild fire. Every supplier seemed to have heard of it, as I had stressed that anyone offering to pay squeeze would lose any future business.

I was having trouble with the electrical suppliers. Their rates were far above what they originally quoted, and, though they gave me a whole ream of reasons why, I was sure it was because they were beginning to understand that this was a major production, and that they could soak me for more money. They never had got over the American company who were quoted in Hong Kong dollars but paid in US Dollars, a huge difference!

I had discovered that Hong Kong was split in two between the Nationalists and the Communists. Many of the pictures made there were for the mainland, so I arranged a meeting with a leading representative of the Communist film industry, a Mr Li (everybody seemed to be called Li, or Lee!) He turned out to be the personification of the inscrutable East. I explained my problems, and he said he would try to help, and then changed the conversation to the weather. I tried to get more information from him like prices, what equipment they had, but, though he was very courteous, all he would say was that he would telephone me later that day, and with great aplomb ushered me out. By the time I got back at the office in Kowloon, a journey of half an hour, he had already phoned. He could supply all my needs and would discuss hire charges the next day in his office.

En route to meet him the next day, I turned over in my mind how far I could trust Mr Li and his Communist bosses. I had not had any dealings with them before, nor had any social contact with them either. Most of my Chinese acquaintances were Nationalists, who told me not to deal with the Reds, and that I would be sorry if I did. However, when I saw Li's prices, which were about half of what I had been quoted by the Nationalist companies, I knew I had to take the risk. Whilst I was studying the figures, Mr Li said he understood I took no squeeze, therefore he had allowed for that in his figures. There and then, I signed the deal, and was never sorry.

Li always kept his word, the equipment was always delivered on time, and in good condition. He was always scrupulously honest in his dealings, and I hired more and more from him. He had only one fault, which was that he would never give me a straight answer. I would arrive at his office in a mad hurry, make my request, and he would say something like, "It's very oppressive weather for this time of year." I learnt to make my request and leave, as he would always have to call and ask someone before he could reply. That was their way and a small inconvenience to pay for the excellent service they gave and the money they saved us.

My personal life was settling into a pattern. I would get up at 7am, have tea or coffee brought by Tom, my room boy, after which I would have my daily meeting with John Stoll. We would discuss the latest problems, and he would up-date me with his progress. Armed with that information, I would then buy the morning paper from the young boy who lived under the arches of the hotel, his bedclothes being the left over newspapers from the day before. Then across the road to the water's edge, where I would catch a Walla-Walla (a motor boat) across to Kowloon and get a taxi to the office in Nathan Road. My busy day was usually interrupted for a business lunch with a supplier, journalist, government official, senior police or army officer, harbour official, and so on, as it was important to know as many people as possible who could help during the shooting of the film.

I rarely finished until late, as there was usually a business dinner or a drink with friends. However, it was not back to a lonely hotel room. Firstly, I would get a warm greeting from Tom, who seemed to be there night and day, and then there would be an even warmer welcome from a happy, smiling, welcoming little darling, Lucy, who was half Cantonese, half Thai. She would wrap her arms and legs around me, give me a big kiss, and then pour me some tea that was always ready, and tell me about her day. She would show me where she had embroidered my name on all my pants, handkerchiefs, and socks. "Make sure boy no steal," she would say. She was on a weekly payment, and was able to send money back to her parents and siblings, who lived in the New Territories. After a hard day's work, she was very relaxing, and her chatter was a welcome change after the effort of haggling all day. We would either go out somewhere locally for dinner, or have it in the hotel restaurant or my room. There was no need to "go out on the town". It was not a love affair, but more like having an attractive housekeeper with special qualities. For instance, she was a wonderful masseuse, and could massage with both her hands and her feet. Mind you, she kept up a constant stream of chatter. The first time we were together she said, "I don't know why Cantonese girl no likey smoke cigar", and come to think of it (and who wouldn't think of it!), it was probably the only time she was quiet!

Soon Lewis came over again, this time bringing with him Otto Heller. It was good to see Lewis again, though John Stoll and I would often say how we were dreading the company arriving and disturbing our pleasant lifestyle! We showed Otto around the various locations, and constantly asked him to give us some idea of his lighting requirements, as all we had to go on so far was my guesswork, and a cameraman I ain't! We couldn't elicit a reply from him, so decided to wait until we had him cornered on the ferry to Macao. But he still managed to dodge the question. He just said, in a thick, mid-European accent and looking around, "So this is the ferry, ya?"

Lewis was starting to get impatient, insisted that we needed to know, so with a weary sigh, he said, "When I started in Prague, they gave me one lamp. Then I went to Bucharest, and they gave me two. Eventually I got to London, and they gave me all the lamps I wanted. Now, here I am in Hong Kong, and you don't want to give me any lamps at all." We never did get an answer, and it was more by luck, and my connections with the Communists, that we got through the shoot without too much trouble.

We were operating with no staff whatsoever. Normally in pre-production there would be a complete art department, with an art director, assistant art director working under the designer, an assistant art director, several draughtsmen, a trained property buyer, one or more set dressers (now called set decorators), and a construction manager. In the production department there would be a production manager (now called a line producer), a unit manager now called the production manager, a secretary (now called a co-ordinator), several location managers, one or more juniors (now called runners), a cashier, a transport manager (now called a transport captain). On a major special effects' picture shooting at the turn of the century in England, in the art department there were 30 people, in the production department 24 and in the accounts 24.

John had only Paula. Later on, his staff was doubled when we brought out a construction manager. That was the art department.

I had a local, untrained location manager. Both John and I drove ourselves, and we had a local girl to do the odd letter and answer the phone. We were cut off from the studio both because of the time difference and because the telephone was erratic, one day one could hear everything, the next day nothing. We had to rely on cables, which was not the easiest way to discuss technical and creative problems.

Seeing what an immense task it was for just John and myself, before returning to the UK, Lewis asked how he could help. I asked him to send us Marguerite Green, which he did. After her arrival things became much easier, and with a proper production office, the burden of paperwork was lifted from my shoulders.

I received a cable from Lewis saying that in London that day Rank's were announcing the casting of both Curt Jurgens and Orson Welles. This was indeed good news. Curt had become a leading international star after the success of "The Enemy Below", and the legendary Orson was one of the world's greats. Lewis had wanted Peter Finch for the role of the tramp, but at the time Curt was a much bigger name, and would greatly add to the prestige of the film. Naturally I thought that after the submarine film Jurgens would be playing the Captain, and Orson the man trapped on the ferry. I was perplexed when I discovered that it was the other way round. I still believe that had it been the former, we would have had a much better picture. Sylvia Syms was confirmed as the young school teacher, leaving just the minor parts to be cast.

One of the casting problems was the role of the Chinese pirate. We just could not find someone who looked right, but could also act, and in English. To cover ourselves, we brought out two stunt men from England. One was Milton Reid, a very oriental-looking villain type, who was actually a wrestler but had branched out into stunt work. He had a magnificent face, and the right body, but he also had the most awful falsetto voice, and every time he opened his mouth he sounded like a chambermaid finding a mouse under the bed. We made a deal with him just as a stunt man on the understanding we might offer him the part as the pirate. Bushel, of course, was the other one.

I was to keep looking for our pirate, which led to my getting a call from Rank's man in Taiwan who told me of an ex-soldier, in fact Chiang Kai-Shek's flag-bearer, now in an old soldier's home in Taiwan. He was seven feet tall, with a physique to match, so I arranged to have him sent over immediately.

The day before his arrival, I received a cable from the Rank man stating, "Giant arriving Kai Tak tomorrow. Please arrange low loader, as he will not fit into taxi"!

At first sight, he looked great, as he was enormous. The trouble was, he couldn't walk, but shuffled. The poor chap had outgrown his strength, and was a pathetic creature. We gave him a few days in Hong Kong, where he never stopped eating. The only time he did was to fuck; he didn't seem to have outgrown that! He told one of our Chinese Assistants it was the best three days of his life.

John was over the moon about Paula, and I got to know her more and more as time went on. She was always the same: immaculately groomed and dressed. She was very polite, spoke only when spoken to and had something important to say. She picked up the film jargon which, interspersed with her pidgin English, was both amusing and attractive. John, she and I would meet for lunch or dinner to discuss the film, how the ship was progressing etc. We were very busy, and these meals together gave us the chance to catch up with each other's activities. All was going well, and both John and I were amazed at the speed with which the Chinese worked, as well as at their skill and ingenuity.

We had received a cable from Lewis saying that he thought he would need a camera crane and, to save shipping, did we think we could build one? John was an artist, a creator, and by no stretch of the imagination could he be called a camera technician, but without a second's hesitation he was soon wrapped up in consultations with the engineers at the shipyard. In no time at all, we were able to confirm that not only could we build the needed piece of camera equipment, but were able to cost it at less than the shipping charges, not to mention the cost of the rental.

I had drawn up plans for the interior of the ship, again with the help of an employee of the shipyard, and we could see all the usual facilities gradually taking shape inside the ship. Paula had made some amazing deals with local companies, so we were able to furnish the principal artists rooms in great style. Marguerite had all the office jobs under control, including training a local Chinese girl. Our reports back to Pinewood were all up to date; we were on our pre-production schedule, and well within our budget. John O'Connel was getting to grips with the job, our locations were being legally covered, nearby hotels and restaurants organised to offer facilities when in their areas. Everything seemed to be under control. It was false security.

Disaster struck – I fell in love.

Working so closely with Paula, it came as no surprise when one day she called me at the hotel and asked if she could come and see me.

"Of course, come over any time."

A few minutes' later there was a gentle knock on the door and there stood five feet of elegant beauty. Shyly she entered the room. "Hi, come on in, it's so good to see you," I greeted her nervously. "How is everything?" I tried to tidy the room up a bit. "Look, why don't you sit here?" I quickly removed the papers off the chair, which she ignored but instead crossed over and looked out of the large window at the fantastic view of the harbour below. I went and stood beside her.

"Wonderful, eh?" I asked. She nodded her head. So far she hadn't said a word. Why was my tummy turning? "Chinese don't say 'eh'?" I asked.

She stood awhile looking out at the activity on the water and then turned to me, and looked me in the eyes. That is when it hit me. I cannot describe it, I cannot even remember how I felt. All I know is that I was gone, lost, finished, kaput, over the moon, besotted! Looking back, I see that I had never fallen like this before. I really loved Peggy, but I don't think I was ever "in love" with her. I had known her since I was twelve and we had a wonderful relationship, but it wasn't the kick in the stomach that this was. Ours had been a fun, warm, and happy companionship. This, by contrast, was a heady, ecstatic, roller-coaster adventure.

When Paula and I consummated our love it was the most thrilling, passionate act I had ever experienced. Whether it was because we were both so in love, or whether it was that, as a daughter of a Mandarin, she had been taught the art of sex, or whether it was the setting, I don't know. All I do know is that it was amazing. We were like one, uninhibited and desperate to take, and to give, the greatest pleasure. The setting, of course, gave a great romantic background to this wonderous love affair, and no doubt added to the emotions of physical and mental attraction.

At the start, Paula would not come to the hotel at night, saying they would think she was a bar girl and lose face. Instead we would go out into the typhoon shelter. Paula owned her own sampan, and the crew (?) looked after it, in return for having the use of the accommodation, which description is a bit of a joke. A sampan is like a bulbous rowing boat that is propelled by a single oar at the back. It has one flat deck underneath which are the sleeping quarters, and this was the accommodation. For the passengers above, there are cushions to recline on, a small wooden table for one's drink and food, and a canvas roof. With this rolled half way back, we would be propelled out into the typhoon shelter and into another world; a very Chinese world. I never ever saw a single European face and I later learnt that very, very few Europeans knew of the amazing life that went on at night.

Out there we would first go to a fish boat and buy fresh fish; we would then be rowed to the cook boat, where we would tie up alongside whilst we waited for them to cook our fish. A liquor sampan would come by and we would purchase beer, and strange Chinese wines and spirits.

When I tried to explain it to my local English friends they would always say, "Oh, you mean the floating restaurants." No, I did not mean that. The floating restaurants were exactly that: large, garish eating establishments anchored close to the coast, mainly frequented by tourists and local Europeans. The typhoon shelter was the opposite. At night it was a mass of little sampans, carrying the local Chinese out on the water to get some cool air in the sultry weather, and have some space after the confines of a tenement dwelling. We would sit there, eating this incredible food and washing it down with either beer or rice wine. Actually I wasn't very fond of Chinese liquor, most of it was far too strong for me, but some of their wines were excellent. I especially liked their rose wine, the smell at first was overpowering, and then it actually did taste of what you expected roses to taste like.

Then would come the fruit boat displaying the freshest of goods. After this would come the singsong boat, which would play a few tunes whilst we finished our meal. I have eaten in some of the greatest restaurants in the world, but I have never enjoyed a meal like the ones I had on the water in Hong Kong. When later on Paula and I took Lewis there, he was so entranced that he changed the script so he could include a scene from this unique place.

When it was time for bed we would be taken out into the harbour and tied up to one of the large buoys used for tethering the large ships. Often we would be under the shadow of a massive vessel. The canvas roof would be closed down, and we would be in our own small world, to begin a night of passion on the waters of one of the most famous harbours in the world. Just after dawn we would be taken back to land, just in time to shower, shave and start a new day. We would part, each of us to carry on our various tasks, longing to meet again at the end of that day.

I never let my personal life interfere with my work. I don't say this with any pride, in fact I am rather ashamed of it and I realise now that this is why I didn't really know my children when they were young. Work came first, even when I was in love, so really we only had the nights together.

Of course, I had Lucy to deal with. Poor, darling Lucy. I still have feelings of guilt about her. I gave her an amazing sum of money and we had one of those awful Oriental farewells. There is something in the character of most Chinese girls that loves an unhappy ending. Their most popular films and books are about unhappy affairs. The business girls, I think, kid themselves that "this is it", and when it inevitably finishes they can indulge in a wonderful heart-breaking scenario.

Soon after this, I had to go to Macao to finalise the plans, including placing the order for the funeral scene. I had spent hours pouring over reference books, and the undertaker's price list, so when I arrived I was in a position to give him a firm order. Paula came with me as the art department representative, which meant that we had a wonderful break of a couple of days working and living together.

Our time with the funeral firm was amazing, so many things to talk about, the number of bands, what they would wear. We discussed the road gods, those large tall papier-mâché figures who would lead the procession and clear the way of any evil spirits, thus giving the deceased a trouble-free ride to Heaven. Everything had to be agreed: the size of the coffin, who would supply the picture of the deceased which would be carried on one of the litters, the type of carrier for the coffin, the number of attendants, how many litters (which are like highly decorated sedan chairs and are carried by two men), how many mourners would be required. And how much it would all cost. We agreed the price, deducted the squeeze, and the undertaker promised me the biggest funeral Macao had ever seen. It's not often you see a happy undertaker, but this one beamed with delight as he bowed us out of his shop.

We went to see the hotel again where we hoped to house the crew, and Paula was horrified. "No good, John, no good." I asked her where she would suggest. She thought for a while, then, "Maybe we could get ship, keep men on ship."

Good idea, I thought, maybe we could find a cruise ship in Hong Kong. I knew that it was no good looking in Macao as we'd be lucky to find a rowing boat there. So we returned to Hong Kong, without having solved the problem of where to house the crew. However, I had put down a little money to reserve the hotel, as a long stop.

Things were beginning to hot up, and the local paper ran a headline "Ferry to Hong Kong Soon To Be On Cellophane". Gift wrapped presumably!

Another major catastrophe occurred. This one a real humdinger.

Out of the blue came a cable that Peggy had been to Rank's and informed them that my son, Gregory, was going blind brought on by my absence, and that I should return home. What was going on? I tried to telephone, but the radio link was going through one of its temperamental phases. I was in turmoil. I didn't believe the story for a second, but on the other hand couldn't take even the remotest chance that it was true.

Of course, Pinewood was happy for me to be recalled and replaced, until Lewis pointed out to them how much personal knowledge I had about the operation, and how impossible it would be to replace me.

I believe that Rank's offered to send Greg to an eye consultant, but his mother turned this down. This made me even more suspicious. Cables went back and forth, getting us nowhere. My days were hectic and full, getting ready for the big day; I was involved in a great love affair; and now this. It was hard keeping a straight head, but I knew I had to concentrate on my work, and plan things so that if I did return to London, then at least I would leave everything in order. I also realised that if I did go back, it would possibly be the end of my career.

I was at a loss to understand Peggy and didn't believe what she was saying. I knew she was used to getting her own way, and lived in a world of her own making. I believed then, and I still believe today, that someone told her about the affair with Paula. This was the only rational explanation. Still, was there an outside chance that she was telling the truth?

Then Lewis came to the rescue. He pointed out to Rank's that they had a charter aircraft to bring the crew out and there were several spare seats. Why not send Peggy and the children over with it? And this is what happened. At least I could get on with the job, without this worry hanging over my head. I never forgot what Lewis did for me, and I remained in his debt for the rest of my working life.

Very soon the "gaffer" electrician, Vic Smith, and his best boy, George, arrived to check the equipment. They were two very suspicious people, and even more so when I explained to them about their accommodation and living. I had always believed in giving the crew a living allowance, so they could go and live where they liked, instead of putting them all up at one hotel where they would have all their meals in the same place with the same people.

Everybody seemed to be opposed to this deal, except for the crews or, more precisely, the crews that had experienced the system. The management didn't like it, objecting that the crew wouldn't get to the location on time. This, of course, was nonsense as they got there when they were living at home, so what was the difference when they were on location? They also disliked it because, with their bureaucratic minds, they liked to keep en eye on everyone. The Unions hated it, and they did have a point, after fighting for years to get their members the best conditions, like first class travel, the best hotels, and excellent food. If their members got the money in lieu then a lot of them would go and live in the cheapest places possible, which would defeat the Union's arguments for the "best conditions".

When I was a junior member of the sound department I really appreciated having the money so I could make my own arrangements. If you work all day and socialise in your spare time with the same people, you never get away from them. Then, what is first class for one person is second class to another.

The British crews in those days were extremely conservative, and liked classic English fish and chips, roast on Sunday etc. I am sure if I had put them in our hotel they would have complained bitterly. With the money they could go where they wanted, eat what they liked and also have a life of their own. This was especially important on this picture where they were going to be away for something like four months.

However, this was not the way they did it at Pinewood and Vic Smith and George were very suspicious. "Try it, and if you don't like it after a week or two, I will put you up in a hotel and go back to the old system." They accepted, and off they went with their first week's living allowance. I had done a very careful calculation as to what it would cost the company, and printed it so any member of the crew could see how their allowance was calculated, and that they were not being cheated.

The next to arrive were the camera crew and the Sound Mixer. It had been decided to shoot the opening Macao scenes with just a camera crew before the Main Unit arrived, but first they would cover, for publicity purposes, the launching of the "Fa-Tsan", our ferry.

After a complete overhaul, it had giant paddle wheels, new passenger decks, plus the re-designed film studio interior. I arranged for a Chinese film star to launch the ship, but first I gave a speech thanking the shipyard for such a fantastic job, on time and on budget. I then said that, apart from Curt Jurgens, Orson Welles and Sylvia Sims, the "Fa-Tsan" would also be a major star in the forthcoming film.

After the bottle of champagne had cracked against the side of the ship, all hell broke loose from the sound of the ship screeching down the rails, but mainly from the thousands of fire crackers let off, which was an awesome sound.

We had a great party, very memorable for me, as I had my first row with Paula. The trouble was that I hadn't introduced her to LiLi Wa, the Chinese star, and she, Paula, had lost face. She screamed at me, and I realised that, like a lot of her fellow country men and women, she couldn't drink!

I learnt a lot of other things, one being that the higher class a Chinese girl, the higher the collar on her cheong-sam. The first thing she does when she gets home is to tear it open, as it is very uncomfortable and greatly restricts any head movement. Rows were saved for home, not to be aired in public, but "when get home, shut door, shit hit fan!"

We rented an unfurnished flat, with two bedrooms. Paula very quickly arranged to rent the necessary furniture, and brought along her half sister to make curtains, bedspreads etc.

Paula's father had six wives, and Paula was the last child of the first wife, but her sister, Dalmain (or Susie) was the first child of the second wife, and therefore held a lower position in the family order. Sometimes she was family, and sometimes she was servant. The only sure thing was that I always got it wrong, and made everyone lose face!

I spoke to George on the phone and invited him and Barbara to share the flat.

Lewis arrived, and we moved over to Macao with the camera crew. With the small numbers, we managed to get everyone a reasonable room. The day before, Lewis wanted to see the funeral procession. I told him there was nothing to see but

I would have it all set up for him the following day. Meanwhile, why didn't we just spot the various camera positions? Naturally, in the way of all directors, one of the main positions he picked was right on the only major thoroughfare in the colony. Our Portuguese Mr Fix-It said it was impossible, as the road would have to be closed, the buses re-routed, police signs set up etc. Lewis turned to him and said, something which I have never forgotten, "My friend, nothing is impossible in films." He then turned to me and said, "John, tomorrow ten o'clock I want to see the procession turning around this corner and travelling up the main road!"

After a long night of many meetings, and little sleep, I had the procession assembled, and, though I say it myself, it was the best funeral I had ever organised! It stretched hundreds of yards long, and when I drove Lewis up to see it, he could not believe his eyes. They were to open even wider when Paula said to him, "Have taken glass out of picture of dead man, so lights no see in glass."

"Christ," said Lewis, "we've been trying to tell the prop departments this for years back home, and they still leave it in!"

At ten o'clock that morning the procession passed into the main high street, a street lined with thousands and thousands of people out to watch the biggest parade the colony had ever seen. The crowds lined the streets for the three days of shooting.

The rushes were sent back to London, and the Pinewood executives viewed them before sending the processed film back to us. But our hard work in Macao caused only consternation back at base, and both Lewis and I received cables. His said how worried they were about the amount of material he had shot, which as Lewis himself pointed out, was understandable considering that it was for only one line in the script, "A Chinese funeral is seen wending its way through the streets of Macao", and he had gone over the top.

Mine read, "Advise cost of Macao operation by return" which I happily did, which resulted in another cable, "Please confirm your figure, and confirm that it covers all costs, especially crowd costs." This I was even happier to confirm.

The truth was that they could not believe my figures, not realising that the men in the procession received something like three to four shillings a day, fifteen to twenty pence in today's money. The crowd on the street, nothing, except for the entertainment they got.

Back in Hong Kong, Curt Jurgens, ever the Prussian gentleman, and his gorgeous wife flew in, and we welcomed them to the colony and to the film. Very soon we had his simple wardrobe requirements under way, and he was able to have a few days' rest before we started filming.

The following day, the charter aircraft from London arrived bringing Sylvia Sims (our leading lady), Hylda (Lewis's wife) and their two boys, John and Stephen. Also on board was George's Barbara, who George had arranged to be Sylvia's stand-in, something which I thought was a big mistake. Then there was the rest of the crew, including Ted Bushel and Milton Reid, and lastly Peggy and the two children.

I had arranged to rent a flat for them on the Kowloon side, and had a car waiting with one of my very good, reliable drivers who I knew would look after them like

Dresden china. I had a happy reunion with the kids, bundled them into the car and told Peggy that the driver would take her to the flat where a girl would be waiting to look after them during their time in the colony. I gave her my office telephone number and sped them on their way, then turned to look after the arriving troops.

Shortly after their arrival, I had a meeting with the whole Unit, explaining that they were booked into the hotel for three nights, after that it was up to them where they stayed. I told them how much they would be getting, and gave them a copy of how this figure was arrived at. I was surprised that there were so few questions, and it was only later that I found out that the advance party had told them what a great deal it was and how happy they were with the set up.

I was surprised that amongst the passengers was Roy Goddard. Roy was assistant to Arthur Alcott and had been sent out to see exactly what was happening. I think the intention was for him to stay out there the whole time. This is not unusual as lots of companies like to have one of their own representatives reporting back to them.

Roy was a dear chap, and one of the few people in Pinewood who had actually tried to help me. He was embarrassed about his position, but I was delighted. With great confidence, I gave him a quick tour of the ship and the various locations. That night Paula and I took him out to dinner, and he told me how very impressed he was with everything he had seen. Furthermore, he showed me the cable he had sent Alcott at the studio, singing my praises in no uncertain language. I was very touched, as I knew how Pinewood would receive this information.

We had a pleasant evening, but early the following day I got a call from Roy saying that he had heard overnight that his mother had died, and he wanted to return to England. We hurriedly got through to our friends at BOAC and got him on the next flight. Paula took him out to the shops so he could take his family back some presents, and she bought him a pair of jade cuff-links as a farewell present. We put him on the plane, a sad, heartbroken little man who had adored his mother. The last time I saw him at a Guild of production executives' dinner years later, he showed me with pride the same cuff-links, and said, "I shall never forget that time, and how kind both you and Paula were." His verbal report to Rank must have been something else, as we never saw a Rank executive again. I have a lot to thank him for.

Then Orson arrived with his wife, Paola, and his daughter, Beatrice. As soon as his ship docked, Lewis and I went on board to greet him, but we hardly had time to say hello before the local and international press arrived. He held a press Conference on board and when asked what sort of film "Ferry …" was, he answered, "A comedy, of course." Well, that was the first time either Lewis or I had heard of it. Never mind, he was in full flood and quite magnificent, answering all the questions easily, and with great charm and wit.

We eventually got him away from the press, especially after the girl from Radio Hong Kong asked the maker of the world classic "Citizen Kane" whether he thought that "Ferry to Hong Kong" would lead him to bigger and better things!

Lewis had decided that he, with his wife and younger son would stay at the Repulse Bay Hotel, which indeed was a very nice hotel, but just about as far away from the location as you could get. Lewis told Curt about it so he and his wife stayed there as well. Orson thought it sounded good, so also elected to stay there. This meant every day that they were on call, they had to be picked up, driven right across the island to the ferry terminal, where a motor boat would be waiting for them to take them to Kowloon. Another car would meet them there and take them to the location. Normally this would not be much of a hassle, but I was learning that with Orson Welles things were rarely normal.

The first thing to throw me was that he had forgotten to bring his wardrobe, which we had carefully arranged to have made for him whilst he was in Los Angeles. No big problem. Hong Kong was the land of the twenty-four hour tailor and we quickly dispatched one to the hotel to measure him up. This is going to take a lot of material I thought, as Orson was the biggest man I had ever seen. Not only was he tall, but, to put it bluntly, he was fat. With a voice to match. He terrified the little Cantonese tailor and his assistants, who scurried about him like so many midgets crawling over a beached whale! This would not have been too bad if he *had* been beached and stood still for a second or two. Instead of that, he paced up and down the room recounting some story about a man he had met on the boat. The poor little tailor trying to measure his trouser length was left kneeling when off went Orson to the other side of the room regaling the assembled company with his escapades, taking a cigar, crossing back to get a match, all the time being chased by the kneeling tailor, who shuffled on his knees to keep up with him. To take his head and neck measurements, the poor chap had to stand on a chair, and no sooner had he climbed up on the chair, tape-measure in hand, than Orson was off again. A great scuffle would ensue as the tailor had to jump off and run after him followed by the assistant carrying the chair.

Orson, I am sure, was well aware of what was going on, and I think, in pity, he suddenly stood still. Here the trouble was that the poor assistant could not hear the numbers his boss was calling out, as Orson's voice boomed all around the room, proving the old sound man's theory that the bigger the speaker the better the sound!

Somehow it got finished, I think Orson got bored. The tailor promised the clothes for the following day, a Sunday. Thank God for Hong Kong, I thought, for Orson was on call on the Monday.

My relief was short-lived because just before I left Orson suddenly turned and said to me, "Have you got my noses?"

"Noses?" I thought, what am I missing here?

"Yes, noses, my noses. You are John Dark?"

Well, this was the only thing I was sure of at that moment, but I had to confess, "Yes, I am John Dark but I am sorry but I have never received any noses."

"Well, I sent them, you'll just have to find them!" Then for a parting shot, "I sent them, John Dark, Hong Kong." And left the room.

It transpired that he nearly always had a false nose when he was working. I think "The Third Man" was one of the few films he performed nasally naked. He had a very tiny nose, which got lost in the mass of his face.

There was only one day to go to shooting, so I went off to town to see what I could do. It was Saturday afternoon, and the post offices were shut. I spent several hours on the telephone, plus visits to Maxim's bar to see who could help. I eventually got hold of the Postmaster General, and after a lot of talk I got his permission to open up the main post offices in the colony.

Several of my colleagues and I searched through all the various bundles of parcels, but with no joy. I spoke to Lewis in the evening and suggested we change the schedule to something which did not require Orson, but he preferred to see what I could come up with the following day. He didn't really want to re-schedule, as it sends the wrong message to the company. I knew what he meant, as the first day, the artists have learnt their lines, the crew have been given the first set-up ... and to suddenly at the last minute change everything sends out the wrong message. It makes people nervous, and apprehensive about the organisation, and the picture in general.

That night I took Peggy and the children out, and after getting them settled, took her aside and asked what was going on. As far as I could see, Gregory had no trouble reading the menu. She insisted that it was true, but I felt more than ever that it was something that she had made up, and now believed to be true in order to justify her behaviour. I said that I would keep in touch, that I was madly busy, gave her a lot of money, and told her that I would not be staying with them. I eventually got back to the flat, and explained the day's happenings to Paula.

Early next day, we started on the cargo stores at Kai Tak airport, and eventually, in the Pan American cargo shed, we found a packet containing the noses. I rushed it up to the hotel and found Orson just finishing his lunch. Beaming with happiness, and enquiring where we had found it, he slapped me on the back, muttering, "Good job, good job." What a difference a pleasant meal can make!

I thought, now it is my turn, called down to the flat, and arranged to have a special pre-shoot lunch with George, Barbara and Paula.

Just as I was leaving the hotel, the manager stopped me and asked whether he could have a word with me. We went into his office and he said, "Mr Dark, The Repulse Bay Hotel is really very proud to have the Jurgens, and Welles' family staying here, very proud, and also the Gilberts, but I must ask you to speak to Mr and Mrs Gilbert and ask them to stop their son shooting the guests with his ping-pong gun. Several of our clients have complained." With a promise to speak to them, I hurriedly left before some other catastrophe struck.

But driving down to the flat, I thought what a little bugger Stephen Gilbert was. I had already heard from the crew about his behaviour on the plane, and I pondered how I could tactfully approach Hylda about her son. I certainly wasn't going to mention it to Lewis, as he had enough worries.

After a sleepless night, the first day of shooting dawned and I was up and about before the sun rose. I was there on the ship ready to greet the early birds: the make-up team, the hairdresser and the wardrobe staff, and have a quick cup of tea with them, served by our catering department already busy getting ready for the day ahead.

Napoleon might have said that an army marches on its stomach, but it was the film industry that gave the world constant eating. In England on location, it was normal for there to be tea, coffee and biscuits when the crew and artists arrived. But over the years this increased to things like egg sandwiches, bacon sandwiches, sausages, and so on. Then, around ten, there would be more sandwiches, buns, cakes, pastries, tea and coffee. At lunch time there would be a choice of menu, usually three courses, plus cheese and fruit. At tea time, the morning menu was repeated, and quite often there was coffee and biscuits at the end of the day (now known as the wrap). If overtime was worked, another hot meal was added. This catering has now grown to such an extent that in America, food is laid out all day long. This is supplied by a separate caterer (now known as craft services) from the one which cooks and serves the main meals (known as the location caterer). No matter where the location, how rugged the terrain, there will be a groaning table laden with every type of snack food you can think of, catering for everyone's tastes. There will be sweet things, savouries, raw vegetables, candy, jams, pastes, white bread, brown rolls … you name it, it'll be there. Our catering was no different, and under the auspices of John O'Connell, our spread was, if anything, above average. On seeing it for the first time, George looked at it all, and in jest said, "What, no Gentlemen's Relish!" About two weeks later a package arrived in my office containing three unmistakable china pots of the missing paste, air freighted from Fortnum and Mason's in London!

The artists started to arrive. I always liked to be there to see them in on the first day. They feel nervous, and a few words, a little hug, a small kiss, all helps to settle the nerves. They all arrived well on time, except for Orson. But as he had said that he would do his basic make-up himself, for which we had arranged a special room at the hotel, I wasn't worried.

The ship's crew were already on board, and when the gaffer arrived, he was able to start up the generators and do a final check. Gradually the crew all moved in and were fascinated to find a working studio at their disposal. It wasn't long before the camera was out, the tracks laid, and the dolly on board ready for the first set up, details of which Lewis had given them the day before.

The first scene was a long tracking shot of the Captain walking along the deck and greeting the passengers, which meant we were introducing the characters to the audience. Each one of the cast had a few lines, so they were quickly established.

All was well, except for one thing: Orson hadn't arrived. To make sure he wouldn't get lost, we had sent not only our most reliable driver, but also a young Chinese Assistant.

I rang his room at the Repulse Bay Hotel, but got no reply. I rang his wife, but again there was no reply.

However, soon Orson's car turned up at the docks where the ferry was moored, but no Orson, just the young Chinese Assistant holding a blood stained handkerchief to his head. After quieting him down, and giving him a cup of tea, we got the story out of him.

Apparently, he had knocked on Orson's door, but was told to go away. Having been given instructions to make sure he brought the actor back on time, he knocked again, but was told to go away once again, although in much stronger language. Then the poor kid made his fatal mistake, for he opened the door, and Orson whipped around and threw a pot of cold cream at him, hitting him on the head!

I phoned the hotel again but was told that Mr Welles was not in his room. I eventually found Paola Welles, who told me that he had left by taxi. We then had to decide whether we waited, or break up the shot and move to some cover shots. We decided to give him an hour, and if he hadn't arrived by then to shoot round him.

The hour went by, but no Orson.

Again I spoke to Paola, asking her if she had heard from him, but she hadn't. Later that day, I got a call from Orson telling me that the glue he had was not compatible with the nose plastic, and he could not get it to stick, that he had been all over Hong Kong looking for the right glue, but not to worry, he would be with us the next day.

However, he wasn't.

It was the third day before we got him on set, and that was after a last-minute drama. We had a car sitting outside The Repulse Bay Hotel with the best driver we had, and as Orson had said there was no way he would have an Assistant travel with him, we also had one in the hotel lobby, keeping well out of the way, to report back to us what was happening. So we breathed a sigh of relief when we heard that he had left the hotel in the car, bang on time.

The only trouble was that he didn't arrive at the location.

The driver phoned in to report that Mr Welles had accused him of driving too fast, and made him stop, then leapt out and jumped into a taxi! I knew he had the address of the location, but would he have it with him? He was on Hong Kong Island, and we were in the docks in Kowloon. Poor Lewis was rapidly running out of work, and his leading actor was lost. It wasn't long, though, before a police car turned up, and out stepped a beaming Orson.

He had arrived at the Star Ferry terminus but, instead of getting on the waiting motor boat, he got on the Star Ferry, the public ferry that ploughs across the harbour between the island and Kowloon. He attracted quite a bit of attention because not only was he a massive figure, dwarfing all around him, but he had stuck on his nose without the make-up! So there was this white proboscis sticking out of the round, rugged face, a wonderful sight for the Chinese passengers!

It didn't help either that when he arrived at the Kowloon terminus, not having a clue where we were, or indeed where he was, he started to shout, "Where movie?"

This attracted quite a crowd, and the more he shouted the bigger the crowd got, until it attracted the attention of a Chinese policeman, who unfortunately couldn't speak English, and hadn't a clue who Orson was. However, he realised he had to remove the cause of the obstruction outside the terminal, so escorted him to his car.

Luckily, an English inspector came along, and solved the problem, rapidly delivered him to the waiting company.

Whilst Orson was getting dressed and his make-up completed, the crew quickly reset the original set up, so by the time he was "on set", Lewis was ready to rehearse. "Right, quiet," shouted Bert, the first assistant.

"Right," called Lewis, "action."

And Orson started his walk down the deck, closely followed by the camera. As he walked down, greeting the passengers, I saw the Continuity Girl studying her script, looking puzzled. Turning, I saw Lewis blinking his eyes in a nervous twitch. I noticed that one or two of the actors were standing with their mouths open.

"Just a sec, just a moment," Lewis called.

"Something wrong?" Orson boomed.

Lewis picked up his script, took Orson by the arm, and walked to the side of the ship. I could see they were having quite a heated conversation. After some time, they came back, and Lewis called the cast together, muttering to me, "He's re-written the scene!" but turned to them and said, "There have been a few changes."

Well, the few changes were that Orson had taken most of their lines and given them to himself! Apart from that, he affected a most peculiar way of speaking in a strange voice that he thought would be good for the part.

As Lewis explained, what could he do? There we were, halfway round the world, so it would take forever to find a replacement. We were already into the third day without a major scene having been shot, and to start trying to recast, with a whole company standing around idle in Hong Kong, was not to be contemplated.

To compound this problem it seemed we had no producer. Even I, who shared a flat and an office with George, only caught passing glances of him. I saw him in and out of the office, but I really didn't have the time to have anything more than a scratch conversation with him. At home, he and Barbara would come in very late, long after we had gone to bed, and I would be out in the morning long before he got up.

Now, I was used to George, as I hadn't seen too much of him on the other pictures, but Lewis and the crew were puzzled not to see him around, especially with such a big problem on our hands. It was left to Lewis to make the decisions. "Look, I know you're busy, but I'm telling you that Orson is your number one priority," Lewis said.

"What can I do?" I asked.

"You can get to know him, spend time with him, cultivate him, do whatever, just make sure you keep him happy, and keep him working."

That is how I came to spend so much time with one of the world's most fascinating men. For he was without doubt one of the most entertaining people I ever met. He was a great raconteur, and he had a fund of amazing stories, all told with great glee in that wonderful bass voice. He would hold court over a restaurant table, telling stories about his life and the people he knew, rocking with laughter at his own jokes. Any interruption was forbidden by the simple expedient of turning up his volume, which very soon drowned out any interjection.

First, I had to get to know him. I had already learnt that he was fascinated with Chinese culture, and adored eating Chinese food, so I played my trump card and introduced him to Paula. She was an immediate success with him, and we started going out at nights, sometimes with Paola, and sometimes alone. Paula went to great lengths to take him to places that would please him, like little restaurants off the beaten tourist track. If he wanted to see a movie, Paula would prevail on the cinema manager to take out the first two rows of the centre balcony, and have armchairs put in, because as Paula explained, "Orson 'fe fe lu' (very fat). Not possible sit on ordinary seat!"

Orson's behaviour did improve, but sadly, not his performance. It was not only his behaviour that improved, but also George's.

We started shooting with Sylvia. Naturally her stand-in was on call with her, and it was no coincidence that her lover was there as well. George never left the ship for two days, then Barbara went sick and we had to quickly find a local girl to take over the stand-in's job.

It is not the hardest job in the world, it helps if you look vaguely like the principal, with the same height, the same colour hair, though I have known plenty of artists who have their pet stand-in who look nothing at all like them. All a stand-in does is to take the place of the artist whilst the scene is being lit. The director "lines up" the shot with the cameraman and the camera operator, and rehearses the actors, planning their moves. Marks are made on the floor to give them their major stops. The stand-in watches all this and when the director is satisfied that he has the scene as he wants it, the principals move off and the stand-ins (usually known as the "second eleven") move in, so that the cameraman can use their bodies to light both the actors and the set. After he has finished, and the principals move back in, he makes his final lighting adjustments with the actual artists. This is especially true with female stars, who to an extent depend upon their looks. Most have a good side and a bad side to their faces, and some are more conscious of this than others. Both the director and his camera crew will be aware of this, and try and plan the set-ups to favour the actress's best side. In the lighting also, the cameraman will take great care to flatter the features as much as he can. Sometimes they will go to great lengths to enhance the face, like putting gauze over the lens to "soften" the image.

A stand-in's job is pretty boring, but they are part of the crew, and important members of the "family". Usually they also look after the actor they are representing, see that they have coffee or tea, and generally fuss over them. Several become good friends with their principals, and often act as companions.

When Barbara went sick, we soon had a replacement. It wasn't a worry. However, at the same time as we lost her, we also lost our producer! Then we nearly lost our leading lady. Sylvia was up in arms, and was threatening to stop work unless Barbara was fired. I thought this was rather an over-reaction, after all the girl had gone off sick, which could happen to anyone. Then I was told that members of the company had seen George and Barbara in several nightclubs, dancing the night away. "Hardly the behaviour of a ... sick person," Sylvia caustically remarked. However, that wasn't the whole story.

Sylvia was exactly one of those who had a close relationship with her stand-in, and before they left the UK she had gone to George and explained the situation to him. As she was going to be alone in Hong Kong for three to four months, she asked if she could take her regular stand-in with her. There was a charter aircraft going out, which meant the company wouldn't have to pay her fare. Sylvia also said she could share her room, so they wouldn't even have to pay for her accommodation. George was very sympathetic, but had told her that they were employing a local girl who was paid a fraction of what a British Union stand-in would get so, sadly, he couldn't help.

Sylvia accepted that, so it was a bit of a shock to her when, sitting next to this blonde girl on the flight out, and asking her what her job was, to be told, "Oh, I'm your stand-in!" There was only one thing I could do. Sylvia had given an ultimatum, which was fully backed by the director, so I had to fire Barbara.

I had to fire a friend, and what is more, it was my boss's girlfriend! As you can imagine, George did not take it too well, but what really upset me was that he said she still had to be paid, and so that's what happened. Every week during the filming she was paid. What made it worse, and what embarrassed the shit out of me, was that George used to pick up her money from the Pinewood cashier himself. You can imagine how quickly that got back to Rank's.

We had very few of what I would call Union problems, and not many gripes with the crew. They all had found places to live, and the majority of them had a girlfriend installed. It was quite strange because usually on a foreign location film, at the end of the day the boys and girls go off and have a drink together, have a meal together, and party together. But on "Ferry...", the cry: "That's a wrap" would mean they would all disperse to their various homes, and were not seen until the following morning. It was the women on the crew I felt sorry for. Usually there is a queue of guys wanting to take them out, but on this one, nothing. They had to find their own entertainment, and what is more, had to pay for it too!

The British and Chinese crews all got on well together in the main. We used to cater for both races and the Brits found the catering excellent. Once we had a problem when they had goulash for lunch. The electrical shop steward complained it was "some strange, exotic, Oriental dish." John O'Connell told him it was not strange, exotic, or Oriental, and that he ate it frequently. The Steward replied, "Ah, yes, but you and that John Dark have been seen eating things off stalls which no white man should touch."

This was because the sparks had come across John and me eating from one of the magnificent food stalls at the end of the harbour.

The one thing that the electrical crew did that was bad was to incite the Chinese electricians to go on strike for more money. One night, when we were night shooting, I was at the hotel, the unit headquarters, when I got the news that the Chinese sparks had stopped work. I leapt into a cab and dashed down to the docks where the crew was waiting, and found the strikers gathered in a group. I quickly got them away from the Brits and into a nearby docks bar. I ushered them into a private room upstairs, and addressed them through an interpreter, the gist of which was, "You want more money, and I am not going to pay it, so we have a dispute. I understand that here in China you settle such a problem with a Yum Sing session." There was laughter, cheers, and a lot of Chinese banter. Glasses were brought up and filled to the rim with either whisky or brandy. I chose whisky. Then standing all together, we raised the glasses and cried, "Yum Sing", and drank the contents down to the last drop, turning the glass over to show there was nothing left.

I cannot remember how many I drank, all I do know is that I saw off every one of the crew. Not one was left standing. For myself, I was as sober as the proverbial judge. It was work, and I had to win.

Afterwards I saw the Chinese gaffer, who had already lined up a replacement crew for the night. I explained to him that I didn't want our Chinese electricians to lose their jobs, as it was not their fault, but had been pushed into it by the Brits. In case there was any trouble with the English crew working with the replacement electricians that night, thinking they were strike breakers, I also spoke to the ETU Steward. I told him that the strike had been settled, but for that night only. They would all be back the next day. He wanted to know the terms reached and why they were all sick. I told him to check with the Chinese gaffer. I entered a taxi a very sober man, and got out of it seven minutes later as drunk as a skunk!

There were some very surprised, indeed incredulous, English electricians when they found out how it had all been settled, and they didn't quite know how to react. It was only the following day, when they had a chance to talk to their Chinese mates, who were adamant that it was all over, that they accepted the outcome. No word of dissent from the Chinese boys was heard again, and peace reigned for the rest of the shoot. Some of the English sparks thought it was a procedure that should be introduced into the next producers/electricians agreement, "providing," as one said, "I can be on the negotiation committee!"

We had one other labour dispute – though, in fact, it was nothing to do with us. We were again night shooting on the ferry, and the film crew had gone off. I went into the hotel to grab a sandwich, and a message came through that the Captain had stolen the ship!

I dashed into my car, which luckily was parked outside, and tore down to the docks. The first thing I could see was all the company standing on the quayside, looking lost. The next thing I saw was the ship slowly navigating its way out of the typhoon shelter. I leapt into the nearest vessel, which happened to be a sampan operated by a very elderly Chinese lady, and shouted the unforgettable words: "Follow that ship."

With much pointing and hand-waving, we pulled away. As the ferry was quite a large vessel, it took time to manoeuvre out of the typhoon shelter and into the harbour, which allowed my sampan time to catch up. We got alongside. I jumped onto the paddlewheel-housing, and started to crawl up on all fours. Halfway I looked up and I could see a man at the top looking down at me. As I got closer, I recognised the ship's Scottish engineer. I could also see that he had a pistol in his hand, which he was pointing straight at me. "If yer make any trouble, Mr Dark, I'll blow your fuckin' head off," he yelled.

The coward in me came right to the fore. "Hi, Jock," I said, as though we were having a cheery meeting.

"Don't fuckin' 'Hi, Jock' me," he shouted, as he staggered about. He was obviously as pissed as a newt, and my fear was that he would pull the trigger more by accident than desire.

Soon I was at deck level, and I stood up and faced him. "What's going on, then?" I asked in as cheery a tone as I could muster.

"I'll let the captain tell you that", and he indicated with the gun where I should go.

It was eerie, as all the ship's lights were out, but I could see he was taking me to the bridge. Once there I saw the Captain at the wheel, in the same state as the engineer.

"What's going on, Captain?" I enquired, as he steered the ship into the busy harbour.

"I'll tell you what's going on, my crew haven't had their overtime, that's what is going on."

I explained to him that his crew were paid by the shipyard, not by us, and if he had a gripe, he should take it up with that company, and not penalise us, the film company, who needed the ship there and then.

Hanging on the wheel more to support himself than to steer, he told me in no uncertain terms that he couldn't care less whose responsibility it was, he wanted their money and he wanted it now. I eventually got out of him how much it was. I told him that obviously I did not carry that kind of money on me, but that I would use the ship to shore phone and get the money sent out. My concern was to save the ship, and to get us back shooting (an unfortunate term in the circumstances).

I got through to the production office, and spoke to Marguerite. "Marguerite," I whispered, holding my cupped hand around the phone as I didn't want the engineer to hear me, "I'm on the ferry, the Captain has stolen the ship, and the engineer is pointing a gun at me."

"Oh, dear," she said. Typical Maggie – nothing would faze her! She would be thinking, inform next of kin, call doctor and undertaker, tell insurance company, advise Rank's, arrange for body to be flown back to England, make note for progress report, "shooting delayed due to murder of production manager."

This all flashed through my mind as I told her to get the money, give it to Ted Bushel, and send him out on a boat so we could pay the captain the crew's alleged overdue overtime. Though it was not our concern, we were suffering the consequences, and once I had the ship back we could argue who should pay what.

Bushel duly arrived in a motor boat, and I handed the money over to the captain, who after slowly counting it, turned the ship around and headed back to the quay. Waiting for us was the American owner of the shipyard, who leapt on board, rushed up to the bridge and knocked out the Captain with one blow. I understood his reason, but the pity of it was that he was unable to take action against the Captain, as the Captain would have had him for assault.

Just another fun night of movie-making!

With all this going on, I still found time to visit the kids most days, even if it was for a short time, with the exception of when they caught measles, when I stayed out of their way until they were declared free. Relations with Peggy were hardly affectionate, but nor were they bitter. As I said before, she had the ability to live in her own world, and to cut herself off from things she didn't like. She treated me as a kind of acquaintance who happened to be very fond of the children. I spoke to Gregory about his eyesight, and he told me that he had some trouble, but it was because he was sitting in the back row and couldn't see the blackboard over the heads of the taller boys!

Talking of children, the cast were very good about helping with the various Hong Kong charities, especially the ones for children. I accompanied them on several occasions to the orphanages, and it was heartbreaking, seeing all those enchanting children who had little hope of ever being adopted, but were destined to spend their lives in drab, soulless institutions. I vowed that if ever I was in the right position, I would adopt one of them.

One member of the cast, Noel Purcell, was especially good with the children. He was a marvellous old Irish actor and one of those actors who everyone recognises, but few, outside his own country, know his name. In Ireland, and especially Dublin, everyone knew him, and so much so that when once he appeared in a big budget film in the capital's main cinema, it was billed, "Noel Purcell in '…' with Elizabeth Taylor and Richard Burton"! He was a lovely man, a great big chap over six feet tall, with a mop of shocking white hair, a marvellous white beard, and big, bushy eyebrows on a craggy face. He was also a great buddy, the only trouble being that, like most of his fellow countrymen, he was one hell of a drinker. Whenever I bumped into him, he would say, "Ah there you are, John, now let's be having a jar." He played the ship's engineer in the film, and took an active part in the typhoon sequence where the ferry sails into a great storm.

It is very difficult to shoot this type of scene on the actual ship whilst at sea, as the camera needs to be off the vessel, otherwise the picture will rise and fall with the ship. It was decided that part of the ferry had to be built on land, in order to simulate the storm. We had to construct two decks, which were built on rockers to roll the ship from side to side and up and down. I knew that hydraulic rockers in England were very unreliable. It was therefore with some apprehension that John Stoll and I placed the order with the shipyard to build such a piece of equipment. Fortunately, like everything else built by the Chinese, it worked perfectly. Even when the cameras were turning!

The set was built close to the sea so that we could pump the sea water up to the giant tip tanks. We arranged for the fire brigade to put a pump onto a small vessel in the sea, sucking up the sea water and sending it on its way.

Everything was going splendidly and Lewis was tickled pink, when suddenly the head fireman informed me that the sea had got rather rough, and he was unable to get the boat out to relieve the men on the floating pump. Furthermore, the pump was rapidly running out of petrol, and there was probably only half an hour of fuel left. Now this was a problem, so I yelled at Bushel to come with me down to the rocky coastline.

It was a bright moonlit night, and we could easily see the pump with the two firemen. We found the boat, with the petrol, and tried to launch it into the sea, but every time we got it to float, the waves just picked it up and threw it against the rocks. I had no idea what to do. However, Ted picked up the jerry can of petrol and walked into the sea. I screamed at him to come back, but he kept going, then dived into the sea with the can in his hand. To swim in that sea was bad enough, but to do so holding a can full of petrol in one hand was suicidal. I could see him being knocked into the rocks as he swam with one arm towards the small boat. At least he was away from the rocks, but my heart was in my mouth, and all I could do was to stand there and pray. He reached the floating pump and I saw the firemen pulling the petrol can on board. He hung on the side for a beat or two, and then started to swim back. As he neared the beach, he was once again bashed into the rocks.

Eventually the fire chief and I dragged him out of the sea, on to the sand, where he lay covered in blood. I went from fear to rage, and called him every name I could lay my tongue on. We felt him all over, and wiped some of the blood off his face and body so we could see how bad the cuts and bruises were. He just looked up at me and said, "Well, we had to keep shooting, mate, didn't we?" What could I say? I just leant over him and hugged him. You should never make a film without a Ted Bushel.

Ted not only did the majority of the stunt work on the picture, but also looked after what I can only describe as "troop's welfare". He collected the English papers, distributed the mail from home, checked that the caterers had all they needed and, as I said earlier, took Beatrice Welles out for a walk. He would also act as an extra help to the production office, and if there was a problem the shout would go up, "Where's Ted?"

The only problem was that he didn't get on with his partner, the other stunt man, Milton Reid. We hadn't been able to find anyone to play the Pirate Chief, so we used Milton. Now I don't know whether this went to his head, or whether Ted was jealous, but whatever it was one morning, just as the sun was rising and the crew were going home after a night's shoot, they had a fight. It was a nasty vicious brawl with a boxer against a wrestler, and they both ended up in a pretty bad state. I had to scare the shit out of them the following day and threaten to send them both home. The truth was we could not afford to lose Milton, but he hadn't the intelligence to work that out, as he wasn't the brightest person in the world. But Ted knew damn well I could put him on the next plane, and when I got him alone, I told him, "You've just got to live with him, eat shit if you have to, for if there is any further trouble it's not going to be Milton, it's going to be good-bye Ted!"

Then it was time to go to Macao. So I called the crew together and told them of the conditions there. We had not been able to find a ship, as Paula had suggested, so it was the Hotel Yuk or nothing. I explained all this to them, and painted the picture a little worse than it was, though it was difficult to exaggerate the appalling conditions. I ended up by suggesting they didn't come. I knew I was taking a bit of a risk because there were some people I really needed, like the camera crew. But there was a lot I could replace with their Chinese counterparts. But I needn't have worried because not one person said they wanted to stay behind. "Okay, but don't come moaning to me when we get there. I don't want to hear one complaint." And to give them their due, there wasn't one. There was one tense moment when the fastidious Marguerite Green sat down at her desk in the temporary production office, and her foot hit a metallic object – a spittoon!

Thank God we only had a few days there, for it was not easy. I made a deal with an Eurasian man called Peter Pagn, pronounced like the famous boy who never grew up. Unfortunately this one had grown up too sharply. He was hired to supply all the crowd we needed, and to that end he did his job. They turned up, but orchestrated by him, they would suddenly demand this, or demand that. They could behave in quite a menacing way to get what they wanted. It got so scary at one stage that Lewis, who was out on a camera boat shooting towards the harbour, wouldn't come ashore until I personally told him that it was safe.

Peter Pagn was a strange character. He crossed the border into Communist China all the time with seemingly no trouble on either side. He had a hold of some sort over the locals, and for one reason or another was given a large measure of licence by the Portuguese authorities, as well as by the Chinese. Crossing the border in those days was no easy matter as it was a very sensitive post on the Chinese mainland and was heavily guarded. Across the inlet one could see a Chinese labour camp, where they were building a massive construction like a damn or an airstrip. I didn't know what it was, and nobody seemed to want to tell me. One could see the pitiful people carrying heavy loads of stone and earth from early dawn to dusk.

After dinner on the first night, Lewis suggested we should go down to the boys' hotel to see what was going on. We entered this concrete mausoleum where the deserted lobby was lit by one bare bulb, which was probably just as well because then you couldn't see the dirt. We went down the long corridor, rooms off either side, with our footsteps echoing off the walls. Lewis shouted, "Bring out your dead", but the only noise we got in return was the sound of slapping and giggles. As we made our way down the bleak stony hall, each room seemed to emit its own sound of sexual goings-on. We left quietly.

The next day, Otto Heller was in a very uppity mood, which was unlike him as he was usually quite jolly, although very mean. Apparently the night before he had succumbed to the charms of one of the girls. He had taken her back to his room, and given her the necessary money. She then bent down, took off his shoes and socks, and then pelted out of the room. "So," he said in his heavy accent, "I pay twenty dollars to have my shoes taken off. Better I take my own off in future, ja?"

I was worried about getting out of Macao, as I had been tipped off that Peter Pagn and his gang were going to hold us to ransom, claiming we had not paid the crowd, which of course was totally untrue. I arranged to move our unused equipment slowly back on to the ferry during the last of the shooting. I also asked Lewis to arrange the shooting schedule so that at the end he was only left with cover shots on the minor artists. We made sure that no one knew what time we would finish, or what we had left to do. We also kept the crowd at another location. At the wrap, the camera crew quickly got their equipment back on to the ferry, and once I knew that everyone was on board, I had the money sent down to pay off the crowd. As I was in the hotel making sure everything was paid, Paula came in and told me we had to leave in a hurry as the Chinese grapevine had told her that trouble was on its way. We rushed up to my room, and as I was collecting my things, we heard a pounding on the door. Luckily we were on the ground floor, so we left by the window and got into the car. Paula pushed me in the back and made me lie on the floor, covering me with a rug. We gave the driver a very large tip, and dashed down to the docks, and onto the ferry. The gangplank was pulled up, and we put to sea, safe in our own ship, glad to be away from Macao and some of its more sinister citizens.

Christmas was approaching, and we anticipated some drama or other. I, and indeed Pinewood, worried about the crew being away over the biggest holiday of the year, a time for families and friends. How would the company react to being away from home at this time? We arranged two big parties, and gave them the customary days off. Not once did I hear a moan, not once did I hear even a sorrowful remark about being away. In fact, the opposite. Several told me it was the best Christmas they had ever spent. One or two of the crew told me, admittedly after several large drinks, that they had been told at Pinewood not to co-operate with me. And further, I was told by someone who was well informed that the reason they passed the budget was they didn't think that I could possibly bring it in for that kind of money.

I spent Christmas running between the kids, Paula and all the various parties we were invited to. Where possible, during the day I was with the children, although it was not easy as Paula was very jealous and resented the time I spent away from her. Apart from doing what I thought was right, I really enjoyed being with the children, so in a way I was being selfish. Peggy and I kept up appearances in front of them, but as soon as they were in bed, I was off. I was still smarting over her behaviour, and how she nearly wrecked my career. On the other hand, she would not forgive me, as we were soon to find out. We didn't socialise together even once. It was Paula who was accepted as my companion to all the parties. The parties we went to were all different.

With the Jurgens, they were very elegant, very correct, and very lavish. We wore evening dress and gathered together for drinks before a wonderful dinner, which was served in a private dining room at the hotel. I was told the Jurgens used to have different kinds of parties on their hired cabin cruiser, but I was never invited to one of them, so cannot speak from first-hand knowledge.

With Orson, it was much more casual. We sat around in his sitting room while he toasted bread on the open fire, and then thickly covered it with mounds of Beluga caviar. I have never eaten so much caviar, or in such a style. Biting into the hot toast, with the sturgeon roe dribbling down one's chin, was unforgettable.

As far as I can remember, Sylvia never entertained; in fact, she was rarely seen after work. I think she went out with the Gilberts, because they have been friends ever since. This was strange, as Lewis never socialised with his cast. He never wanted to do anything to detract from his working association. It is all too easy in a social environment to say something that upsets, give a wrong impression, or seems to favour one against another. Actors are sensitive, insecure, and nervous people, and so it is better to keep them at arm's length.

George and Barbara were rarely invited to any of the private parties, as the cast held them in such disregard. George's standing had reached such a low that both Peter Hunt, the editor, and John Stoll threatened to go on strike unless he was sent back to Britain. It took a lot of hard talking by Lewis and myself to convince them otherwise. With all this bad feeling, I increased my nagging of George for not paying attention to the film, to the cast and the crew. It was true he used to come to the office, but what he did there, I have no idea, and it wasn't long before he had to meet up with Barbara for lunch or whatever. After one of my lectures he asked me what I thought he should do. I suggested he took the cast out to dinner, for a start. He invited the Welles and the Jurgens, but Sylvia turned her invitation down when she heard that Barbara would be there. In the circumstances to come, rather a good idea! I turned up at Maxim's, as usual on time, to find no George. Orson and Paola arrived and then the Jurgens, but still no George. Embarrassed, I did my best to fill the role of host. Eventually George and Barbara arrived, drunk as skunks. We all did our best to ignore their state, and at last we settled down to dinner, George at one end of the table and our hostess, Barbara, at the other. I could see she was not going to be able to cope and I went down and whispered in George's ear. He nodded and came down and gently took her away and back to the flat, leaving me to carry on the producer's party. You can imagine how well this went down. I was desperately unhappy, for I had great affection for George, indeed for them both, and to see them behaving so badly on such an important project saddened me. I didn't mind for myself, as producers can be a bloody nuisance hanging around all the time, but I did expect him to contribute something to the film, especially to be there to back up Lewis. After this we had a row, and I got very mad with him, and told him that he should be at the night shoot the next day. Much to my surprise, he came.

I had a problem that night for I had been unable to get any mobile generators from either Hong Kong or mainland China. In desperation I got through to my American shipbuilder friend who said he could supply me with ships' generators which I could mount on lorries. Proving my lack of technical knowledge, at the last moment I had found out that, unlike the normal generators we use, they were water-cooled. So I then had to arrange to have each generator tow a water browser behind it. I was praying that it would work, and also thinking what an idiot I had been not to have imported one from London. Why did I have to be so cocky?

We did have a bit of a late start, but the genies worked fine and I could breathe again. Then the second assistant director, Don Toms, told me that Curt was asleep in the lobby of a nearby hotel and he was unable to wake him. He suspected that

Curt had been drinking. I shot down to the hotel, and there in the dim night lights of the deserted lobby were both Curt and his wife, fast asleep on a couch. I couldn't reach over to Curt, as his wife was asleep on top of him. "Curt," I said, "Curt."

No response, so to get to Curt I shook his wife gently, which made her, open her eyes. She looked up at me and said, "Oh, you're so sexy", and went back to sleep. Eventually I did get Curt awake, but he was more than six sheets to the wind, and I realised he was in no state to work.

I reported to Lewis who was furious. "Well, what the hell are we going to do? I thought you told me the producer was here," he accused me, and when I assured him that he was, he asked, "Well, where the fuck is he, then?" We all looked around and couldn't see any trace of him.

I shouted for George, and suddenly a very bleary voice from the back of a car said, "Yeah, someone looking for me?"

Lewis marched over and told George, "Look here, we are ready to shoot. It's taken hours to light, and now our star is drunk."

George for once took some decisive action, he shot up, "Well, I'm going to sort this out right away. Where is he?"

"He's in the hotel", said Lewis

"Right, I'm off," George said. And then just as the car was moving, he popped his head out of the window and said, "I really am very surprised, it's just not like Orson!"

We only just managed to stop the car before he travelled all the way down through Kowloon, across the harbour, right across the island to Repulse Bay, to pull Orson out of bed, who wasn't even on call that night! "Why didn't you let him come?" Orson roared when he heard. "I'm going to say that's what happened, and I shall tell how he man-handled me out of my bed, and despite all my protestations, shoved me in the car, drove me through the night to the location miles away, only to find it was Curt who was wanted, not me," and broke into peals of laughter.

I really think that was the end of my trying to get George to face up to his responsibilities, and the end of his position as producer. In George's case he was given it all on a plate, the subject, the money, the director and cast, so he didn't really have to do any work. But what he did have to do was to support the director and give some dignity to his position. He failed on all points. It was very sad.

Somewhere around this time, Orson took me out to lunch, and asked me if I would join him on the next film he was going to make. I was very flattered but also very wary, as I had heard all the stories about Orson's films, and how he left a trail of unpaid bills in his wake. Film-making was like a drug to him. Wherever he was, he was always shooting something. The film vaults of the world must be full of footage that he has shot and then abandoned. I recall him asking me to visit him in his dressing-room, and going in watching him run a roll of film through his hands, holding it up to the light to see what was on the frame and breathing heavily, saying, "I'll shoot this fucking cameraman." However, what he wanted to see me about was his money! He wanted to know how he could get his fees sent to Hong Kong instead of to his bank in Rome. I told him that was not a problem, he just had to sign a piece of paper and the money could be paid to him any where he liked.

"Ah, that's great, just please make sure that no one ever says a word about this to Paola." Poor, darling lovely Paola, who worked so hard to keep his finances on an even keel, was to be left believing that the money was going into the bank every week, only later to find, when the cheques started to bounce, that the money was being spent by Orson on his latest project.

David Lewin, the show-business columnist, visited us, and Orson invited him to go to Macao with him for a weekend. David was delighted to be asked, thinking that all that time with Orson would produce some great copy. However, he found himself being used to hump all Orson's equipment. Orson had bought $10,000 of equipment and had it shipped from LA Poor David was clapper boy, Grip and general dog's body! According to him, all Orson shot was of himself running up and down various streets. I believe that some of this material did end up in one of his films, unlike similar material in other cities.

The other thing about Orson was that he was so amazingly persuasive. For example, he talked the English electricians into working on his film at night, after a day working for us, and then ended up not paying them a cent. British sparks, the most militant Trades Unionists at the time, who got double time *plus* for night work, with long breaks in between, worked for two consecutive nights without a penny! Without one moan! Indeed almost the reverse, as they showed me with great pride the pewter beer mug, that must have cost all of two or three pounds, that Orson gave them, inscribed "With thanks, Orson". No wonder the industry called him a genius!

I started to talk to the various studios about renting stage space for the interior sets that we had to build. At first glance, their quotes looked very good until I found out that it was only for half the stage, as at that time, they would have two films shooting simultaneously on the same stage.

This wasn't the only surprise: this quotation was for an eight-hour day! In other words to have the stage to ourselves for a twenty-four hour day meant that we would have to multiply the original quote by six! I could not get a reasonable deal out of them, so I tried Mr Li, but he told me all his studios were full. So I was forced to go back to the Nationalists where it was obvious that they had all ganged up together and weren't going to drop their prices. I had a meeting with them, and got very mad. I knew they were trying to take me for a ride, and I told them no way would I pay those prices. One enquired in that strange, sarcastic, Oriental way, "What are you going to do, John?" In my rage, and without a second's thought, I said, "I'll tell you what I'm going to do. I'll build one."

Walking down the street afterwards I thought to myself, am I mad? How was I going to build a film studio, and in four weeks? Where am I going to build it? Where will I get the land? First, I went to see my buddy. "John, do you think you could build me a studio?" I asked John Stoll.

Cocking his head on one side, he said, "Oh, how big would it have to be?"

"Look, there are many, many problems John, and we will have to talk about them but, in principal could you do it?" I asked, and then added rather sheepishly, "In four weeks?"

Dear John, nothing threw him. He contacted Ronnie Udell, his Pinewood construction manager, and quietly said, "Ronnie, dear, we're going to build a film studio!" But where? Who did I know who could help? I ended up with the Department of Reclaimed Land. Through them I found some land that had just been settled, but had not yet been approved for building. This was at Deep Water Bay on Hong Kong island, close to Repulse Bay, and was also ideal being completely flat. Through some good friends, I got a very quick response from the government to build the studio on this land, on the understanding that it was for our sole and exclusive use, and that at the end of the film I would take the construction down and leave the site as clean as I had found it. It was a very good deal, especially as they did not charge me a single dollar!

John worked out the size, drew up the plans, the builders were contracted, and work started. Whilst this was happening the sets were being pre-fabricated off site. We not only had to build the stage, we also had to build dressing-rooms, offices, wardrobe, make-up, hairdressers' rooms, prop stores, electrical stores, cutting rooms etc. What an undertaking! Moreover, in four weeks?

On the scheduled date, we moved into the studio, ready to shoot on the first set. The only thing we hadn't had time to build was the restaurant, so we attached a large marquee to the side of the studio. I got my good friend Jimmy Wu, who owned Maxim's restaurant, to give us a very special deal and consequently we had one of Hong Kong's most prestigious restaurants to do our catering. Not for our crew the sordidness of benches and bare trestle tables. We had separate tables for four, starched white linen tablecloths, and napkins, nice cutlery, flowers in the centre, and bow-tied waiters to serve them. The only thing I cursed myself for not thinking of was a string trio!

Most of the cast took it all for granted, but not Orson. For with all his difficulties, he was first and foremost a film maker, and he appreciated what had been done. John and Ronnie were the first to explain to him that it was only possible because of the wonderfully expert and hard-working Chinese construction crew. He praised everyone, though, as he walked around the site, commenting that he just could not believe what had been done in the time. Curt made no comment, whilst Sylvia complained that the flowers in her dressing-room were smaller than those in the boys' rooms!

We soon settled down into a studio routine, and held our schedule. Sets were built, taken down and replaced. Lewis wanted a Chinese girl group, and, though, we hunted all over we could not find one. In the end I held an audition, selected five and started to train them. I first had to find a Chinese song that was pleasing to the Western ear, and out of copyright. I eventually selected a folk song and got a Chinese musician to give it a more modern treatment, though still played on the classical Chinese instruments.

I dispatched the piece to Pinewood, and received a cable back that said that after a lot of research they had found that this was a song sung for children in schools, to which I cabled back to say that our research showed it was a folk song usually sung by girls in brothels!

I rehearsed the girls every day in a room I had taken at The Repulse Bay Hotel, and I would dash down there whenever I had a spare minute. Orson started calling me John Fred Astaire Dark! All progressed very well, the only problem was that Paula accused me of having slept with all of them (I should have been so lucky!). When the time came for the scene to be shot, and they were dressed and made up, they looked like a trained group who had been together for some time, and Lewis was delighted. I was pretty chuffed myself.

We were getting into the final stages of the production and plans had to be made for the return journey back to England. I issued our estimated dates to the Pinewood travel department, and waited for information back regarding the charter aircraft and the intended flight times.

My own personal affairs were getting complicated. Paula was coming back to London with me, but she couldn't go on the charter for obvious reasons. I was going to have to stay on in Hong Kong after the main crew left, to clear up all the unfinished business, see that the studio site was clear and pay the last of the bills. Neither of us was keen to be apart for too long.

I heard back from Pinewood that they had arranged a charter flight for the date requested. The shop stewards asked for more details, including the type of aircraft, its configuration and flight times. Back came the requested information which was far from satisfactory to either the Union members or to ourselves. It was an outdated plane, an Argonaut, which was very slow and obviously took a long time to get back. The crew held a meeting, and unanimously said that they would refuse to fly on such an outdated aircraft, pointing out that the outward trip had been on a modern aircraft. They said that Rank's thought they would fly back on anything, and had gone for cheapness instead of reliability and safety. Even after many cables and telephone calls, the dispute still wasn't settled. Union head offices were brought in to the argument and still nothing was resolved.

Meanwhile Orson asked how much I would charge him for renting the studio for three weeks, as he had a film already financed and ready to shoot. I explained to him that my deal with the Hong Kong Government precluded me from sub-letting, my contract with them was solely for "Ferry To Hong Kong", but I suggested as we needed a narration for the trailer, if he would do it for nothing, I wouldn't charge him anything for the studio providing that he kept it a secret. I would say that he was shooting some extra material for "Ferry...". He was very pleased with this suggestion and he thanked me profusely.

We reached the last shots in the studio, and as Curt and Sylvia were finishing, we had the wrap party there. The next day we started to strike all the interiors, and it was a sad moment when the sets started to come down, to be taken away and burnt.

We still had some night shooting to do with Orson in the town before we finished. About two hours before our start time I got a call from Paola to warn me that Orson was in a towering rage with me although she had no idea why. "What could it be?" I wondered. I thought back to the last few days and could think of nothing that I had done that could have possibly upset him. I turned up at the town location to find that Orson had had a row with a Senior Inspector from the Hong Kong police, and kept on making disparaging remarks about the police in general and the Hong Kong European officers in particular. It took me a long time to talk the police out of withdrawing all co-operation. We were shooting in a main road and we would not have been able to continue. Luckily I knew the Inspector concerned and, after a few drinks together, I convinced him that Orson was mad, and he should treat him as such.

After getting the police back on track, I went over to meet Orson, and as soon as he saw me he started to shout at me, calling me all sorts of impolite things. I was a liar, a cheat, and he went on and on at full volume sitting on the back of a lorry in the middle of the busy street. "What am I supposed to have done?" I asked.

"I made a deal with you, you little bastard, I made a deal with you for the studio."

"That's right, and the deal stands," I said.

"Well Mr clever dick, tell me this," he snorted, "explain this to me: I saw it today being towed away."

"What?" I asked.

"The sets," he yelled

"The sets?" I repeated.

"Yes," he screamed, "the fucking sets."

"But you never asked me anything about the sets," I told him.

"What good is a studio without sets?" he yelled again.

I tried to speak calmly but firmly. "I have no authority to let you have the sets. We would have to get Rank's permission, and I would have to ask the producer."

This set him off again. "The producer? The producer? You mean George Maynard. He couldn't give permission to buy a tram ticket. Since when have you taken any notice of George Maynard?"

I went on trying to explain, but he wasn't having any of it. Days later, I found out the truth. Orson had seen what sets we had, written a quick script, gone to a Philippine company and told them that he had a finished script, he would direct and star, had an equipped studio with the sets already, and all his own equipment. On that basis the company agreed to finance his film. Now, with the sets gone, the whole deal fell apart, and it would just be another of Orson's films that never materialised. Orson didn't speak to me for many years.

The row over the return of the crew was never resolved. Rank's dug their heels in and refused to change the aircraft. I called the crew together and told them the facts. It was on its way and there was nothing that either I or the crew could do to change it. In the end, after a lot of shouting, they accepted the inevitable. Afterwards Lewis asked me how I had convinced the crew, and I told him that I had promised them that his son, Stephen, wouldn't be on the plane!

The last day dawned, I collected Peggy and the children and took them to the airport where a bizarre scene greeted me. For the first time I saw the companions of my colleagues, and there were some fantastic looking girls amongst them, with their slim figures, dressed in their best cheong-sams, beautifully made-up and perfectly groomed. There was a lot of kissing, cuddling, and lots of tears as at last the crew went through passport control. I was left with the wailing wall of China.

I always remember one elderly member of the crew who when he arrived had difficulty getting down the aircraft stairs, and I had thought to myself at the time, "Oh my God, what am I going to do with this old buffer?" Well, this old man had shacked up with a young, nineteen-year-old girl and completely changed, and by the time he left seemed to have shed years, and ran up the aircraft steps and onto the plane. There is a sad end to the story for he kept writing to her after his return home, and one day several years later his wife found one of the letters in his jacket, and divorced him. By which time he was nearing his 70's and his golden wedding anniversary.

Someone who was on the plane told me that it was quite a contrast seeing the pretty, young, sexy girls saying goodbye at one end, and the bigger, heavy English mums with their children in home-knitted pixie hats welcoming them at the other!

We watched as the Argonaut taxied to the end of the runway ready for its take off, and then watched as it taxied back, and the crew disembarked. Engine trouble. After all the cables we had sent saying: "Crew refuses to fly on Argonaut", we were able to send another saying: "Argonaut refuses to fly with crew"! Eventually, after several hours, it took off, though the trip was quite horrendous, with problems throughout the whole journey. In the end, they had to stop overnight in Rome. The final disaster was when the plane tried to land on a road close to London Airport.

Union regulations were tightened up considerably after this, once again proving that management bring a lot of trouble on to themselves, and have no one else to blame when workers demand their rights. Well, at least in some cases.

So I was left with Paula, Marguerite, Bill (our accountant), and about thirty crying girls. Before long it was our turn, and Paula left first, although for the life of me I cannot remember why, and the three of us a few days later. I cabled ahead to my mother asking her to meet Paula at the airport, book her into a hotel and look after her until I arrived. God bless her, that is exactly what she did, without a moment's hesitation or complaint. I said my goodbyes to many old friends, and was back on the Britannia, back to England. Back to what?

CHAPTER 11
EAST IS EAST

Arriving at London, Heathrow, and peering out of the aircraft windows at the typical cold, drizzly day, my heart sank as I contemplated my return and all the trouble that no doubt lay ahead of me.

Then I thought of the excitement of seeing Paula again and my spirits lifted. First I had to get through Customs. During the journey I realised I had nothing that wasn't bought in Hong Kong. Now I am one of those people who are scared of authority. I don't know where I get this from, maybe the army, but people who have you under their control are a problem to me, and Customs' Officers are the worst. They have complete power, much more than the police, and I am just not comfortable with them. Even though I may have absolutely nothing to declare, I always feel guilty. The last profession for me would be a drug smuggler, I'd be dead before I even got on the plane!

Tommy Greene, the charming, lovely Pinewood travel man, who met you in and out, was there to greet me and I quizzed him about the Customs to which he said, "John, this is a Hong Kong plane, and they'll go through you with a fine toothcomb." So I entered the Customs Hall in some trepidation, which increased when I saw all my suitcases piling up on top of each other. Paula had taken me in hand and made me smarten myself up. Consequently I had a lot of new clothing apart from things like radios, toys, jewellery and odds and ends of Paula's. In those days the Customs' Officer approached you with a board on which were printed the various Customs' regulations. So this man approached me, looked me straight in the eyes and said, "John Dark, how are you?"

I responded quickly, "I'm fine, how are you?" – of course not having a clue who he was.

"You don't know who I am," he said, reading my mind.

"Of course I do, it's just … God, I really know your face," I hurriedly answered.

It transpired that we had been rookies in the army together, and in fact used to sleep next to each other! After a brief chat he said, "Look, I'll have to charge you something, what about this pocket radio?" In the end, I paid two pounds and left with all my foreign possessions, having promised to look him up some time.

This is where my luck ran out.

Waiting on the other side of Customs was a man with a sign "John Dark". Thinking he was the limo driver, I introduced myself, but instead of him helping me with my luggage, he handed me an envelope marked "urgent". It was a letter from my solicitor, who I saw was now representing Peggy. In effect the letter said that I was not to return to the matrimonial home, nor to try to take possession of my car, and if I wanted to see the children then I was to ring Peggy to make an appointment.

Standing there I realised that all I possessed was what I had with me: no house, no car, nothing. Well, I thought, that's it, but I have Paula, and that's enough.

My mother had booked her into a very expensive hotel and I zoomed round there, and we had an amazing reunion. I did not stay the night as she had booked in her maiden name and those were the days when you had to put up some sort of appearance that you were married. I didn't want her to lose face so soon in England.

I booked into a hotel in the Cromwell Road very close to Gloucester Road. It was a cold, cheerless, inhospitable place, staffed by ignorant, rude sub-humans. I was frozen in my Hong Kong lightweight suit, as there was no central heating. I looked around and saw a gas fire which I tried to put on, but no gas seemed to come out. Then I saw there was a meter, a goddamn meter into which you had to put shillings to get the gas to flow. Only in England I thought! I got into bed and decided that was the last night like that.

Next day I rang my brother who by then was married to Lynne, an ex work colleague of my mother's at "Time" and "Life", the American magazines. I asked if we could stay with them for a few days, and being the darling that he is, said he couldn't wait to meet Paula. Neither he nor my mother ever really took to Peggy, and I think they were relieved that there was someone else. Certainly Pete and Lynne made us very welcome, and years later Peter told me that he thought that Paula was the most beautiful thing he had ever seen.

First, I had to go to the studios, report that I was back, and get installed into an office there. I met up with Arthur Alcott whose welcoming greeting was, "I suppose you made a fortune out there", implying that I had been taking the kick-backs. This hardly thrilled me after all the care I had taken to make sure that Rank's were not ripped off for a nickel! Despite the fact that we came out on schedule, and within a budget which no one thought we could possibly achieve, not one word was said. The exception was Roy Goddard who, when we were alone, told me what a fantastic achievement it had been, but his position made it difficult for him to say anything aloud.

My time with Rank's was coming to an end, and I had no other picture on offer. I did some quick calculations and realised that after putting down a deposit on a rented flat, buying a new car, paying Peg the money we had agreed, I was going to be in serious trouble if something did not break soon.

Firstly I had to find us a place to live, as I didn't want to abuse my brother's hospitality. So I went flat hunting, and ran in to my first piece of racial discrimination. It was at the estate agent's office in Gloucester Road, where the usual snotty young man took down the details of my requirements and then asked if we were both white. Dumbfounded, I said I didn't know what it had to do with him, but my wife (?) was Chinese. Tearing up the form, he said, "Then I am afraid there is nothing here for you. It's not me, you understand, just our clients", and stood up and walked away.

I was shattered and thought how this cretin, this juvenile upstart, dare think that my gorgeous, refined Paula was not fit to live in some poxy English flat. I thought how incongruous it was, I should have explained to him that the Chinese think of Europeans as red-faced barbarians who smell! The Chinese hate going to Western cinemas because of the offensive body odour.

I had always thought estate agents were at the bottom of the pile, and now this one was denying us the right to rent a flat because of her race! I now regret that I didn't pop him one on the nose. God, it's hell being five foot five some times. However, I quickly found a flat through another agent, a basement flat just off Gloucester Road, ironically just around the corner from the racist estate office. It wasn't the greatest place, but it was central which was very necessary for Paula, who didn't know London at all, and had difficulty in reading English letters. It also had to have two bedrooms, because Paula was anxious to bring over her sister, Susie. Furthermore it had to be somewhere that I could afford. A flat in or near the West End wasn't cheap, so it was difficult to find the right place at the right price and I was lucky to find somewhere that fitted the bill so quickly.

However, looking back I can see it must have been a shock for Paula. In Hong Kong, we had a lovely flat and had an exciting life, with major movie stars as our friends. My job must have looked very important, and it was, but it didn't pay that much at that time. I was earning fifty-five pounds a week. Poor darling, what a comedown for her. It wasn't dirty, it's just that it wasn't in any sense of the word, luxurious.

Once we were settled, I started to make enquiries about getting Susie over. I spoke to a charming woman at the Immigration Department who told me that there was no way she could be brought into the United Kingdom, and it was out of the question. This went on for many months. She was a very pleasant person, and we struck up a friendly telephonic friendship over the many weeks of me nagging her, flattering her, flirting with her. Eventually one day I got the permit. It just shows that you should never take "no" for an answer. I hope she enjoyed the enormous bunch of roses I sent her.

Dalmain (or Susie) travelled to London by ship, so she could bring all Paula's clothes, pieces of furniture, pictures, mementoes and so on. She also brought with her the mink coat that Peggy had bought in Hong Kong. This had not been an easy matter to arrange. Long before Peggy left the colony, she had asked me to get the coat back to England, as she was scared to take it herself because of the Customs' duty. God knows why as I certainly wasn't going to try and bring it in myself. Of course I didn't know how I was to be greeted by H.M. Customs. Every time I saw Peggy she would nag me about it, so when the okay was given for Dalmain to travel, I asked Paula if she would ask her sister to bring it with her. This started a great row, and it was only because she had made so much fuss one night, and was suffering from remorse the next day, that she agreed. For Paula was not easy, and I guess I was not the most reasonable guy in the world either. One of the troubles was that we were living on a great high and still in those early days of love when everything is so intense. We had the most amazing sex life, and with me out of work, and around all the time, we were able to indulge ourselves and enjoy each other to the full.

We also were out a lot seeing old friends like George and Barbara. Now that filming was over, I didn't find it hard to socialise with them once again. I mean, this is what they were good at, and I was fond of them both. If George wanted to wreck his career, that was now none of my concern. Who was I to tell him how to live? Maybe he thought it was worth it. I hope so, for he only made one more picture, and that was a disaster for him, the financier and the public. At the time they were anxious to see Paula and take her to places that they had talked to her about, like Wardour Street, the only street with two shady sides we used to tell her, to the film pub, "The Duke of Wellington", and to Isow's, the film restaurant. We even took her to the old Trocadero restaurant in Piccadilly Circus, where she ordered a dish that we had told her about. We had only told her the Cockney word for it, though. When this Chinese beauty, dressed in an elegant cheong-sam, said, "I have baby's head", the typical English waiter of the time, attired in a black single breasted dinner suit, starched shirt front and black bow tie, did not blink an eyelid, but just said, "Certainly, Madame."

All this was fun, but it was also accompanied by a lot of drink, and as I have said before this was one thing that Paula could not do. What started out as a fun drink would turn into temper, into rage. I was also drinking too much, and wouldn't accept her moods, so the rows started. The next day remorse would set in, and the tears would come, tears so strong that her small Chinese eyes would close right up. Then would be glorious, exciting reconciliation, with kisses, hugs, and promises never to do it again. On top of this she was very jealous, and found it hard to let me be with other women even for a short time, especially Peggy.

I went one day every weekend, and other days during the school holidays to see the children, and naturally I saw Peggy as well. Every week there was tension, but I made it plain that there was no way I wouldn't go to see the kids, even if it meant having to put up with Paula's sulks.

My relationship with Peggy continued in its polite, distant way. We would have a fun day with the kids, a bedtime story, then maybe exchange a couple of words and I was off. Strangely, at that time I had no feelings at all for her. I did not hate her, did not love her, and did not resent her having everything. I certainly did not mind being with her, but I had no desire to stay. I couldn't wait to leave, though I knew I might be returning to a storm. Peggy was a great girl, full of remarkable qualities. I shall always treasure the time we had together, the two children we had, and the happy memories she gave me. Above all, I can never thank her enough for never saying one bad word about me to the children. She was a remarkable, kind and fun person. I don't know why she did what she did;(I await the letters) maybe she was desperate to keep me and went the wrong way about it. Maybe she really thought that Greg was going blind, maybe. But it was over, and the only thing to do was for both of us to behave like intelligent human beings and make the separation as civilised as possible. I hope I did. She certainly did.

Orson led Lewis and Peter a merry dance across Europe whilst they were trying to get him to finish his post-synching (now called looping). This is to correct any sound quality that is not up to standard through one fault or another whilst shooting on location. They eventually managed to record it in some central European studio, but as Orson insisted on doing it without picture the poor editors had a tremendous problem getting his new sound track in synch with the picture. Despite all this, the picture was shortly due to be released, and the publicity boys got to work. Both Orson and Curt were out of the country, and so they had a job getting air and press time with only Sylvia being available. Consequently everyone was dragged in, and Paula got a lot of space, billed as the girl who Orson insisted was in the film. Well, she did have a very, very small part. It was enough to get her pictures in the paper, though they shied off putting her on the interview circuit because of her bad English.

Eventually the press show. The picture was panned by all the critics, but this didn't stop the Rank Organisation holding a large premiere at the Odeon, Leicester Square. With a party at The Festival Hall, and sampans on the River Thames to take the VIP's across to the other side. As we sat down in our seats in the cinema, I just managed to stop Paula from unzipping the neck of her skin-tight evening cheongsam, for shortly afterwards she was introduced to the audience.

At the party, our hosts, John Davis and his wife, greeted us. I am sure they had something to say to each other after we left, as it is not often that a production executive comes back with such an exotic partner. All I can say is that the party was a lot better than the film, but that is saying much. Orson's performance was quite terrible, and Curt was totally miscast, so as the basis of the film was the relationship of these two characters, the whole film collapsed. However, we had one laugh when Paula went up to the show-business correspondent of the "Sunday Pictorial" (now called the "Sunday Mirror") and said to him, "How you write bad thing about film? You out in Hong Kong, eat Rank food, drink Rank drink, then write horrible thing in paper – you really lose face!"

After this I learnt one thing very quickly. There is an old saying in the business that you are as good as your last film. Well, this is always taken to refer to actors, directors and producers, but actually it affects everybody. For instance, a clapper boy goes for a job and is asked, as everybody always is, "What was your last film?"

If he replies, "'Titanic'", he'll get the job. If he replies, "'Ishmar'", he won't. It doesn't matter how good, or how bad, you are, it's credits. If "Ferry …" had been a success, I would have been offered lots of work, but as it was a disaster, nothing. Though I say it myself, I did a fantastic job, much the best job I ever did as a production manager, associate producer or whatever, on any film. Sadly it didn't add up to a row of beans.

With the failure of the film, not having a job and the expenses of running two homes piling up, I was getting to be a basket case. However, I cheered up with the arrival of Paula's sister. We went to Tilbury to meet her, with me full of excitement, though I remembered not to kiss her. With Paula's and Dalmain's curt "hello" to each other, you'd have thought they had only been away from each other for a couple of hours. Back at the flat, she at once took over the household duties, and the smell of great cooking soon filled the place.

Dalmain was a character, a strange person, someone you could not ignore. First she was a wonder in the home, as she could cook anything, be it Chinese, Thai, or Western. Roast beef, Peking Duck, hamburgers, you name it. Not only could she cook it, she could cook it better than anyone I have ever known. She kept the house spotless, she was a fine seamstress, and a clever dressmaker. I cannot think of anything she couldn't do in the house and she soon had our dreary basement flat looking something like a home. She only had one source of enjoyment, and that was the television. Her only objective in life was to make her half-sister happy, for she was devoted to Paula. Dalmain always said she would have liked to be a nun, and it is true she had no interest in men at all. I had to be very careful how I treated her, with no physical touching or any show of warmth. I liked her and, though her English was limited, we had some good laughs together.

Lewis was directing a film for Lord Brabourne, "Sink the Bismark". John Brabourne was an extremely nice man, and, though I never worked with him, he was always most kind whenever we met. His production manager, who later became his partner, was Richard Goodwin, an excellent, well-educated and talented man. They were a great team, and I always had great admiration for both of them. Later Richard and his wife built a studio on the Thames and made several successful Dickensian films. Lewis was very happy being with them, quite apart from having his old friend, Kenneth More, in the lead, a bit different from Orson Welles! As the picture called for extensive model work to depict the sea battle to sink the great German warship, they brought in an expert special effects' man from America. The trouble was that, though he was a great expert in his own field, he thought he was an expert in every field. He soon got up everybody's nose, telling everyone from the runner to the producer how they should be doing their job. This was demonstrated when they were shooting on the large outdoor tank at Pinewood. An electrician got a charge of electricity through the water. They managed to pull the poor unconscious chap out, and tried to revive him. The American came through, pushing everybody out of the way, and leant down and listened at the man's chest. He took his wrist, then looked up and said, "I think he's dead, but I'll see what I can do!"

Around 1959, during the "… Bismark" filming, Lewis phoned me and asked me to go to the theatre with him to see a play he had bought, called "Touch it Light".

It was a comedy of a searchlight crew during the Second World War, a group of men living together in a requisitioned cricket pavilion, operating the searchlight, which was situated on the cricket pitch. It was a lot of fun, very British, and a good laugh. He said that he intended to make this as soon as he could after finishing with John, and asked me whether I would join him as his associate producer.

Now the Hollywood chestnut is, "What does an associate producer do?" The answer is, "He associates with the producer." Well, it is one of those titles that can mean many things. Nowadays I note that it is often given in America to people in the production department who don't have a Union card. In this case, though, Lewis was going to produce and direct, and he would be looking to me to run the production on my own, with the help of a production manager.

Now, it didn't seem to me to be any different from the pictures that I had done as a PM, except I had someone to help me, and I was paid more money! I had never really had a producer, but then the title of producer can also mean many things. There are the active producers, who control everything, from the finding of the property, hiring the director and the writers for the screenplay, to finding the money and supervising the casting. They control the production from the first day to the delivery of the film, and then participate in the publicity and launch of the movie. Then there are, what I would call, impresario producers, people who are masters of raising finance, of getting a package together of artists, directors and story, but take little interest in the actual making of the film. There are producers, appointed by major companies to produce films for them, where the studio owns the subject and have probably developed it themselves in- house. They then hire a producer to make the film from then on. There are producers who get the title for some reason not always apparent, maybe for a legal or other expedient reason like their father owns the property, or it is a financier who will only put the money up if he gets a credit, and so on.

Then there are executive producers, and this too can mean anything. It can mean that he has put up the money, or he is there merely to supervise. It may be that he is actually running the production, but the named producer is not competent, not there, or is lazy. It is so hard to define what these titles mean. I witnessed one scene at Pinewood, I think it was a Warners' film, and the young, bearded, jeaned producer decided that he would like to be in the crowd, which was okay as he wasn't doing much anyhow. The very next day, certain executives of the company arrived for important meetings and found that the producer was stuck on the floor! He had been seen in shot, and was now continuity, and unable to attend the rather important conferences!

The role of the producer in recent years has changed. Where before the producer used to be the person in control, nowadays it is quite often the director. The stars will not work with a director they don't like, or who has no regard for their talent, and as we are in the star-system as much as ever, the director gets control. The other title is "Line producer", and he simply used to be called the production manager!

Whatever the title, it was good news that work was on the horizon. Our lease in Gloucester Road was coming to an end and I had an offer through friends for a furnished flat in Dolphin Square, a massive block of flats on the side of the Thames with its own shops, restaurant and swimming pool. It was through a friend of a friend and it was certainly a lot nicer than the one we were living in, as it was well furnished, with a great bathroom and kitchen, situated on the third floor. There was only one drawback and that was that there was only one bedroom. Paula pooh-poohed this as a problem, "She sleep in sitting room." Well, I wasn't too sure about this, but I had learnt to keep my mouth shut when it came to anything connected to Susie. Thank God I did, because we moved in and all the time we lived there I never saw Susie go to bed, be in bed, or get out of bed. It was as though she didn't sleep there. God knows what time she got up in the morning for, whatever time I left (and movies start early!), she was there, up, washed, showered and dressed. I never saw or heard her in the bathroom, she was like some sort of magical beast that just appeared, and disappeared without even a puff of smoke.

We started to put the movie together. The first thing was to change the title to "Light Up the Sky", and then the script. Lewis always worked with the same writer, Vernon Harris, a shy, quiet retiring man who worked for the BBC and moonlighted on film scripts. He and Lewis were a good team and worked together smoothly, quickly and efficiently. Soon the first draft script was at hand and I could begin. We had already decided to go to Twickenham after the good time that we had there on "A Cry from the Streets". Guido Cohen, an English/Italian, was managing the studio now. He was a delightful man who had produced many small budget films and having been on both sides of the fence, understood his clients. He was not like his predecessor, though, who had practically given me the studio, so we had a little battle over the costs but ended up with a fair deal for both sides.

We were being financed by a new company, Bryanston Pictures, a company formed by a group of independent producers who had joined together to finance and distribute their own films. Sadly it didn't last too long. The Managing director of the company was Max Setton, a nice man. I think he was Egyptian and certainly he was a wonderful linguist, though sadly not one of the greatest geniuses of the motion picture industry. Whilst Lewis was busy putting the finishing touches to the script with Vernon Harris, I was busy with my old friend, Gerry Wheatley, who used to work with George Maynard and Vernon Sewell, agreeing the budget prior to my going to Film Finances to get a completion bond.

The casting was coming along, and it seemed very exciting. First we had Tommy Steele, an immensely popular young rock-and-roll singer at that time, who was branching out into more general entertainment. The other household names we had were Ian Carmichael , a star of so many British films, and Benny Hill who became a giant star in both the UK and the US through television. Wonderful character actors like Victor Maddern, Harry Locke, Sydney Tafler, and Dick Emery, who also became a major television star, in support. The junior member of the team was Johnny Briggs, who several years later took up residence in "Coronation Street", staying there for years and years.

I found a super location for the cricket pitch in a small village called Normandy in Surrey. It was not too far from London, meaning that the crew could get back home after work, saving the company the expense of keeping them overnight. It was the perfect place to make a film, with a wooden pavilion in very pretty grounds, secluded and quiet. I brought in Ted Bushel to run the bar, do some short order cooking to supplement the normal catering, and generally look after the cast. The cricket club was delighted to be able to make some money in the winter time, and used to enjoy calling in for a drink when we were night shooting. Our location address caused a few problems. Johnny Briggs went out and bought himself a lot of lightweight clothes, thinking we were going to Normandy in France!

The days seemed to zoom by with such a cast, and were a lot of fun. There were no tantrums, no egos, just great professionals enjoying their work. There were a few problems, like trying to sort out the credits, which are a producer's nightmare.

Tommy had two agents at the time who said that he had to come first. I explained that in movies Ian Carmichael was a much bigger name, so they agreed that Tommy need not come first, but he could not come second or less. Work that one out! Credits are an ever-growing nightmare. They grow longer and longer, and more and more complicated. The various guilds, like the Screenwriters' Guild and The Directors' Guild, have signed agreements with the Producers' Association both in the UK and in the US. So it is possible for a director to have four credits, "A Film by …", "Directed by…". If the director is also the producer, he gets "Produced by…". Frequently he will have contributed to the script, or even written it, so he gets a further credit! These are Guilds' agreements, and the director as a member is as bound to them as is the producer. It is also laid down where these credits are to appear. The director's credit is always last, the writer's credit precedes it and then the producer's. The last I had from Paramount was that, though there was no laid down placing for the cameraman's credit, he or she should not be too far away from the director!

On a film I made in Canada, because of the nature of the film I wanted to put all the credits at the end, with the stars named last. I think in the end I got Liza Minnelli to sign four separate waivers agreeing to this change in her contract and the Screen Actors Guild (SAG) rules!

But it is the number of credits that are now given that bugs me. When you look at an old black-and-white movie from the 30s or even at a major colour epic in the 40s and 50s, you can see the difference in the number of credits given. The whole thing has gone mad. I think it all started with "Superman One". The film went so far over budget, with numerous private investors involved, that the producers thought if they added a long list of credits at the end, it would, in some way, impress the moneymen. Whatever, it has got worse and worse. We now have the cooks who work on the location kitchens, and the drivers! Where is it going to stop? If the car drivers, why not the bus driver who drops some of the crew off at the studio, or the train driver, or the guard?

I was sitting in my office in Toronto and a man came in and said, "I have just delivered the camera crane you ordered." For which I thanked him. And then he added, "I'd like to discuss my screen credit with you." This discussion did not help my blood pressure, or his ego!

casting directors never used to get any screen credit at all. Now they have to have a solo credit, which means their name has to be on the screen alone, and on the front, a coveted position usually only given to a few: The stars, the lead artists, directors, producers and writers, all go on the front, together with the music composer and possibly the musical director, the cameraman, the production designer and the costume designer, and also certain people that have made a special contribution to the picture, for example the visual effects' designer on "Titanic". All the rest go after "The End", which is a break for the audience who don't have to sit through minutes of meaningless titles.

One of the reasons why people want to be on the front is because they usually get poster billing as well, that means their name appears on all the advertising posters. The real truth about credits is that the audience is only interested in the stars, and in rare cases the director, someone like Spielberg or Hitchcock, or in even rarer cases a writer like Neil Simon. I don't think anyone goes to see a film because the associate producer was John Dark, except perhaps my grocer!

The real headache is when you have two major stars, two stars of equal standing, who have separate agents anxious to show that they are the toughest. Obviously their names will go on the front, before the title, a very important point, and above the title on the poster. But who comes first? Someone has to give, but it mustn't be seen to be a concession. Putting them both on the screen together appears to be the answer, but who goes on the left? The left is the better position, as people read from left to right. After weeks of wrangling, it gets worked out: Actor A will be on the left but lower than Actor B on the right or Actor B's picture will be on the left, but his name on the right, and so on. As I said, it is a nightmare.

On "Light Up the Sky" it was settled by putting them on one card: Ian at the top in the centre, with Tommy underneath but on the left and Benny Hill underneath on the right. Result nobody happy!

That hurdle over, and on to assembling the crew. No trouble with their credits; in those days getting the job was the main thing, and getting the right money. Lewis asked me to take his brother-in-law, Morris Aza, as my production manager and I was very happy to agree, as he was a charming chap and, though lacking in experience, had the right qualities I thought, to make a good PM He was hard working, responsible, totally trustworthy and someone whom I felt it would be easy to work with. His mother had an agency, which eventually Morris inherited, which represented Gracie Fields, one of the biggest names in show business in her day, and Stanley Holloway, who played Audrey Hepburn's father in "My Fair Lady". I believed that his experience would help me in dealing with agents, and helping Lewis cast. It was a happy choice, and, though I don't see him as much as I would like, we are still friends today.

At the Normandy location, all the talk was of the charity football match that Victor Maddern had organised, with our team playing the Show Biz Eleven. Now I am not a football fan, rugby is my game, and in fact almost have a dislike for the game, or rather for certain types who follow it. But Tommy and Lewis were manic football fans, and both enjoyed playing as well as watching. When Lewis found out that Billy Wright, former captain of England, was going to captain the Show Biz Eleven, his enthusiasm knew no bounds, and even more so when he was made captain of our team. He told me years later that after all his awards, he still thought that his proudest moment was when he shook hands with Billy Wright on the pitch before the game. My worry was that there seemed to be more talk of football than film. This was brought home to me when I drove to the location on an amazing sun-drenched day. We badly needed a day like that, for, though, we were shooting in the winter we had certain scenes in the spring and summer to show the passage of time. Such a day was a great relief to me, and I looked at my watch and thought with any luck they would have got at least one scene in the can. So I was more than a bit miffed when I arrived to find them all playing soccer! When I complained to Lewis he said, "We've got to train, John."

"But we've got to shoot the summer scenes, for Christ's sake. What's more important?"

"Don't worry, John, we'll get them," he said as he walked away, then turned and said, "John, you really must get your priorities right."

God, I loved that man. Well, of course, he did get the scenes, and finished the film on schedule and on budget. The football match was another matter, and I can't even remember who won. I also remember that as team manager I had to escort the celebrity to kick off the game, Shirley Bassey, a great person who stayed for the whole match and for the party at Victor Maddern's house. I think the reason I can't remember the score was because it was such a great party.

Paula, Susie, and I settled into the Dolphin Square apartment, which I found very comfortable. However, our rows increased and Paula would often get violent and throw things, many times smashing the windows. We got to know the glazier quite well. We nearly got to know the fireman too, as one day she set fire to many of my clothes! Life was never dull. These were the lows, but there were also many highs, and I still adored her.

However, I was dreading Christmas as I knew that she would resent the time I spent with the children. Peggy and I agreed I should be there first thing on Christmas morning to be with the children as they opened their stockings. I arranged to stay at a pub owned by one of the stunt boys. It was not far away from the house so I was able to get there before dawn. Christmas was a mixture of happy days with the children, and miserable ones in the uncomfortable, seedy and lonely place where I was staying at night.

I got back to Paula on Boxing Day night and she was so pleased to see me she wrapped her arms around me and kissed me all over. It felt like heaven being back with her in the warmth of our little flat, eating the delicious meal she'd asked Susie to prepare. I was also content knowing that not only had I done the right thing, but also that I had really enjoyed being with the kids, and so happy that for once Paula had accepted the situation and made our own belated Christmas so special. Sadly it didn't last and only a few days went by before we had a real bust up, and I left her. I went to live in the Richmond Bridge hotel, a minor, but comfortable hotel close to Twickenham Studios. This gave Tommy Steele the opportunity to engineer one of his practical jokes that he so enjoyed. He had Ted Bushel and Jock Easton dress up as military policemen, and as they already had their uniforms, all they had to hire from the costumiers were the caps with the red covers, and the turned down peaks.

They came to the hotel and asked the receptionist whether she had a Mr John Dark registered there, when she acknowledge the fact they asked for my room number, as I was wanted for desertion. "But he's not in the army, he's in the films, ...I think."

"Oh, they'll say anything," said Ted Bushel.

The door burst open and the two burst in, "Out of there, you," they shouted. I had been fast asleep and didn't for a while recognise them. Before I could take it in, they grabbed me out of the bed and started carrying me out of the room.

"What the fuck?" I shouted.

"Aye, and we'll have none of that kind of language, there are ladies here," warned Jock, and carried me out of the hotel.

The receptionist cried out, "Who's going to pay the bill?"

"Send it to the War Office", Ted shouted back as he bundled me into one of the army cars that we had as props on the film. The car shot off, watched by the gawping hotel clients. Ted and Jock took off their caps, collapsing with laughter. "You bastards, you unbelievable fucking bastards," I screamed. But their laughter was so infectious that I started to see the funny side of it and soon I was laughing with them. I mentioned at the wrap party that I had never realised before in what respect producers were held!

I tried to explain it at the hotel when I got back that night, but they didn't seem to see the funny side of it. It didn't matter as I wasn't there much longer. A few days (or, more importantly, a few nights) away from Paula made me realise I missed her, and we were soon back together again.

Wind-ups went on the whole time. One of the most effective was with Johnny Briggs, who we had already twigged was very gullible. One day Lewis went to him and said, "When you die at the end of the film, I've been thinking that maybe the very last shot should be of you walking up the searchlight beam into heaven."

"Oh, that would be wonderful, Lewis, bloody brilliant."

Lewis went on, "The trouble is, it means you would have the whole of the end of the picture to yourself."

By this time Johnny was peeing himself. "I know, I know, but it's good Lewis, isn't it?"

"It's dramatic," Lewis agreed. "But the problem is the rest of the cast. I don't know how they would take you hogging the very end of the film. You know the old Hollywood saying, Johnny, always leave the last shot on the money, the stars, and you are the junior member of the cast."

Briggs wasn't sure how to reply to this, but finally stuttered, "But couldn't you talk to them?"

"No, I don't think it's up to me, but if you can get them all to agree to the idea, then I'll do it."

Now, of course all the cast had been primed, and it was agreed amongst them that they would all react in different ways, some would agree straight away, some would say they'd have to think it over, but in time all of them would agree, except for one, Sydney Tafler. Poor Johnny spent days locked in conversation with the reluctant ones, sometimes coming away beaming, and other times despondent. Ian Carmichael said, "Wonderful idea, old boy, just the ticket, put me down, yes."

Which Johnny quoted in persuading Tommy, "I mean he's the star, and he's agreed."

To which Tommy replied, "He's one of the stars, and this one hasn't agreed!"

This dragged on for days, and Lewis started to nag him, explaining that it would soon be too late, as we were finishing in Normandy shortly.

At last, Johnny reported back that he had got everyone to agree except Sydney. "He's your brother-in-law. Can't you speak to him?" said Johnny.

"Oh no, Johnny, I couldn't do that. That would be nepotism." So he went back and once again tried to convince Sydney, till in the end Sydney said he couldn't stand any more of it, and we had to tell him the truth. I still think he believes it would have been a great scene!

We had to be careful, though, for they weren't always "wind-ups". As I've said, the guys from the cricket club used to pop in some evenings for a drink and to see what was going on. They were a nice bunch of chaps and the cast didn't seem to mind them being around. After all it was their club.

We told them that before we left we would have to blow up the pavilion. "Oh yes, pull the other one," they said, and the more we told them, the more they thought we were having them on. One day, I told them we would be blowing it up the following night, at which they all laughed and said they would be there. They were all there the following night, beer mugs in their hands, and even when we cleared the building, and made everybody retire behind the cameras, they still didn't believe us. Up went the cries, "Turn Over" ... "Running" ... "Three twenty, take one" ... "Right, action" ... and the pavilion went up.

The crowd stood silent, open mouthed as pieces of wood came raining down, and smoke swirled everywhere.

Finally the Club Secretary said, "Oh well, we always did want it on the other side of the pitch." What they didn't know, was that our art department had put a false front on the front of the pavilion, and it was this that the special effects' boys had blown. This plus the smoke and small controlled flame gave the illusion that the whole thing had gone up. We repainted the pavilion inside and out and handed it back to them in a much better state than when we had found it.

The picture ended and with it the realisation that soon I would be "knocking on doors again", back to selling, though this time the product was myself. Salesmen always say that you're as good as your product – I could see I had a problem.

One day I was in Morris Aza's office and I asked him if he had any scripts. He handed me one called "The Scar", written by Alexander Dore. I took it away, read it, thought it wasn't bad, and would perhaps make a good little second feature. I met Alex and he agreed to let me have an option on the subject whilst I was trying to set it up. An option is a fee paid against the total agreed fee payable to the writer when the picture is financially settled. In this case, the small option fee was very small, it was nothing! This allows the company, or the producer, time in which to assemble the package, and get the finance. I then met Vernon Sewell and asked him whether he would like to direct a film for Cresswell. "Don't be daft, old boy, that's my company."

"'fraid not, Vernon. I bought it."

I had, I'd met George and he told me that he and Vernon had parted, and that he was selling off their company Cresswell Productions Ltd I quickly bought it. Vernon read the script, liked it and was on board.

Next I went to Bryanston to get them to distribute the film. I should explain that in those days financing was one hell of a lot easier than now, though the numbers involved were, even allowing for inflation, minuscule compared to today. Our budget was under twenty thousand pounds, lock, stock and barrel, and included not only the total cost of production, but also the finance charges, interest, insurance, and completion bond. The set up was that if you could get an agreement out of a distributor, you took it to the National Provincial Bank who would advance you seventy per cent of your budget, leaving you to raise the balance, and obtain a guarantee of completion. You could then get from The National Film Finance Cooperation a further twenty per cent, meaning that you privately had to raise the balance of ten per cent, one thousand seven hundred pounds: one thousand seven hundred pounds that I didn't have!

At this time I was being pressured by Peggy's lawyer to hasten the divorce. It was time for me to find someone to argue my legal position, and I was recommend to see this chap, David Holland. Whilst chatting with him he asked me what I did, and what I was up to at that moment. It wasn't long before he had agreed to put up the balance of the ten per cent. It must be the first time that anyone ever came out of a lawyer's office with more money than when he went in! I left clutching his cheque. I think he must have been mad, because it was all done over his desk on a handshake.

Fully financed, I collected all the agreements together, plus the schedule and budget, and went to Film Finances for the Completion Bond. After making a thorough search, they grill you and the director on how you are going to shoot the movie in that amount of time, and on that amount of money. They have to be thorough because if you are wrong it can cost them an awful lot of money. It is easier if they are dealing with experienced people with a good track record, and Vernon was certainly one of those. Luckily, they thought I had done a good job on "Light Up the Sky", so we did not have too much trouble, though they were rather nervous about the size of the budget. They weren't the only ones!

Meanwhile, Morris got Paula an audition for the stage production of "The Flower Drum Song". She had been having singing lessons, and Morris reckoned it was time for her to start getting herself around, and as there was a shortage of Eastern girls, especially singers, she stood a chance. She was petrified, and we thought it would be a good idea to give her a couple of large brandies to settle the nerves, which it did, and we arrived at the stage door of the Drury Lane theatre in quite a calm mood. We then waited and waited, and the effects of the brandy wore off. Finally she was called, and Morris and I watched as this diminutive little figure walked out onto the enormous stage of this large theatre. It must have been the longest walk of her life. To me it seemed to never end. My stomach was in knots, and there were tears in my eyes. I do not remember what she sang or really what happened, all I know is that it was a disaster! She went into a deep depression and back to the old remedy, the bottle. Things got so bad that I rented a flat in Notting Hill Gate, and once more moved out.

Meanwhile pre-production was progressing, but it all took time. We had no money, but Guido was very good to us and let us have a small office for a very nominal fee, (nothing), and Morris, bless him, worked without pay. I had already learnt that producers get nothing until everything is eventually tied up. He not only doesn't get anything, but is expected to pay all the costs until the last contract is signed. Harold Macmillan had recently made his famous speech in South Africa, and as our picture reflected the racial tension in Britain, and as I hated the title "The Scar", I changed the title to "The Wind of Change".

This was 1960 and the movie "Saturday Night and Sunday Morning" was being completed at Twickenham, and I got Guido to leave the sets up for us, so we would not have the expense of building the basic construction. With memories of Orson Welles I knew we couldn't use their exact sets, but with some revamping, we could change their street, for example, to one of our own design. We were in good nick!

I had learnt certain things about Vernon Sewell, and I was determined to ensure that he neither re-wrote the script, nor had a hand in the casting. Therefore, with Morris Aza's great help we started casting. At this point I met an agent, Denis Sellinger, who was to help me enormously in the future. He was a gentleman, and so nice it was hard to think of him as an agent! He had the big names, but also looked after the up-and- coming ones. He was not only the agent of the stars, he was also their friend. At the same time he numbered numerous producers also as his friends, and I was very happy to be among them. After reading the script, he sent it to Donald Pleasance, who at the time was playing the lead in Harold Pinter's "The Caretaker" in the West End, and he agreed to play the important part of the Father. The rest of the cast was coming along nicely: dear darling Hilda Fennimore to play the mother, Anne Lynne the daughter, Glyn Houston the policeman, and the second lead, the son, to be played by Johnny Briggs. I was happy to engage Bunny May also. We had worked together on a commercial years ago when he was still at school and used to come to the studio with a chaperone. I remember it was for Bovril and was always known as "The Boy in the Cold", a title I never let him forget. Bunny was best known for playing "Noddy" in the children's television series, and like the rest was a highly professional actor. This just left the minor parts, which were mainly of young people, for which we had a chance to cast total unknowns.

I also needed a rock-'n'-roll kid, a new teenage boy, who was a bit raunchy, a talented yob. So Morris and I went to see Joan Littlewood's production "Fings Ain't What They Used To Be" which had just been transferred to the West End. As soon as the boy walked on the stage I thought, that's him. Norman Gun was everything we wanted and was so talented that Morris signed him up for his agency. The only trouble was that he not only played the part, but he lived it as well. He was completely irresponsible, and unable to take any form of discipline. One day after we had finished the film, he turned up to see Morris at his London office. The receptionist asked him to take a seat, saying that Mr Aza had asked him to wait a few minutes. A sulky Norman sat down, put his legs up on the table, and watched as the girl started to eat her lunchtime sandwiches. Suddenly Norman leapt up and grabbed all the food from her desk, took the sandwich out of her hand, and stuffed them into his mouth! Not longer after, Norman was found dead, overdosed. Poor fellow, he had a career in front of him but was just unable to accept any form of self-discipline.

A happier story is of a young man who was paid the standard Equity rate of ten pounds a day for a one-day role, by the name of David Hemmings.

The date was fixed, we were cast, crewed, and sets were built. It was at "GO" for my first independent production as a producer.

One day I noticed Johnny Briggs's car, which looked as if it was held together with string. "You intend driving to the studio every day in that?" I asked.

"Well, you can always send me a limo," he said not unreasonably. My worry was that he would not get to the studio on time, so I suggested he came to live with me for the remaining three weeks so I could make sure he arrived there safely. He moved in that night. Mind you, I wasn't so pleased when six months later he came out of his bedroom complaining that he couldn't sleep through the noise of my vacuuming.

John was a sweet and talented man. We had a lot of fun together; he was not only my friend but Paula's, my mothers, and indeed that of most of my family. I became godfather to his son by his first marriage , so it came as a bit of a shock when I picked up his autobiography to see that not only had he ignored me, but had credited the studio manager for giving him the part in "The Wind of Change". Why should that upset me? We had drifted apart, I know, as he was living in the North having taken up permanent residence in "Coronation Street," but I thought friendship knew no time limits. Whatever it was, I am sorry, as I have only the fondest affection for him. I remember when they were doing "This is Your Life Johnny Briggs" they came to me at Pinewood and said, "We hear he used to beg you to give him work". I immediately told them that was not true. I had many stories to tell about him, but that one was not true, and, though I would be proud to be on his show, I could not recount that untruth. They scrapped me on the show, and afterwards Johnny rang me and said, "Thanks a lot for being on my show"!

We made the movie, had a lot of fun, and had the great pleasure of working with Donald Pleasance. Through him I had lunch with Harold Pinter and we discussed making his play "The Caretaker" into a movie. Sadly it never happened. Others made it, and I think it died a horrible death. I am not saying that I could have done any better as it was a very difficult thing to transfer from stage to screen, and Pinter understandably wanted as little change to his original script as possible.

Keeping to the budget was tough, especially when we were on night locations. We used to shoot scenes against the still lit shop windows, or shoot at what is known in the business at the "magic hour", dusk, when we used to bribe the local kids to shin up the lampposts and put the street lights on earlier! We couldn't afford generators, so we were restricted to small lights run from batteries. We had nothing: no catering, no transport, just our own cars and the nearest greasy spoon. No one complained, and everybody helped. When we moved from one location to another all the crew and the cast helped hump the gear. The Unions would have had a fit if they had seen!

In the end we finished under budget with a worthy little second feature of the time. I recently ran it, and in today's world, it is an unmitigated piece of shit. Still it got me started, or so I thought. I searched for new scripts but found nothing I liked or, closer to the truth, nothing on which I could raise money. "Wind of Change" still hadn't been released, as we were waiting for the right film to go with it. Nobody went to the cinema to see the second feature, so its success depended solely on the attraction of the main feature. In those days the second feature got ten per cent of the profit, but at that time there was a British Government subsidy, called the Eady fund, which gave a subsidy to British films based on the box-office take, and gave an extra percentage to movies produced under a certain figure. In the end we did very well with "Wind ...". Everybody, including my new lawyer, David Holland, got his money back many times over.

By this time my money was running out, as my share of profits was yet to be paid. So when Lewis called me and asked whether I would work as a production manager on a new film he was to direct, I wasn't in a position to say no, even though it meant going backwards.

The good thing was that, apart from Lewis being the director, it was to be made for Columbia Pictures and I thought this was a good opportunity for me to be known by a large American major distributor.

The other plus was that the film was to be produced by Victor Saville, a much respected director and producer. At the beginning of the Second World War, he left for America, probably because he had been wounded badly in the First. I reckon he thought he had done enough – it was someone else's turn ... and who could blame him? In the States he made several successful films. One of them was one of my very favourite films, "Good-bye Mr Chips", the story of an eccentric schoolmaster at a British public school, so brilliantly portrayed by Robert Donat.

I didn't know until later that Mr Saville had a terrible reputation. Before the '39 War he had trouble getting crews to work for him, even during the Depression. Apparently he had a ghastly temper and used to hit young Assistants over the head with his walking cane. In my office at Shepperton one day Victor was extolling his own virtues, saying, "All my crews loved me."

At which, to my astonishment, I heard Frank Bush of Technicolor, for the first time in his life, contradict a producer. "Victor, you were an unmitigated bastard and they all hated you!"

Although I was unaware of any of this, I was apprehensive about taking the post. I had never worked with an active producer and was used to working on my own, making my own decisions. I wished that financial circumstances had not forced me to take the job.

The film was based on the Rumer Godden novel, "The Greengage Summer", and was the story of four English children, one girl in her late teens, one girl in her early teens, one young boy about nine, and the baby of the family, a girl of about seven, who were stranded in a French rural hotel. It was a tender, romantic story and

I enjoyed the script immensely. We intended to shoot on location in France and then return to Shepperton Studios.

First, we had to find the right locations in France, and I went out to Paris with Victor to meet Lewis and my old friend John Stoll. We stopped there just long enough to have a fantastic meal and pick up our French location manager, and then off we went to the Champagne district, North of Paris.

The first essential location to find was a French chateau, converted to a hotel, with a greengage orchard in its grounds. Victor took charge, and armed with the "Michelin Guide", he directed the driver. We visited all the chateau hotels in the area, always managing somehow to arrive at the ones with the highest rosettes at both lunch- and dinner-time. Our lunches were such that afternoons were almost a write-off, as we all fell asleep in the car. We found it hard to bond with Victor. For such an experienced producer, and even more a highly experienced director, he had some very strange ideas. We could not find a greengage orchard within the grounds of any of the hotels. Victor said we could shoot the two separately, and then join them together by editing. Though reluctant to accept this, Lewis was prepared to give way, but pointed out that we hadn't yet found a greengage orchard yet. Victor was triumphant, "Not true, whilst you talentless amateurs have been mooning around, I have found one."

So off we went, came to a halt on a busy thoroughfare, and there on the side of the road down a steep incline was a greengage orchard. Victor threw his arm out as though he was introducing a three-ringed circus. We made our way gingerly down through the trees, trying to keep our balance.

"How could we shoot this? How would the actors be able to perform on this steep slope?" I asked myself.

Lewis said, "Well, Victor, it is a greengage orchard, but don't you think that it is a bit awkward?"

"Awkward?" Victor shouted.

"Yes, it's a very steep slope."

"And it's noisy with the traffic so close," I put in.

This set him off. "You're all so bloody negative: 'awkward', 'noisy'. Haven't you heard of post-synch, eh, young Dark, haven't you?"

As we struggled back up the slope, Lewis being conciliatory said, "Well, yes, we could shoot here Victor, but it does have a lot of disadvantages."

"Well, what do you suggest we do?" he asked in the most sarcastic tone.

Lewis quietly replied, "I think we should first find the chateau, and then plant the orchard."

This sent Victor off into peals of laughter. "Oh, that's wonderful," he muttered in-between his guffaws: "Build an orchard!"

As we sped off in the car for another gourmet lunch, he was still laughing. In fact, over the next few days he was still breaking out in the odd chortle. "I've come across a few, but … 'build an orchard'…" and off he would go again, rocking with laughter.

It was the same with the opening scene. Which called for a train to pull up at a small halt to let off a sick mother. An ambulance is waiting to speed her to a hospital, leaving her four children standing there alone watching the ambulance carrying their mother away. Four sad figures abandoned in this desolate foreign spot. So why did Victor pick Meaux Railway Station, the Clapham Junction of Paris? "Isn't it a bit large? " Lewis quietly asked.

"God Almighty, Lewis, do I have to tell you everything? You don't have to show it *all*, you know." He walked towards an advertising hoarding, with his arms outstretched and lectured Lewis on how to shoot the scene. "Look, they come in left, and go out right!"

"Yes, you could do that, but don't you think that it would be better if we looked for a small station somewhere in an idyllic spot, where we can show the kids on a deserted platform watching the ambulance, with their sick mother disappearing over the hills?"

Off stalked Victor muttering about "talentless amateurs" and disappeared into the car to study the "Michelin Guide" for the nearest gourmet restaurant. What neither of us could ever understand was how such an experienced man could talk such rubbish. Was he over his sell-by date? This was the last picture he ever made, and I think it was just our luck to have come across him when he was a little bit too old.

Nevertheless, there was still a film to be made and after our return to London we realised that the only thing we had to show for our French recce were the extra pounds around our waistlines! Convincing Victor that he had no need to return to France, and gathering up Freddy Young, the doyen cameraman, and John Stoll, off we went again. This time it was to find and finalise locations, set up the French crew, and prepare to shoot, rather than concentrating on Michelin's finest eating establishments. With the various delays, we were getting increasingly worried about the weather, and we decided to see if we could find a hotel in the South. After we decided to make our main base at Reims, we dashed down to Marseilles, where the following day we found a gorgeous chateau, an idyllic building set in an enormous garden. It had everything, but greengage trees! But it did have magnificent grounds where we could build our own orchard, and see the Chateau Hotel in the background giving Lewis and Freddy the lush setting they desired.

Columbia pictures at that time had a large European operation, with the head office in London and offices in Paris and Rome. The European boss was an American, Mike Frankovitch, son of the famous comedian Joe E. Brown always remembered for the final pay-off line in "Some Like it Hot". Mike played the role of the movie mogul to the hilt. A big man, he made sure everyone knew who he was. He dressed elegantly, often in England sporting a bowler hat, and was seen at all the society and movie events. He was married to that charming actress, Binnie Barnes, and they were among the leading hosts in London at that time. A monster in the office, he was a charming and generous man outside. He ran the European Columbia production operation with a firm hand, and under his leadership Columbia had a run of big successes. Looking back, it is sad to reflect how the size of that operation has shrunk to nothing. From being a teeming office of executives, including four production supervisors each looking after so many films, accountants, readers, publicity people etc.

This was my first experience of working for an American major, and I had to adapt quickly to their systems. Naturally, all budgets had to be agreed by the company, and an elaborate system of checking enabled Columbia to know what was going on at any time. Before the war, MGM used to boast that they knew where every cent was spent, down to the last nail, until a new whiz kid came in and asked how much it cost to have this information. They soon realised that it would be a hell of a lot cheaper to lose a few nails! Columbia was a little like that, and, though overall the production supervisors were pretty good and didn't get in your hair too much, it always felt as though you had someone looking over your shoulder. In addition, it didn't solve any potential problems, for unless you were actually working on a picture, it was unrealistic to think that you could judge whether a payment was right or wrong. When a Columbia production representative was presented with a pile of a hundred cheques at the end of the week, he was mainly dependent on the honesty of the production accountant, the production manager, and the producer.

The great thing about working for an American major is the back-up you get. There is always help at the end of the phone. On "Greengage ...", we had the Paris office to arrange all our permits, supervise the selection of the French crew, and generally act as our French production office. Unfortunately, the executive in charge, Claude Ganz, unlike his British colleagues, was a pain-in-the-arse. He was determined to make a name for himself, and would waste hours of my time explaining matters of little importance, the phone call costing more money then the query.

Like Pinewood, Shepperton was a fully staffed studio, so one was committed under Union agreements to take their craft grades: carpenters, stage hands, electricians, and sound technicians. To make matters worse, you also had no choice which of these people you took, as there was a rota system and you had to take the next on the list, even if you knew someone was a total incompetent.

Casting was completed, with Kenny More playing the lead opposite Danielle Darrieux, the famous French star, Susannah York playing the eldest of the children, and a new twelve-year-old red-headed actress, Jane Asher, playing the second child. I had never worked with Kenny before, though Lewis and he were great friends, having made the successful "Reach for the Sky", the story of the legless airman Douglas Bader, and "Sink The Bismark".

Kenny was a delightful man and exactly like the character he portrayed in the "Doctor" films. He was always cheerful, full of fun, kind and considerate, he was rather like an enthusiastic college graduate. He was also without doubt one of the nosiest people I ever came across. You never needed to ask the gateman if he had arrived at the studio, as you would hear him. What I really liked about him was his kindness to small- part actors having suffered himself from rough treatment when he was starting up, he always took great pains to put a lesser-known artist at ease. He told the story of how, when he was just beginning, he was given a job replacing an actor in a film already shooting. The part was of a prison warden. The trouble was that the actor he replaced was a giant of a man and Kenny was dressed in his uniform. Nothing fitted, he looked a wreck. There was no time to get him a proper fitting wardrobe. So they pushed him on the set, and for most of the day Kenny managed to hide around the back. Unfortunately, near the end of the day the director spotted him: "Hey you, yes you, big boots." He never forgot the humiliation of that day.

Ken was married to a woman whose character was completely different to his. She was a quiet, dignified lady of the cashmere twin-set and pearls style, quiet and reserved, but nevertheless seemed to be devoted to him. I am sure it must have been a ghastly shock to her when years later he left her for a young, chirpy, fun-loving girl, Angela Douglas, who was one of the girls I had cast in "The Wind of Change". They seemed to have a very happy marriage lasting until his early death.

Danielle Darrieux was to me the classic French woman that men dream about. She was exquisitely groomed and, though by this time in her mid-40's, she still retained her petite, rounded figure. She had a twinkle in her eye, a delicious French accent, and that laugh that only French woman seem to have, a laugh that rolls around in the back of the throat before peeling out. I adored her. Rumour had it that during the war she had an affair with Hermann Goering, and even the thought of that fat ogre humping this delicate beauty could not chill my admiration.

Susannah York was just starting her career, this being her third film and her biggest role to date. She was a sweet girl, and unlike the other actresses of around nineteen-years'-old, she behaved like someone much younger. Young actresses, like most young women try to put on an air of sophistication, and make themselves out to be women of the world. Susannah was not like that, but walked around offering people "sticky sweets" from a paper bag. She dressed very simply, and wore little or no make-up. The trouble was that she dressed like that even when "on duty" in front of the press and the public. I was at the press screening for the film at the Odeon, Leicester Square, when I looked up and saw England's new young star coming down the staircase in a cheap dress, with the hem hanging down at the back, and wearing a pair of scuffed out flat ballet type shoes, and no make up.

Jane Asher was, I guess, every father's idea of what they would like their thirteen-year-old daughter to be. She was perfectly behaved with charming manners and pretty as a picture with her long striking red hair. Her cultured speaking voice reflected the fine family she came from and the education she had received. She told me years later that she was terrified of me. I can't think why, as I thought she was a delight, and I hope I treated her as I would a favoured child.

The rest of the cast and company arrived in Reims ready to shoot.

Before we started, Lewis took me aside and told me my main job was to keep Victor away from the set, and especially away from him. This was a lot easier said than done, for Victor liked to arrive where the action was and play the heavy producer. This would have been all right if he had limited himself to that role, but he would insist on giving Lewis advice, making suggestions to the cast, telling all and sundry how to do their jobs, and even once taking over the supervision of a move from one location to the other, and getting all the various trucks and wagons bogged down in the mud. I did my best to keep him away, even at one time giving him a false "call sheet" and sending him miles away, explaining afterwards that we had changed the "call" at the last moment. I used to suffer his wrath, but at least I managed to give Lewis some help. In the end, Lewis spoke to Mike Frankovitch, who leant on Victor and things got a little better.

Reims was a wonderful place to shoot. Situated right in the middle of the Champagne district, nestling by the side of the river Marne, it was an ideal place. Not only did it have the beauty and the locations required in the script, it was also full of hotels and restaurants to cater for the company. As usual, I was embarrassed beyond belief by the behaviour of some of the British crew. They expected the French boys to do all the heavy work, and spent most of their time eating or drinking. The usual continuous supply of food was available, supplied and cooked by wonderful French caterers, which only brought a continuous stream of complaints about "this Froggy food". At night, after work, the French crew would go back, shower, and change to go out to dine. Many of ours wouldn't even wash or change, or if they did, would come down in open shirts, braces, and no jacket! For, though the Unions had an agreement that their members had to have first class conditions, sadly many of their members were far short of first class manners.

One of our main locations was in the Champagne caves, the underground cellars where the bottled champagne was matured. Each company had its own caves, and my French counterpart had arranged with the Pommery Company so that we could shoot in theirs. I had many meetings with their Managing director, as there were problems with the amount of heat our lights was likely to create. He was the most charming of men, and at every meeting, he would give me various types of champagne not only to taste, but also to drink. It was here that I developed my appreciation of good champagne. I stress "good", as I know little about other wine. I do not understand it, and I think that I am the opposite of a wine snob. But the difference between a good vintage champagne and the run-of-the-mill is vast and hard to explain. Those headaches we have all had after weddings are caused by cheap champagne. The nectar of vintage wine leaves no headache, just an amazing feeling of warmth, wonder and contentment. Who cannot envy the rich man who can enjoy this heaven whenever he wishes?

We had a great time there, and the local people were so helpful. We had no trouble shooting anywhere, including inside the magnificent cathedral – though, there again, I had trouble with some of the UK crew whom I found smoking and drinking tea inside this historic and religious building.

So we were very sad when it was time to leave this beautiful Northern town. I was also worried as where we were going was very different. Bezier was a small town in the South close to Perpignon, and had none of the facilities of Reims. This was the early 60s, the Mercure, or Novotel chains had yet to be established, and the local hotels were, to put it mildly, pretty ropey. Our French location manager had managed to get the main artists and senior crew members looked after, but things were not looking good lower down, and I could see we were going to have trouble.

It was with some trepidation that I took off for the South with the rest of the company.

We had arranged a charter flight to pick us up from the military airport at Reims, and take us to another tiny airport in Perpignon. Kenny was rather worried about the flight. "Don't trust these bloody charter jobs, old boy," he said.

"You'll be all right, I promise you," I said. "You can sit by me and I'll look after you." God knows how sitting next to me was going to help if we crashed, but it seemed to calm him down, and off we went.

It was an amazing flight. Before we took off, they served champagne and canapés, and they just managed to serve liqueurs before we landed, and this was after a three-course gourmet meal they served us on the journey.

I waited at the bottom of the steps of the aircraft as the company disembarked and as Alan Blay came down, I said, "Well, Alan, great flight, eh?"

"Definitely sub-standard travel," he spat out at me.

"How can you say that, Alan?"

Whipping a metallic retractable tape measure from his pocket, he said, "Look, I measured the seat and it was three inches under first class seating as outlined in the Union agreement"

As soon as I got to our temporary production office I heard the rumblings of the English "sparks", and indeed there was a message to say their shop steward would like to see me about their accommodation. There were more urgent things to attend to, so it was about an hour later that I had the time to suddenly wonder why an irate Steward had been up to see me. I went down to their hotel, and found them in the bar entertaining some local young ladies. They greeted me with great warmth, and offered me a drink, which I accepted. I pulled the Steward away and asked him what the trouble was.

"Oh, nothing, John, everything's fine, no trouble", and quickly broke away and back to the party.

This proved to me, once again, that if there are women around, they'd put up with anything. Hong Kong, stinking Macao, not a peep, but in the desert as with "Lawrence ..." ... well, just ask anyone who was there. No women, and you can be in the George V in Paris and you will be in trouble. Crumpet: the great cure for all industrial problems! Well, in the movie business, anyway. I guess it would be a bit of a problem at the HMV television factory!

We were soon back at Shepperton, completing the interiors. We had cast a French boy whilst over there to play the part of the "boot boy" at the hotel. We had been granted a work permit for him so were surprised when we got a call from the Immigration Department saying that they had detained him at Heathrow. Why? His papers were in order, I knew. I couldn't think what the trouble could be. The Immigration Officer said on the phone they thought he was entering the country to take advantage of the British National Health Service. This was a new one, I thought. The Officer suggested I came down to the airport to see for myself. I rushed there, and was taken to a room where our "boot-boy" sat, both arms covered in plaster! He had been in an accident. Eventually I convinced the Immigration

Officials that he was indeed an actor, even if a damaged one. I guaranteed he would return to France at the end of his contract and we would be responsible for any medical bills that he incurred whilst he was working for us. Actually he returned much earlier, as his English was much worse than we had been led to believe, and we had to hastily re-cast him. It was years later that I realised that this rather pathetic boy had become one of France's leading film directors, critically acclaimed across the world for films such as "Jean de Florette" and "Manon des Sources". He was, of course, Claude Berri.

The film was drawing to an end, a happy film for the most part. Victor seemed to have mellowed over the period we had been shooting, or perhaps we all had got used to one another. I myself got quite fond of him and we parted on very pleasant terms. One of the things I was grateful for that came out of this picture was to have worked for the first time with Freddy Young. He was a true master of his craft, and he photographed the French countryside like a master landscape painter at work. He was also a leader, and kept his camera crew under a tight rein: a gentle man with an iron core, an expert technician endowed with great sensitivity. He became my friend on this picture, and it was a friendship that remained until his death in his late 90's.

The film was a disappointment. It looked wonderful, but the trouble was that Kenny, bless him, was miscast. He found it hard to play the lover, and I think it embarrassed him. What the part needed was someone like Laurence Harvey. A rake, a devil-may-care kind of guy.

I would be soon out of work but Paula had got a job! She had been for several auditions, but the trouble was she wasn't very good and very self-conscious. Still Morris Aza, who had become her agent, persevered and got her into "The World of Susie Wong" at the Prince of Wales theatre in the West End. "Wow," I thought, "this will give her something to do, something other than me in her life." And for a while this was true, but then other problems arose. She was working theatre hours and I was working movie hours. I would work from early morning, pick her up from the theatre after eleven at night, and then she would want to eat, and after go out partying. I was dead! The other was her jealousy, she was quite sure I was screwing all the other girls in the show. I'd like to say, I should be so lucky. As it was, I had trouble standing up, never mind *getting* it up.

Then we moved to a cute house near Dulwich. I stopped working so could adjust my hours to hers, and we started going through a calm time. Paula imported a lot of furniture from Hong Kong, and that mixed with modern Western furniture gave us a remarkable looking home, and we were able to entertain our friends in style. A Chinese meal in our house was something that none of our guests would ever forget. It made the best Chinese restaurant in London seem pretty average. For days preceding the party Susie would be busy preparing all the food so that it could be cooked quickly and served. The basis of good Chinese food is that it has to be eaten as soon as it is cooked, and with ten or twelve dishes, the preparation was the secret. Word soon got around, and there was a queue to be invited. Apart from the preparation work, the other problem was that the ingredients were very expensive, and we had to cut back before we went bankrupt. When we first moved in I gave Susie strict instructions never to buy anything from anyone who came to the door. One day I was upstairs when the front door bell went and Susi answered it. I heard a man say, "Good morning, madam, I am from the Dulwich Council and I am here…"

Susie quickly cut him off. "Don't want", she said.

"Let me explain …"

"No want," came the reply.

The man persevered, "I am not selling anything, madam. I just want to explain that you live in a smokeless zone and you must only burn a certain type of coal."

This struck a chord, "Oh," said Susie "want coal." At that point I thought I'd better go and rescue the poor man.

Through my new connections with Columbia, one of their contract producers, Charles H. Schneer, contacted me about making a film in Hong Kong. He had a script with a title like "Mr Wong of Hong Kong" and he was anxious to make the whole film in Hong Kong. The prospect of this delighted me, as well as Paula. He asked where I got my heavy equipment from when I shot "Ferry to Hong Kong" and I explained that I brought it in from Canton, from the Communists. He was at lengths to explain to me that as an American he couldn't possibly do business with a Communist regime. I told him that I understood, but that it would cost him a lot more money, as doing business with the Nationalists in Hong Kong was an expensive affair. "Well, that's a bullet we will have to bite", he responded. It was something of a shock then, when the next day I get a call from him, asking if the Communists were that much cheaper.

Later I found out that Charlie was obsessively mean, not only in his business life but in his personal life as well. He was a very rich man, and had a lovely house in one of the best parts of central London. He was married to a charming woman, who was related to the Schneider family who were the main stockholders of Columbia at that time. He mainly specialised in special effects' films, and his success was directly linked to his relationship with Ray Harryhausen, the doyen special effects' man.

"Mr Wong", though, was not a special effects' movie. I happily started work on breaking down the script and contemplating happily a return to Hong Kong. I had not been with Charlie long when he called me to tell me that Columbia wanted to make a Harryhausen film first, and to drop "Mr Wong …". He handed me the script of "Jason and the Golden Fleece", later changed to "Jason and the Argonauts".

CHAPTER 12
MARRY ME

Jason and the Argonauts? Greek mythology? Jason's search for the Golden Fleece? What did I know about Greek mythology?

To be shot in Super Dynamation?

As I read the script, I realised I hadn't a clue where to even start.

I tried talking to Ray Harryhausen, but found him a very difficult man to converse with. At the time, I thought he just didn't like me but some time later Charlie told me that he had a big problem communicating with his fellow men. I think that was why Charlie never let him direct one of his films. There had to be a reason, as the director was always restricted by Ray's requirements, and it would have made sense for him to have done the whole job. Whatever, I had to get on and to break the script down into some sort of sense, without much success – according to Ray Harryhausen, that is!

He never said anything directly to me, but would make a critical remark to someone in my earshot so I was sure to hear. In the end, we settled down with each other, and after the film even met up at odd times for a meal or a drink.

He was a very tall, lugubrious American who, like many clever people, was totally focused on his job, his creative talents and his technical brilliance. He was not a lot of fun, but I soon found out why he was held in such high regard by both the industry and the public. Sadly the computer has brought an end to his film career.

If I was having trouble with Ray, I was getting on really well with Charlie, but found his stinginess so severe that it was comical. He was planning a TV series of "Gulliver" and employed Sid Cole to produce it. One day Sid got a three page memo from Charlie, not about the show, but about the fact that Sid had left his Vent-Axia fan on all night in the office which was "the height of irresponsibility!" I could see we were going to have fun with the budget.

Charlie had a very small permanent staff, but they were a good and happy lot. He had a good-looking and wildly efficient personal secretary who had him right under control. For example, if he was dictating and paused for any length of time, she would rattle her long finger nails on the desk whilst arching her eyebrows. Once I was in his office and she popped her head in saying, "Would you like a cup of coffee, John?" Which I happily accepted.

As she went to leave, Charlie cried, "What about me? I'd like one too."

"I am not talking to you," she spat out, and left slamming the door. Oh dear Charlie, what have you done? I thought.

Charlie engaged a young American, Paul Maslansky, to read scripts for him. He was a likeable guy, full of wisecracks, seemingly happy with his lot, tucked away in an office the size of a small broom closet and paid a salary to match. Still it was a start, and with his personality, I thought that one day this fellow would make it. I was right. He eventually went back to LA and produced many successful movies, none more financially successful than the "Police Academy" films.

"Jason ..." was to be financed and distributed, like all Charlie's films, by Columbia, and the boys there were able to give me a lot of help in advising me how Charlie operated. On this occasion, he had swallowed his scruples and was making a deal with the Yugoslavian Communist nationalised film industry and they warned me to be careful. The idea was that the Yugoslavs provide certain facilities like sound stages, certain crew, sets, and whatever could be supplied locally, up to a certain financial level. For this they would retain certain Eastern block rights and, more importantly, receive hard currency in the shape of US dollars. The various facilities had to be budgeted at agreed figures, and this was not too much of a problem at the preliminary stage, as the Yugoslavs were so keen to get their hands on dollars they would settle quickly. The trouble came later. What had been agreed was often subsequently disputed, and often items they had agreed to supply never appeared. It was a risky business. However, producers saw a golden carrot hanging there and it was hard for them not to grab it, and worry about the consequences later. There were always rows, and the Columbia accountants were very wary.

First we had to ascertain whether it was possible to shoot the film there, so it was agreed that I should go to Belgrade and Zagreb to see their facilities, and meet the executives of the company.

Whilst in Zagreb, Charlie asked me to speak to a young actor to whom he had offered the lead. So, arriving at the hotel in Zagreb, and finding that this actor was also staying there, I arranged to meet him.

He was a good-looking, fair haired young man and as he came strolling into the bar, I could see why Charlie wanted him. He was easy-going and we quickly felt at ease with each other. However, when I got round to talking about "Jason ..." he very politely said, "I don't know whether you know what they offered me. I would love to do it, but it would hardly keep me in cigarettes."

So we lost Roger Moore, one of the few British actors to become a major international star. Incidentally he stayed the same considerate and pleasant person all throughout his career. The crews loved him, and there was always a great atmosphere on the set when he was on call.

I then met up with various officials of the Yugoslavian film industry, together with our middle-man. There were always several of these negotiators hanging around the Western film industry, and they were usually men who had left their countries years before and settled in the West. They learnt that there were good pickings in arranging finance between the American and British Companies and the Serbs. I found them very dubious, with their over-selling, their insistence that anything we needed could be supplied, and that everything was so much cheaper. Their behaviour reminded me of a shifty second-hand car salesman.

The stages they had to offer were large, but not sound-proofed, and their equipment was antiquated. Overall I was not impressed.

From Zagreb I flew to Belgrade and met up with Charlie in order to meet the Serbian Minister in charge of films. A dinner party was arranged, and I briefed Charlie on how to behave. I told him to accept a drink when offered, and that it wasn't necessary to drink it, but just join in the toast by raising it to his lips. I also told him to keep off politics.

We sat down to eat, with the Minister sitting next to Charlie. He poured some wine into Charlie's glass, saying that it was very special wine, and he thought Charlie would like it. "No, I won't. I'll have a pineapple juice," replied Charlie. They didn't have any pineapple juice, so in the end he settled for a Coke, which much to my surprise they did have. The toast was made, and we settled down to enjoy the dinner. Charlie then turned to the Minister and said, "Are you a Communist?" I could have killed him.

With a shrug of his shoulders, the Minister said quietly, "But, of course".

"Why?" asked Charlie.

"Well," said the Minister, "I think that Capitalism is a case of man exploiting man." I could see Charlie bristle but, before he could reply, the Minister continued, "Where Communism is vice versa."

Charlie's rebuttal got no further than his lips before the meaning sunk in, and the laughter around the table covered his confusion.

I am happy to say that from then on we had a pleasant evening, hosted and entertained by a skilled politician who knew better than to get into a debate on politics with a future investor.

Back in London, and after lengthy meetings with the Columbia boys and the offer of money on the table, it was decided that we would do a full-scale recce of the coastal area. We would find out whether the locations were suited to Ray's work, and the production designer's ideas. It would also give us an idea of how the Yugoslavs worked, and we could test their worth, as it were. Whilst in Yugoslavia I had discussed our locations requirements and they had suggested an area South of Dubrovnik in Montenegro. I had brought back a stack of photos and books on the area and everyone thought that it looked an ideal spot.

The night before I left, Paula and I had a big row, and when I left the next morning, for the first time in our tempestuous relationship, we did not make up; we did not even say good-bye.

Summer 1961 I left for Budva with Ray Harryhausen, the designer, Geoff Drake, his assistants Bert Smith and Jack Maxted. Tickets had been arranged through the Yugoslavian National Airline, JAT, which was an airline on a par with Aeroflot, the Russian airline. The international flights were not too good, but not *too* bad. However, the domestic internal flights were a frightening nightmare! Once, when coming in to land, just as the wheels touched the ground, there was a screeching sound as the pilot put on full power and swooped up into the sky. I asked one of the attendants what was happening, and she replied, "Oh nothing – just clearing the sheep off the runway!"

Our destination was Dubrovnik. But we had to change flights in Belgrade, where we cleared Customs and ran into our first taste of Yugoslavian bureaucracy. It took forever to get through Customs, as they inspected every bit of luggage and were very suspicious of all the cameras as well as the plans and maps of the Southern area. They also searched for money, for one had to declare how much you were carrying. Bert Smith had an unopened leather case with straps, and one of the Customs' Officers just took out a sharp knife and slashed the straps to open it. It was quite unnecessary, as he only had to ask. He was typical of many of the police and other petty officials we came across.

We stayed in Dubrovnik that night (once described by Mel Brooks as a place where half a million people share one electric light bulb), and travelled the next day to where we would be based for the next few days, Sveti Stefan, the pride of the Yugoslavian tourist industry. Being good Communists, they wanted to attract a more up-market type of visitor. To this end, they had developed several five star hotels, and Sveti Stefan was the jewel in the crown.

It had originally been a small fishing village, but they had re-housed the fishermen and their families on the mainland, built a causeway out to the island, and then converted the houses into luxury bedrooms and suites. They turned the shops into bars, souvenir shops, and boutiques. There was also an indoor restaurant and a fabulous terrace restaurant looking out onto the Adriatic. In all it was a unique luxurious hotel. The only trouble was the management.

The director was a party official who presumably got his job because of his political connections, and certainly not through any hotel experience. Nothing ever quite worked, and though most times it was comical and one could have a good laugh, other times it could be tedious and frustrating. For example, if something was not on the menu, you couldn't have it. I once I asked for fresh figs. Which request was flatly turned down. So I stood up and picked one off the tree above me!

Still, it was the most gorgeous place, and the first time I saw it I found it hard to believe that was where we would be staying. It was like a Disney cartoon castle, a brown vision set in a shimmering sea, silhouetted against the blue, blue sky.

As we walked along the causeway, I looked down the beach and a cute little thing in a skimpy pale blue bikini took my eye. I nudged Bert Smith. "I'm going to have that," I muttered, in the charming way that men have when they talk to each other about women. Later that night, after a long tiring day, and with an early call the next day, we all headed for bed. As we passed Dushco's Bar, this girl was sitting outside with some other people, and as we passed, she put her foot out and said in a foreign accent, "Why don't you stay and join us?"

I was tired so I declined the invitation. However, the following night we finished very late, and every one of our gang had gone to bed. I thought I would try to find her, as I had been thinking about her all day. However, my luck was out, and I guessed she must have gone to bed too, so I sat in Dushco's empty bar nursing a drink, and nursing something more than that as well. Dushco, the barman, spoke little English so conversation was not exactly flowing. However, he got the gist of my predicament. He made a telephone call, and shortly after took me down to some gardens and introduced me to a sweet little Serbian girl who worked in the hotel. Well, it wasn't what I had had in mind when I started the evening, but at least it was going to solve one problem. We sat on some rocks while she explained to me in her sparse but pretty English that we would have to wait until they closed the office and the director went to his room.

She was really very cute, with a great big flowing bosom, yet so tiny. As we sat chatting, I was aware of something, perhaps an animal, moving in the bushes. My companion didn't seem to notice anything as she was too busy talking, and getting to know me. Suddenly out of nowhere appeared the bikini girl. "Mind if I join you?" she asked chirpily.

Well, then I was in the shit. There I was, about to get laid, and up pops a girl I fancy. It was an impossible situation. Firstly, I felt embarrassed; secondly, I was dying to get to know the bikini girl – but, boy!, it would be good to be in the sack, and I had a guaranteed lay.

However, I need not have worried, because the two girls took over, and started chatting happily together, so much so I felt right out of it. I think at one time, I even fell asleep. I know we saw the dawn up together, and then my little Serbian friend thought she should catch a few hours' sleep before she had to start work.

My bikini girl, a Dutch girl called Ineke (an impossible name which I never could remember), decided to go for a swim. And what a swim it was! We rushed down the beach and into the sea. The rising sun's bright red rays slanted across the sea, flashing like some electrical fusing creating turmoil of colour. Just the two us, alone in the sea, cavorting like two inelegant dolphins as we swam together, diving down into the clear water, our solitude only broken by a passing turtle.

"Did you see that?" we shouted in unison, which made us laugh and added to this magical moment in time.

We held onto each other, hugged and kissed, breaking away, only to rejoin quickly as though scared to let each other go. Little did I think that those salty kisses were to be the start of a life-long love affair, which time and age have only deepened.

This was August 1961. And two days after we met, I asked her to marry me.

What made me so sure? After all, this was my third attempt. How did I know, in such a short time, that this was the woman I wanted to spend the rest of my life with? I shall never know.

Two-and-a-half days later, she accepted. Again I cannot fathom out why. I think I give the credit to the turtle!

Well, this caused something of sensation. Charlie spoke to me rather like a father, certainly not like an employer. "John, having a bit of a fling is up to you and her. But asking her to marry you … that is something else! Are you serious, or are you just trying to get her into bed?"

He was a very moral man, kind and thoughtful, and he wasn't going to have one of his gang treat this or any other girl badly. I respected him for that. Once I convinced him that indeed it was for real, things changed and he could not have been nicer to the two of us. Whenever we stopped for lunch, Charlie would send the car back so Ineke could have the midday meal with us. Everyone thought Charlie was cold and thoughtless, and I wished others could see that other side of him. He was a strange mixture, and I think he wanted to be like the late Harry Cohn, the ogre and President of Columbia. The trouble was, Charlie was a nice man, and Harry Cohn certainly was not.

Ineke was a girl from The Hague, the daughter of an artist and architect. She used to talk about their butler and I thought for a crazy moment that I might be marrying into money. Sadly for all concerned, the money had run out a long time before. The reason she was in Yugoslavia was that her brother (actually her step-brother, both her parents having been married before) and his two children lived in Belgrade. He was divorced from his wife, and Ineke had gone there to make sure that the children were being looked after. Whilst in Belgrade, she met up with a young American family who asked her to join them on holiday in Sveti Stefan.

The young father was in the American diplomatic service, and worked in the embassy in Belgrade. There was quite a large number of them including his wife's father and mother, the two of them and the four children. They were a wonderful Bostonian family, and in many ways more English than the English. The father told me proudly that he only ever smoked Craven A cigarettes. I hadn't the heart to tell him that no one any longer smoked that brand in England, and in fact I was surprised that they were still made. The young father, Douglas, was educated at both Eton and Harvard, and it would be hard to think of a more prestigious education. (I suppose some would say Harrow and Yale!) Though Douglas and his wife divorced, we have remained friends with him and the children. After all, if it hadn't been for them, Ineke and I would never have met.

Despite my new love, there was work to be done. As soon as we had covered the land locations we were to go to sea to study the coastline for the many scenes aboard the Argos, and another big sequence known as the Clashing Rocks, where Neptune holds the sides of the rocks up so the Argo can sail through safely. These scenes were mainly the concern of Ray and he needed to settle on a suitable and interesting location so he could recreate it exactly in the studio. We would shoot the boat entering the narrow channel on the location, and shoot the rocks falling, and Neptune rising out of the sea to hold them back on a miniature set in the studio.

We hired a fishing boat and crew and gradually made our way down the coast almost to the Albanian border. The fishermen were great guys and we soon fell into their evil ways. They had said it was best to make an early start, and not to have breakfast as they would supply that on the boat. We set sail, and it wasn't long before there were cries in Serbian that breakfast was being served. One of the crew appeared with a loaf of bread under one arm, some local ham under the other, and a wicked looking knife in his right hand. He hacked off a large slice of bread, and taking the ham from under his arm attacked it with the knife. I thought Charlie was going to throw up, and he declined to even have a taste.

This was quickly followed by another crew member who handed out glasses and poured large amounts of white wine from a plastic container, similar to a jerry can. It was the final straw for Charlie, and he went off with his fellow American, whilst the rest of us and the crew sat around on the deck, having a magnificent start to the day. Mind you, I had the intelligence not to eat the red peppers we were offered, but poor old Jack Maxted dived in, and nearly exploded. It was impossible for him to stop drinking for hours, and despite having, as he said, a cast iron stomach, he never ever again ate a red pepper. Charlie never came out with us again, and returned the next day to London.

We continued the search for the right spots, and got into a daily routine, with numerous stops at small coastal villages to study the terrain and replenish the wine container. Ray would study the rocks and ask anyone who happened to pass, regardless of their nationality, "Have you seen any interesting rock formations?"

We would stop for lunch in small villages, eating and drinking whatever was put in front of us, except for Ray, who was strictly a meat and potatoes man. After lunch most of us had a siesta, including the crew. On several occasions Ray woke the Captain up when he realised that the boat was heading out to sea with no one at the wheel!

We had an interpreter with us, and we had plenty of time to talk to these tough fishermen. The interpreter was a young Serbian from Belgrade and was a lot of fun, unlike the mainly dour ones that I had come across before. We talked about the war, and their total hatred for the Germans. I pointed out that they were their friends now, with all the East German tourists in Budva, which was fairly close to Sveti Stefan. Without any embarrassment, she said, "Ah yes, good for fucking." It seems that the fishermen would go along with their boat close to the shore, scoop up two or more girls, take them out to sea, have their way with them and, bringing them back, throw them in the sea. From what I have heard of the general treatment of these East Germans, this was only part of what went on. The Captain told me that the girls used to wait in the sea for them, and it was the high note of their holiday. It was just sex, sand, and slivovitz.

Slivovitz, plum brandy, is a particularly foul alcoholic drink. It smells of old socks and in my opinion tastes like them too! One night Ray and I and our girl interpreter were in town called Titograd. I stayed up drinking slivovitz with a party of Serbs, finally tottered to my room, undressed, brushed my teeth and collapsed into bed. What seemed like seconds later, I found myself lying on the floor. I thought, "That bloody slivovitz", and got back into bed and fell fast asleep again. Then bang, I was back on the floor again. I crawled back to bed thinking, "Never again, I shall sign the pledge, no doubt about it", and fell asleep.

Going down to breakfast, I spotted Ray in the cavernous dining room, already tucking into a plate of eggs, and looking indecently healthy. I sat down with him, but could only face a black coffee. We sat in silence for a while until Ray suddenly said, "Looked for you in the park last night."

"Why the hell were you looking for me in the park?"

Finishing the last of his eggs, he replied, "When they evacuated the hotel when the earthquake hit."

"What earthquake?"

He looked at me in disbelief, "You don't know about the earthquake? Look up there." He pointed to the large staircase where a huge crack split the wall. He could not believe that I had slept through the shaking, the noise, the cries of the staff clearing the hotel, the klaxon blaring. I didn't like to tell him the reason!

Back in Sveti Stefan the romance still bloomed. Ineke sent a cable to her parents in Holland saying: "Engaged to John Dark of London. Please try and delay family reunion so both he and I can attend."

On the work front, on the other hand, things were not good.

I was becoming more and more disenchanted with our Serbian colleagues. The estimates were coming in from our female construction manager, and we could have rebuilt Dubrovnik for the money. In addition, the quality of the workmanship was not to the standard required for a first feature American production. If we ever so gently pointed out some of this, I would get back a lot of gobbledygook like, "We have seen your American films, and our quality is better." And that would be that. In no way did they want to either learn, or even agree that the man who pays the piper might be allowed not only to call the tune, but also to even ask for a change of melody.

The high costs, the quality and their obstinacy made me more and more nervous. I called the Columbia office in London, and voiced my apprehensions. I pointed out that time was getting short, we would miss the weather and have to postpone shooting until the following year. They were supportive, and were not surprised by my report. We discussed what we could do, and I suggested that we could possibly make the film in Italy, where Columbia had their own offices and had made many movies there. I then rang Charlie, and went over the same ground. As he had been there himself, he was able to grasp the problem quickly, and when I gave him some of the Yugoslavian quotes, he realised that the money invested by the Yugoslavs would not compensate for the added expenses. He agreed that I should go to Italy.

I left Paul Maslansky in Sveti Stefan, with a couple of the art department, the rest having already gone back to London, and I set off for Rome. In Italy I met the local Columbia production man, an Englishman called Roger Good, and their accountant, Giorgio Migliarini. I discussed with them the budget, and got comparative figures so I could estimate the difference in costs between the two countries. I immediately felt happier. We had the opportunity of getting expert film makers at every level, plus we had the back-up of the local Columbia office and staff.

But where in Italy could we base ourselves?

After pouring over books, photos and maps, we settled on an area in the South. What attracted us there the most was that there was an ancient Greek temple there, which would save building a big and expensive set.

I made a lightning trip down to the area and quickly realised that we could find all the locations we needed there, the rocky coastline was ideal for Ray, and the temple was marvellous. I quickly called London and said that there were some shortcomings, like hotel accommodation and other general facilities. But for the look of the film it was magnificent. That night we moved out of Yugoslavia.

I returned to London, and stayed at my mother's flat. Paula and I, as I said, had had a row the night before I left, and for the first time in our relationship, we didn't make it up before parting. I do not know whether this had anything to do with it, but she somehow did not seem surprised when I phoned her, but she did insist that I see her and tell her to her face. We met at Genaro's restaurant (now the Groucho Club) and had a tearful, unhappy meal. Genaro, the owner, always gave his female clients a rose, and when I said good-bye to her at the stage door and as I turned to walk away, she called out "John", and as I turned back, she threw the rose at me, and entered the theatre.

Poor darling Paula, it was a wonderful romance but it was doomed to fail. We were like two fireworks, but when the noise, the excitement, the sparkle died, we were like two empty firework *containers*, with nothing to fall back on. We had our love, and we had passion, but in the end, that was all, and it wasn't enough. I shall always have a very special place in my heart for her. She did many things for me, and helped me a lot in my career. She smartened me up, always inspecting me before I left for work. She entertained my colleagues and friends. She was more than kind to my family. Peter, my brother, was especially fond of her. Unlike my mother, on the other hand, who was fond of quoting "East is East and West is West and never the twain shall meet". Maybe she was right. Anyhow, we still keep in touch, and I have great warmth and love for her. She has been happily married now for a long time to a rich Norwegian and lives in Oslo. She has two grandsons and is as happy as she can be, I think, living outside of the East.

I flew to Holland to meet all Ineke's family, who were coming from as far as Brazil for a once in a lifetime family reunion. Ineke met me at Schiphol airport, and told me later that she was worried she would not recognise me! Ours was such a whirlwind romance, in such a romantic setting and as she said, there you could fall in love with a hunch-backed dwarf!

As she drove me to the family home in The Hague, she gave me a rundown of who would be there. She also scared me by saying I would have to formally ask for her hand in marriage, adding, "Just think yourself lucky. When Loek, her brother-in-law, proposed to my sister he not only had to come and formally ask, he had to dress up in a morning suit, complete with top hat!" My God, I thought, what kind of bourgeois family am I getting into?

Her parents lived in a large impressive house, and I was greeted there by these charming people, and made to feel right at home. Before I could hardly open my mouth, her father was pouring me a large drink. This wasn't just hospitality I found out later, but an excuse to have one himself. Now, if any man deserved a drink it was him.

Ineke's father had been a prominent figure in the Dutch underground in the Second World War, until he was captured. Firstly he was sent to the local prison less than a mile away from his home, where life was not too bad. His wife used to smuggle his Dutch gin to him by pretending it was cleaning fluid, which he needed to paint the guards' portraits. This didn't last for long though, and he was all too soon sent to Buchenwald concentration camp in Germany, where he spent the next four years. This small, dapper man was always formally attired in a three-piece blue suit, a gold watch chain adorning his waistcoat. He breathed bonhomie, and exuded warmth, kindness and compassion to all who came into his orbit, loving the world and the people that populated it. His family and friends adored him, and it was hard to reconcile this sweet man with an underground guerrilla leader. Even after his arrest and deportation to Buchenwald, he still kept up his illegal activities – illegal to the Germans, that is.

I suppose the real story of Henri Pieck will never be told. By the time I met him his mind was already beginning to go, and I was only able to piece together the vaguest of stories. However, some things I did know. I knew he was a Communist, and had always been desperate to see a better balance in the world between the rich and the poor. To this end he studied Marxism and in the 20s travelled extensively in Russia. He made many contacts there, but all both Ineke and I really know is that long after the Second World War, John Kennedy, then President of the United States, had him flown to Washington to help his government understand the Russian leaders better. Poor darling, by this time he was well over the hill, and I am sure they can have gleaned nothing from him. On the other hand, he had a whale of a time, especially as because of bad weather they had to land in New York and spend the night there. Most people would never stop bitching about it, but the old man said, "It was fantastic, there I was going to Washington, but I got to see New York as well." His cup was always half full, never half empty, a trait inherited by his daughter, Ineke.

Stories from Buchenwald were sparse. It wasn't that he was reluctant to talk about his time there, it was more, I think, that he wasn't terribly keen on talking about himself. It was through his paintings and his sketches that I was able to piece together certain things.

Buchenwald was a concentration camp supplying labour to the armament factory next door, and not a death camp like Auschwitz. It housed underground offenders like Henri Pieck, undesirables like gypsies, gays, Russians, and Polish prisoners-of-war, who under the Geneva Convention should never have been there at all. The Russians seemed to have been treated the worst and few survived. Each country and each group had its own leader, and they held frequent meetings to see what could be done to help each other, or to frustrate the Germans. One way, my father-in-law told me, was to pander to their self-importance. An example of this was when two of their friends, two Polish soldiers, were due to be executed. Henri went to the Camp Commandant and told him that the two men were meteorologists, and that he found it amazing that Buchenwald had no meteorological station. He pointed out that every camp, including all the American ones, had one, but not Buchenwald. The execution was stopped, and the two men spent the rest of their time in the camp sitting under a thermometer. My father-in law painted the scene, and it now hangs on our sitting room wall in our house in Spain.

Apart from working in the factory, they also produced serum for the German Army. Now this was a wonderful thing as it gave the prisoners two great advantages. One was that the Germans were scared stiff of disease, so the prisoners put up numerous signs saying: "Warning! Contaminated Area" and they were more or less left alone. The second was that they said they needed rabbits to make the serum, and this gave them a constant supply of fresh food. Mind you, he never ate rabbit again after his release.

Another amazing thing about Buchenwald was that the prisoners freed themselves. They used to smuggle back bits from the factory, and reassemble them in the camp, until they had quite an armoury. Once they heard the Allied troops were in the area, they emerged with their guns, and the Germans fled.

As he was the leader of the Dutch underground in the camp, Queen Wilhelmina, the Dutch Queen, sent her own plane to pick him up and bring him home. He was a brave, clever, dedicated man, who seemed to be without bitterness. I told him that I couldn't imagine what he went through. "Well, I must say it was a very interesting experience." As I said, it was hard to reconcile this kindly, warm-hearted man with a leader in one of Germany's infamous camps. But then he was a man of great contradictions, being not only a Communist but also a Monarchist! He soon had my admiration, and over a short time had my love. The sad thing was that at the end of his life he realised that Communism had not brought about the justice and well-being for all that he had hoped for. Rather it had become just another way of oppressing the people it purported to serve. To that end I think he died disillusioned politically.

The dinner party went off well with the big family gathered around the dining table. Even the old butler came back specially for the night. Just before the meal, I whispered to Ineke, "There are not going to be any speeches, are there?"

"No," she assured me.

But we had hardly sat down when one of the family got up to speak. I quickly realised that I would be expected to say a few words as well, especially as they all spoke in English out of courtesy to myself. The time came, and I was at a loss for a minute until I remembered a film that I had worked on as a kid many years before, called "Dear Octopus", based on the play by Terrence Rattigan. I stood up and gave the speech from the family reunion scene. Did anyone have a better speech writer?

My new Dutch family was more than impressed, and I think her parents thought that the right man had been found for their daughter. Ineke and I returned to London after a happy weekend. She was pleased that I had got on with her family so well, and so was I, for finding how good it was to be with my new love and her delightful family.

Then off to Italy. Rome was a lot of fun. "Cleopatra" was being filmed and the city was full of British and American film-makers and actors. We all used to congregate in Dave Crowley's bar.

Dave was a British boxing champion, turned stunt man. He had been a great friend of Errol Flynn's and had a hundred stories of their exploits together. He knew most of the people in the business, because as soon as one arrived in Rome, it was off to Dave's Bar to catch up on the gossip and find out who was in town. It was a great meeting place, and you could meet everyone there, from the Burtons to a stunt man.

"Cleopatra" certainly added to the gaiety of the city but it also brought with it many problems. It was such a gigantic production, with a budget to match, that it had virtually monopolised the whole of the Italian film industry. My Italian costume designer reported to me that there were no period clothes, like Roman soldiers' uniforms, for hire as "Cleopatra" had the lot. We had to resort to various illicit methods to get the materials we wanted. Money changed hands in the middle of the night, trucks were parked down dark alleys, and bit by bit we put the clothes together.

These kinds of escapades were always difficult to explain to the accounts' office in Los Angeles. Despite both the Rome and London offices trying to explain the Italian way of doing business, they still insisted that you had to have receipts for everything. The "black" economy was still a mystery to them, and they just thought that the production was ripping them off. These arguments used to roll on for years. It was hard enough in Italy at the best of times to operate without resorting to "black" money, but in the "Cleopatra" days it was impossible.

At this time, the director, Don Chaffey, came on board. He was an ex-production designer and had directed several films, none of them of any particular note. Technically he was very proficient, but he was not especially talented. What he lacked in flair, he made up for in noise.

He and Charlie never got on, and this caused a strain throughout the picture. Charlie could be difficult and there is no doubt he was pound-foolish. However, he bent over backwards to help Don but only got firmly kicked in the rear. There again, nobody ever said you had to love each other when you make a picture.

Charlie flew in with his family, his wife Shirley and their three daughters. We had a pleasant night out in Rome, and I found all four female members of the family charming. I took them around several of the more famous places and got a horse-drawn carriage to take them back to their hotel. The children were agog with the wonders of the city, and thrilled by their transport. Unfortunately it was ruined by Charlie constantly asking, "How much does this cost, John?"

I was sitting up with the driver and just ignored Charlie's repeated question. As we pulled up in the Via Veneto, I quickly slipped the money into the driver's hand, and leapt out of the carriage. Charlie stood up, "How much is it, John?"

"Don't worry, Charlie, it's all paid for."

Even when I was across the road I could still hear him, standing up in the carriage saying, "John, how much? You're embarrassing me, John."

A few days later I was sitting in the foyer of the Jolly Hotel in Salerno, trying to make a deal with a boat owner to rent his vessel as a camera boat, when I heard the front door open, and a familiar voice saying, "How much for a chicken sandwich?"

"Que?" the puzzled doorman replied.

"A chicken sandwich, how much do you charge?" I didn't need to turn, it could only be one person. Not getting anywhere, Charlie spied a waiter, "Hey, could you tell me how much for a chicken sandwich?"

The waiter gazed at him, not understanding, "*Signor?*"

"Chicken sandwich, how much? Where's the manager?"

The waiter understood the word "manager". "Pliss," the waiter replied, knocking on the door of the lobby, which was opened by the manager.

After a few words from the waiter, the manager turned to Charlie and in perfect English asked how could he help.

"How much do you charge for a chicken sandwich?"

The manager was rather puzzled. "Well, let me see, I think we charge about two thousand lire, *signor*. One moment." And in Italian he asked the waiter the cost, which was confirmed at two thousand lire.

"Right, how much for six?" asked Charlie.

"Well, that would be twelve thousand lire."

"That's ridiculous." And he then started to give the manager a lesson in retailing. Charlie had his family and driver outside in the car, and he was negotiating for their lunch. Though I found it hard to believe, I also thought that at least he was the same at home as he was in the office!

Casting was completed, although it was not very inspiring. The role of Jason went to a young American actor, Todd Armstrong, who was under contract to Columbia, and supporting him was another Columbia contract artist, Nancy Kovack. Neither of them achieved much in the future, but quite honestly neither of them deserved much either. Both were good-looking, and that was just about it. A substantial number of the cast came from the "Cleopatra" repertory company, consisting of a group of British actors who had been engaged to play any part that might come up! Most of the time they just sat around enjoying the Eternal City. The money was good so there were many talented people amongst them. Though it wasn't the most exciting job in the world, it gave them an opportunity to see Rome at the company's expense, and put some money in the bank at the same time.

Charlie was over the moon as he was able to make a deal with several of them, engaging them at the local rate, which was much lower than he would have to pay if we brought them out from England. Also, he didn't have to pay their air fares because they all held return tickets from "Cleopatra". He told me that he wasn't going to pay them any living allowance, with which I disagreed, for, though I could run a very tight ship, I also knew when you had to pay money. I pointed out to him that even if we brought actors, Italian or foreign, down from Rome to the South, we would have to pay them either an allowance or alternatively house them and feed them. He wouldn't have it, and insisted that that was the deal he had made with them, and the deal that they had accepted. I warned him it would cause trouble, and pointed out that you couldn't have one group not receiving a brass nickel when the rest of the company were in receipt of a big allowance. For I had made a deal with the British crew that they would receive the same allowance in the South as they got in Rome, compensating them for the bad living conditions on the Southern location. This was the cause of our very first row, but I had already done the deal so there was little he could about it. I promised him it would pay dividends in the end, and this certainly proved to be more than true, for the boys and girls had a really tough time, but never once complained.

Well, I won that one, but lost the argument over the actors.

When the British actors arrived, amongst them eminent names like Laurence Naismith, Nigel Greene, and Gary Raymond – to name just three – and they found out that they were supposed to pay for their own accommodation and food, we very nearly didn't have a cast. A quick call from Mike Frankovitch to Charlie settled the dispute, and we were able to get going.

We were based in a small village, Palinuro, South of Salerno. It had one hotel, and two restaurants, and living conditions were pretty grim. Ineke and I had a room in an unfinished house – so unfinished that the staircase upwards was just concrete steps, no banister. Not that it mattered, as it led to nowhere: the upstairs never having been completed.

Most of the artists, Charlie, and Don were in the hotel and the rest of the crew dotted around in various houses all over the place. The roads were terrible and it was difficult to get to the various locations. However, the scenery was magnificent, with miles and miles of unspoilt beaches with not a soul on them, for the very good reason there was no way of getting on to them. We used a lot of donkey transport, including sending down bottled water as the company was shooting in the hot sun. Several loads never arrived and the following day there would be a different donkey crew. When we asked where the others were, they just shrugged their shoulders. In the end a meeting was arranged between me and the local Mafia chief. He was a funny little man, not like a gangster at all, more like a comfortably off peasant, and very polite. I asked for his support in getting the co-operation of the local people, and said that we would be engaging a lot of them for the film, and hopefully bringing a little temporary financial benefit to the local area. I also assured him that we would be giving him a sum of money for him to donate to any charity that he liked. From then on we had much less trouble.

Not only was it a tough location, with bad accommodation, but the choice between the two restaurants was of little consequence as they both served the same food: pasta and veal. The day they killed the pig in the village was a red letter day, we all ate pork that evening and did so until it eventually ran out and we were back to veal. The weather was hot, the shooting all day long, and because we had no caterers, the crew brought their own lunch and snacks. I can't imagine a modern day crew putting up with such conditions.

Shooting with Ray Harryhausen taught me a lot. He had perfected the system of marrying live action with puppets. In today's world of computer technology, it all seems very antiquated and the results poor. However, there are many science-fiction fans who still think that Ray's work has never been surpassed, and he certainly was a master of this particular field.

I think that "Jason …" will always be remembered for the skeleton sword fight, where six skeletons fight six of the Argonauts. Ray and the Stunt Arranger choreographed the fight using six stunt men, dressed in white as the skeletons, and a further six stunt men doubling for the actors. When the plan of the fight was finalised they brought in the actors and then decided which parts of the fight they could do and which parts the stunt doubles did.

On the day of the shoot, Ray would first of all shoot the fight in black-and-white, with the six stunt men still dressed in white playing the skeletons. Then the stunt men would step out, colour film would be loaded back into the camera and, having memorised the moves, the actors would then fight the imaginary skeletons.

It is has to be said that it did look rather comical, with Argonauts slashing away at seemingly nothing. The Italian audience, who gathered everyday to watch our antics, loved every minute of it, and used to roll about laughing watching these mad foreigners battling away against nothing.

Back at the studio, in his own little stage, Ray would have the piece of film with the stunt men doubling the skeletons so he could match the miniature skeletons.

In a way, it was an actor's nightmare, and some were much better at it than others. Sadly, one of the worst was our leading actor, Todd. He just wasn't cut out to be a period action artist. Except for one day, whilst I was watching, when he suddenly turned into a frantic Errol Flynn. I wondered what had got into him, then as he was slicing away into the thin air, I heard him say, "Fucking wasps!"

One day our Italian production manager told me that I had been summoned to appear before the local council. On enquiring what it was all about he said, "No idea, but I bet they're after money. It's just a case of how they intend going about getting it."

We were soon to find out.

Leon and I duly turned up and were confronted by about twenty men, all in their Sunday suits, looking very serious. The Leader of the council got up and talked for about half-an-hour. The gist of which was that the council was going to sue us for the damage that our trucks had done to their roads, but before they took legal action, and in a spirit of goodwill, they wanted to hear what I intended to do about it.

Through Leon I said that I appreciated their consulting me first. I pointed out the economic value of our film to their area, the money spent locally, the numbers of unemployed people given work and so on. I ended by saying that it was strange that they should think of suing me for the damage that our trucks had done to their roads, for only that morning I was seriously thinking of taking action against the council for the damage that their roads had done to our trucks! This brought an amazing response, as they all burst into laughter.

As the meeting broke up, they came over to shake my hand, slapped me on the back and we all retired to the local hostelry. Oh, I do love the Italian people.

Every village has its idiot, and Palinuro was no exception. He was a big fat boy who had outgrown his strength. He was the butt of the locals, the recipient of taunts, the victim of the local bullies. We were always very sorry for this kid, and whenever we could, we would give him a day's work in the crowd. Unbeknown to us, he had never drawn any of his daily fees. On the last day he drew all the money that he was owed, and that evening walked down to one of the two restaurants, put the pile of notes on the table, ordered himself a gigantic meal, a bottle of wine, and sat there like a king. He ordered the staff about in dictatorial manner, calling them every name under the sun. "Hey, shit-bag, bring me more steak!" he would shout.

The staff hurried around him, whilst the local villagers gathered around outside the café, and watched as the boy ate through the pile of notes. Probably for the first time in his life he wasn't hungry, not hungry and not abused.

The next day we moved back to Rome for the interior sequences, back to civilisation with its wonderful restaurants, great hotels, and to the city I loved so much. All too soon, we wrapped up in Rome and moved back to Shepperton studios for the travelling matte work, which we were unable to complete in Rome as they did not possess the equipment or the technical knowledge.

We were shooting on the largest stage in the studio. We had a full size replica of the Argo mounted on hydraulic rams to simulate the rocking of the boat. The blue screen background would be replaced later with scenes that we had shot in Italy. One day I was standing on the set high up in the air when I was aware of someone whispering. I turned and saw the Chief shop steward, who had climbed up a tall ladder to talk to me.

"What?" I asked.

"The Bovril," he replied.

"The Bovril?" I repeated with some incredulity.

"Yes, John, the 'ot Bovril. When shooting on this stage in the winter, you 'ave to supply 'ot Bovril." I knew I was back in England.

With the main shooting completed, it was time for Ray to retire to his magic room, with just one electrician, in order to supply the exciting elements. There he would start to marry the film with his incredible miniature figures, shooting a frame a time. Each frame is slightly different from the last, so in the end you have the continuous movement required. It was a highly skilled task, requiring endless patience. When on occasions I asked how he was doing, he would say something like, "Good, shot twenty frames today." Well, as film goes through the camera at twenty-four frames a second, you get some idea of how tedious his work was.

When I saw "Jason ..." after it was completed, I thought Ray had done an amazing job. The skeleton fight especially came over so well. I think that this was because his technique of stop-frame photography suited the jerky movements associated with skeletons. In the same way with any fur covered four-legged creature the mechanical movement detracted from the lithe movement of the creature. Whatever it was, I was always grateful to Ray for teaching me so much, and giving me the opportunity of working with a master.

Columbia were over the moon, with the picture coming in well under budget, which originally was thought too tight to be met. Charlie was delighted and gave me an amazing paper thin Piaget watch. After thanking him, I couldn't help adding, "God, Charlie, how many sleepless nights did you have over this?"

So, there I was again, out on the street looking for a new film. Also getting ready to take on a new wife. My divorce with Peggy was through, thanks in large part to Ted Bushel!

I had a meeting with the divorce detectives who told me that it was no longer necessary to go away with a girl, and let one of their men take photos of you both in bed. All that was needed was to get a girl to sign a confession that she had slept with you. So I went to Bushel (who else?) and told him to find out how much one of the tarts (now known as hookers) would charge.

He came back a few days later and said, "Well, guv, the cheapest one was a tenner. But I tell you what, the old women will do it for a fiver!" Hence my divorce was for committing adultery with Mrs Bushel!

I was free to marry again, the date was set: June 16, 1962, and I rang Peggy to tell her.

Much to my surprise, she asked me if I would like the children to come, which proposal I gratefully accepted. The only proviso was that I should tell the children myself that I was getting married.

I arrived at her house in Albany Street, and was greeted by the children with great excitement.

"What is it? What is it?" they cried, having been primed by their mother that I had something to tell them.

After the kisses and the hugs, and with the two of them dancing around me, we sat down in the sitting room and I said to them, "I have come to see if you would like to come to my wedding on Saturday."

"Don't be ridiculous," said Gregory, giving us the benefit of his eleven years of experience, "that's bigamy!"

"No, darling," said Peg, "Daddy and I have been separated for years."

Greg threw himself back in the chair, "That's the problem with this family," he said with an air of resignation, "nobody tells me anything!"

Peggy asked to meet Ineke, so we both went and picked up the children for the ceremony and the reception. They were both charming to each other, though Peggy did tell a friend afterwards, "I give it two years."

How wrong can you be!

I asked Charlie to be my Best Man, which he was kind enough to accept. He gave us a set of beautiful carvers, and I made the mistake of not giving him a penny. It is said that you should never give a friend a knife. You can sell it, but not give it, or the friendship will be cut.

It was a simple wedding at the Kensington Registry office, with a small reception at the "22 Restaurant" in Dover Street. Ineke's two sisters and brother-in-law, Loek, came over from Holland, which was so good for Ineke. The children seemed not only to enjoy it all, but also seemed to get on with Ineke very well. There was no way that we could have a honeymoon: I had to find work.

Luckily that did not take long. Columbia called me and asked me to work on another film for them. They said there was good news, and bad news. The good news was that the film was to be directed by Carol Reed, a director I had long admired for having directed such wonderful films as "Odd Man Out", "The Fallen Idol", and of course the amazing "The Third Man". The bad news was that there was an associate producer involved. Carol would produce as well as direct and he had an Associate. I was not happy with this at all as I had always been on my own, no matter what credit I had, so I turned the job down. Columbia then put pressure on me by increasing my money and telling me how good it would be for me to work with a director of Carol's standing. Well, I had a divorce to pay, alimony payments to be met, a new home, and nothing else on offer. Apart from the money, I liked Columbia and I certainly did not want to upset my good relationship with them.

The movie was entitled "The Running Man" with Lee Remick and Alan Bates. The locations were in Spain, but as the leading man, Laurence Harvey, could not work in the UK for tax reasons, the studio work was to be in Ireland. This meant that I would be away with all my expenses paid for something like six months, and so I could save most of my fee. I accepted. What I couldn't understand why they were so keen to have me when they had such an experienced production trained associate producer, but I was to find out!

What I never ever found out was what he actually did. He certainly never gave me any advice, help, or instructions. Now and again he would give me a message from Carol, and that was about it. Whenever trouble loomed, he would depart for somewhere else. What was worse, he never backed me up when I had trouble with Carol.

And trouble I had in spades! He rode the shit out of me: if it rained, it was my fault … nothing was ever right. Luckily I had good allies in the lighting cameraman, the famous Bob Krasker, and also Bert Bates, Carol's editor. Both of whom had worked a lot with Carol, and were very close to him. They were my defenders against Carol's constant criticism.

Both of them were experts at their jobs, yet very different. Bobby was gay and very aesthetic, whilst Bert was a bluff, hearty, "a spade is a spade" type of Englishman. Bobby was born in Australia, studied photography in Europe, then moved to England and became one of Britain's, indeed one of the world's, great Cameramen. He won an Oscar for his work on Carol's "The Third Man". We became great friends, but he was not always easy.

He dreamt up a system of "bouncing" light through plate glass, and wherever we went in Spain we had to move these giant panels of glass about on low-loaders. Getting fed up with the cost of transportation and storage, especially as we had never used them, I told him I was going to get rid of the glass. He looked daggers at me and said, "You do that and I shall go straight home." So we carried them around for another few days until he tried the system out, found it didn't work, and that was that.

He was an expensive cameraman, but so good. Actresses loved him, for no one enhanced their beauty better than he did. I always thought it sad that he was not interested in them other than as a job.

My favourite story of Bert Bates was when leaving New York, his American colleagues turned up at the airport to see him off. The plane was delayed and several bottles of champagne were consumed before the time came for him to board. In those days the Strato-cruisers had sleepers. So, on boarding, Bert asked the Flight Attendant if there was a spare one, and because of a cancellation, he was in luck. Bert got into the bunk and before the plane took off he was fast asleep. He was woken by the most awful screeching noise, with the plane shuddering. He broke out in a sweat, pulled the curtain back, and yelled for the Flight Attendant, but nothing happened. He climbed out as the noise and movement continued, and looked down the plane. It was empty. Not a person in sight! He walked slowly down the aisle in a state of complete shock. Finally he spied a man in a pair of white overalls, bending down holding a large pneumatic drill. He was in the hangar at London airport!

It transpired that as he had taken over an empty bunk at the last moment, the cabin crew had forgotten to put a card on the outside, and he had been forgotten! But he never forgot the nightmare of what he described as "his near-death experience".

I had another friend, another defender, in Laurence Harvey. He was a really nice person, and for some reason latched on to Ineke and myself. We had many great evenings with him, often with his latest conquest.

Not long before we started, Harry Cohn, the President of Columbia, and probably the most hated man in Hollywood, died. His wife, Joan, inherited his estate, including his Columbia shares. Now Joan had been kept very much in the background of Harry's life, leaving him free to screw everything he could lay his hands on. With him dead, it was her turn to be free, and she very quickly flew out of the cage and straight into Larry's arms. Although middle-aged, Joan was still a good-looking woman. With his looks, his charm, and possessing one of the greatest speaking voices, Larry could have had any girl (or man, because he could swing both ways) he fancied. Together they made an odd couple.

Joan joined us in Spain, and one evening during the annual Malaga Feria, we went out for dinner, where many of the diners recognised Larry. Joan was a lot of fun, and she really enjoyed the excitement of this very Spanish annual event. She was besotted by Larry, although he treated her most of the time in a very off-handed way. That evening Joan could hardly keep her hands off him, but Larry was not in the best of moods and kept trying to push her away. She twittered and whispered in his ear, until in the end he turned round to her and said in that cultured, golden voice, "Look, Joan, when are you going to understand I only fuck you for your Columbia shares?"

It didn't phase Joan one bit, after all she was trained by an expert, known by all in Hollywood as "Harry the Horror". She just said, "Doesn't he say the cutest things?"

Joan used to visit us at constant intervals, sending the Columbia offices in both London and Madrid into turmoil. Joan was a major stock- holder of the company, and they used to get themselves into a state of nerves whenever she visited. On the other hand, we used to enjoy her visits, and she and Larry threw some great parties. The end of the story was that they married, then divorced, but I don't know who got the shares. Dear Larry was to die of cancer at the age of forty-five.

I wasn't the only one having trouble with Carol.

Lee Remick was a very unhappy girl. First of all, she had her husband and young baby with her, and the marriage seemed to be a bit rocky. On top of that, Larry was notorious for not getting on with his leading ladies. She and Carol did not hit it off either, and here I think the real problem was the script. That master, John Mortimer, wrote it from a novel by Shelley Smith. The basic story was pretty slim, and the characters lacked any depth. Lee realised she had made a mistake in taking the part. She seemed to withdraw into herself and just turned up, hit the marks, and said the lines. Carol obviously wanted to get more out of her, and this is where the conflict started. She was a very nice person, and I knew from experience how difficult Carol could be, so I felt for her.

Also in the cast was Alan Bates, a lovely person. He wasn't over- enamoured by the story either, but had a different way of coping with it. He just went with the flow, kept up his enthusiasm, and did his best. He was a great actor and a great guy. Unfortunately I never worked with him again.

We were based in the Hotel Miramar (now a government building) and, as the Feria was on, the leading bull-fighters of Spain were there, most of whom stayed at our hotel. One day I was standing outside the front door of the hotel, watching the matadors and their attendants leaving for the fights, when a carriage stopped and out stepped Orson Welles.

The last time I had seen him was when we had that blazing row in Hong Kong. As he entered the hotel, he glared at me, then recognised me and threw his arms around me, greeting me like a long-lost friend. What a strange man. I have to admit that I was happy that we were back on speaking terms as he was without doubt one of the most interesting and entertaining men I ever met.

Very soon after that we moved to San Roque, a small village close to both Gibraltar and Algeciras (now a thriving tourist area complete with a golf course and a five star hotel). As we were moving, our Spanish production manager, Robert Roberts, asked Larry whether he would like to stay in a hotel or a villa.

Larry replied, "I only live in palaces."

Of course he stayed in a suite at the hotel as happy as a clam, and we never heard any more about the palaces. It was just Larry. Carol told me that he had first met Larry when he was still a student. He came up to Carol at a party and said to him, "Mr Reed I am going to be a film star, what would you suggest is the best way I go about it ?"

The main unit was shooting on the mainland, and we had an aerial unit shooting in Gibraltar. My office was in San Roque itself, in an old house we had rented for the few weeks. I used to go over to Gibraltar most days. The Gibraltarians only allowed you one visit a day, so I had to plan it quite well. I hated the place, as it had all the worst attributes of a British naval town, but I had to be nice to the officials for obvious reasons.

I made one good friend there, the Officer in Command of the RAF. He was a nice chap, who helped us immensely, especially when our camera plane crashed off the Gibraltar coast. Luckily I hadn't been to Gibraltar that day so I had no trouble at the border.

Until I got to the airport I had no idea how serious it was. There were two on board, the English pilot and our camera operator, Johnny Harris. Johnny's wife and three children were with him in Spain, and they lived above us. I hadn't told his wife, as I thought it best to first find out how serious it was. The RAF boys were waiting for me, and told me that the pilot and Johnny were already in the military hospital. Both were still alive, but they didn't know how serious their injuries were.

I immediately called my secretary and told her to tell Ursula Harris that he was alive, and to send a car to bring her to Gibraltar. Whilst we were waiting for news from the hospital, the airmen told me what happened. Our camera plane was coming in from the sea and approaching the runway, which is on the edge of the rocky coast. As the plane got closer, its engine stopped and the aircraft crashed into the sea. Three RAF boys were water skiing nearby and they quickly raced to the spot where the plane crashed. Two of them dived down and managed to free them both. The chaps in the control tower had witnessed it all, and quickly called the air force ambulance, so by the time the rescuers got them back to land, the ambulances were waiting to take them off straight away.

The report from the hospital was very encouraging and, by the time Ursula arrived, I was able to tell her that her husband was not seriously hurt, and should be released in a few days. On the other hand the pilot was in a pretty bad state. It seems that as they were landing, Johnny Harris wanted to get another shot and unbuckled his seat belt. The pilot had his done up when they crashed, and the buckle went into his spleen.

It truly had been a lucky escape, as had they been a few yards nearer, they would have been into the rocks; a fraction earlier and they would have been in deep water, and very unlikely to have got out. The military hospital was fantastic and they could not have been better looked after.

Our main problem was that the girl staying with the pilot was not his wife, and he was anxious that I should contact his real wife before she read about it in the papers. "She'll want to come out," he whispered. "So, can you get rid of the other one?" By some strange coincidence, the real wife arrived at Gib airport on the plane that was to take the girlfriend back to England and they literally passed each other in the airport building.

My next contact with the RAF was right at the end of the shoot. One day Carol said he had changed the ending, and the following day wanted an RAF rescue launch on the quayside at La Linea, and stalked off! Oh, nice one, I thought. First I had to get the RAF to lend me one. But the really tricky one was to get the permission from the Spanish Government for a British military boat to come from Gibraltar and land in Spanish territory! This was during the Franco regime, and Gibraltar was, in the parlance of their national sport, like a red rag to a bull.

I called the AOC in Gib and put my problem to him. He said there was no problem in letting me have a boat, but that it would need Air Ministry approval. However, for it to land at La Linea, we would need the approval of the Spanish. He gave me his home telephone number and said I could call him at any time. Then we had to start the wheels in motion.

We got Roberto to call his brother, Luis, who was also a production manager and had brought many large American films to Spain and consequently had close contacts with government officials. At the same time, I spoke to the Columbia London office and asked them to contact the Air Ministry and use their clout. There were only a few hours left before the London offices closed. Later that evening we finally had permission from both the British and Spanish authorities. When I spoke to the AOC, he had just received the news, "Congratulations, John. You know the Air Ministry has left it to my discretion?" There was a pause. He continued, "I need a favour in return. We have just built a new gymnasium, and I would like you to get Laurence Harvey to officially open it for us."

There was no way I could get hold of Larry quickly, and I had to have the boat the following morning. "You got it, give me the date and time and he'll be there."

The next morning, history was made when a British military boat from Gibraltar landed on Spanish soil. The one thing the Spanish authorities insisted on was that no airmen were to get off the boat. So, of course, the first thing I saw when I arrived was the crew of the boat all sitting on the quayside, but as they were talking to the Spanish Guardia Civil, I just ignored the situation. What I did not ignore was getting Larry to open the gym. Being the lovely guy he was, he agreed straight away, and not only performed the opening ceremony, but spent time with all the airmen and their wives.

The next day we left for Ireland. This was a worry as the Spanish Customs were notoriously difficult in those days. All our equipment was brought in on temporary import licences, and you had to prove that you were taking out what you had brought in. We had already had trouble with the film stock because when Ted Bushel was in Gibraltar he noticed that a consignment of unexposed film had arrived for us from London. Thinking he was doing us a good turn, he smuggled twenty thousand feet of film over the border in his car. Later that day, coming into my office I saw the film in the outer office. When they told me Ted had brought it over from Gib, I went spare. "Get me Bushel," I yelled.

When he arrived I explained that we had to prove where every foot of film went. Our camera sheets, and our daily reports were all checked by the Spanish Customs to see that what we brought in was taken out. "Now, you have brought in twenty thousand feet of film which hasn't been checked into Customs' records, so what are you going to do?"

He cut me off. "I know. I've got to smuggle it back into Gibraltar." He was right, as we couldn't afford one slip up. He somehow managed to get it back.

I viewed our departure from Malaga with some trepidation, just prayed that the Customs' men were going to be in a good mood, for you never knew, sometimes they could be real bastards and pick on every minute detail.

At the start, everything went smoothly. The company all arrived at the airport on time and with their passports (usually there is one who forgets), and Roberto told me that Customs had already cleared our equipment and it was ready to load. The KLM charter aircraft, fitted out with first class seats, arrived on time.

The only problem was that Lee Remick's baby was sick, and the father was kicking up a lot of fuss, especially when Roberto said he would get a doctor to look at the little one. "I wouldn't let any Spanish doctor near my child," he shouted, which went down really well with the local people, including airport officials, police and reporters from the local press, most of whom spoke excellent English. And, of course, the Customs' officials!

I tried to calm everyone down, and told Lee that I would get the pilot to call ahead to have a doctor standing by at Dublin airport, and that we would be there in just over a couple of hours.

At that moment, one of the KLM crew came up to me, and whispered that there was a problem. It transpired that the editing machine would not go through the cargo door. I told them not to worry about that as Roberto could send it on the next cargo flight available. Thinking the problem was solved, I went to tell Bert Bates what had happened, but as he was busy with Carol, I let it go. All I needed at that moment was for Carol to think up something to complain about. I noticed that he was drinking pretty heavily for that time of day, and then I remembered that he was petrified of flying.

At that moment an agitated Roberto arrived. "It's the *Aduana*, the Customs. They won't let you leave the Steinbeck behind."

"Why ever not? They have already cleared it for export, they can hold it in their duty free area until a suitable flight can be found, so what's the problem?"

He replied, "The problem is that they say you either take everything, or nothing." Then hoping, I suppose, to shift the blame, he shouted at me, "And I don't believe these Dutch people. If there is a weight problem why not take off some of the petrol?"

I didn't have time to tell him that it was nothing to do with the weight, for I could see that the "brothers" had got wind that something was up, and there were little groups in tight conversation. I suddenly had an idea, and told Ineke the problem, "Go and speak in Dutch with the Captain, and see what he can do to help us, promise him anything , even your body, we've just got to leave."

Off she went, just as Carol literally rolled up. "John, dear, don't take any petrol off the plane." I promised him I wouldn't!

I was then accosted by Lee's husband, who wanted to know what was going on. Then, after calming him down, I went to see the Customs' men myself, but that got me nowhere, just a lot of stony faces who refused to be moved on their decision. Ineke came back full of admiration for the pilot and started to tell me all about him. I asked her to leave the personal details till later, meanwhile could he do anything? She said he had an idea and was talking to his loading official at that moment and that she had just come back to tell me what a lovely guy he was. It turned out she was right, he *was* a lovely guy. They found out that they could get the machine through the front cabin doors, and, though it was against regulations, he was prepared to do it, but he pointed out it would mean that there was no room in the front for any passengers.

I could see a crowd of brothers' faces, and the shop stewards edging forward. I explained what had happened, and that some people would have to be left behind and flown out later to London, and then on to Dublin the next day. I said the wives, three of four of them including Ineke, would have to be the ones left behind. What had been a rather bolshie crowd suddenly changed, as they realised that the ones left behind would get a night at their homes in London. Then it was less a question of persuading some to stay, but rather of disappointing the ones that were coming. Eventually we got the numbers right, and the company started to board.

I said good-bye to Ineke, and was about to go through Immigration when Roberto came up – to say good-bye, I thought.

"No, no. Good-bye *problem*!"

"Oh Christ, what now?"

"The Captain, he has found out that Ineke is not coming, and he say if she no come, he is not going to fly!" In the end she joined me.

On board everyone was seated comfortably in their first class seats, but the front cabin had not only the Steinbeck, but also all sorts of other equipment. There were no seats left, so Ineke and I sat on top of this machinery, heads almost touching the roof, all the way to Dublin. We were quite happy as the Chief Purser was so embarrassed with our treatment that he plied us with champagne and caviar the whole trip.

Shortly after take off Carol came careering down the plane, and grabbed me affectionately round the legs. "That was a horrible time for you, dear John." And turning to Ineke said, "We are so lucky to have him." Sitting there, I suddenly thought, good God, he called me "dear". From that moment, I could do no wrong. In the future, being a very large man, he would bend down and kiss me on my head, and I would say, "You know, Carol, I liked you better when you hated me!" Which wasn't true because I had great affection for him.

He would say that I should be a producer, and in some of the dark days ahead I often thought back on his advice. Sadly, I never worked with him again, though we used to bump into each other, and he always seemed happy to see me, as I was to see him.

Dublin was a joy, and time passed too quickly. Joan came over for Larry's birthday, and threw a hilarious party at the Shelbourne Hotel.

All too soon it was time to go. We had a great Irish wrap party, with lots of tears and promises to write, but our main goodbye was going to be at the docks. I had brought my car over so Ineke and I had to leave Dublin on the ferry. I thought it would be a good idea to invite my numerous Irish friends to a farewell drink on the boat. We got down to the docks early to load the car, and I said to the guy at the top of the gangplank, "My name is John Dark and I have invited a few friends to have a drink with me before we leave. Would you direct them up to the bar?"

"Ah now, that'll be a bit of a problem."

"What's that?" I enquired impatiently.

"It's not open".

The thought of an Irish bar not being open amazed me. "And why not?"

"It be the Customs."

"And what customs would that be?"

"Ah, bless you sir, it's not *our* customs, oh no, far from it. In fact, no sir, it be *the* Customs, sir. The bar is duty free so it's not opened till after the ship has put to sea."

Now this threw me into a quandary. "What am I going to do?" I asked the man. "I've got all these people coming and, well, they'll be expecting a drink!"

"Ah, that they will, that they will," he said, shaking his head, the full horror of the situation sinking in, and he sighed at the mere thought of people turning up and finding no drink. Suddenly he clapped his hands together, "I've got it, I tell you, I've got it. Look, see that pub across there," and pointed to a quay-side pub, "you go over there sir, you go over there and when your friends turn up, I'll send them across to you."

What a brilliant solution. I slapped him on the back thanked him profusely, passed a few notes over, and Ineke and I crossed over to the pub.

Now, apart from certain pubs in the centre of towns, Irish pubs on the whole are pretty basic. It's the drinking that's important, not the surroundings. This was a dockers' pub, and to call it "basic" would be to flatter it. Bare walls, dirty tiled floor, a few rickety tables with chairs to match, the whole dominated by a long bar. We pushed our way through the throng, and waited for our guests to arrive. I was a little concerned because I knew that a few of them were going on to a "do" and would be wearing evening dress, and I didn't know how this would be received. I need not have worried. No one took a blind bit of notice. They were too busy drinking!

Slowly my friends started to trickle in, and I would wave, greet them and order them a drink. Standing up at the bar asking for "Two gin-and- tonics, large scotch on the rocks ... you know, with ice" when I felt a nudge against me. It was a big burly docker who was holding his empty glass. "Would you care for a drink?" I asked.

"Oh, t'ank you, I'll be after having a jar ... and my pal Ned here, he'd like a jar too."

Ned leant round my tall neighbour, beaming with his empty glass in his hand. "Bless you, sir, bless you," said Ned.

And I replied, "And I suppose *you've* got a friend too?"

"Well, as a mater fact ..."

I interrupted him turning to the barman, "Give the pub a drink!"

In the end I suppose I must have bought the pub about a couple of times, but it was whilst I was busy talking to my friends that trouble struck.

I felt myself being grabbed from the back and lifted up into the air. "Jesus Christ," I thought, "it's the IRA. They're going to kill me!"

I was plonked down on one of the tables and as I was released from the grip around me I looked back and saw this massive docker and my worst fears were confirmed. Then I heard "shush". Turning back I looked down and saw a small wizened old man going "shush, shush" and attempting to quieten the heaving crowd.

"Quiet," he shouted, and the noise started to abate.

"I know, it's a kangaroo court," I thought.

The old man, nodding his head and fluttering his hands. "That's better," he muttered. Then, raising his voice, he addressed the baying multitude, "Now listen,

listen, listen to me. We've seem 'em come, and we've seen 'em go, but none of them has ever bought us a drink before." A tremendous cheer went up, and turning to me, and looking up he went on "Sir, we are only common working men so we can't buy you a drink, but we'll give you a song." And the whole place sang to me.

I don't know how much it eventually cost me to get out. Whatever it was, it was worth every penny. They all accompanied us to the boat, and sang us off, what an amazing farewell. One of the ship's crew said he had been working for many years on the ferry and he had never seen anything like it.

Back to the Smoke (Cockney for London). We rented the cutest house, a converted chapel situated in Hollywood Road, just off the Fulham Road. I still had some work to do for Carol, mainly shooting the background for the titles, down at my old stamping ground, Brighton. Well, to be exact, Shoreham airport.

We had rented a flat in Brighton not long after we had met, and used to spend our weekends there. However, with going abroad so much and being so busy, we had not been through the door for nearly two years, and had been trying like mad to get rid of the lease. Whilst having a drink with one of the local journalists at the airport, I happened to tell him this. They must have been short of news that day, because the "Evening Argus" came out with the story. Driving back to Brighton that night I was taken completely by surprise when I saw the billboards, "Film Man Hasn't Been In His Brighton Flat For Two Years". It was a bit of luck really as through the article I managed to rid myself of the place.

The film came out, and proved Lee Remick right. It was not by any means a Carol Reed classic. I was sorry for him, but it was only two years later in 1965 that he directed "Oliver", for which he deservedly won an Oscar. He made only two more films after that, and died in 1976. Like many others, I mourned his loss. Though my brief experience of working for him was not always happy, I am pleased that we ended up on friendly terms, and I am grateful for all that he taught me.

CHAPTER 13
FOREIGN AFFAIRS

Peggy had let our house in Molesey and moved to Regent's Park, but I had kept in touch with my old neighbours from that time, the lovely O'Neills. One day when Ineke and I were visiting them, we came across some new flats being built at the side of Bushy Park, at Hampton Court. It was love at first sight (we were good at that!) so we put a deposit down on the unfinished property. Heaven knows where the balance was to come from. What with renting furnished accommodation, paying the alimony, and supporting my mother, which I had done for years, finances were tight. I reckoned either God or Columbia would provide. Well Columbia let me down, for despite being top of their list, they just had no new movies, so it was down to God, and he, she, or it, didn't let me down! One Saturday the phone rang, and it was Bud Ornstein, the head of United Artists in Britain.

I had met Bud at a party, and had broached him about the film that Lewis Gilbert was to direct for his company in Malaya. I was desperate to make this film, firstly because of the director, secondly because the designer was my old friend John Stoll, thirdly because Morris Aza, another old friend, was the production manager, and because it was to be made entirely overseas. Last but by no means least, because I was broke.

However, he told me that the film was already set up by Charles K. Feldman, with Karl Tunberg producing and an associate already on board.

This was a big disappointment to me, and I was kind of surprised to get his call for that was some time ago.

He said, "Listen, I'm in trouble, it's Lewis's film. Charlie Feldman has sacked the producer and the associate producer has resigned. We're due to start shooting in a few weeks time, and to get right to the point, can you take it over?" (They say God moves in a mysterious ways!) I told him I would be delighted (over the moon would be more precise).

Minutes after I put the phone down, Lewis came through fromLA, welcoming me on board and telling me how relieved he was that I was there. I then spoke with Charlie Feldman, a man I did not know at all, but he was full of charm and flattery.

Next day I met with the departing associate. We knew each other, but we were in no way friends. He said that although things were a mess in London, he promised me everything in Malaya was ready and on schedule. I thanked him, picked up the script and the budget, and hid myself away to read it all before meeting the "brass". The script was by Karl Tunberg (the fired producer) and was based on the novel "The Durian Tree" by Michael Keon.

It was a romantic adventure set in the early 50s about the Communist rebels at the time of the British withdrawal from Malaya. It was to be shot entirely in Malaya and starred William Holden, Capucine, Susannah York, and Japanese star, Tetsuro Tamba. I was only able to read it through quickly and glance at the budget, before I was due at the Ritz.

I met Arthur Krim and Arnold Picker. Mr Krim was President of U.A. and Picker was his most senior executive. Mr Krim, a very small man, greeted me warmly and sat me down in the sitting room of his suite, whilst he sat on the other side of the table, immediately disappearing behind an enormous basket of fruit which dominated the table.

He asked me if I had read the script, but before I had time to reply, he popped up at the side of the fruit basket offering me an apple, and then a pear. It took us a quite a while to work through all the fruit in the basket, and by the time we got to the grapes Arnold Picker came in. He was a big man and as different in personality as he was in size from Arthur Krim. There were few preliminaries, just a quick, strong hand-shake, then "You got the budget I see, so what you think?"

"Well, Mr Picker, you won't make this script for this budget," I said.

Luckily the room didn't have a fan as he went off like I had stuck a firework up his arse. "I don't get it. Jesus! I have a friend who made a film in the Far East for one million," and he went on and on.

When he had subsided a little I quietly replied, "Well, Mr Picker, I'll make this film for any price you like. I can stick a few trees up at Shepperton and I'll get Lewis to shoot it in four weeks. However, I don't think you will like it very much and I doubt if Mr Holden would agree. If you want to make this film …" raising the script in the air "… as an international film to the standards required by your company, then I am afraid you will have to increase this budget."

Just then another U.A executive entered the room, and he too had studied the budget. "Well, what do you think?" Arnold Picker growled.

"It's not enough," he replied.

Then Picker and Krim explained to me what a jam they were in. The stars had all been contracted, the subject purchased, and they were past the point of no return. They were worried that we would not be able to start on time, but I told them I had been assured by the previous associate that all was ready in Kuala Lumpur, and I had no reason to disbelieve him. The crew had already been engaged, so I couldn't see any reason why we shouldn't hit the date. "You know what any delay will cost us?" was Arnold Picker's parting shot to me, which was not a question but a threat.

I hurried to the temporary London office where the pre-production team was based, and studied the crew list, and this was of concern to me as one always likes to have people you know, and who you can rely on. I was more than happy to see that Freddy Young was the cameraman, and Harry Gillam the camera operator, though a bit perturbed at the electricians, who numbered amongst them a well-known trouble maker. Well, it was too late to do anything about them. But my main concern was the young accountant, whose name I didn't recognise. I checked up and found out that he had only ever worked at Pinewood in the Rank budgetary department.

Now the accountant is one's right arm; you depend on him to keep you advised not only on what has happened, but more importantly to sense what the future holds. I knew he had left Pinewood to take this job and would find it tough to find another one quickly, so I met him, and found him a very likeable fellow, who seemed to know what he was talking about. So, a few days later he and I flew out to Malaya. We had a really nice trip and got on well with each other. He told me that he was married, had two children and was sorry he was going to miss the cricket season! He added that he hoped we wouldn't be away too long. Not in my wildest dreams did I think that this unassuming young man, Paul Hitchcock, would become not only a vice-president of Warner Brothers, but also the producer of such films as "Mission Impossible 1" and "...2". A lovely guy, who remained as unassuming later in life as he was then. We have been friends ever since.

A story that I love about him ... well, actually about his wife, Beryl, is when Paul was having a beer and sandwich with Clint Eastwood, another unassuming man, in a pub near Pinewood Studios. When Clint heard that Paul lived about five minutes away, he suggested Paul should ring his wife and invite her to join them, which he did. He said, "I'm here at the Black Horse having a bite of lunch with Clint Eastwood and he suggested that you might like to join us."

Beryl quickly replied, "Oh Paul, you know it's Monday and I've got a pile of washing."

He reported this to Clint, who said, "Well, that sure keeps things in perspective!"

We arrived in Kuala Lumpur and were met by John Stoll, Morris Aza, and an Indian who turned out to be the local production manager. After saying "Hello" in that unmistakable accent which sounds like an excitable impersonation of a Welsh Dervish, he said, "Now I will get you a very nice suit, hand stitched, no trouble, fit you like, how do you say, yes, like glove. My brother very fine tailor."

"Ay-ay," I thought, "this one has to go."

They rushed me through Customs and back to the local office, a room in The Federal Hotel, where they were all staying. I asked Morris to send in his secretary, as I wanted to send a telegram to London. A sweet little shy Chinese girl came in, and I dictated a short cable. I then turned to the two boys and asked how it was going.

"Well, it isn't," said Morris.

"What do you mean, 'it isn't'?" I asked with a certain amount of alarm.

"It isn't because we have been told to do nothing, by your predecessor"

"So, what have you been doing all this time here? Don't tell me, nothing!"

I turned to John Stoll, "The sets? None?" He shook his head.

At that moment the little Chinese girl came in, handed me my cable, and rushed from the room. It was gibberish! The poor little thing could speak English just about well enough to answer the phone, but by no stretch of the imagination could she be called a secretary. I turned to my colleagues, "Let me get this straight: we have no sets, no offices, no staff, no local crew, the wrong local production manager, no locations, no permits, no accommodation for the company, no transport ... in short, nothing!" They nodded in agreement. "We have just a few days before the crew and artists arrive including, I might add, one of the world's highest paid stars." They all nodded again and shuffled their feet in embarrassment. "Right, I have told U.A. that we will start on the scheduled date, and we will. So, gentlemen, let's all go and have some lunch, because this is the last time any of us is going to have time to eat for weeks to come!"

I called Lewis in LA and Bud in London, and informed them of the situation. I told them not to worry, that we would get ready on time. "How?" they both asked.

"I don't know," I replied, "but we will."

The picture had to be re-scheduled in order for John to get the sets up. Luckily both John and I knew what the Chinese workmen were capable of, so he went steaming ahead. Next, Paul and I had to issue a new budget, and Morris had to find new staff. I found an excellent European woman, the wife of a senior English police officer. (This was 1963, when Britain was relinquishing its power, and British civil servants and police were handing over to their Malayan counterparts.) She was a godsend, a professional secretary, who was very knowledgeable about the country. She was immensely helpful and it was she who advised me to take on a Malayan production manager rather than a Chinese or Indian one, as he would have much more influence with the local government officials. This confirmed my action in sacking the Indian guy.

Mind you, Freddie Young arrived shortly after, and he and I had quite a set-to when he criticised my firing the poor chap. I loved Freddie dearly, but he was a bit of a martinet who liked things to go his way, and he had taken a liking to the Indian on a previous trip. Perhaps his brother had made him a suit!

Lewis arrived, and I met him at the airport where I filled him in on the state of affairs. Neither of us could understand how my predecessor had put the picture in such jeopardy, "But there you go, Lewis, it's no good wondering why, we have just got to make sure that we catch up."

The days flew by at a terrifying rate, and it wasn't long before William Holden arrived with his secretary. He had decided to come in early, and I thought, "Great, that's all we need." However, he arrived with a minimum of fuss, and seemed to be happy with all the arrangements made for his comfort. Stars are spoilt, and you never know how they are going to react. When there are no complaints, agents on the phone, screams, or tantrums, we all breathe a sigh of relief.

Holden was not like that, but it wasn't till the next day that I found out just what a regular guy he was. I was in my office when he came in so I naturally stood up and introduced him to the staff. When we sat down he said, "Don't worry about me. I have heard what a jam you are in, and I'd like to help. I'm not much good at most things, but I could stick stamps on envelopes or something."

I looked at him in utter disbelief and said, "Well, if you really do mean that, you could help with one problem. I haven't yet got all the permits and permissions, the use of the Malayan army, the police force and so on. If you would come around this town with me, every door would be opened. They're not interested in John Dark, but in William Holden. Christ, you are one of the most popular stars in the East!"

All he said was, "Happy to be along."

So that is what happened. It was like arriving with Ali Baba, but instead of "Open sesame!" I just said, "William Holden." The doors to all the local authorities were flung open and full co-operation offered to us, or rather to him, on a plate.

Capucine arrived shortly after Bill. It was obvious that there was a thing going on between them. Like everybody else, I had heard the stories that she had been a top model, and that she was a man. If she's a man, he's the prettiest one I have ever seen, I thought. Tall, elegant, softly spoken she was a charming person, and I liked her from the start. So we had our first break in having two lovely people as stars and felt we were doing okay.

Of course I already knew Susannah was a darling, so it only left the Japanese actor to worry about.

Tetsuro Tamba, unlike most Japanese, he was a tall man. He spoke little English and on arrival could only say, "Where Tunberg?" We had great difficulty trying to explain that Karl Tunberg was no longer with us. As Tunberg was the only person he had met, and as he had no understanding of the English language, the poor chap must have thought he was on the wrong picture! We hired a dialogue director for him, and he soon started to get to grips with the script, and becoming one of the most popular people in the company.

Through one of our young Malayan production assistants, a very well educated, enthusiastic kid, I arranged a meeting with the President, Tunku Abdul Rahman, the father of the new Malaysia. He was a very busy man, and I was very flattered that he gave up some of his time to meet me. He could not have been more charming, and asked me many questions about the production. He said how very pleased his government was that we had come to Malaysia to make the film, and that he wanted the fullest co-operation from all his departments. Before I left he handed me a slip of paper with his private telephone number, stating that it went straight to him, and I could call if I was in trouble. He added, "But, please, John, only if you have real trouble."

I was flabbergasted and amazed, that with all he had to do, he would even consider giving me direct access. But he wanted personally to help. I used it only once. This was when, many weeks later, I wanted to use the main law court to shoot the trial scenes. I met the Chief Justice, a lugubrious Englishman who looked just like a bloodhound, with long sagging cheeks, and soulful eyes. He greeted me by telling me that he hadn't seen a film since they added sound, and hadn't thought much of them then. He continued in the same vein rather as though he was sentencing me to ten years. The upshot was that he flatly refused my request, and told me I was impertinent to even ask!.

I returned to my office and immediately rang the Tunku's private number.

He answered immediately and I briefly told him the story. "Leave it to me, John," he said.

About ten minutes later a messenger arrived from the courts asking me to return to see the Chief Justice. When I went into his office, he asked me to sit and then said, "Look, I've been thinking about your request a bit more, and really I cannot see any reason why you shouldn't use it. However, I must make one thing very clear, there is to be no throwing of custard pies in the court!"

The crew arrived with the rest of the cast, including some stalwart British actors like Michael Goodliffe, Alan Cuthbertson and Sydney Tafler, Hylda's brother.

Sydney's arrival brought the members of the Gilbert family up to seven. There was Lewis, his wife Hylda, their two sons, John and Stephen, and Morris Aza, his brother-in-law, with his wife Sheila. When another brother-in-law came to visit, it made eight.

On the same plane came the U.A. executive I met in London, Oscar Danziger. They were so worried, they sent him out to keep an eye on things. He was a very nice man, but contributed nothing. He spent all his time at the Lake Country Club. He made the odd, rare visit to the office, usually suggesting something which we would convince him was impractical, and he would disappear back to the club muttering, "Wrong again". He wrote the occasional letter to Hollywood, mostly praising me. As I said, he was a very nice man! Also on the plane was Ted Bushel. Of course!

We started on time, mainly due to the skill of John Stoll, the expertise of the Chinese workers, the great local team we had built around us, and the co-operation of the Malayan government, not forgetting the help of our leading artist.

The first day's shoot was in the night club of the Federal Hotel, for which we engaged both European and Oriental crowd. During the morning I started getting the wrong vibes, and soon found out that a European man was stirring up trouble over the fact that we were paying more to the Europeans than we were to the Chinese and Malays. I went down to see Lewis at the shoot and whispered in his ear, "It's possible that all your crowd will disappear. If they do, please keep shooting, even though we might have to retake at a later date."

Back came the reply, "All right, boy." And he went on with his job. That's Lewis: no questions, no arguments. He knew I must have had a good reason to say that, and there was no point in wasting time. In this case my reasoning was that in a potential strike situation, the main thing is not to be intimidated.

I quickly met with their self-appointed representatives who included a Charlie Wheeler type, who was very obnoxious. I explained the reasoning behind the difference in pay scales. It had nothing to do with what we were being accused of, racialism, but was a case of supply and demand. There was a mass of unemployed Orientals dying to work, but the Europeans had to be lured out of their air-conditioned houses to sit under the hot lights for ten or twelve hours a day. I also pointed out that in London when they had made "The World of Susie Wong", it was the other way round, and they had to pay the Chinese crowd more than the going rate to get them to give up their waiters' jobs. It soon blew over. Our friend tried to continue it, but was fighting a lost cause as no one would back him up.

The next day the front page of the local paper had a large picture of me, and the story of the strike that never happened. Bill Holden and the rest of the cast had no idea what was going on, as Lewis hadn't said anything or given any indication that there might be trouble. He had just quietly got on with the job in hand. Bill was so impressed that he insisted that we send a cutting to Charlie Feldman in LA, which I thought couldn't do any harm. Charlie never mentioned it, as I don't think he was in the slightest bit interested in the day-to-day problems of film making, but quite rightly expected you to handle the problems without worrying him.

Two days later the company were due to shoot outside. Morris had organised everything: the transport, the logistics, the permissions, the police, the fire brigade, everything but one, the caterer. As I have said before, catering on a film shoot is a big number, and heaven help you if you get it wrong. Morris had met the Chinese caterer who had promised to bring his mobile kitchen up for him to see. It was always coming up from Singapore, every day it was coming, but it never appeared.

The night before exterior shooting, Morris came excitedly into my office, "It's here, the truck, the chuck wagon is here." I jumped up and together we rushed outside to the car park to be greeted by our caterer, grinning from ear to ear. With a flourish he took us to an open three ton lorry which had a tent erected on its back. Inside the tent there were four chairs around a precisely laid out table, complete with four place settings, salt and pepper shakers, wine glasses and a plastic vase holding a bunch of artificial flowers! Morris and I looked at each other. "But where's the mobile kitchen?" we asked. The caterer beamed and once again indicated the truck. It was too late to do anything.

The next day after the company left, I said to Mo, "Stand by for the first radio call." We were linked to the location by radio, as this was years before the mobile phone when communications were a perennial nightmare. But it was strangely silent. Being a coward, I suggested to Morris he went there to see what was happening. Off he went, but still silence.

Maybe the radio is broken, I thought, and decided to venture there myself. The crew were shooting in a jungle river, and I was just in time to see the caterer wading out to Lewis and the camera crew with a tray of coffee in one hand and a biscuit tin in the other. I watched as he passed Lewis a china cup of coffee then proffered the sugar. Everyone seemed very happy, not a moan to be heard, and even the electricians' shop steward was quiet.

The caterer turned out to be one of the best I ever had on a film! I have no idea how he did it, he appeared to have nothing more than two gas burners in a cardboard box. He cooked the crew whatever they wanted, but where it all came from I have no idea. There appeared to be many little men scurrying around all over the place who somehow brought along the required produce. But it was that first remark that told you all. Standing in a jungle river, it was not just, "Would you like a biscuit, Mr Gilbert?" but "Would you like a Huntley and Palmer biscuit, Mr Gilbert?" This was a class caterer.

The company quickly settled down, and from the start kept up with the schedule. Everyone seemed to be getting on with each other. Susannah was a bit of a pain-in-the-arse, as she didn't seem to have grown up at all since I worked with her on "Greengage Summer". She still walked around in short skirts, with scuffed moccasins clutching a bag of sweets. I think she was a bit lonely. Bill and Cap were a number, Tetsuro hardly spoke a word of English, and the rest of the cast kept themselves very much to themselves. Sydney Tafler had his family, and most of the boys soon had a little Oriental companion. So poor old Sue didn't have a friend, and possibly this made her a little churlish. I think she might have had a thing for Bill. The very mild love scene she had with him triggered something bizarre. John Stoll had built Bill's Malayan bungalow home inside the local studio but, as we had to shoot at both day and night he took out one of the walls (it was built out of corrugated iron!) and laid out a garden on the other side of the terrace. We were just about to shoot when Capucine, who was not on call, turned up dressed in the shortest of dresses and flat shoes, in fact a total caricature of how Susannah dressed. She took a chair, plonked it by the side of the camera, sat down, took out a baby's dummy and stuck it in her mouth. We all tried to ignore it, but as Bill came off the set he whispered to me, "How do I get out of this?"

Location shooting is a strange thing. It is like a large family, working together and playing together. Affairs start, marriages break up, it all goes on. At the end of a day's shooting, with no home to go to, most of the crew and artists have a drink together, before plans are made for the evening. There is a bond between everyone, and though a certain amount of bitching goes on, heaven help any outsider who tries to criticise one of the company. Our chippie summed it up one day when he told me someone had come to see me. "Was he one of the crew?" I asked.

"Oh no," he replied, "he was a civilian!"

I remember Shirley Maclaine saying that there is always one person on every location that everyone hates. I think there is a certain amount of truth in that, though thinking back I can only think of one example. Usually there is a certain amount of class division, and the manual grades like sparks, chippies, props, painters etc. tend to band together.

Like shipboard romances, some affairs start and last the length of the location. Others continue, and divorce is frequent, not helped by the forced separation, as I can personally testify. There are many parties and everyone is invited, even the wives, some of whom can be a real pain-in-the-arse on location. They sometimes treat the production office like a combination of a travel agency, Citizens' Advice Bureau, crèche, tourist information centre, complaints desk and general "can you help me" centre. If one is not careful they can interfere with the essential work of the office, arriving on the location and expecting to be fed with the crew, taking up seats in the transport.

One who I had to take off the plane from Malaga to Dublin on "The Running Man" I met years and years later, when her husband, the cashier on the picture, became a minor executive at Twickenham Studios. She screamed at me for having dared to take her off the flight! The company paid for her seat, did she expect that we would take off one of the crew, thereby stopping us from shooting the next day? Another example was on "Darling Lili" when they were moving from Dublin to Brussels, Blake Edwards, the producer/director, had the cameras taken off the aircraft so that his family's bicycles could be transported. But that film is another story.

In Malaya our electrical shop steward lived up to his nickname, "General Strike". If he could find something to complain about, something that he could make money out of, he would be in the office, and he really led poor old Morris a dog's life. One day I was having one of those even- more-busy-than-usual days, and nothing was going right. As I was leaving the location, Len, the fearsome Steward stopped me, saying he wanted a word.

Oh God, I thought, what now? "Well, Len, if you want to talk to me, you'll have to come into the car because I am late for my next appointment." So together we took off. "Well what is it now, Len?"

"Well ..." and then paused. I thought that's funny, as verbal hesitation was not one of his characteristics. "Well, it's like this, governor ..." That was something else odd, as usually he wouldn't use any word that might denote even the slightest hint of respect. He twisted around and stared into my face in his usual belligerent way, his shaggy beard bristling, his lips curled tightly over his missing teeth, shoulders hunched, for all the world as if he were about to launch himself onto my body and bite my jugular vein out. Finally with some effort he spat out, "I'm getting married." And collapsed back into his seat.

We both sat there in silence for a while, then, recovering from the shock, I said, "That's wonderful Len, marvellous. Congratulations."

"Then, you don't mind?" Mind, I thought, *mind?* God, I had thought he was going to call a strike or something. Jesus, he could marry an orang-utan for all I cared. Then guessing my thoughts, he said, "She ain't a bar girl, you know. She's a real nice girl, Chinese."

"Well, that's great, I had a Chinese girl for many years. I wish you all happiness."

"Thanks, John, thanks, but you got to help us."

Then it came out. With her being a Malaysian citizen and Len a British subject, they had run into the usual bureaucracy, the upshot of which was that there was no way they could get married before we were due to finish in Malaya. "Leave it with me, and don't worry!"

I phoned a few friends in the right places to check out the girl. She had led a blameless life, had been at one time in the police force and was well thought of. She was well educated, and a good-looking girl, and the only worrying thing about her was why she should want to get married to Len! Anyhow that was not my problem, and within a few days I had all the paper work arranged and obtained the licence for them to marry. As can be imagined, Len was over the moon, and changed from being my "bête noire" to my biggest fan! The date was fixed, a reception arranged, and then Ruby, the bride, asked me if I would act in place of her father and give her away. As I said at the reception, I never thought I would end up as Len's father-in-law! The joke amongst the crew was that when Len asked "What's for dinner," she would reply: "Number 12, 26, 30, and a bowl of fried rice."

It was a true romance and the bride turned our Len into quite a smart man, with a trimmed beard, and new teeth. She was the perfect wife, and they had two children and as far as I know, lived happily ever after.

We had been shooting for about a month when news came through that our famous producer, Charlie, was going to visit us. Lewis had explained quite a lot to me about him, of how he had been orphaned at an early age, and he and his brother were brought up in an orphanage. One day a couple came to adopt a boy, but they only wanted one and had to choose between the two brothers. As they couldn't make up their minds, they decided to hold a running race between the two boys, to be held in a local grocer's shop. They marked out the start and finish line and like a scene from a Western movie, the two boys lined up, determined to win. They were running for their future on a race track of bare boards, against the sacks of rice, potatoes, and tins of molasses. A heart-rending race, with so much at stake. Charlie won and was adopted. He never saw his brother again. He was brought up by the couple, given an excellent education, and became a lawyer. He changed professions and became the president of Famous Artists, one of the biggest agencies in Hollywood which represented at one time or another nearly every major star. He had recently produced films like "A Streetcar Named Desire" and "The Seven Year Itch." We knew that he was Bill Holden's greatest friend, and wondered if Charlie knew about Bill and Cap, for Capucine had been Charlie's girl friend! Life, we thought, could become interesting.

What is it about successful men that gives them that unmistakable aura of money and power? Charlie was far from being the best dressed of men. In fact, I rarely saw him in anything other than a blue blazer and grey flannels, same type and colour of shirt, and same tie. But as he came off the plane I could pick him out straight away from all the other passengers. A handsome man in his late 50's, he stood out against all the rest which included his lawyer and a few friends who had accompanied him. Naturally we had organised it so we could meet him straight off the plane, and we escorted him and his party through Customs and Immigration, leaving one of the production staff behind to pick up their luggage. We returned to the suite we had booked for him at the Federal Hotel.

After a few drinks with Bill, Cap, and Lewis, I left to return to work. I hadn't been there long before Morris came to tell me that Charlie had requested a masseur. "What do you think he wants, a genuine one, or one of the girls?" he asked.

"I don't know. Why don't you ask him?"

"Shit, John, I couldn't do that. I mean, I don't know the man. Why don't *you* ask him?" So I got him on the house phone and put the question to him.

"Oh no, I want a real massage."

"Morris," I yelled, "straight one."

A few minutes went by, my phone went and it was Charlie: "Better send up one of each."

"Morris, one straight and one bent!"

For Kuala Lumpur was not Bangkok, and did not display or advertise sex like the Thai capital. Nevertheless, like most Eastern countries, there was an abundance of pretty girls making their living, and supporting their families, by selling their bodies. The trouble for them was that there was also an abundance of "talented amateurs", especially around a film company. I guess they were the early "groupies". The next day I got another call from Charlie, and without any preamble he said, "What you doing about Cap's bunnies?"

I racked my brains. "'Cap's bunnies'?" I thought, "What the fuck does that mean?"

Charlie continued, "You got the bicycle scene coming up, and that's when they're due." The penny dropped, it was Capucine's periods. Charlie went on, "I think we should have a meeting." And so that night, Lewis, Freddy Young, Morris, John Stoll and I met in Charlie's suite, where we discussed her condition, how badly she got them, how regular she was and so on. The upshot was that we had a contingency plan to rearrange the schedule if necessary. But the great thing from all this was that we never heard another word about it.

As Morris said, "Either the rumours are true and she is a man, or she's pregnant!"

Charlie made one trip out to the location and said, "It's a piss poor country", and left.

During the shoot, Bill Holden had not touched a drop of alcohol. He had a reputation of being a very heavy drinker, which resulted in him continually getting presents of booze, which he always sent down to me with the same note, "Think of me whilst you are drinking this!" He and Cap were very close and spent all their free time together, rarely going out in the evenings. If they had a day or two free, they would immediately go off somewhere. They seemed to have an insatiable desire for travel. A strange thing they did on a few occasions was visit a Chinese death house. This is a place where terminally ill people go when they are near death. It was hardly the most entertaining place, and I can only think that being movie stars they had experienced everything and so that was a novelty to them.

Bill and I had shared a mutual passion for Africa. He and his oil magnate friend bought the Mawingo Hotel in Nakuru, Kenya and changed the name to the Mount Kenya Safari Club. He spent many of his holidays there. I knew this hotel from when I was working there, and always tried to make it my last call before going home, as it was so beautiful. One day Bill told me that he had been approached by the production company which made "The Big Wide World of Sport" to make a programme on a safari in Africa. He asked me if I would like to make it with him. Can a duck swim? I leapt at the opportunity to be with one of the nicest of men, working on a programme in one of the nicest of countries. Sadly, in the end the whole thing fizzled out because they could not agree dates. I shall always be sorry that it never happened.

I was running into the first political problem. The government heard that we were building a village, which had to be burnt down in portraying a sequence in the film showing the British sniffing out the terrorists. They wanted me to assure them that this would be a Chinese village, and not a Malayan one as, they pointed out, there were no Malaysian terrorists, only Chinese Communist guerrillas. I did my best not to guarantee anything, pointing out that, though what they said was probably historically correct, they had to understand that we were making an entertainment movie, a film that would be shown all over the world. I asked, did they really want us to show a shitty Chinese village, when they could possibly have a pretty, attractive Malaysian one? Well, this didn't quite win them over but they said they would like to think about it.

I left the Government office and drove back to the office at the Federal Hotel, where John Stoll was standing on the steps outside. As I got out of the car, John said in his funny squeaky voice, "You know, John, I am building a Malaysian village, not a Chinese one." How had he heard? I had only just left, and nobody knew beforehand what the meeting was about. That was not the point just then, and I heatedly told him not to build anything until I gave the word. He got very hot under the collar and we had a few words, and it ended up with him hitting me. It was a very small hit, but was something I never let him forget. In the end he got his way and, with the Government's blessing, he built a beautiful Malaysian village. It was so lovely that we could hardly bear the thought of it going up in flames.

The due day dawned, a dull, grey day, overcast with ominous signs of rain. I arrived at the location to be greeted by Lewis saying, "We aren't going to shoot today and that's a fact."

I pointed out it was only ten o'clock, and he reluctantly agreed to wait. The rain started to fall softly. I sent for Kip, our young Malay production assistant, "Go and see the Bomoh, and ask him what we should do."

The reply came back, "He says he'll stop the rain at twelve, but he cannot hold it up later than five."

I went to see Lewis who wanted to return to the hotel. "No, Lewis, it's going to be all right, it's going to stop raining at twelve and we have until five, which will give us plenty of time to get the day's work in."

"Where did you get that from, the Met. Office? They're always unreliable."

"No, the Bomoh."

"The Bomoh?" he asked incredulously "Who the fuck is he?"

"He sort of controls the weather." He looked at me, thinking the sun had obviously got to me. I explained to him that the Bomoh was an old hermit who lived out in the countryside and it was thought he had mystical powers over the weather. He was always consulted by the Royal Family, and the Government when parades, weddings etc. were planned. Even the Europeans used him when they were playing important cricket matches.

"Okay, we will wait till twelve." And shaking his head went off in search of the chuck wagon, muttering to himself, "A bloody witch doctor!"

Twelve o'clock came and the rain still fell. "Right," said Lewis from the back of a truck where he was sheltering, "that's it, I'm off." But before he could move the rain abruptly stopped.

"Right, gel up."

"Do you think that's wise?" Lewis asked.

In those days to burn a large set like that, first the special effects' boys coated the set with an inflammable gelly, then left it for an hour before setting it alight. The problem was that, once having put the gelly on, you had to set fire to it. It couldn't be left for another day for it was so combustible that the slightest thing would set it alight. "Just because he was right once, doesn't mean…"

"It will be all right," I interrupted him, fingers firmly crossed behind my back. Oh ye of little faith, I thought, as I anxiously watched the scurrying special effects' men spreading the gelly over John Stoll's brilliant set. If I was wrong, or rather the Bomoh was wrong, it would mean building the whole thing again at vast cost. I didn't want to even contemplate it. It would mean extending the schedule, and like night follows day, the budget would be blown apart.

Once again, like so many times in my life, the gods were kind and everything went smoothly. Lewis called a "wrap", at five to five, and at five the rain started again. Believe it or not, these are the facts!

Actually the Bomoh had been on the pay roll for some time due to my superstitious nature. I don't know whether it is because I have no religious beliefs, or whether I picked it up from actors and entertainers, as so many people in "show business" are notoriously careful not to tempt Fate. My motto is, don't take a risk, so don't cut your nails on a Friday, mention that Scottish play, walk under ladders, see a magpie look for another, the list is endless. Also I never messed with the natives beliefs. In Kenya I always respected, and paid, the local witch doctors; in Hong Kong I went most days to the temple and offered up an incense taper and a prayer. Movies are fickle things and you can't take a chance!

However, this payment to the Bomoh caused quite a stir amongst the accounts' department at United Artists in Los Angeles. As I explained earlier, everything on a movie is budgeted, from the stars' salaries to the materials for the cleaners. Each item has its own number and its own place in the detailed budget. Based on this, we received a cable from U.A.'s Accounts department, "Explain role of Bomoh."

We cabled back, "He controls the weather."

Back came the reply, "Re. Bomoh and your reply, in that case he should be put under 'Meteorological'."

To which we responded: "Re. Bomoh, no, he does not forecast, he controls the weather, that is why we have put him under 'location facilities'." This correspondence went on for some time, with them never querying the payment, just its allocation! In the end, we compromised and put it down as a 'Religious Contribution'!

There was one major battle scene for which I had arranged to have the Malayan Army as the Communists, and the Australian Army as the British. Those Aussies were something else: a real tough bunch, but with amazing good manners and kindness. Morris came to me and said they had requested beer instead of the soft drinks that we supplied to all and sundry. We had a deal with the local soft drinks company to not only supply us drinks at the wholesale price, but also to give us a truck and two men to hand out the refrigerated drinks to the whole company. I said I didn't mind them having the beer, but I was buggered if I'd pay for it. So we started selling them beer, the profit from which ended up paying for all our soft drinks. As one U.A. accountant said, "You have created movie history." Normally this account goes wildly over budget. So, apart from being the best collection of stunt men I ever had and being really nice guys, the Aussies also saved us a small fortune on our catering account.

Work was tough; it was hot, it was sticky, and the script was hard to film. In addition, we were always fighting the loss of preparation. But at the end of the day, when we had finished work, we had some great times. The girls were great and you never had to worry about having a date for the evening. So I was surprised when two of the British Police Chiefs came to me one day saying the Police Chief of Singapore was coming to K.L., and would I throw a party for him. I replied that as police bosses, they must know a thing or two about parties! But they insisted that I was the one that would know how to entertain him. So I got hold of my good friend Seow, our local Chinese Mr Fix-It who was already on our pay-roll, and told him to find me the best-looking, most fun girls in town, and with the least hang-ups, as I didn't know what his tastes were.

I then arranged for our wonderful caterer to make some very special Chinese delicacies, filled my sitting room with champagne, got the latest records, and I was ready to rock-and-roll! Though I say it myself, it was one hell of a party.

All the girls had been paid for in advance so there was no haggling, every cherry was for picking. Unknown to me, in the room next door was an airline pilot trying to get some sleep, who kept ringing down to reception to complain about the noise. After several futile attempts to get someone to take action, he yelled down the phone, "If you don't stop it now, I am going to call the police."

To which he got the reply, "No good, all police at party!"

The next day, the guest of honour said to me, "John, being Police Chief of Singapore is not a bad thing, and I've been to a few parties, but yours was the best, the very best." He then gave me a present of a bottle of some strange Chinese medicine, saying, "We all need a little help now and again, if you know what I mean, and this is a specially strong and reliable aphrodisiac." I thanked him, but thought, that's one thing I don't need. In any case I had once read that there was no such thing (this was the days long before Viagra), and put it in my medicine box. First Aid, you know.

One of the Far East's top singers arrived in Kuala Lumpur for an engagement at one of the hotels. I went to see her and was knocked out. Apart from being a great singer, in several languages, with a wonderful stage presence, she was also a fabulous looking girl. I had to meet her, but despite all my entreaties she would not accept any of my invitations. Seow, my go-between, explained to me that in the East girl singers are expected to mingle with the clients, and it may not stop at a "mingle". Singers like her, highly professional recording artists, made sure they weren't put into the same bracket as the less talented. They went to great lengths to protect their reputation so that not a breath of scandal was associated with their name. No way would she meet me. This was now a real challenge. I managed to find out that she was attending a government party, which even she could hardly refuse to attend. I knew the Minister involved and arranged to attend this formal function. I spotted her as soon as I entered the room, but deliberately steered clear of her as I went around greeting the various officials I knew. Finally I got someone to introduce her to me. "Ah, Mr Dark," she said as she held my hand, "and what are you doing at a Government reception?"

"Why, hoping to meet you, of course," I replied.

She threw back her head and laughed a deep throaty laugh. I was entranced. I did my very best to be as formal as I could, but at the same time leaving no doubt about my great interest in her. We seemed to be getting on really well, and being used to Paula, I was surprised at how well she spoke English. All too soon she said she had to go. "Show time," she explained.

I offered to escort her to the hotel which she declined. All hope was gone when she whispered to me, "Call me", and slipped a piece of paper in my hand with her telephone number.

After making several calls, and sending bunches of roses to the hotel, she at last agreed to meet, but it all had to be done in a real cloak-and-dagger manner. She did not live in the hotel but had a bungalow in the grounds. I was not to breathe a word to anyone other than my driver, who was to be sworn to secrecy. He was to drive me to the front door at precisely 1 am, which she would leave open, and I was to go straight into the bungalow.

I followed the directions precisely. The only trouble was that I took with me some champagne and some lobster. As I have explained, I am cack-handed and, as I got out of the car, I dropped the silver dish which made enough noise to waken the dead. Eventually I got into the house where she was waiting for me. "I don't know why you didn't bring some trumpeters to herald your arrival," she said smiling. "Next time you just come, okay, no champagne, nothing – just you."

Well, I thought, at least there's going to be a next time.

Our romance lasted a short time, as she had to go back to Hong Kong to do an American Special TV show. I promised to go to her last night in K.L. After her introduction she said to the audience, "I hope you'll forgive me if tonight I just sing to one person."

Unbeknown to me some of the crew were in that night, and at that point they stood up, and turning to me, cheered. Oh, my God, and we thought no one knew.

The next day I saw her off at the airport.

It just so happened that the Tunku was returning from abroad that morning, and a guard of honour was lined up ready to greet him. I had arranged with the airport authorities that I could take her to the steps of the plane, and as we crossed the tarmac I noticed the guard was headed by Jimmy Ismail, an old mate. As we passed he brought the guard of honour to attention and gave us a smashing salute. At the foot of the stairs, we parted, a quick last kiss, and she was up the steps, where she stopped, turned, and said, "You needn't have bothered with the army I would have gone anyway!" and she was gone.

I was sad she had gone but also, in another way, happy. I loved and adored my little Dutch dish waiting for me back in London, and I didn't want anything to interfere with that. My Chinese song bird was the type of person that I could have become more serious about, and despite myself, I might just have fallen for her and wrecked the only thing that really mattered to me. Maybe I was maturing at last?

I decided on a course of action. I knew myself too well to think that I was going to live without the comfort of a companion, so I decided to find myself someone I knew would make a fine friend, but with whom I would never fall in love. In actual fact she found me. She was a little Eurasian girl, a secretary in the Malaysian National Health Service, and in fact just crowned as "Miss Insurance". And you don't get higher than that! She was great, and we had a lot of fun together until the day I left.

Paul and I stayed on for a week, clearing up, paying the last of the bills, and making sure we left everything in apple-pie order. We said our farewells to the various people who had helped us so much. And to our local production staff.

The exception was Seow. He drew no pay until the very end, when he had come to me and pleaded with me to let him come back to England on our charter plane. He explained that he had left his job at the Federal Hotel to work for us, and if we all left and he stayed behind, he would lose face. As the flight didn't cost any more with an extra passenger, he was able to leave with his head held high, and his face very much intact.

At Heathrow, my darling wife was there to meet me, and we hurried back to our first real home together. She had done a brilliant job, and it was everything I had hoped for. Seeing her there in our small nest I realised how much I had missed her, and how much I loved her. Nine months later our son Daniel was born.

Later that day I was having a bath, and I told her about "Miss Insurance" and that she had given me a present which she had had put on the seat in the plane. "And you see, darling, she earned so little money, it must have cost her more than she earned in a week."

I looked up and saw the tears streaming down her face. "Oh, that is so sweet," she sobbed.

"You silly darling, you're supposed to throw things at me, divorce me, not cry about how sweet she was." But that was, and is, Ineke – whose heart is so big it is a wonder it fits in her body, and whose mind so wise it makes the rest of us look stupid.

We had talked often about our beliefs, and, though she was deeply spiritual and I wasn't, we understood each other and each allowed the other to have our own beliefs, our own mental space. Ineke thought that it was not feasible for a man to be away from his mate for a long time and not seek sexual gratification. She felt amazed that women could throw their lives totally away, and jeopardise their children's happiness over their mate's indiscretion.

I agreed that tolerance of infidelity was the same for both, and she shouldn't be treated any differently from me. Now, I know probably most people disagree, but we have stayed married, blissfully happy all these years.

Back to Shepperton for post-production, for which I had budgeted twelve weeks. I hadn't allowed for Charlie.

The first thing we did on Charlie's instructions was to engage Maurice Binder to create the titles. Maurice was a "titles' genius", and created the titles for all the "Bond" films, as well as many other famous movies. He was a likeable person, short, bald, and a little plump, always smiling, and rather like a cheeky gnome. He was American, but had lived in England for many years, carving himself a very special niche, and was a major contributor to the British Film Industry. I knew him and liked him very much, but I had never worked with him. I discovered that darling Maurice, like many talented people, had little sense of time.

An example of this many years later was when I was crossing the Champs Elysées in Paris and met Maurice carrying a film can under his arm. After greeting each other, and making all the usual comments about "how funny!", "what a coincidence!", he suggested we had a cup of coffee. We sat at one of the outside cafés and whilst chatting away, I noticed a man rushing down the road looking for someone like "a pregnant ferret in a forest fire". He spotted Maurice, almost leapt on him, and panting and screaming in French he dragged Maurice off. Later I learnt that the poor man had arranged a viewing of his new film, and Maurice had the titles in the can under his arm!

Maurice started shooting our titles and it seemed to me that at that time he had no real idea of what he wanted. He wasn't helped by the fact that Charlie kept changing the title. In Malaya we shot under the name "The Year of the Dragon" but he changed the title every other day, till it ended up as "The 7th Dawn". Someone had told Charlie that it was lucky to have the number '7' in the title! So Maurice shot and shot, then decided he needed a tank to hold water, and a dead Chinese soldier. We brought in our old friend, Seow, who lay in the water for weeks, whilst Maurice tried this idea and that. I had many rows with him, for by then we were weeks overdue, and consequently way over budget. I need not have worried.

Charlie came to London, and we met up in Soho where we had a very pleasant lunch. Whilst walking down Dean Street, he put his arm around my shoulder and said, "Now, John, I just have one thing to say to you: don't finish this picture quickly!" And we didn't!

During this time, April 1964, Daniel was born.

We had always promised my mother-in-law that he would be born in the family home in The Hague, so shortly before the time Ineke flew to Holland. I kept in touch by phone. Finally I received a call that it was on the way, and I caught the next flight to Rotterdam. On the flight over I was congratulating myself on not being there at the birth but would arrive to see mother and baby both looking snug in bed, and ready to be kissed by a loving husband and doting father! I had a few glasses of champagne at the airport to celebrate, and a few more on the plane. I got a taxi from the airport to The Hague, only to be greeted by the fact that the baby hadn't arrived yet. I went in to see Ineke who looked quite wonderful and more beautiful than ever. "What happened?" I asked.

"I wanted to wait for you," she replied. I just hugged her, there were no words, but boy did I feel a shit. "Now I'm going to go to sleep, and Bouricius (our doctor) and I will arrange to have it in the morning", and with that she kissed me and turned over and went to sleep.

I left the bedroom and joined the family group including Bouricius, who explained that he had given her a sedative and confirmed that the baby would be born in the morning.

"Well, I think that this calls for a drink," said my father-in-law.

To which my mother-in-law replied, "You're not drinking here and making a racket, you can go out."

So Vadertje (my father-in-law's family title "little father" which I always thought sounded a bit twee in English, but somehow sounded okay in Dutch), my brother in-law, Loek, and I left for the local pub. I asked Bouricius to come, but he said he wouldn't be leaving the house until the baby was born. What a doctor to have!

My brother-in-law was a very interesting man and that night we formed a friendship that lasted till his early death. We had nothing in common, as he was a medical professor specialising in cancer research, and a most highly educated and literate man. One day at his house he said, "John, I'm so pleased you've come as there are a couple of clues I can't answer in the 'Observer' Crossword!"

Me? Crossword puzzles? I can't even do the children's one in the "Evening Standard"! And I felt ashamed that I was unable to help a Dutchman in my own language.

It always amazed me how well the Dutch speak English. I would see the little two- and three-year-olds prattling away in their own language; and then, it seemed on the next trip, they would be talking to me in English. How do they do it? Wouldn't it be a good idea if they taught our teachers how to teach foreign languages? I suppose it's not so much that they speak English, it is that they speak English better than the majority of the English.

I am reminded of the Professor Higgins' song, "Why Can't The English Teach Their Children How To Speak?" Now, at the turn of the century, we have a race of non-communicators. With their inverted snobbery, they actually think that it is right to speak badly. I am not referring to regional accents. I love some more than others, and an accent lends flavour, but speaking badly just means you're lazy, incompetent and ignorant.

Next morning I woke with a ghastly hangover. Things were beginning to happen I was told, and nobody really had any time for me. The medical team had been increased. There was Ineke's uncle, a retired G.P., two doctor friends of Vadertje, and Loek and they were all talking and all seeming to have a different idea of what to do. One thing was for sure: they didn't have any interest in easing my post drinking pains! I found myself a chair in the corner and sat quietly there, till Bouricius came in and said, "You have a son."

The birth of one's child always produces a great surge of emotion, another Dark, another life, another joy. I was dispatched with Loek to register the birth. I always wanted to call the baby Toby, but Ineke had wanted Daniel, so Daniel it was. Later in life he told me that he was very pleased I had lost the argument. Ineke stayed in Holland for ten days, then they both flew back to join me back in London, where I was still on the United Artists pay roll, playing with the film.

Charlie used to edit the picture over the phone, usually to me and I would pass the comments on to the editor, John Shirley. Lewis by this time had gone on to another project. Charlie's main concern was whether Capucine should die at the end or be executed. Through process photography we had poor Cap in the cell, out of the cell, behind bars, against a wall, in the clouds, in the clear sky, and so on.

Christmas came and went, and at last we engaged the composer, a young up-and-coming musician, Riz Ortolani. Charlie arrived with a new member of the entourage, John Shepbridge, a charming Hungarian, but what his function was I couldn't begin to guess, and when I did find out all I wondered was where does he fit in the budget.

They were soon joined by Warren Beatty, referred to by Charlie as "the kid", as he was Shirley Maclaine's young brother. Charlie explained to me that there were two pictures he wanted to make. One was an original comedy for Beatty called "What's New, Pussycat?", which was one of Warren's favourite sayings.

Charlie said he had a new writer and "You shove him in a broom closet, take him out two days later, and he hands you the finished script!" This was Woody Allen. The other subject was the only Ian Fleming Bond book not owned by Harry Saltzman and Cubby Broccoli, "Casino Royale" .

So whilst we were finishing "The 7th Dawn" we started work on the other two projects.

Now I understood why Charlie didn't want us to finish the picture quickly. The thing is to set up your new picture on the back of your old film. Your offices and staff are all paid for, all your own producer's expenses are charged to the existing project, and in this way you can reduce your pre-productions cost quite considerably.

Charlie told me he was having trouble with "the kid", as he couldn't get him to agree to any of the casting suggestions for the girl. I was asked to get together with him and make up a list of three girls he would be prepared to work with. So arming myself with "Spotlight", the British book of talent, and "The American Players", I found Warren who I soon realised was in a devilish mood. Like Bill Holden, he was a charming guy, with no bullshit, and so used to fame that it didn't appear to affect him. He was just a nice, fun person to be with. He rejected the American book, but went through "Spotlight" carefully.

"Poor old Charlie, we're going to have some fun here," he said. "What do you think of her?" he'd ask, pointing to some one like Rita Webb, a wonderful character actress who made her living playing fat, ugly Cockney woman. In the end Warren made up a list of similar actresses and sent it through to Charlie, who, to put it in Americanese, went "ape shit".

Not long after I learnt that Warren had left the project. Personally I don't think he ever had any intention of making it, but I was sorry to see him go.

In the meantime the search for a director began, and this is where I saw Charlie at his best. He exuded magnetism when interviewing possible candidates. I remember taking the director Michael Anderson up to see him. On the way up in the lift Michael said to me, "You know even if I wanted to do this picture, I couldn't because I have another commitment."

I asked him why he was going to see Charlie then. "Well, he's a big man, and I thought it was only courteous to accept his invitation." About half-an-hour later I took him down in the same lift, after he had given Charlie an undertaking to do the film, even though Charlie had given him nothing – no offer, no commitment, nothing.

When Lewis was asked by a journalist if he would do another film for him, Lewis replied, "No way, unless of course he spoke to me for five minutes!" He was a man of hypnotic power, and it is no wonder he had been the top agent in Hollywood. He used that power on me more than once.

The next thing I learnt was that Charlie wanted to make both films in Italy.

"The 7th Dawn" was just about wrapped, and it was time to say good-bye to Morris Aza, a sad good-bye for I was very fond of him. I was going to miss him because, apart from being a good production manager, he was a delightful friend. Also, he was very useful because he looked so like me that I used to send him to meetings in my place! I asked him once where the name Aza came from? He explained that his father was a member of a musical group, who had a new act but didn't have the money to pay for new costumes. So they wrote to the manufacturers of Chillproof saying they would call themselves the Chillproof Four if they would pay for their costumes. They got a positive response, but the manufacturer pointed out that the name Chillproof was well launched. However, they had a new product coming onto the market and if they called themselves by that name they would finance the clothes. That is how the Aza Four was formed, and how when the war came, and National Registration was launched, the name became official.

This was Morris's last picture as a PM and he went back to running the agency that was originally owned by his mother. She was a formidable lady, who represented some of the top talent in the UK of that time, including Gracie Fields. I suppose Gracie must have been the biggest star by far in the country then, and I used to love to hear Morris's stories about her. My favourite was that when she was starring at the London Palladium she used to go back home after the show by bus! If no one recognised her, she would sing her signature tune, "Sally", at the top of her voice.

So it was good-bye to Morris, and many other old friends. Seow was still living in England, and somehow or other was very friendly with one of the executives of the Football Association. He used to get VIP tickets to all the major matches including the Cup Final, which really pissed off my football fan colleagues. Never underestimate the Chinese! He stayed in England for several years, married a Chinese girl and had a son, and, though Seow went back to Malaya, his son completed his education in England and the last time I heard had an important job in the City.

"The 7th Dawn" opened and closed very quickly. The best things about it were the titles!

We packed up, and Ineke, Daniel and I drove to Rome. It was so good to be back.

We all loved Rome, and of course it was Daniel's first time, but he took to it at once. Maybe it was all the attention he was getting, as Italian men are crazy about babies. Nothing typified this more than the scene of an amazing white-suited and helmeted Roman policeman, standing on his podium in the middle of a busy junction outside our hotel, directing the traffic like an extrovert conductor performing a major symphony. In the middle of all this confusion and cacophony, he would spot Daniel's pram coming out of the hotel, and would leap off his podium to rush over to wish him "Bon giorno." To hell with the traffic, that could wait, this was much more important!

Another day Ineke was driving through the centre of Rome, and aware that the traffic was even more congested than normal, and realising she would not get back to the hotel in time to feed the baby, pulled into the side of the road, unbuttoned her blouse and served lunch. A policeman appeared, blowing his whistle, and shrieking at her that there was no way she could park there. He became quite hysterical and threatening, until he peered in the car and saw what was happening. Immediately his whole attitude changed, and most apologetically explained that she couldn't park there. He then walked in front of the car and indicated that Ineke should follow him, and he personally guided her to a quiet spot at the back of a building. With a big smile, and a smart salute he wished her a quiet time and the baby a good appetite. Later we found out there had been a big state funeral of a leading Communist politician, and all of Rome was brought to a standstill.

I started to set up our Italian organisation.

First I engaged Giorgio Migliarini to act as our administrator and accountant. Next was the production manager, and I was lucky to get the wonderful Maurizio Lo de Fe, the son of an Italian father and an English mother. Dear Maurizio was more English than the English. A tall, distinguished, grey-haired man, with a faultless educated English voice, he had served during the war in one of Italy's upper crust cavalry regiments.

"Wasn't that difficult for you, fighting against the British?" I asked him.

"Oh no, old boy, I never did that, I never fought against the British."

"How did you manage that?" I questioned.

"Oh, quite simple really, as soon as the British came into any operation they would post me to a different area. No never fought the British. The Americans, yes, but never the British, old boy!"

Whilst this was going on, Charlie was busy enlarging his entourage. Apart from John Shepbridge, we had Norman Foster, a most delightful man who was an actor turned director. To me, his main claim to fame was that he had once been married to one of my all time favourite film stars, Claudette Colbert. I never did find out what Charlie had in mind for him, all I knew he was ensconced in a suite at a top hotel at our expense.

Another member of the team was Richard Sylbert, a leading American production designer who had designed so many great American movies, including "The Graduate" and "Walk On The Wild Side". He was a great friend of Warren Beatty, but sadly he didn't have the same pleasant personality. In my stupidity, I thought he was going to design one of our films, but, no, he didn't have a title, he was just one of the gang.

One day, Maurizio and I were having lunch in a restaurant when Charlie came in with some friends. He came over and sat down at our table. Seeing his chance, Maurizio asked, "Charlie, I wonder whether you would be so kind as to tell me exactly who actually is the producer of these films."

Without a pause Charlie looked straight at him, "Why, you are, Maurizio." Six foot Maurizio suddenly grew to seven feet. Then Charlie continued, "And Johnny here, and John Shepbridge over there. You got to understand, Maurizio, I only employ producers." And got up and left.

One day we were all sitting in Charlie's sitting room in his suite at The Excelsior Hotel. He was pacing up and down, smoking furiously. We were discussing casting, and were still looking for a leading lady. Charlie was getting more and more uptight, several names had been mentioned, but turned down out of hand. "Come on, you guys, what do you think I pay you for?"

One suggested Jane Fonda.

"Hank's little girl, forget it." ..."Sophia? Too old." ... And so it went on till finally Charlie turned on us and spat out, "Listen, you guys, will you not mention anyone I don't like!"

About this time he left for LA leaving me with this collection of expensive executives (I suppose that's the word) and no money. Giorgio came to me one day, and said we had hardly a single lira left and had all the hotel bills, the office rentals, wages etc. to pay.

After some time, I managed to get hold of Charlie and tell him of the situation, "Don't ring me about money. I'm not United Artists. Get hold of Ilya Lopat."

In retrospect I can understand. He still had no deal. He had a script, and he had a stand-up unknown comic, Woody Allen. He had lost Warren Beatty, he had no director and no major star signed. There was no budget, for we had no details, no locations, no designer, no sets, no studio! Just producers! Maurizio and I had put together some sort of below-the-line figure which was entirely based on experience and guess work. That's all Charlie had to help him, and the last thing he needed was a phone call from me asking for money.

However, at that time all I could see in front of me was the inside of Italian prison, and as an Italian friend once said to me, never go into an Italian police station for you'll never come out! I wondered how long you got for debt! We had already borrowed some money off the manager of the Excelsior hotel on Giorgio's okay, so we really were in desperate straits. So there was nothing else for it but to speak to Ilya.

Now, Ilya was the head of European production for U.A. in Europe (excluding Britain), an ex-White Russian, and a monster to boot. U.A.'s Publicity director, Jerry Juroe, once said to me, "After meeting Ilya, you realise what a good thing it was that the Reds won." So, taking my life in my hands, I rang the Rome U.A. office only to find he was on holiday, and no one would tell me where he was.

I then spoke to his production chief, Lee Katz, in the Paris office, who was full of sympathy, but could do nothing. The only person who could okay an advance of money was Ilya, and Lee, like everybody else in the office, was under pain of death not to divulge where he was staying. As I hung up, I saw Giorgio's and Maurizio's long, grim faces.

Then I had a flash of inspiration and rang Bud Ornstein at the London office, and after the usual greetings, I posed the question, "I don't suppose you know where Ilya went on holiday." He did.

I rang the hotel and asked to speak to him and was told that Mr Lopat was on the beach, but if I held on they would get a message to him. I waited for ever, and I could visualise him being pulled away from his latest amore and summoned to the hotel phone. The beach must be at the other end of the town I thought. At last I heard: "Lopat. Who's that?"

"It's John Dark," I replied.

"John Dark? John Dark?" I realised he was trying to place the name for I had only met him quickly a couple of times.

"John Dark, Charlie Feldman's Associate," I explained.

"Charlie Feldman? Is he dead?" he queried.

"No, Mr Lopat."

"Then, what the fuck are you doing ringing me here?" And before I could explain, he carried on, "I told everyone I was not to be disturbed. Not to be goddamn disturbed, do you hear me? How did you find me here? How the fuck did you find me?" His temper was increasing and he was having trouble getting the words out of his mouth, but he still didn't wait for a reply. "I told them, all of them. I'm on fucking holiday, for Christ's sake. Who told you I was here? I'll have his balls. Who was it, eh?"

I told him that it was the London office, and I had to wait several minutes while he blasted off about Bud, and the whole English operation. Then at last he said, "Well, what do you want? And it better be good."

I then explained to him our financial situation, to which he responded in a voice gradually raising to a crescendo like some grumbling volcano slowly waking up before spewing out its fire. "Let me get this straight, you have inveigled my hotel address out of some stinking British moron, and despite all my instructions, you have disturbed my annual holiday. You have dragged me not only from the beach, but also from my companion and my lunch, and now you tell me you want money. Well, go and fuck yourself, do you understand? Fuck you and fuck you hard, and I'll see you in my office in Rome." And the phone went dead. I saw what Jerry meant.

I phoned Charlie expecting him to say close down, but all he said was, "Oh, don't worry. That's just Ilya, it'll be all right."

And it was.

The next day Giorgio rang me to say he had a cheque from U.A. What had happened? I reckon that Charlie had done some sort of deal in LA and got them to phone their Rome office to release the money. So we were still in business.

Ilya returned to Rome after his holiday and I never heard another word. In fact, the first time we met afterwards he could not have been nicer to me.

I never really got used to this type of row. Charlie would quite often have a violent and vitriolic argument with a major executive in which I thought they were going to kill each other, and suddenly they'd put their arms around each other and go off to dinner.

Once I witnessed an argument between Ilya and Charlie in the lobby of the Excelsior Hotel in Rome, as they came out of the elevator. Charlie went to speak to the concierge and Ilya, fuming, waited for him by the reception desk on the opposite side of the lobby. Suddenly Ilya could contain himself no longer and shouted, "The trouble with you, Charlie, is you know fuck all."

Hardly bothering to turn, Charlie shouted back, "And the trouble with you Ilya is that you know fuck all about fuck all!"

These were not probably the words of greeting that the party of rich American clerics, waiting to check in, were expecting on their first visit to the Holy City. In fact, I was expecting one of them to say, "We need never have bothered to have left home!"

I got used to Ilya after a while, and whenever he started to have one of his tantrums, I would just say, "Did you get laid last night Ilya?" A smile would break out on his face, "Did I get laid?" He would then describe to me the girl he had, what he had done to her and how many times he had fucked her. Now I don't know how old he was at this time, I would say somewhere in his mid-50's, early 60's, and, though in truth I found him a really dirty old man, I nevertheless at that time thought it sort of gave me hope for the future!

Things settled down a bit. Norman Foster left us. I guess he'd had a good holiday at U.A.'s expense and had judged the situation for himself and decided to go home. On the other hand, we had a visit from our scriptwriter and star, Woody Allen.

He arrived with his agent, or I should say one of his agents, Charlie Joffe. Like a lot of comedians, Woody was a pretty serious chap, although I think Charlie Feldman was a constant source of amusement to him. This was because Woody was both appalled and amused by the Hollywood scene and Charlie Feldman was the very essence of that scene.

It was Woody who said that the only thing that California gave to the world was to be able to turn right on the red (meaning that at a red stop light, if there was no traffic or pedestrian to impede you, you could turn right. Of course, in Britain this would mean turning left). To this day, none of his amazing films has ever been made on the West Coast. He has always ignored Hollywood, even refusing to turn up at the Academy Awards when he was nominated for an Oscar as best director.

However, in those days, he was still only known as a New York stand-up comic. Who would have guessed that he would become one of the world's most inventive directors? I suppose I should have had a clue to their future when Charlie Joffe said to me, "Do you mind if I sit in your office and see what you do?" but at the time I thought that's all I needed!

As everybody knows, Woody is a tiny chap, the opposite of Charles Atlas, the one that gets sand kicked into his eyes. But he could give Joffe an inch or two (maybe that's why he had him as an agent). The three of us used to go out and have a few meals together, and walking down the road the Italians must have wondered who were these three midgets? Woody was totally unknown to the Italians, and all they saw were these three funny little men. No one would have thought that two of them would become the most prolific and successful film-makers in the States. With his partner, Jack Rollins, Joffe produced nearly all of Woody's pictures. No wonder he wanted to sit in my office. Probably to find out what not to do!

We were now well ensconced in the studio. The "… Pussycat" offices down one side, "Casino …" the other. I sat in the middle. Secretaries were being hired, cashiers engaged, and a lot of the day was spent interviewing different crew members. We were gradually starting to look like we were in business, so much so that "Casino …" had a director, an Italian. Charlie called me and told me he was going to Paris for the week-end, so I wished him a good time and told him not to eat too much, put down the phone and thought about how we would spend our own week-end.

Daniel loved the beach and as the restaurants were prolific at the coast, it was no great hardship to go there. Children, and especially babies, were not only welcomed but positively spoiled. So we had a great time and I arrived at the studio on Monday morning relaxed and ready for the fray. Later that morning Charlie rang and said, "Where are you?"

I thought this was a pretty dumb question, as after all he had rung me, but nevertheless I answered, "At the studio."

The next question really floored me. "No, which *country* I mean?"

"Well, Italy, of course."

With a great laugh, he yelled, "Then, you're in the wrong goddamn country." He explained that we were going to make both pictures in Paris, and that I was to get there on the next plane. I tried to tell him that it wasn't as simple as that. The Rome operation had to be closed down, people paid off. "Maurizio can do that, you get your arse on the next flight. I need you here urgently."

I hurriedly explained the situation to Maurizio who quite naturally was crestfallen. I then rushed back to the hotel after having rung Ineke and told her the situation. She had a bag packed already ready for me.

"I'm afraid you'll have to drive up to Paris on your own with the baby," I said, concerned.

"Don't worry, darling, you go and catch your plane. We'll be fine." An extraordinary girl, nothing fazed her, everything was an adventure and a long drive across Europe with a young baby was just the thing to get her excited. Driving was not so simple in those days, as it was before the time of the motorways.

On arrival in Paris I went straight round to the Plaza Athénée to find out what the panic was, to find every one had gone to lunch, as it was now well into the afternoon. At a loss, I contacted the U.A. office and spoke to Lee Katz. He came and collected me and we went to the studio, where I was very surprised to be introduced to the French production manager and all his team.

It soon became obvious that U.A. had taken over the running of the film under Lee Katz, the practical Head of Production for U.A. He was one of America's most experienced production managers who had worked on such prestigious films as "The Longest Day" and who earlier in his life had been the first assistant director on "Casablanca", so I could hardly complain that we didn't have a highly-regarded production chief running the film. However, it was a big blow for me, for how could I be responsible for the control of a film when I hadn't even had the opportunity to discuss the choice of critical staff? Was it that or was it my ego? I could see that Lee had everything under his thumb and I was not going to be involved in anything on the physical production side. He and his team were nothing but charming to me, but as far as they were concerned I was part of the Feldman entourage and only needed to be told what they decided. Not speaking the language didn't help, and I had no old friends there like I had in Italy.

I told Charlie my misgivings about how I would not be able to run things as I would like, and indeed as he would want me to do. "Look, kid, ..." putting his arm around me, "... fuck 'em. Let them do it, and when it's a fuck-up, that's their look out. Look, we got plenty to do. I've signed Clive Donner to direct, and got Peter Sellers and Peter O'Toole." In his inimitable way, Charlie convinced me that indeed I had nothing to worry about, and for a while I forgot my apprehensions. I would go to the studio where, although everyone was very nice to me, they kept their cards very close to their chests.

I would meet up with Clive Donner, a very likeable man but to me a most amazing choice as director. His background hardly fitted him for directing a zany Hollywood multi-star movie. His films to-date had been more noticeable than successful, and certainly weren't in the international American style. He was obviously enjoying the life style that Charlie lavished on his directors, with a suite at The Plaza Athénée, and dinners at "Maxim's"; nothing was too good, and who could blame him? The whole entourage flattered him and welcomed him into their circle.

I used to try and explain things to him saying, "One cold winter's day, Clive, at eight o'clock in the morning, you will walk out on the set with a crew you don't know, many of whom won't even speak your language, and you know something? All your present buddies will be asleep in bed. You'll be on your own!" But Clive was too immersed in the heady Hollywood scene, and didn't really want to know the facts of life!

Ineke had an uneventful drive up, and we were all ensconced in a service apartment off the Champs Elysées. Daniel, who had been very happy in Rome, didn't take kindly to the colder Parisian air. I wasn't very happy because of the situation on the film, and Ineke wasn't happy because we weren't happy.

Things did not get better, and I could see that if I wasn't careful I was going to be just one more "hanger-on". I had a row with Richard Sylbert as I couldn't understand how a man of such talent was content just to lounge about and contribute nothing to the film.

But wasn't I as bad ?

So I decided to quit.

But first I went to see Ilya Lopat as I couldn't afford to upset U.A. He could not have been nicer, and said, "John, I would much rather lose the others, but I know how you feel, and I admire you for it. You go with my blessing and, believe me, if we have anything at U.A here, I will be in touch." He bid me a fond good-bye, probably thinking that at least that was one less on the budget.

Charlie was another matter. He was furious, went red in the face, swore at me, and walked out of the room in a temper. It was just as well, because had he stayed, knowing him, he probably would have talked me back into it. Back at our apartment, I got a call from Lee Katz who said how sorry he was that I was leaving etc. but that he had a problem with which maybe I could help. He said that Paris hotels were all full and he had Terry Thomas arriving, so would it be possible for us to leave on the following day so he could have the flat. I was only too happy to oblige. Next day we left for Holland.

We arrived at my in-laws' charming house in The Hague, and were greeted in their usual sweet, hospitable, and loving way. I had hardly entered the house when a call came for me from an American producer who was going to produce "Khartoum" for U.A. starring Burt Lancaster. He asked if I would join him as associate producer. I don't know why, but I didn't immediately leap at the chance, and asked him if I could have a day or two to think it over.

I had hardly put down the phone when another call came in for me from Columbia; would I join them under contract as a floating production executive? This sounded very attractive to me, but I pointed out that I had received an offer from U.A. and I would have to think it over.

Not waiting for me to call him, the very next day Julian Blaustein called again and I told him about the Columbia offer. His response was: "Look, John, whatever they offer you, I'll give you half again."

I told him I'd think it over, but he kept ringing me throughout the day and each time offered me more. Eventually he said, "Look, every man has his price. What do you want? An apartment in London, a house, what?" A great offer ... but I took the Columbia job.

Before I went to London to take up my new appointment, I went to see our wonderful Dutch doctor whom I always consulted when I was there. He was a brilliant man who had become a friend. I had an ulcer which he had been trying to cure for years, but I wasn't a very good patient! After exhaustive x-rays, he told me that it was still there, adding, "I am always telling you to eat a proper diet, to stop smoking and to stop drinking, but you carry on in your own mad way and you can see the result. You still have a nasty little ulcer down there. Now, it's no good me telling you to change your life style because you won't. However, I am going to tell you what you have to do. You have a choice of three things. You have to take up either flying, sailing or horse-riding."

I looked at him, "You're going potty, Bouricius, you're mad."

"Listen to me," he said. "Taking part in any of these activities on a daily basis, for a short time each day, you have to put your mind onto other things than your work, your personal life, your love life, or whatever. For a short time your mind needs to be focused on to only one thing."

"And what is that?" I queried.

He looked at me and said, "Survival."

In the end, I bet him double his fee or nothing that no horse-riding was going to cure my ulcer.

We returned to London, and I reported to Columbia where I was greeted like a long-lost son. I signed the contract and was taken for a long lunch to celebrate. When we got back to the office, I asked them what they had for me and was told there was nothing then, but there was a lot in the pipe-line. They suggested I went home and they would ring me as soon as there was something!

We lived near Bushy Park, at one time part of Hampton Court Palace, so I took this rare opportunity of paid idleness to take up Bouricius's challenge and go riding every morning. Well, it was not exactly riding, rather what is known in the trade as "hacking". I must say I enjoyed it, and I could see what the good doctor meant whilst I was trying to steer my nervous horse round Hampton Court roundabout, with lorries huffing and puffing all around. It was then into the peace of the park and a sedate walk until my Cockney girl tutor issued the command to trot! Or even worse, to canter! I would hang on for dear life, trying not to get too involved with the deer! A little trot, a little canter, even a little jumping (very low jumping !), then back to the stables and a few jars in the next door pub. Life was good. I used to call into Columbia once or twice a week, usually accept an invitation to lunch and then back home and a little siesta.

After six months, I returned to Holland, and unbelievably my ulcer had totally disappeared! Well, I have never been a lucky gambler, and I was very happy to pay the wager.

During this time Ineke and I started looking for a bigger place to live. The flat was great but Daniel was growing, and we had talked of a second child. Over the years we had discussed what I had seen in Hong Kong and my desire to adopt a child from one of the orphanages there. We both agreed that we could not cure the world's problems, but that if we could take just one child it would be one child less living in a ghastly orphanage. We started to make a few enquiries, but little did we realise at the time how long and how difficult it would be.

Life was exceedingly pleasant. I had time to be with Daniel and to enjoy some of our neighbours, amongst whom were a young doctor, a businessman in the upper end of the carpet industry, and a police Sergeant. In a way we represented the younger element in this collection of pretty flats, for mainly they were occupied by people much older than ourselves. Daniel was the only baby, but was mainly ignored other than by our friends, as the English on the whole are not taken with other people's children. Gregory and Vicki would sometimes come and spend a day with us, and even my ex, Peggy, came over once.

"Very mature," Vicki said, years later.

All good things had to come to an end, but I never dreamt it would happen like it did. I got a call from Columbia to go to the office, and when I got there I was given a cable from the studios at the coast which read: "Have today signed Charlie Feldman's 'Casino Royale'. Feldman insists John Dark be his Associate." Signed Mike Frankovich.

CHAPTER 14
THE CIRCUS

I spoke with Ken Maidment, Columbia's very pleasant and very efficient company secretary. I explained my situation with Charlie Feldman and how I had resigned from "… Pussycat" and the reasons why. I said I thought that in the circumstances it would be better if I opted out of "Casino Royale".

"Well, that's too bad, you are under contract to Columbia. And as I understand it, you, John Dark, are written into Feldman's contract, so you have no choice. Mike says you are to do it, so that is that. They're sending you the script over and you can get straight to work."

I left Maidment's office knowing that I was caught, and there was no way out. I then started to think that maybe it wasn't such a bad thing. Why Charlie should want me after our unhappy parting in Paris I couldn't fathom, but in a way I found it rather flattering after all that happened he should still want me. I also felt that it didn't do my standing with Columbia any harm either. Then, on second thoughts, I pondered, maybe it is just Charlie: he always has to win.

So I went home to have a few days off and await the arrival of the script which arrived by courier the next day. I immediately settled down to read this James Bond script, penned by one of Hollywood's greats, Ben Hecht. I wasn't exactly bowled over by it, but it was as professional as one would expect from such a respected writer. Then I had another meeting with Ken Maidment to discuss the budget so we knew what we were in for. Although I knew there were re-writes in the mill, I thought it prudent for Columbia to get some idea of their commitment. Much to my surprise he told me they knew what they were committed to, three million dollars. "But that is impossible, Ken," I said.

"It's written in the contract," he replied.

"But has anyone done a budget or has someone just guessed the figure?" I asked testily.

"Look, as I said, it is in Feldman's contract, and if it goes over that figure he will be responsible for the first half-a-million."

"Ken, have you any idea who you are dealing with?" I asked, which seemed to really irritate him.

"John, we have dealt with them all: Otto Preminger, Sam Spiegel – we are used to these people. Now leave me alone, I'm busy."

I got up and walked to the door, and turning said to him, "Ken, I'm going to tell you something now, believe me when I tell you, you will never make this film, this script, or any other forthcoming Feldman script for three million dollars. And if you think that you will get a brass nickel out of Charlie, let me tell you you've got more chance of getting blood out of a stone. I'm telling you this now, so don't ever come to me at any time in the future and ask me why we are over budget." Much to the credit of him and the rest of Columbia, they never did.

This was the start of the three-ring circus that was "Casino Royale". The three rings were situated in Britain's three largest film studios at that time, Shepperton, Pinewood and MGM (closed for many a long year now). We had five ringmasters (or directors) plus two action directors, and a cast of international stars. The budget soared. Few people actually know the final cost as I think there was some creative book-keeping at Columbia to cover up the truth. I do know that the British below-the-line costs were close to thirteen million dollars, and this did not include any American costs, costs of stars, all of which were paid directly by Columbia. I have heard the budget was in the region of twenty-eight million, and I think that is not far from the truth. This was 1966 and I can't say what the cost would be today taking into consideration inflation, except it would be mammoth. Originally scheduled for three months with one unit, it eventually took over a year with two.

The first indication that we were in for a long haul was when I heard that Charlie had rented a large house in South Audley Street, very near to John Shepridges's charming cottage type house. Before he arrived he sent a list of changes he wanted made to this rented furnished house, so I called in a top set decorator, Peter Howitt. I knew money would be no problem so I told him to spare no expense in making the place look as wonderful as they could, but abiding by Charlie's detailed instructions.

Peter was a delightful, funny and talented man, and he relished his gay sexuality, and had the humour that so often seems to go with these guys. One story he told was of when he was working on Richard Attenborough's "A Bridge Too Far", Peter went up to Dickie just before the big assault scene and said, "You know, Richard, today is my birthday."

And Dickie replied, "Yes, I know Peter and very soon I am going to give you your present. In about half-an-hour I am going to push a button and three thousand men are going to drop out of the sky."

"Oh," said Peter, recounting the story, "I love him so!"

Which I think is true for so many people in the business.

Sadly I have never worked with Richard Attenborough, but I have always been impressed by his talent, his commitment, his generosity, his energy, and his amazing memory for people. A few years ago I passed him in the corridor in Twickenham studios, surrounded by an entourage of cutting room bodies. As I passed by, he stopped and said, "How are you, John, dear?" God knows how he remembered, but I was very flattered and left thinking what a lovely man, and what a memory. I have a hard time remembering the children's names!

Three weeks later Peter had finished "tarting" up the Mayfair house, and as his property buyer said in his camp accent, "It's just like 'My Fair Lady'."

Charlie arrived accompanied by his latest love, a gorgeous tall French girl. I was immediately struck by how much she looked like Capucine. Funny how so many men fall in love with the same type of women. Charlie arrived, settled into his new house, and the fun began. He was the same old Charlie, dressed in his usual blue blazer and grey slacks, a subdued tie and a button-down shirt. He greeted me as though we had never parted. Neither Paris nor our previous relationship was ever mentioned.

First of all he brought over several new scripts that he had commissioned as, like me, he had not been too impressed by the Ben Hecht one. However, he was not happy with these either, and when I read them I could see why. So we had no script or director, but there was one good thing we did not have, the entourage of producers that we had on "...Pussycat": there was Charlie, myself and John Shepbridge.

The latter was a weird guy, a Hungarian charmer, I was told he had been Darryl Zanuck's procurer. Well, one thing was for sure, he was always surrounded by the most gorgeous girls, and his pretty little house was always alive with amazing looking creatures. I always had the feeling that if you were lost in the middle of the Sahara desert with John, he would take his little black book out of his pocket and say in his strong Hungarian accent, "I know some great broads around here", and over the sand dunes several beauties would come slinking over! The one thing about John was he never interfered, he never even made a suggestion or discussed the film, nothing. It was as though we were all on some wonderful extended party. I liked him very much except when he fell asleep in my office and snored!

Charlie was desperate to get Peter Sellers, but Peter was playing hard to get and implied "...Pussycat" had been enough of a Feldman experience for him. Charlie was not going to let go, though, and had many meetings with Peter's agent, my old friend, Denis Sellinger. At the same time the hunt for a James Bond started. This confused me, as I thought that was the role Peter was going to play, but every time I quizzed Charlie about this, he got irritated and told me to wait for the new script, and to keep on looking for a good-looking young man who could play the part. We went through "Spotlight", the casting directory, on a daily basis, but Charlie rejected all suggestions.

I remember Ian Hendry being considered and George Baker, but they didn't even got as far as being seen. I would get a call from Charlie. He had seen a news reader on the television and would I see him. I would see the poor man, who was very flattered, but said he had no acting experience, and indeed would be terrified by the idea.

My old friend, Morris Aza, at this time had a job as a casting director and I talked to him about a possible James Bond. He came up with a guy by the name of Terence Cooper, a good-looking, well-built guy but with limited acting experience. Anyhow I took him round to see Charlie who was quite taken with him. After several more meetings he was signed up. Charlie sent him off to Dougie Hayward (tailor to the stars), Turnbull and Acer for his shirts and ties, and in fact gave him what has become known as "a complete make-over". I'd like to say that Terry was good, I would even like to say he was well-behaved, but unfortunately he was neither. With the role, with his new wardrobe and with a contract in his pocket, he was the man about town, and the booze got to him.

He used to meet Charlie in an up-market restaurant and abuse him. Charlie would call me. "Your boy ..." he would start. Whenever Terry behaved badly he was always "my boy" so I knew I was in for a tirade. I would have Terry in the office for a dressing down, and he would promise to be a better boy. He would be fine for a while, then he would break out again.

At the same time Charlie was talking to writers and directors. Columbia used to ring me and ask how the planning was going, and I would point out that it was a bit difficult to plan without a script and a director. I met Max Setton who had taken over from Mike Frankovich as head of the London office. Max complained that he could never get hold of Charlie and that he never returned his phone calls. He asked me to tell him that he would like him to call round to the office to discuss the film. I passed this message on and the only response I got was, "Tell him I never go to offices." And he never did. Columbia were in the dark from the very beginning.

I had moved into Shepperton Studios taken on a top class secretary, Phil Russell. I also arranged for an ex Columbia production girl to work for Charlie in town. I knew we were going to need the best people we could get, as it was going to be important that I had a system of communication between Charlie's office and my own so I had some idea of what was going on. I then hired a production accountant and basing it on one of the old scripts, concocted a budget coming to three million dollars. Of course, it had nothing to do with the facts, but we had to start somewhere.

At this point Charlie told me that he had achieved a break-through with Sellers, but that one of his conditions, apart from the usual things like his own stunt man, own driver, own stand-in, own make-up man and hairdresser (this was before they had dreamt up their own cook, and their own trainer!) was that he could nominate the director.

Charlie asked me if I had ever heard of a director called Joe McGrath, and I had to confess that I hadn't. So I rushed back to the office, and looked him up in the directory. I could find no trace of him, and it seemed he had never directed a feature film. I then found out, probably from Denis Sellinger that he was a television director, and mainly known for directing a comedy series, "A Square World".

As soon as I could, I voiced my misgivings to Charlie. Here we had a major American feature film with a major star on board, with others waiting at the docks, and it was going to be handed over to an inexperienced director who had never made anything but television comedy, and was not used to film technique or helming a large and complicated shoot. Charlie seemed to agree, and I left him feeling better and waited for the next suggestion. It wasn't long before I heard that he had signed Peter and agreed to all his demands, including the choice of director.

At my weekly meeting with Columbia I was able to point out that, though we still had no script, we did have a director, and although he had never before made a film, at least we had someone's name to put on the chair. We also had a star, but they should bear in mind that his fee had taken up a third of the budget!

I met Joe McGrath, and found him a very likeable, short, energetic Scotsman, and excited as a child at Christmas. Everything was funny to him, and as he made suggestions, he fell about laughing. Well, I thought, maybe this is what this script needs, a young, vigorous new approach, and maybe Peter is right. Let's give the guy a break, surround him with the best talent we can get, and be at his side to help. He and I became quite close. At the same time writers were coming in and going out almost as quickly.

One addition to the writing team was John Law who had been such a contributor to the highly successful "That Was The Week That Was". Here again we had a highly talented person who was most charming, and I soon began to enjoy his company also. The trouble was both John and Joe were half-hour merchants as that was their background, that's where their talent lay. They were used to television, the small screen, and the half-hour format. A movie that lasts anything from one-and-a-half to three-and-a-half hours is a completely different thing. This was way before the talented Richard Lester moved from television to feature films with the Beatles' films, and disproved this theory. Sadly John died before we started. I missed him, as he had become a dear friend.

Then at last we had a break. Charlie signed Wolf Mankowitz whose credits included feature films like "A Kid for Two Farthings" from his own novel of the same name, "Expresso Bongo" from his own play and so on. He was not what I would call a top-class features' writer, but at least he had experience and talent, albeit limited.

On the other side, I engaged some major talent including Oscar-winning cameraman, Jack Hyldyard; production designer Michael Stringer; doyen casting director Maude Spector, another Oscar winner, Julie Harris, as costume designer; and my old friend, Dougie Pierce as production manager. At Joe's request we also engaged an editor, Bill Lenny. This was the team that went through the whole film. Others joined us for short periods, coming and going, but the fabulous six stayed with me for over a year.

We had a start date, which had to fit in with Sellers's schedule, but unfortunately not with ours! We were starting to get set and costume designs, but we were still working on a script that changed with every day of the week. I used to meet with Charlie in town and try and get some sense, but usually we only managed a few minutes together. His house was always full of people, as the major talent of the industry were always popping in to say "hello". Producers, directors and actors were all bustled in and out.

I met up again with Orson, who seemed to be even larger than life, as well as size. He again greeted me like a long-lost friend, and I must say I was delighted to see him and spent a pleasant afternoon in Charlie's sitting room listening to him recount some of his latest exploits.

Another afternoon I remember with fondness was when Shirley Maclaine visited. She and Charlie were very old friends, and I mean friends! She was as delightful in person as the one she often portrayed, and I could have fallen for her many times over. I always hoped we would get her in "Casino ...". Sadly that was not to be.

It was certainly pleasant meeting all these people, but it meant I had precious little time with Charlie. He liked me to go out at nights with him, which meant dining at one of London's top restaurants then onto somewhere like "Annabel's", then to a casino. Not being a gambler, I was very bored by this. It was also very tiring. I had to be at the studio early in the morning, overseeing the thousand-and-one details of pre-production. Even though we had no script, there had to be some sort of plan and stage space had to be booked, sets designed and built, crews hired, Unions consulted, casting completed, so that costumes could be made, and so on.

After several weeks of late nights and early mornings, in the early hours of one morning, I told Charlie I was going home. He was not pleased, and in fact my relationship with him was never quite the same from then on. Charlie liked his retinue around him at all times, and you didn't go till you were told, and he had retired to bed with his latest companion. Also Charlie had no understanding of the mechanics of film making, consequently he never understood other people's problems, just ploughed on in his own way without worrying what effects his decisions would have.

We were spending money at a fast rate, so I issued a cost report showing our current financial position. That evening at my usual nightly meeting with Charlie he asked me to explain the cost statement to him. "Well, Charlie, this column shows what we have spent to date, this shows our budgeted figure and the end column shows what we forecast our final position will be," I explained.

"But how can you forecast when you don't know what I am going to do?" he asked.

"That is the truest thing you've ever said," I replied.

"Well, if you don't know, what is the use of this piece of paper?"

"Well, we have to give Columbia a weekly report, to give them some idea of their financial commitment."

"No way," said Charlie. "Don't send any more of these out." And we never did.

We went through the whole film with Columbia having no idea of what they were in for. Indeed at one time they were quoting a figure for the total cost which was less than what we had already spent when we were only halfway through!

Charlie was always full of surprises. One day he rang me and said he wanted me to set up a magic department. "What's that for?" I asked.

"You'll find out" he growled.

I signed up a well known, wonderful magician, David Berglas. A lovely man, he was a great manipulator of playing cards, which made it rather ironic that he lost all his own money gambling. We never did find out what the magic department was supposed to do. Charlie got mad when he found out that there was only one person in that department, so I had to get David to sign up another two magicians. True, at the end of the film Le Chiffe performs magic tricks, but as this part was played by Orson, a pretty good amateur magician himself, and not one to take lessons from anyone, none of them was ever called to perform any magic on the film at all.

However, David was to earn his keep because, being a gambler, he was an authority on casinos, and became our technical advisor as well as playing the part of the chief croupier.

I liked David a lot, and we spent some fun evenings together, when he would use his mastery of magic to totally dumbfound waiters, hat check girls, and members of the public who were bemused when he did things like tearing up five pound notes and then finding the complete one in someone's pocket.

One night he asked me to go with him whilst he drove from the Royal Academy in Piccadilly to Pall Mall. The next day he was appearing on a television programme for the BBC about extra-sensory perception. He was going to be blind-folded, then a black sack, which had been laboratory tested, would be put over his head, then he would be taken to a car he had never driven before. He was to drive out of Burlington House into Piccadilly, around the Circus, down the Haymarket and park the car in Pall Mall. He and I travelled the route, and I noticed him taking note of certain landmarks. The programme was shot the next day under the supervision of three eminent scientists, at the end of which they asked him if he possessed certain powers.

"No," he replied, "it's a trick. But you find out how it is done!"

The day came when we actually started shooting. It was a very unromantic spot: a car-wash in Shepherd's Bush, one of the uglier parts of outer London. For two days, Yootha Joyce and several good-looking girls dressed in black plastic uniforms crawled all over Peter's car as it went through the wash. The girls were soaked, so their figures left little to the imagination. After that we moved into the studio.

From the start, Peter's behaviour was erratic. He was accompanied by his little group consisting of his chauffeur, valet, right hand man, Bert Mortimer, and his stunt double – who, like his stand-in, didn't even vaguely look like Peter. Then there was his make-up man who had little work to do as Peter didn't do too many of his famous disguises in this film. He also had his actor chums, like Graham Stark and David Lodge, for whom parts had to be found. Peter would arrive late, then find something to delay him further, and often the crew and fellow artists would wait hours for him.

However, at that stage, that wasn't my main worry.

I knew we would be needing the girl very soon. The "Richest Girl in the World" looked like she was going to be "The *Invisible* Richest Girl in the World"!, as so far we had no one. So I looked to see what else we could shoot, but no sets were ready for use, and no casting had been done for the available locations. At the last moment Maude Spector rang me to say that Charlie had cast Ursula Andréss, a non-UK citizen who would need a work permit.

This was a tedious procedure through the Home Office, who in turn consulted the corresponding Trades Union, in this case the actors' Union, Equity. I spoke to a charming woman at the Home Office and explained my problem. She promised to speed things up, saying that as far as she was concerned I could have the permit immediately, but the Unions always seemed to lose the documents, or were on holiday, anything to slow the process down in the hope that the producer would give up and cast a British citizen. This was the start of my long relationship with the Home Office and in the end I applied for work permits for not only Ursula but Orson Welles, Joanna Petitt, Daliah Lavi, William Holden, Woody Allen, Charles

Boyer, John Huston, Kurt Kasznar, George Raft, Jean Paul Belmondo and Barbara Bouchet, as well as the Action director, Richard Talmadge. All of them wanted as of yesterday! I have to say Equity was very kind to us and in the end I only got refused one, and that was for Charlie's girlfriend. As she had no acting experience at all, it was hardly surprising, but Charlie liked to think it was my incompetence!

The script was an on-going nightmare, pages would arrive the night before we were to shoot, and even on one occasion the day after! Two weeks after the start of principle photography, the heavies from Columbia arrived, Ken Maidment, Andy Donnelly, and Don Romney.

"John," Ken started, "you have been shooting now for two weeks."

"Right," I responded.

"But on your Progress Reports you are showing that you are two weeks over schedule."

"Right again," I replied.

"But you must have shot something?" he pleaded.

"Ken, we have quite a few minutes actually, the only trouble is we haven't shot anything that was in the original script. It is my understanding that these scenes are still to be shot, so you can see why we are two weeks over."

Poor Ken, off he went with his troops, back to his London office to report back to his masters in Los Angeles.

We were soon into the casino set which occupied the whole of one of the largest sound stages at Shepperton. Apart from the principals, we engaged numerous great-looking actresses to play what were really crowd parts. It was a good idea, because not only did we have the best looking of the available girls, but we also had trained actresses who could react to the action going on around the gambling tables, something that few extras were able to manage successfully, bless them. The idea was to sell the film on gorgeous girls, and I guess they had a point as there was pretty little else in the film.

We had a tie-up with "Playboy" and Hugh Heffner came for lunch with us one day. He was a strange, rather boring man, I thought, and I couldn't recognise the man I read about in his monthly magazine. I guess he was tired out with all that humping of the centrefold girls.

With all these girls and the "Playboy" tie-up we were surrounded every day with stills photographers. As Jack Hyldyard said to me, "This will be the first film in the history of the industry to have exposed more 'still' stock (film) than movie stock !" Sadly, I was too busy to give them even a cursory glance.

One day Phyl, my secretary, came in to tell me that there was a Mr Murray in her office asking to see me.

"Show him in!" I said, for Chic Murray was a famous Scottish comic, a comics' comic, admired by so many professionals. Chic had a special brand of humour, and it was his deadpan strong Scottish accent, so beloved by every amateur mimic, that gave his ridiculous patter its comic edge.

This tall man entered the office and I jumped up to greet him, apologising profusely for not having seen him before, sitting him down and offering him a drink.

"How long have you been with us?" I asked.

He replied, "It'll be four weeks now."

"God, that makes it even worse. There really is no excuse for me not having greeted you before."

"Oh, please don't apologise. I know how busy you are."

I asked him if everything was all right, if his dressing-room was okay. To which he replied everything was excellent and that he shared it with Jonathan Routh. However, there was one favour we could do: could he go on set to see what was happening?

Poor chap, not only had he not been used all that time, but he hadn't even got onto the stage!

The script called for Ursula to enter, held aloft in an elephant's trunk. We engaged a small circus, but as there was no stabling at the studios it was decided that the elephant would come up every morning. Each time the circus was on call, the elephant would leave its quarters and travel to Shepperton. Every morning the circus was cancelled, and Dougie would call the police in Esher to stop the elephant at the A3 roundabout. One morning the elephant keeper had had enough, and ignoring the police message, came on to the studio. That day a charming woman from Constance Spry, the Knightsbridge florist, who was carrying an enormous bunch of expensive flowers, stopped the studio manager to ask him the way. She was rather attractive and Andy Worker took her to his office and rang through to the Property Master to find out which film was expecting delivery of the flowers. On being told that he had no idea, Worker gave him a bollocking and told him that it was his job to know. To which the Property Master replied, "Sorry, guv'nor, but I didn't even know about the elephant."

We never did shoot the circus.

It was the same with "Super Pooh".

Peter had the idea that instead of Winnie the Pooh we would have an over sized teddy bear "Super Pooh". As we had no script on this creature and no one knew where he fitted in, Super Pooh was on call every day. For weeks, the poor guy in the Super Pooh costume completely covered with the exception of his head, used to wander around the studios, like some decapitated monster. Again, this over-sized teddy never did get in front of the camera and none of us knew what he was going to do if he had.

Despite the never-ending script changes and Peter's behaviour, we continued to shoot, albeit in a rather erratic way. From the time the clapper board went in till long after the "Cut", whilst watching the rushes, our director was convulsed with laughter. Though most of the cast and crew didn't see the joke, Joe's laughter was so infectious that we all started to guffaw as well. "Well that went down well," he would say in his strong Scottish accent as we left the preview theatre, not for a moment realising that it was his infectious laugh they were reacting to, not the rushes!

Ursula was the opposite of Peter and on the days she was on call the morale of the unit shot up. She was a darling, and I soon fell in love with her. The great thing about her was she didn't take herself seriously. I remember doing a stills session with her, when the stills' man wanted her to take different poses. She bent over and looked at her crutch saying, "Hello there, you little money spinner, you!"

Similarly when she was in a film in Ireland, "The Blue Max", starring opposite George Peppard, the director insisted she do a love scene in the nude, much to her great annoyance. At midday she came into the restaurant at Ardmore studios. "That director," she fumed, "has photographed my crutch from seventeen different angles," and then putting on that sweet smile of hers said, "and I know it only looks good from four!" What a darling.

In contrast, Ian Hendry, a very good actor, was on the point of being cast when he turned up drunk as a skunk, and that was the end of that. Poor Ian, he was such a good actor, and had starred in notable films like Sydney Lumet's "The Hill", but he could not control the booze. The really sad thing about him was that he was married to a fine young actress, Janet Munro, who also had a drink problem. They loved each other, I am sure, but they should never have lived together. Married to other people they might well have conquered their addictions, but as it was they both died tragically young.

Another addition to our cast was my old friend Orson Welles. After his appalling behaviour during "Ferry to Hong Kong" I was expecting the same sort of thing. However, after a few days I realised that here we had a completely different Orson. This Orson was the professional, a good time keeper, an actor who listened to the director, knew his lines – in fact, one could not have wished for a better behaved star.

One day, standing on the side of the set with him, and after studying what was going and muttering "fascinating business," he quietly whispered to me, "Mr Sellers is not very professional, is he?"

As Peter became more and more difficult, so Orson became more and more co-operative. Peter hated him. This came to a head over the Princess Margaret incident. One morning the studio manager called me referring to a call from Scotland Yard about our lunch guest. "Hold on a second, what lunch guest?"

"Oh, I thought you knew, it's Princess Margaret. And Mr Sellers has booked the studio boardroom for lunch."

I knew she was a friend of Peter's as one day earlier on he said to me, "I don't mind fucking her, but I do resent having to call her ma'am whilst I'm doing it!"

I caught up with him on the stage. "Yes, she's been nagging me to come down, so I thought just you, me, Joe, and John Law could have a bite with her." Then throwing me a piercing look, "I don't have to invite Ursula or Orson, do I?"

"Well, Peter, it's your party," I replied, "but they are your co-stars and it might be…"

But he quickly cut me off: "Well, I don't think I have to." And stormed off. This went on all day. He must have changed his mind four or five times. But by the time she arrived they were on the invitation list.

Conspicuously absent, and not even mentioned, was Charlie Feldman. He rang me that morning and asked, "Who is coming, the Queen or the Princess?"

"The Princess," I told him.

To which his only response was: "Big deal."

Orson was aware what was going on, and was highly amused by it all. Our lunch was very fraught as Orson did not abide by protocol. When she was talking about Danny Kaye's classical concert which she attended at the Albert Hall she said, "He was so far away I couldn't really appreciate his style of conducting."

To which Orson remarked, "Well if *you* can't get a good seat, who *can?*"

This sort of remark didn't faze her at all, but enraged Peter who wanted to be the only one on chummy terms with her.

Although a life-long Royalist, I did not take to her at all. I had to escort her around the studio and take her on the set and I found her hard going, and far from the attractive person I had always thought her to be.

From then on, the relationship between Peter and Orson got even worse. Things finally came to a head one day when a furious Peter barged into my office shouting, "John, I will not work with Mr Welles anymore."

"What do you mean exactly?" I asked hesitantly.

"What I mean 'exactly', is that I will not work with Mr Welles any more!"

"But, Peter, you haven't finished your big casino scene with him yet," I explained.

"Well, you will have to shoot it without me."

"But you're both in the scene together," I pleaded.

"Do I have to tell you how to make films?" he raged. "You shoot Orson, then turn the camera around and shoot me, got it ?"

Well, of course, you could shoot them separately and then cut the two together, but it was hardly the way to approach a major scene in a major movie.

I talked it over with Charlie, but as Peter had left the studio, we had no choice. I explained the situation to Orson and he simply said, "I always thought he was a goddamn amateur!"

So we shot the scene with the Continuity Girl reading Peter's lines. Orson was finished. And we had an early rushes call the next day so that he could leave the country.

Peter arrived, on time, and seemed to be in a good mood, so I breathed a huge sigh of relief. However, my euphoria did not last long. I got an urgent message to go to the set. When I arrived, the director whispered to me, "He's changed the script."

"What do you mean, he's changed the script?" I asked in bewilderment.

"He's changed the script, and written his own version." And that is exactly what had happened.

"It was crap, this is much better," he said.

I pointed out that we had already shot Orson with the original script, and his new dialogue would not match what we had shot.

"Well, that's your problem. I won't use that script, I will only shoot this one," he replied.

"But, Peter, we can't re-shoot Orson because he's left the country!"

He just shrugged.

So the scene was shot and the editor did his best, but the end of the film is a bit difficult to comprehend to say the least. But this was "Casino Royale" and I think that by the time the audience had sat through over two hours of equal incomprehension, it really didn't matter much!

The next day – as always – the main gate rang me when Peter had arrived, and I was happy to note that he had arrived once again bang on time. My tranquillity was short-lived. Bert Mortimer rang me to say that Peter wanted to see me.

"Oh my God," I thought, "what now?"

I walked up from my office to his dressing-rooms in the Old House and as I entered his make-up room, he leapt out of the chair, almost foaming at the mouth. "I am really mad," he said. And I thought, "You're absolutely right!" He raged around the room, "Do you know what that Assistant said to me? Do you know what that Dominic said?"

"No, Peter, what did he say?"

"He said 'we're ready when you are, Mr Sellers.' 'Ready when you are'!"

Knowing that there was no point in arguing I said, "He didn't?!"

"He bloody did: 'ready when you are'," he repeated.

"Then, in that case, he is fired."

This seemed to calm him, and he sat back in the make-up chair still muttering, "'ready when you are'."

I said, "I am going to see to this right away, you stay there. I am fucking furious and heads are going to roll, 'ready when you are' indeed!"

I left the room and hunted out the second assistant, "Listen, Peter is having one of his fits, and it is your turn, so take a couple of days off and come back on Monday." The next Monday when he came back to work, Peter didn't say a word. There was never any logic to his behaviour.

Whenever he wanted something, a new camera, or a tape machine, he had to have it immediately. Once he wanted a set of drums, and people were dispatched in fast cars to town. They were set up in one of his rooms, he came in, banged away a few times, and that was that. The drums were packed away the following day, never to be seen again. The same fate awaited all his toys which were brought on to the set to be demonstrated, holding up shooting, and then ignored. He was the typical spoilt child who breaks all his toys and like a spoilt child he could be very vicious, often picking on one of the crew and having them removed from the set.

One day Peter arrived in my office saying, "I just want you to know that Joe is getting too big for his boots." He then phoned Charlie and said that if we didn't change directors he would not work any more. So the man who Peter had insisted direct the film was to be fired because Peter would not work with him.

Poor Joe was sacked that very day. Not that he would have to worry too long for on Sellers's next film, "The Magic Christian", Sellers once again insisted that Joe directed. And once again the film was a turkey.

In came director number two, Robert Parish, a charming American with a background as an Oscar-winning editor. For many years he was the editor for the legendary director John Ford. He later became a director himself and brought his technical prowess to the floor. However, he never realised the potential envisaged by the industry. He was a strange choice, because what was needed at the time was not so much a technician, but a director who understood comedy and had experience in major feature production handling major stars. But Charlie had been pushed into a corner by Peter, and he did not have the time to search the world for a replacement.

Bob was a lovely man, and I found life a lot easier with him because he was such an old hand at the game. Once again we settled down, or so we thought. But it wasn't long before Peter was up to his old tricks, and things got slower and slower. Charlie rang me one day and said, "Listen, kid, I've got an idea how to cope with Sellers. Why don't we make him the producer and see if that helps? You don't mind, do you?"

"Charlie, I'd agree to anything that would solve our problem," I replied.

So it was announced that Peter was now the producer. It was like the old movie chestnut about the girl on "Cleopatra" who said to her friend on the set, "Who do you have to fuck to get off this film?"

Incidentally, I told this once to Orson Welles and he had never heard it before, and was very miffed when after recounting this to his friends to find out that they had all heard it years before.

So Peter became the producer but nothing really changed, although there was a slight increase in output. I don't think he even knew what a producer did, his one and only instruction was when my door was flung open and Peter shouted from the corridor the immortal lines, "John, forget the octopus, but I want a hundred massed Scottish pipers."

I sat at my desk and repeated out loud, "Forget the octopus, and get 100 Scottish Pipers." What was going on? Was it all getting to me? There was nothing in the script that called for such an item, but Peter was allowed to have a free hand in his new capacity as producer! I asked Dougie to try and find the pipers. He came back to me with the dismal news that the army had only a handful in Britain, most of them being spread around the world. Then I came up with one of my better ideas: Chic Murray!

Chic knew anyone who was anyone in Scotland. He not only knew them but was admired by most of them. He was my man. Bless his heart, he didn't hesitate for a second. He was on the next plane to Scotland and a few days later rang me to say that he had got The Edinburgh Police Band, The Glasgow Police Band, and several coal-miners' pipe bands. We chartered an aircraft to fly them down. Michael Stringer, our over-worked designer, built a white backing right around one of the stages, and painted the floor white according to our producer's instruction. Special effects were alerted to supply "mist". So, we had the cast, we had the set, we had the hundred pipers … what next?

The full contingent of pipers fell into line in the studio car park, and were a magnificent sight. They tuned up – a ghastly sound – and then, under the Senior Pipe Major's command, marched off and did a tour of the studio circular road. It was a rare sight even for a film studio, and it brought out everyone from their offices, cutting rooms, everywhere. Then they marched onto the stage, and paraded around whilst the final lighting adjustments were made.

Ready to shoot.

A red light was called for … "Roll 'em" … the clapper board went in … "Action."

The parade took off, and after a while Peter came in and sort of shook his hands at the pipers and then retired. He repeated this several times until "Cut". This went on for two days, only spiced up by Peter O'Toole, having made the mistake of popping in to say hello, being co-opted into the pipe band. Chic Murray and Jonathan Routh also made brief appearances.

On the second day I asked Bob Parish what it was all about. "Is it supposed to be funny, dramatic, what?"

To which he replied, "I am sorry, John, but obviously you don't have a sense of humour."

Ah, I thought, Sellers has got at him. For Peter could, when he wanted, charm the birds off the trees and could flatter people into thinking that he was their very best friend, until he got bored and then it was "chop of their heads!"

After this, his behaviour quickly returned to being unpredictable, and his producer's role came to an end by some unsaid mutual agreement. Things returned to normal, but help was at hand.

I was in Charlie's house when he was on the phone to the chief executive of Columbia, Leo Jaffe. "Listen, Leo, Johnny Dark has just come in. Now look, *he* can't control him, *I* can't control him, so if you're so fucking clever why don't you come over here and control him yourself?" Turning to me with a big wink he went on, "Oh, you will? Good. Look forward to seeing you, Leo." He put down the phone, "He's coming over on the next flight." And so he did.

A meeting was hurriedly arranged for the following day with Charlie, Ken Maidment, Max Setton (from the London office), myself, and Leo. We all assembled in Charlie's house, and started to discuss what could be done about Sellers's behaviour. Leo, a very small man, was sitting on a hard-backed chair, his feet hardly touching the ground when suddenly I saw him go pale and he said, "Just a moment, I think I've made a terrible mistake."

Apparently he was met at the airport by the local Columbia brass and taken to the Dorchester Hotel. He told the entourage he would meet them in the lobby. After sprucing up, he caught the lift down to the lobby and as he came out, he almost bumped into someone he knew. He put out his hand and said, "Hi, Woody. I'm Leo Jaffe." The only problem was that it wasn't Woody Allen, it was Peter Sellers!

Poor Leo. He caught the next plane back to LA. And Peter couldn't stop laughing because he knew full well what was going on, and realised with Leo's mistake he was once more off the hook.

About this time, the family and I moved to a great house in Molesey, very close to where I used to live with Peggy. After our tiny flat it was like Grand Central Station.

We also continued our search for an organisation that would let us adopt a child from a Third World country. All avenues were closed either because we had no religion, or no secure employment, or we were too old, and on top of that I was divorced. Never mind, we were determined to continue the struggle. It seemed strange to me then, as indeed it still does, that with thousands of children in the world needing homes, desperate children living in horrifying conditions needing care, attention and love, that it is so difficult to take them into one's own family. I understand that they have to be protected from nutters, slave dealers, paedophiles etc., but we were two fairly respectable people with a lovely home, anxious to have one of those kids as part of our family. But we did not fit the ridiculous rules dreamt up by bureaucrats.

The other sad thing on the home front was that I was forced to part company with Ted Bushel, as he had taken a big dislike to Ineke. I think the trouble was that he was jealous of her. He had been so close to me for so many years that he resented her, and saw her as an intrusion in my life. He tolerated Paula to a certain extent but then we weren't married and, anyhow, we had a pretty rocky relationship. But my marriage to Ineke was different and he did everything he could to break it up. Poor old Ted, I still feel sorry. I don't think I had any alternative, but I have a little guilty feeling in my stomach when I think of him. He had been a fantastic friend.

At one of our nightly meetings, Charlie handed me a bunch of pages of script and explained that this was a new section of the film that he wanted to start almost immediately. Well, this was a new one on me, and I didn't at first grasp what he was up to. It seemed that this section, or episode, was only vaguely connected with the other script. It would be entirely separate and have a different director and crew and be shot whilst the Sellers section was being completed.

Charlie had already signed the director, Ken Hughes, an experienced man who had come up the hard way, and like me had been a sound engineer, in his case with the BBC. In the army he was sent to an Army Film Unit, where I guess he learnt to become a director. After he was demobbed he started to direct documentaries, shorts and eventually 'B'-movies, until he got his break and directed the first class movie "The Trials of Oscar Wilde". Ken was a lovely man, and I became very fond of him during the time we worked together. We were friends for a long time, up until the time that he went to California when we lost touch.

I had to explain to him some of the problems that we had, the biggest being space. Space was a problem because when I made the original booking it was based on a script that never really existed from the start. However, business was booming, studio space was at a premium, and, though I leant on Andy Worker, there was not a lot he could do about it as stages had been already contracted to other companies. The stage where the casino was built was coming to the end of its already extended period, and there was no way I could get a further extension, even though we were far from finished with the set.

The heavy guns at Columbia were brought in to try and solve the problem, so much so that they tried to get Fred Zinnemann to postpone his film. In fact, if his contract had not been signed and sealed there is no doubt that Columbia would not have gone ahead with his project, and the world would have been deprived of "The Man for All Seasons".

In the end we were able to get just enough stage space for Ken's section in the silent stage, so called because it was not sound-proofed and was not normally used for filming with direct sound. Space being what it was, I took a long option on it so that when I had to release the stage where the casino was, I had somewhere to move to – not ideal but a case of necessity.

I got a call from Charlie asking whether the new stage was bigger than the one we were vacating and, on being told it was, said, "Make the set bigger then."

"I don't think the continuity is going to look too good," I said.

"Forget the continuity, I want a bigger set."

So we built a bigger set.

One day going up to this new stage, I noticed a large black Daimler parked and as I drew alongside, the window lowered and a hand came out beckoning me. I walked to the car and peered inside. Sitting there was America's number one gangster. Well, I should qualify that statement: it was *Hollywood's* greatest gangster, George Raft.

"Get in, John, and shut the door," he said. I did as I was told and sat nervously beside him. Nothing was said, except George felt in his pocket! For what? Suddenly he pulled out a bag. "Have a candy."

At this time I was working night and day, Saturdays and Sundays, to somehow run two different films at the same time, arbitrating between the two about things like who would get David Niven or some other leading artist on a given day. It was not made easier by the ever-changing script.

Ineke was always a marvellous support, and just took it that she and Daniel would hardly ever see me until the movie was over. She worried that I was over-working and that if I wasn't careful I would get over-tired and make a bad mistake, or even worse it would affect my health.

One night after a bad day where nothing had gone right, I was really pissed off. I went to the studio bar to have a couple of drinks before I went home and met this cute girl and, to cut to the chase, ended up getting home about four o'clock in the morning. I took off my shoes in the darkened hallway, quietly climbed the stairs, and opened the bedroom door. A ghostly figure rose from the bed. "Where have you been?" she asked accusingly.

"Darling, let me explain. I had a terrible day, just awful, met a girl in the bar, went up to town got pissed and ... well ..."

"Oh no, you didn't, you've been working!" What a girl! I will never get over her. What other woman would take that attitude?

We settled into our new house, and I heard that my matrimonial home with Peggy was empty. She had rented the Molesey house and in turn rented a Crown Estate house in Regent's Park. Her tenants had done a runner. Dennis Speed, the local estate agent, and an old friend, went with me to see the house.

It was in a terrible state, dirty, doors scratched by the children, windows broken, a disaster. Dennis suggested cleaning it up, repairing the worst of it and then put it on the market to see what happened. Before we could do a thing, Dennis rang me and said he had a buyer. This guy had heard the house was coming up for sale, went to see it, opened the garden gate and said, "That's it, I want to buy it." So we sold it before it was ever advertised and before any repair work had been carried out.

The buyer was an actor, Keith Baron, who later starred in several TV shows including "Lucky Jim". During what were known as the Molesey floods, the whole area was flooded and his house in particular. I waded down there to see my friends who lived next door to him, and shouted out, "Oh Lucky Jim!"

And he sarcastically replied, "I'd kill you if I could swim!"

From my share of the sale of the house I was able to buy my mother a new house that was being built on the border of our garden.

Around this time, Charlie, continuing his policy of employing producers, added an American, Gerry Bresler, whose credits included such notable films as "Gidget Goes Hawaiian"! Gerry was a talentless, ineffectual idiot, and why Charlie ever gave him a job I shall never know. We needed someone else, but we needed some one with talent. Columbia was violently opposed to the appointment, but that had no affect on Charlie other than to make him more determined. Columbia expected me to resign, but I had got used to Charlie's circus of producers. I also thought it might give John Shepbridge someone to talk to! Furthermore, I couldn't abandon the crews who had been so good to me. In any case, I knew Charlie would somehow or other get me back on board. I also felt that I owed it to Columbia, a company that had been so good to me. Mind you, at that time I did not know what a prick the guy was.

Even that nicest of men, the most professional, best-behaved actor there has ever been, David Niven, made a complaint against the asshole. He asked me, "Please, can you do something? Just as we are about to shoot, a bald head appears in front of one of the lights and asks me if I have heard who has just died!"

I don't know whether or not it was Jerry's arrival, but one day Peter packed up all his things, including the expensive wardrobe that the company had paid for, and left. His role unfinished, without a word to anyone, he just left, never to be seen again. Personally, I was glad to see him go. I understand the insecurity of an artist, I can imagine how hard it must be to live with one's own talent, but I found him an impossible, vicious bully, with no regard for anyone other than himself. He used his power to attack people who could not fight back. In the end he even turned on the person who had always remained loyal: his confidant, his dedicated employee, Bert Mortimer, whom he fired after years of dedicated service.

Part unfinished in any other film would be a catastrophe, but on this scriptless, rudderless film it didn't even cause a hiccup!

On the other hand, we had David Niven who was a real gentleman, and a true pro. One day I found him wandering around the back of the studio, and knowing he had been called three days and not used, I went up to him and said, "I am so sorry David that you have been called for three days, made-up, dressed and then not used."

"Do you know," he responded "I've just been standing here thinking how wonderful it is that I get paid all this money for doing nothing?"

Another sweet man joined us an American Action director, Richard Talmadge.

Now, Talmadge was a little bit of Hollywood history. He started in movies as Douglas Fairbanks's stunt double, and then began to make his own films with himself as the leading man, and doing all his own acrobatic stunts. But with the advent of sound and his rather heavy German accent, he was forced behind the camera as an assistant director, and then became a successful Action, or Second Unit, director.

Bob Parish's section finished early due to Peter's departure, and Richard took over shooting action material for the end of the film. This included red Indians, cowboys, sea lions, horses, large numbers of crowd, and every stunt man in the country. He was shooting all the stunt work that was being dreamt up on an hourly basis. He was a very sweet man, but he was an old man. He would have been about seventy at the time, but he acted much older, and Lewis Gilbert seemed younger at eighty than poor Richard at seventy. It was sad, but he had gone past his sell-by date.

One day we had to shoot on a Sunday and the first assistant director would not come in, so I said I would do it myself. It was a job I always loved so I did not think it was any special hardship. I thought it would also give me the opportunity to see how he worked, because the crew had been complaining to me that they could not understand his directions. So, that Sunday, with a large crowd and dozens of stunt men all on double time, we started. "So, what's the first set-up, Richard?" I asked.

This is the moment that the director sets out the next shot. "Well," he said, "let the guys come in and then ... whammy bammy." And retired back to his chair at the side of the set and alongside his sweet wife.

Now this is not exactly the instructions an assistant needs, and I could understand the frustration of Richard's crew. Poor Richard, he was in another world. We shot many more weeks with him, and things did not improve. It only shows that we all need to know when to give up, but will any of us ever admit it? If the phone rang now to ask me to go to Timbuktu to produce the re-make of "Gunga Din", I guess I'd go. So I certainly don't blame Richard in any way. He was offered a job and he did it to the best of his ability. Sadly it was just another factor in this mish-mash of a film.

I got the buzz down the grapevine that another separate section of script was on its way to me. Each time these sections popped up it meant virtually starting a new film, with all the attendant complications of artistes required on the same day for two different shoots etc. This script was something completely new and was mainly set in Scotland, with a new cast. I wondered who was going to direct this: Ken Hughes? Bob Parish? Who? And it turned out to be the legendary great John Huston! Going from Joe McGrath to John Huston was not even like going from cod to caviar. I wondered why on earth this great talent wanted to get involved in this travesty of a production.

It was not long before I found out. When I quizzed Charlie about it he said, "Money."

Apparently John was a great spender, a great gambler, and, in spite of all the great films behind him, was always short of money. Like Orson, he had to take jobs to "pay the rent".

There certainly was no stage space at Shepperton and as this sequence was isolated from the remainder of the "story", I rented space at Pinewood, engaged a production manager, took Jack Hyldyard and his camera crew from Shepperton and replaced them with a young cameraman, Nick Roeg, who became one of Britain's leading directors.

Pinewood was a very civilised place and I had many friends there from the days of "Ferry to Hong Kong". The tales of that location were part of the Pinewood legend, as the boys who had been with us never stopped recounting the stories of the lives, the loves and the wonderful time they had in the East to their less fortunate colleagues. As time went by the tales of the romances and the life style became more and more exaggerated. It was hardly surprising they came down from the rails whenever I went onto one of the stages. The studio management had changed, Arthur Alcott had left, and the days of contract production staff and technicians was over; changes I am afraid initially caused by me.

Deborah Kerr, the nicest of screen ladies, joined the nicest of actors, David Niven, and they were supported by a bevy of gorgeous girls.

Once again I did not understand the script but felt that John Huston knew a lot more about it than I did. He was a strange man, but very likeable. There was an aura around him which said, "I am someone special, talented and not to be fooled with." I remember the day before shooting started he arrived on the set with all the usual hubbub going on. The sparks still putting up the last of the lights, the props placing the furniture, the chippies, the painters, the riggers all making the final touches, all making a hell of a racket. John came in, took a chair and sat down and looked at the set without saying a word. Very gradually the noise abated till in the end you could hear the proverbial pin drop. That is what I mean by his aura.

It also had its downside. I could never find out from him what he was going to do, and every time I posed a question he would reply, "I really don't know!"

All the exteriors were in Scotland, so we had location people there to take photographs for John to look at. I then got a message from John Merriman, the Huston production manager, that John wanted to go to Ireland. I hurried over to Pinewood to see him, and tried to explain the problems of making Ireland look like Scotland. The script was all about a grouse shoot, and I tried to explain there weren't any grouse in Ireland. Taking the cigarette out of his mouth, he bent down from his great height, and said in a very low voice, "Then you'll just have to send some over there, won't you?" And that is exactly what we did!

Apart from this, the shooting went very smoothly. With a talented director, professional actors, and top crew it was a dream and in complete contrast to what we had at Shepperton with dear old Richard still shooting lighted arrows into the crowd, blowing up the wrong car, and keeping highly paid stunt men standing around doing nothing.

The next to arrive on my desk was a new script for another segment, to be directed by Val Guest. Again, he was a lovely man but he had mainly directed 'B'-movies. Another strange choice, I thought. I knew Val would bring it in on time, and run a professional shoot, but would he deliver first feature material?

After reading the script I knew there wasn't much help there. I asked myself what Charlie was up to. Here was the man who had produced such films as "The Seven Year Itch" and "A Streetcar Named Desire", had worked with the best, represented the biggest stars of Hollywood, counted every major executive as a friend, spending millions on a fractured script and, with the exception of John Huston, leaving it in the hands of people who were far from the front rank of helmsmen. I think I discovered the reason much later.

As usual there was a problem with space, and this new piece of script needed a lot of it. Pinewood and Shepperton were both full, so I took myself off to MGM at Borehamwood.

I had used this studio before for some exterior scenes for the Ken Hughes' section, where I had built on their back lot. I knew they were not easy to make a deal with, but I had nowhere else to go. The trouble was the studio manager knew this as well. I was forced to pay the full rental, without the concessions that are normally included. In fact he took me for a ride. So I reluctantly signed the contract quickly, as I was aware with stage space so short I might lose even that, and then we would have to go abroad or stop shooting.

Meanwhile Ineke had a chat with a local vicar to whom she poured out our tale of woe in trying to adopt a child from overseas. He gave her the name of The Agnostics Adoption Society. So without much optimism we took ourselves off one cold winter's night to a small office in Bethnal Green, not the most salubrious part of London. There we met a delightful woman, Kirstine Richards. After listening to us carefully, she told us that they were such a small organisation they just did not have the finance to keep agents in foreign countries. We thought that once again we had come to a halt, so thanked her and got up to go. She then said, "The problem with adoption in this country is that whilst there is a long queue of people wanting to adopt, they all want little blue-eyed girls. But what about the mentally or physically handicapped, what about the black babies, the cross-breed babies? There's no long queue for them."

After a quick look at each other we said that we would take the next baby, no matter what it was. We then had to fill in a lengthy form with all our personal details, including my profession, what income we had, our medical history and that of our parents, what sort of house we lived in and most importantly why we wanted to adopt.

Kirtsine said, "Now it is up to the committee to approve your application. I will be only too happy to endorse it."

Years later I found out exactly how much she had helped. The committee had not been very impressed and could not understand, if Ineke could have more children herself, why we should want to adopt. She replied, "Why shouldn't people want to adopt, as they put it, 'to do one small thing to help'?"

Her argument won the day, though it was several weeks later that we knew.

Before we left that first night she asked me one final question: Did I have anything to do with a film called "Half a Sixpence"?

"No," I laughingly replied. "I have enough trouble with 'Casino Royale', though it is being produced by a friend of mine. But why do you ask?"

"My daughter is a dancer in that film and we have to be so careful about accusations of collusion," she said.

We left that night feeling good, and that at last we were getting somewhere. Kirstine Richards made such an impression on us that we felt we were in the best of hands.

Next day I got an urgent call from the MGM studios. The American boss was over and needed to see me urgently regarding a problem with our contract. I said I would come over immediately, and smelling trouble I contacted the company lawyers, Dental Hall, and summoned Peter de Berenger to meet me at the studios in Elstree. There I was told they had a big problem. They recognised that I had a signed contract, and a deposit paid, but the picture now occupying that space was going months over schedule and would not be off before our contracted date. Having suffered by their treatment of me, I was not in a mood to help, quite apart from the fact that Columbia would not thank me for jeopardising their mammoth investment.

There was nothing that MGM could do but they had stages full of sets and a director who was not worried about the time it was taking. They begged, literally, and said they would do anything, agree to anything, if only I would give them some extra time. Whilst talking I said I had thought of a way that we could possibly delay. "Yes?" the guy nearly leapt on me, eyes bulging.

"There may be a way, but it would be very costly."

"Don't worry about that, we will pay, we will compensate you for any additional costs or inconvenience you have. Just tell me that you can help."

I came out with the best deal any producer ever had, including a gigantic discount on the stages, an agreement that I would never pay any overtime on the construction labour, free use of the back lot, and no extra charges on any other facilities or rental on any MGM owned equipment in the studio. Everyone was happy: MGM were happy, I was happy, Columbia was happy, even Stanley Kubrick was happy that he could finish his film!

And so the circus rolled on: new pages, new artists, it seemed never ending, but like all movies eventually it did come to an end. After a gigantic wrap party, I contemplated my future. I reckoned there would be about six months post-production and I wondered what Charlie would then have up his sleeve. I also wondered what plans Columbia might have for me. I knew that at that time I was very much their "flavour of the month", and they were very grateful that I did not resign when Gerry Bresler came on board.

So, after nearly three long years, the first thing I had to do was take Ineke on a short holiday. Poor darling, she had had such a tough time with me nearly always being at work and I was looking forward to making it up to her.

One Saturday I got a phone call from Bud Ornstein, asking if I would have a drink with him in town. Now I knew that Bud had left United Artists and was now Head of Production in Europe for Paramount. Ineke was very suspicious. "I'm just going to have a drink with him," I said.

"Oh yes! Why should he suddenly ring you on a Saturday?"

"Look, he's a big man, an important guy. I can't say 'no'."

"That's what worries me," she said: "You can't say 'no'."

Bud lived in Arlington House, one of the most prestigious block of flats in central London, situated just behind the Ritz, and housed one of London's leading restaurants, "The Caprice". Bud's apartment covered three floors, which gives an idea of how well-heeled he was. Although we had got to know each other during the Malaya film, we had never spent too much time together. However, he greeted me like a long lost friend.

He sat me down with a large drink and explained that he had inherited a movie that was in dire trouble. This was "Half a Sixpence", and because of penny-pinching by the producers, the film was way over budget and behind schedule. I listened as he went into a lot of detail. I knew the producer well, and it sounded like classic Charlie Schneer behaviour. The problems had now reached a crunch where the American director refused to work with Charlie anymore, and it was a question of "either he goes or I go".

Director George Sidney had major credits including "Anchors Away" with Frank Sinatra and Grace Kelly, "Show Boat", and "Annie Get Your Gun" to name just three. And he was one of the industry's most experienced directors of musicals. Paramount had little choice.

"Well," I said, "you certainly have problems."

Bud looked straight at me, "Don't give me that shit, I haven't got problems, *you've* got problems."

"What do you mean?"

"You know damn well what I mean. You are going to take over producing the film."

"Whoa … hold on a bit. I'd love to help you, but I have all the post-production on 'Casino …', I'm taking my wife on holiday, and Charlie Schneer is a friend of mine, so it is impossible for me to do it."

"Have another drink." He grabbed my glass and I followed him into his walk-in bar. "Look, you can take your wife on holiday after the movie. Paramount will pay for you to go anywhere you say. Next, Charlie is going to be fired whatever happens, or I ain't got a director. Third, I have already spoken to Charlie Feldman and he says he will release you."

I found out later that when Bud had been appointed to his Paramount position, Feldman had written him a letter of congratulations and added that if he ever could do anything for him not to hesitate to ask. So when trouble broke, Bud rang Charlie and said, "I'm ringing to cash in that favour: let me have John Dark!"

I did manage to hang on for about a couple of hours, but in the end he wore me down, and so I agreed on certain conditions. The first was that I would go to see Charlie Schneer before making a final decision. Secondly, that I would go on holiday as soon as the movie stopped shooting. And thirdly, that Paramount would give me a letter giving me personal control of the film. So I met Schneer, who was very sweet saying, "I am going to be fired anyway and I would rather it be you than anyone else."

Bud wanted me to fire the production manager as well, but I thought that unfair and that there had been enough firing. It was probably a mistake on my part as he was very loyal to Charlie, and certainly not to me. Understandable, but not very helpful.

Back home, I explained everything to Ineke, who was not a happy bunny, but when I told her that at the end of shooting I would take to her Brazil to see her brother, she cheered up slightly. But, typically, she said, "It's not for me. I worry about you. You need some rest." I did, but the thought of a new challenge got the adrenaline pumping, and I felt very fit.

I said good-bye to the boys and girls left on "Casino …", and told Dougie that he would be in employment until the end of post-production. I got the blessing of Columbia, who raised no objections. I think there had been some back street work going on there, as they seemed to know all about it.

Much to my surprise I received a personal letter from the President of Columbia, Leo Jaffe, which read:

Dear John

I was sorry to learn that, because of a very important offer that had been made to you by Paramount, you deemed it advisable to take an assignment with them for the next two years. I just want you to know that we liked having you with our company and sincerely hope that your new assignment will be a happy and fruitful one.

I also want to take this opportunity to thank you for your efforts on behalf of CASINO ROYALE. Despite our many problems, we still feel very strongly that we will have an outstanding picture, and we know that your contribution was an important one. Warmest personal regards,

Sincerely

Mind you, it was soon forgotten when neither I, nor any of the British crew, was invited to the premiere until I called the Columbia office, and got tickets for Julie Harris, Jack Hyldyard and myself. Even so, we were still not invited to the party.

Instead of kicking up a fuss, Julie Harris threw a small party for the gallant few who had suffered such torment. We at least had a happy time, despite watching a load of total crap, a feeling obviously shared by the first-night audience. We also suspected that it was Jerry Bresler who drew up the lists for the premiere and party.

It would be like him, for he had tried to reduce my credit, but Columbia put their foot down and insisted that I was given credit according to my contract with them.

The film got the worst reviews ever, and was a complete disaster; though Columbia always insisted that it made money. I think they had to say this, and with the help of a bit of creative accounting prove that their decision to make the film was vindicated. In all fairness, I have to say after all these years, it has for some strange reason become a cult film, and is a healthy seller on DVD

So one cold Tuesday morning I officially joined "...Sixpence".

I met George Sidney the previous evening, when he poured out all his problems to me. He was a strange man, but then weren't they all in this business? Whilst talking to him I just thought of all the wonderful films he had made. My first job at this stage was to get close to him, to get him to trust me, and to address the gripes that he had. The next was to make sure that the company were not going to be disturbed by this sudden change of producer.

It was a lucky break that the film starred Tommy Steele, whom I had worked with in the past you will remember. I got on well with him, but I was well aware of his devious behaviour.

On that particular cold morning, the company were shooting one of the big musical numbers at the Wimbledon Theatre. I walked down the centre aisle of the theatre with all the usual noise going on around me, lights being man-handled into position under the shouted instructions of the gaffer, cameras being positioned, dancers rehearsing in a corner, people chattering, the usual noisy start to the day. As I walked down, the noise gradually died down. This may remind you of John Huston's visit to the "Casino ..." set, but let me tell you that was in respect of his great talent. In this case it was, "What the fuck have we got here?"

Up on the stage I was greeted by Tommy, and after a quick shake of the hand he came straight out with, "You know they cut the 'Flash Bang ...' number, what ye'r going to do?"

"I'm putting it back in," I said.

A cheer went up from the assembled dancers and cast and the tension was broken. I did not know at that stage that it had been cut. I thought it a strange decision as it had been the most popular song in the stage show. By agreeing to put it back I had in one stroke got the company with me. If at a later date I found that there was a good reason for the decision I reckoned by that time I would have won the trust of the company.

Next day in the office, the last cost return signed by Charlie Schneer dropped on my desk. He had plastered all over the front page how much extra my services were going to cost the film. I really did not care, but I thought it rather petty. Then my phone rang and it was Schneer himself. We started a perfectly friendly conversation for I was genuinely fond of him, then he started giving me certain instructions. "Hold on a bit, Charlie," I said. "I have taken over now. I must run it my way, and that is what Paramount is paying me for."

I took out the letter I had from Paramount spelling out in no uncertain terms my position. I read this to him, and he put the phone down. I am afraid that was the end of our friendship. Sad, but I had no alternative. I had insisted that he kept his credit, and all his fee, so I didn't feel too bad about it, though I would have preferred to have kept his friendship.

So began my time not just on "Half a Sixpence" but also with Paramount. I had a joint contract with that illustrious company, both as a producer and as an Executive of the company, which hit the front page of the trades.

Paramount had recently been taken over by a major American conglomerate, Gulf and Western (nothing to do with the oil company). Its President was an energetic mid-European, Charles H. Bludhorn, who was determined to turn this rather staid and old-fashioned company into a modern vibrant one, and to that end had engaged a team of new executives. Bud headed Europe, and Robert Evans America. I was very happy to find that Michael Flint (late of Denton, Hall) was running business affairs. He had represented "Casino Royale" for Columbia, and was an old and trusted friend. I didn't meet Charlie Bludhorn (I seemed to be surrounded by Charlies in those days!) or the American team until much later.

In London, Bud did gradually build up his team. He engaged Jerry Juroe as a production executive, an excellent publicity man but with little knowledge of production. At a later date, he engaged Steve Previn (brother of André), who again was a very nice guy, but a lightweight. To head publicity he brought in my old friend from "Ferry to Hong Kong" days, Gerry Lewis, who not only was a nice guy, but was also a top class publicity chief, later to become head of publicity for Stephen Spielberg. Of course all these people in turn engaged assistants, secretaries and so on.

The offices in Wardour Street were dank and depressing, so architects and designers were brought in to completely change them.

The first day Bud went into his new office, he pulled the curtains and they fell down – rotten through age! When he asked for a drink, the only thing they could find was some brandy in the first aid box! Things were about to change.

Whilst all this was going on, I was busy getting "… Sixpence" back on the rails. George and I struck up a good relationship. We not only worked well, but most nights went out to dinner and socialised a lot together. On the floor everything was swinging and the company seemed to accept the change at the top. However, in my review of the costs and the schedule I came up against my old enemy, stage space. There was not enough stage space to complete the film. So once again I went to Andy Worker (the Shepperton studio manager) for help. He did try to help, without success.

After a week, Bud asked me to come to a meeting at his flat with the previous Head of Paramount in London. Also in attendance was an American old-timer who had been put on the film by the old regime to represent Paramount.

As soon as the meeting started this guy started to attack me for the way I was handling my job. I let him rant on until he ran out of steam then said, "All that may be true, it is a matter of opinion, but what concerns me, and I would have thought would have concerned you, is that because of falling behind schedule, the contracts on the stages are going to run out before we are finished."

There was a long silence, then Bud's predecessor piped up, "Well, I knew that." Another long silence. I never saw either man again.

This was Paramount. When I asked who counter-signed the "... Sixpence" cheques on behalf of Paramount, I was told it was the company secretary.

"But what does he know about film production?" I asked. "How often does he go to the studio?"

"You don't understand. He *doesn't* go to the studio. You see, he has a bad heart condition, and this is a job he can do sitting down"!

By some tricky juggling, and the cancellation of a small film, we just about had enough space. However, there was no way that we could afford to go even a day over-schedule, and did not allow for the shooting of the "Flash Bang Wallop" number. Bud agreed with me that we should try and find a way of including this number in the film, as the audience would feel cheated if it was not included.

On the personal front, it was back to long seven-day weeks. Apart from being at the studio from seven in the morning till late, Bud liked me to go to town to tell him how the day went, and more importantly to discuss future projects. We used to speak to both New York where Paramount Head Office was based and also to studios in LA.

Bud was a hell of a drinker, and one of the first changes in the offices was to make sure there was always a large supply of liquor. After a long meeting accompanied by large drinks, we usually would go out to dinner to somewhere like "The Mirabelle", "The Caprice" or "The Ivy". Then it was back to his apartment where we would continue our discussions about the future which, as they were through a haze of alcohol, probably made no sense whatsoever. Bud lived an opulent life style. His amazing apartment looked out onto Green Park.

Bud was a lovely American who had spent many years in Europe. He was especially fond of Spain, where he had been Mr United Artists in Madrid for many years. He always carried with him a silver framed picture of Franco, who we used to argue about in the middle of the night. He was a strange chap in that he did his best to make people think he was not Jewish, something else we would discuss when the wine had flowed. Bud was married to a darling woman, Gwynne. She was the niece of the legendary silent movie star, the Queen of Hollywood, Mary Pickford, who was the first of the major international film stars and also the founder, with Charles Chaplin, of United Artists. At the age of five, Gwynne was adopted by her grandmother, but when she died Gwynne went to live with Mary, and to all intents and purposes was brought up by her.

I loved Gwynne, though at times she could be little vague. One of my favourite stories about Gwynne was when Bud had an answering service fitted to his phone, in those days something of a rarity. He forgot to tell his wife so when the phone rang and she answered, the phone said, "This is Mayfair 0629. ..."

"Oh, no it isn't," said a indignant and swaying Gwynne, "that's my number."

"... The home of Mr and Mrs George Ornstein ..." it continued.

"For God's sake, that's me!"

"... If you wish to leave a message, please speak after the tone."

"Why on earth should I want to leave a message for myself?"

We used to re-play that tape many times.

Bud and Gwynne had three children, the eldest girl was married to one of the Beatles' entourage, and was already married when I met them so I really hardly knew her. The second daughter, Mary, was a sweet girl, with a wonderful face, good-looking and full of character. The son was a fairly useless guy at that time, but then his parents did not give him much attention. Indeed they did not give any of their children much of their time. I don't think Bud had a great deal of interest in them. He just loved his work and sitting around with a few buddies drinking into the early hours. I loved both Bud and Gwynne, and I spent many, many happy hours in their company.

Luckily I had put Billy Willmot in the contract, so I never had to drive myself. I would leave Arlington House in the early hours of the morning. As Billy said, the milkman was his best friend at the time. Dear Billy; I would get in his car and fall fast asleep till he woke me up when we arrived. He was from a bygone age, dressed in dark blue suit, white shirt, dark blue tie, and cap, and he always insisted on getting out to open the door. He was a friend and a buddy, loved by me and by my family. When things were quiet we would go out and have a few drinks together, but he never took advantage. I would say to him, "Billy we got to go and see so and so, it's a cap job." This meant a bit of bullshit. We worked together on or off for over forty years, and I considered him one of God's real gentlemen.

Now, if I was not with Bud, I would be with George. He was the most generous of men and there is no doubt we had some great times together. He lived at Claridge's but he did not like the way his suite was furnished so he hired new furniture of his own. We always dined at the most expensive restaurants. His girlfriend was an ex-Bluebell girl (the most beautiful show girls in Paris) who was wonderful fun, but also one hell of a drinker. One night she changed around all the shoes which had been left outside the various rooms, not a new caper but very damaging to London's leading hotel.

George lived in some strange world. One day he didn't turn up for work and when I eventually got him on the phone he said, "Do you know who is staying here?" he asked.

"No, George, I have no idea." I replied tetchily.

"Only the Russian Head of State!"

"Well, Heads of State always stay at Claridge's, George, it is quite normal."

"Normal!" he yelled. "Supposing someone takes a shot at him and misses and kills me! What about that?"

I changed my tone, "Well, George, if it worries you, why don't you come down here to the studio, where you will be safe?"

After a very long pause, "Okay, but I hope I'll get out alive!"

Another time we were sitting in the monitor room at a music session when he suddenly took his pipe out of his mouth, leant foreword and said quietly, "Have you heard of the atomic bomb?"

"Of course I've heard of the atomic bomb," I answered. "Why?"

Pointing the stem of his pipe at himself, he mouthed, "Me."

"You?" I asked in some amazement.

He nodded.

"What do you mean, George? You built it?"

He nodded, "Supervised it."

As I said, he was on another planet. I had to bear this in mind when dealing with him. I never argued with him at the time, but would talk to him later and gently bring him around to reality. He was a master at directing musical numbers, and used to use multiple cameras on dollies to interweave with the routines, crossing each other at times, thus knowing that he had a mass of material to use in the cutting rooms. I ran all the material they shot, and I must say that I was very impressed with the dance numbers, and thought the music was delightful.

The picture looked lush, mainly because they had a great cameraman, Geoff Unsworth. Gentle Geoff went on to light such great films as "Superman" and "Cabaret". He was married to our Continuity Girl (now called Script Supervisor), Maggie, a highly experienced, talented and educated lady. After Geoff's tragic death she became personal assistant to David Lean.

The choice of designer was a mistake. He was American, and talented but, like so many Americans I met, he did not function well out of his own territory.

The real talent was the choreographer, Gillian Lynne. She was a small bundle of amazing energy, and had been leading soloist at the Sadlers Wells' Ballet, and star dancer at the London Palladium. She worked in movies with the great and legendary Errol Flynn with whom she had an affair. (Which I think secretly she was very proud of.) I asked what he was like as a lover, and she said he was terrible because he drank so much. So, why did she sleep with him, I asked. "Because he was Errol Flynn," she replied. And why not? He was the most fantastic looking, charismatic actor ever: the truly definitive film star, perhaps the greatest ever.

She danced all over the world, winning awards in London, Broadway, Australia and France. Her talents have been used in musicals, opera and ballet. On television she is best known for her work on "The Muppet Show" and in that medium she has also directed straight plays. She is a BAFTA winner, but probably her greatest achievement was winning the prestigious Olivier Award for "Cats". In the year 2000 she was decorated by the Queen with the OBE for services to dance.

She is also one of the nicest people in show business. With charm and personality she gets the best out of her dancers, and not for her the bullying tactics of choreographers like Busby Berkeley, she builds a close relationship with each one, so they want to do the very best for her.

Sometimes she would use character actors in certain of the numbers, picking them for their looks even if they had no dance training at all. One of these in "... Sixpence" was an actor, Georgie Moon, who I had worked with at the Bush when he played second lead to Tommy Handley in a terrible comedy film "Time Flies".

Georgie was that typical all-round English character actor, who did not get too much work other than summer season, pantomime, and the odd days in TV. Always dependable, but never to gain the heights again that he had when he starred with

Tommy Handley. I think he liked me because I always treated him, as he still was in my eyes ... a star.

Gillian took Georgie and several other character actors and carefully choreographed a dance sequence they could manage if they really worked, and – golly! – did they work. Georgie told me he would never have taken on the job if he had known in advance what was expected of him. He also confessed that he was in love with Gilly and did it all for her.

Darling Gilly, my very special friend then, now and forever!

Backing Gilly we had another talented person: American musical director, Irwin Kostal, a gentle, talented professional with credits such as "West Side Story", "The Sound of Music", "Mary Poppins" amongst many. This is someone else who remained a friend up until the time of his death. The relationship between these two was what created the magic.

Not many people realise how a dance number is created. First, there is the song, then the choreographer designs the dance. Once that is constructed the MD scores the tune from the base line that the choreographer and the dance pianist have written. Then, and only then, is the music actually scored.

Musicals are always tricky to schedule for time must be allowed for rehearsals and recordings. Invariably the lead artists are in the majority of the scenes, so they are wanted for rehearsals but at the same time required to be with the shooting crew. As it is too expensive to keep the crew hanging around with nothing to do whilst rehearsals are going on, the production manager and the first assistant have to do some pretty tricky juggling.

Despite the producer problem, the cast and crew worked well together and were a happy band. Tommy could be a pain-in-the-arse behind the scenes, but on the floor he was a hard worker, very pleasant to everyone, and a great professional. All the cast took the lead from him and there was only one problem, a girl who always turned up on the set late. But after a few well-chosen words from me she was soon back on track. Oh what joy after the problems on "Casino ...".

The cast came over well and Tommy was, of course, Tommy. You either bought him or you didn't, but he had starred in the stage show, which had been a success on Broadway as well as London. I worried whether the American audiences would understand his Cockney accent. Broadway is not America. I discussed this with George who didn't see it as a problem, but at the time George was totally won over by Tommy who could do no wrong in his eyes. Julia Foster was the female lead, a darling, sweet, talented actress who played that difficult part with what I thought was great charm. In contrast to Tommy, for some reason George could not stand her, and the poor girl could do nothing to please him.

The head of distribution called me saying all the Paramount European bureau chiefs were coming in for a major conference at which the plans for the new Paramount would be announced. Would I run some of the film for them and throw a small party? I explained that they would have to come to the studio, as the film could not be played properly anywhere else. We hired a London double-decker bus to bring them to Shepperton, then we took them into the largest of the preview theatres and plied them with drinks before running a couple of numbers from the film. After that we took them into the square in Shepperton Village, which the police had cleared of cars at my request. We dressed it as a Victorian market, complete with crowd artists in costume. I rented a large room in the Anchor Hotel and covered the floor in sawdust. Earlier we had taken all the staff, including the landlord and landlady to the studio to be dressed and made-up. We served fish and chips, saveloys, meat pies, and all sorts of ghastly, typical Victorian Cockney food. We got the brewery to brew some special beer from a recipe of that period. For entertainment we had a piano and banjo player playing old English Music Hall songs. Tommy led the French, the Germans, the Italians, the Spanish and other nationalities in singing all the old numbers. The party was a wow, and I was told they were still singing when the bus arrived back at their hotel. Previously the best they could hope for was a glass of warm sherry. It was such a success that its fame spread all over the Paramount empire. I received an excited call from the president, Charlie Bludhorn, and more fuss was made over that than my success in straightening out "Half A Sixpence".

On the personal front, I had to confess to Kirstine Richards at the Adoption Society that, though I was not connected with "Half A Sixpence" when she first asked me, I was now very much connected with it. I spent the whole film pretending that I did not know that the pretty dancer with the long legs was Kirstine's daughter. Apart from this, though, things at last seemed to be progressing. Kirstine reported that two students – she, a white New Zealander and he a black African – were having a baby. There was no way they could marry, as he had to go back to his tribe who had funded his education, and she would never be accepted in his village, and neither would he be accepted at the family's fruit farm in New Zealand. So we waited.

Vicki was at boarding school in Seaford on the South Coast and I used to go down to see her on the odd Sunday when I was not working. One such Sunday, the headmistress called me into her office. "Mr Dark, when the girls have birthdays here, it is a tradition that the parents or guardians send a birthday cake so the whole school can join in."

I quickly defended myself and said I was sure I had sent one the previous week for Vicki's birthday.

"You not only sent a cake, but *cakes*, plural, Mr Dark – together with pies, tarts, jellies, sandwiches, the contents of a whole bakery!"

I remembered, yes, I had asked my secretary to send some goodies down to Vicki for her birthday. It seems a large van from "Fortnum and Mason's" had arrived, loaded with a children's banquet. The headmistress might have been upset, but the rest of the school seemed to enjoy it, and as Vicki said, it did her reputation no end of good.

Shortly after that, she left there and went to the Arts Education School in London, which she found much more fun. She once had a party at our house and invited all her friends from the school. These cute, cheeky little things arrived, each one in her own mind already a budding actress. As I was the only adult male around, and also a film producer, there was some childish flirting going on, nothing physical, of course, just with the eyes. Until the dancing started when they all insisted on dancing with me, which was all right until someone turned off the lights. I shouted, "Ineke rescue me!" I could hear the prison gates closing around me!

But back at the ranch it was a daily battle to keep to the schedule, and with our studio contract stop-date hanging over our heads, there was many a sleepless night. Especially as certain of the still-to-be shot numbers had to be abandoned, and new songs and dance routines devised and written. I was still spending evenings and week-ends on other Paramount business, and soon realised that what was needed in the London office was someone who really understood the nuts and bolts of film making.

I persuaded Bud to hire Paul Hitchcock, my accountant from the Malaya picture. He did not have a very happy start, and Bud was not impressed with him. In fact he said to me, Paul would never make an Executive. How wrong can you be? Years later Paul left Paramount, and went on to head Warner Brothers' European operation. He then became a very successful independent producer with major block-buster credits to his name. He always said he got started because of me, but actually it was all his own doing, and I merely opened the door for him.

Paul never changed over the years, and although he dressed better, had better haircuts, drove bigger cars, he remained a cricket-playing, feet on the ground, English guy surrounded by his wife and family. Paul also had great wit and I loved the story of how Sean Connery summoned him to his dressing-room whilst filming for Warners'. Sean complained about the unprofessional behaviour of the producer, and said he would leave if he ever again came on the set again. Paul promised to deal with it. As he was leaving, Sean said, "I will never work again with an untalented director or producer."

Paul just looked back and said, "Pity this is your last film!"

We moved the "… Sixpence" company over to ABPC studios at Elstree, where I had obtained stage space once I had Paramount's okay to shoot the "Flash Bang Wallop" number.

Meanwhile on the 11th of February 1967 we heard from the Adoption Society that our baby, a girl, had been born, and we could pick her up in a few weeks' time. So great excitement as a new nursery was prepared, clothes bought, toys collected and all made ready for the great event. Then, after five weeks, Ineke, Daniel, Billy and I travelled to the halfway house where she had spent several weeks, to pick her up.

We had received a sweet, sad letter from her mother saying how happy she was that she was coming to us. Kirstine had told her all about us and she felt that she and the baby were very lucky. Her mother had called her Helen Susie, and although we weren't too keen on Helen, we wanted to keep close to her mother's wishes, so we just switched the names around to Susan Helen. She was always just plain Susie, or Sue.

We peeked into her carry cot and saw this tiny little thing. I have never found new-born babies particularly attractive and this one was no exception, but I looked at this piece of chewed string and fell in love. And so Sue came into our lives, and we took her home just like any couple bringing their baby home from the hospital for the first time. And just like any other baby we fussed and worried over her. She was a funny looking little thing, coffee coloured and with a mob of straight black hair.

Little did we think at the time that this caterpillar would turn into a ravishing butterfly and that this little scrawny thing would grow into an elegant, intelligent, great-looking woman. She is a television executive and producer, happily married and with a little "Susie" of her own, Grace, and for good measure, to complete the family, George.

From the beginning, we never felt that she was any different from the other children. There is no difference and the love we felt for her on that first day remains and will do so until the day we die. Ineke and I will never forget the Agnostic Adoption Society (now called The Independent Adoption Society) for being brave enough to let us have Susie as our daughter. One day, she was talking about it with her friend, Dr Rajendra Sharma, who said that the relationship of an adopted child with its parents is completely different from that of a naturally born child. Susie took great offence and argued fiercely that there was no difference. I suppose it is only different when the parents want it to be different. As far as we are concerned, she is our daughter, and we are rather miffed when people refer to her as our "adopted" daughter. Neither of us ever feels that she is not of "our blood". In fact, we used to say stupid things like, "I really think she's got your nose".

As she got older she would have the same traits as one of us, and again we would say, "Well, of course, she gets that from you!"

We were really upset when the Tory government suggested that white parents should not be allowed to adopt black, or mixed blood children. Apart from the fact that there are few ethnic adults that want to adopt, the whole idea was dangerous nonsense. I don't understand the Black Militants when they talk about these children being denied their own culture. Is Susie's culture African, New Zealand? No, her culture is British, the culture that she had been brought up in. When African Americans go to Africa to find their roots, they very quickly realise that they have nothing in common with the people living there. In the UK, in order to satisfy their own political and intellectual ideals, it seems that the militants and the intellectuals would rather these children be brought up in orphanages than in happy homes.

I was so incensed that I wrote to Virginia Bottomley, the Health Minister at the time:

9th February 1990
Dear Mrs Bottomley
  Re: The Government Advice to Councils on Adoption of Black Babies
  How sad, how very, very sad. Our small family read your report with horror for our "baby" of twenty-two years is black, and as we read your advice we realised that, had you been in power all those years ago you would have denied us a loving daughter, and denied her not only the love of a

family, but an international education, allowing her now to hold a senior position in the Television world.

You would have instead have had her brought up in an orphanage ill educated, another unemployed black, bitter against white society.

We adopted to make one less in the institutions, our reward was this successful, beautiful, well-adjusted daughter.

Your advice ma'am is wrong. Not only wrong but in actual fact completely wrong, for the reverse of your advice is the right way – to integrate totally.

You say that the child's interests are paramount. Agreed. How many children have you spoken to? I fear you have fallen victim to black militants (whites don't have a monopoly on racialism), welfare workers and intellectual theorists.

As I said, how sad. How sad that you being a politician won't say "I'm wrong". How sad you won't meet my daughter who would be able to tell you herself how being brought up in a white family helps you cope with racialism.

On March 23rd I received a reply from Richard Brunskill of the Community Services Division of the Department of Health, which included:-

... Mrs Bottomley takes the view that race and culture are important factors in seeking foster parents and adopters for children in care; she supports efforts to encourage people from ethnic minorities to come forward, so that more families are available which will reflect the racial origin and cultural background in need of placements.

However, she does not agree with any rigidity and dogmatically applied policies which place racial and cultural factors above the wider interests of the individual child. Nor would such policies or practices be in accordance with the law, which requires courts and agencies to give first consideration to promote and safeguard a child's welfare throughout childhood, taking into account the child's wishes and feelings, having regard to his age and understanding. A placement with a family of different race can sometimes be in a child's interest, where the family is able to understand and meet all the child's needs, including those arising from his racial and cultural background.

The Department guidance to local authorities and child care agencies follow these lines, and we are considering what amplification is needed.

Thank you for your interest.

Naturally it was a typical politician's reply, not coming down on one side or the other, with the exception of their belief that a baby is born with a ready-made culture Many years later Susie lent me that wonderful book by Sebastian Faulks, "Birdsong", that we both so enjoyed reading. There was one line in it that I think sums up what we both think, "Love is more important than the flesh and blood facts of who gave birth to whom."

Shooting on the film was nearing completion, and I had promised to take Ineke to Brazil where her brother Han lived. We were going for a month which would give George and the editor time to get the film into a first cut state, and ready for a heavy post-production period. The problem was that Susie was not yet legally our daughter. We had to go through a six month probationary period to see how we got on with each other, and this meant that we had to get her natural mother's written permission and obtain a passport for her. Thus her first passport was in the name of Reid.

So, we wrapped the film, and we took off for Brazil. We were to stay in Han's house which he had built in the countryside outside Sao Paulo, and from what he had told me it sounded a fantastic place. We flew to Rio and then changed flights for Sao Paulo where Han met us. He was his usual excited self, and told us that he had finished building a wing on his house just for us.

Well, his house was quite pleasant, not grand, but not without taste. We were shown the new "wing" and it was just big enough to hold a small double bed and a cot. The cement walls were still wet and it was a disaster. I should have walked out there and then, but I did not want to upset Ineke who had been looking forward to being with her big brother after so many years. I was to find out that this "brother" was the most selfish man I had ever met, and still to this day cannot believe how he behaved towards his sister who had so admired him. He was a liar and lived in a Walter Mitty land, and continued like that for the rest of his life. The whole holiday was a grim experience. We went out on Han's yacht, but the sea was so rough that I became violently ill and threatened to throw up over his shiny boat if he didn't turn back. In the end we moved out and took an apartment on the coast.

Except for Sue, who slept through most of it, we all hated Brazil. The people we met were unbearable, mostly trying to impress us with how much money they had. There were also a number of grey-haired Germans whom we both viewed with a certain amount of suspicion. At one party I was introduced to the Chairman of the Volkswagen Company in Brazil who asked me, if I made a picture in Brazil, would it be a Brazilian film?

I replied, "It will be as Brazilian as the Volkswagen is Brazilian."

To which he screamed in his heavy German accent, "The Volkswagen _is_ a Brazilian car!"

I had promised Bud to investigate the local scene as he was anxious to make a film based on the book "Woman on a Horseback". This told the story of the Irish mistress of one of the Presidents of Paraguay. I flew to Rio to meet local producers, suppliers, lawyers, government officials etc. and to suss out the local scene. I was interested in finding what facilities were available if we were to shoot in Brazil, or Paraguay.

Brazil had quite a thriving movie industry at one time, and indeed quite a number of British technicians used to work there. But, for whatever reason, that had all died out years before. The studios were empty shells, just bare brick walls as every bit of equipment had been stripped, even down to the sound proof cladding from the stage walls. There was practically no equipment of any sort in the country, except for that serving the local Newsreel Company and a few documentary producers. The Customs' people were most unhelpful, and the government not much better. After meeting me, one producer said to a friend, "I have just met a man from the moon," such had been my questions regarding the facilities we would require. Still, I quite liked Rio, the girls were fantastic looking, the restaurants were good, and my new companions were fun. Unfortunately, I had to leave after a short time, but I was there long enough to know Brazil was out of the question.

Our favourite time was when we went to Paraguay to investigate the possibility of shooting there. As we had been able to obtain a really good nanny, Ineke was able to come with me. Our Brazilian friends (sic) all took me aside and said that I shouldn't take Ineke as it was such a rough country. Well, that was a laugh for we found it the most beautiful country, full of charming people. Unlike its larger neighbour with its background of Western pop music, it had its own music. The government was mad keen for the film to be made and I left with their guarantee of 100% co-operation, including the use of the Paraguayan army. Sadly the film was never made.

We returned to Brazil, but thankfully our time was running out and we would soon be returning to London. I would never forgive my brother-in-law for not only giving us the worst and most expensive holiday ever, but for behaving so badly to his sister that she sometimes was reduced to tears. We said good-bye to him in San Paulo, and caught the flight to Rio in order to catch our British Midlands flight to London.

We had a short hold-over in Rio, but we sat and sat and there was no sign of our plane which was coming from Buenos Aries. After frequent enquires to the ground staff, in the end I said, "Look, this plane is coming from Argentina, you must know whether it has left. I have two young children and I have to know what to do with them." They could not give me a reply so I tried again. No one seemed to know anything, so in desperation I went on, "If you don't do something I am going to take my family and sit on the runway." This seemed to gear them into some form of action. "I give you ten minutes to come up with an answer." And stalked back to where the family were sitting.

Within ten minutes a man came up and said, "A coach is coming and we are going to take you to a hotel."

I said, "Let's get this straight. My family and I are not going in any coach, and there are only two hotels that I will agree to stay at," mentioning the two most expensive hotels in Rio. Much to my surprise, as we watched all the other stranded passengers get on a coach, a limo pulled up and took us to our chosen hotel where we stayed for three nights.

On the first day, I walked round to the local Paramount office and sent a cable to Bud in London, just saying, "Stranded in Rio." As I had been robbed that morning on the Copacabana beach, I collected some money from the office and settled down in the sun for British Midland to sort out the problem.

In the end, and several days later, we came back on the Brazilian airline, Vargas. We arrived back at the airport in a limousine courtesy of British Midland, and as we entered the departure hall all the Brazilian airport staff stood up and applauded us! This was the warmest and nicest thing that happened to us on our miserable Brazilian visit. On eventually getting back to the London office, the only comment I got from Bud was, "Stranded in Rio! Of course, you couldn't get stranded in some arsehole place, just in one of the world's great fleshpots." Little did he know.

I was dismayed to see what little progress George had made on the editing, and the crew were getting frustrated at the continual changes. Instead of making a full assembly, then going back and fine-tuning, George would get stuck into one number and play around with it to the exclusion of all else. This meant that the Sound editors and Music editors were all sitting around with nothing to do.

I respected George's experience, but as time went on, I was getting more and more worried. Publicity was building up, and dates set. At the rate we were going we wouldn't open till the following year. I did not seem to be able to get through to George that we had to make some drastic decisions if we were to have any hope of meeting the scheduled premiere date, but all to no avail. Dear old George went plodding along in his own happy way and refused to face up to facts. In the end I was forced to go to Bud at Paramount and tell him that unless we could get George to behave, he would have to go, or they would have to cancel the release date. This threw a real spanner into the works, as this date was set in stone and the whole publicity campaign geared to it. Sadly, but inevitably, George was sent home. Now it all rested on me. I quickly got the boys working night and day, seven days a week and achieved a sort of first assembly. At that time the fashion was to have road show films lasting two-and-a-half hours or more, but with an interval in the middle, for what the Americans referred to as "a comfort break!"

Then I began with the editor, and in a couple of weeks I thought we had something that I could show Bludhorn and the other executives at Paramount. I had sent my dear old friend the respected leading cameraman Bobby Krasker, to shoot background titles, and in his usual brilliant way he brought back exquisite scenes of "Old England".

When I ran the film for Charlie, at the end of the titles he leant over to me and said, "So far I like it!" Charlie loved the film and consequently so did the other execs.

But I thought it was too long, as it had too much of Tommy, and the audience needed a break from the smiling, toothy face. So I went back into the cutting rooms, and first of all cut out the first number, and whenever possible I cut away from Tommy, not as easy as it sounds as he was in everything. I then shortened the dance numbers, which were too long. There were a couple of senior execs in town from the New York office and I ran this version for them. They went wild about it, and thought it was a fantastic achievement. "At last we have a movie," said one.

Next day I got a phone call from Tommy's agent, the creepy Ian Bevan, asking to see the film. I had no power to stop him as he had a clause in Tommy's contract allowing him to view before release, so we ran the film for him and the proverbial hit the fan. Tommy went straight to Bludhorn accusing me of ruining the film. Of course, having a bigger ego than Maria Callas, he did not like my reducing his presence. Charlie called me, screamed down the phone , told me he had to have a two-and-a-half hour road show film, and ordered me to put it all back. So we went back to almost the original length, though I did manage to keep a few of my short original cuts.

We were fast approaching our dubbing date. Which was so close to the first press viewing, it was far from funny. To add to our problems, it was a complicated dub because the picture had been shot in wide screen on thirty five millimetre, but was going to be printed up to seventy millimetre, allowing us to record in seven track stereophonic sound.

Towards the end, I had the lab print up a seventy married print (this is when the sound track is added to the picture) so I could run it in the West End cinema where the premiere was to be held. It was a disaster, and I felt like throwing myself off the balcony of the Astoria.

Firstly, it sounded as though it had been recorded through a sieve, and the principals could hardly be heard. Then as the picture had been enlarged, the cuts in the negative flashed on the screen.

Luckily one of the senior people from Rank cinemas was there and he asked the projectionist to come down from his box. A senior Hollywood producer said to me once, "Always remember that the projectionist is not a master of his craft." And never was this more evident than on that day. For a start they did not have a test track, but eventually the Rank man found one for us. Meanwhile I was huddled with the Technicolor representative trying to solve the problem of the neg flashes, because every time there was a change from one piece of film to the other, there was a big flash. As always, everyone blamed everyone else; the lab said it was the cinema, the projectionist the lab, whilst all I could see were the big signs on the buses: "Yum Tidilly Um Pom Pom (part of the lyrics from "Flash Bang Wallop")......Coming Soon." We got the test roll and found the cinema speakers were balanced incorrectly. The outside speakers which carried the chorus track was drowning out the inside speakers which carried, for the most past, the principals. The only comment the projectionist made was, "That's all right. That's the way we always have it!"

I had to get a special aperture made for the projectors to cover the bottom of screen and thus hide the flashes. I realised that I was going to have to nurse this film into the cinema, and that's just what I did. I attended every press or trade showing, always in touch with the projection box.

The opening was to be a Royal Premiere in the presence of Her Royal Highness, Princess Alexandra, but first I had to show the finished film to George who arrived back from LA well in advance of the first night. It was a nervous time for me, much worse than the English press showings, for here was the man who I had got rid of, and this was my cut not his. Being the sweet man that he was, he could not have been nicer and thanked me for a job well done. Few men would have been that generous.

On top of everything else, it was decided that I should arrange the party. Usually this is done by the distributors' publicity department, but such was my reputation it was handed over to me. I could have done without it. I had trouble getting the right venue as all the top hotels were booked up for that night. In the end I took two floors at the Café Royal, with the reception on the first floor, and dinner and dancing on the floor above. I asked my old friend Patrick McLoughlin to decorate the two floors including the staircase which he turned into a tunnel of fresh flowers. There were three different bands, and the menu was British style; roast venison, beef, steak, kidney and oyster pudding etc. No money was spared.

Charlie Bludhorn and his senior executives, including his vice president, Martin Davis, came over for the opening. Much to my surprise, Charlie Schneer also advised that he intended to be there, and was included in the royal line-up. When Princess Alexander passed down the line of assembled Paramount executives, George Sydney, Tommy, and myself, she apologised for the absence of her husband. Bludhorn quickly cut in, "What's he got? The same thing as me? Diarrhoea?"

The press reviews were mixed but not bad on the whole. The premiere was amazing. Before the start, I warned George that English audiences were not like American ones, who stamp and cheer, but were on the whole a pretty cold bunch. I could not have been more wrong. From the start they clapped and cheered. I have never experienced such an amazing reception on an English first night. At the end it got a standing ovation, and I thought to myself how wrong I had been. I was soon to learn that maybe I wasn't so daft.

The next day George and I flew to New York for the New York premiere.

I left George at the hotel and went round to the boys at the head office, 1501 Broadway. By this time I had got to know most of them and found them a good bunch. Martin Davis was a bit of a strange guy, always very quiet, unresponsive and terse, in direct contrast to Charlie who was loud, excitable and never stopped talking. Charlie spent most of his time on the phone playing the stock market, and had a phone in his car (very rare in those days) so he could continue doing so whilst travelling. His chauffeur, Oliver, used to drop Charlie off, then immediately get on the phone to his own stockbroker. If Gulf and Western bought into a company, then like night follows day the stock would increase. Oliver was the richest driver in New York.

Arriving at the office, I went straight in to see Charlie. It always amazed the other executives of the company that I could walk straight into his office, as they could wait days to see him.

"How do you do it?" I was asked.

"I don't know, I just go in and sit down."

"Well, when we open the door he tells us to fuck off."

"Oh, he does the same to me, but I don't take any notice." For some unknown reason I had this special relationship with him. For a start I liked him, and I admired his achievement from being a penniless refugee to the head of one of America's giant conglomerates. We would row, he would get stroppy with me at times, but we always talked as equals, and I was always able to say my bit even if in the end he over-ruled me.

For lunch in his office, an outside caterer would bring in an excellent meal for just Charlie, Marty, Bud (if he was around), and maybe one of the other executives. In the evening we would go to the "21" or the latest fad restaurant. Whilst in New York my time was totally taken up with Charlie and Marty, and I must say it was no hardship.

This time when I got into his office, he said to me, "Have you seen the sign?" I looked blank. "Goddammit, I've bought the biggest sign ever seen on Broadway, go out and look at it."

I went out into the street and looking up I saw this gigantic sign: "Half a Sixpence". I crossed to the other side to get a better view, and such is one's ego that my eye immediately went to my name in gigantic neon letters with "champagne flowing through". That old song went through my head, "When your name goes up in lights on old Broadway". Yes, I thought, you've made it. Once again I was wrong.

The opening was a disaster. And the sign came down two days later.

The terrible reviews said it was too long, too English (they couldn't understand Tommy's Cockney accent), too boring and so on.

The next day, George and I flew to LA for the opening there. If New York was bad, this was a disaster. Some genius had the idea of having the Milton Berle show on before the film, which went on for an hour but seemed like a day! By the time the two-and-a-half hour film started, the audience was already tired out. It bombed, they hated it!

There was the usual party afterwards, which was more like a wake. Gillian Lynne had joined us there, and she and I quickly escaped. We were staying at the Wilshire Boulevard hotel, so we had a couple of drinks in the bar then went upstairs, got into bed and watched the television (this tells you how depressed we were!) On the box was an amazing comic, Don Rickles, whom neither of us had heard of before. His whole act consisted of being rude to everyone – the Jews, the blacks, the rich, the poor, celebrities, whoever. He was Jewish himself, and so brilliant that it was impossible for anyone to be offended by him. I met him years later and told him the story, explaining, "We were so depressed, yet despite that you made us laugh, and no greater proof is needed of your amazing talent."

A little tear appeared at the corner of his eye, and I saw the real Don Rickles as he said, "That's a wonderful story and I especially like the bit when you got in bed with the choreographer!"

In London, the film was still doing well. It appealed to English audiences, and of course was helped by the popularity of Tommy Steele. However, I would never forgive him or his agent, Ian Bevan, for the influence they put on Charlie to make me put back those thirty minutes.

I returned to the London offices which had been transformed from being dingy, dowdy, and dirty into delightful places to work. Bud's office in particular was impressive, done out in light oak panelling, with antique furniture, complete with electrically operated curtains, which he demonstrated to whoever happened to drop in. Had the films been as good as the offices we would have been all right.

Ever since Charlie Bludhorn had discovered how much Lewis Gilbert's "Alfie" cost, and how much it made, he was convinced that this was the recipe for success. It took him many years to discover that there is no recipe. Consequently a row of low budget films were put into production, and one of these was "The Bliss of Mrs

Blossom", starring Shirley Maclaine and Richard Attenborough and directed by my old friend, Joe McGrath.

It was produced by Joe Shaftel, a rather odious American with very little talent and even less charm. He had no idea how to deal with Shirley. As she said to me, "He's shit scared of me." And that's how she treated him – like shit!

It was so good to see her again, for she was a really nice person who did not suffer fools gladly. When Joe showed us the rough cut we were all dismayed. I had hoped for Joe's sake especially that it would be a success. It died on its first run.

Another was "Two Gentlemen Sharing" – on which Gregory, my eldest son worked as a runner. Another disaster. This was directed by a Canadian, Ted Kotcheff, who went on to direct many international movies. The trouble again was it had a novice producer, although this one was at least a charming guy and was grateful for help.

Even the tried, tested and talented couldn't bring success to the European office of Paramount. "The Assassination Bureau", produced by Michael Relph and directed by Basil Dearden, was a monumental flop, and you could not get a more experienced pair than those two with a long list of successful films to their credit. Ken Annakin tried to equal the success of his "Those Magnificent Men In Their Flying Machines" with "Monte Carlo or Bust", without success.

Actually, whilst in New York I pleaded with Charlie not to make this film, as by its very nature it could not be cheap, and I had read the script and found it particularly unfunny. I even went down on my knees to Charlie in the corridor of 1501 Broadway and *begged* him not to do it! But he had the bit between his teeth and so it went ahead.

"Barbarella" was shooting in Rome for Dino De Laurentiis, and this I guess was the start of the love affair between Dino and Charlie. Despite the fact that he was cheating on us throughout, Charlie wouldn't hear a thing against him. The film did quite well, and I suppose was one of the few European films that did. I had dinner one night with Jane Fonda, who starred in the film and Roger Vadim, the director. Previously he had been married to Brigitte Bardot, but by now he and Jane were wed, and I must say they made delightful dinner companions. Jane was a pretty tough cookie and used to give Dino a hard time, which I am quite sure he deserved, but am also sure did not worry him one little bit.

It was during this picture that Dino's dislike of me began. I was sure there was a fiddle going on, and did my best to find out where it was, but I never found the last set of books. It is hardly surprising that he resented me.

The LA Studios were also busy under the leadership of Bobby Evans, who was tall, good-looking, handsome, beautifully spoken, smartly dressed and rich. He was what every man dreamed of being and had the pick of the Hollywood girls. Bud hated him but I found him a delightful person. In the end Bobby was the one who was the success in the company. He commissioned "Rosemary's Baby" for which he had to fight Charlie every inch of the way. Charlie hated the script, hated Mia Farrow, and especially hated the director, Roman Polanski. Bobby also gave Paramount its first hit under the Bludhorn regime, "Love Story", starring Ryan

O'Neal and Ali MacGraw whom Bobby eventually married. He also had the "Godfather" films. In all, not a bad string in anyone's language, and it made the European contribution look pathetic.

I had managed to avoid getting an office in the Paramount building, instead they rented a furnished flat for me in Kensington, where I ensconced myself, complete with a new secretary. This soon became a handy spot for old buddies to drop in, have a drink, and chew the fat. A constant visitor was Maggie Wright, the statuesque ex-Parisienne Bluebell and ex-girlfriend of George Sydney. Maggie was a darling, but did like the bottle a bit too much. On my first day in the new place the front door bell rang and when my new Sloane Ranger P.A. answered, Maggie literally fell in, then looked up at the girl and said, "For fuck's sake, help me up." Poor girl, what a first day!

I did not get much work done there, but I was always hearing from Bud, asking me to look at this film or other, or from Charlie asking me to fly over to New York to see him. (Bludhorn didn't think you were working unless you were in an aeroplane!)

One day I got a message asking me to attend a meeting in Bud's office at six o'clock that night. As we already had our weekly production meeting the day before, I could not figure out what it was all about. I rang around and discovered that the whole team had been summoned, but no one knew what it was all about. I duly reported, and found everyone already gathered in Bud's office. Whilst I grabbed a seat, Bud said, "Great, now Johnny's here, we can start. Now, you guys, I've got something to tell you. Today I've had an ice-making machine put in this office. Now, let's sit here and see if we can out-drink it!"

That was Paramount in those days: long lunches, busy evenings either at a premiere or a party, or just dining out. There were trips abroad, always first class, with limousines to pick you up at either end, and always a little man waiting to greet you with a packet of money for incidental expense (never once did anyone ask me to account for this money), and five star hotel suites. Life was luxurious, but tiring. If Ineke and I got a night at home alone, we would think ourselves lucky!

It was about this time that I went to LA with Bud and Gwynne. Unlike many people, I really liked the place. I know I led the fat cat life there, but I loved the film buzz around the place. Everyone had a script to sell, every waiter was an actor resting in between film roles, and the conversation was all about movies. Apart from that I liked the weather, the food, the fun restaurants, and I loved the girls with their long, sun tanned legs, and big boobs. No wonder it is called tinsel town. As a film man it was rather like an Arab going to Mecca. On that trip we were booked into the Beverly Hills Hotel, but after a couple of nights Bud said that the guest house at Pickfair was empty, and we were moving there. Oh my God, I thought, Pickfair, the most famous house in California, the house built by Mary Pickford and Douglas Fairbanks Snr., legends of Hollywood.

With great excitement we pulled up to Pickfair in Mary Pickford's Rolls which Bud had borrowed. The guest house was built in the grounds, and very close to the main house. It had a terrace, a large sitting room, with kitchen off, and two large double bedrooms. Various members of the family and old friends came and went. Gwynne told me that Mary was almost a recluse, that she kept to her own suite in the house and spent most of her time in bed. However, Bud was determined that I should meet her and indeed a day later the phone rang and it was for me. A voice said in a whisper, "This is the butler. Don't tell anyone, but Miss Pickford wishes to see you, so come out of the house and meet me at the third bush on the left." And the phone went dead.

Putting the phone down, I looked at the chatting group, and walked to the door, thinking that with a bit of luck they wouldn't notice I'd left. Just as I opened the door, someone asked me where I was going. "Oh," I said, "just getting a breath of fresh air, it's the air-conditioning." And left hurriedly. I heard them laugh and someone say, "The Brits!"

At the third bush on the left I was duly met by the butler who escorted me into the main house, where most of the windows were shuttered and the place was in semi-darkness. In the sitting room I noticed a portrait of her hanging over the fireplace. We went up the carpeted stairs to the first floor, and the butler knocked on a door. A strong voice said, "Come in" and I entered the room.

There was this elderly lady sitting upright, perfectly but lightly made-up, and posed as if she were waiting to have an official photograph taken. Her pale green full length housecoat, more like a negligee, was folded carefully, and in retrospect I realised that she must have gone to a lot of trouble. The first sight of her still lives in my mind, and when she held out her hand and I took it and said, "It's a great honour." I meant it.

We had such a wonderful chat together, with me flattering her outrageously, though how you can flatter one of the biggest stars the world has ever known, I'm not sure. I told her that she ought to come to England again.

"Do you think they still remember me?" she asked.

"You'll never be forgotten," I replied.

She constantly brought her ex-husband into the conversation, referring to him as "My Duggie" and it was very obvious that she was still in love with him.

At the end, when she started to tire, she said, "Did you see the bar I built for Duggie on his birthday?" And when I said I hadn't, she summoned the butler and told him, "Take Mr Dark and show him the Western bar, and show him my museum as well."

We said our good-byes, and I left her feeling as though I had had an audience with the Queen. We went up into the loft, and displayed there were all the gifts she had been given when she toured around the world. It was an amazing collection of priceless mementoes. I looked down one of the rooms and the butler told me that they were storage rooms, and asked if I would like to see them. There were racks of silverware, plates, dishes, bowls, with golden statues in the middle, and rows of amazing silver and ceramic ware. In another room were racks holding her collection of fur coats. From there we went down to the ground floor and off from the sitting room entered a pine panelled corridor. Pushing one of the knots in the wood, a secret door slid back revealing a full Western bar. He told me that Miss Pickford had bought an actual Western bar and he showed me the bullet holes in it. In a way it was a sad place, for obviously it had not been used for years, and it hadn't even been looked after. It wasn't very clean, and paintings had fallen off the wall and broken out of their frames.

When I got back there was a chorus of: "Where have you been?"

"I went for a walk," I said.

"Don't be silly, no one goes for a walk in Beverley Hills, not even an Englishman."

Back in London, Bud and I got a call from New York saying they were thinking of making a movie from a book entitled "The Cold War Swap".

This was a fictional tale of an escape from East Germany into the West via the Underground railway system. I was asked to go to Berlin to see if it was possible, and to talk with the German authorities, especially the management of the metro system, to see what co-operation we could expect. This was around 1967 and the demise of the wall was just a dream.

On arrival in Berlin, I was struck by the language. It was nonsense, I know, but the sound of German made me feel uncomfortable, and I could feel my hairs rise. However, I got used to it, and the people were so nice to me I soon settled down.

I engaged a young Berlin production assistant to show me around, make appointments, and act as my interpreter. I soon got to like the city. One of the first things I wanted to do was to see the East, so on my first full day there, we went to the viewing platform that had been erected on the West side in the very centre of the city, rather like Piccadilly Circus, or Times Square. Though I had read so much about it, and watched the television reports, I still was not prepared for the total desolation and emptiness, with no traffic, and no people except for armed border guards. There was the wall, then a strip of land occupied by German Shepherd dogs, leashed to a wire and patrolling up and down. After that were several rows of barbed wire, and then nothing. All the buildings close to the wall had been destroyed, with not a brick left standing. The only buildings were the observation towers manned by the border guards.

I had always hated Communism, even as a little boy. At the height of pro-Russian feeling in England during the war, I used to get into heated arguments with the pro-Soviet English. I viewed the scene in total disbelief as I watched rabbits running across the empty land that had once been the busy centre of one of Europe's greatest capitals. I felt sick when I thought of all the pro-Soviet Communists I had met, and wished I could have brought them out to see how the system worked in reality. I heard it said so many times, and it was so true, that for the first time in history a wall had been built to keep the people in, not to keep the invaders out!

The following day, my young assistant fixed me up with a chauffeur-driven car that would take me into the East. The driver was an Arab and held a special permit allowing him to cross "the border". We drove through Check Point Charlie with a cheery wave from the G.I. on duty, then confronted with the strict formalities of the East Germans. Our car was searched as indeed were both the driver and myself.

We were forced to change a certain amount of money, and then scrutinised very carefully by the Immigration Officers. No one smiled, there were no greetings, and other than to utter some gruff orders, no one spoke at all.

Once through, we drove around the miserable looking streets, and I was amazed by the lack of noise, the absence of advertising hoardings. There were no parking meters for which there was no need as there were so few cars. We stopped at a hotel to have a cup of coffee, and entered this large vestibule full of people sitting at little tables. Speaking to each other in almost whispers. The service was sluggish and surly until I tipped the guy a few dollars. My paternal grandfather always told me that it was as bad to over-tip as it was to under-tip. Well, I have been over tipping all my life, and do you know, nobody yet has seemed anything other than happy about it! Outside, I told my Arab friend I had seen enough, and to take me back to paradise, back to the Hilton with its chromium plated cocktail bars. We crossed back with the same level of security and I did not breathe properly until we crossed Check Point Charlie. I was never so happy to get caught in a traffic jam, to hear the cheery greetings of the hooting cars, and sense the hustle and bustle on the pavements, see the glamorous shop windows and above all the sparkling neon signs. Back at the hotel, I bought my Muslim friend a Coca-Cola and myself a champagne cocktail. Ah, the nectar of freedom.

I had put out calls to the headquarters of the underground system, and soon I had a call back from the senior manager of railway operations. Knowing that without his help there was no way we could make the film, I invited him to lunch so I could explain exactly what we needed. I expected an aging, portly German official and was happily surprised when he turned out to be a young man, blonde hair, about six feet tall, charming and helpful. We had an excellent lunch, and like most people he was fascinated by the mechanics of film making. He left saying he would get back to me in a couple of days. He explained that the line went through the Western section, then into the Eastern section for three stations, and then back again into the West. He was in direct communication with his Eastern counterpart, and together they had set up a system to deal with any problem which might arise. To demonstrate this, he took me down into one of the Western stations and, as the train came in, hurried me into the driver's cab. I was disturbed, to put it mildly, as I knew this train was headed for the Eastern sector and I hadn't got my passport with me. He told me not to worry about that. However, I was still anxious as I had seen the other side, and I had read the reports of visitors being accused of spying and locked up.

My anxiety grew when he pointed out the iron rolled up gates in the roof of the tunnel, that the East could drop down at a moment's notice, if there were any infringements of the contract between them – or indeed if anything out of the ordinary occurred that made them suspicious.

The next tummy churner was when we started to slow down, but my railway friend explained that, according to their agreement, they had to drive slowly through the Eastern stations. We crawled past the platform empty except for one border guard whose face I still remember. It was the face of a non-human: expressionless, with glazed eyes, and a facial structure suitable for a Hammer film. As we cleared the station and started to pick up speed again, came the clincher. My railway friend said, "Now, don't get nervous if you see rather a lot of activity on the platform when we go through the next station. Our friend back there will have phoned through that there are extra people in the driver's cab." Don't get nervous!! I was only in East Berlin without a passport or any other means of identification! I didn't know how I was going to explain it to the hotel laundryman! We got through the next station and back into the West where I staggered out of the driver's cab, and being the coward that I am, sank on to the nearest wall to recover.

I presumed we would have to shoot at night when the trains weren't running, but my friend explained that they had a short branch line, which since the partition they didn't use, and he could see no reason why we couldn't use that. Perfect, I thought, he had already offered me a train, now we had the track, and we would not be involved in night shooting.

When the London office rang and said the director and associate producer were coming out to Berlin, I was happy to be able to tell them that from a German viewpoint, there was no reason why the movie could not go ahead. Bud told me Steve McQueen's production company, Solar, would be making the film for Paramount, and the director was one of McQueen's protégés.

The two guys arrived and naturally I was excited to show them all the facilities the Germans were offering us, the locations, and to take them down the subway. However, they didn't want to know, and spent most of the time talking quietly to each other, hurriedly breaking off whenever I appeared.

Well, bollocks to this, I thought, and caught the next plane back to London. Bud was surprised to see me, but when I explained he was mad. Anyhow, the film was never made and I never saw the director again. I did, though, meet the production manager years later, when he was the Vice-president of production managers at the Paramount Studios at the Coast.

Then came "Roman Holiday". Someone in the States had suggested that this brilliant film directed by the talented craftsman, Willy Wyler, starring Gregory Peck and launching into mega-stardom Audrey Hepburn, should be re-made as a musical. The Sherman brothers, Bob and Dick, were approached to write the score, with Franco Zeffirelli directing. It was mooted that I, together with Dino De Laurentiis, should produce, and a deal was struck. It was a bit embarrassing when Bud said to me, "You realise that you're earning more money than me now."

The first meeting was in Rome in Dino's office. Dino had built this large studio outside the Eternal City. In reality it was an impressive front block, with a wonderful studio restaurant and some stages at the back. There was no carpenters' shop, no plasterers' shop, or any sound back up – nothing, just bare stages. There was no power supply and you had to bring in your own generators. Dino worked on the principle that senior movie executives did not look into the details. In the lobby he had built a magnificent display of model soldiers lined up in the battle of Waterloo formation advertising his forthcoming production (he hoped), "Napoleon". He had an amazing restaurant, designed like an Italian farmhouse serving the best of food, where he would entertain his guests. By the time they got to his office they were suitably impressed.

Apart from Bud and myself, there was the head of the Rome office, Luigi Luraschi, and his newly appointed assistant my old friend, Maurizio Lodi Fe. With us came Bob and Dick Sherman who were in Rome to pick up the atmosphere.

The first thing Dino did was to try and get the Shermans to give up their credit on the film. His reason was so he could put an Italian's name on the credits and thereby qualify for an Italian Government subsidy. Though I understood the reason why, I also knew that you don't treat two famous songwriters in that way. It would be rather like asking Tom Cruise to say he was Bernado Luci. That morning we nearly lost the Shermans, but after some quick talking from Bud, and Luigi explaining that Dino's English was not very good (which it wasn't when he didn't want it to be), they managed to calm them down.

At this time I had lined up, but not engaged, Gillian Lynne and Irwin Kostal, the team from "Sixpence", and the best in the business.

Dino had given me an office at the studio, and had also given me a secretary, Mimi Gnoli. She explained to me later that Dino had given her to me so that she would report back to him whatever I was doing. She also warned me about using the office phone for anything confidential, and sending any telegrams from the studio. The wonderful thing about Mimi was that she was the double agent, for what he didn't know was that she hated him and so kept me abreast of all his little tricks.

One thing was for sure, Dino was determined to get rid of me, and went to great lengths, including lying to Charlie, to accomplish that. Dino told Bludhorn that I was anti-Italian and I might have been in trouble if it had not been for Luigi saying I was the most pro-Italian Englishman he had ever met, and one of the very few that took the trouble to learn the language. Now that Paramount knew the truth, Dino did not worry me much, and the fact that I had Mimi telling me what was going on actually made the whole thing quite exciting.

At the time Dino was trying to make deals with the Russians, mainly so that he could get the use of their army in his "Napoleon" film, and so he was anxious to use a Russian dance company in "Roman Holiday". My point was that until we had a script, and a girl to play the Hepburn role, and we had the approval of Franco Zefferelli and the choreographer, we were not in a position to make any sort of commitment to the Russians. This, of course, did not stop Dino continuing to negotiate with the Russian dance troupe.

Mimi was a darling girl, not pretty exactly but with a wonderful strong, dark complexioned face crowned with straight dark hair. She was a striking looking woman. From a very upper class family, her mother a genuine *contessa*, her family stretching back for years. She had a good figure and the most riveting personality. One thing she wasn't was a secretary, but she was a great photographer, great interpreter, and was wonderful at steering me through the minefield of the Italian film industry.

She also could be very funny. One story she used to tell in her very slight Italian accent was the horror of staying in an English country house. "I was staying in this beautiful house in mid-winter. My bedroom was freezing cold and I woke up because I just had to have a pee pee. So I put on my overcoat and crept down the drafty corridor to the bathroom, only to find that the pee pee bowl was totally frozen, so I used the bath. What I did not realise was that the pipe from the bath was also frozen and there, in the bath lay a puddle of yellow liquid. I did not know what to do, so I took a towel and mopped it up and threw the towel out of the window. The next day I was forced to join in one of those ghastly English customs, the walk after lunch. Coming back we came across the frozen towel, and my companions thought I was a very bad sport in not joining in their game of throwing the towel at each other."

I was too fond of Mimi. We never had an affair, for that could have ended up in a tragedy. She knew I was married and had two children, as she was a regular visitor to the house, and she knew I could not love three people more, consequently neither of us was prepared to jeopardise that situation. I will always think of her with great affection, and it is good to look back and remember the warmth there was between us.

We had moved into a furnished house in The Apia Antigua, a four-bedroom villa complete with two swimming pools, one Olympic length, and a floodlit tennis court. We had engaged a nanny, Annie, in London, and had a wonderful local cook. Our old friends from the American Embassy in Belgrade, the Hartleys, now posted to Rome, used to use our tennis courts and in return kept us in booze, which they got through their PX Store.

The house soon became the place where film folk would drop in, and every day we would entertain not only the Paramount people, but anybody who had the slightest connection with us. Every night was party night and it soon got known as "the last of the dolce vita". We had only one house rule and that was that after midnight nobody was allowed to wear any clothes, swimsuits, briefs, bikinis, in the pool, except for Ineke who was allowed to keep on her necklace when she swam out with the drinks.

Paul Hitchcock recalls telling a friend after visiting us in Rome, "When I arrived there was a barbecue, and John was wearing an apron, but that's all, an apron!"

I got a call from Bud saying, "Do you think we should make 'Oh! What A Lovely War'?"

"Wow, that's a tough one."

"I didn't ask you whether it was a tough one. Should we make it?"

I replied, "Well I think on principal, if it's a tough one, a challenge, then you should bite the bullet, but you would have to make it on a very low budget because I doubt it will have a major international appeal."

It was not till my next visit to London that I found out that Richard Attenborough was going to make his directorial debut on it. Nor did I know that he was going to take this one-set show, with a small group of unknown actors dressed as Pierrots throughout, and turn it into a massive, wide- screen epic, with a cast of Britain's finest classical actors headed by Laurence Olivier.

Let me say, I thought that Dickie did a fantastic job, but the budget was far in excess of what even the greatest optimist could expect to get in return. It bombed, and did not even get back its prints-and-advertising. It did start Dickie's directing career, though, and for that we have to be grateful.

So, life was very pleasant, except for the fact that Paramount, despite the fact that I was supposed to be producing "Roman Holiday", kept wanting me in different places. And once again I seemed to spend my time on aeroplanes.

On one of my visits to LA, I met up with the Sherman brothers, as I had an idea that I wanted to try out on them. I had not spoken to anyone else about it and I was anxious to get their reaction. We met in the "Brown Derby" on Wilshire Boulevard (no longer there), and I explained, "At the end of the film after the press conference, Audrey Hepburn says good-bye to the press and Eddie Albert gives her back the photos. We cut outside the palace and see Gregory Peck walk down the steps, look back, then turn and walk off, and then 'The End' credit comes on. So, why don't we play it exactly the same way? Hold it, see Peck walk off and then the music rises up and we see the princess running down the steps of the palace after him?"

The boys shouted with glee, and Bob got up and did a little dance around his stick. We left that lunch full of excitement.

Back in Rome, I met an Italian script writer Ennio De Concini who had an idea about a man who lived in Selfridges. I thought the idea good, but suggested that he change it to Harrods'. Ennio was a very successful comedy writer, with such films as "Divorce, Italian Style" to his credit, and I thought that not only was it a good idea but that he would be the right man to write the script. Ennio said that he would not write a word unless he got paid, and I told him that Paramount would pay him if they wanted to develop the idea. He said he would insist on entering into a full agreement which would give him guarantee of payment. I did agree a figure of five hundred pounds for the first draft, a pittance, so I rang Bud to get his okay and he told me to meet him in Paris.

"But, Bud," I said, "it would cost more for me to fly to Paris than what I am asking you for."

"Listen, kid, if you want this money then you come to Paris."

So next day I flew off to Paris.

On my arrival at the Plaza Athénée, I bumped in to Bud's chauffeur, "What are you doing here?" I enquired.

He told me that he had driven from London so he was able to pick up Bud at the airport in Paris.

"And are you staying here as well?" I asked.

"Oh no," he replied, "I'm staying at the George Cinque!"

I next bumped into Tom Carlyle, one of the Paramount publicity men. "Hi, John," he greeted me. "So you've been called to this meeting too?"

"No," I replied, "I don't know of any meeting. I'm here to see Bud."

I got to the desk to check in and there was a note for me from Bud: "Do not check in, but come straight to the terrace." I got to the terrace and was surprised to see Bud sitting at a large table surrounded by numerous members of the London office.

"Come and sit down, we've been waiting for you, so now we can start." In some bewilderment I sat down on the only vacant chair, and wondered what was going on. "Now, you guys, to save time, I'm going to order for us all, so if there is something you really don't like, just shout." He then proceeded to order a very expensive lunch, with wines to match. He then addressed us, "I've called you guys together to tell you we're spending too much money and it must stop. From now on, no limos, you can grab a cab at the airports. You must also watch your expenses." He went on in this way for some time, "Now, have you guys any ideas how we can cut costs?"

To break the deadly silence I said, "Why don't we sack Billy?" This was our office boy in London who earned about five pounds a week, or about what each glass of wine was costing.

"There you go, you guys: Johnny's come up with something. Now how about the rest of you?" glaring at them all.

Oh boy, was I the flavour of the month! I had only meant it as a joke, and was horrified to find out later that they had actually sacked the poor kid, and it took me several phone calls before I got Bud to rescind it.

After lunch, I tried to get Bud to one side, but he was having none of it, "I'm going to lay down for a few minutes and I suggest you do the same. We've got a heavy night ahead of us." And swept out.

I checked in, and then got up to my suite. From there I rang through to Bud, "Sorry to wake you, Bud, but this is really important. I mean, I know we are economising, but do you know my suite only has three bathrooms?"

The whole Paris trip consisted of boozy lunches running into boozy dinners. Every time I tried to get Bud to okay the payment for the Harrods' script, he would dodge the question. And in the end I got fed up and returned to Rome.

When Mimi asked if I had the okay, I felt a complete idiot when I tried to explain to her what had happened. "In other words," she said, "you didn't get it. So, shall I tell De Concini?"

"No," I said, "this is ridiculous. Let me ring Bud."

Which I did, thinking probably he couldn't dodge the issue so easily on the phone. When I rang him and explained that we had never discussed what I had gone to Paris for, he said, "You're right, Johnny, so come straight back and we'll sort it out."

"But why can't we sort it out now, on the phone?"

"Listen, kid, if you want the money, you have to come here. If you come here, I'll give you the money."

"So, if I come to Paris, you'll okay the deal?"

"Yes."

"And pay the money?"

"Yes, with one proviso."

"And what's that"

"That you bring Ineke with you."

So I arrived back in Paris, this time with my darling wife. Another round of partying ensued, but this time Bud lived up to his word, and agreed the deal.

Before I could sign the deal with De Concini I had to get the agreement of Harrods'. So I flew to London and met with one of the directors, but in the end it took six months to get their agreement. One of their worries concerned the possibility of someone actually living in the store, but eventually they gave their conditional agreement. One of those conditions being the approval of the script as it affected Harrods'.

For me personally, one of the side benefits of these negotiations was that I was given a conducted tour behind the scenes of the store. Harrods' had always been a part of my life. In fact, Susie, my daughter, always says her first memory is of going up the escalators in the store. It was fascinating to see the under belly and I was amazed to find a network of tunnels and storage rooms in the basement. These went under the Brompton Road and surfaced on the other side of the street where the delivery vans were garaged. I also found that Harrods' had its own well, and there was the fascinating story of an Agricultural Show in Hyde Park one year, when the pigs refused to drink the London water. Someone had the bright idea of using the pure and uncontaminated well water from Harrods'.

I was sure we were on a winner with this idea, and started turning over in my mind who we could get to play the lead. I thought we could have a musical number located in the piano department, and that Danny Kaye would be ideal. I also thought that once we had a script I could talk to Lewis Gilbert about directing it, and how good it would be to be back working with him.

Back in Rome, we signed the deal with De Concini and waited for the first draft of the script to arrive. When it did it was late at night before I had a chance to study it, and my first reaction was that I was not taking it in, I was too tired. So I left it till the next morning, and then to my horror I found that instead of writing us an outright comedy, he had written an anti-consumer society film. I found out later that he was a member of the Italian Communist Party. Can you imagine Harrods' reaction if they had read that script? I reckon my family and I would have been banned from the store for life! So that was that.

As our house in Rome was close by, I often walked over to see Franco. I used to go early in the morning so I could catch him before his busy day began. I would have coffee with him, and try and get his ideas about a writer, but he was very difficult to tie down, and didn't want to commit himself to anyone in particular. I was anxious about the script, and wanted his input. However, we never got past ideas like the ballet sequence that he wanted to shoot on the top of cars that were locked in a traffic jam in the Via Venito. Though this was an interesting concept, it really didn't help me much at that stage. My other main worry was the girl. Where, oh where, did you find another Audrey Hepburn? Here Franco did help me by introducing me to one of his close colleagues, Dyson Lovell, who later produced for Franco. We engaged Dyson who in turn engaged other casting agents across Europe to look for the girl. Franco wanted to hire his designer with his team, which I was against, but Paramount agreed as they were so anxious to keep Franco. So we had two producers, one director, one choreographer, one musical director, two composers, and now an art department – but no writer and consequently no script!

However, this situation did not last long. For one morning I walked across to see Franco and found out that he had left for Mexico City where he was going to direct an opera. In reality I don't think that Franco had any intention of directing the film, and this explains his rather bizarre behaviour. It was a great loss, as he was, in my opinion, a man of great talent and would have given us the creative leadership that this project needed.

I immediately thought of Lewis but he was already committed to another Paramount film, "The Adventurers". At the same time I got news that Paramount New York had engaged a writer who was arriving in the next few days. So Fred Segal, a very likeable, cheery, young American came into our lives. I couldn't find out anything about him except that he was the brother of the actor George Segal. So we lost a director, but gained a writer!

I thought we would give him a couple of days to acclimatise himself and rest after the long flight, before we got down to work. This guy had never been out of the States before, and just fell in love with Rome. As the Americans say, "He went ape, totally ape-shit." So instead of resting he went out and partied.

I sent a car for him to come up to the house and he arrived looking like he had just got out of bed. Which, of course, he had, because the driver told me that he had a job waking him up, and as soon as he got into the car he fell asleep.

At the house, and after numerous cups of coffee, he looked around and declared that this was where he would like to work. He said he could not type very well, but could dictate! I rang my girl in London, Rosemary Marks, and told her to fly out. Two days later we, or rather he, got started.

We got rid of the kids, and gave him space in the sitting room, but after a while Fred decided that he would work better outside, so we moved a desk and Rosemary's bits and pieces, shorthand book, typewriter etc. out to the back of the house where it was very quiet and shaded. Then he decided to have a swim first "to blow away the cobwebs". From the pool he shouted, "This is it, this is it." He had decided that was the place, he would write from the pool. And that is how it began. He would lie on an inflated bed and dictate to a bikini-clad, gorgeous-looking Rosemary sitting on the pool side, pencil poised above her notebook. He would very slowly dictate for about fifteen minutes, then fall in the pool and say, "Well, I think that's a pretty good day's work!" We were not even getting two pages a day. Most days he was late, and it took him a long time to begin. He would dictate a few stuttering words, then, "Am I going too fast for you, honey?" he would ask Rosemary.

I reported all this back to Paramount but they took no notice. At the time they were having a real problem with a Blake Edwards' movie "Darling Lili", starring his wife, Julie Andréws. They were miles behind schedule and as Charlie was in Europe he decided to pay them a visit.

Unusually for Ireland, it was a beautiful sunny day and as Charlie swept into Baldonal airport he was hoping to find them busy at work, catching up on lost time. What he found was the British crew playing cricket, the Americans playing with the Frisbee, and the Irish sitting in the shade watching the lunatics sweating in the rarely seen Irish sun.

Charlie was ready to blow a gasket, but worse was to come.

"Oh, hi, Charlie," greeted Blake, not even bothering to get up from his chair.

"How you doing, Blake?"

"Oh, pretty good."

"So, why aren't you shooting?" queried Charlie.

"It's the weather," responded Blake.

Charlie looked up into the blue sky. "The weather?" He shrugged his shoulders in dumb amazement. "The fucking weather is beautiful."

"That's the trouble," Blake said.

"That's the trouble?" Charlie asked.

"Yeah," Blake responded in his laid-back way, "we're waiting for a cloud."

"You're waiting for a cloud? How long have you been waiting for this cloud?"

"Oh, I don't know," said Blake, getting pissed off with all these questions, "you'll have to ask my assistant. Hal, how long we been waiting for the cloud?"

"Three days," came back the answer.

"And the budget, how's the budget?" Charlie asked, on the verge of a nervous breakdown.

Blake shook his head and said in exasperation, "Look, Charlie, stop asking me all these questions. You want to know the schedule, go ask the production manager, you want to know the budget, go ask the accountant." And stood up and walked away, picking up a Frisbee on his way.

That night in Italy I got a call from an irate Paramount President, going mad and screaming down the phone to me, "You get yourself on the next plane to Ireland, and you take over that fucking film. You take it over, do you hear? Sort out this son of a bitch."

I let him go on, although to tell the truth there was no stopping him. Finally I managed to say, "Charlie, listen to me, it won't do any good and anyhow I am working on 'Roman Holiday'."

"Forget 'Roman Holiday'. We're losing millions on this goddamn film, and, Doctor Dark, you've got to sort it out."

"Look," I said "you're not going to change Blake, he's not going to listen to me."

He interrupted, "If he doesn't do as you say, then you sack him, you have my authority to sack him."

"Charlie, he has a contract as both producer and director."

"So, I'll get the lawyers to break his contract."

I quietly added, "You forget that the leading lady is his wife, you don't think she's gong to stay once her husband is fired?" The phone went very quiet. Blake had us boxed in and Charlie knew it, and what was worse, Blake knew it. So I missed out on an Irish holiday and it was back to "Roman Holiday".

I used to run the Willie Wyler movie, and ask myself how could we top it? Where did we find an Audrey Hepburn who could act and dance? Singing could be fixed, but there was no way round acting and dancing. Dyson and his team had not come up with anyone who fitted the bill. There had to be a girl somewhere, but where?

We were in a pretty poor state. However, the Sherman boys sent me a tape of the first three songs they had written, which I thought were delightful. However, Charlie said he couldn't tell anything from a piano track, and needed a complete orchestration, so I contacted Irwin Kostal to score the three tunes and Ineke and I flew back to London to attend recording session. Together with a fifty-piece orchestra, it was the most amazing and wonderful music. I was ecstatic, and I returned to Rome full of renewed excitement.

However, things were not good there. Our writer had gone completely over the hill. We were without the key elements of a director and writer, and had just three great songs and some pretty pictures painted by Franco Zefferelli's art department.

Then Bud called me to meet him at the Cannes Film Festival in the South of France. I had no idea why, but as Bud pointed out, "That's where you're wanted, so that's where you're going, okay? Tell us what flight you're on and we'll have you picked up at the airport."

I arrived at Nice airport and there sure enough was a limo waiting which drove me to the Hotel Du Cap, one of the most expensive hotels in one of the most expensive parts of Europe – and even more so at that particular time of the year.

At the hotel I was greeted by Bud and Gwynne, and as always it was so good to see them. With them was their twenty-four-year-old daughter, Mary. Mary and I were old friends, and it was especially good to see her again.

The hotel was gorgeous, especially the seaside area named "Eden Rock", with its pool built into the side of the rocky coast line, and had an excellent gourmet restaurant. The only thing I had against it was that it was some way from the centre of Cannes where all the action was. But Bud was eager to point out to me that there was a Rolls standing by to take us anywhere at any time! Of course, silly me.

However, before the festival could get into gear a general strike was called, stirred up by left wing, militant French film-makers – one of the leaders being my old friend, Claude Berri, from "Greengage Summer" days. Not only were there no films, there was no transport, no planes, no buses, and we were stuck.

But what a place to get stuck! We could have gone out on Sam Spiegel's yacht, but Bud reckoned it would be over quickly, so we pigged it out at the hotel. It was whilst we were having a lobster lunch on the terrace at "Eden Rock" that Ineke managed to get through on the phone. There had been so much news about it, and she was worried that I was hungry.

"Darling," I said, "last night they had no caviar. Would you believe it? Those fucking Union peasants, they just don't care who they upset. They should be shot!"

So, the four of us sat for two days, getting fatter and fatter, as the only thing to do was to eat and drink. Mary did try and get me out to play tennis, but firstly it was too hot, and secondly I can't play. I am uncoordinated, so when I serve I throw the ball up in the air, it disappears, and I don't find it till I hear it bouncing on the ground several feet away.

One day, a German film producer invited us out on his yacht. When his enormous craft pulled up at the "Eden Rock" jetty, Bud muttered to me, "Can you imagine what he would have had if they had won the war?"

It was a beautiful boat, and crewed by an all-English crew. I asked the owner where he kept it and was surprised to be told that it stayed at the Cannes Yacht Club. I asked him how often he got down to France. "Vell," he said, "I try to get down two weeks in the year. Once I managed three." And I looked around at the British crew and thought, if he has it for two weeks a year then they have it for fifty. Somehow it didn't make sense, but I felt very happy for the lads.

Eventually Bud decided we would leave, and suggested that I get my car and another car to meet us at the border town of San Remo. We would take the Rolls from Cannes and switch cars there.

With Bud in the front with the driver, and Gwynne and I in the back with Mary between us, we set off. At one point Gwynne said she was feeling cold, so we put the rug over us.

That rug was the start of my demise.

J. D. flirting with Julia Foster and veteran director George Sidney expressing his view "Half a Sixpence"
1967

J. D. and Ineke at the premier of "Half a Sixpence" 1967

J.D. with Doug McClure, Peter Gilmore and Lea Brodie "Warlords of Atlantis" 1977

J. D. with Mickey Rooney "Arabian Adventure" 1979

J. D. and Ineke at the premier "Morons from Outer Space" 1985 with daughter Susie in the background

J. D. with director Lewis Gilbert and Pauline Collins "Shirley Valentine" 1988

J. D. with Pauline Collins on location in the Greek Isles "Shirley Valentine" 1988

J. D. with chums Mel Smith and writer Willy Russell at the premier arty of "Shirley Valentine" 1989

J. D. on the set of "Stepping Out" with Andrea MArtin and Liza Minnelli 1990

Royal Premier of "Stepping Out" J. D. with HRH Diana Princess of Wales 1991

CHAPTER 15
THE PRODUCERS

Back in Rome, I was trying to get sense out of someone, anyone. Looking back, I realise the writing was already on the wall then. I could not get any answers from anyone about the stalling on "Roman Holiday". Fred Segal had gone totally "ape", we'd lost Franco, and no one wanted to discuss his replacement. I wrote making several suggestions, but got no reply.

Bud was strangely quiet, so in desperation I went over his head and rang Martin Davis, the vice president of the company. "What you ringing me for?" was his charming greeting.

I explained the whole sad situation, and at the end he grunted, "So?"

"So, what do you suggest I do?" I said.

"I suggest you go out and get yourself laid." And put the phone down. Well there's not a lot one can say to that.

Marty was a funny chap, very quiet, always hiding himself behind his pipe. We had a strange relationship. I remember him saying to me once, "You think it's a lot of fun being the vice president of the company."

"I never said that, Marty, but the money's good!"

You'd have thought a time bomb had been lit under him, and for the first time I saw him lose his composure. "I don't do it just for the money," he yelled.

I let him rant on and just said quietly, "Well, I can't understand why you do it, then."

He pulled himself together and suddenly said for no apparent reason, "Listen, John, I'd like to be like you, but I can't."

To which the only reply I could think of was, "I'm sorry!"

Meanwhile back at the villa, time was running out. European production was slowing down, money was getting tight, and "Roman Holiday" was one of the abandoned productions. The Rome office was being scaled down, and we were soon to leave Italy. With sadness, I said good-bye to Luigi and Mauricio, and with a heavy heart, the darling Mimi.

Lewis and Hylda Gilbert took over the house, whilst he was shooting "The Adventurers". In contrast to us, they had a really miserable time there, especially as Hylda was robbed of her precious jewellery.

Back in London, things were fast falling apart. The European operation had not had one box-office success. In complete contrast in Los Angeles Bobby Evans had a string of great successes. Jerry Juroe left, and returned to what he was really good at. He took over as head of publicity at Eon on the "Bond" movies. My main concern was getting the money that Paramount owed me from my signed contract on the aborted "Roman Holiday". To this end I had a big row with Marty, but in the end won.

Although we were sad to leave Italy, which we loved, and all our Italian friends, it was good to be back in our own home. The only fly in the ointment was when Gregory advised me that he was marrying Annie, our nanny. This I thought was disastrous, for, though he was of a legal age, she was much older and also more mature. He had only just left school, for God's sake! Nevertheless they married, and Ineke and I went to the ceremony. The marriage did not last very long, and they soon parted. Later, Annie had a baby by one our friends, and we visited her in hospital, but that was the last time we saw her. This was 1969, the year the first man landed on the moon.

I was approached by Harry Booth, a director who had a reputation on shorts and rather bad English comedies like "On the Buses", which although quite awful, made money because of the success of the show on television, and the popularity of the "stars". Anyhow, Harry approached me as he knew that Paramount were making some support shorts, and he had a script which Michael Bentine (one of the Goons) had written, in which he wanted to star.

Now the thing about shorts at that time was that they attracted double Eady money. Eady money was the subsidy for British pictures where you got a percentage of the box-office take from the government. The great thing about it from a producer's point of view was that the money was not subject to any distribution charges. The budgets were minimal, and I thought it would be a challenge to make an entertaining comedy for such a paltry sum. So, I made a good deal with Paramount which gave me practically no fee, but a large slice of the profits, and we went ahead.

I took on John Seeley as production manager as well as doubling as editor. He had been a small-time editor but was keen to move into production, and really anxious to work with me. I then did a deal with a little commercials' company that had a really tiny studio near Walton. They would supply the camera and the crew, headed by Sam Martin, who was a director of the company and also the lighting cameraman. I had worked with him in the past when I used to work on commercials in-between movies. We had no money so the minimal crew all worked for basic. We used our own cars, except for one truck, which contained the camera and accessories, the lights, the wardrobe, and a refrigerator which contained the unit catering. Each night it was charged up and then the following morning the food was put into the then cold fridge, which kept it cool till lunch time. The van also doubled up as a changing room.

In addition to Michael Bentine, we had a strong supporting cast of Bob Todd, Una Stubbs, Norman Vaughan and my old friend Georgie Moon.

We took terrible liberties, like when I rang Norman Vaughan who was due on location the following day and asked him if he had a big car. "Oh yes," he said proudly, "I've got a Bentley."

"Oh great," I replied, "would you mind stopping off and picking up some props and bringing them down with you?" Anything to save money.

On this type of budget you have to fight for every shilling, it was like making another "Wind of Change". John Seeley was great at getting free props. From Sainsbury's, the grocer's, he not only got two of their large vans for free, but got Sainsbury's to pay us for putting them in the film. Family were pulled in, and Ineke, Dan, and Sue all appeared as extras.

We needed a traffic jam, so we contacted the British car manufacturers to ask them to lend us some cars, but to no avail.

So I rang up the editor of the Business section of "The Times" and told him the story, ending with "... so it looks as if this pretty English village will be full of Japanese cars!"

He told me to get back to the British companies and tell them that I had spoken to him and that he was very interested in the outcome. We got all the cars we needed.

We also played our parts: Harry Booth played the ferry Captain, I played an irate motorist, and so on. We paid Gus, Bentine's son, to drive Michael to the various locations, for one of our problems was that Michael was also in a show at the theatre in Brighton, so had to leave early each day. By having his son drive him, the responsibility for getting him back and forth on time was his, not ours.

Michael was a strange man, well educated, intelligent, and a man of many talents. I don't think he really liked performing but was much more interested in restoring old paintings, and in his collection of antique fire arms. He also enjoyed practising with explosive special effects. His neighbours in Esher were not too happy by the periodic explosions emanating from his house, with smoke drifting over their carefully tended Esher gardens.

He liked radio, and I think it was because he did not have to be seen. He was one of "The Goons" with Peter Sellers, Harry Secombe and Spike Milligan. It's sad that in retrospective publicity, his name was rarely mentioned, and, though he never referred to it, I am sure it was very hurtful to him. Michael was proud of being Peruvian, though my Peruvian daughter-in-law, Greg's second wife, said no one in Peru had ever heard of him. When his son, Gus, was tragically killed in a light aircraft crash, I rang him with my condolences. He told me not to worry, that he had spoken to him and that he was fine. He was a great spiritualist as well as a fine comic. On refection, maybe that is not so strange after all!

He was also a great snob, never more demonstrated by the days we shot at Fort Belvedere. We had to shoot a nudist colony. I have to stress that in accordance with my contract with Paramount, the film had to have a 'U' certificate, so it was the old "beach-ball cover-up" scene. We had to find somewhere private that wouldn't be accessible to the public. Harry came up with Fort Belvedere, a mini castle surrounded by acres and acres of protected land. He had shot there before when he made a documentary about Edward the Eighth, who had broadcast his abdication speech from there. He knew the present owner, the Honourable Gerald Lascelles, who quickly gave his permission.

The day we arrived Michael turned up wearing his Old Etonian tie and when Gerald Lascelles came to greet us Michael made a great play of straightening it.

Lascelles, in his open necked shirt took no notice whatsoever when giving him a brief but warm handshake.

In the end, Michael was forced into saying, "I don't think we were there at the same time, were we?"

Lascelles turned, "Where?"

"Oh, you know, Eton."

"Oh, there. No, I don't think so." For Lascelles had other things on his mind: the girls.

When I booked six gorgeous girls, I stressed to the agent that, though this was a 'U'-certificate film, the girls would have to strip off, and I pleaded with him not to send me any shy or prudish ones. Well, they were gorgeous and I could see that our host was very taken with them, and this was when we had just arrived and they were still clothed! What was it going to be like when we started work? Well, Lascelles never left our side for the whole shoot. The girls were great and totally stripped off and, as it was a wonderful warm day, they didn't bother to put their clothes on even when we stopped for coffee. After the initial interest, and because the girls were not in any way embarrassed, the crew took not a blind bit of notice of their nudity. They chatted with them about the previous night's television, and other mundane subjects. This confirmed what I always thought, that the less fuss made about it, the less anyone takes any interest.

With the exception maybe of our host, who said, "This place has seen many extraordinary sights, but none as great as today's!"

In confirmation of what I have just said, at the end of the day, Nobby, our sole electrician, was loading the lights onto the truck with the driver whilst the fully clothed girls were sitting on the bank waiting for the car to take them to Virginia Water station. All day long Nobby had been looking at the nude girls, and as he lifted the last light stand onto the back of the truck, he nudged the driver and said in a stage whisper, "Hey, Bob, I can see right up that bird's kilt!"

Another example of people's strange attitudes concerns the respect the British have for authority, even in the most bizarre circumstances. We were shooting at the Ferry Terminal at Newhaven, and Bob Todd (who was playing a policeman) was, for reasons of the script, dressed in his helmet and jacket, but no trousers, just long-johns. Some of the people boarding the ferry would stop to ask the correct way. They would pull up, notice that he had no trousers, avert their eyes, but continue to ask their question. They just pretended not to notice that this policeman, this symbol of authority, was without his trousers!

Actually it is not only comic figures of authority that they ignore, but anyone who does not conform. Everyone buries their heads in their newspapers when hippies or punks get in a train. There was a man in Soho who for years wore a bathroom tap sticking out of his forehead and no one ever took any notice! For some extraordinary reason Bud Ornstein once bought a First World War German Officer's dress helmet with a spike coming out of the centre. As we walked down Wardour Street, he put it on my head saying, "See what they make of that." Again they just looked the other way.

My relationship with the Ornstein family came to an end after an affair with their twenty-four-year-old daughter was discovered. The wax moustache was twirled, and I was thrown out into the proverbial snow! I don't want to write much about this, not from my point of view, but I have too much respect for her. She was a sweet girl, and I only hope she is happy in the marriage that she was pushed into. The only thing I would say is that it was not all my fault, but nevertheless the man takes the rap, and on that score I certainly did.

Bud moved to Warner Brothers taking Paul Hitchcock with him, the Paramount European office was practically closed down, and I was out of work.

Worse was that I was persona non-grata with all the American companies. There is none so puritan as the sinner when someone else is caught out.

My short was released and as it went out with "True Grit". A huge box-office success, it too was a success. Thank God, for that is what kept us alive. I took an office at Shepperton, which I still think is the best office in the studio. Through the conservatory, there was an inner and outer office, high ceiling with a fan light, and a door that leads out onto the lawns at the back. In those days, there was a wondrous cedar tree, which was the studio symbol, but sadly at some stage it was cut down. There I was ensconced, looking for anything to save the day.

At the same time we moved from Molesey to St. George's Hill in Weybridge, the "Beverley Hills" of England. With the money I made on the Molesey house, I was able to get rid of my mortgage and move into this millionaire enclave. When you're down you have to look even bigger.

About this time I met Anne Burnaby again. Now, Anne had been a woman of great importance at Associated British, one of Britain's leading film companies with their own studios at Elstree. She was the head of the story department and wielded great power. No one, not even directors, could change a word in the script without her permission.

However, Anne had a couple of problems, because despite being married and having two children, she liked her drink, and she also liked the attention of male companions. One day in a drunken mood she had a row with her current lover, picked up a pair of scissors and stabbed him in the arm. The lover left the flat rapidly, and Anne went to bed and fell fast asleep, until she was woken by hammering on her front door, and a voice saying, "Police!"

The lover had gone straight round to the police station and made charges against her. She was eventually taken to court and accused of causing grievous bodily harm, found guilty and sentenced to a year's imprisonment. Whilst in prison she was visited by the head of the company, Robert Clark, a man not known for his generosity either financially or emotionally. He used to say to her that she looked so good he was going to put it in future contracts that she spent so many months each year in the nick! He paid her all the time she was inside and made it plain that her job would be waiting for her when she got out.

However, when she did get out, she did not go back to the studio, but wrote a television play based on her time in the First Offenders' wing of Holloway prison, entitled "Girl in a Birdcage". It was directed by Charles Jarrott who later became a features director, ("Anne of a Thousand Days", "Mary Queen of Scots") for the doyen American producer, Hal Wallis.

The play was a critical and public success and the film rights were bought by Lewis Gilbert. He had done nothing with them so I asked him if he would be willing to sell them to me. He said that he would discuss this once I had a deal in place, which was okay with me. Naturally I hoped that he would direct it as well.

Despite its success, I always thought that what actually happened at the end was so much better than what was in the play which ends when she is sent to an open prison. What actually happened was that she never went back to Associated British, nor did she go back to her husband and children, but shacked up with the female warder who had looked after her in prison! And if that was not enough, the girl had to give up her job when she went to live with Anne but found that she could not take life outside the prison service, so left Anne and went back to the nick!

When I met Anne again she was living with a strange little woman called something like Twinky. Anne supported them both by playing the piano in a pub in the East End of London. She dragged me there one night, and I spent a jolly time joining in the singing of all the old songs which Anne hammered out on a tinny piano, which she somehow managed to combine with drinking the vast numbers of pints of beer bought for her by her adoring audience. Naturally she was excited about making it into a film, and wanted desperately to be involved in writing the script. I started my quest for finance, and had discussions with Peter Eade for his client, Glenda Jackson (who became a Labour M.P.), to play the lead.

I heard that Sam Arkoff, the head of American International Films, was in town and I made an appointment to see him at his suite at the Savoy Hotel. I arrived at the appointed hour, knocked on the door which was opened by the great man himself. Well "great" really was not the word to describe him, as he was very short and not helped by not wearing shoes or socks, and for being rather rotund.

"Mr Arkoff, I'm John Dark."

"Oh, *you're* John Dark. Well, I'm going to sue the shit out of you, come in."

What he was going to sue me for I never found out. I think it was just his way of unsettling you before you had even started.

Anyhow, I told him the story and he was more than interested. At the end he excitedly jumped out of his chair saying, "We could have an Attica ending. ..." An Attica ending? What was he talking about? "... And they can fire their machine guns, and we can have close–ups of the blood oozing out of their tits." And then I got it: Attica was the American prison where there had been very bad riots and the police and the National Guard had massacred a lot of the inmates.

After Sam had exhausted himself with describing his gory ending, and sank back into his chair, I said, "But, Sam, they don't have machine guns in Holloway Prison. And I doubt they have even rusty knitting needles."

I wanted to say it wasn't a riot film, or even a brutal or sadistic one. If anything it was a kind of love story, but he cut in, "For Christ's sake, who cares? No one's heard of Holloway, so forget it. Write in some action and send it to me." I never did.

I met him later on in life and, though he was a tough old sod, I quite liked him. He was the boss of his company and he ran it on a day-to-day, hour-to-hour basis, and you could always get hold of him. Of course, in return he liked to rough you up, he'd phone you and berate you about something or the other, in fact anything, then would say, "That scared the shit of you," and laugh. He did it so many times, it lost its effect, but you never, if you were wise, let on to that.

Times were tough with the major Americans out of the ball game. Quite apart from my indiscretion, all the companies were reducing their UK operations. Columbia, for example, which had been the biggest operator in England, had reduced their office to practically zero.

So I turned my attention to the British companies. At that time Shepperton Studios were owned by British Lion, and through the studio manager, Andy Worker, I got to meet the Boulting Brothers, John and Roy, who were the two great characters of the British Film Industry.

They were twins and were rarely separated, either producing or directing their own films. In their early days they made several critically acclaimed films including "Seven Days to Noon", "Brighton Rock" and "The Magic Box". However, I think they are best remembered for their later comedy films, especially "I'm All Right Jack", a brilliant satire on the British labour scene which gave Peter Sellers probably one of his finest roles as the militant shop steward. Amongst others they also made "Private's Progress" and "Brothers In Law". They were great characters, and physically very alike, so people often called them by their wrong name, which did not amuse either of them. They also spoke alike on the phone, so it was impossible to tell which one it was. They affected the most strange, strangled upper-class English accent which worked for them, and indeed was imitated by a lot of people, including myself. The best stories about them are those told orally, for without the accent lots of the humour is lost.

It was always said that you could not get on with both of them, and there was a certain amount of truth in that for each one of them they had their favourites. I never experienced this myself, and got on with both of them. In fact one day John said, "I really don't know why Roy and I are so desperately fond of you. I suppose it is because everyone takes the piss out of us behind our back, but you do it to our face!"

At this time John had taken over as Managing director of the company, and I therefore saw more of him than Roy. After what seemed to be numerous meetings, some of which necessitated the consumption of vast quantities of alcohol, he offered me a job as his eyes and ears on a film they were shooting which was heading for trouble. (Send for Dr Dark again!)

This film was Joe Orton's black comedy "Loot", being shot as a film and directed by Silvio Narizzano, starring Lee Remick, Richard Attenborough, Hywel Bennett and that lovely Irish actor, Milo O'Shea.

After my first day there I rang John and expressed my view that the film was a disaster. "The trouble is," I explained, "Orton's play is a black comedy based on seemingly normal looking people in a normal looking setting doing the most appalling things. As Silvio has set the film in a crazy set, and dressed the characters bizarrely, the whole humour of the action is lost, especially as he has all the actors playing it over the top, thus losing the subtle comedy in Orton's play."

The only thing to help was to stop and start again, but they were too far into production, and the Completion Guarantor would not pay for that and a small company like British Lion certainly could not afford it. So all I could do was to see that they kept to schedule and spent as little money as possible.

Hywel Bennett was under contract to the Boultings, so when John came to Shepperton (usually at the end of day when he was on his way home), Hywel would join us in my office. John loved to sit and drink, chew the fat, or to be more precise, to argue. The arguments would get more and more vocal the more the scotch went down.

One evening Chic Murray came to visit me, and got caught up in all the lively debate, but not lively enough to stop him from falling asleep. John was haranguing Hywel and myself and shouted so loud that he woke up Chic who had been asleep for some time. "And what do you thing about it?" John asked the blinking Chic.

"Oh, I quite agree with you Mr Boulting!" said Chic.

"There you are!" shouted a jubilant John Boulting, then seeing Chic had fallen back to sleep asked, "Who is that man? Most intelligent."

The producer of the film was an extremely nice American man, Arthur Lewis, who had lived in England for years. He was mainly a stage producer and in fact I don't think he had produced a movie before "Loot". I guess it was through his theatrical experience that he got the rights to the Orton property. I liked him a lot, and we used to keep in touch. At one time he had the rights from the Great Ormond Street hospital of "Peter Pan", and I spent a long time with the script working out how best we could make it. I was sorry that he never managed to get the deal together. When I was a child my mother used to take me every year to see it on the stage, and it has stayed in my mind as I think it is the greatest of children's stories. When Spielberg made "Hook" I could have cried. For once I think he missed the whole charm of the story, and despite an all-star cast and a budget of millions, it was a turkey. Arthur remained a friend, and I have a wonderful painting on my sitting room wall painted by his talented wife.

At this time I was represented by the most famous of agents, the William Morris office, and they had a call from the mighty Sam Spielberg, producer of "The Bridge On the River Kwai" and "Lawrence of Arabia" amongst many others. He was after me to be his associate producer on his soon-to-be-made "Nicholas and Alexandra". At the same time John came up with a counter-offer to produce a film in Australia based on the two explorers who opened up the interior of that great country. What was really compelling was that the script was by the great playwright and screen writer, Sir Terence Rattigan. Films based on his own plays include "Separate Tables", "The Winslow Boy" and "The Browning Version".

His Australian script was called after the two men, "Burke and Wills". I did not want to upset Spiegel, as he was an important and successful man, and I didn't know when I might need him in the future, so I told the Morris office to out-price me. He accepted this fee, so I then made some other demands and he eventually gave in.

John said, "You can't really go and work for the frightful little man", so I accepted the British Lion deal. This was that Lion would finance the film fifty-fifty with an Australian company. It was to be directed by Lionel Harris, whom I had never heard of but who was hailed as a great genius by John and his fellow board members.

The plan was that Lionel and I, together with a production designer, would carry out an extensive recce in Australia. Whilst there, we would view the area that had been set aside to build a British Lion Film Studio, and give any advice or help on this plan to the Aussies. Meanwhile Andy Worker, the Shepperton General Manager, had already been out there.

I was lucky in having my dear old friend, John Stoll, come with us as the designated production designer. I met Lionel Harris, and found him a pleasant enough person, small, bald and rotund, and with his great big eyes he looked like an overweight "bush baby".

So Lionel, John and I caught our first class Qantas flight to Sydney. There we met the Australian lawyers who were representing the consortium. They were very special people who could not have been nicer to us, though I did have to put my foot down on the necessity of taking an Australian location manager with us. We would be returning to London and we needed someone with movie experience we could contact when making our preliminary plans. So another John joined the team.

Later I discovered the reason there had been so much opposition was that the Australians were running out of money. Thus far, they had financed all the domestic costs, including the air fares for John Boulting, Andy Worker and our group, and they had yet to see any money from Lion even though, according to them, they were supposed to be equal investors. That was not my affair, though I made a note to discuss it with John when I got back to the UK.

My main problem was that I could not get Lionel out of Sydney. Now don't get me wrong; I have absolutely nothing against gays, in fact I am all for them, they usually have a great sense of humour and anyway they cut the opposition down and leave more women for the straight guys! However, Lionel was having a great time with the lads in this very gay city, and it took me days to prise him away from the fleshpots. Eventually, and after a further row because I would not fly in a single engine aircraft, we took off in our chartered plane for the interior.

The night before we left for Australia, Ineke and I had watched a "Whicker's World" programme about a place in Australia, Broken Hill, which gave a terrifying portrayal of this mining town, which boasted of being the largest city outside a capital city in Australia. Alan Whicker described how the town was run by the Unions, and specifically the Barrier Industrial Council. The city was situated in the bleak desert of the interior, where they mined all sorts of different minerals, and the miners there were the top paid miners in the world. The power of the Council was everywhere – for example, insisting that every miner take the miners' newspaper every day; so, if there was a father and four sons working in the pits, then that household would take five copies of the paper.

Once a month, it was badge day and every worker had to wear his Union badge. One day a guy's house burned down and he arrived at his place of work without his badge, where he explained what had happened. That was no excuse and he was sent home. The pubs in New South Wales are closed by law on Sundays, except in Broken Hill. It was the same with the gambling game, the "Two Up" game, illegal everywhere except in Broken Hill where the police helped you to park your car at the selected venue. All the boys know that when they grow up they will get a job down the mines, so they are unruly and don't give a damn. As soon as they are old enough, they buy a second-hand American gas guzzler and charge out to the desert with a stock of beer and some girls, and try and out-race each other, then come back into town and make trouble.

Married women are not allowed to work, so the girls know that they have to make hay while the sun shines. When they are married they have little to do, nowhere to go, so spend their time playing the poker machines (fruit machines) in the RSL club. The RSL clubs are ex-servicemen's clubs, and are the centre of attraction in many Australian towns and cities. In Broken Hill, it is practically the only place to socialise outside of the various pubs. It is also a brutal place. They don't take kindly to strangers or to criticism. Alan Whicker didn't dare show his face in the town again and, as it was, one of his crew was beaten up and had to be put in the Flying Doctor hospital.

On seeing this Ineke said, "If that's Australia, there is no way you are going there." I pointed out to her that Australia was a massive country and that our plans did not take us anywhere near Broken Hill.

We assembled at the airport, our location manager, John, the partner and sister of our lawyer friend, John Stoll, the pilot, and myself. Lionel turned up dressed for the Outback in green shorts, green long socks, desert boots, and a matching cotton top. A kind of green bush hat, complete with a black veil, covered his face. No longer a bush baby, more a green dung-beetle!

"Well, you can laugh," he addressed the open-mouthed gang, "but wait till you see those flies."

"But, Lionel, we're still in Sydney," someone said.

"I know, but I want to be prepared. And another thing, I'm just warning you if I sit anywhere but in the front, I'll be sick. It's up to you. I don't mind, but if I sit at the back, be warned."

So we flew off with Lionel in the front.

The plan was to follow as far as possible the route taken by Burke and Wills. We had not been in the air all that long, when the pilot turned to us after talking on the radio and said, "The weather's a bit crock, so I am going to have to divert and land for a while till it clears up. There's an airport near here so we should be down in about ten minutes."

"Where's that?" Lionel asked.

"Broken Hill," he replied. It had to be!

Well, I thought, maybe it won't be as bad as the television show, they always exaggerate. Well, this time they didn't. If anything it was worse.

It was rather like being in a bad Western, "We don't like strangers in this town, mister." Everywhere you went you met there was an air of hostility. The people in the motel where we stayed were just about civil, but were keen to tell us what would happen if Alan Whicker ever came back. We were allowed to use the RSL club, which was my first experience of the place. On the first night I suddenly heard a bugle playing and noticed everyone became quiet as they stood up. I wondered what on earth was happening. Afterwards I found out that they played the "last post" every night in memory of their soldiers who never returned from the two World Wars.

One of the more charming experiences that night was when I ordered a vodka and tonic. Whatever they gave me certainly wasn't vodka nor was it tonic. I can't swear to it because I don't know what it tastes like, but I am pretty sure it was pee! The food was ghastly. We found a small restaurant which looked clean at least, and I decided to order something simple, something they couldn't fuck up. So I ordered eggs and bacon, and was offered mushrooms. I thought that might be nice, and that was my big mistake. When my food came it looked like a plate of axle-grease with a yellow eye looking out of it. The mushrooms turned out to be some pulped, tinned variety and they tasted as bad as they looked. After over three years in the army I had eaten some pretty awful things, but that ranked as the worst meal I ever ate – or more accurately didn't eat!

After a few days, the weather changed and we managed to escape. To paraphrase those famous American travelogues, "As we say good-bye to Broken Hill, we remember the miserable time we had and the most unpleasant people we ever came across."

The people in the Outback on the whole were very unfriendly. After flying for hours over the deserted red desert, and then seeing some blinking lights ahead which turned out to be the sun reflecting on the mounds of beer cans heaped outside a settlement, I used to think these people are going to be pleased to see some new faces. We would troop into the town bar, and as soon as the locals who were lounging over the counter saw us, they would spread themselves out so we couldn't get to order easily. They thought we were "Sydney poofters", which is just about the worst insult you can call anybody in their lingo. God knows what they would have thought if they had known we were "poms"!

We landed at a small place called Cooper's Creek, and watching us as we got out of the plane was an old man obviously wondering what on earth was happening. When he caught sight of Lionel, he blinked and said, "I've never seen anything like this in all my life. Wait a moment whilst I go home and get my camera. I won't be a sec, promise me you'll wait. I've got to have a picture of this, no one's going to believe me!" And off he dashed.

As this was one of the more important locations, John Stoll and I started to look around, take photographs, and make notes. John had already started to make rough sketches. We said, "Aren't you coming Lionel?"

"Oh no, you go on, I've been here before" was his reply whilst sitting himself on a log.

"I don't believe him," I said to John. "He never discusses the script, or what he intends to do. He doesn't look at the locations, make suggestions, never answers a question, nothing."

"I don't think," John added, "he's ever made a film before, so why would British Lion employ him?"

"Probably because he owned the script and conned the Aussies into putting up some money, I don't know."

Our mystified elderly local soon returned, panting heavily, camera in hand. "Good on yers. Just had to have a picture of this." Then, pointing the camera at Lionel, who preened himself with all the attention, said, "Now you, the one dressed like a sheila, hold still."

Why he thought he was dressed like a girl, I don't know. Maybe that was as far as his imagination could go, or maybe it was just because of Lionel's behaviour!

We used to stay at strange hotels, more like hostels, sleeping in dormitories, and using communal ablutions facilities. When the sheep- shearer guests saw Lionel flouncing into the wash house in his silk dressing gown and his array of perfumes, soaps and creams, they had something to talk about for a long time to come.

One day we visited an Aboriginal Education Centre run by a charming and dedicated Welshman and his wife. The aim of the centre was to teach the indigenous people how to cope with the modern Western world. We were standing in a dried-up river bed filled with giant boulders, and looking for a way out so as to get back to our car. The kind Welshman shouted out, "Come this way, Lionel, and I'll give you a good route."

Lionel burst out laughing. "Oh, I can't wait, he's going to give me a good root," and dissolved in peals of laughter again. This went on for the rest of the day. The Welshman was embarrassed. The wife didn't even understand why Lionel thought it was comical, and the rest of us just wanted to drop through the floor. But Lionel did not always enjoy references to his sexuality. Every time we got out of the plane John, our location manager, would shout, "Have you got your handbag, Lionel?"

Lionel complained to me, "I can definitely detect a swish of the skirt!"

Instead of being a fascinating and wonderful trip, it turned into a nightmare, and somewhere along the line I had enough. We arrived at a place where Lionel had insisted we land, and I asked, "What are we looking at here, Lionel?"

He replied, "There's the most marvellous view from the top of the hill."

"Yes, but what exactly do you want to shoot here?"

"Oh, I thought it would be good for some of the trekking scenes."

"Well, let's go and have a look and you can show us exactly what you mean."

"Oh no," was the reply. "It's far too hot. And as I said, I've seen it before."

There was no point in arguing, so the two Johns and I climbed this steep hill in the middle of the day, in the burning heat. Well, it was certainly a view that could possibly have been used, as one could see the red desert right up to the horizon, but you see the same thing wherever you stopped. I tried to explain to Lionel that we would have to bring everything, not only all the crew and cast, but also all the equipment, and as there was no hotel for miles we would have to build camps for people to live in.

Actually I hated the thought, even hated myself for having the thought. I reckoned you could shoot a great part of the movie based on Broken Hill. At least there was some accommodation, there was an airport, it was close to Sydney etc. etc. To me one part of the Outback looked exactly the same as the other, except for some really dramatic places which we would have to travel to in any case. Because of their isolation and to avoid blowing the budget into outer space, these would be kept to a minimum.

We got back from our hilltop recce, soaked in sweat, to find Lionel sitting in the shade consuming the last of the water! That's when I blew my top, and ended up accusing him of knowing nothing about film-making, and from the way he behaved was never likely to. We now had a truly sulky and petulant director. His camp behaviour became even more pronounced, and when we asked him a question, he would shrug, and turn away, then look back at us over his shoulder and with a soulful glower from his pop eyes walk away – a style of rejection enjoyed by Greta Garbo in her silent movies.

On our way back, I was anxious to see Birdsville, which was mentioned so often in the script. The pilot told me that as the heat was so intense there, and as there was no landing strip, just the packed sand of the desert, we would have to go in either early in the morning or late in the evening. We decided to take the early turn. We came down low over the little settlement, which with just a few corrugated iron huts and one or two stone ones, was too small to call a village. We landed and as the door of the plane opened thirty thousand flies attacked. For the first time I understood Lionel. We battled our way across the gritty sand, and as we got closer I could see a stone building with a creaking sign swinging in the heat outside, The Birdsville Inn. As I entered I could see nothing, it was just black, and it took several minutes for my eyes to adjust. The place was devoid of light other than some rays of sun which shone through the slats of the shuttered windows. The place was empty except for a few wooden tables and chairs, an ancient poster for Schweppes Indian Tonic Water, and a counter behind which there was the usual array of bottles.

Eventually an old crone came out from the back of the bar, and greeted us in that well known Outback greeting. Well, the one thing I had learnt in my travels in Australia was that wherever you went you could always get a cold beer, served in a sparkling clean glass, so I ordered one. Whilst I was waiting for her to pour it into the glass I ventured, "Wow, this weather, it is unbelievable, how do you put up with it?"

And passing the glass over she said, "Yeah, I know, it goes on and on. Sometimes I think winter will never end!"

From Birdsville, we travelled down to Gosford, a small town slightly North of Sydney, and the location of the proposed British Lion studio. We were met by a member of the Gosford council and taken out to where they intended to build. As we stood in the middle of this large tract of land, the details of the studio were pointed out, "Over there will be the initial two stages, and at the side will be the carpenters' shop and the prop store ..." and so the list went on. There were no plans, just a verbal description of this dream. We met other members of the Gosford council in the RSL club where we had lunch, and were made honorary members.

I felt sad, and I felt guilty, for I could see that this was never going to happen. If you were going to build a studio in Australia, why on earth would you want to build it in Gosford? Studios need to be close to facilities and to where the technicians and actors live. This idea would mean being away from their homes for weeks on end, and knowing a little about Australian Trades Unions, that would cost money. It would probably mean keeping the whole company on per diems, paying for their transport from Sydney and so on. The Gosford people were so nice and so excited at the prospect of a large English company coming to their town to make great international films. I knew absolutely that this was never going to happen.

I left Australia shortly after and insisted on getting out of the country on either a British or American airline. I can still remember my happiness on boarding an American Airlines 747 and being greeted by a cute Air Hostess in that happy, breezy American way. I'd had my fill of the "yep" culture, and was much happier with the "have a nice day" one.

Back in England, I met a hostile John Boulting who had been telephoned by Lionel telling his side of the row we had back in Australia. John was in one of his I-know-best moods, and nothing one could say would make him change his mind. In the end I left, saying on my way out, "If you do go ahead with this man, I promise you, John, you will be making the biggest mistake of your life." I always seemed to be making doom-laden prophecies from doorways.

Two or three weeks later, John began to tell me that Lionel was an idiot, completely ignoring the fact that he had blasted me for daring to suggest that Lionel was not a genius.

Lion had no money to put up for even half of the budget, so with no director and no finance, the project died and I was out of work. When John told me this he added, "Well, the one thing you can never accuse me of is talking you into this." That was John.

So joining the ranks of the unemployed, I continued my hunt for a script or a book on which I could raise money. Through Desmond Elliot, a literary agent, I got a deal on several books. Desmond had a good list of clients, headed by Leslie Thomas, a lovely man whom I greatly enjoyed meeting. One of his books, "The Virgin Soldiers", had been made into a film by Columbia, and had a limited success in the UK.

So I took his book "Orange Wednesday" to Columbia, whose story department gave it a favourable report. However, they were reducing their European operation and dickered and dithered around with it for months, so when Roy Boulting asked me to join him in a new movie he was making, I jumped at the chance

I signed a contract with British Lion to act as executive producer on a film entitled "Bread, Cheese and Kisses". John would have credit as producer, but, as he was still acting as MD for British Lion, he would in fact be producer in name only (well I was used to that). The script was to be another vehicle for Hywel Bennett and Roy's baby bride-to-be, Hayley Mills. It was to follow their two previous films for the Boultings, "The Family Way" and "Twisted Nerve". I read the script and thought it very lightweight, but charming in parts. Set against the enchanting Tuscany scenery, it might well turn out to be a popular film. Whatever the eventual outcome it would be a pleasant picture to work on, and hardly going to tax my brain.

The fee was up to the usual British lousy standard, but there was nothing else on offer and I really did like Roy. I liked John as well but I would not be seeing much of him on this one. Hywel was a lot of fun and I had met Hayley with Roy and found her a bubbly, easy-going girl. There was no doubt that Roy was crazy over Hayley, though their relationship caused a furore in the tabloid press, and they had to put up with the usual sick diatribe published by the British press. But it wasn't only the press, it was also her parents, for Roy was about the same age as her father, Johnny Mills.

Ineke and I bumped into Johnny and his wife at the "Complete Angler" at Marlow. I didn't tell him that I was in any way connected with Roy, but when we parted he said to me, "If you ever bump into Hayley, do what you can to break it off with that terrible man." Several years later, I was witness to that break up.

Hayley was in a play in the West End and Roy had been nagging me to go and see it, so we made a date and arranged to meet at their house, then Ineke and I would go on to the theatre and meet them both afterwards for dinner.

That morning I opened the newspaper to see the headline, "Hayley Leaves Roy Boulting." God, I thought, what do I do now? So I rang their joint agent, John Redway, to explain the problem, and he said we had to go. So we duly arrived at Roy's opulent London home at the appointed hour.

Roy Boulting had aged forty years, looking haggard and grey, with the flesh seeming to droop down his face. He was leaning on the back of a chair as we entered the room, distraught, and almost unable to talk. He had been robbed of his dignity and manhood which was unthinkable to anyone who had known this proud man. Ineke was at her best as she tried to console him. Roy never forgot her help, and from that day till the day he died she was one of his favourite people. I would have loved to have hugged him, but even at this desperate time you didn't hug a Boulting!

He begged us to go on to the play, and made us promise that we would go backstage and see her afterwards. I have no idea what the play was about because all I could think of was what I was going to say to Hayley. The curtain came down and we made our way backstage. I think she was surprised to see us, and asked us to stay for a drink, but after a quick "you were wonderful, darling" we left, saying we had to relieve the baby-sitter.

We leapt into a taxi and drove straight to the "Trattoria" in Romily Street and ordered two large drinks. It seemed only a matter of minutes before Hayley came in with the new boyfriend. We spent the rest of the evening ignoring each other.

I left for Pisa to find locations and start the preliminary Italian plans for "Bread and Cheese". I arranged for Giorgio Migliarini to meet me there so I could brief him and get him to prepare the Italian budget. We had a lovely time in Tuscany, Georgio found us a lovely hotel near the centre of Pisa, where I was amazed by the American tourists and their punishing schedule, "If it's Tuesday it's Belgium!" It was so tight they could have dinner or they could see the Leaning Tower, they could not do both. But what really astounded me was that when they did have dinner, they all changed into elegant clothes. I would have neither dined nor gone sight-seeing, but gone to bed!

We found several villages that would fit the script, and armed with stills and Giorgio's first figures, I returned to London. I am just a lousy photographer, and Roy was far from pleased with the results. However, I was able to explain to him that everything was there and we could have an easy and cost effective shoot in that area.

Back home I got a call from John Boulting, and when I hurried to town he told me that they were not going ahead with "Bread, Cheese and Kisses". My stomach turned. He then proceeded to tell me that he had signed a deal with Columbia and Mike Frankovich to make "There's a Girl in My Soup" with Goldie Hawn, and would I be agreeable to changing my contract to fit these new circumstances?

I replied, "I would work for nothing to work with Goldie Hawn. Just kidding, John, just kidding."

The only fly in the ointment was that the male lead was going to be Peter Sellers. When I voiced my fears about him John said, "He's only like that with your bloody American friends. We've worked with him for years with no trouble. He's not only talented but a good chum, now don't give me any more of that talk."

I went to see the stage show, which I thoroughly enjoyed. So, apart from Sellers, it looked as though we were going to have a nice time, with locations in the South of France, and Goldie Hawn on top.

John Seeley was still with me, a hangover from the short, so I took him along with me as production manager. This was a mistake, as Roy hated him and wouldn't talk to him, therefore adding to my work load.

Roy had special chums whom he always worked with, like the Wardrobe Mistress, the cameraman, and especially the two Stand-by Prop men, Chuck and Bobby. These latter two were the characters at the studio. Chuck was a rotund cheery Cockney, and Bobby was a tall, softly spoken gay. Chuck was straight but they just had this strange relationship and always worked together. The artists loved them and it is true they used to keep the floor very happy, but I have to say they were very bad prop men, and often it was necessary to get in extra guys to get the job done. They were legends in their own lifetime, and the stories about them were numerous. My favourite was that Bobby did have one woman once in his lifetime, and that woman was Ava Gardner – not a bad single to notch up if it was true, which I doubt!

Like Pinewood, Shepperton was fully staffed with the craft grades and the sound crews, and there was a rota system to allocate the employees to the various pictures.

When it was a location film there was great excitement, for the boys earned a lot more money. Theoretically the producer had no choice who his crew would be, though there was always a bit of wangling. Mainly you were stuck with whoever was top of the list, and you could find yourself lumbered with a bolshie incompetent, out to make trouble and to do as little work as possible.

One of these was Bert Kent, a painter, and a pain-in-the-arse. His great claim to fame, of which he was very proud, was that Peter Sellers had based his role in "I'm All Right Jack" on him. He was too stupid to realise that the role was actually taking the piss out of such people as himself. Some of his remarks were legendary in the business, as on one Spanish location when offered some "extra money" for the tough location, he remarked in his strong London accent, "There's no amount of pesetas that will compensate the bruvvers for the inconvenience."

However, his most famous remark was on "The Guns of Navarone" when at a crew meeting with the producer, Carl Foreman, to air any complaints, Carl said, "Is there anything else?"

Up shot Bert Kent. "Yes, it's the laundry."

"What's wrong with the laundry?"

"It's a disgrace, ain't it? Look, sometimes it comes back dirty, sometimes it comes back wet, and sometimes it comes back missing!"

I was determined we should not get lumbered with him, but Roy heard about it and both he and John told me that this was Bert's last film before he retired and he was a very decent chap! Sometimes I wondered what world the two of them lived in. So there was no way of getting rid of him as the Boultings not only were the producers of the film but were directors of Shepperton Studios as well.

The next personnel problem I had was with the production designer, Roy's man, who in my opinion, was a real second banana, though Roy wouldn't hear a bad word about him. So he was engaged and completed his first set designs which I thought were quite awful. I took them to Roy and said, "You can see what a load of crap he is intending to build." But Roy would not have it, and insisted that with a few colour changes they would be very good sets. It was not until we were near our start date, and the sets were built and dressed that Roy realised how ghastly they were.

We had to fire the poor guy and bring in some talent to make some vital changes. We brought in a couple of buddies, top designer John Howell and set decorator Patrick McLoughlin, who with their great expertise and by working day and night, saved the day.

The point of this story is that neither John or Roy, in my opinion, had any visual sense. They were literary film makers and if one looks back at their work this is what stands out. They were brilliant at what they did, and in the opinion of most people they did their best work in the days of black-and-white.

Goldie arrived with her husband, Gus Triconis. They seemed a very ordinary couple, sweet and unsophisticated, just like two tourists on their first visit to Europe. She proved to be the darling that I had always suspected, and it was great to welcome her and Gus to London.

We'd been shooting for a few weeks when Peter came into my office and said, "You'll have to do something." My heart sank. "I'm not right for this part, you'll have to recast."

"But, Peter," I stuttered, "we've been shooting for days, we'd have to start all over again."

"I can't help that," he replied, "I can't get to grips with it, and that's that." And left.

With Peter you never knew.

We quickly arranged meetings and eventually he was persuaded to stay. Looking back at it now, and looking at the film, I really think he was right, he was miscast.

After this little crisis, shooting went easily, and things settled down in a happy and efficient manner. I don't think Goldie cared for Sellers, and with Gus around, thankfully he kept his hands off her. She complained only once, which was more a plea for help: She hated kissing him because his breath smelt!

We left for Cannes in the South of France. I had been lucky in getting a great guy as our location manager, Tim Hampton, who became the Head of Fox in London. He was a real charmer, and very reliable. He had everything organised and I had little to do. I was staying at the Carlton Hotel as we had a deal with them to shoot inside and outside the hotel. It was good publicity for them, and a great location for us as well as giving me a splendid room at a very special price.

One day we were on a pretty little beach at the top of which was a fantastic restaurant. I invited Goldie and Gus to lunch and arranged a great menu with some very special wines. However, both Goldie and her husband ate French fries with tomato ketchup and drank Coca-Cola. All she spoke about were her worries about leaving their home in New York. I doubt she is like that now, but it was refreshing to have such a darling, talented and unspoilt star. I had a great lunch!

The crew were staying at a lovely hotel, where I came across Brother Kent one morning sunning himself on the outside terrace, dressed in his thick London trousers held up with a pair of what looked like army braces. "Everything all right, Bert? Nice room? Had breakfast?" I stupidly asked.

"I must say, it is a nice hotel," he reluctantly replied.

"But what about the breakfast?" I enquired – now this was really pushing my luck.

To which he replied, "Ah, breakfast, ah now, that's another matter."

"No good?" I asked

"No condiments," shaking his head in despair, "no condiments!"

We came back to London, and Peter worked until the end and on the whole did not behave too badly, except for the usual whinging about this person and that. He took the piss out of little character actors that he had taken a dislike to, but on the whole was not too bad. Goldie was the same darling throughout and I said good-bye to her with great sadness.

At the end of the shoot Brother Kent made his retirement speech, "I've had a very good time in my life 'ere, and I was very proud to have been asked by Mr Peter Sellers to be his technical advisor. Also I 'ave been proud in my capacity as Chief

Steward, to 'ave fought and won for betta' conditions for the workers 'ere. It therefore was with great sadness that on my last picture on the French location in the South of France with John Dark and Tim Hampton, after all I 'ave fought for over the years, that there were no mobile toilets." I thought he was going to say no condiments.

At the end of the film, John and Roy decided to make a short to go out with "Soup". On the film Roy had a very experienced and efficient Assistant, David Tringham, who made no bones about the fact that he wanted to be a director. We had already sent him out to France to shoot some shots of a wine festival that we could fit into the film. So Roy gave this short to David to direct saying, "Let him have a go. Maybe he will find out that it is not as easy as it looks."

I am not quite sure who had the hold on the property, David or the Boultings, but it was a short story by the famed writer John Fowles, entitled "The Last Chapter", and was to star Denholm Elliot and a new young rising actress, Susan Penhaligon. Though I was credited with the title of producer, I really had nothing to do. The money was there, the script was there, the film was cast, so it was a case of "let's shoot". However, what it did do for me was to introduce me to Susan Penhaligon, and also to Elliot Scott, the designer who later became Spielberg's designer.

We had great fun making this little film, and I thought David did a pretty good job, though to my knowledge he was never to direct again. It is such a big leap from editor, assistant director, actor, cameraman, writer to director. It is tough, and you need to be lucky. The only exception is when you are a leading actor, a star, when the company is so anxious for your services they agree to your demands some of whom become amongst the best like the great Clint Eastwood.

After this, British Lion had nothing for me, and I never worked with John or Roy again, though we remained friends until both their deaths. They made one more film, "Soft Beds and Hard Battles", which luckily I was unable to accept their offer as I was busy on another project. It was a financial disaster and they both lost a lot of money. They did not obey the principal law of film-making: never put your own money into your own films.

John died long before Roy, who ended his days living alone in a miserable council flat outside Oxford. Ineke and I used to visit him there and take him out to lunch. He was quite amazing, never complained about his situation, or was in any way bitter. Ineke asked him once how he managed to cope and he said he coped by looking back at the wonderful life he had led. He was a wonderful man, a super friend and I am filled with sadness when I write about him. Then, like him, I look back at the fun we had together, the warmth that surrounded our friendship and the amazing films that he and John had made.

It puzzles me how the industry allowed him to end up in such poverty. I know that he was a proud man and refused charity, but there must have been some way to have helped him. In America, a director like Roy would have been protected by the Directors' Guild, but here in England, the Unions and the guilds are more interested in politics than in their members. One would have thought that his fellow directors, some of whom were receiving major fees for their work, could have helped. It doesn't say much for them, for BAFTA, and all the other worthy organisations that abound.

So, once again I started to set up my own projects.

The role of an Independent producer is tough. In fact, Barry Spikings the head of EMI films, one day said to me that it was almost impossible. Unless you are a rich man, or have some back-up, it is very, very difficult. You have all the expenses with no guarantee of any return.

You have to buy the book, the play, the idea, and you then have to develop it, and pay writers. At the same time you must pay for your offices, your secretary, phone calls, and travel, which often means getting on a plane and going to LA. Many people have gone bust in the attempt. In one way I was lucky as, through my relationship with Desmond Elliott, I had the rights on numerous books.

With two children at private schools, alimony, and my mother to support, it was a worrying time. You never know when something might break but you always go to bed wondering, worrying. As part of my separation from Peggy she took over the "Football Results Service", the only remaining asset left from the press Agency. When she moved to Regent's Park, she decided to give it up, and kindly offered to give it back to me. At this time it was not making much money, and I really did not have the time, so I asked my mother if she would like to run it. She leapt at the idea, and for many years she used to see that it got out every Saturday night. It was amazing really, as it paid for the early school days of Gregory and Vicki, and then went through the family, till in the end it reached the eldest, and kept her in a little pocket money and also gave her an interest in her life.

At this time, with the near collapse of Columbia in England, many of the staff were looking for work. Amongst them was a secretary I had lusted over for years, though never got anywhere. I have remarked before on how lucky I have been, and this is especially true regarding who are known nowadays as personal assistants (which actually I think is a correct title). Whatever their title, I have had so many great ones. I often ponder how many executives like me have been quietly nudged in the right direction by their assistants. They have saved my neck on many occasions, and stopped me from making an idiot of myself, as well as reminding me about birthdays, anniversaries, and who should be rung, written to, or bought a present for. I had had so many wonderful ones and I was to be blessed again when Diane Furnberg came to help me through the Amicus Affair.

She was five feet of energy, pretty as a picture, with years of experience with Columbia, and had the sweetest personality. Her identical twin was so like her it was spooky! She could have sent her sister to work with me and I would not have known. However, when Diane first approached me for a job things were not looking good, and I had nothing to offer her. Then the accountant, Arthur Cleaver, introduced me to Max Rosenberg, an American who ran a small British production company with his English based but American partner, Milton Subotsky. He asked me if I would like to join their company, Amicus Productions. I can't say I leapt at the chance, but it seemed to be the only game in town. At times like this you have to bury your pride and just think about the money.

In any case, people in the business all know what it is like and think no less of you when you accept things that maybe you shouldn't. Most film people I have found to be kind, understanding and generous.

The first thing I did was to call Diane and she was to stay with me until ... but that's a later story.

Max said he would like me to improve the look of his films, which after running a couple I didn't think would be too difficult. What I did not know at the time was that Max and Milton did not like each other.

Milton fought against my appointment, and resented my presence from day one, which he did not try to hide.

Our first real brush was when I found out that the company was bankrupt, and Technicolor had frozen all the company's negatives through non-payment of outstanding bills.

I met the Managing director, Bill Ingram, who was a great hulk of a man who I thought was going to try to intimidate me with his size. We had quite a stormy meeting. In the end, he said he would un-freeze the material if I would give him my personal guarantee that the bill would be paid. He would not accept the company's guarantee or Milton's, it had to be mine. Stupidly I guess, I gave it. Some time later, luckily the currency for once went in the right direction, and consequently brought down the cost of one of our independently financed films, so I was able to pay off the lab's debt.

This was the first of many occasions when Subotsky and I crossed swords. He said it was immoral, but I said, if the currency had gone the other way we would have had to pay the money, so there was nothing immoral at all. When I asked him how he would have paid it, all he did was to bluster. Of course, he wrote several letters to Max about it, but Max was only too delighted to have access to the company's films again.

If I sneezed, he would write to Max that I was spreading germs! He would stop at nothing to either discredit or abuse me. Also he was a liar, which is the hardest thing to cope with. There are so many occasions when it is one's own word against someone else's. However, in my case, I think the reaction of Technicolor to Subotsky and myself sums up the general opinion of the industry.

Being associated with Subotsky was a nightmare. I thought back to all the wonderful people I had worked with in the past, the great relationships I had with the major American companies, from their Presidents down, I realised how far I had sunk. I tried to be pleasant to him, but to no avail, he was unapproachable. To this day, I consider he was the only person in the whole of my career in the film business that I actively disliked, even hated. I did not like Sellers, or the way he behaved, but he was talented. I guess if it had not been for Max, I would have quit, but as he backed me on everything I decided that I would not let this creature beat me.

Three films were on the books at the time, all horror subjects.

One was a film called "Madhouse" starring the delightful Vincent Price and Peter Cushing and was to be directed by Jim Clark, one of Britain's leading editors.

The next was "The Beast Must Die" to be directed by Paul Annett with Calvin Lockhart, Peter Cushing, and Charles Grey.

The third was "The Tales from Beyond the Grave" to be directed by Kevin Connor starring once again Peter Cushing, Donald Pleasence, David Warner and Diana Dors.

Jim Clark's film was already set up and crewed, but I was able to arrange an American-style house near where I lived for one of the main locations. We used my house as the production centre, and Daniel was the runner, cycling messages on his racing-bike between our house and the location. Subotsky, of course, could not bear the fact that I lived in such an area, but as he never visited the location I was saved the embarrassment (his not mine) of inviting him home. The only good thing about him was that I rarely saw him, his office was at Twickenham and, of course, I was at Shepperton. Our differences were mainly conducted on the telephone, and on his side by letter.

It was a delight to work with Vincent Price and Peter Cushing, both of whom had exquisite manners and were the opposite of Subotsky. Jim Clark was such a nice man, though he never managed to make it into being a leading director and he went back to being a top editor. I visited most days, saw the rushes, checked the costs, visited the set and left. As to the film itself, I can't remember seeing it and I have been unable to find it in my reference books.

Back at Shepperton, I was meeting with Paul Annett who had an excellent reputation in television, and through that brought together an excellent cast of Calvin Lockhart, Charles Gray, Michael Gambon and Peter Cushing. I signed up Jack Hyldyard as director of photography and John Stoll as designer, both Oscar winners. Great cast, great crew, poor script, and a director who was not happy in the film genre, and worse of all he would not listen to the good advice being given to him. Here again Subotsky wrote a letter criticising the photography and the sets. It was a pity that he did not wait a little, at least until the letter arrived from the main distributor in the States thanking me for the wonderful production values, and adding that he had no idea how we could get such quality on such a low budget.

Then we had "Tales From Beyond the Grave" to be directed by Kevin Connor. He had been Richard Attenborough's editor for years, so came to us with a welter of feature experience. My first meeting with him was a complete disaster as he resented my position and my power. To this day, I don't know whether Subotsky got to him, but the meeting ended with him throwing a ruler at me. I think that was the only row we had over all the years we worked together. He was a lovely man, who brought great happiness to my life.

We also shared the saddest of times when his little five-year-old boy slowly died of leukaemia. It was inevitable, unlike today when the recovery rate is so high. My heart bled for him when the little white coffin was carried into the church.

During the shooting of Kevin's directorial debut, Max sent me a script written by that well know sci-fi writer, Michael Moorcock. He and James Cawthorne had scripted an Edgar Rice (Tarzan) Burroughs' book, "The Land That Time Forgot".

Now this was really something, a well-written script based on a great piece of Burroughs's hokum, far removed from the usual Amicus nickel-and-dime horrors. It was a difficult film, full of special effects, and calling for pre-historic monsters. It was a challenge, but it would take Amicus out of the dead 'B'-movie market.

It was becoming increasingly difficult for Milton and me to work together, and his relationship with Max was also deteriorating. After much discussion, Max and I agreed that I would produce "Land ..." and he and Milton would act as executive producers. Max was keen for me to use Paul Annett as director but, though I thought he was a man of talent, he was not, to my mind, sufficiently experienced to take on a special effects' film with a budget that in no way reflected the complications of the script.

So we plumped for Kevin Connor.

Max had made a deal with American International (my old friend Sam Arkoff's company) for what is known as "domestic", that is America. And with Rank for the UK and Commonwealth territories. As it was Rank it meant moving to Pinewood. This was no hardship as I loved Pinewood, had a lot of old friends there, and all of my enemies had left. It also had an outside tank which was very useful for the exterior submarine scenes.

Whilst all this was happening, we were enjoying our life in St. George's Hill where we had many old friends, like Dick Emery who after our movie had gone on to bigger and better things and was by this time a leading television star. The place was full of people from the entertainment world, amongst others, Cliff Richard. We met Sarah Miles, as her son, Tom, went to the same school as Susie and, as she lived nearby, she and Ineke would share the turgid school run.

At the time Sarah was married to Robert Bolt, the amazing playwright and script writer, who wrote some of Britain's greatest films, including "A Man for all Seasons" (both play and film), "Lawrence of Arabia", "Dr Zhivago" and "Ryan's Daughter". A double Oscar winner. They lived in a Manor House, complete with a Mill House, where Robert had his study. There was a river running through the grounds and Ineke and I and the two kids spent many a happy weekend day there, punting up and down and even swimming in the not too clean water.

Robert was the least pompous academic you ever met. There was no bullshit, no conceit, no pretence. Lunch there was NAAFI type sandwiches and rough white wine. It was so relaxed, no airs and graces, just a bunch of friends enjoying this magic spot and one another's company. We became very friendly with the two of them and also with Robert's three children by his previous marriage.

Sarah Bolt, or Miles, was one of the sexiest women I have ever met. She wasn't the greatest looking, but by God she oozed sex. I think she radiated such sex because she was so horny herself. I remember once when she was staying with us, all the males in the house were going mad. Sarah personified the power of sexy women.

I remember having lunch one day with Mia Farrow, who at the time was married to André Previn. We were sitting at a round table in the Pinewood restaurant when I said something which made her turn and look at me. It was like two searchlights sweeping across the table and resting on my eyes. At that moment if she had said "Let's go", I would have stood up and followed her to ... wherever! They're scary.

About this time, not long after "Ryan's Daughter", Sarah went off with Robert Mitchum, leaving a very upset Robert. For, though he did his very best to conceal it, he was hurt. During his other disastrous marriage, and his many affairs, we used to say to him, "You are still in love with Sarah", which he always vehemently denied. It was a happy day when they got together again, and lived happily until Robert's sad death.

Whilst living near us, he became interested in the politics of the technicians' Union (the ACTT) where for years the Trotskyites had been gaining influence. In fact, most of the various committees were dominated by the far left. What made me sick was the fact that the last thing they thought or cared about was the interest of the members. One glaring example was the lack of a pension scheme, and I personally know great technicians who ended their days with just the state pension, and perhaps a little hand-out now and then from the Film Benevolent Fund.

The contrast with the American Unions which have had wonderful pension schemes for years is immense. The Directors' Guild of America not only looks after directors but also assistant directors and production managers, and not only in retirement, but also in cases of illness too. Again, there is just no comparison between Equity and the Screen Actors' Guild in the States. Why? Because the Union leaders in England were, and I am sure still are, in it to feather their own political nests.

Robert decided to stand as President, and I and a number of my colleagues used to turn up at the various meetings to support him, and at the same time fight all the various left-wing groups. Most of these meetings were deadly dull, but then this was one of their ploys to get you to leave. So, we used to hang on until the bitter end, just in case they tried to pull a fast one.

Mind you, they did get more exciting when the Trots realised they were starting to lose the arguments. They used to snaffle the microphone and refuse to give it up, so fights would start and there was uproar.

One day one of our group got up to speak and we all groaned, for although he was a sweet chap, he was such a bad speaker that he usually managed to give the other side the benefit of the argument! He started to speak, "All this reminds me of the migration of the birds ..." A look passed between us. "... It was winter, and they all started to fly off to warmer climes. Except for one little bird which thought to itself, 'God, I just can't face up to that journey.'..." We were bewildered, but he certainly had got the attention of the hall. He continued, "... He said farewell to all his family and friends, waved them good-bye, and settled down in his nest. Then the winter came, and, though he settled further and further down in his feathers, he was frozen. He thought, 'I have to go, I can't stand any more of this,' so he took off to fly South. But when he was up in the air his wings started to freeze, which caused him to crash land into a field, into a cow pat! 'Oh, how disgusting,' the little bird thought, but after a while he started to get warm, and being warm again made him happy, so happy that he started to sing. Which attracted the farm cat who came over and gobbled him up. ... Now, what can we learn from this story? One, those who drop you in the shit aren't necessarily your enemies. Two, those that pull you out of the shit aren't necessarily your friends. And three, if you *are* in the shit, don't sing!" The meeting collapsed.

Robert became President, and there was a brief period of sanity. At the Annual General Meeting where he was elected I was a delegate, and as I entered the main door of the TUC headquarters I was greeted by my old friend, Charlie Wheeler. "P'uck me," he said, "Johnny p'ucking Dark. I never fought I would live to see the day 'e entered the 'eadquarters of the TU p'ucking C." Some things never change.

Meanwhile we were busy getting into pre-production on "Land ...".

I was lucky to sign Maurice Carter, probably the most experienced designer on special effects' films in the country, and through him I met Derek Meddings, who became head of our special effects' department.

Derek had just come off Gerry Anderson's "Thunderbirds". He went on to lend his great talents to the "Bond" films and others like "Superman". He was the leader in his particular field, a lovely man, a dear friend who sadly died at much too young an age.

One of our biggest problems was how were we going to make and shoot the various pre-historic animals that the script called for, and in the confines of our budget. This was before the days of computers, and we were forced to go with very sophisticated puppets which were made brilliantly by Roger Dicken, a young, eccentric puppet-maker. Together with a combination of back- and front-projection, we had just enough confidence to think that it would work. We were really reaching into the unknown, and just crossed our fingers that it would all be right on the night.

As the film was to be financed between American International and Rank, everything was planned for Pinewood, but I was unable to get a definite answer from their head of distribution, and he kept delaying the signing of the deal. So, when British Lion approached me with a much better offer, I did not hesitate to accept. Shepperton Studios and its parent company, British Lion, had been sold to new owners, and they were desperate to get a picture into the studio, even at a give-away price. This was going to be of great help to our budget.

I told Max, who was delighted, even though Rank's were bleating. They were so used to treating independent producers badly, making them wait for an answer, and changing parts of the contract at the last moment, that it came as quite a shock to have the tables turned on them for once.

I could only see one problem and that was that Shepperton did not have an outside tank. Maurice Carter suggested we flood the silent stage. This in actual fact would be better than the Pinewood outside tank, more under control and not dependent on the fickle British weather.

I signed the deal with Lion International (British Lion's new name) and also with Shepperton Studios.

With this under our belt, we were able to complete the budget for submission to Film Finances, the Bond of Completion company. Now, I knew this was going to be a bumpy ride, because the budget was much too low for such a picture, we were also entering unknown territory. It would not take long, I knew, for their senior production executive, John Croydon, to fathom that one out. He was a wily old bird, and after a lifetime of working in production on feature films, spent his time studying the viability of budgets to their scripts. Like that of most independent companies, our problem was that it was all the money we had, and there was no going back and asking for more. We had to have a bond of completion, for that was written into both the American and British distribution agreements. So we had to get the bond come hell or high water, even if it meant cutting the script, something I was loathe to do.

The meeting with them did not start of too well, as John Croydon opened it up by holding the script in one hand and the budget in the other, saying, "This is impossible."

It took us many long hours proving that we could do it, as every special effects' shot was explained, and each day's schedule analysed. Eventually, John and his colleagues said they would give us a bond only because of the people involved: Maurice Carter, Derek Meddings, the stalwart cameraman, Alan Hume, and John Peverall, our production manager.

John had been the assistant director on Kevin Connor's first picture, but was a very experienced PM as well. They also said they had taken into account Kevin's handling of his first picture. Finally they said that they had been swayed by my own reputation, but added they still thought it was impossible.

And a few days later I nearly agreed with them!

I got a call from the studio manager Andy Worker asking me to meet him for a drink. I was up to my eyes at that time, and asked if I could have a rain-check, but he insisted. So, sensing something was afoot, I went round to his office.

"What's up?" I asked nervously.

"Have a drink first, you might need it," he said ominously. He then said, "We are going four-wall."

My heart sank. "When?"

"We are putting the men under notice this week."

My heart sank further. As I explained earlier, up till then all the major studios carried their own labour force, including all set construction staff and electricians. Going "four-wall" meant that the studio would hold no labour and we would have to engage our own construction crew, props and floor electricians, which in turn would mean us having to completely reassess our budget. Also I did not know how the brothers would react: Would they picket the studio? Call a strike? What?

I met quickly with the Unions and I gave them an undertaking that we would immediately engage any of the redundant workers that wished to join us. This meant that the workers would get their redundancy payment on the Friday, and would immediately be re-employed by Amicus on the following Monday for the run of the picture. After that, they would join the pool of freelance workers. This system was becoming more and more popular, and now there is no studio left in the country that does not operate the four-wall system.

From being what I thought was going to be a disaster, it turned out to be a great benefit. The boys and girls in the studio were happy and I suddenly became the flavour of the month, especially when I said that no one would have to clock-in or -out. I always thought it was completely unfair that the craft grades, who had been through a lengthy apprenticeship, should have the indignity of clocking-in, when a fresh faced kid working as a runner with no training whatsoever, did not. It was discriminatory and divisive, so I stopped it. George Robinson, the Chief Electrician, was soon in my office.

"I hear you stopped them clocking-in."

"That's right."

"But what if they are late? What do we do?"

"It's very simple, George, we sack you!"

I had often watched the American television series "The Virginian" and been impressed by a young actor who played "Trampas", Doug McClure. We needed an American lead, so I suggested him to Max. A few days later he said Doug had turned the part down, and so he had signed Stuart Whitman. Now, I don't want to be cruel to the poor chap, but firstly he was too old; secondly, he seemed to be in every 'B'-movie ever made; and thirdly, I was trying to move Amicus away from this type of thinking. I voiced my objections in no uncertain terms.

"But I've signed him," bleated Max.

"Well, you'll have to unsign him."

"We'll have to pay him."

"So we have to pay him. Listen, Max, this film could change the whole of Amicus's reputation. The market for low-priced horror films has collapsed. Hammer has closed down and if you want this company to have any future then we have to get away from the Whitman way of thinking."

"Well, who should I get?"

"Get Doug," I replied.

"But he's turned it down."

Employing a lesson that Charlie Feldman had taught me, I said, "Go back, Max. You never know, his tax demand might have just come in."

A few days passed and Max rang, "I've signed him."

Guess dear old Doug must have just heard from the Internal Revenue Service!

Now I was able to get on with the rest of the casting. There was no money for names, just good actors. We signed the girl from the British Lion short, Susan Penhaligon, and John McEnery to play the U-Boat Captain.

I suppose looking back, this last one was a mistake. I was so keen to get away from the obvious that I don't know whether I was right about him. He was mainly a Shakespearean actor, and I thought he gave a very interesting portrayal of a German submarine commander. It was different from the usual movie character German who was usually portrayed either as a sadist or a comic buffoon. In the end, Sam

Arkoff (who as we know was not endowed with too much taste) made me re-voice him, and I got my old friend Anton Diffring to perform the job.

Anton was a sweet man, and always played the German Gestapo agent or the SS Officer. The interesting thing is that he was a Jew. I think I should have played him in the part.

Then we contracted Keith Baron who starred in many television shows and incidentally was the guy that bought my house in Molesey. Luckily, as long as you don't need "names", England is full of great character actors who are prepared to work for almost the basic Equity rates. So we were able to fill the other roles with good solid character artists.

John Stoll once said that you had to be strong enough to take one major disaster every day. The silent stage was flooded, the submarine exterior built, and we were almost ready to roll, when the next blow fell. This was mine, and a big one.

British Lion management had been changed again. Barry Spikings and Michael Deeley, with the backing of EMI, the musical and electrical company, were to take over. I was assured they would honour all existing contracts. However, when I got a call from Michael Deeley I was apprehensive. After the usual pleasantries Michael said, "John, we would like you to move your film to Pinewood."

I paused, "And how would you like me to move the water from the silent stage? In plastic bags?"

Of course he had no idea what was involved and how close we were to shooting. It was obvious to me that he wanted us out of the way so that they could close the studio down and go to the planning authorities to get permission to build houses on the site. What other explanation could there be? I told Michael in no uncertain terms that we had a contract with the studio and I expected them to live up to their announcement that they would honour all existing contracts. He said he would get back to me.

Sometimes you have to sup with the devil, and so I rang the two Unions involved. They were horrified at the prospect of Shepperton being left empty, and the possible consequences. They said they would give me their full backing. I knew this could be a costly battle, and I wanted to move fast and have all my troops lined up. I alerted our lawyers and also Film Finances, and spoke to the local shop stewards to get them to keep the pressure on their head offices.

I also spoke to Andy Worker, who was in a difficult position being an employee of the new British Lion. He took a tough line, though, and told me that he was pointing out to the new management the consequences of their actions. When it came out that they wanted to move this film out of the studio into another studio everybody would ask why. As I said, you didn't have to be Einstein to work that one out. Andy warned it could mean a national strike affecting all the studios. After a few days, they capitulated, and we had the green light to go ahead.

We started shooting the dinosaur material, which would be used later by various different types of process shots. Roger Dicken had excelled himself in the manufacture of the hand puppets, and we were about to see how he would control them, and how they would look when blown up on a large cinema screen. The ultimate test would be not only the combination of two pieces of film, but also the combination of the talents of the puppeteer, the designer, and the special effects' department which had to match and build the model set so it would cut in with the full scale set or location. Important too was the talent of the lighting cameraman, who had to light the two separate shots so, once again, the two pieces of film were identical in their lighting mode.

With the main shooting date fast approaching, plans were made to bring Doug McClure over from LA There were discussions with his agent as to where he would like to live and any special air-line he wanted to travel on. For, though on our budget we could not afford all the crap that surrounds major artists, we did want him to be as comfortable as possible. After all it was his first trip to England. Though we found out later that his mother had been born in Canterbury – a fact that none of us is ever likely to forget, as he reminded us at every opportunity!

When he arrived, we sent an Assistant director, the driver and the American car we had hired for the duration of his stay to meet him.

When he arrived in my office I jumped up and greeted him, "Welcome to Shepperton. I am John Dark and I want you to know what a thrill it is to have you join us." Nothing. The man never said a word. So I continued to blabber away. Nothing, no response. "Can I get you anything?" Silence "Please sit down." And he did, so I thought at least he could hear even if he couldn't talk. "How was the flight?" No reply. "Guess you're tired, would you like to go straight to the hotel?" He stood up and opened his briefcase. We're getting some response, I thought, perhaps I should just keep quiet. He burrowed in his case and looked up at me and said, "Where am I?"

This is the actor I had fought for, had threatened to give up my job for, that we'd had to pay Stuart Whitman off for. This was the man that was due to star in our picture starting in two days' time. This was the actor written in to our distribution contracts. "Where am I?" Well, if he didn't know where he was, I knew where I was: In the shit.

I didn't tell anyone, swore my darling new secretary to secrecy, and prayed. Two days later we started shooting. Doug arrived punctually, and I walked with him down on to the set where I introduced him to the crew and his fellow actors. The lights were burning, and Kevin started to get his first line-up on the conning tower of the submarine. It was a tight squeeze there, so I left and walked back to the office.

I hadn't been there long when I got an urgent call to come up to the set. Trouble. When I got there Kevin pulled me aside, "He's not talking."

"What you mean, he's not talking?"

"Well I called for a rehearsal and he just mumbled. What do I do?"

I thought for a minute, and then, "There's only one thing you can do. Shoot, go for a take."

So red light ... turn over ... running ..."Slate 35, Take one." ... "Action." At the end, "Cut and print."

The crew all applauded, for they knew full well what was going on. Kevin looked at me, shrugged his shoulders, then smiled as Doug, word perfect, gave a professional performance.

When we got to know each other better, he explained it to me. He said that being on a long-running television show like "The Virginian", and shooting at the speed demanded by the network schedules, you have to pace yourself, and you don't begin to perform and give it your all until the camera turns.

"Well, Doug," I said, "that explains that, but what about the 'Where am I?'"

"Jesus, I guess I must have been in some other world!"

I think that was true because in those days he was a pretty heavy drinker, and not averse to pushing some powder up his nose, or smoking some wacky backy. This, plus jet lag, probably did push him into outer space. However, we were to became good friends and he fitted into our movie family well.

By this time we had become a tightly-knit group, including several people from Kevin's first film, especially the camera crew headed by Alan Hume, who was to light every film I produced from then on.

But Doug could be an awkward child. He would be as good as gold, then "wham". He was very professional, always on time, and always word perfect. Having been in a long-running television show, he found the slower pace of a feature almost relaxing, especially on a special effects' movie where there were always long hold-ups whilst the technicians coped with their complex problems. So, we would chug along happily and then suddenly he would erupt.

One day he burst into a production meeting and shouted at us, "If you guys think that I am going to fuck Susan Penhaligon, then you better think again." And rushed out, slamming the door behind him. What was that all about?

We never heard another word on the subject, and he and Sue got on well, although there was never anything between them. As I was to tell one of my colleagues, "Woman have one period every month. Doug has two!"

Another time he was in one of his orbital modes, shouting at me in the office, and he threw a punch. Now, I am sure he did not mean to aim for me, but I didn't hang about to find out. All I remember is seeing this great cowboy fist heading my way, so I threw myself down on the floor. I felt it go past me and land with a crash on the office wall. Silence. "Where are you, John?"

"I'm on the floor, Doug."

I cut out the part of the wall with the hole in it ,which Doug signed, and I had it framed.

From then on if I had any trouble with him, I would just point at the framed hole, and he would slink away. Despite all his ups and downs, we became friends, for in his more sane moments he was the most likeable of people. He never stopped telling us how much he enjoyed working in England, and in particular working with us. He made no demands and was a great favourite with the crew. What sort of actor was he, though? Well, he was Doug. He was like an old-fashioned movie star, you gets what you pay for, that was Doug McClure. If you wanted an actor then you hired John Gielgud.

Shooting progressed smoothly, keeping to schedule and on budget, much to the relief of the Completion Guarantor. We practically never saw Milton, but we did have a visit from the lawyer for the Edgar Rice Burroughs's estate. The estate was protected by very tough lawyers, mainly I think to protect the Tarzan name. We showed this guy some footage, and he seemed delighted with what he saw. He said in front of the crew that he had to have a credit or his mother would never forgive him, and then took off in his helicopter with his girlfriend to enjoy some days (and nights) at the Savoy hotel, and we did not see him again.

I hardly ever heard from British Lion or EMI. Someone used to counter-sign the cheques and that was that. I did not know Barry Spikings at all, but had a brief knowledge of Michael Deeley. Later Michael asked me why I told everyone that he used to sell spacing (unused film used in the cutting-rooms for fillers) in the corridors of Pinewood.

"Well, Michael, I tell them because I am so proud you have come so far!"

"And you tell them I'm known as 'Devious Deeley'."

"All I can say to that is, you are!"

Both of the boys came to the studio to see a rough cut. They were very polite but did not say much but the driver reported back the next day that they thought it was a pile of shit!

So, it was with some trepidation that I took the finished film to EMI and ran it for the distribution team. At the end, the lights went up and the head man said, "Now I can do something with that."

It went down a blast, and was to take far more money than any of the other EMI films. Max was delighted. But – of course – there had to be a letter from Milton listing all the things I had done wrong. It didn't worry me any more.

On the whole, it got pretty good reviews. One critic criticised "the wholesale slaughter of pre-historic animals", which at the time I thought rather strange but, on reflection after many years, I now take as a compliment.

There was something of a soul in the hand-operated puppets. Roger Dicken's face when he was operating one showed the intensity that he put into his work, and consequently into his hands. In a way his feelings were transmitted into the "animal". Many people have commented that, though the computer-generated creatures in films like "Jurassic Park" are mind-blowing, they do lack a certain living presence. One enraptured critic wrote about "Land ...", "Even the dinosaurs are lovely."

Another critic wrote, "One of the best special effects' pictures to have come out of America in years."

This brought a storm of protest from the crew, but I told them, "That's great, let them think that. We are holding our own against the best."

I got a pleasant call from Sam Arkoff saying how pleased he was. Michael Deeley said there was no justice in the world, as the film he produced for EMI had bombed.

On top of this, the Burroughs's estate was happy. They had always hated the way Hollywood had portrayed Tarzan, so we had all been nervous of their reaction.

It was good news when they gave their okay to proceed with other Burroughs' books.

I wanted to make "People That Time Forgot" (the sequel to "Land…"). But Max, for some reason, was more anxious to make "At The Earth's Core", so we went ahead with planning this.

Arkoff and EMI were anxious to star Doug in it, to which neither Kevin nor I had any objection, indeed we had got used to him, and what is more important he had got used to us. My objections lay closer to home. Max, Milton and I had a meeting with the lawyers where it was agreed that this would be the last film that Milton would participate in. He would get a Presenter's credit, shared with Max and Sam Arkoff, and he would also get the normal Screenwriter's credit, but no other. He would have no control, and not be allowed to interfere. Out of courtesy he would be allowed to see the final film at the end and make any comments. He still made trouble, but more about that later.

With "At the Earth's Core" I was worried about our "monsters". The trouble was that by enlarging these miniature creatures and projecting them onto an enormous screen, we got increasing grain problems, which increased when you came to re-photograph it with the main action. In other words the main shoot was first generation but the special effects were second generation.

For some reason, I remembered working as a journalist on "The Recorder", and covering a demonstration of Paramount's new wide screen process, VistaVision. The whole basis of this system was that the film went through the camera vertically instead of horizontally, thus allowing an increase in the negative area exposed. So when you projected the positive of the film onto a large screen the grain problem was drastically reduced. I knew that Rank's had gone into this system, so I rang up Charlie Staffell at Pinewood and asked him if the VistaVision cameras were still around.

A few days later, he rang back and said he had dug one out, covered in dust and cobwebs, which he was testing. We used this camera from then on for all our process work, and now most companies do the same.

Several things combined to make me realise that we should use Pinewood for the next film. However, I did not want to jeopardise our EMI investment. So I had a meeting with Barry Spikings, whom I had got to know over the past few months and whom I had found to be always charming and polite, in complete contrast to our other investor, Sam Arkoff of AIP. I explained to Barry that not only had Pinewood the right cameras, but also the equipment necessary for our special effects' needs. Also they were going through a bad patch, and as they still retained their own labour, had offered me a deal that would be impossible for Shepperton to match.

Barry at once understood the problem and, though he found it almost comical that now I should be insisting on going to Rank's studio when on the last film I had insisted on staying at Shepperton, he agreed that we should sign with the opposition.

So we moved to Iver, and, though I was sorry to leave my office at Shepperton, I was looking forward to being in England's most pleasant studio.

The Studios were based around an old Manor House, Heatherden Hall, which stood in attractive gardens in an estate of 156 acres. The manor house was used as offices, and housed a magnificent, wood-panelled restaurant, the panelling having come from the old passenger ship the "Mauritania". I soon had my own table and lunched happily there for several years to come. Off from the restaurant was the busy bar, whose French windows led out onto a terrace overlooking the formal gardens. Ah, the number of evenings I spent hanging over that bar, gossiping with friends, discussing with colleagues, and entertaining guests.

This bar horrified visiting American producers, as all American studios, like their ships, are dry. Mind you, most executives there keep a bottle behind a locked door. Once they get to know you, they bring it out surreptitiously and, like a naughty schoolboy, pour a shot into a paper cup, and hand it to you with a nervous glance at the door.

The Pinewood bar was a civilised place, all wood, chandeliers and precious rugs. British drinking was done openly, though at times abused. Many a career has ended there, and woe betide an actor who took one too many before returning to work on the set.

But it was the stories, the characters that one met. For instance André de Toth, the Hungarian director, most famously known for being the one-eyed director of the most well known 3-D film, "The House of Wax". I am sure he would not have been so well known if it had not been for the fact that he had only one eye, and therefore was incapable of seeing the 3-D effect himself!

He was a charming man, and I used to bump into him at various parties and the houses of film people. He was a Hungarian by birth and had led an exciting life: part-time cowboy, pilot, racing driver. He was kidnapped in Egypt when the terrorists mistook him for the Israeli, Moshe Dayan. After pistol-whipping him, they stripped him, only to find out that he wasn't even Jewish!

I did not really get to know him until I moved to Pinewood, and we spent many happy hours in each other's company. At the time, André was trying to set up his own movie based on a story about the British Navy nuclear submarines, one of which he had sailed on.

One day he introduced me to the Flotilla Commander who told me a delightful story. He said in the 80s he and his fellow officers were discussing mess nights, and the fact that women, wives and girlfriends were never invited as it was strictly stag. One day they decided to break with tradition and invite the ladies to the next wardroom dinner. As Flotilla Commander he had to select a wife to reply to the toast, and he chose a young wife who had been on the stage and who, seemingly, could stand up and say a few words of thanks.

The night was a great success, and after thanking her hosts she went on, "This makes such a change, normally one bathes the kids early, and puts them into their night-clothes. You then go into the bedroom and help your husband finish dressing by tying his bow tie, putting in the cuff-links, then holding up the blue jacket with the golden emblems, a final brush- down, then a check in the mirror to see if it is all immaculate. You then slap on some lipstick, grab the kids and stick them in the back of the battered old Morris Oxford. You then drive your man to the docks, praying that no one sees you. When you arrive and he gets out and walks down the dockside, you watch this handsome god-like creature with a sigh, with a note of pride. Then one of the kids pipes up, 'Mummy, why is Daddy so rich and we're so poor?'"

André was never able to get a deal on his submarine film. In fact he had a pretty rough ride after 1968. Before then he had been busy making numerous Westerns, and also tight little dramas like "Monkey on My Back". After that he kept busy as a Second Unit, or Action, director, and contributed to films such as "Lawrence of Arabia" and "Superman". He died in 2002, after having been married seven times and fathered 19 children. It is sad to think that, after a lifetime in films, he is best remembered for the fact that he had only one eye.

Gossip and stories about movies abounded in the bar, for if there is something film people like more than making movies, it is talking about them.

I loved the story that a well-known cameraman Paul Beeson told. In 1972 Alfred Hitchcock was in England shooting a movie, and was irritated by the fact that all his rushes were coming back from Technicolor with a strong magenta bias. He issued instructions that on the following Saturday morning he wanted all his rushes assembled and the top man at Technicolor in attendance. By chance, both the Managing director and his Number Two were out of the country attending urgent meetings elsewhere. The next man in line was Frank Bush, a delightful man, who although middle-aged, dressed and spoke more like a junior army officer in the Pay Corps. So, on the Saturday morning Frank duly turned up and all the terrible colour rushes were run. At the end not a word was spoken until, after an embarrassing silence, Hitch said, "Well Mr Technicolor, what have you to say about that?"

Frank stood up and addressed the great man, "Well Mr Hitchcock, I am so pleased that you asked me that, because I did think that Miss Whitelaw was a bit over the top in that last scene!"

Whilst at Pinewood there always seemed to be a "Bond" about. The producer, Cubby Broccoli, was a charming man, in complete contrast to his partner, Harry Saltzman. Probably the best thing that happened was when they split up. Though I had little to do with Cubby, he was always helpful, and his crew would always help out if we were in trouble. They had all the money and therefore the clout, but they never abused that position, and there was never any conflict sharing the same studio. His daughter, Barbara, continues with this pleasant way of working.

At this time Roger Moore was starring in the film, and I hate to say it but he was another very nice man, always polite and always fun. I know the crews adored him.

The new 007 stage was built, and Ineke and I were invited to the opening ceremony. It was a great movie party, especially for us because we spent the afternoon with Kingsley Amis, whom I knew from my Paramount days, and dear Kenneth Moore. What a couple of fun guys. Ineke, who was rarely impressed by "stars", had one of the nicest days of her life.

At the same time, we were busy getting the next Edgar Rice Burroughs' subject ready. Sadly, it was not scripted by Michael Morocco, but basically it was the same crew with the exception of the production manager. The budget was even tighter than for "Land …", and despite its success I was unable to screw more money out of Lion, and Max had the same trouble with AIP. The profits were good, but they were not sure whether spending more money would necessarily mean that they would gross more. I think they were wrong, proved by the later success of the many pre-historic movies made.

My choice of PM was going to be vital. I was wary of getting an old- timer who was set in his ways, which I often found unacceptable. I then thought of the second assistant that we had on both "The Beast Must Die" and "Land …"

One incident which stuck in my mind was when we were shooting "Beast". I found out that both dear old Charles Gray and Calvin Lockhart were bringing alcohol on to the set, and sitting there drinking it. I told this Second to go and stop it.

Next day I noticed that neither of them were drinking any more, and asked him how he achieved it. "Oh, I told Charles that we had no objection to him drinking on the set, but that Calvin had a drink problem. 'Say no more, dear boy,' replied Charles."

"But what about Calvin?" I wanted to know, who wasn't so easy.

"Oh, I told him Charles had a drink problem," he replied.

I thought then this boy was going places. Graham Easton joined me as production manager, and spoiled me for all time as he took over all the production problems on a day-to-day basis. It was a tough film for one's debut, as the script called for so much and the budget placed such tight restrictions on how it could be achieved.

This led John Croydon of Film Finances to say, "This is impossible."

"But you said that last time, John," we all chorused.

"Yes, I know I did, but this time it really is."

As I said earlier, he was a wily old bird. Now Graham is the Managing director of Film Finances throughout the world outside of North and South America.

Doug arrived this time with wife in tow. We did not see much of her, and she seemed to live a fairly independent life. She was an amazing looking woman, part Indian, a real beauty, but she was a very cold person and reminded me of the wooden Indians they used to have standing outside tobacconists.

Doug himself was a different person from the one who had arrived on "Land…" Even though we had changed studios, he knew where he was, and one look at the studio bar made him feel very comfortable indeed.

Poor Graham's first crisis was when Doug asked him for a bar in his dressing-room. Knowing his liking for the bottle, Graham asked me what to do. I told him to say that no way was he going to set up his own bar in his dressing-room, as it's against studio regulations. A little later Graham came back rather shamefaced, "He wants an *exercise* bar."

Of course, Doug thought it was the funniest thing ever. "I wouldn't want a bar in my room. What do you take me for? Some kind of lush?"

As always, casting was a difficult task, but one role was easy, that of the professor, and once again I had the delight of working with that gentleman of the horror world, Peter Cushing. Why was it that screen horror stars were always such nice men, from Boris Karloff to Vincent Price? As a change, this time he was playing a potty professor, supporting Doug's macho man. The only worry I had was how they would get on with each other. Peter was very religious, reserved, punctiliously polite, and hated anyone swearing on the set. In the end they got on just fine, and Doug was obviously upset when Peter's part was completed and they said good-bye.

We had a tough shoot, there was so much fire, so much action and so much process work. We regularly set off the studio watering system, and also worried both the studio management and the insurers. The only accident we had, though slight, was very sad.

In "Land ..." we had a little chap, Bobby Parr, playing a Neanderthal man, which he did very well, and endeared himself to all. He was just a sweet, simple guy who I came across one day sharing a tin of stewed steak with his dog, with the same spoon! In a fight scene, Doug accidentally cut off two of his fingers. We always had a nurse standing by on the set and she took care of him straight away and rushed him to the nearest hospital, together with the missing digits, but all to no avail. They were unable to sew them back on.

Of course I was desperately worried, and rang our insurers to see what they could do. They told me that he would have to sue us for the damage and then they would pay the awarded amount. Dear Bobby hadn't got a nickel, so I rang Equity on his behalf and explained the situation and ended by saying, "In other words you have got to help Bobby sue us, then he will get his compensation and you will get your costs back, for there can be no argument that he was injured in the course of his work." Equity never did take up his case, and Bobby never did get any compensation.

I think that is a pretty awful indictment against this so-called caring Union and is another reason why I hate the way British Unions are run. The really sad part of this story is that in the summer time Bobby used to work as a Punch and Judy man, but with two fingers missing he was no longer able to perform. No great credit to Equity.

One day I opened the trade magazine "Screen International" to read a letter from Milton saying something like "... just to inform the people at Pinewood Studios that John Dark is actually not the producer of the film 'At The Earth's Core'. ..."

Everyone at the studio was outraged, and I pondered my reply. In the end, on the advice of friends, I ignored it. The next week someone unknown to me in person, Brian Clemens, the writer and the man who thought up "The Avengers", replied saying that as far as he could see J.D. was *certainly* the producer and was every day at Pinewood. He said J.D. seemed to be doing a producer's job, and that no one else had appeared on the scene, certainly not Mr Subotsky.

I then had a series of visits from organisers of the technicians' Union (the ACTT), representing their member, Milton Subotsky. His complaint was that I had in some way denied him his right to work, and his rightful credit. I think they came down more in the hope of a boozy lunch than anything else because I knew all these guys well. After a couple of fruitless visits, I got really pissed off and rang Alan Sapper, the general secretary of the Union, and told him in no uncertain terms to call his dogs off me.

"I don't know how you can take up the case of this evil man," I shouted.

"You mean that, John? An evil man?"

"Too bloody right I do, and I think that you have a nerve to attack me who, I might remind you, has been a member of your Union since 1943." I never heard another word.

Also I never heard from Milton again.

We did run the finished film for him, and he did write pages of criticism to Max, but I never heard or saw him again.

The only rider to this is that I had always wondered what made him tick, why he was like he was. After all he was married to a child psychologist (rather appropriate, I thought) and had two children. I knew he was an American living in England and admirer of the British Labour party. I also knew he had some strange habits, like disappearing into the men's loo for hours with a game of ludo. But one day I was talking to Desmond Elliot and he told me that he had just got back from Puerto Rico and in a bath house frequented by people of the same persuasion as himself. "And do you know who I saw?" And he told me.

Of course, I thought, a closet queen. Maybe that explains it.

Maybe he wasn't bad, just sad.

Poor old Milton.

We had a good start to the shoot until we hit a major problem. One of the monster effects, the flying Mahers, just were not working.

We had struggled for a long time how we should create these, and had eventually come to the conclusion that "men in suits" would be the best way.

Maurice Carter designed some magnificently spooky creatures, and had them moulded in rubber so that stuntmen could work them from the inside. They were very effective, and all was well until we tried to fly them. With the best wire-men in the business, they would just drop like a stone, or hang in the air, legs down – not the best position for a stuntman after a heavy lunch. On our tight budgets, we didn't have the luxury of going another way, or taking another line of action. We only had one bite at the cherry, and even with careful planning, things did not always work out the way they had been planned on paper.

It took months for them to get Superman to fly, and on "Jaws" they had so much trouble with the prop shark that they very nearly abandoned the film. We were trying to fly heavy unbalanced weights in a *day*. Well, we took several days, without much success, and I was struggling to think what we could do.

Here I really missed the experience and talent of Derek Meddings, who was now in the big time. However, we had one great asset: an experienced editor as a director. Kevin shot whatever he could get, and also covered each shot with numerous close-ups, a wing, a claw, a head, an eye, and then in the cutting room cut the scene together so we could see if it would work.

He was helped by having a wonderful dubbing editor, Jim Atkinson, the creative man in charge of the sound effects, and certainly the best I ever worked with.

He was one of the industry's great characters. On paper he did not exist, as I don't think his mother had ever registered his birth, and he had no social security number. He had no family, and lived alone. He only worked for people he liked, but you never really knew him, other than that he was a lovable man, with amazing creative talent. Most dubbing editors are more mechanic than creator, but he was the exception. So, between him, Kevin, and the editor they turned disaster into triumph. Several critics picked out "the evil of the brooding Mahers".

Talking of Superman and the trouble they had getting him to fly, a series of special effects' men struggled for months on the problem. Poor Christopher Reeve hung in the air for hours at a time, without a moan, and behaved so well. This was only to be expected by the people who knew him and like them I found him the most courteous of men. We were all horrified by his riding accident, and so admired his constant fight to overcome his injuries. When I saw him battling to walk, struggling to breathe, tears came to my eyes. Just as he took so long to fly, we all hoped that he would eventually learn to walk again. His death affected so many people. A gentleman, a fighter, a charmer, a star.

On "Superman", I got to know the director, Richard Donner. He was a lovely man who proved you can have talent and still be a nice guy. One of my sorrows is that I never worked with him.

I love the story of when he heard that Johnny Dark had been shot in a night club in London he told his secretary to send a wreath. He then found out that this Johnny Dark was a well-known gangster. My family seems to specialise in getting flowers to our own funerals, and in my own case having a rather unpleasant namesake!

We finished on schedule, and just had to get through the post-production period. This wasn't helped by Sam Arkoff sending over one of his Executives to see whether it was suitable for the American market. I thought it a good idea, as it is hard for an Englishman to understand all the nuances of that all-important market. The trouble was that I don't think this guy was very clever, as he cut a lot Peter Cushing's humorous ad-lib lines which gave the film that "tongue in cheek" feel.

I would have liked to have had two versions; one for the States and one for the UK and the rest of the world, but we just did not have the money. British Lion wouldn't put up any more, and we could not go to Film Finances because we had already drawn back our "no claims bonus". So sadly, the American version went out across the world. However, it was greeted by good reviews on the whole, and it is funny how often the Mahers are mentioned.

Perhaps it is worth quoting from "The Daily Mirror": "Winning Monster Magic. …It is imaginative, eye-boggling science-fiction … If you want to give your kids a treat take them to…"

And from other critics: "All mayhem and monsters", "A Terror Trip, but the kids will love it" and so on. Naturally there were the knockers saying it was too frightening, too dull, scary monsters, loveable monsters. But even the bad ones were kind to us and, despite the American alterations, Peter's character got well mentioned.

The business lived up its reviews and we had another winner.

Consequently we went ahead with "People That Time Forgot", the sequel to "Land That Time Forgot".

In my opinion, Max made a big mistake here by taking on Brent- Walker, a small distributor, to release in the UK. We had good deals with Lion, and built up a good relationship, but Brent-Walker was an unknown factor. In America, we were still with AIP, and so our funding was complete.

At this time I never saw Max. I liked him and kept on telling him that he should come to London, but for some reason he was loathe to come, so all our business was carried out over the phone or by letter. There are times when these methods of communication are not sufficient. One of the things I wanted to discuss with him was my share of the profits. I knew the money that had been made but, apart from one cheque, I had seen nothing from Max. What made it worse was that I had agreed to give Kevin and Maurice Carter a share of my share. Maybe this explained Max's reluctance to come to the UK.

I sent Graham and Maurice Carter to Spain to look for possible locations, but after a week they said they had found nothing that was quite right. They wanted to go to one of the smaller Canary Islands, La Palma, which being a volcanic island, had some extraordinary sites.

They came back to London full of photographs and enthusiasm, and it was settled that we would go there. Casting was complete, budget agreed, bond in place, and shooting date established, when we found we had a real problem getting us all to the island. The airport there was only used for two engine aircraft, and, though it was technically possible for them to land a four-engine aeroplane, no one had done it before, and none of the usual charter companies was prepared to take the risk. In the end, and just before we were making plans to tranship at Linarite, an aviation company was found that would do the job.

So we took off, and eventually arrived over the island of la Palma. The plane banked over so we could all see this dot in the ocean. We got closer and the pilot made a couple of runs over the airstrip so we could see how small it actually was. We landed and the plane managed to stop a few feet from the end of the runway and the end of the island. It was the first four-engine plane to land there, and history had been made. There was a welcome burst of applause from the waiting spectators.

The island was a delight, very few tourists, and very unspoilt. The locals were friendly, so friendly in fact that they practically never left our side, especially when we let off explosives. On one occasion we caused a minor panic when we used dynamite and smoke bombs in one of the dormant volcanoes that dot the island, and some of the islanders thought it was active again.

These old volcanoes were incredible, and I found it quite spooky when you dropped a piece of paper on the ground and it immediately burst into flames. The plant life was extraordinary too, and botanists came from all over the world to study it. In fact, the local government was worried that we would damage these rare plants and we did take great care whenever we shot near them. The air was so clear that the Spanish government built a mega-telescope at the top of one of the mountains. When we were there it was only in its planning stage, and in fact we had a waiting astro-physicist working in our catering department!

Well, "catering department" is a bit too grand a title. Actually it was Jean out of the canteen at Pinewood, as we could not afford to bring location caterers with us. Normally a large mobile kitchen would either be shipped over, in this case from Spain, or be brought from the UK. The Spanish caterers were very experienced in supplying food to both nationalities, Spanish and English. I remember on "Lawrence of Arabia" in the desert, the caterer was serving salads from his refrigerated truck, which caused trouble with the "brothers" who wanted steak-and-kidney pie!

Not for us such riches, we just had Jean. She would organise food from the nearest restaurant or café near to where we were shooting, and if that was too far she would make a barbecue and cook it on the spot. We never had any complaints, but maybe that was because Jean was used to dealing with the boys, and if they made any trouble, she would tell them to "fuck off" and bash them with a ladle! Her highly educated assistant learnt another side of life.

Our team was nearly the same as on the previous two films. The cast was made up of Patrick Wayne (John Wayne's son), Sarah Douglas, a very English brittle actress, and Dana Gillespie who was mainly a blues' singer.

Dana had to play the part of a cave girl, and was she built for the part! In fact we had trouble with the American censor regarding the size of her boobs. Pretty silly, really. These films were made for a family audience and we had to be careful, but after all this was the way she was built and she was always fully covered. She was a lovely girl, and I became very fond of her, although she was something of an exhibitionist. I remember her turning up for the shoot on the first day, dressed in a cotton top and a pair of mauve Janet Reager panties. We always had an audience of locals with us which increased whenever Dana was on call.

Then there was Thorley Walters, a reliable character actor, who I had worked with before but became a real pain-in-the-arse when on location. As Shirley Maclaine said there always has to be one person on every shoot that everybody hates and Thorley was ours.

Doug played his "Land …" character, and joined us later in the shoot. He was to land at Lanzarote and change to the two engine aircraft that shuttles between the islands. There is La Palma and La<u>s</u> Palma<u>s</u>, and I told Diane he would never get on the right plane. Not many foreigners want to go to the former, and when you go to take that flight the staff query, "You sure you don't mean Las Palmas?" So I thought it better if I sent Diane over to meet him and get him to us safely. This I think was the start of the love affair.

I had been anxious to find Spanish-speaking Assistant directors – not easy. And then, with a certain amount of reluctance, I took Gregory as the Second.

The shoot went very smoothly. There were the usual cock-ups caused mostly by the language. On the first day, the prop truck driven by a Spanish driver, was late turning up and that evening a humiliated Property Master (the lovely, efficient, conscientious Bertie Hearn) arrived at our nightly production meeting full of apologies. We calmed him down and sent him on his way, but, as he got to the door he turned and said, in his version of Spanish, "What really upsets me, though, is that I told the driver specifically, not once but twice: location-o, seven o'clock-o!"

Patrick turned up with his model girlfriend, and who could blame him? Patrick was a nice boy but sadly was not one of the world's greatest actors. However, on this type of film with a slender budget, we were forced to take someone whom the Americas would accept, and whom we could afford. Poor Pat, he went through life living off his father's name.

The film was released, and once again, we did very well in the States but very badly in the UK, owing to having the wrong distributor. It was no epic, but it needed the kind of selling that we had with British Lion and EMI.

At this time I was getting more and more frustrated with Max, as not only did he not appear in London, but he studiously ignored all my letters regarding the money that was owed to myself and others in England. Kevin said there was not much point in carrying on, if we were never to receive the money contracted, and why didn't I sue him? I spoke to Michael Flint about it and his view was that as Max had a partner in New York who was a smart lawyer, they would keep us tied up in the courts forever, and we would be in for all our legal fees, a case of throwing good money after bad.

Barry Spikings invited me to lunch with him where he offered me a contract with EMI to make films for them. I asked him about Max, and he replied that there was no deal for him and that as far as he could see, apart from getting finances, he contributed very little. I left it like that with Barry and wrote Max, outlining what had happened. I also said that if he wanted to continue our relationship, he should get the money owed to us by return, otherwise I would think myself free to accept the Lion deal. Hearing nothing, I signed with Lion.

I never heard from Max again, and never saw a dime either.

Now we were on our own, with no more Burroughs' books. EMI were anxious to have a picture as soon as possible, so the first thing was to find a new property. I had had dealings with a young writer who I thought had the right type of skills for our type of movie, so I commissioned him to write an original to be based on the legend of Atlantis, the underwater city.

That is how "Seven Cities to Atlantis" started, but there was a conflict with another movie of the same sort of name, so it was eventually entitled "Warlords of Atlantis". The film was to be released by EMI in the UK and Commonwealth, and by Columbia in the Americas.

Doug was to return to play the lead, backed up by Peter Gilmore, the star of "The Onedin Line", a highly successful television series at the time. We also had that wonderful actor, Daniel Massey, and the legend of Hollywood, Cyd Charisse.

One of our problems was getting American artists, so when a scruffy young, ugly-looking American actor came into my office, I looked up and said, "You're booked". This was Johnny Ratzenberg who became the postman in the hit television series, "Cheers". I also booked Hal Galili, an American actor who had lived in England for many years after having served with the Israeli army, but who had never lost his Brooklyn accent.

The crew was basically the same, with one major exception: I changed designers. I loved Maurice but I felt that we needed a new look to our films, and also I found out that one of Britain's best designers, Elliot Scott, was available. I asked him to work with us, although I knew that we would only be able to pay him a fraction of the kind of money that he earned when he was working with people like Stephen Spielberg. However, I also knew that the money was not his major concern in life.

He was a strange man in many ways. He lived simply but well in a house which was a wooden structure in the middle of a wood. His wife could only be described as eccentric. She believed electricity hated her, and only recently had some electrical appliances in the house, although when Scotty was away she never used them. In the middle of winter she used to sleep out in the garden under blankets topped with a plastic raincoat, and think nothing of arriving at Victoria station with a bag on her back and booking a third class ticket to Beijing.

Scotty used to arrive at the studio about seven o'clock, and I remember one of his assistants telling me that Scotty was the only person who made him feel guilty when he arrived for work half-an-hour before his call! They were both delightful people.

The other change was the special effects' Chief who, with our dependence on visual effects, was of the greatest importance to us.

Here again, I was lucky to get John Richardson who I had worked with in Malaya, where he was Assistant to his father, Cliff.

Over there, poor John, as a young, healthy teenager, was forced to share a bedroom with his father, thus unable to take advantage of the local girls who were so attracted to this good-looking boy. John had been my friend since those days, and now had taken over his father's business, making a great reputation for himself. So I was lucky on two accounts, having an old friend, and one with great experience and talent.

After a careful recce, we decided to shoot in Malta and to base ourselves on the tiny off-shore island of Gozo for the sea sequences, before returning back to Pinewood for the interiors and model shooting.

Malta is not one of my favourite places. Like Gibraltar, it is "Portsmouth with sun" and is a rocky, barren place on the whole, with towns made for visiting British sailors.

Another film crew was staying at the same hotel as we were, working on Alan Parker's "Midnight Express". I really did not know Alan at that time, although we were studio acquaintances. He was a quiet almost shy man, and I never thought he would become such a wonderful director. He has directed such a range from films like "Bugsy Malone", "Evita", "Angela's Ashes", "The Commitment" and "Fame". What a talent. They say he is feisty now, and if he is I am sure it is because he is so talented and does not, quite rightly, put up with fools easily.

Whilst in Malta, the Prime Minister (to all intents and purposes the Head of State) was a left-wing thorn in the side of the British Government and a great friend of Gadaffi the controversial Libyan leader. Anyhow, he, Dom Mintoff, approached me and Alan's producer, Alan Marshall, to make a documentary of the island. Well, I knew my budget could not stand that, so I told him documentaries were not my field, but Alan was an expert at that type of film. I never did know how he got out of that, for the next day we left for Gozo.

However, I did have several more meetings with Mintoff over the years. I used to go to his beach-house, where he insisted on doing the cooking himself, and served the worst of Maltese wine. It was difficult to decide whether to push the food down with the wine, or the wine down with the food. He used to get mad with me because I was such an aficionado of Gozo, which I loved, unlike Malta.

It is funny how it turned out, for both Graham and I were worried about this tiny off-shore island. We did not know how we were going to be treated and how efficient the locals were. As far as we could see they had fishing and tourism and a bit of farming and that was that. We were so worried that initially we took our drivers with us from Malta. We soon discovered how wrong our apprehensions had been. Far from being backward, the people were a lot more on the ball, and certainly a hell of a lot pleasanter than those on the main island. In fact, very soon many of them became friends, especially the Portelli family, the biggest family on the island. They owned a large chunk of Gozo including the hotel where we stayed, the Hotel Calypso. This was known by the crew as the Hotel "Collapso", and it was far from the Ritz, but the people were so nice and so helpful that no one cared.

Gozo was a strange little place, and for example we were surprised to find two giant cinemas. One of them had boxes on either side rather like an opera house, and in fact they did quite often stage operas, bringing over the cast from near-by Italy. However, the strangest thing about these places was that they were both owned and run by local band clubs who hated each other, similar to the way of certain football clubs in England. However, I never ever saw or heard of any violence between them. Each club had its own saint and on the relevant saint's day each club would parade and shout abuse at the other's headquarters. Rivalry was taken to great lengths, even to the extent that one band on tour in Italy arrived at their hotel to find that the booking had been cancelled!

It was a happy shoot, and a lucky one also. The sea behaved itself, and was like a mill pond every day when it so easily could have been a raging storm, making it impossible to shoot. Naturally we had our problems, but as we had a great crew and a great cast, they were soon ironed out. We never heard from EMI, which led me one day to ask Graham if they knew we were there. "Well, they keep sending the money!" he replied.

Here again we did not carry the usual baggage of caterers, caravans, or stopped-for large lunches. The hotel supplied the food and drink, but it was all eaten on-the-hoof, as it were – though we never abused the crew's co-operation and always finished shooting early. This way, we had continuous shooting, for having a break always seems to take the steam out of it. I was asked by the representative from Film

Finances what facilities we gave the cast. I told him they had a chair and a towel, but if they misbehaved we took the chair away! It was all a bit different from the large trailers that even the minor artists demand these days.

All too soon, it was time to return to Pinewood and continue photography there.

However, we had the pleasure of looking forward to working with Cyd Charisse, and what a pleasure it turned out to be. I am sure she hated doing what she had signed to do. After being a major star in Hollywood, it must have been a horrible comedown to be working on this low-budget British film, but she never for one second gave any indication of this, and was just a sweet, and professional working actress.

There was just one embarrassing moment: and that was when Kevin and I took her and her husband, the aging singing star, Tony Martin, out to dinner. The orchestra leader spotted Tony and asked him to sing, which at first Tony declined, but without much persuasion quickly hurried to the stand. The trouble was not getting him to sing, but getting him to stop. He went on and on until the band took a break and he was forced to return to the table. Where I loved her, I did not take to him. I think that he found the lack of fame much harder to cope with than she did, even though he had never been as successful as she had. His first wife was Alice Faye, a major star of the 30s and 40s, when he himself made a few low budget 'B'-movies. After marrying Cyd, they did a double cabaret act together, which I am sure she only did to support him.

We wrapped up on schedule and on budget. I rang Barry Spikings and asked him if he would like to see the film before we started dubbing. He thanked me but said he was very busy so I suggested we could take it to town for him. "That really is nice of you, thank you," he said, a little different from Sam Arkoff!

Barry was a gentleman, and, though he attracted a lot of flak from the press and criticism from people in the industry, he was always very nice to me. He was very honest, and one of the few people whose word you could take without the back-up of contracts. Once again, we had a super response from Barry and his distribution chief, and we returned to Pinewood to complete the post-production.

During this time, we moved house once again, this time to a four bed-roomed country house standing in six-and-a-half acres. The house had been owned by an elderly couple, and was a bit short on creature comforts. We ripped the whole place apart, replaced the small windows with big patio doors, knocked down walls to give space, built wardrobes, cupboards, installed central heating, and ended up with the perfect home, set in a jewel of a garden, surrounded by its own woods, and orchards. It was approached down a private un-tarmacked road, and gave us complete privacy. It was a little piece of paradise. The only trouble was the children's schooling.

Dan had been very happy at his school, but had now outgrown it. It was a Christian Science school, Fan Court, but they did not push their philosophy down the children's neck. It gave the children an excellent education, and on the last day of term, when the boys realised that they would not be together any more, and certainly not see their teachers, they broke down and cried. That is a testament to a great school.

After this, Dan decided he wanted to go to boarding school, so we got him in to Seaford College, a typical British public school. He only lasted two terms. I had a telephone call from him, "Daddy, get me out of this horrible place." Remembering how much I hated boarding school, I did not hesitate. The trouble was, where now?

We tried one prep school in Weybridge, but it was hopeless, and we were forced to accept the only option left, which was the local state school. It was a horrible decision, but, though hampered by his dyslexia, at fourteen I thought he was a strong boy, and might learn something. In any case, he didn't seem to be getting very far in the very expensive private schools I had sent him to. I have always carried a great deal of guilt about this decision, but Daniel has always said that he is grateful for the time that he had spent there, for now he is able to be at ease with all the different classes in England, and has friends across the whole spectrum. I myself hated the place, and thought the head master an ignorant fool, who would have been better off running a third division football club. The school itself was impressive with magnificent facilities but, with such leadership, the children were, on the whole, destined to fill the lower jobs in the country. Here again was another example of teachers completely letting down the ones they are supposed to prepare for life ahead.

On the other hand, Susie embraced the state system. Whilst we were living in Surrey she had been at yet another Christian Science school, which by coincidence just happened to be the best school in the district. She had been wildly happy there, and she was sad to leave because we moved out of the area. She sat the exam for the High Wycombe Grammar School and, being bright, passed. This school was excellent, and gave the best education to the brightest, regardless of class or money. Of course, being the best, it was hated by the Socialists and it was only in areas where the Tories controlled the councils that they still existed. Another example of the Socialist determination to dumb down, rather than build up. The side benefit of all this meant that my school fees had suddenly dropped to nothing.

Dan survived the experience and stayed there until he was sixteen. At the end of the last term, he threw a party at the house, which his class mates managed to trash, which just about summed up the level to which this school had educated the children. Just one last comment on this: One of his female teachers came to the party for a brief visit and when I heard she was walking home got the car out to give her a lift. As I drove up the road, I saw her and Daniel in the lights of my headlights: Daniel with his tongue down her throat! I wonder whether it was a coincidence that she was the only teacher to give him a pass mark in his exam tests.

This seems to be a good time to talk about Gregory and Vicki. After his education at Colet Court and St. Paul's, Greg went as a student to the Royal Court, and ended up directing a play at the Theatre Upstairs. He directed plays at various small theatres, and also got his Film Union ticket. About this time, he had a contract with the British Council to go to Peru to direct plays there. Out there he met and married a very clever Peruvian girl, Clara, whom he brought back to

England. An amazing girl, she got a lowly job at the BBC World Service but ended up years later as one of their most senior executives. She and Greg had a baby, Lyubov, a Russian name, which tied in with their far-left political views. She grew up into a gorgeous woman and changed this name. I am happy to say she did not adopt their leftwing ideas.

At this time I suppose I should have noticed how much Greg was drinking, but we used to meet and have a few drinks together, chew the fat, and off he would go. He was always secretive about what he was up to, so really I did not see too much of him. However, Clara got fed up with his constant drunkenness and they separated, and in the end divorced.

Vicki also divorced her barrister husband and went off with another barrister. They were going to go to South Africa, which maddened me. This was the time of apartheid, and I said to her, "How can you go to a country where your own sister could not come and visit you, or stay in the same house as you?" Despite this they left. I felt very sorry for Chris, her divorced husband, for, though he was a rather dull person, I had got to quite like him. The new one I could not stand, and how right I was proved to be in the future. I think this is the only real row that I have ever had with Vicki, as we have always been close. She did not have such a great childhood as her mother put all her ambitions and interest in Gregory, and, though she undoubtedly loved Vick, she was pushed on the side-lines, as it were. I think she bears the scars of this to this day. She always says that, though she was young when I left her mother, in some strange way she understood.

"Warlords of Atlantis" finished and once again EMI was delighted. I don't think Barry Spikings really understood this type of film, but was just happy to have some financially successful films under his belt.

My next job was to take the film to Los Angeles to show to Columbia. Now, this was a completely different Columbia from the one I had known, and I don't think there was one major executive left that I knew. On top of this, the Head of the Studio had recently been found guilty of forging an actor's cheque to pay himself.

With the usual butterflies in the tummy, I showed the film to the caretaker boss, who brought along his PA. She proved to be my best friend when she jumped out of her seat at the entrance of the monster.

"Oh, for Christ's sake, it's only a movie," said her boss in a bored tone. At the end they swept out, he without a word, but she turned and gave me a lovely smile. I had gone with EMI's LA lawyer who said to me afterwards, "Jesus, John, what a fantastic reception." Well, I thought, if that was a great reception, what must a bad one be like?

I loved being back in California and managed to see old friends, including Doug, who in his usual style kept me hanging around waiting for him, when I could have been with Cyd Charisse. In the end I ran out of excuses to stay there, and returned back to London to start our next project.

It was around this time that Kevin Connor's little boy, Daniel, died of leukaemia. We had known for a long time that he had this dreaded disease, but it was still ghastly when the funeral day eventually arrived. The night before, I had got the

Property Buyer to get a dinosaur made out of flowers, as Daniel was always excited that his father had them in his films. However, I woke up in the night and thought I had just done the most tasteless thing and didn't sleep for the rest of the night. Thank God everyone thought it a wonderful idea and a fitting tribute. My heart bled for my partner and his wife. There can be nothing worse than losing one of your children.

Today the chances are he would have survived as the mortality rate has dropped dramatically with the ever increasing success of cancer research.

Kevin and I started to plan our next and most ambitious project to date. We had the same team of writer Brian Hayles, designer Scotty, Lighting Alan Hume, with a new boy heading the special effects, George Gibbs, who after this first film as Chief, went on to head some major international films.

We embarked on a sort of "Thief of Baghdad"- or "Aladdin"-type film which was technically very daunting. We had to make several carpets fly in the same frame and we planned an Arabian aerial battle.

Whilst the technical boys were working out how to achieve the various effects, we were busy casting. Doug was mad with me, as there was no part for him in the film. Not only was there no part for him, but there was no money to pay for him. Pissed off with me, his romance with my lovely right hand, my PA, Diane, increased. She eventually told me that she was going to get married to him as soon as he could arrange a divorce. I was dumb-struck. I mean, it's one thing to have an affair, quite another to get married! And who should know better? Anyhow I played the heavy father, "Do you think you are doing the right thing? ... You'll be a long way from your family ... Hollywood marriages don't last etc."

Her reply was, "If I don't, I will always regret not doing it." She never did have any regrets. I was the one who suffered, and making a film without my personal assistant was not going to be so much fun, and certainly a lot harder for me.

Casting started. First, we needed the wicked Caliph, and here we had a bit of luck. "Star Trek" was the hit TV show of the time, and I thought Leonard Nimoy who played Dr Spock would be marvellous. EMI okayed. He read the script and said he would be delighted to play it. I think it was a case of anything to get away from those big ears. He even agreed the money! Well, I thought, that's a great start.

A week or two later, I got a call from him and he told me that initially he had turned down "Star Trek, The Motion Picture", but they had now offered him so much money that it was just impossible for him to refuse. Our dates clashed so it was impossible for him to do both.

"I feel so bad about it, John, I feel terrible. But this means financial independence for me and my family." Sadly I thanked him for calling me, as most actors would have got their agent to do it, but Leonard Nimoy was a gentleman.

The next choice was one that I really wanted to dodge. It was my old friend, Christopher Lee and I thought it was too much type-casting. I knew he could do it standing on his head, and as Barry seemed excited to have him, we signed him for the part.

Next, we needed his side kick, the Caliph's P.A. As it was mostly a comical role, and knowing that the "Carry On" cycle was coming to an end, I rang Kenneth Williams and arranged to have lunch with him. I always enjoyed his company, and he never failed to make me laugh so I looked forward to our meal together.

I explained all about the film, and the role I would like him to play. He was worried about being uncomfortable, and asked me questions like what sort of clothes he would have to wear, would he be involved in any fight scenes, and so on. I had to tell him about the flying carpets, and that he would certainly have to be on one or more of them, flying through rain, storms and wind. I also said I didn't want him to camp it up too much. When I got back to the office, his agent was on the phone saying I had cast doubts about his acting ability. A strange, sad man. Anyway, he turned the part down.

Next I approached another old friend, the wonderful Irish actor, Milo O'Shea whom I had originally met on "Loot". He accepted, and so the next thing was to cast the young prince and the princess. I had met and been impressed by a young actor who was desperate for the part, and who had great fencing training. I was on the point of signing him when I got a call from Barry who said he would like me to use Oliver Tobias.

Now, Ollie had been a big success in sexy films like "The Stud", hardly a great recommendation for this very family film. Anyhow Barry rightly thought that he was a very well-known name in the UK, and he would really like me to use him. What could I say? This was the man that had backed me all way through, so I signed him. The trouble was that at that time I didn't know that he couldn't act!

Next on the list was the little Asian boy. We were using the offices at EMI for our auditions, outside which was a long queue of Asian families with their kids in tow, all amazingly quiet and well behaved. Telling parents that their child is not right for the part is difficult. Turning people down at auditions is never easy, and I hate it as much as they do, I am sure, but with kids it is that much worse. We eventually came across a pair of brothers whose father was an actor, and the children had a little experience. One of the two, the youngest, was a good-looking boy, unfortunately much better looking than his brother. We played along for a while saying we were having a hard job deciding which one too choose, so as to lessen the blow to the elder brother. The day came and the loser broke down in tears. There was no way out. We gave him a small part and also made him his brother's stand-in. Little Puneet, of course, was the happiest boy in town. He was a talented little actor, and both children were very well behaved and a credit to their father and mother.

The hardest job I had was finding a gorgeous, young, innocent girl. We tested God knows how many, and I even flew to Italy to see if I could get the right girl. We were getting worried, as we were getting near to our start date, and we still hadn't got the girl. One did stand out, a young extremely pretty girl who was the daughter of Michael Samuelson of the highly respected Samuelson family. They had the largest camera equipment hire company in Europe, and Michael had his own lighting company. Sydney became the first London Film Commissioner, and was honoured by the Queen and made a knight.

I had checked at the beginning that all the girls we tested had Equity cards, but after I had signed Emma, and shortened her name to Samms, she confessed to me that she had not got the vital Equity membership. I was in the shit, as the time was fast approaching when we needed her. I immediately called Equity and told them the problem, that she had said she was a member, how we were already shooting, and so on. To their credit they responded quickly.

Not to their credit was their answer, which was an emphatic "no".

The next move was to go to a conciliation meeting where both sides meet. A producer's representative, the producer (me), two from Equity, one official and one member. The member was Kenneth Williams.

Now, I did not know how he was going to react, but I need not have worried. We had hardly started when he went into full flow Kenny Williams mode. "I don't understand. I mean, where are they supposed to get a sixteen-year-old *experienced* actress? It's ridiculous. You want them to play some old bag? An experienced virgin is a contradiction in terms. I say …" The official tried to get in every so often, but Kenny would have none of it. We could not have had a better advocate, and of course Equity signed her up.

In due course, we were lucky to sign Peter Cushing, my dear friend Capucine and, most exciting of all, the legendary Mickey Rooney.

Our tests for flying the carpets turned out fantastically, and I took them up to show them to EMI, who were happy to have one of their worries solved.

We were ready to shoot.

The first day sets the tone for the rest of the filming, and I told Kevin to always get a shot in before ten o'clock, and to keep a tight pace for the rest of the day. "I don't care if we have to shoot the whole day's work again, this sends a message to the crew." So, we had a good start and everybody settled down.

The only problem was our male lead, who was a lovely chap but had no idea how to act. I used to say to him, "Oliver, you are supposed to be a prince, not a second-hand car salesman." But all to no avail. To give him his due, he did work hard and took fencing lessons every day under the tutelage of our stunt arranger, Alf Joint.

Another old friend joined us, my darling Gillian Lynne, who came in as a favour to me to design the brief dance at the front of the movie.

Emma looked everything we wanted her to be, but sadly her inexperience showed and in the end we had to re-voice her. Milo, of course, was great, but with the speed at which we had to shoot Kevin never really found time to cover his work. Dear Peter Cushing came in and word perfect as always gave a nice beginning to the film.

Then Cap arrived: Capucine.

What a pleasure it was to see her again. We went out to dinner and we had a wonderful time talking about our time together in Malaya, and of all our mutual friends. We, of course, talked about Charlie Feldman, and I was not surprised when she said to me, rather wistfully, "He was the best." She also told me that Charlie knew he was dying whilst we were making "Casino Royale", which at long last explained his strange behaviour. What a sorry story it all turned out to be: Charlie dying of cancer, Bill Holden falling down the stairs and bleeding to death, and Cap herself committing suicide in Switzerland. I was so fond of all three.

The day came when Mickey Rooney arrived and Andy Hardy Meets John Dark. This was the man who had kept me enraptured since the age of eleven, the partner to Judy Garland in so many films including the memorable Andy Hardy series, singing, dancing, and wise-cracking his way through all fifteen of them. He was the number one box-office star of the world in the 40s. It was a thrill to welcome him to Pinewood, and an honour to have him in our film. I walked across to his dressing-room and brought him and his manager over to my office. In the five-minute walk, he told me the plots of three films that he wanted to make, an idea he had for marketing special coins (I never did understand what it was about, hardly surprising as it was all spoken at the speed of a machine gun), and the show that he wanted to bring to London. He was seven years older than me, but he left me breathless.

He only had a few days' work with us but behaved impeccably, though at the end I did get the feeling that over a longer period he would probably not be as easy. All the time he was with us he was wonderful not only on the set, but on all the chat-shows he did, and always gave the film a great plug and was very generous to both Kevin and myself. His wife was with him (number eight, if I remember rightly). He used to say that he had a wedding licence made out "To Whom it May Concern"! She was a sweet, very un-show-business type girl, and Kevin, Mickey and I, with our respective wives, had a memorable dinner one night in Windsor, near Eton College.

Mickey was worried about being recognised, but he did not have worried, for no one knew who the plump, balding little American was. He soon let them know though! When we said good-bye and I thanked him for everything, he said, "I'll give you one bit of advice, John: They say they want this type of family film, but believe me they don't." He must be surprised at the success of the "Harry Potter" films.

It was around this time that catastrophe struck.

For some unknown reason, the technical system we were using to "fly" the carpets stopped working. We were picking up the mechanism that lifted the carpets, we were also seeing the tiny motors that made the fringes flutter and no one could understand it. All the technical guys would meet in my office and talk "techno-speak". This is always one of a producer's nightmares, when your leading technicians have different ideas and you, not having a clue yourself, have to make a decision.

We tried everything and would meet at the processing laboratory at six o'clock in the morning to see the results, but nothing they did helped. We were in bad trouble. Graham did some rapid re-scheduling to give us time to see what we could do. It was obvious that we had to make a major change, and in the end had to sacrifice certain shots, and simplify the system. We still had not finished the battle scenes when the two sides fight each other on the carpets. It was still very effective, but not what we had planned.

At the completion of Main Unit shooting, but leaving the visual effects work still to be shot, I was asked to take the film to LA to show Barry and Michael and the other EMI executives there. Then the plan was for me to go to New York and run the film for the American distributor, Orion. This was a new company set up by the ex-executives of United Artists.

The LA running went well, Michael Deeley saying, "Well, John, you've done it again."

The New York one, though, was a disaster. They hated it from the first minute. It wasn't helped by the unfinished special effects and a temporary dub. Nevertheless they suffered in silence, including leaving at the end with not one word. Let me say this would not have happened at Paramount under Frank Mancuso. No matter how bad the film, they always left with a thank you, a little applause, and a handshake. Just good manners, that's all.

I reported back to Barry, who told me not to worry as he had other distributors up his sleeve. I got back to London, very depressed, but determined to put even greater effort into the finishing. I consequently approached Bob Mercer who had previously headed EMI music before transferring over to the production side of the company. I spoke to him about getting some of their top talent on the record side to compose and play the music for the film, thus giving us a record deal up-front. I thought with a combination of pop and classical Arabian music, we might have an intriguing sound. Well, this was another disaster. EMI kept me waiting and waiting, and eventually sent me down a couple who they said were going to be big. Well, they weren't and with us they were useless. By now I was running out of time, so I got hold of Ken Thorne and asked him if he could do the job in two weeks, which he did.

Whilst all this was going on, I had said to Kevin that there had to be a better way of collecting money for the Leukaemia Charity than what we had been doing to date with charity football matches, fetes, and so on. I suggested that I talk to Barry about having a Charity Premiere for the film and he agreed. When we talked to the charity, of course they were over the moon, but said that they were a very small organisation and did not know how to run such an affair. So we contacted the Variety Club who said they would help if we would split the event between the Leukaemia charity and The Great Ormond Street Hospital for sick children, to which all the parties agreed. We used to meet at the hospital under the chairmanship of Mrs Callaghan, the wife of the ex-Prime Minister, a most charming woman, and a very effective chairman (oops, sorry, chair*person* or even *chair*!!). One day, I was able to read out to them the most wonderful review in "Variety", headed "Star Wars with Flying Carpets".

We then entered the Cork Film Festival. The organisers rang me to ask if I could bring a celebrity down who could actually "do" something, like sing, dance, bird imitations, anything. They were pissed off with people arriving and standing around like zombies. So I took Dana Gillespie who sang at the opening and was a great success.

On the morning of the showing of the film, I was late from giving a press interview, and as I got nearer to the cinema I could hear the audience of children screaming. We had the best audience ever. It was fantastic. At the end, I was presented with a trophy for the Best Children's Film of the Year. I then did a press conference which went really well. Ken Maidment of Columbia said afterwards, "I don't know how, John, but apart from making a great film, you also actually managed to wake the press up!"

The premiere loomed, and soon the reviews came out. They were terrible. "Never mind, these films aren't made for critics," I told Kevin. Princess Margaret and her son graced the event, allowing us to add "Royal" to the word "Premiere".

Because of Emma, the Samuelsons installed live circuit television, and the cast, crew, and other celebrities were interviewed by an old friend, David Lodge, as they arrived, and screened to the waiting audience inside. Amongst those interviewed were the widow of Brian Hayles, the writer – who sadly died shortly before – and Jim Callaghan, a very nice man, very much like his wife whom I had come to admire over the various meetings we had together.

All premieres, or nearly all, go down well, and this one was no exception. However, that was the last breath of success. It died.

And together with it, my career.

Never was there a truer expression than: "You're as good as your last film."

CHAPTER 16
TAKE THE MONEY AND RUN

I had thought "Arabian Adventure" business would pick up, but it didn't. Kevin and I, and the team of Graham and Scotty had started on the next venture, a pirate picture.

We had found a small peninsula in Gozo where we intended to build the pirate ship, which would enable us to shoot almost to three hundred degrees out to sea. All the miniature sailing shots would be done on the excellent tank in Malta. This tank was constructed in such a way that the sea itself was the backing, thereby saving the expense of a painted backing like the one at Pinewood. However, we never made the film. We had the script, the budget, the set sketches, the locations, but Barry did not like the script. It was a shock to us, for we had never had such a situation before. Of course, had "Arabian Adventure" made money we would not have had this reaction. There you go!

I said a sad good-bye to Scotty, and then later to Kevin who decided to try his luck in Los Angeles. He had a tough start, and I think he had got down to his last hundred dollars before he got a break to direct a TV film, and has never looked back since. Sadly he split up with his wife and married the girl that had taken over Diane's job. It was sad to see Kevin go, for after a shaky start we really got on well, and we had such a lot of fun together. He did the right thing, and I could not be happier for him now that he is a successful and sought-after TV director.

So the only one left with me was darling Graham. He and I worked really hard in trying to launch a new project, but all to no avail. It seemed EMI was going through a bad patch too, and I could understand why Barry did not want another "family" film after the disappointing results of the last one.

I think that it was about this time, 1979, that Barry and Michael Deeley split up. I don't know what caused it, but I know it was a far from amicable parting. John Cohen had been brought in to run the LA office and Barry was spending more and more time there. I had always liked Barry, and I thought we had a good relationship, and he was always, as I have said before, honest and pleasant to work with. Later I was surprised by some of his decisions, especially after reading minutes of meetings that I should not have seen. My newspaper training came in handy at times, especially reading papers upside down! I had also started to like Michael, and after our first inauspicious start, he had become a big supporter of mine. That is no surprise, as everyone loves you when you are making money for them. I remember going to Barry's wedding and as I walked down the stairs, Barry looked up and said to a group of people standing at the bar, "Ah, here comes the man that makes us all the money."

Lewis always says a successful film has many parents, and a failure is an orphan.

I am not going to go through the number of deals Graham and I tried to put together, all to no avail.

We had a fun script, a sort of spoof on "The Land that Time Forgot" but we could not sell it to anyone. I had the rights on several books, but got close a couple of times but for some reason or another the deal fell through.

One last story before Columbia packed up its London office. As I have said, Max Setton took over when Mike Frankovich returned to America. Whilst under contract there, I put up an idea for a television series, based on an American family on holiday in England who win millions on the football pools (which would now be the lottery). Unable to take the money to their home in Oklahoma because of currency restrictions in those days, they decide to buy a boat, and the series is of them travelling around Europe. The format would change all the time, sometimes being a travelogue, another time an adventure story, or a comedy. For example, we would see them sailing up the Seine and going to the theatre in Paris and we would see the actual show they have gone to watch. Next week, it could be a love story in Rome with the daughter falling in love with an Italian football player, and so on.

At this time I was seeing a lot of Norman Wisdom, and for those who are too young to know, Norman was England's most successful screen comic. At one time, Norman used to haunt my office, and when he heard about this idea he wanted to sell me his beautiful boat. Well, I was not in the market for buying boats at that moment, but I did talk to him about renting it, and with him playing the deck-hand, in order to give us some comic relief.

The idea went in to the Columbia office and that was the end of that. To tell the truth, I had forgotten all about it, till one day Max Setton called and said on going through the files in the office, he had come across the idea. "And I have the very man for you to play the lead," he said.

"Oh wonderful, who is that?" I asked.

"Rex Harrison," he replied.

Rex Harrison? I thought he must have read the wrong treatment, but he was serious. I tried to explain that the idea was about a middle-class American family from the mid-West, and Norman Wisdom. But he would have none of it and told me that he had already arranged a date for me to meet up with the famous man.

This is another fine mess you've got me into, I thought. I grabbed a writer friend and we quickly wrote something which would fit our new potential star, although I knew whatever we wrote he wasn't going to do it. Of course he didn't, though I must say he was very gracious about it. I felt like a lemon. The point of this anecdote is that I don't understand how people like Max get into such high positions knowing absolutely nothing. The doorman at Pinewood would not think about playing Rex Harrison in a Norman Wisdom role, but Max was obviously in a different world from the rest of us.

Back in the real world, we battled on, remembering Barry Spikings words to me once, "The role of the independent producer is hard, and so difficult that some way should be found to help." This was before any subsidies, lottery money, or tax deals. As an independent, you were on your own. Each deal takes so long as you are in the hands of the money men and they don't rush. A large amount of it is at stake and they're not going to make any hasty decisions. I have always tried to get a deal with a major distribution company for, though you rarely ever see any profits, at least you are only dealing with one investor and you can sleep at nights. With the multiple finance deals, every investor has a lawyer and an accountant, the papers are always somewhere in transit from one place to another, and you spend your life chasing them. Then you are still left with getting a distribution deal.

Barry left EMI and moved permanently to the States. Verity Lambert was appointed in his place.

I had met Verity before but didn't really know her. I had tried to sell her a TV series idea when she was the very successful head of Euston films which made so many great shows, including "Minder". She was also the first producer of "Dr Who". She was obviously a very successful woman with a great track-record in television. But how she would fare in the different world of features was anyone's guess.

Whilst all this was going on, I had various jobs offered me, and one was to take over producing "Wagner", a television series starring Richard Burton. It was a big project, woefully under-budgeted and due to start shooting within a few weeks. I was unable to take my own people with me as the show was fully crewed, neither could I re-budget or be allowed to cut the script to fit the available finance, so I declined. Looking back, I suppose I should have just taken the money and made it. But that's not me. I can't pretend, and I am not clever enough to lie.

After this, Graham was offered the position of production chief with the new regime at EMI, and I said good-bye to him with sadness. They were wise to offer him this position because in my book he was the best – the nicest, most honest, most efficient, most educated person in the production side of the business. He was so loyal to me and so, though devastated to lose his companionship, I was happy that he had landed such a good job. I knew that being as close as I was to that family, I would be seeing a lot of him.

After Graham left, another job came along through Pierre Spengler, who was one of the producers of the "Superman" films. "Superman's" main producer was Alexander Salkind, a mysterious man who seemed to roam the world raising money to produce films. His son was in charge of making it, and Pierre was there smoothing things along, especially when the money didn't arrive, which as the budget escalated and the schedule increased, was quite frequent. In fact, it was so often that he was one of the busiest guys on the show!

One day Pierre told me there was a subject that for years he had been trying to make in his native Russia. As luck would have it, he had just signed to make "Santa Claus" when his film was given the go-ahead. It was to be financed with private money and by the Soviet government, and was to be shot entirely in the Soviet Union. Would I take it over?

Now, this was more like it, and I jumped at the chance. I read the script and my mind was blown away. It was enormous and would make "Superman" look like a second feature. It would take months to prepare and months to shoot. It was one of those scripts that would necessitate sitting down with the director and top technicians and going over each scene carefully before it was all put on a storyboard. I hardly had put down the script when Pierre rang and said, "It is urgent that either you go to Russia or the Russians come to the UK."

I didn't understand the hurry, but am a great believer in making initial meetings in one's own back-yard, so even though I really wanted to see Russia, I said, "I think they should come here." That was a mistake for I still have never seen that country.

I had so many questions for Pierre, not least who was going to direct this epic, but he always made excuses and dodged the issue. Michael Flint did make a deal with him to cover my initial work, and also set out the basis of a deal for the movie. This was big bucks.

One morning the Russians arrived at Pinewood, and Pierre organised a lunch for them. I turned up at the "before-lunch drinks" to find the Russians there, but no Pierre, so I found a girl translator and I went around introducing myself.

Amongst the group was a production designer, a cameraman, an Optical special effects' man, a sort of production manager, and another two technicians. There were also two other men, and I later learnt that one was a political beast, and the other a KGB man. Pierre eventually turned up and made a welcoming speech in his mother tongue, Russian, and we had a pleasant lunch. It was then agreed that I would meet our guests at nine o'clock the following morning.

I entered the board room on the first floor of the Admin block at Pinewood and the entire Russian team, plus two girl translators, were already seated. As I made my way to my chair at the top of the enormous table, I could see piles of paper piled up in front of my chair. As soon as the morning pleasantries had been exchanged, the political head said that before anything else I must sign the papers, indicating the piles of paper stacked up on the table. "What are these?" I enquired and was told that they were the prop and set requirements for the whole film. "Just a second, you mean to tell me that with no discussion, no director, and at our very first meeting, you want me to sign to say how many pencils we want on the General's desk?"

"Exactly," they replied.

They explained that as we were going to shoot in a few months' time they needed confirmed authorisation immediately. I was bewildered and holding my head in my hands said, "There is no way you are going to start shooting in a few months."

This created an uproar as if I was going to start the Third World War! They finally said that we had to start then as the major sets in Moscow had already been built. I was then completely lost. "Who authorised the building of sets?" I enquired.

Another long Russian discussion then, "You do not understand, they had to be built in order to meet the start date."

"But who said we were going to start then?"

More discussion then, "We have to start then because we need the stages later for another major film."

I knew how Alice felt when she fell down the rabbit hole!

And it was true they had started building. It also transpired that there was not enough stage space in Moscow to accommodate the needs of the film, and therefore they were also intending to start building in Leningrad (now once again St. Petersburg). I tried to find Pierre to tell him what was going on, but he was always in heavy meetings for "Santa Claus".

However, I got a message saying there would be a party for the Russians that night. This was the first of the many amazing parties we had. Every night that the Russians were in town we would meet somewhere different but with one thing in common, they were all very expensive.

Money seemed no problem, and we wined and dined on the best. I enjoyed the Russians ... well, the Russian technicians, that is. The KGB and the politico were harder going. I especially enjoyed the designer, who was a round, grey-haired, jolly little man with a big grin, who just loved life – especially, I fancy, life in the West – as he ate and drank in true Henry the Eighth style.

I did eventually get hold of Pierre and arranged a meeting with not only him, but also with the money man.

We met at the Carlton Towers, Sloane Street, where I told this charming Persian exactly what I thought. I said that the film was a major special effects' undertaking, would cost millions, take months to prepare, and that the schedule could also last that long. I added that the Russians had already built the sets, even though we had no director, no team, nothing. I strongly advised him to burn his bridges: He should write off the money he had spent to date, and cancel all the work in Russia, pending appointing a director, agreeing a realistic start date, and giving us time to organise ourselves in a professional manner. I said I would cease work, and forget what money was owed to me, then come back when the necessary ingredients were put in place. They begged me to stay on, and I agreed but I wanted them both to know that I thought it was madness to be talking at this stage about how many candles we wanted on the cake!

So began a series of meetings with my Russian colleagues. I tried to go through the script with them, trying to fathom how they worked. I wanted to know if there were any English-speaking actors there, what crew should come from the UK, how long a pre-production period to allow, and so on. There were to be some major scenes on an oil rig, so I asked where the crew would stay when we were shooting there. They replied they could stay on the rig itself. I could just imagine an English film crew living on a Russian oil rig! When I suggested hiring a cruise ship, it started a major debate, and Moscow had to be rung. Every time we came to a point that needed a decision the answer would be "niet", followed by a long debate, then Moscow would have to be rung whilst we waited for the answer.

I once said, "We will shoot six days a week."

"Niet." In Russia it seemed they only worked five days a week.

So I said, "Well, that is all right for your Russian boys, but what are my English crew going to do over the weekends?"

And the politico said, "They can go to the museums and the ballet."

To which I replied, "I am afraid my crews aren't the ballet-, museum- going types. They are more likely to get drunk and beat up the hotel."

"Then," said the KGB man, "we will put them into prison."

"But we will need them again on Monday morning."

"Then," he replied, "we will take them out of prison"!

The next hurdle came after we had agreed the number of Brits we needed to bring out. I asked about the wives and girlfriends as everyone had to have a special visa.

"Niet."

This started a long argument. My point was that as some of these people could be away for a year or more, it was unlikely that they would agree to come at all if their close partners could not visit them. In the end, Moscow was rung and it was agreed that wives or husbands could come. The thinking, of course, was that they would be spending hard currency.

The next question I raised was the gay partners.

"The what?" they queried.

"The gays, the homosexuals," I replied.

Well, the fuse really blew this time, as the KGB man shot off his chair and ranted, "Niet, niet, niet."

Practically foaming at the mouth, the politico said, "There are laws against this in Russia. It is an illegal activity."

"Well," I turned to the KGB man who was holding his head in his hands, "Boris, you'd better give me a kiss and we'll forget it."

After a few days, I got a call from Pierre to say that they had taken my advice, the Russians would be going back, and we would re-group at a later date. We had a big party at the "Coq D'Or" in Jermyn Street, where my designer friend ate a dozen oysters before we had even sat down. Poor people, they took everything: the napkins, the book matches, and they especially loved the little paper umbrellas that came with some of the drinks. They used to order these cocktails not because they liked them but because of the decorations! I had enjoyed their company and I was sorry to see them go. I had a feeling that I would not see them again, nor would the film ever get made. I do not know what was behind it all, what scam was going on, but perhaps it was something to do with currencies, with the Russians putting up funds in order to have a share in an international product sold for hard currencies. I don't know, all I do know is that we had a hell of a job getting the money they owed me!

Another deal which nearly came off was "The White Witch of Rosehall." John Davis, my colleague from the past, came to me and told me that he had this contact, a rich American property developer who had bought land in Jamaica – in Montego Bay, to be precise. Much to his surprise, on this land he found this house, "Rosehall". Further to his surprise, he found that there had been a book written about it. A book written by H.G. de Lisser, who had been the editor of "The Gleaner", the main Jamaican newspaper, for some forty years.

John Rollins was a self-made man, and was married to a woman much younger than himself and also from an opposite upbringing to her husband. She spent years restoring the house to its former glory, and furnishing it with the antiques that she had scoured the world to obtain. I think it was at this point that John decided to make a movie of the story so he bought the rights to the book, and contacted John Davis.

John Davis invited me to join him to produce this film which would be financed a hundred per cent by John Rollins's company. We had a meeting in London with Mr Rollins and his Chief Executive where it was agreed to hire a writer and then the three of us would fly to Jamaica, and carry out a detailed recce to enable us to develop the script, and arrive at a first budget. It all sounded so simple.

Jamaica, though, was far from simple.

The restored "Rosehall" itself was great, and perfect for shooting the interiors as well as the exteriors. The other locations were all accessible, but the violence and the attitude were not helpful.

Like when we first got there we stayed at The Holiday Inn, which was leased from John Rollins. The place was surrounded by a strong wire fence and the poor Jamaicans used to look in at the rich tourists enjoying the fleshpots of their country which seemed to be denied to them. After a few days here, we moved to a private bungalow which again belonged to Rollins. Here we had armed guards at both the front and at the rear. What worried me was who watched the guards, for I have never seen such a pair of villainous looking men. The domestic staff were not much better, and at the best very surly.

One day whilst looking for a certain location, seemingly in the middle of the jungle we came across ... wait for it ... a film studio! Two stages, and all the normal facilities of an active studio. Indeed in one stage all the lighting equipment was lined up, and in the other all the location transport including a mobile kitchen – also a motorised camera crane mounted on a four wheel vehicle.

I said to the jovial caretaker who had shown us around that I would like to see this piece of equipment in operation

"Ah," he said, "dat needs Henri."

"Well," I went on, "maybe you could ask Henri to come and demonstrate it to us."

This elicited the fact that Henri was not there but lived further away. "But don't worry, on Tuesday morning, nine o'clock, I have Henri here. He show you, don't worry."

So on the Tuesday we dutifully turned up sharp at nine to be greeted by the caretaker, but with no sign of Henri. "Is Henri here?" we enquired.

"No."

"No?" we questioned.

"No, he come yesterday, but he don get hungry so he went home."

This was Jamaica, but despite this kind of thing John and I thought with enough UK guys we could make it work.

After a few more days here, we returned to London, via Delaware to report our findings to the big man. Everything seemed rosy and we said we would be able to give him a fairly accurate budget after a few weeks. Which indeed we did, and Mr Rollins dispatched his chief executives to meet with the Completion Guarantor and us to confirm the budget.

Soon after his arrival in London, there was a currency change, raising the budget quite considerably, and this gave Rollins time for thought. Somehow he had the original figure in his brain, and he could not accept a dime over. He said on a telephone link, "I think I need to take in a partner." I knew at that moment we were finished. He never did find a partner, and it is still a great subject ready to be made.

At EMI, Graham was settling in, and Bob Mercer was acting as a sort of Assistant to Verity. Together they announced a series of films that they intended to make during the coming year. They offered one of these films to me. It was based on a highly-trained chimpanzee that gets up to no good. I thought the script was truly pathetic, but my main worry was what would happen if the chimp stopped co-operating. The animal was in practically every scene, and I knew all about animals in films: They were okay until you wanted to shoot, then they would decide to play silly buggers. My question to Verity was who do we sue if the monkey stopped working? Also I had made some enquiries about the producer/director, which I did not like so I turned it down.

It was a desperately unhappy film, as although the chimp behaved beautifully, I'm afraid the producer/director did not. And it was a complete disaster at the box-office, and it would have been better to let the chimp direct the film.

Mind you, I was pretty bloody stupid for I needed the money. With a wife, two children and a mother to support, life was tough. So, when a developer made a substantial offer to buy our house and land, I accepted. They had already spoiled our six-and-a-half acre garden by building on our borders, so it wasn't the same, anyway. Our plan was to move abroad.

Ineke and I had often discussed leaving England one day, and our dream was to live on a mountain in the South of Spain. This was before that area had been invaded by Brits in their thousands. Not knowing where or when we would have another home, poor darling Ineke saw her home sold. With sad hearts, we left this little piece of paradise to the ravages of the developers. We rented a furnished house nearby, put our furniture in Malcolm's barn and made plans to move abroad. We had discussed which country to go to, and seriously thought about going to Italy, which we loved. When we looked at the cost of the air fares, and because I still lived in hope that I would get work after we moved, we discounted it. We thought about the South of France, for we wanted to go somewhere warm, and we both loved France. Despite what every Brit says, we both got on well with the French, and Ineke spoke the language. However, we had heard about French bureaucracy and the cost of air fares from Nice, so thought we should look at Spain first before making a decision.

Then, before we could arrange a recce, EMI called me saying they had a movie in trouble, and could I take it over as they were going to sack the producer. I said I would, as long as the original producer got the credit and my name did not appear anywhere. The film was eventually called "Morons From Outer Space" and starred Mel Smith and Griff Rhys Jones, two highly successful entertainers. The director was Mike Hodges who had directed the acclaimed and successful "Get Carter" with Michael Caine.

The film was in a bloody mess and, like all these jobs, there was little that one could do. The script had been accepted, the cast established, and the director and crew in place. All you can do in these cases is pull the reins in, install some discipline and make sure no more bad decisions are made that delay the finishing of the film. The designer had already been fired, and his wife, the costume designer, resigned the day I took over.

My first task was to get together with Mike Hodges, to become working partners so as to get the film back on track. The next was to regain the confidence of our two leading actors. I liked them both very much from the start, but naturally they were worried as this was their first film, and to use that old American saying, "Their asses were on the line." However, I also knew that we had to make some pretty drastic cuts to get us into a better cost situation, and I knew they were not going to be happy about that.

I was not helped by a very poor production team, including an unknown production accountant, so I called in the EMI auditor to go through the accounts. I also brought in my dear old friend, Ron Allday, to inspect the books. Both gave me the okay, and it was only later after I left that a lot of bills had been put in a drawer and never been paid. How do you check things like that?

At the end of photography, I left, as my job was done.

During this time my old friend, Malcolm Cockren, had been handling my affairs especially regarding the tax man. With the sale of the house and the land I was due to pay tax on everything except the house and one acre. Despite my accountant's advice that it was not possible to make a deal with the tax man on capital gains, Malcolm did. He had already turned down the tax man's estimate, so he and I met up with the Tax Assessor in High Wycombe and put our case. He did not agree, and we left without the figure being resolved. A few days later the Tax inspector rang and said to Malcolm "I understand that Mr Dark is prepared to make an offer?" We eventually settled for half the original claim. Neither of us will ever know why they were prepared to accept such a big compromise, for really we had no case as the law stood. Let that be a lesson: always try, you never know it might come off. This was another example of Malcolm's great help to me. He was indeed a wonderful friend and still is to this present day.

Ineke and I travelled to Spain and decided it was the place. We rented an apartment near to Puerto Banus, arranged an international school for Susie, and returned to England to pack up and leave the UK. By this time, Daniel had left school and entered the same business, starting as a runner on a Sean Connery film, and then joined John Richardson in the special effects' department. When we told him we were leaving for Spain, he said fine and moved in with his girlfriend in her mother's house. When I rang him to see how he was getting on, he said, "It's much better than home, her mother brings me tea in bed in the morning!"

Susie, on the other hand, was furious and quite naturally did not take kindly to leaving all her friends behind.

We packed up our Citroen Safari car, and then Verity gave me a script for a film to be shot entirely in Japan.

It was written by Nancy Dowd who had written one of my favourite films, "Slapshot", an ice-hockey film starring Paul Newman. She also had won an Academy Award for "Coming Home". I have to say the script was a bit disappointing, but the thought of spending a year in Japan was an exciting prospect, quite apart from the thought of getting paid. I was to leave immediately for Los Angeles, meet up with Nancy there, then travel together to Tokyo.

Poor Ineke would have to make the trip to Spain just with the teenage Susie as companion. I arranged for my good friend, Gregorio Sacristán, to meet them in Madrid, arrange a hotel and generally look after them. From there they would travel to Marbella. Ineke told me later that Susie kept her Walkman on the whole journey, and it wasn't till they got to Puerto Banus, and she saw the lifestyle there, that she began to cheer up. Whilst they were wending their way down the roads of Europe to Spain I was up in the sky.

In LA, I met Nancy, a strange, cookie lady, who displayed all the signs of being difficult, although I felt she was someone that I could get on with. On the journey to Japan, she told me that the script was largely autobiographical, and based on her experiences in Tokyo when she was there teaching English in a language college.

We checked into the Imperial Hotel, a skyscraper building in the centre of the city very close to the Imperial Palace. Nancy was eager to show me the locations mentioned in the script, I was also keen to meet up with some Japanese producers to see if we could make some form of co-production. But it was not easy and, unlike in most countries where people come flocking in once you have arrived, no one made contact.

We hired a charming Japanese girl who spoke fluent English, for, though Nancy spoke a little of the language, it was not sufficient to cope with the complex business dealings that I hoped to have. Through her we made a date to visit Tokyo's leading studio. We were not greeted very warmly, in fact the studio manager actually said that they were not very interested in having foreign companies renting space. He seemed to think that they were too much trouble.

We also met two of Nancy's Japanese friends, a professor and his wife, who both spoke perfect English. The first time we met, he came to the hotel dressed in classical Japanese style, and they wouldn't let him in. They said the slats across the bottom of his shoes cut the carpets in the hotel! He and his wife were a lovely couple, and we were honoured to be invited to their house for dinner. The fact that they had a house at all was amazing by Japanese standards, for property is at a premium in the city, and if you have a house it has usually been left to you by a relative, as in their case. The truly amazing thing was that this place had a garden, admittedly not big, but nevertheless there it was at the back of the house for the enjoyment of their four delightful children. The house had two bedrooms, one for the children, and one for our host's mother. Our hosts slept on the floor in what I can only call the living room. We had dinner there that night, sitting on the floor, a position I had always found most uncomfortable. The food was excellent and the companionship warm.

I poured out my troubles, and my host explained that there were two reasons people had not approached me. One was that if I did not want for some reason to do business with them, they would lose face. The other was that if I did, and they did not, then they would worry that *I* would lose face. I was told to get a middle person so any embarrassment would be avoided. It is hard for us to understand Japanese customs. He said that he hated exams, for if he had to fail a student he was worried that they would commit suicide.

I remembered Lewis Gilbert telling me about his experience on the Bond film "You Only Live Twice" which they made partly in Japan. Cubby had cast a Japanese girl and the Japanese press made a big fuss of her. But when they got her to England and in front of the camera, she couldn't act, or at least could not act in English. Lewis was in quandary how to tell her as gently as possible, so he got hold of our old friend from "The Seventh Dawn" Tetsuro Tamba, and asked him to explain the problem to her, and tell her she would have to go. Reluctantly Tamba agreed, and as he was leaving Lewis asked him, "She won't be too upset, will she?"

Tamba shrugged, "She will just kill herself!"

In the end, they did not sack her. She played out her contract and they just gave her a little non-speaking part. Tamba explained that there was no way she could have gone back after all the press attention and tell the waiting throng that she had lost the job. Death was preferable!

We got our break when somehow Toshiro Mifune heard we were in town and invited us to join him for dinner. Mifune was the best known Japanese screen actor abroad, having shot to fame after starring in "The Seven Samurai". He then went on not only to star in numerous domestic films, but also Hollywood epics.

We met in a charming building, and Mifune greeted us with the extreme courtesy expected of someone of his standing. We went in to dine, and the usual low table set ready, and I viewed the usual low table setting, knowing that we were in for a long evening and wondering how I would fare on the floor. Our host sat in the middle, his back ramrod straight, as he viewed his ten guests, one of whom was his son, Shiro. Like his father, he spoke English, though was more "Western" than his famous parent.

Halfway through dinner, I realised I was in a Geisha House when some of the entertainers came and sat with us. The experience was far from pleasurable, as sitting down has always been a problem for me. I have no bottom and sitting on hard chairs is agony enough, but on the floor it combines a pain in the *butt* with a pain in the *back*. How I lived through it I do not know, and when we eventually left, and the girls were sitting in the hall to bow us good-bye, I had a hard time walking. I thought, this is not the best place to be seen crawling out of: a Geisha House.

Mifune's generosity was staggering. This was 1983, and by this time Geisha Houses were unbelievably expensive, so expensive that most customers rented by the hour. My Japanese friends were amazed when I told them we spent the whole evening there.

Other fun places Nancy and I visited were the love hotels. These are not brothels, but places that husband and wives, boys and girls can go to make love.

They vary in style and the equipment they provide. One we were in had the usual Jacuzzi, the mirrored floor in the tub, a chair designed to make for deeper penetration. And a television running porn, the funny thing being that it is heavily censored! Japan has some strange laws. For example, "Playboy" and "Penthouse" are sold, but all the genital shots are blacked out.

But, at Nancy's insistence, we went to a live sex show, where the girls entered fully clothed, lifted their skirts to display their naked charms, and then went around letting the men feel them. I have to say that they were all very delicate about it and seemed to approach it rather like a watch-mender might approach a Cartier watch. This was the opening act before the top of the bill where a man was taken out of the audience, obviously a plant, and is ravaged by a striking looking girl. At the end, the girl held up the condom to display the evidence of the completion. No simulated sex here.

Nancy had been going on for days saying, "When can we see people fucking?"

When we eventually got into a place which (surprise, surprise!) was full of men, she whispered nervously in my ear, "Supposing I get raped?"

I answered, "Then I'll put you in the show."

So, back at the love hotel, we are both lying on the round bed looking up into the large revolving mirror above (although let me say that neither of us fancied each other and there was nothing between us), when Nancy said, "I wonder if I could ever fuck in a place like this." I did offer to try and find a partner for her, but I don't think she ever found anyone she fancied on that trip.

Japanese culture fascinated me. Just getting in the lift at the hotel was a drama. The lift captain (I'm using the American title for we don't have such a person in Europe) was always a lovely looking girl, who would bow to you as you entered the lift. I always thought it was only polite to bow back, which meant that she would bow back again, and so on. In the end, I had to get in like everybody else and accept the bow with a nod of the head.

Talking about customs, one day I had a nail in my shoe, so I asked our girl where I could get it taken out. She told me that the cobblers worked on the streets but, as it was raining, they would all have gone home. I looked rather downcast, and feeling sorry for me, she said, "Why don't you go down into the basement of the hotel and ask the shoe-shine man there if he can help you?"

Now, the basement of the Imperial Hotel was like an expensive shopping mall, with every type of luxurious product on sale. I descended the lift into the soft carpeted basement, and found the shoe-shine area, a roped-off spot with several raised chairs, and found the shoe-shine man reading a newspaper.

He put down the paper when I approached, so I displayed my shoe and said, "Have nail in my shoe, can you fix?" pointing at him and miming pulling the nail out.

This led to a torrent of Japanese. I have to say I thought he was rather uncooperative, so I persevered. "Look," I said, taking hold of his hand, "got nail in shoe." And made the mistake of pushing his hand down the shoe so he could feel where the nail was.

He reacted as if he was having a brain-storm. He shot out of the seat, threw the shoe to the floor, screamed something at me, glowered and let out a tirade of angry abuse. I thought he was going to hit me, but I was saved by a little Japanese man in a red coat with blue lapels, who managed to calm my attacker. I later discovered that my "shoe-shine man" was an important executive with the Toyota motor company, and the real shoe man was the fellow in the red jacket!

Next day I went back with our translator to express my apologises. She explained to me that Japanese do not like touching foreigners at the best of times, but to have one shove one's hand down his shoe was an incredible insult.

Back to work … None of the producers introduced to me by Shiro Mifune was interested in the script. Several of them queried aspects of Japanese life which they said were not true. Such remarks would send Nancy into a fit of rage, and she would rant on about them not admitting to what she fucking knew. Nancy had a choice form of expression, and hated anyone querying or questioning anything she wrote. Our poor little translator stopped a few beauties when she pointed out certain inaccuracies regarding Japanese etiquette in the script. Nancy wouldn't have it, and threatened to sack her.

Nancy and I got on quite well, for at this stage there was little for us to argue about. We did have one short blast and that was when she did not want to get out of the car to look at a possible location. I explained to her that was what you did on a recce, you kept searching for the right place, to which she replied, "If I want a lecture, I'll ring my father!"

Our real row happened on the way back to London. We had completed our task and, armed with photos, pages of costs and details of locations, we flew back. All was well till we changed planes at Singapore. Nancy lost her bracelet. She was flapping around screaming at all-and-sundry, and I could not see how I could help. This pissed her off, and she refused to speak to me although we were sitting next to each other on the long flight to London.

As soon as we landed, she was on the phone to Verity, who very wisely pointed out that people in the middle of the night on a long flight do not always behave as they should.

Nancy's next target was Verity herself, whom she hated, for introducing Stephen Frears to her as a possible director. At that time, Stephen had not had the success that later he would achieve. Nancy took an instant dislike to him and accused Verity of trying to push a television director onto her eminent feature.

Anyhow, she never forgave me, and in the end mellowed towards Verity, probably because there was no other company interested. Not that it mattered, for EMI was unable to raise any American investment and another project hit the dust.

I returned to Spain, and we rented a large house about ten minutes' drive from Marbella. The house itself was delightful but we did not like the area, as it was a large urbanisation full of foreigners. In fact, it was hard to find a Spaniard on the whole complex. Still it was a good base for us to start looking for a house to buy. In actual fact, it really did us a good turn living there as it taught us very quickly what we didn't want. House- hunting at the best of times is a soulless occupation, and we had done it so many times – or, to be exact, Ineke had done it so many times.

She sorted out the possibilities for me to look at. For a long time we could find nothing we liked at a price we could afford. We realised that living at the Coast was not for us, with its tourists, pollution and all that goes with it. It was several months before we started looking up in the hills. We investigated the Ronda road, which was very nice. But it was a long way from the airport, and as I was still hoping to work it was important that I could get back to London quickly.

We were then introduced to an English estate agent who operated from the mountain village of Mijas. We immediately loved the area, and started the hunt in and around this village. We found two places we liked, both very close to each other. One was owned by a delightful German/ Danish couple who were selling up to return to Germany. It was an old converted *finca* (farm) building, which had been not very well converted, and would need a lot of building to make it into anything like what we wanted. It was set in the most delightful garden, and also had the benefit of a guest house which we thought would be great for visitors.

The other house was totally different. It was a modern construction, built on the top of a hill looking down across a valley to the Mediterranean. It was a soulless place owned by an English KLM pilot and his wife. She could not take the hot weather and they wished to return to Holland. Ineke liked the first and I the second, though it was a lot more money than I had intended to spend. But isn't that the norm? You nearly always go up on the price you can really afford, but as property prices normally go up, this is a good thing.

In the end, Ineke eventually agreed after I pointed out what we had always said, you can change the house, but you can't change where it is: location, location, location. The major problem was that it was a long way from Susie's school. After a long discussion we came to the conclusion that Susie, now sixteen, only had two more years at school and it would be silly not to take the place that we felt was right for us. We would just have to put up with the inconvenience of trekking to Marbella twice a day.

So we bought "La Peninsula", and started turning it into the place that we had always dreamt we would own. Not that all our houses hadn't been fantastic, but this one was in the sun, with its own swimming pool, and space for the family to come and go. It also had a garden that went almost 360 degrees around the house, giving us total privacy. All this with the backdrop of the Mijas mountains, and a view down the valley and to the Mediterranean. There was a lot to do to make it our dream home, but we had the time to do it, if not the money.

Ninety per cent of the houses in the area had white walls and ceilings, with brown wooden beams. Our house was no exception, if anything more so, for very soon we discovered the previous owners had a "brown" complex, as everything was brown: brown kitchen, brown bathroom and even things they left behind, like paper napkins, were brown. We recalled they both always wore brown clothes. I am ashamed to say that after twenty years there are still traces of brown left.

We had hardly settled in when a call came from London about a new picture for EMI. This was a property which had been brought to Verity, via Bob Mercer, by two commercials' boys, Terry Bedford as director, and Gower Frost as producer.

They were both partners in a very successful commercials' company based in the UK and the States. As Gower had no experience in features, Verity wanted me to produce the film and have Gower as my Associate. I accepted with the one proviso, that as Gower and Terry had paid all the development costs, Gower should share the producer's credit with me.

I thought the script was a pile of shit, but this time I told myself to just take the money. Stop being so precious! Get control of it and see that they don't get themselves into trouble!

During the various script meetings my fears were in no way allayed. I thought the writer was in another world. Bob Mercer's talent I had always found minimal, even though he was a delightful person and I really liked him. When I heard him describing "Slayground" as the next great British movie, my fears were confirmed. Later Verity told me that she wished she had taken notice of the fact that I had fallen asleep in one of these meetings! You can take just so much crap.

How Bob got a job on the movie side is beyond me. He had been with EMI records, but whether he was any good there I am not competent to judge. It was Barry Spikings who gave him a job on the feature film side.

When EMI eventually closed, Bob got one of the best jobs in the entertainment industry – a job in a million – as manager to Paul McCartney. It was well paid, and it seems Paul was a very nice boss. In fact, there were only two rules in his office: one was that everyone should have lunch in his wonderful suite of offices, complete with its own kitchen, and the other, that under no circumstances were there to be any drugs in his offices. Being Bob, he ignored both.

One night, a few months after he got the job, we all met up to celebrate his getting this fantastic appointment. He was late, as usual, but when he did arrive it was obvious that he was more than eight sheets to the wind. Roaring with laughter and grabbing a drink, he told us about his busy day. It seemed it was Paul's birthday. "So, I rang him up to wish him a happy birthday," said Bob, in his mild North country accent. "But, strange bloke that he is, he didn't want to know anything about it. Just ignored it and went on talking business. So, when I put the phone down, I thought, fuck it, maybe he's not celebrating his birthday, but that doesn't mean that I can't. I went out and had a great lunch with a few mates, rather a late lunch, come to think of it. Anyhow, when I got back to the office, I told the gang there it was Paul's birthday and we should celebrate. I sent out for some champagne and it was a hell of a party, I can tell you. You won't believe this, but there was a row and one of the girls threw an empty bottle of champagne at someone. But the bloody thing missed and went straight through the windows – you know, those long windows he's got in his office – bloody things cost a fortune, had them specially made. But that's not the funny bit ... You've no idea where it landed. You know the ACTt (the technicians' Union at that time) offices are just down below. And who should be going in at that precise moment but Alan Sapper (the Union's general secretary)? Fucking bottle missed him by inches, but he did get a nice shower of glass." Then laughing loudly, "Nearly got rid of him at last." McCartney fired him the next day.

However, during this film Bob was a senior executive of EMI Films, and we were about to make an expensive piece of crap. Enter the director.

He was a sweet young man with a highly successful commercials' career, but with no features experience at all. Now, a lot of successful directors have come from that area (the wonderful Ridley and Tony Scott to mention just two), and I would not criticise Verity for giving him a break. He did not take to the features' world, though, and he certainly resented any advice.

First of all, I think he selected the wrong script, the wrong subject for his debut. It was a frail story at the best of times, and it needed an immense amount of director's input to make it into anything. Maybe that was what attracted him to it. What made me first suspicious was on our recce around England looking for suitable location sites, we discussed the use of a fairground. I said, "The best fairground will be the one we will build in the grounds of Pinewood studios. There we will have the choice of whatever attraction you want, but also the use of all the studio facilities."

"Oh no," he said, "I must have the smell of the sea!"

I didn't know that we were making a "smelly". Actually we were making a stinker.

I poured out all my misgivings to Verity, from the script to the director. I did not think we had a chance and, though the company was already into some heavy commitments, it would be a spit in the bucket compared to the cost of an unreleasable film.

Verity, remember, had only been in the job a short time, and she felt we were too far down the line. Also she was getting this upbeat chat from Bob Mercer who really thought we were making "Gone With The Wind"! To sum up, we went ahead. This time, as I have said, I was going to take the money. God, how I hated myself.

The casting did not cheer me up either. The American lead everyone was keen on, and who was willing to do it for the right price, was someone completely unknown to me, Peter Coyote. "Well, that's really going to get them queuing up," I said. I was told that he was in the great big box-office success of the year "E.T.", and arrangements were made for me to see the film, which I loved. But when we were near the end, I realised that we hadn't seen anyone who looked remotely like Peter Coyote. Then, in the scene where they capture the alien, a man in a contamination suit enters and, on looking closely, I thought this could be our star! And it was! He had five minutes' screen time, and for most of that he was wearing a helmet! However, I was told that the LA office said this actor was going to be a big star, and we were getting him at just the right time, as soon we wouldn't be able to afford him.

Then we had some good news: we got Billie Whitelaw. Heaven knows why, I reckon her tax demand came in that morning!

Then someone had the great idea of casting Mel Smith as a sort of heavy. Now I loved Mel and also had great respect for his talent, but in no way was he right for the part. So another row. Then the usual, "He's another name."

"*Another* name," I shouted "we haven't got one name, never mind another."

Then came the rejoinder, "All the more reason to have Mel!"

EMI seemed happy to finance this disaster, and I am afraid I could not help thinking bitterly of the scripts of mine that they had turned down after the failure of "Arabian Adventure". Despite all my misgivings, my rows, my often repeated reservations, we began. And we began in that most miserable of places, Blackpool, a monument to the taste of the British holiday-maker: candy-floss, kiss-me-quick hats, fish-and-chips, and dodgem cars, together with rude stall holders and miserable hotel staff. Why do the Brits put up with it? Well, of course, the answer to that is that they don't any longer, they go abroad.

I begged Verity not to come on the first day of shooting. The first day is nearly always a mess; things get mislaid, the crew have to settle down working with each other, the artists are nervous and the last thing needed is for a heavy to come down from the front office. But no, she insisted, and so she arrived the night before. This, of course, turned it into quite a party. Mel and Bob were much to the fore, and no expense was spared. I made a mental note to see that it didn't get on to my budget, for, though in the end the company put all expenses onto the film, at least I could control the production side of it and make sure I retained my 100 per cent track record with Film Finances.

Luckily for me, all my big budgeted films that got into trouble were made without a bond, the American company taking the risk themselves.

I promised our young director that I would keep Verity out of the way, so early in the morning, after checking that there were no major shocks, I took her off to see all the other locations, and ended up having a pleasant lunch in a fairly civilised restaurant. This was the first time I had really been with her on my own, and I must say that I took a immediate liking to her. We got on just fine, and by the time we got back we were like old friends, so much so that standing in our crappy little production office she whispered to me that she wanted to go to have a pee, but as the loo was practically in the middle of the room, and its walls made out of thin plaster board, she was scared of making a noise. So I had the room cleared, but as I went out I said to her, "Of course, Verity, the best way is to put one leg in the bowl and then pee down it!"

Somehow we stayed on schedule. Terry brought some of his crew with him, which caused another row, as I thought he needed experienced feature technicians but, again backed by Verity and Bob, he won the day. We completed the English locations with some pretty dismal material, despite the Blackpool air, and returned to Pinewood for the interiors. I left for New York to make sure all was in order there, and to see to the American casting.

Bob had gone ahead of me with his wife and baby, I can't remember why for he had nothing to do. However, he was the company man, and therefore it had nothing to do with me. He met me at Kennedy airport, and I was amazed when I found I was travelling in the most luxurious stretch. I hate money being wasted on unnecessary transport, but when I raised an objection all Bob said was, "Think big." And helped himself from the inboard bar.

"Oh fuck it," I thought "if you can't fight 'em, join 'em!" And swallowed the proffered drink.

We had made a deal with the Mayflower hotel on Central Park, and here I had another shock.

After checking in, the bell boy took my bags and said, "Oh Mr Dark, you're with Mr Mercer, aren't you? Would you kindly tell him that I have got his pot." This is great, I thought, now we're using the hotel staff to get our drugs. As soon as I could, I collared Bob and gave him the message, but before I could question him, he said, "Good, it's to warm the baby's formula!"

They had taken offices in an old piano factory which had been converted to offices on some floors, and to small factories on others. The building was located in the dock areas, not one of the more salubrious parts of New York. I arrived one morning and found the main door shut, and thought the janitor hadn't yet opened. Several factory girls turned up, and, as it started to snow, it was not the most pleasant of places to be. In the end there was quite a crowd of us. I was thinking about writing letters of complaint to the building management, when someone turned up, ignored the waiting crowd, and pulled the door open! I knew the Americans drove on the right-hand side, but had forgotten that their doors opened outwards!

Shooting went as well as could be expected, and we were lucky, we had an experienced first assistant director, who kept things rolling.

Peter Coyote was a decent chap, very professional, and I think enjoyed being the lead actor. Certainly he was no trouble.

Of course, there were the usual problems that all films seem to have. The casting director was a disaster, and even managed to double-book an actor for the same date.

There was the undisciplined actor needed for night shooting and found at the Oscars' ceremony in Los Angeles. On the whole, it went well, with the New York crew and the Brits seemingly getting on okay. Also I found the American production team very efficient. Soon it was the farewell party and back to the UK, then onto Spain and home.

The film had not been a happy experience, and I was uncomfortable on it the whole time. It finished on budget and on schedule, and that is the only good thing about it.

Well, that is not fair, for I also made some good friends like Gower Frost and Mel Smith. The trouble with my relationship with Mel was that I could not keep up with his life-style, his boozing and snorting. I was forced to break off my relationship with him, which was a real shame, for he is the most likeable of men, talented, a great comic, and now a leading film director. How he manages to do it all is beyond me, but he does and it couldn't happen to a nicer guy.

This seems a good time to get up to date with family affairs: It is clear that I was always absorbed in my work, and sadly there was little time left for my children. Poor Vicki had a rotten childhood, her mother and Gregory were such a close pair and somehow she just hung on the edges of that relationship. She told me recently that her mother had complained that she did not participate in the family, but Vicki said, "They were the family, Mother and Greg. I was never included."

During her second marriage and after having two children, she got very ill whilst in Africa. She realised at that time that the marriage was a disaster and returned to London with the two children, and nothing else, penniless. She managed to get an unfurnished flat in a dreary part of London. I still had quite a lot of furniture left in Malcolm's barn, so we were able to help her. Despite all her problems back in England, she was so happy to be away from Africa and the life she led there.

I think our relationship can be summed up by a paragraph from a letter she wrote me in the year 2000: *"You have always been there for me, rescuing me from various scrapes and unsuitable marriages, illnesses. A shoulder to cry on, someone to talk to, somewhere to go when the world gets too tough. A voice at the end of a telephone, that makes me feel warm inside."*

Darling girl, she makes me feel less guilty about my role as a father, in contrast to Gregory, who was much more distant from me. His far-left political views made our relationship, how shall I put it ...nervous. Well, for my part, anyhow. I blame myself for not noticing his drinking before it got so bad, as after all I come from a family of drinkers. I myself was a heavy drinker, but never in any way an alcoholic. I was a social drinker, and never drank at home unless we had guests. I guess I was a pretty useless father but, to be honest, I have never known how to deal with him. I did have one pretty tough warning session with him about his drinking, whilst we were still living in St. George's Hill, but I think the bug had already got to him.

The other children, Dan and Su, were so different. Like Vicki, they were close, warm, and a joy to have around.

Daniel was working on all the big movies, still with Richardson's special effects' crew. I was not happy about him doing this job, because unless you're the boss it is a pretty lousy occupation. You get covered in filth, you carry great weights, and you are always liable to injury. However, apart from learning how to blow up a bridge, you do start to learn how a film is made. I always wanted Dan to go into production, but his dyslexia held him back. Our personal relationship, though, got closer and closer the more we got to know each other in adulthood.

Susie got over her dislike of moving to Spain, and in fact enjoyed it immensely. With twenty-two different nationalities at the school, she learnt the world did not stop at Dover. She began to enjoy the more Latin way of life, like kissing everyone when they arrived at school, and kissing them again when they left. She made some great friends, many of whom she still has today. She learnt the language, and enjoyed the fleshpots on offer. I don't think she did as much work as she probably ought, but she had a grand time. As a teenager, she was a real pain-in-the-arse. I used to say to her, "I doubt you will live through this. I will probably murder you, and the judge will let me off on the grounds of justifiable homicide." You see, adopted children are just the same as blood ones There is no difference: It's sometimes good, sometimes bad.

1983 and 1984 I seem to have spent travelling between London and Spain, discussing future projects with Verity and others. One I was especially enthusiastic about was a film for John Carpenter, "El Diablo", a Western. It had a good script, and a good and experienced director.

My intention was to make it in Spain, and I called in my old friend, Gregorio Sacristán, to do a budget and schedule. Armed with these and some pretty spectacular location stills, I went back to London and presented them to Verity and her colleagues.

The London office was excited about the project, and very soon after, Verity and I left for LA.

We were not alone as the previews of "Morons ..." were going to be shown, and we were accompanied by Mike Hodges, the director. He was a sweet and talented man, but not right for this type of film. He told me on the flight that he had repeated the funniest bits at the end of the film (well, what he thought were the funniest bits!). I told him that I thought it was a very bad error. Poor Mike, I wish I had not said it, as it was too late to do anything as the print was in the cargo-hold, and there was no way it could be re-cut.

Unfortunately I was made to go to the first (and last) preview. It fell on stony ground. At least in England the audiences knew Mel and Griff, and knew that they were supposed to laugh. In LA they hadn't a clue who they were and what they were supposed to be doing. On the audience reaction cards the nicest comment was: "This film sucks."

I was keen to get on with "El Diablo", so a meeting was set up with EMI's lawyers. At that meeting, it transpired that EMI no longer owned the rights, as they had expired some time back. It was a case of the left hand etc. Oh shit!

Back to London. Then back home and the Malaga/London air commuting continued. On one of these trips, I bumped into an entertainment lawyer I knew, who told me that he had been busy building a film studio in Norway with EEC money. I thought it a strange place to build a studio, and Spain would be a much better place as at the time they hadn't one film studio (as opposed to television). So I flew to Madrid and once again met up with Gregorio Sacristán, who was still working for what had been Mole-Richardson, but was now owned by the Lee Brothers.

John and Bennie Lee were two Cockney guys who, starting as film electricians, built themselves quite a little empire, and had bought Mole's. Together with their own equipment, they became by far the leading film electrical company in the country. I think I was the only person who did not like them. Everybody else thought they were great, generous clowns, but I viewed them with suspicion.

Gregorio thought it was a great idea and that we should approach the Barcelona Town Council. He also confirmed to me at this time that he had the same arrangements with Lee's as he did with Mole's, that he could take on outside work. Appointments were made and we flew to that great city, had an excellent meeting which resulted in their taking us to some land they could allocate to us for the studio.

They were as excited as we were, and I was happily surprised by these local government officials who were so helpful, supportive and enthusiastic. We had several meetings, and started to make approaches to the European Union to assist in funding the operation. Plans were being drawn up indicating the intended size, and content. We had already got the approval from the Barcelona City to fund the initial expenses, and things were going well.

Suddenly I got a call from Gregorio to tell me that the Lee Brothers had found out what he was up to, and had gone to the Barcelona Government Trade Commission and said that they could put the money down on the table straight away. They showed them the size of the company and convinced the Council to go into business with them, cutting me right out.

I was stunned and could not believe their behaviour. I had never trusted them but this was such an underhand trick. I did not think that Gregorio had behaved well either, as he told me nothing until it was all over. It did no one any good, for shortly after that the Lee brothers ran out of money, and the whole thing collapsed. I certainly was not going to get involved again. It takes only a few short lines to explain, but it took nearly a year of my life.

It was not the only thing to collapse. Verity's reign at EMI came to an end. The office was cut back, and a new executive was appointed. Bob was made redundant and Graham, whilst losing his job, was given a film to produce, as a sort of golden handshake, I guess.

It was 1986 and life was very depressing. I got a call from Lee Katz in Los Angeles telling me that he was now working for the Completion Bond Company of Los Angeles.

Now, Lee was my old adversary at United Artists when I was with Charlie Feldman in Rome. From there he had become Head of Production for U.A. at the Coast, and was in charge of all their epic films, including "Heaven's Gate" (if only they had listened to him!).

He told me there was a film shooting in Almeria which they were bonding, and which they were worried about. Would I pop along there and give him a report on what I thought? This was a very low budget British film directed by Alex Cox (who had had a success with "Sid and Nancy") and produced by Eric Fellner, who also produced "Sid and Nancy" and became one of Europe's top producers. With his partner, Nick Brown, and in his company "Working Title", they went on to make numerous highly successful British and international successes.

I thought a trip along the coast would be fine, and then Lee added they had another film shooting in Madrid which was okay, but I might like to drop in and say hello.

In Almeria, I found everything well under control, and though they had had some problems, they had been quickly sorted out by Eric Fellner and they were now running smoothly, and on schedule.

I left them after a day, and headed for Madrid where I was met by the associate producer. It transpired he was the son of George Brown, the producer, and the brother of the famous Tina Brown the editor of "Vanity Fair" and "The New Yorker". I knew his parents as they lived near to me in Spain, but sadly this boy had not inherited any of his father's talents – all of which, plus some, had gone into the daughter.

On reaching the Madrid studio, I found an anxious English production manager waiting for me, who hurried me into a room and slammed the door. It transpired that the producers had run out of money, and the previous day, Dusty, the PM, was so worried he had stopped the crew going out to work. So much for "well under control".

At this time Dusty was a comparatively inexperienced PM, though he had served for many years as a successful first assistant director, and later was to become a senior executive in the trade. I calmed him down, and told him that getting the money was not part of his job. The important thing was to keep shooting until I could find out exactly what was going on.

I contacted Lee Katz and reported to him this worrying situation. I quickly met with the production accountant who reported that some money had just come in. So, for the moment things were back to normal.

It was a strange picture with a strange set-up. It was entitled "Siesta" and had an amazing cast of Ellen Barkin, Gabriel Byrne, Jodie Foster and Isabella Rossellini leading the way.

The trouble was the script and the director, Mary Lambert, who was making – as far as I could fathom – an experimental film! And I am not sure that this is what the producers wanted. To give some idea of what was going on, when I first walked on the set, I was greeted by the English sound recordist, an old acquaintance, with the words, "Welcome to the Madrid School of Film Making." The trouble was, the leading pupil did not want to learn!

I read the script, looked at the budget and progress reports, and reported to Lee that they had changed the script so much there could be no come-back against the Bond Company as none of these changes had been notified to his company.

My work was done and I returned to my home in the South.

I had hardly got in the front door when I got a call from Barry Spikings in LA. "Do you know anything about a film shooting in Madrid called 'Siesta'?"

Did I!

I filled Barry in with what I knew and he commented they were after them for money, and did I think they should put any in. I explained to him that my previous visit had been on behalf of the bond company, and the creative side of the film was none of my business. However, I did explain that I had reservations about the script and the amateur way it appeared to be shot.

He said, "Would you mind going back there and having a look at the rushes, re-read the script and then giving me a call to advise me what you think?" So, back to Madrid with a new mandate.

I looked at the material, and was not impressed. I couldn't help thinking what a waste of talent. As instructed, I re-read the script, but whilst having a drink in the bar that night with some of the crew, I found out that the script I was reading was not the one that they were using to shoot the film. I called Barry that night and checked what script he was reading and – surprise, surprise! – found that it was the same one as I had. I gave him my opinion of the rushes, and advised him to keep his money.

I left the next day. Months later, I got a call again from Barry telling me that he was just going to see a running of the film. Oh my God, I thought, it is going to turn out to be one of their biggest grossers of the year.

A few hours later, Barry rang again, "Thank God you kept us out of that!" It was one of the *stinkers* of the year and had a pathetic release.

Back home, life had changed.

Susie was eighteen and left school. She did not get as many passes as her ability suggested, and without them she would not have been able to get into a university, even if she had wanted to. Instead, being a typical Dark, she was anxious to start work in the television industry. She was keen to go back to London and start a career. We agreed, providing she first went to a really top secretarial college and learnt shorthand and typing, and all the things needed to make a top secretary. We explained that even if she never used these talents, they would always find them useful, and also she would never need to be out of work.

Ineke took her to London and booked her into a girl's hostel, and into a top college. So, she was the last of the chicks to leave the nest. (Well, that really is a totally untrue statement, because I left the first two chicks, and Ineke and I left our eldest, so Susie really was the only one that left us.) She settled down well and, when she finished her course, got a job as a secretary at London Weekend Television. After a short time there, she got a job as a production assistant with newly formed Sky Television, and settled down to an exciting life in the television world, soon becoming a production manager, and then going on to produce shows like "The Comedy Awards".

I am immensely proud of her, as she has overcome problems that would have fazed many people: she is adopted, and she is black. At no time did we ever think of her as anything but our daughter and I don't think that she ever thought of us as anything other than her parents. Both Ineke and I could not love anybody more, even though she was a typical teenager, and impossible. The day they leave you forget all those times, and all you are left with is a gaping hole in your tummy. You know life will never be the same again.

Her colour was never an issue, but whether or not she worried about this, I have no way of knowing. We were never made aware either by her or by other people of any problem.

There was only one incident she told us about, when she applied for a temporary job after seeing a notice in a shop window. When she went in, she was told that the position had been taken. But the following week she saw the notice was still in the widow. "I did wonder if it was because I was black." Certainly she gives no sign of having any qualms about it, and sails through life giving the impression of supreme confidence, though I know she sometimes was a bundle of nerves, rather like her father.

Talking of fathers, she quite naturally wanted to meet her biological parents. She managed to track down her father, and she met him on a few occasions when he was visiting England. They seemed to get on well with each other, but sadly he died not long after they met. On the other hand, her mother in New Zealand made it clear that she didn't want to know anything about her. It is sad as I think she would have been very proud of her. However, I can understand it as she was probably married, with other children, and did not want her past to interfere with her present life.

Someone asked me whether it worried me, her seeing her biological father, to which I replied, "Good God, no. The fact that he had something to do with her delivery does not change the fact that she is my daughter, and has been all her conscious life."

Shortly after returning from Madrid, I got a further call from Lee Katz who told me that they were about to start shooting a film in Florida, which was to be directed by an Englishman, Ken Annakin. I knew of him, though we had never met.

My connection with him was that he married a girl I had some mild designs on. Sadly, Pauline went on a film to South Africa and met the director, and married him – which was Ken, of course.

The Florida film was entitled "The Further Adventures of Pippi Long Stocking", based on a children's book of the same name. Lee explained that it was a Columbia pick-up deal, and they were very worried about it, as they all thought that the budget was much too low – all, that is, except Betty Smith, the boss of the company. Would I go down there and keep a very close eye on it?

At that moment I would have gone to Alcatraz, and the thought of Florida was appealing. I asked when they wanted me and "Yesterday" was the reply. I agreed to go, and arranged the money, the living allowance, and the first class travel. The accountant from the firm called about my details, and warned me the film was a disaster and Betty Smith, the boss, had no right to give it a bond. Well, that's a good start, I thought.

I was going to Jacksonville and then on to Amelia Island where the company was based. At Jacksonville airport, no one was there to meet me. Another good start, I thought. Never mind, I'll get a taxi. No taxis! An airport without taxis is like a restaurant without food.

Eventually, a young assistant did turn up with a lot of pretty poor excuses, and I thought if he was an example of the crew, then we were in for a bumpy ride.

There was a meeting the next day with the whole crew, at which Ken went through the script, and answered questions. I kept my comments to myself, as what I wanted to say was not to be said in front of the whole gathering. I read the script and looked at the schedule and budget, and after a discussion with the production manager, I met Ken. I told him that he had only one chance of getting through on time and said, "You will have to push as much of the special effects' shooting as possible over to the Second Unit."

Now, at that time the Second Unit comprised of a cameraman (lighting and operating) and a Camera Assistant.

He then asked me if I would take over directing the unit. Well, I knew that they couldn't pay me as there was no allowance in the budget for that, but I also knew that I would rather be doing that than sitting around counting up how much they were going to run over, and therefore have a claim against Betty's company. So I agreed.

"… Pippi Long Stocking" was the story of a young girl with magical powers, and contained the three worst things a film can have: children, animals, and special effects. This was compounded by the fact that the budget was too low for the script, and no allowances had been made for the things that could go wrong. If that wasn't bad enough, the Effects' chief, who had worked with Ken years ago on "Those Magnificent Men and their Flying Machines", had got a lot older and he really was no longer up to it. Ken had complete faith in him, but I was always scared for the safety of the children in the film.

Trouble started from the beginning. Because the film had been delayed so many times and for so long, the girl playing Pippi had developed a very admirable, but unsuitable, pair of breasts. These had to be strapped down.

Actually it was the *girl* we should have strapped down, for she soon was flirting with the guys on the crew. There were some scenes of her and a palomino stallion, but once the girl came on the set, the horse would go mad. In the end, it had to be taken to the vet and be neutered, poor thing. It was a pity we couldn't do the same thing to certain members of the crew!

I used to bolster my little unit by borrowing off the main crew, and one of our main jobs was to cover the monkey, which played quite an important part.

This monkey, which was supposed to have been well-trained, was owned and supposedly trained by a late middle-aged lady, and they both shared a minute caravan. The trouble was that the monkey was very temperamental, and its training seemed to be confined to taking its hat off, which even that simple exercise was dependent on how he woke up that morning. One thing for sure, he would do it off-camera brilliantly, but get him in front of the camera and it stayed on his head as though it had been fixed on with super-glue. The woman treated the animal like a recalcitrant child.

I like animals, but after a day of frustrating shooting, with "Take your hat off, darling. Mummy give you a lovely banana …" and so on, I could willingly have murdered the little bugger.

As I said, I used to beg and borrow crew, but when we were night- shooting a model ship on an improvised tank we had to have sparks, special effects' guys, extra grips and so on and, as I was still light, I recruited the girl in the accounts' office. She would work all day on the figures and all night with me on the tank.

Blue was a real Southern gal and I still love her to this day. There was nothing she would not do. If someone had to go into the water it would be her, if someone had to drive back to base for something, Blue would be there and back before you knew she had gone. She was also a great character, great fun, and totally devoted to film making.

Her boss, Duke, our accountant, was another character. Duke had once been a croupier in a Las Vegas casino, and it was a great sight to see him pay out the crowd as though they were their winnings. I have never seen a crowd paid off so quickly. He explained to me that in the casino, they are given just so much time to pay out and get the next game going. These were the days before computers, and he did all the paperwork, all the cashier work, supported by just Blue. My main job was to see that we were travelling along on sound financial rails and I could never fault him. He was always up-to-date, and able to reflect exactly what was happening in monetary terms.

When computers came in, the idea was that they would cut down the number of people you would have in the production accounts' office. Exactly the opposite has happened, and the accountant's department has grown. Of course they are a great help, but it is not total progress. For example, if I want to know how much we have spent on sets to-date, the computer can quickly tell you – if it is not busy doing something else. In the old days, all you had to do was to look it up in a ledger … which was *never* too busy.

I find that computers tend to put out too much information. Sheets and sheets of paper arrive on your desk, covered in numbers, and tucked in there somewhere is what you want to know. Fine for an accountant, but for a busy producer, or production manager, all he wants is a quick answer to a simple question.

Of course the studio, the Head Office, loves all this information flowing back from their numerous productions, never being out of touch, creating the opportunity for more people to be taken on to cope with all this information. All this then can be transcribed onto a different format and distributed to the other executives. More people mean a bigger department, which means more power. More power means gaining more and more control till eventually you are running the place. This is what so many people say has happened to Hollywood today.

Duke was from a different era. It is sad that the individual accountant, the one that could smell trouble as he entered the figures, has been taken over by the system. Ron Allday always said he could feel trouble in his pen. Computers don't have that sensitivity

Apart from Duke and Blue, we had a wonderful cameraman, Bob Jessup, on the Second Unit and, if any credit is due for our work, it all belongs to him. I just would shout, "Action" and "Fuck that monkey!"

But, apart from these guys, I was not very impressed with the American crew. Which is odd for, on the whole, I have always found them very professional, even if they did have some strange ways … well, to a Limey, that is.

I liked the production secretary who was a rebel, and married to a black Trades' Union leader. This sorted her out from her fellow crew members, especially being in Florida where so many were from the South. I remember how she laughed for days when I sang her my favourite version of the Red Flag:

The Working Class
Can kiss my arse:
I've got the Steward's job at last!

Talking of the South, you did have to be careful. The Rednecks did not like us and several of our boys got threatened.

Then there was the Law.

A policeman came down to check the security in the accounts' office and was horrified when he found out that we didn't have a gun. He insisted we have one, and then said, "I want to tell you all that if you catch a mother here, make sure that, when you shoot, you empty the chamber into him. We don't want no wounded!"

One day, the main producer was driving down to the South. He had heard how the "one-light" towns lived off traffic fines. So, when driving through, he kept strictly under the limit.

When driving through one little place, as he came out of the speed zone, he started to accelerate when he heard the police siren. A speed cop pulled him over, made him get out of the car, and told him he was going to give him a ticket for speeding. The producer exclaimed, "But I was driving way under the speed."

Before he could say any more, he was over the bonnet with a gun at his head. "Are you saying I'm lying, son?" the policeman asked. He was carted off to the local judge, fined, and sent on his way. Welcome to the South!

The producers were two strange guys, the main one seemed to have a little experience, which was more than his buddy had, but he had put some money into the film. The principal guy was totally under the domination of his wife, a scary Jewish lady, whose scarlet painted talons seemed to get longer every day and which I thought might attack at any second. There was the usual once-a-day panic about something or another and we needed to meet. Our producer made it clear that he couldn't come because his wife was waiting for him. And I didn't blame him, she was one tough lady and very much the power behind the throne. She was a successful business woman, and ran a company that sent out presents. In Hollywood presents are big business, as people and companies are always sending them to each other, so she was on to a good thing. I should imagine she was a great sales' person, and one look at those bejewelled hands closing in on you would make you buy anything!

Ineke joined me out there, and we had a cute apartment close to the production office. We seemed to be getting on top of things and I started to enjoy the experience. That's the trouble with movies, you should never relax, as there is always a problem waiting to pounce around the corner. In this case, it was the looming directors' strike.

This was a real dilemma for us, and indeed for the Completion Guarantor, for the film had no big company behind it to take care of any overages. The deal with Columbia was a pick-up deal which meant that they had the film for a set price. Normally, a major company like Columbia would not take a bond, they would take the risk themselves (as in the case of "Casino Royale"). However, "... Pippi ..." was outside their usual pattern of finance, and they did not come in till the end. The money was raised through banks and private investors against the guarantee from Columbia, and backed up by the bond of completion. So, if there was a strike, and if the contingency had either already been spent or already committed, where did the money come from? When, through industrial action, you are forced to a halt, who pays the costs? You can certainly reduce your costs, but there will inevitably be costs.

I thought there was only one place they could go, and that was to the company I represented. I had a meeting with Ken, our genius producers, our production manager, and Duke to decide what to do. We had tried to call Columbia, but nobody there wanted to talk to us. I think they had their own problems to worry about and were not very interested in a crappy kids' film down in Florida on a pick-up deal.

The strike actually only affected Ken. I say "only", because it was his film and, to all intents and purposes, he was not only the director, but the real producer. The other two were too busy wetting their pants to add anything very intelligent. The other members of the DGA were not affected, likewise none of the other Unions were involved. Was there any way we could keep going?

Could we bring in an outside director who could work under Ken's instructions?

At this point Ken said, "If we get to that, then I want to make it clear there is only one person that I will agree to acting as director, and that is John Dark."

I was really surprised, as I was unaware that he held me in such esteem. So, it was agreed that if the worst came to the worst, we would keep shooting, with me standing in for Ken after having been briefed by him.

Worst didn't come to worst, and the threatened strike never took place. Everybody breathed again, and no one more so than Betty Smith.

The remainder of the film went as smoothly as could be expected. Ken kept to the schedule and we just scraped in under the budget. On the whole, I had a really good time.

As I said, I loved Blue who eventually came to visit us in Spain, and is now married to a civilian working for the US military stationed in Hawaii.

I would miss Pauline, though she had become rather grand – or maybe it was my memories of her living in a council flat married to a school teacher, that clouded my judgement. How could she be the same, married to a film director, living in California, with her friends drawn from the top echelons of the film industry? It was amazing that underneath she was the same Pauline, a really sweet girl that I knew arriving at the studio in her crash-helmet on her scooter. I was very happy that her life had turned out so well. We used to chat in Ken's trailer when he was night-shooting, going back over the old days.

I also got to like Ken, though I always think he was suspicious of me. He once said to me, "Pauline tells me you taught her all she knows. I don't know quite what to make of that!"

On that note I will leave "… Pippi Longstocking", only to say that my grandchildren, Rebecca and Tom, found it on television one day, and sat engrossed through it all. I saw about ten minutes, which was quite enough.

Poor Ken. It never did get a theatrical release, and went straight to video and the dreaded box.

Ineke and I left Florida, she to return home and I to LA to visit Barry Spikings to see if he had anything going, but he hadn't. I visited the guarantor's offices and basked in the glory of getting them through what they thought was an impossible situation. I really liked Betty, and, though she was as tough as nails, there was a charm about her. We said good-bye but I was to hear from her sooner than I expected.

Back in Spain, my old friend, Lewis Gilbert called me to say that he was making a film based on the hit play "Shirley Valentine", which he was going to produce and direct, and would I like to join him as executive producer?

You can imagine my excitement at being offered the chance to be back with someone who had been a part of my life for so long, the man who probably saved my career when I was with him in Hong Kong. Of course, I jumped at the chance.

He told me they had to wait until the leading lady was free. At the time, I did not know who that was going to be, and in my pleasure I forgot to ask. He said he would call me as soon as he got some news.

Shortly after this surprise call, I got another. This time from Verity in Melbourne.

After leaving EMI, Verity got her Australian film financed by the Cannon company. It was the strange story of a woman convicted of murdering her infant child, her defence being that a dingo (a wild dog) had snatched it. This was a major movie for her, and I was very excited that she had such a big one for her first feature credit as a producer. She also had a great Australian to direct it, Fred Schepsi, and the star was that superstar, Meryl Streep. So, our Verity was flying high.

She phoned to tell me she had a problem, saying, "John, you have to help me. It's about the completion bond. There is no one here who can sign off the budget and schedule, and I can't get the money released until I have the bond signed."

I queried which company it was and found that it was Betty's. Verity asked if I could fly out. I explained to her about Lewis's film and that, as much as I loved her, I could not take the chance of screwing up on his film. She asked me if I could check straight away and see if it was possible. I have to say that the last place on earth I wanted to return to was Australia, after the miserable time I had there last time, but it was Verity, who was a great chum. And so I called Lewis who said there was no problem as there was still no date set.

Just as I put the phone down to him it rang, and it was Lee Katz asking me whether I would go to Australia to sign off the budget on Verity's movie, and added, "You know that, if you go, we would want you to stay there till the end of shooting as we are more than a little concerned?" As usual they wanted me to leave "yesterday".

I had to get a visa, and Lee told me that Verity's London office had some connections with the Australian embassy, but when I rang them they said that it would take about ten days, so I packed my bag and left for Madrid. At the consulate, a delightful woman said she would speed it through, and I could pick it up in a couple of days. But after pouring my heart out to her, I got it in two *hours*. So, I was off that afternoon on my way to Melbourne.

It was lovely seeing Verity again, and I soon had all the information I needed about the script, the schedule, and the budget. Verity had stressed the urgency of the situation, which was confirmed to me by the Cannon representative, Ronnie Yakov. So my first day in Australia, I read the script, studied the budget, held a meeting with certain department heads, met with the director, and that evening committed the Completion Bond Company of Los Angeles to the movie.

The following day, the money flowed in and the film had the green light and was ready to start.

My work really was now over. I had done my thing. All that was left for me to do was see that the production kept its pledges, watch the rushes to make sure that what was being reflected was actually being shot, watch the schedule, and study the cost statements. It was not the most interesting, but neither was it the most time-consuming. I was lucky that the Production Supervisor was an old friend of mine, Roy Stevens.

He had been David Lean's right hand man for many years, starting as his Assistant director on films like "Lawrence of Arabia" and ending up as one of the producers on "Ryan's Daughter". So, with Roy there, I did not have any day-to-day worries, and I knew he would alert me if he could see any trouble ahead.

When I first arrived, I stayed with Verity in her rented house, which was fun, and, though we used to have almighty rows, I did enjoy her company, and became more and more fond of her, in a totally platonic way. We became almost like an old married couple, and took turns in cooking. One evening in rushes, in the company of the director, the crew and artists, I suddenly remembered something and, as I crept out, whispered in Verity's ear, "I left the curry on the stove!" That just about summed up my role on the film.

And it was a strange role for me who had always been so actively involved. I had very little contact with the cast or the crew. Meryl hardly recognised my presence. The male lead, Sam Neill, was a sullen, private man, and except for his relationship with the Japanese make-up girl, did not socialise. We were on nodding terms with each other, which I respected, as why on earth would he want to waste his time with me?

I also respected Meryl. Until the fiasco with the Australian Prime Minister. His aide enquired through Verity if Meryl would like to join the PM and a small group at dinner one night. Meryl said she would be delighted, so an official invitation was sent, which accepted. On the day of the party, she decided that she did not want to go and, despite Verity's pleas saying it would be seen as an insult, she still refused, and indeed did not go.

It's this kind of behaviour that I find sickening. They get paid a fortune, a small part of it for being an actress but the majority for being a star. Certain things are expected of a star, one of them not being rude to the leader of the country in which they are lucky enough to be working. It was quite unbelievable arrogance, and I thought of people like David Niven and Bill Holden who were always so gracious to people, and would never embarrass themselves or the company they were working for.

This period was enjoyable, but uneventful. Ineke joined me out there and we had a wonderful time. We travelled to Alice Springs, where I was told, "We've got a traffic light in town since you were last here." We then went to Ayers Rock, the spiritual home of the Aborigines.

Before they would let us shoot in this area all members of the company, without exception, had to attend an indoctrination meeting at which a film was shown showing the history of the strange red rock dominating the surrounding flat landscape. A talk was given by an Aboriginal warden, which no one understood a word of. This was followed by a talk by one of the European women who acted as supervisors on the Aboriginal enclave, the gist of which was that if any of us bought alcohol and gave it to an Aboriginal, our permit to shoot would be revoked immediately.

I always used to feel such a heel when these guys approached me to get them some booze. I knew it was bad for them, but I thought it wasn't too good for any of us either, and it did rather smack of racialism.

From Ayers Rock, we went to hot, humid Darwin, before heading back for Melbourne and the studio. At Christmas, the company took a two- week break and, after having a wonderful family party at Verity's house with her father present, Ineke and I took off for a fabulous week on Turtle Island in Fiji – probably the only real holiday alone we had ever had.

It was a dream holiday on an unspoilt, but luxurious, isolated golden island reached only by sea plane. It catered for just eight couples, and no children, and was the ideal place for a restful holiday. As we had never had a honeymoon, we treated this holiday as ours, even if it was about twenty years too late! We revelled in the tranquilly of the remote beaches, the warm sea with its abundance of tropical fish, the Fijian people, the great food, the snorkelling, and the water sports. It was delightful living in a typical Fijian hut, but with up-to-date modern fittings. We were sad to leave.

Back in Melbourne, we soon had the wrap party, and it was time to fly home. I really enjoyed Australia, and the Australians. What had happened in the years since I was last there? The country had changed its immigration laws and instead of immigration being restricted to Brits, it was now much more open. I personally think that made the country so much more alive and vibrant.

The other factor was that this time I was with people that I knew, liked, and respected, rather than the clown I was with the last time.

The picture wrapped on time and on budget so there were no claims on the bond company. The film was well received on the whole, and I thought that nice man, Fred Schepisi, did a really good job, and Meryl Streep gave an astonishing portrayal of an Australian woman. I don't think it did great business but then Ms. Streep's films rarely did. I also think Verity came out of it with great credit, as she found the subject, the cast, and the money, all the things a producer has to do. She had got it made.

It is a marvellous country, and a fantastic place for young people to make their lives: "Go South, young man, and young woman."

Back to our lovely home, to find there had been a large fire whilst we had been away, and we lost a lot of our garden. Luckily there was no damage to the house, but we were left with a garden of a lot of burnt stumps. However, with a lot of money, lots of replanting, and a lot of water, it did not take long for it to recover.

In the meantime, my connection with Australia continued. I was approached by an Aussie, James Todesco, who had lived in Spain for a long time, and who spoke and wrote fluent Spanish. At one time, he had been in partnership with the actor, Stewart Granger, in a real estate business. He showed me some land he owned not far away from where I lived, and suggested that we build a film studio there.

Now, two things I had learnt about Southern Spain were that someone always wanted to hold a film festival there, and someone always wanted to build a film studio.

I told James that I thought he was out of his mind, and explained that film makers came to Southern Spain for the location, not because there was a studio there. If they want to shoot an interior, they find a warehouse in which to put the set. In addition, the Costa del Sol had no real technicians and, although there were a few commercials' companies, they brought in their crews from far and wide. I told him that it takes more than four walls and roof to create a studio. Madrid or Barcelona would make sense, as there was a pool of film workers, actors, and musicians. I told him to forget it, but he insisted on taking me to some other land, an enormous tract of pine forest.

"You own this?" I asked with surprise.

And he said, "No, but the Town Hall of Coin will rent this to me for a peppercorn rent."

"So, what are you going to use it for?"

The only reply I got was, "I have no idea, but it's a bargain."

"A bargain is only a bargain if you want it," I caustically replied.

So, that was the first of my many meetings with James Todesco.

CHAPTER 17
AS GOOD AS IT GETS

A call came from Lewis: "Amber light".

This meant that the film had been approved but no money had been allocated so far. I caught the next flight.

There was nothing to stop me as I had nothing to do in Spain, other than convincing James not to build a studio!

I had already completed my deal with Paramount, not the greatest deal in the world, but okay. The best thing about it was that I insisted on a living allowance all the time I was away from Southern Spain, they also agreed to pay all my return air fares, and Ineke's. She would join me after a couple of days.

So, there I was, knocking on the front door of Lewis's Kensington house, being greeted by my old mentor, friend and boss from long ago.

After a hasty but warm hello from Hylda, we were off to the office.

Being Lewis, and as the money had not yet come through, this was the tea shack in Holland Park. It was a rather basic, dreary, wooden construction, serving the usual British snack food of bad tea, undrinkable coffee, sticky buns, and sandwiches made of white bread and razor thin slices of ham or cheese. It was typical of Lewis that we were setting up a major American movie huddled over a bare table, surrounded by mums with their babies, nannies from the wealthy homes around Holland Park, a generous mixture of office workers, teenagers, road workers, and senior citizens – in short, a motley crew. None of them perturbed Lewis, as he discussed the film and asked my reaction to the script.

I told him that I was over the moon about it.

It was written by Willy Russell, who had previously written a film for Lewis, "Educating Rita", based on his own stage play, starring Michael Caine and introducing Julie Walters.

We then discussed the budget, which I had already studied. Lewis told me that Paramount in LA said it could not be done for that figure, that it was way under-budgeted.

"Lewis," I said, "if you're happy with the schedule, then I am happy with the budget."

For the most part, it was a very straightforward location and studio film and, after the special effects' pictures that I was used to, it looked a doddle, with locations in London and Liverpool and a few weeks location shooting on a Greek Island. I could not see what Paramount were worrying about.

He then went on to explain the position with the cast. The leading actress, Pauline Collins, had been agreed. She was an actress well known to me but no way a household name. She had starred in both the West End and Broadway versions of the play. Paramount initially had wanted Cher, but Lewis persuaded them to come to London and see for themselves. They arrived one day, saw the show, and left the next, agreeing that Pauline Collins should have the part.

Pauline was what is known as a jobbing actress, going from the stage to television to the theatre. She had starred in several television shows, notably as the maid in "Upstairs, Downstairs". She was one of those people whom everybody in England knew, but most did not know her name. She was known for her cheekiness, her sense of humour, and was one of those people you want to pick up and hug. Her performance in the one-woman stage show "Shirley Valentine" brought her numerous awards. Alone on the stage for two hours, she held the audience in the palm of her hand, whether cooking the evening meal ("I like a glass of wine when I'm cooking the evening meal") or sitting on the beach in Greece talking to a rock. Alone up there on the stage, she transported the audience into Shirley Valentine's world.

Pauline was the only one cast so far, so, with Lewis's agreement, I engaged an old colleague who I had used on my EMI films, the casting director, Allan Foenander, and gradually the parts started to be filled.

One was Shirley Valentine's friend. For which we employed Alison Steadman, that wonderful actress who starred in one of British television's most successful plays, "Abigail's Party", directed by her then husband Mike Leigh. Also there were great artists like Julia McKenzie, Joanna Lumley, Bernard Hill and (from our days on "Ferry to Hong Kong") Sylvia Syms. We were assembling a very strong cast, though we all recognised that we had no "star" to pull in the punters. The film itself would have to do that.

The one part un-cast was the role of the Greek fisherman, Shirley Valentine's lover. The hot favourite for the part was Tom Conti, but he was nervous about accepting, so to persuade him Lewis and I flew to Zagreb in Yugoslavia where he was filming. Well, he did not take much persuading, and after a short talk he accepted. We flew back knowing that there was nothing to stop us.

I say that, but the truth is you never know, as so many films collapse at the last hurdle, even after they have started shooting. But we had every reason to be confident as we were making the film for an American major, we would not be chasing around various financing houses, distributors, or having to place a completion bond. Just one company would finance and distribute, and this company was not only American, but it was Paramount, with which both Lewis and I had so many close contacts.

True, the company had changed enormously. Sadly, Bud had died. Bobby Evans had gone into independent producing, but got himself in trouble with his first film, "The Cotton Club", and developed a taste for drugs. More importantly, Charlie Bludhorn had died, and much to my surprise Martin Davis had taken over as President of the company. "Well," I thought, "*that* ain't going to do me any good", remembering our last meeting.

Head of the Studio now was Frank Mancuso, but the executive in charge of our production was a charming man, Gary Luchasi. Now, I don't think he knew an awful lot, but he was one hell of a nice guy, and he made all our discussions, meetings, even disagreements, very pleasant.

The London office had dwindled to just a few offices in the United International Pictures building in a depressing part of that city. UIP was the distribution arm of both Paramount and Universal. In charge of the office was a young man, Michael O'Sullivan, who had been with the company some time but had joined after I had left. He also was a very pleasant person, and we were able to settle everything very quickly so we could be funded.

There is nothing like the time that you get the first money. As Bud often said, "Talk is cheap, but whisky costs money."

I got hold of Ron Fry who had been my English production manager on "Slayground". I thought he needed a nice one after that! He brought with him his Co-ordinator, an efficient lady but not one of the world's nicest people. Next I wanted Lewis to meet another of my old group, my cameraman, Alan Hume.

Alan had lit every special effects' film I had produced, and, though this was another cup of tea, I knew that with his speed and expertise he would fit in well with Lewis. We then added our dear old friend John Stoll as the production designer. Lewis brought with him his Assistant, Michel Cheyko, a bilingual Frenchman, always known as Mishka, whom I found not only a quite excellent A.D., but also a very charming man. Lewis also wanted his costume designer whom I did not know but who had done several films with Lewis, and I had no reason to doubt her competence.

One day I bumped into Billy Willmot, who had left Michael Caine not because he didn't like him, he just could not take the hours any longer. I signed him up immediately. He was the best driver in the business, always reliable, always pleasant, and always looked after whoever he was driving. Soon his first job was to drive Lewis and myself to the airport to catch a flight to Athens to start our recce in Greece.

There we met up with our Greek production manager, Dimitri Dimitriadis, who had been recommended to me and whom I had engaged over the phone. He was a delightful man with a string of credits to his name, and we soon felt at ease with him. It is funny but after a short talk with anyone in the business you soon know whether they know what they are talking about. We also engaged a young, bilingual assistant director, Panos Thomaidis, who was not very experienced, but extremely enthusiastic and spoke excellent English (unlike Dimitri whose English was voluble but not always intelligible).

I was happy to leave Athens, a polluted, noisy, unpleasant city. The four of us flew to Rhodes, but that was not right, so we went on to Crete, which was no good either. So we visited several of the smaller islands by boat until we came to Mykonos.

There it was, as though the art department had laid it all out: the taberna, the beach, the hotel, all together just as in Willy's script.

Mykonos was a strange place, its only existence, apart from a little fishing, was tourism. Originally a gay holiday resort, in recent years it had attracted the straights as well, but its main attraction was still sex. There was one beach where the authorities let people sleep at night, but you had to get there early to find a spot. Known as the Mykonos Hilton, it was one writhing mass of humanity late at night. I understand that it has become a more up-market holiday resort, but I am sure its main attraction is still the basic one.

In those days, 1988, there was only one five-star hotel on the island. It was a strange place, with the main body of the hotel on the top of a hill which housed the restaurant, bar, swimming pool and the hotel offices, then lower down the hill were not unattractive individual bungalows. The trouble with the hotel was that, though perfectly situated, with a great view looking down across the island to the sea, it was run by amateurs.

On checking in late on the first night, there were no sheets on my bed, and we could not find any one to deal with this. When we did eventually find someone, he did not have the key to the linen room. In the end, at my suggestion, he took the sheets from an unoccupied room. Breakfast was a disaster so we gave that up and used to eat in the village. It was such a shame as, sitting on the balcony of the bungalow looking out to the setting sun, it was a truly idyllic spot. When I got to know some of the government people in Athens at a later date, I told the Minister for Tourism, who promised to look into it. Whether he did or not, I don't know, as it did not improve whilst we were there.

In fact, Ineke used to organise Lewis's breakfast. I didn't care about it, but as Hylda said to me before we left, "I hope you remember, John, what a monster he can be if he doesn't get fed!"

I was in contact with the government as I was determined to get them to pay for our transport costs to and from Greece. I pointed out to them the huge impact a feature film can have on tourism. It has much more effect than any advertising campaign, and does not cost a penny. It is very like the benefit of editorial mention in the press against display advertising. I was able to convince them of the desirability of such a film, and they did indeed pay for all our passenger and cargo costs, which made huge savings on the budget.

Once back in London, Lewis and I left for Liverpool to visit Willy Russell, and look for locations. He had booked us into the Adelphi Hotel, Liverpool's leading hotel.

If this is their leading hotel, I thought, God knows what the worst must be like. It was incredible as it was dirty, and it smelt, and really I hated getting into the bed, and certainly I kept my socks on when walking on the carpet. There was only one word for the place, and that was seedy. The food was also unbelievably bad. On the first day, our first mistake was having lunch in the hotel. We had grilled herrings, and I thought, they can't fuck those up. Wrong! They came served with a red paste over them, and the heads were still clinging to the body of the fish. I say "clinging" because they had not been grilled, but crucified! It was the worst meal I have ever had outside of Broken Hill, Australia.

Actually, Willy did take us to a restaurant which was not too bad.

Willy himself was a strange man. After reading his script and watching "Educating Rita", I really admired his talent and I expected to find a fun person, witty and entertaining. Instead I found him morose and, if anything, dull!

In spite of all the money he had earned, Willy still lived in a grotty house in one of the poorer areas of the city. His children went to the local school, and from what little I saw of them, they reflected this place of learning. However, he always stayed at the Athenaeum Hotel when he came to London, and I could never understand this sort of double life that he led. I was to find out more as I got to know him better.

This is not to say I didn't like him, because I did. Though why, I am not quite sure.

Back from Liverpool, we were a few weeks off starting to shoot in Greece before returning to Twickenham for interiors and the English locations. We had practically cut out going to Liverpool as anything we wanted there, we could find in the Greater London area. We appeared to be well organised when the dreaded Co-ordinator went sick.

We just got over that shock when Ron Fry, the production manager, had a heart attack. So, there I was, about to take off for Greece, and no production office.

I rang up an old friend of mine, Roy Stevens, the PM on the Meryl Streep film, and asked him if he knew of anyone good, and available immediately. Thank God he said he would do it himself. As his co-ordinator was not free, I called in another old friend, Lorraine Fennell, very experienced and, unlike the other one, a darling girl.

We were back under control, though poor Roy had a lot to assimilate in a short time. I had decided from day one not to take the English PM to Greece, as I had a perfectly good one there, but I would take the co-ordinator to keep all our records straight. This gave Roy a chance to catch up.

Neither was I taking the designer as for what we had to do in Greece it was not worth it, and anyhow he had all the sets to build whilst we were away.

We had a few interiors to shoot in Mykonos, so we decided to take the artists in these scenes with us, so that if we hit any bad weather we had good stand-bys. The cost of paying them and keeping them there was good insurance. For, in my opinion, if you keep on schedule, you will roughly keep on budget. As it was, we had perfect weather the whole time, and we did not shoot the interiors until the very end. But I am not a prophet and I didn't have a Malayan "Bomoh" on hand.

So, the company left by Olympic Airline (the Greek National Carrier) for Athens, then transferred to a small two-engine aircraft to Mykonos. This is always a nightmare because so many things can go wrong, especially as Olympic was giving all this for free. Now, this is where you need a top co-ordinator, for they have to plan how they are going to get sixty people who have travelled in a large capacity aeroplane onto a plane whose total capacity is nowhere as big. But it all went well and very soon the crew were in their hotels, unpacking the equipment to be ready for shooting the next day.

Pauline was flying in a day later, accompanied I might say, by Ineke!

Tom Conti arrived about a week later when we were well in our stride. He, Pauline, and I met for a drink.

Now, I had already had trouble with his agent, who had insisted that he have a trailer. As there were no such things on the island, and I wasn't about to import one on our budget, I told the agent that we would supply a hotel room near where we were shooting. I had had a further cable from the agent saying that he had been told that there *were* trailers on the island, and I replied saying if he could find one I would not only rent it but I would *buy* it.

So, when Tom said, "I presume I will have a car and driver on twenty- four hour stand-by", I just kept quiet!

Two days later, I saw Tom in his self-drive jeep, giving a lift to the Greek construction crew. "Oh," I thought, "he's got the message."

What a lovely man he was. He had been used to the big American films with all their facilities, but as soon as he saw how we operated he joined in, and was just one of the company.

So many times actors have been taken for a ride and find themselves treated like second class citizens, whilst the producers and director swan around in luxurious style. Consequently they demand this and that, but if they see that everyone is being treated equally, then they are happy to join in. Well, perhaps not all of them are like that, but the majority are, especially the British. In Hollywood even the stunt men have to have their own trailers on location according to Union agreements. Major stars, of course, have almost run out of ideas of what they can demand: double-size trailers, flush loos, cars with drivers, chefs, trainers, personal make-up artist, hairdresser, secretary, quite apart from the normal stand-ins and stunt doubles.

Once at Shepperton, I remember that Elizabeth Taylor used to bring her butler to the studio; and when her driver lost his licence for some reason, he in turn was chauffeured down to the studio each day.

The trouble is they all have their own people and so, in making a deal, it is impossible to negotiate, as the retinue can ask for whatever. The star has insisted they are hired, they know that, so you are buggered before you start.

We had none of these problems on our film and shooting went like a dream. I had almost forgotten what an easy director Lewis was. He always did his homework, arrived on the floor knowing exactly what he wanted, knew each set-up and exactly where he wanted the camera. He had an easy relationship with his actors and left them room to work, only guiding them if he thought it was necessary. He rarely needed more than a few takes, and did not use video assist. (This is a video camera, attached to the top of the film camera, which shoots in unison so that the director can see immediately what he has got on the screen. It is like seeing immediate rushes.) Lewis's objection to this system is that it is not only the director who gets to see it, but all the actors crowd around to watch, and start to change their performance based on what they have just seen. Not having the experience or talent to relate the performance to the whole sequence, it is human nature that they only look at their own performance. Lewis always shot the day's work, never worked late, was economical with the film stock, had an easy atmosphere on the set, and never shouted or screamed or blasphemed. Altogether, a dream.

Pauline and Tom both were giving great performances, and the British and Greek crews worked well together. There were two disasters.

There was a minor one on the Greek side, as the Greek art director really wasn't an art director at all, but a set dresser. Unfortunately he had no taste, and we had to change some of his more bizarre prop dressings.

The major one was on the English side. Lewis's costume designer, firstly, wasn't a designer, she wasn't even a good dresser. In fact, was just hopeless.

I spoke to Lewis about it, but he wouldn't have it. "She's good, ask Bill Cartwright." (Bill was with Lewis on "Educating Rita") Who, when asked, told me she was even worse than what I thought. It is a rare man who has no faults and if Lewis has one, God bless him, it is that he picks up people he likes, or more likely who Hylda likes. I suppose you could include me in this collection! Anyway we were saddled with her, and somehow we got through. As I said, it was not a difficult film, and the costumes were very simple.

When we got back to the studio, though, we shot a scene there that whenever we ran the film I always closed my eyes, I could not bear to watch it. It was the scene when Shirley Valentine's neighbour, played by Julia McKenzie, brings her a present to take on holiday to Greece. It is supposed to be a very sexy, diaphanous, see-through garment, something like you would buy from Anne Summers. Our genius designer supplied a floral flannelette beribboned night-dress, the kind of thing you would buy from the Co-op! What is worse is that Lewis accepted it!

Willy paid us a visit accompanied by his wife and his agent. Willy had the bungalow next to ours. The following day after his arrival, Ineke wanted to go into town. So I suggested to her that she ask Willy if he could give her a lift, which he kindly did. I was to find out later how careful in life one has to be. Willy only stayed a few days, but it was good to see him again and get to know him better. It was a great location, though the crew didn't earn the kind of money they usually got on a foreign location. Lewis was not a believer in shooting long hours, and anyhow there was only one week of night-shooting. This was the week the crew picked up some real money. It was also when our poor little make-up girl went sick, and missed the gravy week.

Going through the accounts, I saw her time-sheet where she had put down "sick" for that week, and a memory came back to me. On the film in Italy where I was the junior on the sound crew, I had gone to Rome for the weekend to pick up Peggy. When I came back, I asked the PM, what I should do with my time sheet, and he said, "Book the same as the rest of the crew." I had never forgotten what that meant to me, so I sent her time-sheet back with the same instructions. The next time I saw her she was almost in tears and she hugged me around the neck. It also went around the crew like wild-fire, and it once again proved that a small gesture repays you many times over.

One of the cameo performers was Cardew Robinson. Now, Cardew was an amazing person, for he was one of the worst comics ever with his schoolboy act known as Cardew the Cad, yet he was also one of the best known, for he was in a weekly comic publication called "Film Fun" for years. Everybody seemed to know him, and he earned his meagre living giving after-dinner speeches at events like tennis or cricket clubs. He was lucky to have been in the Air Force with Lewis, who always tried to find a small part for him in his films. In "Shirley Valentine" he had the ideal two-liner as an English tourist who hates the Greek food and just wants chips and egg!

Tom Conti turned out to be a smashing bloke, but he did throw one wobbly. He did not like the girl we had cast in England to sit with him at the bar while he flirted with her. We explained that she had no lines and we would only see her back, but, no, he was adamant. He wanted Dimitiri's wife(!). So I had to tell the poor girl that we were sending her back home without being used. I assured her that she would still be paid, and her agent told her that the director always had the final choice and can change his mind if he so wants. I promised both her and her agent I would try and find another part for her when we returned to London.

That part came up soon after we got back, and it was a much better part, paid more, she even had a little dialogue and her face would be seen, on top of that the scene she was in got one of the biggest laughs. She was so excited and told me, "I never believed for a second you would give me anything else." I was just happy for her that we did have something that suited her.

Soon it was our time to leave Greece, and surprisingly the planes from Olympic arrived on time and we were back in London. John Stoll and Roy Stevens had things well under control, so that we were able to start shooting the day after we arrived.

The additions to the cast were great: Joanna Lumley (playing a high-class hooker) was a darling; Julia McKenzie and Bernie Hill professionals to their fingertips. The girl who played the young Shirley Valentine, Gillian Kearney, went on to bigger things when she was an adult, including her acclaimed performance in "The Forsyte Saga". We finished photography, and under the fine editing of Leslie Walker, we were able to start dubbing very soon after.

Willy wrote the background music but Paramount would not agree to him writing the title song, which eventually won the film its only Oscar. One of my few disputes with Lewis was over the title designs. He got another of his cronies to sketch them, and I thought they were quite terrible. But he was the boss and anyhow they did not damage the film one jot. The film was an amazing success.

Lewis was away, so I ran the film for Frank Mancuso and his wife. When the lights went up it was obvious that Mrs Mancuso was crying and her mascara had run. Frank said, "That's some film!"

And that it was.

It won so many awards in Britain, including the best Comedy Film award, when Lewis and I got to stand on the stage of the London Palladium. It also won the "Evening Standard" Award for Best Actress, Best Script and Best Film. In Willy's acceptance speech, he remarked on the public's view of writers and continued, "Mrs Dark thought I was a driver!" That teaches you something – never ask a writer for a lift!

I learnt another lesson at the BAFTA awards, where Pauline won Best Actress, and Lewis won the Lifetime Achievement Award. Paramount's Gary Luchasi and the new President of the company, Martin Davis, flew over. I had no idea how Marty was going to react at seeing me, for the last time we had been together we had had a big row. Well, I need not have worried, for he greeted me like his long-lost son, and we sat next to each other during the whole ceremony, and as anyone who has ever attended one of these events knows, that is a very long time.

Later that, month I received a letter from him:

Dear John

It was great to see you again.

I just want to remind you of our joint commitment of getting together next time you are floating around New York, and I, of course, will do the same in London.

Looking forward to reviving old memories and with every good wish

Warm regards

Marty

President and Chief Executive

The lesson I learnt: don't take too much notice of fights and disagreements in the movie business, it is all part of the job.

I also realised what an idiot I had been. As soon as Marty became President I should have gone to see him in New York. For I realise now that when he said he would like to be like me, it was sincerely meant. I am sure he would have given me a deal at Paramount, but there again I am not very good at asking people for things. I never want to put them into the embarrassing position of saying, "No."

It was a great night. They played clips from many of Lewis's films, including a scene when he was a boy actor with Laurence Olivier. He was presented with his award by Princess Anne, and made a charming speech. I was so happy to be with him on this special night.

There were many more special nights throughout the amazing success of the film, including a wonderful London premiere.

Walking into Leicester Square for the press show, I saw the neon sign outside the Empire, "Tonight, the Royal Premiere of 'Shirley Valentine' in front of the Princess of Wales". After the rave reviews, this was the crowning moment. I was lucky to be involved in this piece of magic.

I will always remember that night for seeing the Princess of Wales up-close for the first time. What a woman! She had the most amazing presence, was so beautiful, wearing a brilliant green dress that looked as though it had been sprayed on. One could see that her body was as ravishing as her face was beautiful. When I was introduced to her, I realised that she was one of those people that have the ability to make you think they are really only interested in you. She was regal, yet she still exuded sex – sex with style, sex with glamour … Royal sex. What could be more of a turn-on? Oh, what a woman!

After the amazing reception, there was a great party with many old friends there, including my old mate, Mel Smith, and even Willy was on good form. It was nice too meeting Pauline's husband, John Alderton, again whom I knew slightly from drinking together in Gerry's. The great thing, though, was that Susie, my daughter, met her future husband, Kevin Lane, that night.

He had been our second assistant in the cutting-rooms, and somehow or other Leslie Walker, our great editor, found herself with a spare ticket, so she invited young Lane. They met that night and are still together as I write. They have a lovely house in Fulham and, best of all, Grace and George.

At the end of the evening, as we had given up the flat in Twickenham, Paramount gave us a suite at the Grosvenor House Hotel in Park Lane, which was better than the YMCA, and so big that both Dan and Sue spent the night there with us. I think this was the last night that the four of us were alone together.

A few days later, Lewis and I left for Los Angeles, and the opening of the film there. Frank Mancuso had been so impressed that he had allocated a massive sum to launch a gigantic publicity campaign. We woke up in New York and were staggered that there was three whole pages of display advertising in the New York papers. After all, this wasn't "Ben Hur", just a small British film – a very good one, but we couldn't help thinking that it had been blown out of all proportion.

Sadly we would be proved right, as the film did little business in the States, and certainly did not recoup the vast amount of money spent on the campaign. This was despite Lewis and myself doing a major tour across the States and Canada. Had Pauline won the American Academy Award for which she had been nominated, it might have helped, but she lost out to Jessica Tandy for her part in "Driving Miss Daisy". (In which, incidentally, I thought she was miscast.) I think it was what is known as the sympathy vote.

The really sad thing about it was that if the picture had not been released in America, it would have made money. As it was, none of us would see a nickel. Not that that worried me, as Paramount had given me a nice bonus, and I had an amazing trip around America and Canada.

We went as far up as Montreal, where we opened the Montreal Film Festival, but where I am afraid Paramount dropped a big clanger by not putting French sub-tittles on the copy shown. Few people could have had such a trip, with five-star hotels, first class travel, limos waiting at the airports to whisk us into town, the best restaurants, and the attention of the Paramount local publicity staff to pander to our every whim.

Back to London, and back to reality.

I had one of my many get-togethers with Verity Lambert, and discussed, amongst many things, the idea of making a television series in the South of Spain.

My idea was to make an English language series based around Puerto Banus and Marbella. We would show the large yachts, the elegant houses, the swinging night clubs, the glamorous brothels, the gourmet restaurants, and the five-star hotels with their sun soaked beach clubs, and amazing golf clubs. There would be people from all over the world, all intent on having a wonderful time. There would be the crooks, the dope smugglers, the slave-traders bringing in refugees from Morocco, the criminals hiding from the law in their own countries, the Mafia, Italian and Russian, the sex-traders bringing in girls from the East, the international jet set, the golden beaches with the bikini-clad girls, the second-rate entertainers not able to find work elsewhere, the luxury yachts, the night clubs, discos, all-night bars all swinging till the early morning. We would also show the Spanish people tolerating this tidal wave of humanity engulfing their country, tolerating it for the money, but secretly hating most of it. The scripts would vary, one week an adventure story of smuggling on the high seas, another week a romance, a comedy, and sad stories. There are a thousand stories – all set against the richness and culture of Spain, with its flamenco, bull fighting, great-looking men and pretty, sultry Spanish girls.

Verity never seemed all that enthusiastic about it, so when she rang on my return to Spain, I was surprised to be told that the BBC was looking for a new programme. Should she put up the Spanish idea to them? It transpired that Terry Wogan wanted to give up his programme and they needed something to fill in the space. I replied, "Why not?" And promptly forgot all about it.

At that time Gregory's drinking problem had become really serious, and he was no doubt an alcoholic. His brother, Daniel, almost frog-marched him into a rehabilitation residential complex, a sort of Betty Ford clinic in the South of England. Gregory's relationship with a lovely girl he was dating broke down because of his drinking, but I had hoped that the clinic would cure him and he could get together again with her.

The other members of the family were doing okay, though.

Vicki had got married to a brave man who took on not just a wife but two kids as well. She went to live in the North, practically almost in Scotland, and it seemed almost as far away as South Africa.

Daniel continued in special effects, working on big films like the "Bond"s and "Alien"s.

Susie had moved as a secretary from London Weekend and joined Sky as a production assistant, working on a nightly chat-show. Lewis very sweetly went on it to give her a bit of a boost.

I hadn't been long in Spain when Lewis suggested I go to the South of France where he has an apartment, and read a script that he thought would make a good follow-up to "Shirley Valentine".

Well, it is always nice to go to France and, despite their reputation, I have always got on well with the French. I like looking at their women and eating their food. We knew the hotel we liked in the middle of Cannes as we had stayed there on several occasions. It was unlike the Carlton, and even less like the Hotel du Cap, but about a quarter of the price and was a small but comfortable place. In Cannes, Lewis gave me the stage script of "Stepping Out", the story about a collection of no-hopers who join a tap- dancing class.

I told Lewis that I thought the storyline was too thin for a movie, but over dinner he and Hylda worked me over until I conceded that it was worth having a film script written. At this point I was told that the property was owned by the Stage producer, Bill Kenwright, and that there was a script in existence which he also owned. Back in London, we had a meeting with Bill who said, "Well, I have never been able to set it up, so I'm happy for you to have a go."

We then met Richard Harris, the writer of the original stage show and also of the movie script. It was agreed that he would make the changes that Lewis wanted.

Riding on the success of "Shirley Valentine", Paramount gave a nervous nod for it to go into development. Discussions then took place regarding the lead. Lewis wanted Liza Minnelli, which I thought was a great idea, but Paramount were, let us say, a little apprehensive. The trouble was that Liza had been in so many bad films. However, Lewis talked them into it, and we sent her the script and arranged to meet her in New York.

And meeting her was a great thrill. I had been a great fan of her mother, and of her too ever since "Cabaret". In person she was a normal, feet-on-the-ground type of person, very unlike the character she so often played, and also the reputation that she had. She loved the script and seemed delighted to be approached to play the part of the dance instructor. If anything, she seemed humble, and prefaced her observations with phrases like, "Well, *if* I was to be offered etc. etc."

When Lewis did offer her the part, she seemed genuinely thrilled. Later she told me that when she left our hotel suite, she danced down the corridor saying out loud, "I've got a job!"

Lewis returned to London, and I left for LA to discuss details with Paramount.

I don't know why people don't like this city, because I love it. I know it's a bit garish but that is one of the things I like about it. I love the weather, the shops, the restaurants, Beverly Hills with its large mansions, its hotel that carries its name and contains the Polo Lounge. Rodeo Drive, Santa Monica with its long-legged beautiful girls swaying side to side on their roller blades. There is valet-parking, frozen yoghurt, cinemas without commercials, and turning right on a red. And the service! America is the only country I have been where you get great service without servility.

You know that you are in the Mecca of the film industry, where everybody seems to be in the business, where every pump attendant has a script in his pocket, and every waiter is a resting actor. Nobody is what he seems, though more likely, everybody is actually *exactly* what they seem to be. They live in a fantasy world, but then the whole place is built on a fantasy.

I always remember explaining all this to Ineke when I first took her there. The studio limo picked us up at the airport, and on the way the driver leant back and said, "I'm not really a driver, just helping a buddy. I'm a writer."

We exchanged looks: "Welcome to Hollywood!"

I also love the way they talk. I know Europeans get fed up with "Have a nice day", but I think that is vastly preferable to the grunt of the English, and they have such a descriptive way of talking.

I was trying to buy a pair of jeans one day, and here I have to confess to a physical problem: I have no backside, no "ass", and after trying God knows how many pairs, I gave up. Next day, I was in my favourite coffee bar in Westwood village, drinking my low-fat cappuccino and listening to the chatter in the crowded café. I heard someone shouting and I looked up. It was the girl from the jeans' shop, "Hi, there, you." I looked around to see who she was waving at. "You! You, pancake-butt!"

It was good to be back, and I happily checked into the Westwood Marquee, much favoured by film folk, collected my rented car, and went off to the studio. There I met Gary Luchasi, the lawyers, the accountants, and the business affairs guys.

That is another thing about working for a major, they do a whole lot of the work for you. Contracts for artists, producers, and directors are handled by business affairs, the budget by the accounts' department; the music department clears the copyrights, the production department does a preliminary schedule and cross-plot, and so on. All these things you normally do yourself.

The vice president of production management was Bob Reyea, whom I had not seen since I was a Paramount executive, and he was a production manager for Steve McQueen's company. We had not got on when we met in Berlin, but now he was very pleasant, and very helpful.

Paramount thought to shoot the film in Canada where costs were much lower, and this made sense to me. The story originally had been set in England but, to be more attractive to US audiences, it was decided to set it in Buffalo, just across the border to Toronto. So before we could move any further I made contact with the Toronto Film Commission.

Now, Canada did not become a major centre for making American movies just because the costs were lower. It was the main reason, but not the only one. The assistance and co-operation you get there was another factor. You sent them the script, and they in turn sent out one of their location managers to take stills of various sites, so that by the time the producer or director arrived, they could quickly show you a selection. They helped in many other ways, like booking hotels at very special discounted rates, taking you to the various studios, getting roads closed, obtaining shooting permits, and liaising with the police. One way and another, they are of a tremendous help. And they were certainly like that with me.

They met me at the airport, and held my hand until I was sure we would have no trouble shooting the film there. I quickly found a two-and-a- half stage studio, built in one covered building which housed everything, including offices, dressing-rooms, cutting rooms and so on. With the amount of rehearsal needed I thought it was ideal, as the artists would never have to go outside into a different temperature, and the half-stage would make a great rehearsal room. In actual fact, we only really needed one stage, but it was better to take the whole place so we were completely private, and we would be able to control who came and went. Which was a consideration with an artist of Liza's fame.

Before leaving the UK, we had to decide what crew we should bring from England, and the fewer the better as far as the budget was concerned, although it was important that we had a few principals who were known to us as after all we were going into unknown territory. Actually with hindsight, because of the

433

experienced people there, we could have taken less. Obviously the production manager would have to be Canadian, but the designer, cameraman, assistant director, and the choreographer should come from the UK – as well as ... wait for it ... the costume designer.

On Paramount's recommendation I took on board a Canadian production manager, a woman, who seemed pleasant enough, and highly experienced at making American movies in Canada.

Our biggest problem crew-wise at this stage was the production designer. Lewis and I had lunch with John Stoll in London before we left, but the poor chap was not well, and had trouble walking, relying heavily on a walking stick. It was with great sadness that Lewis and I realised that he was not up to it. It would have been difficult for him in a studio in London, but across the other side of the world, with new people, new places, we did not think that we could take the risk. Poor John, he died whilst we were shooting. So we engaged Peter Mullins, who always worked with Blake Edwards on the "Pink Panther" films, whom I knew but had never worked with.

We had agreed that Alan Hume would be the cameraman. This left the choreographer, and I naturally immediately thought of my old friend Gillian Lynne, but sadly she was already committed to a show and could not accept. So we decided to wait and see who we could get in either Canada or the States.

Luckily we were able to engage our favourite Frenchman, Mishka, again to be assistant to Lewis.

Normally we would have taken a camera operator as well, but Johnny Harris, Bobby Krasker's old operator, lived in Canada so we were able to pick him up there.

This just left the costume designer. I tackled Lewis early on about this critical appointment, saying, "You can't really think in your wildest dreams Lewis, that 'Candy' could cope with a film starring one of the world's great stars?"

But he could and he did.

I think the only thing Lewis and I seriously argued about was this woman. She was an acute embarrassment throughout the whole shoot. How Liza put up with her I shall never know. Thank God we had a wonderful Canadian Wardrobe Master who managed, somehow, to pull us through. Candy had no shame, and accepted all his work as her own.

Back to LA to complete the budget with Grace, our PM, and the Paramount budget accountant. We went through the usual exercise of "But it *can't* be that much!" or "Can you get it lower?"

Then back to Toronto but, before I had unpacked my bag, I got a call from Gary to come back to the studio. When I got there, Gary had been called away, but left a message I was to wait for him. So I spent a pleasant few days going to see old friends, including Doug and Diane.

Doug greeted me in his usual way: "Where am I, John?" Which had been a long-standing joke since the first time we met. Poor old Doug, he had not been having an easy time. He had starred in an ill-fated television show, and did some small parts in the odd movie. Times had changed and there were not many parts for aging cowboys. It wasn't just the money, it was the ego as well. People did not remember him anymore. He went from being the star of one of the world's most popular TV shows to being forgotten. One day he rang a restaurant to make a booking, and they asked him to spell his name. "I'm Doug McClure or, if you like, Trampas (his character's name)."

"How do you spell that?" they asked.

He put the phone down. The only good thing in his life was Diane, who from being a top secretary had become a great wife. Which was proved later when Doug caught cancer, and she nursed him night-and-day through all that terrible time, until so very sadly he died.

Gary returned and we had a nice meeting about nothing and I returned to Toronto. This happened three times, and each time it was something that could have been solved over the phone.

Lewis joined me in Toronto and was very happy with the set-up there. The casting director was a real find, and we started to finalise the casting.

We had filled all the major parts, but there were still the minor roles, and one very important role, the part of the cantankerous pianist, for which in the end we were brave enough to sign Shelley Winters.

The budget was approved and we had a firm start date. We again had a lucky streak when we found a great American tap-choreographer, Danny Daniels. He and his wife, Bea, are my friends to this day. Liza had worked with Danny Daniels before, and was thrilled that we had him with us. This also made us feel good as it was so important that they felt comfortable working with each other, and her excitement endorsed our choice.

For, in a way, Danny was the key to the film. He had to turn non-dancers into, first of all, an amateur, sloppy dance group, and then into looking like a top professional group. Even worse, he had to show them gradually progressing under, seemingly, Liza's tuition. On top of this, he had to create one solo number for Liza.

At the beginning I had allowed a three-week rehearsal period for Liza alone with Danny, but Liza came to me and asked if she could have another two weeks, quickly adding that she did not expect to be paid for this. I, of course, agreed, even if it did mean back-dating Danny's contract and adding to his expenses in New York.

Next, we met with John Kander and Fred Ebb, the wondrous writers of so many of Liza's songs and shows, including "Cabaret" and "Chicago". "Music by John Kander and Lyrics by Fred Ebb" put the stamp of excellence on any show, and their music will, I am sure, live on long after we have all gone. It was a great thrill to go to Fred's apartment in New York and hear the number "Stepping Out". I have to say at this point that I was not over the moon about it, it was all right, but in my opinion not the hit number that we needed for the film. But both Lewis and Liza loved it, so I thought, if Liza thinks it will work, who am I to disagree?

The five weeks were soon up, and came the evening when we all met for a get-together in the Hotel Kempinski in Toronto. The whole cast was there, with exception of Shelley who was to join us later. There was Lewis, Danny Daniels, Bill

Orlowski (Danny's Canadian assistant), Peter Howard (the dance music arranger), and myself.

Unlike what most people assume, the dance is arranged first, then the music is written to fit the dance. This is done by the choreographer planning the movements. The dance music arranger, having the top line, works with him (or her) and the dancers, gradually building up the music to match the dance. At a later stage, the music scorer comes in and starts to work with the dance team. So, the dancers are dancing to a piano track, until fairly near the time that they are ready to shoot.

In our case, we had decided that the stand-ins for the artists should also be dancers, so that if one of the principals could not perform a tricky step, for example, we would have someone trained ready to take over. This is one of the reasons why we carried an assistant choreographer, as he trained the stand-ins, or doubles, in the wake of the principals.

He also gave one-to-one rehearsals for the artists as they became available from the Main Unit shooting. For, though there would be a rehearsal period at the front, the rehearsal would be going on through the shooting period, gradually bringing them up to the standard required.

At the drinks party that first night in Toronto, I think Julie Waters summed it up when she said to Danny Daniels, "Do you like a challenge?" For Julie, like most of the others, had no tap-dancing experience at all, and the others very little, including Liza.

They had to learn three routines. One, when they put on their first show in front of an audience, and they are not very good. The second when they are up to professional standards, and the third when they take their bows at the end with the credits over.

So the rehearsals started, and very soon the cast settled down with each other. It was rather like a boarding school, with Liza as head girl, Danny Daniels as the headmaster, and Peter the music teacher. It was tough, and we even had to bring in extra air-conditioning as the exercises plus the Toronto heat were proving too much. I used to sit and watch them and think they would never make it in time. I wondered whether we should talk to Danny and make the routines easier. But they worked at it – God! how they worked – and at the end of a session came off covered in sweat and exhausted.

Carol Woods, with all her weight, was the most amazing, as she was always there, never complained, but came for a break, shattered. But it was not all misery, for they did enjoy each other, and they did laugh. But they were soon put back in line by Sergeant-Major Daniels.

I remember one time when they all crashed into one another and fell down on top of one another. Laughing bodies were strewn all over the floor and Liza sat up saying, "Oh my God, I think I peed myself."

Just then the cast noticed a puddle on the floor, and there was a second or two when the laughter stopped and they just stared. Then a little voice said, "It's me. I didn't pee, but it's me!"

It was a forlorn Robyn Stevan, and it transpired that when she first put her rehearsal costume on she noticed it exaggerated her flat chest, so she took two balloons and filled them with water. In the crash the inevitable happened, one burst.

Meanwhile, the sets were being built, and Grace and I were busy engaging the Canadian crew. We found the Canadians excellent. I don't know if we were just lucky, but we could not have had a better bunch, and really we need not have brought so many Europeans, probably with the exception of Mishka, who was so used to Lewis's way of working that it made Lewis's life a lot easier.

I did have one problem at the beginning: Lewis and I wanted to work French hours, that is start at twelve midday, after everyone has eaten, and finish at seven-thirty. This gives you seven-and-a-half hours of continuous shooting. Stopping for lunch always breaks the momentum, quite apart from the fact that the artists invariably have to go back into make-up and hair afterwards.

In the end, we came to a compromise which was that we would give them lunch on arrival, but before shooting, and then shoot straight through to the wrap. It worked well, and the whole company was happy with this arrangement, especially the artists, make-up folk, hairdressers and wardrobe, who did not have to get up in what always seemed like the middle of the night.

On Monday August 27 1990, we started Principal Photography, and because of the rehearsal period everything went amazingly smoothly. There was no settling down period for that had been done during the rehearsal period. Grace turned out to be a very good production manager, and the secretaries could not have been better.

Our main accountant, Brian Wensel, was a Paramount employee, and another great guy, even if he was very much the trained studio accountant.

After taking the cast out to dinner one night, I put my expenses in the next day. It wasn't long before Brian was in my office saying, "You have to write down what you discussed at this dinner on these expenses." So, I duly took the paper and, a bit later, sent it back to the accounts' office.

It seemed only seconds before Brian was back. "No, John, you can't put down that you discussed Geoff Kelly's sex life." (Geoff was a young Paramount executive.)

"But, Brian, that is exactly what we discussed."

"But you can't put that down, you have to say something like we discussed the script."

"Oh," I replied, "they want me to lie? I don't get it."

Similarly, when we were doing the budget, I told them not to forget the wrap party, but was told we couldn't put that down.

"You don't have wrap parties?" I asked.

"Oh yes, we have them, but they must not go down as such in the budget. Put an allowance in for extra timber or some other thing, anything but a party."

To me that makes the whole costing system a joke. Everybody knows the truth but everybody plays these idiotic games.

Everything was progressing well. Frank Mancuso rang from the studio to say how pleased he was with the "dailies", but Lewis said, "This can't continue." And like the clever old bird that he is, he was right.

A shadow fell across the company with the arrival of Shelley Winters. When Lewis and I met her in New York, I was shocked by her appearance. She seemed not so much to have aged, but to have let herself go. At that meeting, Lewis had made a big point of the fact that she was to behave, he didn't want the trouble that he had with her on "Alfie". She promised him to be as good as gold, but she wasn't.

Maybe it was the fact that she had engaged a girl to be a kind of companion/ secretary/ helpmate, whatever. But on the first day the poor girl drove Shelley's car out of the garage and right over her boss's foot! So that was her career in show-business over! And another girl was hired – whose main job now was to push Shelley around in a wheel-chair! Maybe this is what caused her bad temper, but I don't think so. I think if it hadn't been that, it would have been something else. Thank God she did not have to dance. For the most part, she just had to sit at the piano in the Church Hall where she played the music for Liza's classes.

Her role was not only that of piano player but also as Liza's cantankerous critic. Well, this was pretty true in real life as well, for they did not like each other. Shelley would yell across the set, "Minnelli, come over here and give us a song." This did not go down well, although Liza was always polite and kind to her. I think she realised that it was hard for her, after being one of the sexiest stars in Hollywood, to be reduced to this fat old lady who looked more like one of those bag ladies who push their entire personal belongings around in a supermarket trolley. I don't think she could adjust to her years. She said to one of the young prop boys one day, "Joe, have you ever had a woman of my age?"

She always had a list of complaints, and most days when she arrived at the studio she would enter in her chariot in Boadiccea style and shout, "John Dark? Where's that John Dark? I want to see him." The whole studio would ring to my name.

But I soon got to know how to handle her, and used the Ilya Lopart technique. I would meet her in her dressing-room, where usually she would be lying on the couch. With a wave of her hand, she would send her entourage away, and when they had gone start her latest diatribe. I would let her go on till she had finished and then I would bend over her and say softly, "Shelley, tell me, did you really make it with Montgomery Clift (or Clark Gable, or some other major star, it didn't seem to matter for she had had most)?"

Her whole manner would change, her eyes would light up, and one could see again that gorgeous girl now hiding in the body of this old lady. She was very difficult, and sometimes I could have killed her, but I also felt sorry for her. She was old and she was nervous and, before any big scene, she would call in sick, mainly I think because she had trouble remembering her lines.

We were shooting in the Elgin theatre, and every day Shelley had called in sick. Finally we had shot everything but her scenes, so I rang her up and told her that she had to come in, saying, "Look, Shelley, I do not have the theatre after today, you have to come in. I'm sorry but I have no alternative than to insist." Well, she arrived, entering from the wings and onto the stage like a galleon in full sail going into battle, with me as the target.

"Where's that John Dark? Where is he? Oh, there you are. Well, I have been onto my agent and my manager, and soon my lawyer. I'm going to sue you. That's what I am going to do."

Somehow Make-up and Hair got her ready and, with Mishka's charm, he got her in front of the camera, still muttering. She then noticed there was no one else about. She was the only one of the actors there, and all the attention was on her. She blossomed, hitched herself up, and performed. After the first rehearsal she said to Lewis and the crew, "John Dark said, if I came to work I'd feel a lot better, and you know something, he was right!"

And you know something else? Shelley added spice to the film. She kept me on my toes, as you never knew when this volcano was going to erupt.

With Liza it was so different, never bitching, never complaining, always on time, always generous to her fellow artists, pleasant to all the crew, and a delight to the Production staff. If she wanted something, she would ask politely, like the time when she was not on call for a few days, and she asked if she could go back to the States to visit her sister. I was only too happy to let her go, and she became very excited as her sister had just given birth, and she was eager to see the new baby. Then, for some reason or other, we were forced to change the schedule, which meant that she couldn't go. When I told her I was expecting her to say something like, "Well you gave your permission" or "I am sorry I have already made my plans", but no, not Liza. She said, "Oh well, it is probably for the best, it's a long journey."

If Shelley was the spice, Liza was the heart.

When tragedy struck and Julie Walters's daughter was diagnosed with leukaemia, it was Liza who led the warmth and support that we all, especially the cast, gave Julie. I told Julie to take time off, but she was another trouper, and wanted to continue working. In fact, she said afterwards when the worst was over, that it was work and her fellow artists that kept her going. Julie had a great partner, and we did not see him much. He was a bit like Ineke, in that he kept out of the way. It was he who looked after the baby, and was an amazing father. I was really happy when I read years later that they had got married.

The other news was that the baby completely recovered, and I should record what an amazing hospital "Sick Kids" in Toronto is. Though it was very unfortunate that the child caught such a terrible illness, it was also lucky that we were so close to such a great hospital. The staff, the doctors and the nurses were, like so many Canadians, not only efficient but also such nice people.

Liza bonded the cast together, and this was apparent when we recorded her song and several of the cast turned up at the session. On their day off, they came along just to be with Liza. We all sat in the monitor room, till Liza called them into the recording booth. She wanted them close to her, and they all sat around the floor as she sang into the microphone.

The day we received the music tapes, we were shooting some scenes but Lewis suggested we play the tape for the kids. (We were very much the parents of this group!) Up to now, all that they had had to dance to was dear old Peter's piano track.

So the music started and as the cast sat around listening, Liza picked up a cane and started to dance. One by one the rest of the cast joined in. It was quite extraordinary, no one asked them to do it, after all they got few breaks during the day, but there they were giving it their all. At the end, Liza and several of the others burst into tears. I can't explain it, but a little bit of magic fell over the set that day.

The time for my tears, tears of pride, was the day they came out from the wings of the Elgin Theatre, lined up in the classical chorus line, strutting out and dancing with the perfect precision of the Tiller Girls. I knew the blood, sweat, and pain needed to turn actors into dancers in a few weeks. It sounds silly, I guess, but I was very proud of them. Sadly, we were nearing the end, and soon I would be saying good-bye to them all. Most of them I would never see again, although I watched their careers avidly.

One day, four or five heavies from the Paramount accounts' department arrived when we were shooting in the Elgin theatre. After a friendly greeting, they said rather ominously I thought, "We need to talk to you, John. Where can we talk privately?"

This was a bit of a problem as we were using up all the space, but I managed to find a store cupboard, where we all crammed in. It began to resemble the cabin scene in the Marx Brothers' film "A Night at the Opera".

"Look, John," the main man said, "we don't want another 'Shirley Valentine'. For God's sake, don't come under budget. You have no idea the trouble it causes. Just spend the money." So, that is what I did.

I made sure that we had some decent titles. We had shot the backgrounds in Toronto and I wanted the lettering to be of the same standard. We had fun perfecting them, which used up some of the spare budgeted money, but sadly I was not able to help them much, and once again we were comfortably under-budget.

But what an attitude, and it made me feel I wish I had stayed being an executive of the company. Such stupidity, such sad thinking. You mustn't say the truth, and you mustn't save money. Yet they insist on having a representative on each film to make sure no one is stealing. However, we did not have one of these on our shoot, on orders from the very top.

We got out of Canada on-schedule and went back to Twickenham for post-production. There we dubbed and got through, despite the best efforts of the Music editor, who was very grand and considered our film below his talents.

The first thing he said to me was, "Miss Minnelli is off-key in several places. What do you want me to do?"

You can guess my reply: "Leave it alone." Actually I should have done without his talent, as he was obviously not the man for the job.

I was anxious about the sound of the taps because, for obvious reasons, they have to be put on afterwards. The taps had to be more in synch with the music track than the visual. One strived to get both, but it was the combination of taps and music that was all important. For this reason I wanted the Music editors to be in charge of these, rather than the Effects' boys. However, our grand Music editor felt this was below his talents and, unknown to me, had passed it over to the Effects' department who I found out – to my horror – had intended using a Foley artist.

Now, a Foley artist is someone who puts the sounds of footsteps on a post-recorded scene. They are not by any stretch of the imagination dancers. It was almost impossible to get the whole cutting crew to understand that the taps were part of the music.

I was helped when Peter Matz, the music scorer, arrived and took over the problem. Peter composed and conducted all the title and background music. I would have liked him to stay for the dub but he had other commitments, and we missed him.

We took the finished film back to Paramount who had numerous previews, some of which were given an extraordinary rapturous reception. There was also one in Chicago, where it received a much cooler reception. So, what was one to make of it?

It would be a wonderful ending if I could report the film was a success. But it wasn't. They always say happy films never make box-office films. Sam Spiegel once said, "Films that run smoothly are colourless, and only those produced in strife have outstanding merit." Well, it couldn't have been a happier shoot, and I suppose we paid the price.

But there were other reasons. Firstly, the management of Paramount changed and, despite having fantastic American previews, they booked us into lousy cinemas. New management always hates the product of the previous one. Then, we had a long post-production period and, in all honesty, I think that Lewis over-cut the film, and he took the heart out of it. Next, Liza is just not a film box-office star. She'll pack any theatre – indeed whilst the film was playing in London she was packing them in at the Albert Hall – but not the Odeon in Ruislip.

How sad.

We did have a wonderful premiere though, attended once again by the Princess of Wales. Liza was there, of course, and Julie Waters and many old friends. That night, I thought, "Well, maybe it isn't a success but could anyone ever have had more fun?"

I didn't realise it at the time but it would be my last film, and I could not have gone out with better memories

I never saw Liza again. I did go to her show "Liza is Back" but I did not go backstage to see her. I think I wanted to keep my memory of one of the greatest performers in the world, a wonderful professional, a sweet girl, and what I can only call a dear friend.

Poor dear Liza, she was so hopeful that the movie would boost her cinematic career but, like me, she will probably never make another film again.

It was sad for Lewis, it was sad for me, but it was a tragedy for Liza.

CHAPTER 18
TOTALLY FxxxED UP

So many times in my life the phone has rung and changed my life. 1991 was not different, except for the fact that before it had changed for the better. This time it was another matter, another show another medium.

Verity rang me and said that the BBC was interested in the Southern Spain idea. However, they insisted on certain things. That it should be a "soap" not a series, and that it should be produced by Julia Smith, and that Tony Holland should head the writing team.

Verity told me that these two were the King and Queen of Soaps, (actually Queen and Queen would be more appropriate!). They were regarded as the most highly talented in this field of entertainment throughout the television industry, having worked together on the BBC's biggest shows, including the amazingly popular and never-ending "East Enders".

The other proviso was that we would have to guarantee that we would be ready to transmit on July 1992, to follow on immediately after the Terry Wogan show finished.

Strangely – and so unlike me – I did not feel excited at this news. Pleased, yes, but not excited. I wonder why. Was this an omen? "Well, where does this leave us?" I asked Verity.

And she answered, "You and I will be the co-executive producers and your Spanish company and my British company, Cinema Verity Ltd, will be the joint production companies."

Well, this sounded all very good to me and, as I knew nothing about television, I was very happy that the BBC was insisting on an experienced television "soap" producer.

Everything was okay, except I did not have a Spanish company. So I rang James and after telling him the news and, coping with his excitement, I told him to get hold of our mutual lawyer, Fernando del Valle, and form a company with forty percent to each of us and the remaining twenty percent to Fernando, thus making sure that we had an arbitrator if there were any disagreements between us.

Verity and I met Julia and Tony, and I can't say that I was very taken with either of them. However, I thought I often didn't like people on the first meeting, and they later became my best friends. I hoped this would be the same, though I found it hard to believe, as Julia was a difficult woman and brusque to the point of rudeness. A date was made for us to meet in Spain so as to give them the opportunity of getting a sense of the place, visiting possible locations, and meeting the local people.

Before I left for home, Verity called me to tell me that the idea of the series had been changed, and instead of my idea of an upmarket show, it was to be about working-class people who had moved to Spain. I was more than a bit miffed by this, and felt it was wrong. I had envisaged the viewer sitting in England in the cold and the wet watching people frolicking about in the sun.

"Why do they want to go this way?" I asked.

She explained that, according to the BBC, American audiences like up-market soaps, and the Brits like working-class ones like "Coronation Street".

I pointed out that "Dallas" had been a big success in England, and that was about as far from working-class as you could get. I was told not to be difficult.

I was pissed off, and I it still think it was wrong. But I was also a realist and thought they should know, and anyhow if it runs as long as "EastEnders" and "Coronation Street", that is my pension taken care of. I decided to take Verity's advice and not argue.

There was another factor, a personal one that I kept to myself, though, no doubt, other people realised it. This was that I was a different person from what I had been. Gone was the fighter, the tough man ready to do battle, to meet challenges head-on. In its place was the weak man, the apprehensive one, the doubter, the coward. I don't know what happened, and I certainly was not proud of this new personality whose characteristics I tried to hide from everyone.

Mind you, at one stage, I did find out that they were thinking of calling the show "Little England", and I had a good fight over that, and for a change won. This was, though, a rarity, and on most matters I seemed to give way. This was not always for the good of the show. I remember after it was all over doing an interview for, I think, BBC2, when I told the interviewer that I thought we were all to blame, and he asked me, "What do you think that you did wrong?"

I replied, "I wasn't tough enough."

I realised later that this was the start of my medical troubles.

Back in Spain, James and I looked at various places where we could base the show, including the forest land owned by the town hall of Coin, inland from Marbella. "Look, James, we don't want to build. I know Julia does, but I think it is madness. What we need is to shoot on a building estate (known as an "*urbanisation*" in Spain) already built. And then, after a year, if the show is a success, we can build, knowing we have many years of work ahead of us. And if we do build, then the last place we would want to build is in the middle of a forest, miles from anywhere, with bad roads."

Well, you can guess the rest. Julia insisted on building, despite the fact that we showed her excellent sites, one with finished apartments, right next to a hotel where we could house the crew and the artists. The flats themselves would be used as interior and exterior sets, as well as housing the dressing-rooms and make-up, hair, and wardrobe.

I discussed this with Verity but she once again explained that if we wanted the deal, we had to have Julia, and whatever Julia wants, Julia must have! And, of course, we built in the forest.

The next piece of troubling news was that Verity and Julia had interviewed prospective production managers, and had chosen Gregory, my eldest son. This was a worry both on a personal level and also a business one.

My first concern was that the stress level of a recovering alcoholic must be kept to a minimum. Secondly, I really did not think that Greg was qualified for the job, even though he spoke fair Spanish. Furthermore, I am not good at working with my own family, and I always regretted having him on the picture in the Canaries. However, the deed had been done and he arrived in Spain. I knew everyone would think I had got him the job, but that was something I could do nothing about.

I have to say that, at the start, it was fun having him around, and he got on with James and our adorable Spanish secretary, Inma. At that time we had rented a small commercials' studio, just one stage and a few outbuildings, one of which we used as a restaurant run by a lovely Belgian woman, and we had some jolly times there. I did notice that Greg had started to drink again, but he told me that he had it under control – I believe this is normal with alcoholics.

Julia and Tony came out, and that was the end of the happy times. She was a monster: rude, aggressive and generally unpleasant. She was not too bad with me, but with James, and Gregory especially, she could not have been more loathsome if she tried. I later learnt she believed in stress management. She knew that she had the backing of the BBC, and knew she could ignore me. This was one of their numerous mistakes and we should have been together, making sure that the right decisions were taken.

Then came the next shock. She had appointed a BBC production designer who had made a model of the set to be built. It was enormous, and included a modern *urbanisation*, a Spanish square, a petrol station, swimming pool, shops, police station, a theatre, and a two-storey supermarket. Many of the sets were for shooting inside, so in many ways we were to build an actual town, to be built out of bricks and mortar and to last for at least thirty years! In addition, we would have to build the support buildings, offices, wardrobe, make-up, hair, camera rooms, dark rooms, electrical storage, property department, drapes, stores department, and a large restaurant.

I had a fit when I was told that Julia intended to cast forty-two actors, and therefore would need forty-two dressing-rooms. I just could not believe this, and voiced my worries. Did the BBC really want this size operation before they knew what the success of the show was? After all, not one script had yet been written.

On top of this, I found out that Julia wanted, not only to shoot everything in Spain, but also complete the post-production on-site too! This meant building what was virtually a complete television studio, a working studio.

We hardly had time to put up the buildings, never mind fitting in the necessary technical equipment, and the time to test it all. Time was something we just did not have. Not only were there no scripts, there was no budget. Then came my next shock.

Gregory, who at that time was not computer-literate, had hired his brother, Daniel, to work with him on the budget. Now, I did not know that Dan knew anything about computers, but it appeared that as soon as computers came on the market, Daniel realised that this would solve his dyslexia problem, as the computer would correct his mistakes, and he quickly took advantage of it, and became skilful in its operation. And indeed his life was to change from that moment, and he became an important member of the team.

With James he produced a budget which was accepted and approved by the BBC. So then we had to get the final agreement with the Town Hall. Despite the fact that they had been crying out for something on this land, now we had produced something it was as far away from their aspirations as can be imagined. When the time came to sign the papers, they started to play silly buggers, coming up with one objection or another. One of the troubles was that, in this little town, there were numerous political parties, and they all wanted to have their say.

I explained to them, with James translating, that the BBC was one of the most admired and honourable broadcasting companies in the world, that they had nothing to do politically with Gibraltar as they were politically neutral as decreed by UK law. James was brilliant with them, but when they continued to be difficult, I told James to tell them either to sign or we would take the show elsewhere, and added that the Mayor of Mijas would give us land straight away. They signed that day.

Our concern was whether it could be done in the time. We had one hundred days to build the set and the studio, and be ready to shoot so that the BBC could have the soap on air straight after the last Terry Wogan show, and continue twice nightly from then on. Our concern was not allayed when, at the first practical meeting with the BBC production designer, he got up and said, "Before anyone says anything, I have one statement to make. ..." We waited. "... This is impossible."

"Well, thank you for that," I replied. "Now, I think we should get started. What do you think, James?"

"It'll be all right, don't worry, you don't know the Spanish worker, we'll do it." Ever the optimist, I thought. This same designer really worried me. After his statement about "being impossible", I thought he was hardly the man for this responsible job, and the more I got to know him, the more I was convinced.

So I took Julia out to dinner one night and explained my worries to her. She listened carefully and at the end we parted the best of friends with the understanding that we would replace him. I even rang James to tell him. The next morning, Madame was in a rage and refused to talk to me. In desperation I cornered her in an office to ask her, "What gives?"

She turned on me like a stuck alley-cat, saying that she had no intention of sacking the designer. "If he goes, I go," she said. I think that was almost the last real conversation (if you can call it a conversation) that we had.

James, Daniel and the Spanish boys started clearing the sight the next day. I had little to do, other than attend meetings in London with the lawyers whilst the papers were being drawn up. Once again I was represented by Michael Flint, who so impressed all the Spanish lawyers.

Which is more than can be said for the BBC representatives, who I found were a woeful lot.

As an example, James and I wanted it put in the contract that a very small part of the land be designated for our own offices, and we would pay the construction costs ourselves. One woman from the Beeb was deeply concerned, and this one question took up all one afternoon. She would not agree to this clause, even though it had no effect on the BBC costs. In fact, the opposite was the case, for if we did not build then the BBC would have to find us accommodation at their own cost.

Days were taken up in fruitless conversations and objections like this, with highly paid lawyers representing all parties, including two Spanish lawyers covering matters pertaining to Spanish law. The BBC lawyer was an old friend of mine, who had been the lawyer for EMI when I was making films there. After one meeting, he nodded for me to follow him upstairs and over a drink told me, "I really don't know what I am doing, John. They just won't brief me, and I am flying in the dark." I was to find this was typical of the BBC.

One exception was our main contact man, Peter Cregeen, a delightful, honest and professional person. He was so good, he would come down to see the progress of the site, and get the Spanish workers together, have a glass of wine with them and, through an interpreter, thank them on behalf of the BBC.

Well, these guys were not used to such courtesy. They were just grateful to have a job, as Coin was what is know as a Red area, meaning it was one of the worst areas for unemployment. It did wonders for morale. Peter was fully aware that James was the power behind the rapid building, and the fact that he stuck rigidly to the budget. I had already decreed that no one was to be given a commission, and any one found receiving anything would be fired: a practice unknown in Southern Spain.

Gregory had been commuting back and forth to London, as that was where the scripts were being written and the casting done. One day whilst I was in London myself I got a call from Verity asking to see me urgently. She came to my hotel where, with great embarrassment, she told me that Gregory had to go. His drinking was now obvious, and Julia could no longer continue his employment.

I cannot say this surprised me, and I felt sorry for Verity being put in this position. She and I had no secrets, for she was almost like one of the family herself, and I knew how difficult this was for her. She offered to see him herself, but I thought she had been through enough and told her I would deal with it that day. When I informed him, he did not seem the slightest put out, and in fact seemed to welcome it. He said, "I feel a great knot has unwound in my stomach." Once after Julia had given him another hard time. He said, and I quote, "I could swing for her." Later he became her champion. That is Gregory.

James was so furious about his sacking that we took him on in our Spanish company, and I paid him out of my own pocket. Another great mistake.

One of Verity's contacts came in as Line producer (another name for production manager) who seemed a likeable lad, and as he would be working with Verity, he seemed a good choice. One of the last things Gregory had done before he was sacked was to engage an engineer to purchase and fit-in all the technical equipment. I found this guy objectionable, but, my God, was he efficient!

I think that Arthur Tarry, the accountant, summed it up when he said, "It is incredible that the equipment was unpacked, installed, and it all worked first time. It must be a record."

It is hard to explain the complexity of the technical operation. A dubbing theatre had to be installed complete with a soundproof booth entirely lined with lead for post recorded dialogue. Cutting rooms have to be built and equipped. Cables were laid underground so that all around the site the camera could be plugged in to the link with the mobile recording trucks.

Another example of how the way the BBC works: as the OB trucks are so expensive, I asked the BBC whether they had any in stock, thus saving the cost of building them. We were assured that they had none that they could let us have, so we went ahead with their blessing and placed the order for two, one small and one large. A few weeks later, as we neared shooting time, we had a call from the appropriate department saying they now had two that they could let us have. Of course, by this time we were almost ready to take delivery of our own.

Work went on apace at the site: roads had to be built, water found (Ineke went out with a dowser stick and found a mass of underground water), a reliable power supply installed, and a lake built so to give a vast water supply in case of fire. Daniel bought a second-hand small fire engine from Pinewood, and had our security men trained in fire-fighting.

Dan again was a great help with his knowledge and experience in special effects, and handled all the problems with the insurance company. Luckily the BBC broker was our old friend Malcolm Cockren.

Uniforms had to be designed and made for the security men, who had to guard the set, which was obviously going to attract a lot of attention. They would man the front gates, patrol the fenced perimeter that we had erected, and also regularly inspect the dressing-room areas and the interior and exterior of the whole set on a twenty-four hour basis.

The crew started to build up. The art department increased and it was good to have a couple of film draughtsman there whom I knew and could trust. The buildings were going up with the Spanish workmen working like demons. I just cannot stress too much how wonderful they were, and I had not seen people work like that since my days in Hong Kong. Odd bods started to drift in, but as they were from the television world I did not know any of them. Apart from the lighting cameraman, I did not take a liking to any of them either.

One person I did know and who I was both pleased and surprised to greet, was the BBC representative on the show, my old friend who was the production manager on the Madrid film "Siesta", Dusty Symonds. How he became the official representative, neither he or I had the faintest idea, as he, like me, had no experience of television! I suppose that is why they chose him!

Now and again, the BBC did send down people with experience, and one was a girl from the budget department. We entertained her on her first day as it was her first visit to Spain and, as I said good-night to her, I said, "We'll go over the budget tomorrow."

To which she replied, "I'm going shopping tomorrow."

Which she did. And left the day after.

In retrospect, I do in a way understand, as their usual contracts called for the producers to be responsible for any overage, therefore it was of no interest to the Beeb in seeing that their outside produced shows were keeping to the costs. Obviously the budget department had not read our contract. In actual fact, at this time I don't think the Beeb understood the role of an outside production company, and the whole thinking at Television Centre was buried in "what had always happened". Or maybe I am being nice to them.

It was a kick, bollock and scramble to get finished in time, and we had to take some short-cuts like buying six Portacabins to house the various offices. The large restaurant, equipped to serve two hundred people a day, was never even drawn up on paper. James drew an outline of it on the ground.

This restaurant was the scene of one of the few happy times at Coin City.

Daniel got married on its roof, and the reception was held in its interior. I said in my speech that there was a connection between the studio restaurant and the wedding: They were both held in a frantic hurry. Julie, or Red as she is known to us, our darling daughter-in-law, was four months' pregnant. The restaurant's loos were only completed after the bride had left for the wedding.

The wedding was amazing. The roof had a view over the surrounding countryside, and the local nursery had put arches of flowers for the bride and her father to walk down, the seated guests filling the large space on either side. The bridal car entered the studio grounds where the security men lined the route, smartly saluting as the car passed by. The Coin town band, in their smart red uniforms, played a fanfare as the car reached the bottom of the steps, and then into the bridal march as Red and her famous stunt man father, Rocky Taylor, made their way down through the arches to the waiting Daniel, and the good-looking, young female judge who performed the ceremony.

The reception afterwards was the first test for our catering department, which was headed by a Spanish chef I had known for years. The food was fantastic, the party a wild success, and I hoped that this was a good omen for the future.

After this happy time, when even Julia seemed to relax, came reality with the fast approaching start date. I was given the first script and I thought it was dire, but it was the same old story when I voiced my concern. I was once again told I did not know what I was talking about, that "soap" scripts take time to settle down, the characters have to be introduced to the audience before the story-lines can be developed. My concern increased with the arrival of the forty-two members of the cast. They were a mixed bag, which, of course, was necessary to portray the inhabitants of this *urbanisation.* What did surprise me was that amongst the wonderful character actors there were a sprinkling of totally untrained people. Knowing the tight schedule, I wondered how the directors were going to get a performance out of these amateurs.

During all this build-up, the press were taking more and more interest, and it was obvious from the start that they were against it. I was never sure why. Was it because they saw it as a run-away production? Was it that they were just anti the BBC? *What* was it?

Whatever it was, they were their usual inaccurate selves, writing whatever served their purpose. One national paper screamed out that we were "raping the Spanish countryside" under the photo of a swathe cut through a hillside forest. If they had taken the trouble to check, they would have found that the swathe was, in actual fact, a fire-break that had been there for years. Things were not helped by the BBC press Office, who were scared stiff of the media, and when I spoke frankly to them they got into an awful huff.

It was the same with product-placement. We erected a large bull, the trademark of a leading brandy distiller. The Spanish countryside is littered with such Spanish symbols, but the press Office made us take it down, even after I said we were not getting any money for it although we were not paying for the actual "bull sign".

The BBC seemed confident that we would hit the date and, though we did not share their confidence, we were determined to do all in our power to be on time. We had to live up to their trust despite having no help from our producer or her designer.

The day came for the official opening. We erected flagpoles to carry the flags for Spain, Andalucia, JDyT (our company), Cinema Verity and the BBC. The latter had to take the BBC flag from the top of their building in Portland Place as it was the only one they could find.

It was a great day, attended by the Mayor and his councillors, the head of the Guardia Civil, the chief of Police, the local press, Peter Cregeen and several of his colleagues from the BBC, the cast, and whatever crew had arrived. Somehow the buildings were up, the power on, the water flowing, the lake full, and all the technical equipment installed and tested. All this was a great credit to many people, but especially James and the Spanish workers, and the various English technicians.

Now that we were assured of shooting on time, the bosses of the BBC arrived, and threw a dinner party for the cast. It was obvious that James and I were of no interest to them at all, and they ignored us, almost to the point of rudeness. I suppose I should have walked out, but I thought, what the hell, I have little to do with the making of this piece of crap, and ignored them.

James, on the other hand, was another matter. Not that he cared for himself, but he was always very protective of me, and also very sensitive to any slight against Spain. He felt we had been insulted by their treatment of us and the Spanish company we headed.

Now, let me say from the start, James was not the most tactful or diplomatic person in the world, and it took me some time to quieten him down. Really this was the start of the bad relationship between James and Verity. He was not used to working with lots of people, he did not understand the television industry, and very soon there were rows between him and Verity. He did seem to get on well with Peter Cregeen and the odd body who came down from Television Centre.

He would also row with me, but I would just slam back and he would retreat. He had a bad temper, but it lasted for a very short period and then he would be completely contrite – very like me, in fact.

We had one amazing fight sitting in his stationery Range Rover. It was over his time-keeping, as he was always late. I told him, "If you are going to continue to be unpunctual, then this partnership is over."

We rowed so much that the Guardia Civil came up to see what was happening. "Oh, it's nothing, Officer. My partner is just complaining I'm late."

"Oh," said the Guardia, "We thought you were killing each other!"

There were other problems, mainly caused by the differences in the ways of Spain and Britain. For example, the BBC wanted the accounts to be documented in the usual UK way. However, because these accounts were handled through the Spanish company, Spanish law decreed that they had to be done in the regulation Spanish system. The production accountant was a highly experienced man, well known to me, and whom I trusted completely, but an argument developed between him and the Spanish legal team.

I blame myself a lot for this, as I should have foreseen it. I don't know why it did not occur to me that on features shot in Spain, the accounts are done either in the American or the British way and, as it is not usual to shoot more than a few months in any foreign country, you are in and out before any bureaucracy catches up with you. It would be unusual for such a foreign company to be operating through a Spanish one.

This caused great problems, with everyone blaming everyone else. James was not used to this kind of corporate problem, and reacted badly. Verity, not unnaturally, took a dim view of his behaviour and I was always getting lengthy phone calls from her as to what was going on. She suggested that we should have a private arrangement between the two companies that her company should have control of running the whole operation. I readily agreed. She stressed that this agreement, which would be formally drawn up into a legal document, would have to be a secret between our two selves and our closest advisors. Again I agreed. This document was eventually drawn up and to all intents and purposes we abided by it, though, actually, it was never signed.

The first episode was in the can.

I had not seen any rushes so I went into the viewing room with some apprehension, fearing the worst, but hoping for the best, as after all it was my future livelihood that was at stake.

It was even worse than I thought possible. It was sheer unadulterated crap.

So much so, that I went to Verity and said to her, "You must cancel the transmission date, this is wholly unacceptable."

To which she replied, "You're the only one that thinks that. The BBC and I are very happy with it!"

This statement was only topped when the first transmission date was nearly due, and the BBC threw a big press junket, flying out a plane load of journalists. Jonathan

Powell said at the press conference, "You can all see the wonderful acting and great scripts."

Well, the reviews are history, and it was one of the entertainment industry's great disasters.

But nothing changed: a few odd cast members left, but basically it was just the same, and the characters were as unattractive and charmless as before. Mind you, the poor darlings were having to struggle with terrible scripts.

Well, I thought, there ain't much I can do here, I think I'll go to LA and see what's cooking there. So Ineke and I took flight. We had a pleasant stay at our old haunt, The Westwood Marquee, spoke to a few people, and saw old friends. But everything seemed very quiet there, so we decided that we would take a trip up the Pacific highway. Wherever we stopped, there were calls waiting for me, mostly from Verity complaining about some piece of Spanish bureaucracy, but mostly about James.

When I arrived in San Francisco, I got a call from the London "Evening Standard" telling me that they had just run a piece about James Todesco revealing that he had been barred from practising the law in Australia from some infraction of legal ethics there, and also referred to a land deal that he had made with the actor Stewart Granger. I was on the phone to them for hours, and the owner of the hotel said that they had never had such a long international phone call. As this hotel was The Inn at the Opera, situated just around the corner from the San Francisco Opera House, where some of the most famous opera singers in the world stayed, I found that hard to believe.

Anyhow, there was not a lot that I could do about it, and I felt, whatever the truth – and I have to say at this point I take everything I read in the British press with a large pinch of salt – I had to leave it alone and back James. He was the only contact we had with the local government, he was the only person we had with fluent Spanish, both spoken and written, and he and Fernando coped with all matters pertaining to the law, and the Spanish media. If it had not been for him, the set would never have been built on time, on the budgeted figure, and on a large acres of land at a pittance of a rent.

Naturally I got calls from both Verity and the BBC. Actually the Beeb, in the guise of Peter Cregeen, was very good about it, and played it down, whereas Verity was the opposite, for which I don't blame her, but she did not like him and that feeling was mutual.

I don't want to harp on their distrust of each other, but it ran deep on both sides. Suffice to say, it never was resolved and maybe – just maybe – was one of the factors that brought the show to an end.

Our American break was not completely spoiled by the reports from Spain, but I realised I had to get back, before murder was committed. We returned to LA and, after a quick visit to Paramount and to Spikings and a tearful farewell to the McClures, we flew back to Spain and all the troubles.

Which were plenty.

Everyone was arguing with everyone else: the Madrid lawyers with the London ones, the BBC ones with our Marbella lawyer, the accountants with everyone, and the trouble between Verity and James continued to such an extent that, in the end, Verity wanted to take legal action to move him off the show. The lawyers had a field day over this one, I can tell you.

Things were not helped by Verity's business affairs woman, who had been troublesome to all of us from the start. Michael Flint had warned me she was dangerous as, he said, she had a limited knowledge of the law, and was also ambitious.

The other factor was Julia Smith who continued her policy of "stress management". The poor Line producer was not of much help either for I think he was scared of Verity and her business affairs woman, and told them what they wanted to hear. There was a lot of, let us say, playing with the truth, which is very hard to deal with.

The good news was that the show went out regularly and the studio and the technical facilities all worked well, which was a credit to all concerned especially, I ought to say, to the Line producer who had a tough job. It was just a shame that it wasn't very good, even though – very slowly – the viewing figures started to rise.

Some time previously, on the advice of the Pinewood studio doctor, I consulted a cardiologist, who diagnosed a very high level of cholesterol and put me on pills and a low-fat diet.

I consulted him regularly from then on, and he thought I had it under control, though warned me that, in spite of this, two minutes later I could drop dead!

With that consoling thought in mind, when we moved to Spain I consulted a local man, who had been trained in the United States, and also had practised there. I felt more comfortable having someone local that I could call on, even though I always checked in with Roger Blackwood when I was in London.

But my peace of mind was short lived, as the local doctor disappeared, and no one seemed to know where he had gone.

The reason I raise this at this juncture is because I was not feeling well, and the constant strain of troubles was starting to affect me Every day I would wake up wondering what disaster would strike. Greg had handled matters on my behalf whilst I was in the States, but now I was back, I had to be the "man". Dan was a great help, a shoulder to lean on, and as he had been involved with the building of the studio, had developed a close relationship with James, and knew what his contribution had been. He was able, therefore, to help keep the peace.

At this stage, there was some good news for a change. The BBC at last agreed with what I had always said, got rid of Julia Smith, and brought in a new producer, another woman, Corinne Hollingworth. There was an immediate change and for a start everyone was much happier. More importantly, the script got better, and there was an air of optimism. Sadly it was a little too late for me.

I was walking down a street in Fuengirola saying to Ineke, "I just don't feel well", when looking up at a nearby high building, Ineke spotted a sign: "Dr Jalili" – the long-lost cardiologist.

We went straight up to his surgery and he explained that he had gone back to America to continue his work there, but his wife wanted to return to Spain. I explained how I felt, and he had me on the treadmill and on the ECG machine immediately. At the end he said, "You have got to me just in time. You have unstable angina, and you have to go straight to hospital. Go home, collect your things and I will make the arrangements."

So, I was rushed into the Marbella clinic – a private hospital, but outside of Calcutta you could not find a worse place. The nursing staff were, with the exception of one Irish sister, hopeless. I broke the drip bottle one day, and the broken glass lay on the floor for twenty-four hours. There was only one good thing about it and that was the food, which was delicious – and one other thing: the loo paper, quite the softest I have ever found! The intake and the outtake were fine, it was just the bit in the middle that was so poor!

Before I left for the hospital, I called Roger Blackwood, who after listening to me, said, "If you have unstable angina, the best place for you is hospital." My doctor did not like surgery unless it was absolutely essential, and treated me with drugs. After about two weeks, he declared me fit to go home, and as soon as I was allowed, I travelled back to England to see Roger.

He was shocked, as indeed were both Lewis Gilbert and Morris Aza whom I saw the day I got to London. They took one look at me, and both exclaimed that I looked like death. Roger told me in no uncertain terms that I had to give up the "El Dorado" job. In fact, he wrote me a letter saying, "This is not a suggestion, this is an order."

I then went to see Verity, and told her I had to resign my position as executive producer. She was very sweet, and very concerned. I also said that I would, of course, not expect to be paid after that day. Everybody was most kind and, when I returned to Spain, went out of their way to commiserate with me.

The trouble was that, though I had resigned as executive producer, I was still a director of JDyT, and consequently just as involved as I was before.

On the personal side, good things were happening. Gregory set up home with a delightful woman, who had been his councillor in the detox clinic in Spain, and was a recovering alcoholic herself.

The other major event was the birth of my darling granddaughter, Rebecca, who brought us so much delight. She was a darling girl from the day she was born, and much fussed over by the whole of the village.

The show was coming to the end of its first year and the whole company was buzzing as to whether the BBC would renew its contract. The viewing figures continued to climb, which gave us some hope. James and I were worried that if they cancelled the show how would we be able to make certain that all bills were paid before they pulled out.

In turn, the BBC was going through changes. Jonathan Powell left and Alan Yentob became the Controller of BBC One.

It was a strange choice, as he had always been more on the arts' side than on popular television. We were told that Peter Cregeen was flying out to tell us of

Yentob's decision, but when he arrived he himself had not heard what it was. He then made a phone call to Television Centre and was told that they would not be extending the contract. It was a strange decision. They had already paid for the building of an enormous standing set, and the rental was minuscule, the technical equipment was paid for, all in place and working. The Spanish boys and girls were quickly learning the technical and production jobs and soon we would be shedding the expensive Brits and using Spanish ones who would not have to be paid living allowances. In addition, negotiations were nearing completion for the BBC to receive grants from the Spanish government for creating employment in a an area with high unemployment). On top of this, the ratings were reaching more than respectable figures.

This strange decision can possibly be explained by Yentob having to make such a decision soon after being appointed to the post. He was not the type of person who would have watched the show and probably all he knew about it was what he had read in the press which, to say the least, was always negative.

I don't know whether Verity wanted the show to continue, I really don't. According to newspaper reports, Yentob offered her a six months' stay of execution. If this is true, I have to say, it was extremely disrespectful of her that she never discussed this with me. Had she done so, I would have persuaded her to accept, hoping that, over the six months, Yentob would see the success of the show, and change his previous decision. At the worst, the local boys and girls would have got six months' more work.

At this time Verity and I had remained friends, and I like to think good friends. However, it was the wrap party that pulled us apart. From the word "go", I (and indeed James) were very conscious that the Coin set-up would be a marvellous thing for the local people. To this end, we had established a film school in the studio to train up the young people. We thought that it would be marvellous to give the kids a chance to have a future in something other than being a waiter or a chambermaid. So, when the show was cancelled, we felt it not so much for ourselves, but for those kids.

So, when Verity decided to have a wrap party, in all good conscience, we could not accept. We felt it was not something to celebrate, and therefore declined.

Verity wrote me a bitter letter and that, as they say, was that. Our friendship was over. Verity paid for the party but the BBC flew over several BBC executives with gifts of wine! I could not understand why they would waste the Corporation's money in this way. But I was getting used to the way the BBC dealt with the nation's money.

James and I went to see Alan Yentob in London. We knew we had no chance of getting him to change his mind as, once he had made the announcement to the press, there was no way he was going to recant.

What we wanted to discuss was the future of the plant. We were anxious to make sure that the Beeb left with no unpaid bills, and also that we should jointly try and find other business for the studio.

Yentob was a strange man. I don't think he looked me in the eye the whole time we were there. He didn't say much, and other than agreeing that we should start tourist tours of the site. We came out with nothing, although I did feel that he was not anti us.

Back in Spain, things were worrying. Basically, the trouble was that Verity's company and ours had no trust in each other. The accountant changed, and the banks changed, though I really don't know why, because neither James nor I were signatories on the account. Various BBC staff came to Spain, we would have a pleasant lunch, go over our worries, and, though they would assure us that all would be well, they would leave and we would never see the person again. I don't think we ever saw the same person twice.

At one of those meetings, I suggested that they take the large OB truck back as they are expensive pieces of equipment and I felt sure they could use it back in the UK. A few days later, they came to collect it. They drove it to a garage in Malaga and, to the best of my knowledge, it is still there.

We could never get any concrete information out of their British firm of accountants, not that I blame them as I reckon they had the same problem as the lawyers, they were never briefed properly. I was so worried at what was going on I faxed the Board of Governors, saying I would like them to authorise a private established firm of auditors to come to Spain to examine the books. We would abide by their rulings and would expect the BBC to do the same. I never had a reply.

The tourist trips started and were a great success. Coaches arrived every day packed with fans of the show, all complaining that it had been stopped, and some were quite belligerent thinking that it was our decision. Not only did they like the show, but thought it was much better than "Coronation Street". They also loved the tour and the money that it brought in just about kept the ship afloat, but there certainly wasn't enough left over to share out in profits. We knew that these trips would only work for a short while, until the memory faded.

My health did not improve, and I said to Ineke, "I think I should go back to London. But we won't have the car so we can't get to Roger Blackwood's surgery at the back of Pinewood, and his hospital is some miles away in the country. I think we should call Rajendra and get him to make an appointment with a cardiologist based in central London."

Here I should explain that Rajendra was the son of our original doctor, DrChandra Sharma, who actually was more Ineke's doctor than mine. He was a homeopathic doctor who had helped Ineke amazingly, and also performed a great miracle: he stopped me from smoking!

Actually I had come across Sharma before I even met Ineke. This was the doctor I had so much trouble with on the Max Bygraves' film. He was never my own doctor, though he did become a good friend, and I enjoyed his company. I think he was, for some people a good, possibly a great, doctor, especially as he firmly believed in plenty of sex! My problem was that I could not buy into homeopathy one hundred per cent.

When he died his son, Rajendra, took over his practice, which was sad as he was not able to finish his internship. So, although he passed all his exams and was entitled to call himself "doctor", he is not accepted by the insurance companies. In my opinion, Rajendra is a better doctor than his father, for he is not so strict in sticking to the homeopathic code. He would prescribe antibiotics if he felt they were really necessary and there was no effective alternative.

He also cured Vicki, my daughter, of M.E, which orthodox doctors had told her could not be cured. I picked her up, an old lady, from Euston station, hardly able to walk and, after four weeks with Rajendra treating her daily, I put a young girl back on the train.

So, Rajendra became my personal doctor, and he arranged an appointment for me with Dr Graham Jackson at The London Bridge Hospital. A charming man who after a few minutes diagnosed a leaky valve and possibly some blockages as well. Later this was confirmed and I was operated on, and my poor old valve replaced with a pig's one. I also had three bypasses.

I have to say loud and clear that the operation and the recovery were a doddle. I had two days in Intensive Care, a day in post, and then I walked back to my room.

The worst part of it was the waiting beforehand, and that was only a few days. I thought of all the people that could not afford private medicine and had to wait months, in some cases years.

My days of waiting were eased by my main prop in life: my Ineke. In so many ways it was worse for her than me, as not only had she to cope with my fears, she also had to hide her own anxieties. The two children, Daniel and Sue, were always there on hand to help us both. I will always remember Susie cooking me a "last lunch". For some reason, all I wanted was fish cakes! On the day, the four of us went to the hospital and they stayed with me till I was wheeled down to the Operating Theatre. Their concern and their love were, as so many times in my life, the thing that brought so much joy. It was consoling knowing that they would be there for their mother if I should not pull through.

The other person who was wonderful to me was Rajendra Sharma, who insisted that I have an infusion before I had the "op". He said he was going to fill me up with goodies to help me through it, and I am sure this is one of the reasons why I jumped back so quickly afterwards, and I was released in ten days.

Back in Spain tours came to an end, there was no other business, and the BBC did not appear to have any interest in sending down any other shows. James and I could not afford to keep the place running, paying the staff, the rent, utilities and so on. The BBC gave permission to the original Installing Engineer to take out all the technical equipment, which he did with great thoroughness and stripped the place, so it could no longer be used. Why, I have no idea, for outside it was only worth the scrap price. Within the buildings, it formed the basis of a working studio, but outside it was worth almost nothing. So that was the end.

Well not quite for I did join Lewis on "Annie Two", a follow up to the awful John Huston film for Ray Stark, but with a nice trip to LA and a recce to East Germany just after the wall had come down it all came to nothing

Lewis was to make another film, this time in the Isle of Man, but I was not involved. I don't know what happened to it, but I think it must have fallen at the first jump.

He continued to get awards, the latest being the Film Critics' Award. "That's it, boy," he would say to me: "lots of awards, no films"

CHAPTER 19
TIME FLIES

So, it's hey-ho: the big eight 0!

Time speeds up the older you get. One guy described it as having two breakfasts a day.

So I contemplate the time ahead.

But how much time ? That is the problem. How do you plan for an unknown period? Will I have enough money to see us through? The dollar is down, the markets are down, interests rates are down. Our income has plummeted. The old money bogey is there again to haunt me. It seems some things never change, and worrying will be with me till the end.

I am already worried about the funeral. Who will know? *How* will they know? Who will audition the undertaker? What happens if I die in Spain? ('Cause they dispose of them quickly here!) Ineke doesn't want me to be cremated until after three days, something about getting prepared. I don't begin to understand, but that is what she wants, so be it. With no religion, who would lead the ceremony? Maybe they could get Stephen Fry, he always does the BAFTAs well! But that is a pretentious idea. The music? The flowers? The transport? Wonder if Willie of "Willie's Wheels" will still be around? Who will do the catering? Maybe they can get Location Caterers? I wonder whether I should leave a note?

Actually I'd really like to see a Call Sheet before I go!

This, of course, presumes I go first – which please let that be! Ineke agrees, she says she will cope with it better than me. As usual, she is dead right – excuse the pun!

I always thought, once I stopped work, I would stop worrying. No longer having to worry about finding the money, the cast, the budget, all the thousand and one things involved in making a movie. But no, you just worry about other things: you worry about whether you locked the back door, lost your car keys, put out the cat! (Haven't got one of those, so that's one worry less.) The list is endless, and the fact that most of these worries are trivial doesn't seem to lessen the intensity of the concern.

Old age creeps up on you, you don't recognise the signs at the beginning: the loss of memory, especially people's names, searching the house looking for your diary, your cash, whatever. You especially know when travelling and you spy a lovely girl, or a fascinating woman. In the old days, you'd indulge in a little "eye flirtation". You'd never seen her before and you'd never see her again, but it past the time happily. Now you find out that they hurriedly look away or, what is even worse, stand up and offer you their seat!

Another thing is realisation that people are not listening to a word you are saying. My mother always used to say that the worst thing about getting old is that people ignore you. This was especially tough for me who was a great talker, and I always felt people were entertained by my conversation. Let's face it, any success I did have was by my having the "gift of the gab". But old people can be very boring. I understand that, but it is nevertheless disconcerting when you are in full flood and they walk away with your words floating in the air!

Actually, and let's face it, old people are a pain-in-the-arse. They occupy housing whilst the young wait in queues. They clog up the hospitals, they severely damage the economy, and they're a worry to their children. Mostly they just sit around whingeing about how life was better when they were young. Let's face it, we oldies all do it, and the ideal solution would be to do away with us. No pain, no dribbles, no incontinence, just a pill ... wouldn't it be wonderful?

Not that it will ever happen, and, in fact the reverse is true and the problem will get worse. God help future generations who will have greater numbers of old people than young.

In my case, I think I have become, as I've got older, an easier person. I hope a more mellow one, probably not so much fun, but assuredly a much nicer one. Someone who sees that there is life outside the film world, accepts that the busy times are over, that the fascinating work has ended. Gone are the interesting people, the celebrities, the parties, the premieres, the luxury travel, the five-star hotels, the chauffeur-driven cars, gourmet restaurants, exotic wines. Hanging over bars with chums, chatting up the girls! All gone!

Do I miss it?

I don't really know. Maybe. I certainly relish the memory, but life has moved on and I am too busy enjoying this period to waste it on living in the past, even if it is the last reel.

Now I have the time to enjoy my family.

They all live in England, but they visit whenever work or schools allow. They all have such busy lives, and now that I have the time they don't. But on those days, when they are here, that is the time that I can enjoy my children and dote on my grandchildren, especially the younger ones, for the older ones already have their own lives, either working or in the last stages of academia. The little ones still enjoy your company, and express their love with cuddles and kisses and words of sweet adulation.

Daniel's, for example: Rebecca, who now is of an age to travel down to Spain on her own, and who is so proud of being born in Spain, and just loves coming to stay with us. Recently after a school trip to Northern Spain she rang me and said, "Every night I went out and looked up at the sky and blew you a kiss"; Tom, who is so affectionate, and, though a Rugby-playing ten-year-old, loves to cuddle up to his aged grandparents.

And then there are Susie's two: Grace, at six, a piece of sheer heaven, bright and studious at present learning touch typing and Mandarin. George, the baby, can't talk yet, but seems to find the world a comical place and never stops laughing.

These are the great gifts to cheer up ones sunset years. Sadly, Vicki and her two, Richard and Simone, rarely now come. She is always busy and has poor health. Her children busy in their budding careers and home building.

So, for the most part Ineke and I just have each other, and that is no hardship for me for I revel in her company. Though I may have become a bit of a bore, at least I am easier to live with, and she no longer has to take the strain of my stress, my temper and my wild life. No longer do I disappear early in the morning and return late at night, or go on location for months on end, only to reappear with stories of all the women I had met. This unique woman who, when once again was asked by one of her female friends why she did not complain about all my other women, replied, "I'm just grateful it's not boys."

Nowadays we are never apart, and I am happy to be still so in love with this remarkable woman, and have the time to enjoy her constant companionship. Though Dutch, she is a very patriotic Brit, a great admirer of the British Royal Family, a lover of England, the English and especially the English countryside. Most importantly, a keen Rugby fan and was as excited as I was when Johnny Wilkinson's drop-goal gave England the World Cup in 2004. Unlike me, a very spiritual woman, a kind person – certainly the kindest person I have ever known, always there ready to help anyone who is going through a tough time. An amazing healer: I have never believed in such things but one tough day she cured my gout, one of the most painful of ailments. I am no longer sceptical.

A wife whom I always see as a mechanical genius, plumber, mechanic, carpenter, painter. Nothing seems to faze her and if she hasn't got the right tool she will improvise. During the Molesey floods, not having a boat, she used the children's paddling pool and beach spades to canoe down to take hot food to our flooded friends. Nothing will defeat her. Kevin Connor never forgot arriving at my house in Buckinghamshire only to find the drive blocked by a large hole. But he was even more surprised to see Ineke appear out of the hole ... topless! She thought the plumber had quoted an exorbitant amount so decided to mend the leak herself! Kevin was used to her home maintenance and all he said, " Wow, you're well stacked!"

She could cope with the hard times, keep the spending down, like she would paint a whole house inside and out, not only paint it but paint it so much better that any professional painter we have ever had, and hell of a lot cheaper. Yet she also could handle the good times: the premieres, the parties, and the dealing with major players in the movie trade.

Today she still looks so good, especially since she stopped dying her hair, she has turned into a blonde! People often ask (not knowing I was connected with the movies) whether she's an actress. Even when she was on crutches after a hip operation, someone stopped her in the street to say, "Oh, you look so glamorous." As the time goes by, she gets just a tiny bit heavier, but what she has never lost is her smile – a smile that lights up the room, and lights up my early mornings when she opens her eyes and sees me at the start of day. A day that we will spend together, rarely apart, never bored with each other. People ask, "Don't you ever run out of things to talk about?" I don't think we ever do.

She was, above all, the anchor in my life, an anchor on a long chain which would let me float away but only so far. She knew when the time was to "up anchor" and hold me tight. I am still tempted to stray, but an old man chasing young girls is not only pathetic but also distasteful. So I stay in the safety of the bay and watch the action from the harbour wall

My problem is that I don't really like this "me", the old man that I have become. I no longer have any balls and I will now run away from confrontation. More and more I let, indeed encourage, Ineke to handle any difficult problem. I know that I can't take stress, and maybe I hide behind that. What I do know is that I have a very low regard of myself.

Vicki says I have become a "pussycat". I am not too sure I like being a domestic feline. I think I preferred me when I was a Rottweiler. Well, not so much a Rottweiler, but certainly a Terrier.

I do miss work, or rather what my dear old friend and production manager, Ron Fry, calls "the buzz". I am lucky that I have family and friends in the business to keep me up-to-date. Daniel and Susie both.

Well, Susie is in television, managing director of a major American company in the U.K. Her husband Kevin gave up as a music editor on large features to become a freelance editor in television – wise boy! Though, latterly, he has edited his first feature film and is now directing his first television programme. He has a brilliant career in front of him.

Daniel has his own studio consulting company, and has been responsible for turning Leavesden from an aircraft factory into a major film studio. Under his management, he has had in the studio a "Bond" film, a "Star Wars" film and, more recently, all the "Harry Potter" films. He is also consultant to a London studios, and has been advisor to numerous other British and foreign studios. I am very proud of him. Then I have a nephew, James, an up-and-coming major TV director and a dear boy.

I try and see as many films as possible, we have several excellent cinemas down here which run original language films, there is also DVDs and when we go back to either England or the States, we see as many films as possible. Usually by the time the BAFTA awards come around, I am pretty well briefed.

So, here we are living in the sun, on top of a mountain looking down to the Mediterranean and over to North Africa. Can't help thinking if you have to get old, what better place to spend the last years?

I enjoy my lovely home with its all-round garden giving us complete privacy; views on one side down the valley to the sea, on the other to the mountains. A little piece of paradise. I love the wonderful Spanish people. Appreciate not having to get up early in the morning. Enjoy sitting outside my favourite café in the village, the "Fiesta", sipping one or two glasses of "*tinto de verano*". Chatting to the local boys in my appalling Spanish. For the language has defeated me. French, Italian, I can hear the words and in Italian especially, which I learnt to speak badly but volubly. But Spanish I just can't get the music of the language, especially here in Andalucia where the accent is so bad. Anyhow, I think it is probably better if you don't speak a language too well. You need enough to get around, do a bit of shopping, order a meal, make fairly basic chat but to go much further is asking for trouble. Without a fluency in the language, one lives in a warm vacuum. You miss all the arguments, the rows, the panics. You even miss any abuse. You think that everyone is lovely and that they all love you. Oh, I would hate to lose that possible illusion.

In the "Fiesta", in the bar, a favourite haunt of the locals, we get on well, and I am on friendly terms with all of them.

The "Fiesta" is a strange place in many ways. I have known it since it first opened in 1986. In fact, the owner still has a five hundred peseta note which I gave them the day they opened, and this was the first money they had ever taken. What is great about it is that it is one of the few places where the Spanish and the foreigners frequent, though I have to say, few of the latter ever mingle, and they keep themselves apart in the restaurant. I always say to people, I don't know why I keep going there. It certainly is not the food. Well, it is rather like visiting your mother: you never know what you are going to get, one day it will be good, sometimes even very good, but sometimes bloody awful.

No, it is just that it has a certain soul about it. I know I can wander into the kitchen and see what is the least of the disasters, which really is an unfair remark because some things they do very well. *Gambas pil pil* (prawns and garlic fried with spices), great barbecue, wonderful steaks. It is on the daily specials that you can get led astray, but also you find some treasures of Spanish cooking. Another reason why I like it, they do not serve English breakfast, or have HP sauce, or tomato ketchup on the tables indeed on the premises. One of its greatest assets is that it makes the best coffee, something that I so miss when I am away.

It is almost our second home. They cash our cheques, even lend us money, and come to our aid when we're in trouble. The owner, José, is a great friend of Dan's. He used to go shooting with them until he found they all stood in a circle around some unfortunate creature like a baby rabbit, and let blast – in a circle? They are amazingly kind (unless you're a rabbit!) and nothing is too much trouble for them. I can't say I am treated with respect. In fact, my favourite waiter often takes the mickey out of me, but it is done in a marvellously warm way, nothing malicious. Well, I hope so, anyhow for, as I said, I cannot always understand the joke. Thinking about it, I realise that what the "Fiesta" is, of course. It is a Spanish equivalent of an English pub.

Other things, we are so lucky here that we can get British, as well as Spanish television, which keeps us up to date with the world news, and a constant source of entertainment. I love reading and have shelves full of books. Skinny-dipping in my own pool, eating out, eating in and cooking the food that I like. (Ineke will eat anything as long as she doesn't have to cook it herself!)

Life is very good, and I am getting used to it.

People say to me, "But what do you do all day?" I wish I could answer, I don't know I am always busy, but doing what......?

When I go back to London, I meet up with old friends like dear Graham Easton, now Managing director of Film Finances, who takes me to lunch and fills me in with the latest movie news. Still the sweet boy he always was, and the success I always knew he would be. At BAFTA, I bump into old friends, who always seem to be genuinely pleased to see me. With my Spanish sunshine tan, and the fact that I am still slim, usually means that after saying, "Good God, John Dark!", they say, "Well, you *are* looking well."

Which used to please me till I remembered Bob Hope saying that there are three ages of man: young, middle-aged and "aren't you looking well".

I still stay in touch with Lewis Gilbert, and we have the odd lunch together. We eat alone so that our trip down Memory Lane won't bore our companions, and we won't have to make excuses for our delving into the past. Also Michael O'Sullivan, Paramount's man in London, is a good buddy and we have long lunches together when we put the world to rights (the movie world that is).

I also keep in touch with another special person, Paul Hitchcock, now an independent producer after leaving Warner Brothers.

Then there is dear Malcolm Cockren who has been such a good friend to me over so many years. He has done me so many good turns over the years that it would take a book longer than this to list them all. We have had a couple of disagreements but, like all good friends, those are forgotten in the weight of the years of happiness. We meet when I am in London, and it's always so warming to be in his company again.

Then there is a very special person in my life, my lawyer and my friend, Michael Flint, senior partner at Denton, Hall till he recently retired. He steered me through many a bad time.

Amongst old friends, I had a wonderful dinner with Mel Smith and Griffith Rhys Jones in 2004 and it was good to be in their company again. They are both now rich after selling their successful commercials' company. Mel looking better than I have ever seen him, now more interested in directing than performing after the success of "Mr Bean". I would so have liked to have produced a film that he directed. They are both very flattering to me, and at this age I can confess to rather liking that. So many people, so many friends like Maurice Aza, my colleague and friend for so many years

Then there are the three special women in my life , Diane McClure, who stayed in Los Angeles after Doug McClure sadly died, and who had been a friend up until the end. Luckily she does come to Europe quite often to see her family, and we meet up and the years roll away.

The other, is Gillian Lynne. Dear, darling Gilly OBE, a very special friend for over thirty years, still working as hard as ever even, though she is about the same age as myself. Now very rich, money made by being the most successful choreographer in Europe, money earned literally by her own sweat. We meet infrequently, sadly, and it is always a total joy to be with her. She is trying to set up a feature film with herself directing. She is the only one that could pull me out of retirement.

And now down here in Spain I have lovely Aurora, our lawyer, who not only looks after us but also is a very special friend.

Writing this book has been a painful experience, something that I have not enjoyed at all. First of all, I found it a lonely occupation. but more importantly I realised what an idiot I have been. How I screwed up my life, and how I could have done so much better. I had the ability. My trouble was I liked to play too much. When I was explaining all this to a friend he said, "Yes, you really did screw up. Look at you: a lovely family, perfect wife, beautiful home in a wonderful country which you love, enough money to live in contentment. Yes, you really should be ashamed of yourself."

And, of course, he was right. But what is it that makes us dissatisfied with ourselves? Would I have been happier if I had gone to Hollywood with Paramount? Stayed an executive of the studio? How does anyone know?

What I do know, is that I have been incredibly lucky, had some unhappy times in my life, but for the most part I have had a very happy life. I *should* have been happy for, on reflection, I have always been spoiled. Whether it was in childhood, the army, marriages, work, or retirement, there has always been someone around who made my life pleasant, eased my path, and held my hand. I am so grateful to all of them.

I was not so lucky in my relationship with Greg. Our political beliefs intruding in our lives and keeping us apart, me to the right and he to the left. I am, though, proud of him, having cured himself of alcoholism, and got his first book published, "The Prophet of the New Millennium". He kindly gave me a copy but said that I wouldn't like it. Well it is beautifully written and proves once again that he is a master of words. Do I like it? Well, it is not, I think, a book to be enjoyed, more a book to make you think.

In more recent times, we have been getting on better, much better, and I certainly enjoy his company, and look forward to his weekly visits when we talk about movies and laugh a lot about our different experiences. A love that lay dormant has been rekindled, and a son returned.

We also talk about his lovely daughter, Lyubov. I see her rarely but when we do meet they are happy moments which I treasure. Sadly she has little connection with the rest of the family. I find that sad but that I think is her choice and I do not get into it with her.

It was only a short time ago that I realised that Vicki had had such a sad up-bringing. Her mother put all her love and attention into Gregory, and Vick was just someone who came tagging along. The death of her mother though has brought her brother and her together.

Not only her mother's death but also the fact that she has, and still is, fighting against the dreaded cancer. Greg has been there to help her through the ordeal The past months have amazed us all as to her bravery, her courage and her acceptance of the constant and increasing pain. Her acceptance of the inevitable, and her concern for others has been so very moving.

We talk on the phone on a daily basis so, though I see her the least, I communicate with her the most. She is still great fun to talk to and has a sharp wit. Like when her present husband asked her whether there was a Viagra for women. To which she replied, "Yes. It's called a Platinum card!"

Vicki and Susie are great friends, and keep in close touch. There is nothing better than when your children get on with each other. People ask me how Daniel took to Susie when we adopted her. Which I find a funny question. He took to her like any other baby who is born into a family. Why do people think there is any difference? He was three at the time and thought she was some sort of new toy. As they got older, growing up together, they behaved like most brothers and sisters. Fighting like cat and dog one minute, laughing together the next. Now and again, they meet up and have a quiet and lovely chat with each other. What is for sure, if anyone said a word against Susie, Daniel would rise up in fury. When London had the bomb attacks in 2005, Susie was the first person Daniel called.

Dan and I are very close, though we are not alike in many ways, and I find it difficult to chat with him. Light conversation is not his forte. When I talk about his latest movie in the studio, I want to know about the cast, the director, and the crew. He really is only interested in the construction and running of the studio! Having said that, we have total honesty between us. To quote him, "There is nothing that we can't say to each other." He is amazingly generous both with his time, and his money. I also know that if ever we were in any kind of trouble, he would be the first one there to protect us. He is the perfect son, and I love him to bits. As Vicki once said to me, "You always feel very safe when Dan is around."

He is married to a sweet, great-looking girl, whose father and grandfather were both top stuntmen, so she was also brought up in the business. She is a darling to us, and looks after us so well when we stay. Though the marriage has not been without its problems, it now seems happy and successful. For which I am so grateful for I love her dearly.

Dear Rebecca, when she was about eleven, her parents were going through the bad patch and had split up – for, like two days! At the time, she said to her mother, "Look at it this way, Mummy, now you've got the use of the carport!"

Then there is Susie. As I have said before, I have always been lucky and never more so than on the day we adopted her. That was a fight that at one time I thought we would lose, and I am sure with the new regulations about adopting we would have certainly lost.

Though the orphanages around the world are still full, every obstacle is put in the way of people wanting to adopt. Sure, safeguards have to be put into effect to make sure that undesirables don't get hold of children they might harm. But what about the children who are abused in "care"? What about the children in safe places like the Scouts, the Church, and the children's homes? No, there are evil people everywhere, but too many restrictions, rules, regulations are put on well-meaning, good, honest people who wish to adopt meaning that the "in-care" population remains high.

To me, one is too many.

Let me assure everyone that there is no difference between a child of your own blood and one of someone else's. I fell in love with her on the first day, a love that even survived her adolescence, a love that continues, a strong, close, enduring love which is probably why Ineke and I resent people talking about "your adopted daughter". Susie is our daughter, and how she arrived is of no consequence. You do not talk about "your Caesarean child".

One day when Grace was three she said to her mother, "Mummy, why are you browner that I am?"

And Susie replied, "Because Mummy has African blood in her, and you have African blood in you ...and Daddy is just a poor little white boy!" Nothing more to say really, except to add that Sue and Kevin, after having Grace, decided that they, like us and for the same reasons, wished to adopt. They have a lovely home in Fulham, they have an excellent housekeeper and a full-time nanny. Brilliant parents, and have a sample to demonstrate the fact. They are financially secure and Grace is educated at a very good private school. They have the resources to educate another, so one would have thought the ideal people to adopt what, in adoption talk, is called "hard-to-place children". But no, every obstacle was put up –including Susie being told she would have to go on a course to learn how to look after an adopted child. Of course, the truth is that it is Susie that should be the one giving the course. They gave up, now have a second child of their own: George. Though we are thrilled to have another grandson, we cannot but feel sad that there is another child still in care who does not need to be there.

My life is made easier, and happier, by the two Spaniards who help us with the house and garden. That is Marie and José. After many years I cannot remember a day when they were bad-tempered, out of sorts or a bit grumpy. The days that they are with us are the days when laughter fills the house. And, though my Spanish is still pathetic, somehow they understand me. They are indeed part of the family.

Ineke and I have a great relationship with the folks in the village, in the pueblo, and I enjoy my daily walks through Mijas and being greeted "Hola, Juan." They are super people, and, though I know their life has been for the better since the growth of the tourist trade, I also know that this prosperity has come with a price: In many ways it is like Britain where the schools are swamped with immigrant children. Here it is the Brits that are the immigrants, and the Spanish teachers are forced to teach these children the Spanish language – this to the neglect of the Spanish children. There are areas where a Spaniard feels as though he is a foreigner in his own country, streets where the bars and restaurants are British-owned and the only language seemingly spoken is English.

On top of this, the Brits do not behave. What's new? They don't behave properly in their own country, so here where the wine is cheap and with the hot sun, they get inflamed even quicker. Still, as one of the village elders said to me: "Before the foreigners came, we used to starve." And a little tear appeared in his eye.

As I write these few last lines, I now know that Vicki is terminally ill, the cancer has spread, and despite everything that can be done is being done, she is still in pain. We talk and I visit. It is so very hard to watch one's darling daughter lying there under constant attack of this dreaded disease. You watch and think, "what can I do?", knowing full well there is nothing. In 2000 she wrote me "you have always been there for me ---- A shoulder to cry on ---- someone to talk to, somewhere safe to go when the world gets too rough."

And now in her hour of deepest need I can do precisely nothing, how tragic is that. All I can do is to talk, chat, and be what she once wrote "A voice at the end of a telephone that makes me feel warm inside."

As for me my own death I am afraid of just one thing: and that is, despite not having a religion (in fact, hating organised religion), I will, at the end, ask to see some sort of frump of a priest.

On reflection maybe that won't be such a bad thing as I will I be the sinner that repenteth at the end, and then allowed into, if there is such a place, the Kingdom of Heaven.

Maybe I'll meet Cecil B. De Mille

ଚ୍ଚ The End ଓ

FILMS WHOSE TITLES I ROBBED

A CHILD IS BORN   1939
PROD   SAM BISCHOFF
DIR   LLOYD BACON
STAR   EVE ARDEN

THE DARK PAST   1948
PROD   BUDDY ADLER
DIR   RUDOLPH MATÉ
STARS   WILLIAM HOLDEN
              LEE J COBB

THIS HAPPY BREED   1994
PROD   NOEL COWARD
DIR   DAVID LEAN
STARS   ROBERT NEWTON
              CELIA JOHNSON

MEMORIES OF ME   1988
PROD   ALAN KING
DIR   HENRY WINKLER
STARS   BILLY CRYSTAL
              ALAN KING

YOUNG & WILLING   1942
PROD/ DIR   ED.GRIFFITH
STARS   WILLIAM HOLDEN
              SUSAN HAYWARD

O.H.M.S   1936
PROD   GEORGE BARKAS
DIR   RAOUL WALSH
STARS   JOHN MILLS
              WALLACE FORD

WHAT HAVE I DONE TO DESERVE THIS?
                                    1984
PROD   TADEO VILLABLA
DIR   PEDRO ALMADOVAR
STAR   CARMEN MAURA

BACK TO THE FUTURE   1985
PROD/ DIR   STEVEN SPIELBERG
STARS   MICHAEL J FOX
              CHRISTOPHER LLOYD

THE WAY AHEAD   1944
PROD   JOHN SUTRO
DIR   CAROL REED
STAR   DAVID NIVEN

CHINA GIRL   1943
PROD   BEN HECHT
DIR   HENRY HATHAWAY
STARS   GENE TIERNEY
              G. MONTGOMERY

EAST IS EAST   1999
PROD   LESLEE UDWIN
DIR   DAMIEN O'DONNELL
STARS   OM PURI
              LINDA BASSETT

MARRY ME   1949
PROD   BETTY BOX
DIR   TERENCE FISHER
STARS   DEREK BOND
              SUSAN SHAW

THE CIRCUS   1928
PROD   CHARLES CHAPLIN
DIR   CHARLES CHAPLIN
STAR   CHARLES CHAPLIN

FOREIGN AFFAIRS   1935
PROD   MICHAEL BALCON
DIR   TOM WALLS
STARS   TOM WALLS
              RALPH LYNN

THE PRODUCER   1968
PROD   SIDNEYGLAZIER
DIR   MEL BROOKS
STARS   ZERO MOSTEL
              GENE WILDER

TAKE THE MONEY AND RUN   1968
PROD   CHARLES JOFFE
DIR   WOODY ALLEN
STARS   WOODY ALLEN

AS GOOD AS IT GETS   1997
PROD/ DIR   JAMESL BROOKS
STARS   JACK NICHOLSON
              HELEN HUNT

TOTALLY FXXXED UP   1994
PROD   ANDRÉA SPERLING
DIR   GREG ARAKI
STARS   JAMES DUVAL
              ROKO BELIC

TIME FLIES   1944
PROD   EDWARD BLACK
DIR   WALTER FORD
STARS   TOMMY HANDLEY
              GEORGE MOON
SOUND LOADER JOHN DARK

Lightning Source UK Ltd.
Milton Keynes UK

176541UK00005B/27/A